Encyclopedia of Physical Education, Fitness, and Sports

Philosophy, Programs, and History

James S. Bosco and Mary Ann Turner

Volume Editors

Thomas K. Cureton, Jr.

Series Editor

Sponsored by

The American Alliance for Health,
Physical Education, Recreation, and Dance

BRIGHTON PUBLISHING COMPANY
P.O. Box 6235
Salt Lake City, Utah 84106

ENCYCLOPEDIA OF PHYSICAL EDUCATION, FITNESS, AND SPORTS
Volumes in Print

Volume 1: Philosophy, Programs, and History
Volume editors: James S. Bosco and Mary Ann Turner
1981. ISBN 0-89832-017-8

Volume 2: Training, Environment, Nutrition, and Fitness
Volume editor: G. Alan Stull
1980. ISBN 0-89832-016-X

Volume 3: Sports, Dance, and Related Activities
Volume editor: Reuben B. Frost
1977. ISBN 0-89832-018-6 (previously 0-201-01077-1)

Library of Congress Cataloging in Publication Data (revised)
Main entry under title:

Encyclopedia of physical education, fitness, and
    sports.

    Vol. 1 published: Salt Lake City, Utah:
Brighton Pub. Co., 1981.
    Includes bibliographies and indexes.
    CONTENTS: v. 1. Philosophy, programs, and
history.   v. 2. Training, environment, nutrition, and
fitness.   v. 3. Sports, dance, and related activities.
    1. Sports—dictionaries.   2. Physical education
and training—Dictionaries.   I. Cureton, Thomas
Kirk, 1901-

GV567.E49   796'.03   76-46608
ISBN 0-89832-017-8 (v. 1)   AACR1

About the Alliance

Since 1885 when the original organization was founded by a group of people interested in "physical training," the American Alliance for Health, Physical Education, Recreation, and Dance has been the professional home of educators concerned with physical activity, health, and fitness.

Alliance sponsorship of the publication of this *Encylopedia* crowns more than 95 years of program efforts devoted to professional development, research, and scholarship.

In that time the Alliance has provided numerous vehicles for the growth and dissemination of the knowledge base of the profession. These include an Alliance network of periodicals reaching all members and many segments of the public; professional meetings and conventions; professional books and reports; and collaboration with the professions, government, business, and media.

The Alliance has been attentive to the responsibility of providing reference materials representative of the profession. These materials have helped members initiate, develop, and conduct programs in health, leisure, and movement-related activities for the enrichment of human life.

The AAHPERD *Journal of Physical Education and Recreation* has been the major journal of the profession for nearly 50 years. The *Research Quarterly* has been published since 1929. *Completed Research in Health, Physical Education, and Recreation* was started in 1958 and is published annually. *Health Education* has been published since 1969. The annual convention of the Alliance provides continuous reporting of current research, with abstracts available in an annual volume since 1971.

The educational world is just awakening to the importance of motor behavior. For eons the cognitive aspects of scholarship were explored with great emphasis upon the history and heritage of knowledge. As the world recognizes greater responsibility for motor behaviors as well, the area of physical activity assumes its rightful place in the education of human beings.

For many years the Alliance has recognized the growing need for a compendium of knowledge related to physical education, sport, and fitness. Students, teachers, leaders from other disciplines, the Alliance Research Consortium, the American Academy of Physical Education—all have encouraged the development and publication of such a reference.

Yet, perhaps like most achievements realized through group effort, one individual can be pointed out as primarily responsible for bringing this *Encyclopedia* into being. Dr. Thomas K. Cureton, professor emeritus of physical education, University of Illinois at Champaign, has been the conscience of the profession in promoting, preparing, and urging its publication. Under his determined and persevering leadership, the idea of the *Encylopedia of Physical Education, Fitness, and Sports* was initiated and the volumes organized and published.

As meaning and ideas are gleaned from this work, future scholars will be in debt to Dr. Cureton and to the hundreds of other professional women and men who have contributed to these volumes. It is with a sense of great achievement that the American Alliance for Health, Physical Education, Recreation, and Dance joins with the publisher in the presentation of a reference unique in the annals of physical education.

With the publication of these volumes, at long last an inclusive analysis of the areas represented by the art and science of movement-oriented activities will be available for use. It should be a valuable asset to the professional libraries of Alliance members and will undoubtedly become part of the professional collections of most university, school, and city libraries.

The American Alliance for Health, Physical Education, Recreation, and Dance is a voluntary, professional organization presently made up of the following seven associations: Association for the Advancement of Health Education (AAHE), American Association for Leisure and Recreation (AALR), the American School and Community Safety Association (ASCSA), Association for Research, Administration, Professional Councils and Societies (ARAPCS), National Association for Girls and Women in Sport (NAGWS), National Association for Sport and Physical Education (NASPE), and National Dance Association (NDA).

The purpose of the Alliance is to support, encourage, and assist member groups as they initiate, develop, and conduct programs in health, leisure, and movement-related activities for the enrichment of human life. Headquarters are in the AAHPERD Center, 1900 Association Drive, Reston, Virginia 22091.

Series Editor

Thomas K. Cureton, Jr., series editor of the *Encylopedia of Physical Education, Fitness, and Sports,* is professor emeritus of physical education at the University of Illinois. He retired in 1969. He has, however, continued to speak, write, study, work, and spread the gospel of physical fitness.

Educated at Yale University, Springfield College, and Columbia University, Dr. Cureton's contributions to his profession and his influence on the lives of those with whom he has come in contact are immeasurable. His inspirational teaching, his passion for research, and his untiring pursuit of knowledge have brought him fame and appreciation. During his long professional career, thousands of graduate students have come under his guidance. Through their accomplishments as well as his own, his influence in the field of physical education and fitness is felt worldwide.

Dr. Cureton has contributed more than 50 books and monographs and at least 600 articles to the professional literature of his field.

He has been honored by many organizations in the areas of health, fitness, and youth leadership. He has served as consultant on fitness to the President's Council on Physical Fitness and Sports under three United States presidents. He is a Founding Fellow of the American College of Sports Medicine. His contributions to the YMCA program have been recognized by the Roberts-Gulick Award for Distinguished Leadership. The American Alliance for Health, Physical Education, Recreation, and Dance has accorded him its highest honor—the Gulick Award.

Dr. Cureton is still a vigorous participant in physical activities. In 1973 he broke four national records for his age class in the National AAU Masters' Swimming Championships. He continues his active professional life as Director of the Physical Fitness Institute at the University of Illinois.

Volume Editors

Dr. James S. Bosco is a professor of physical education at California State University at Sacramento, where he served as Chairman and Dean of the Division of Health, Physical Education, and Recreation from 1971 to 1975. He received a B.S. degree from Springfield College in 1951 and an M.S. degree (1952) and Ph.D. (1962) from the University of Illinois. He has taught, coached, and served as administrator at the elementary, junior and senior high school, and university levels for over twenty-five years. He was a guest researcher with NASA, Moffet Field, California, for eight years.

Dr. Bosco has held many offices in state, district, and national associations of health, physical education, and recreation, serving as president of the California Association in 1976-77. He has also served as an officer in Phi Epsilon Kappa and the National College Physical Education Association for Men.

Dr. Bosco has presented numerous professional and scientific papers throughout the country. He has authored or coauthored over thirty articles. He served as research editor of *Modern Gymnast* magazine from 1964 to 1971 and as editor-in-chief of the *American Corrective Therapy Journal* from 1967 to 1970.

Dr. Bosco's many honors include citations from the National Association of Gymnastics Coaches, the Amateur Athletics Association of the United States, the American Corrective Therapy Association, the Tae Kwon Do Association of Korea, and the California Association for Health, Physical Education, and Recreation. A recipient of a number of research awards, he was elected a Fellow of the American College of Sports Medicine and a Fellow of the American Academy of Physical Education. In 1967 he received the Distinguished Teacher Award from the California State Colleges and was listed in *Who's Who in the West* in 1973.

Dr. Mary Ann Turner received the B.A. degree from Wilmington College in 1952, and the M.A. and Ph.D. degrees from the Ohio State University in 1958 and 1965 respectively.

She has taught physical education and English at Versailles High School in Ohio, and was chairman of the girls' physical education department and director of girls' interscholastic sports at Fairmont High School, also in Ohio. From 1961 to 1964 she was an assistant professor at the University of Iowa, where she supervised student teachers. In 1964 she supervised student teachers and directed the undergraduate professional preparation program at the University of Colorado. She has been at California State University at Sacramento since 1965, where she is presently a professor of physical education and supervisor and coordinator of student teachers in girls' secondary-level physical education.

Dr. Turner has been active since 1969 in the California Association for Health, Physical Education, and Recreation (CAHPER). She has chaired numerous committees, including resolutions, honor awards, and professional advancement. On three occasions she chaired or cochaired the annual state conference committee. She has served as president of CAHPER at the district and state levels.

CAHPER has not failed to acknowledge her contributions. In 1975 the Northern District presented her with their CAHPER honor award. That same year, she was honored by the California Legislature Rules Committee with their recognition and commendation award for outstanding teaching. In 1976 she received the CAHPER Honor Award, and in 1979 CAHPER presented her with its highest award—the Verne Landreth Award.

Dr. Turner has contributed to the profesional literature through articles in *JOPER* and in other AAHPERD and CAHPER publications. Her paper entitled "League Constitution and Bylaws for Girls' Interscholastic Programs for California GWS" was adopted by AAHPERD.

Preface

This first volume of the *Encyclopedia of Physical Education, Fitness, and Sports* undertakes the ambitious task of attempting to identify the scope and breadth of physical education in the United States. It does this by addressing the questions: What ought to be, and why? (philosphy, aims, objectives); What has been? (history); and What is going on? (programs, schools, military, related and affiliated organizations). The order of the above questions reveals this bias of the editors, who assume, albeit naively, that philosophy (thinking) precedes program (action) and that history essentially records these actions.

Of course, there is widespread disagreement within the physical education profession as to its own definition, let alone what philosophies, sets of objectives, and programs should predominate—an affliction common to most viable professions. For the purposes of this volume, however, the editors will brave the contention that physical education is the art and science of human movement as expressed through participation in exercise, games, sports, and dance.

At the risk of oversimplification, it might be said that philosophies don't change much—only the extent of their application (and the language used to express them); and that the extent of application of philosophy is conditioned by changing social and political forces. Thus, no new philosophies of physical education will be uncovered in this volume.

The two major philosophies vying for ascendancy today are those discussed in Section 1 by George Leonard and Delbert Oberteuffer. Expressed in nontechnical language, they are:

1. The "natural" approach—that it is enough for physical education to be personnally enlightening, self-fulfilling, and in harmony with nature and the universe.
2. The "get fit quick" philosophy—that physical education should be indulged in only to meet immediate objectives such as preparation for war.

Both philosophies concede the physiological benefits that accrue from participation in physical education, and neither disputes the proposition that it should be participated in throughout life.

The history of physical education from the early Greek period to the present reveals that indeed the two philosophies above have prevailed periodically—early Greek society embracing the "natural" philosophy, and present American society embracing the "educational" philosophy. Sections 1 and 2 make some mention, but little space is devoted by the authors, to the fact that at least two additional philosophies of physical education have prevailed over the centuries. Again, expressed in nontechnical terms, they are:

1. The "body is bad" philosophy—that physical education is a matter of the flesh and should therefore be avoided.
2. The "get fit quick" philosphy—that physical education should be indulged in only to meet immediate objectives such as preparation for war.

The purpose of the sections on programs and administration is to present the kinds of physical education programs commonly found in American school and military establishments today, and to identify the kinds of administrative structures in which they are conducted. The vast majority of the programs in the schools appear to be based on the "educational" philosophy. The program aims and objectives listed by numerous authors in Section 3 correspond quite well with those suggested by Oberteuffer in Section 1. It is also quite clear that, in general, schools attempt to meet those objectives by making it possible for students to participate in a wide variety of programs given such names as movement education (predominantly at the elementary level), physical fitness, basic sports skills (including dance), intramurals, interscholastics (athletics), and adapted physical education.

The aims and objectives of physical education, and the kinds of programs conducted in the military establishments as reported in Section 4, are surprisingly similar to those of the public schools—with the possible exception of movement education and adapted physical education. The difference is in the emphasis they place upon the various programs. Ultimately the emphasis placed on any of the programs is largely a matter of local determination in both the public schools and the military. Throughout this volume a number of authors recommend a shift in emphasis from the "educational" philosophy to the "natural" philosophy championed by Leonard in Section 1. The magnitude of the impact of that thrust upon American physical education during the past few years and in the immediate future remains to be assessed.

The purpose of the chapters on related and affiliated organizations is to point out that the physical education profession has been instrumental in the development of a number of related professions, and that it maintains a cooperative relationship with numerous others; and in this country, in addition to the schools and the military, literally hundreds of organizations (public, quasi-public, and private) support, conduct, or are otherwise associated with various kinds of physical education programs serving millions of citizens of all ages.

Selection of chapters for inclusion in this volume was necessarily arbitrary. Inevitably, important areas were either omitted or slighted. Some may have been overemphasized. It is hoped that the final materials contribute in some degree to a better understanding of the scope and breadth of physical education in the United States. Other volumes in this series will supply extensive coverage of selected areas such as physical fitness, sports, and research.

The fact that authors were given autonomy, and that some articles were written originally for other publications, will explain why considerable inconsistency exists in format and writing style. It should also be pointed out that significant events have transpired recently that would cause some articles to appear somewhat dated. These are discussed in Section 7 and include the advent and interpretations of Title IX of the Education Amendments Act; and the advent and interpretations of Public Law 94-142, the Education for All Handicapped Children Act, and Section 504 of the Rehabilitation Act (Public Law 93-112). Other important recent changes that will affect some of the chapters in this volume are the name change of the AAHPER to the American Alliance for Health, Physical Education, Recreation, and Dance (AAHPERD) recommended by the Alliance assembly in March 1979; and the merger of the NCPEAM and the NAPECW in June 1978 to form the National Association for Physical Education in Higher Education (NAPEHE). Nevertheless, it is believed that these factors do not detract appreciably from the primary purpose of this volume.

It is impossible to name in this preface all of the individuals who have contributed significantly to the completion of this project. However, sincere appreciation and admiration must be expressed to Dr. Thomas K. Cureton, Jr., series editor, for his valuable assistance and determination to see this work to its conclusion; to the chapter and section editors and authors, who gave unselfishly of their knowledge and expertise; to Raymond Ciszek for his constant support, encouragement, and sympathy; and to the Brighton Publishing Company staff for its technical assistance and cooperation. Special appreciation and affection is expressed to Mariana Bosco, whose unwavering support, patience, and understanding were matched only by her untiring assistance with editing and typing.

Sacramento, California   J.S.B.
November 1981   M.A.T.

Contents

Section 3

SCHOOL PROGRAMS

CONTENTS

CONTENTS

Section 5

THERAPEUTIC EXERCISE AND PROGRAMS

Section 8

RELATED PROFESSIONS

Section 9

AFFILIATED ORGANIZATIONS

PHILOSOPHY, AIMS, AND OBJECTIVES

Introduction

Section 1 contains four chapters expressing, in each author's opinion, *what ought to be* the aims and objectives of physical education and what types of programs and/or activities might best achieve those goals. Since no single philosophy is embraced by all in physical education, authors of national repute and from diverse backgrounds and experiences were solicited.

Leonard relates the most recent trend in physical education philosophy, namely, that participation in physical education and sports should be personally enlightening, individualistic, self-fulfilling, and in harmony with nature and the universe. The author virtually advocates a return to the time-honored trilogy of body, mind, and spirit.

In the second chapter, Oberteuffer agrees that participation in physical education should be personally liberating rather than confining, but it is not enough for physical education to be self-fulfilling in the bodily sense. He also includes a theoretical analysis of the term *education* as used in physical education. It is not enough for participation in physical education to produce a sound body in which to house a sound mind. In addition to physical (physiological) values, additional outcomes should include knowledge, emotional stability, social consciousness, problem solving, decision making, and ethical behavior. Finally, physical education should be participated in so that it enhances democratic values and ideals.

In the third chapter, Holbrook places physical education in the light of total life experience. She identifies aims and objectives of life in general and suggests that participation in physical education should contribute to those objectives. Basically, her aims and objectives for physical education correspond well with those of Oberteuffer.

In the fourth chapter, Zeigler defines physical education, outlines its scope, discusses the social forces that influence it, and suggests common denominators underlying various philosophies of physical education. Rather than champion a particular philosophy, he produces a chronology of philosophies and claims about physical education from a historical perspective—leading nicely to the next chapter on history.

Finally, it is debatable whether any of the philosophies discussed can be considered "modern," since the "body-mind-spirit" philosophy can be attributed to the ancient Greeks, while the "education through the physical" philosophy can be traced at least to the early 1900s in America (see Section 2).

JSB

Section Editor

Dr. Leona Holbrook, prior to her death in 1980 was professor emeritus at Brigham Young University. She had a full perspective of the concept and activities in physical education. She had been a teacher at all levels and in many phases of the program in physical education and recreation. She had been an instructor, a supervisor of student teachers, and an administrator.

Dr. Holbrook was a leading scholar in the areas of philosophy and history and had expressed her thoughts both in writing and speaking. She was affiliated with several of the professional organizations in the field of physical education and gave special attention to the area of philosophy.

Dr. Holbrook wrote numerous articles and contributed to professional publications and books. Many of her articles have been published in scholarly proceedings. She prepared working papers and materials for, and participated in, the UNESCO First International Conference for Ministers of Education and Senior Officials Responsible for Physical Education and Sport in the Education of Youth (Paris, April 1976) and the Interim Intergovernmental Council (Paris, July 1977). Dr. Holbrook was a past president of AAHPERD and a member of the American Academy of Physical Education.

1
Physical Education for Life
George B. Leonard

In the time of the early Greeks, we are told, there was originally no concept of the body as separate from the mind and spirit. The tingling aliveness of every limb after a run might trigger an intellectual discussion, no less alive and tingling. The flight of the javelin was akin to the flight of the spirit. Life was whole and unified, and we still admire that classic unity in the masterpieces of Greek sculpture.

But then the great games at Olympia and Delphi, Nemea and the Corinthian Isthmus, fell under the spell of professionalism. The pressure for winners became intense. Bribes became commonplace. Olympic victors were given the most extravagant prizes and privileges. The ancient ideal—the unity of body, mind, and spirit—was degraded beyond repair.

By the time of Alexander the Great, Olympic athletes were generally held in disrepute. Finally, under the Romans, the Olympics themselves were disgraced. The Emperor Nero was allowed to enter the Games (which had been put off for two years at his request) as a chariot racer. He fell out of the chariot twice and finally had to give up, after which the judges awarded him the olive crown of victory.

Our present big-time sports have not descended that far, but we of the West have never regained the ancient ideal of body/mind/spirit, pure and whole, and that loss is not merely a theoretical one. As a matter of fact, our present fragmented approach to physical education and the body imposes serious handicaps on every administrator, teacher, and student in our school systems today.

Today's Education, NEA, September-October 1975, pp. 75-76. Reprinted with the permission of the National Education Association.

SCHOOL PHYSICAL EDUCATION MISDIRECTED

Too often, we tend to think of our elementary school children as little bundles of thought and emotion who also happen to have bodies. These bodies are often a nuisance to us—squirming and moving around when we want them to be still, having to "be excused," hitting out at other bodies.

We find ourselves thinking of physical education or play period as an alternative or corrective to sitting still. The children line up at the door, then explode onto the playground. They run around "releasing" their physical aggression.

Sometimes they are actually encouraged in combativeness through the traditional "games and relays" approach to elementary physical education. Yet, we find it strange when they reenter the classroom even more restless and troublesome than before. We are slow to recognize that, far from releasing physical aggression, the traditional approach is likely to *teach* physical aggression.

At the intermediate and secondary school level, physical education may be almost totally cut off from the rest of education. At worst, it is preoccupied with dress regulations and showers to the detriment of all else. At best, it probably plays second string to the extramural athletic program, which benefits only a minority of the students. Again, this program is probably justified, not as an end in itself, but as a corrective, a way of "keeping the kids off the street."

For many of the boys and most of the girls, traditional P.E. is merely something to be endured. In the longer view, however, it may have more serious consequences. Wherever it concentrates on the competitive team sports that most students will not be playing later in life, it helps create passive spectators rather than lifelong participants. Wherever it reinforces the current nonsense that winning is "the only thing" and that everyone except "Number One" is a loser, it increases the number of "losers" among us. To this extent, school varsity programs are joined with what is worst about the professional sports boom, a boom which could turn out to be a health hazard. It might be said, in fact, that—

Our current overemphasis on competitive team sports is making us a nation of weaklings.

Our current overemphasis on winning is making us a nation of losers.

Before we can regain the ideal unity of body, mind, and spirit, we must renounce the idea of the body as instrument, something to be used, to be viewed as if from a distance. We do not *have* bodies. We *are* bodies. The success or failure of the first graders sitting in a semicircle around the teacher depends not just on mental abilities. How can they learn to read if they don't know how to sit comfortably, to relax, to breathe easily, to move gracefully and efficiently?

We do not take leave of our bodies when we perform cognitive tasks. Success in the three R's involves perceptual motor skills as well as health, endurance, and the ability to relax under pressure. And there is reason to believe that even the highest abstract reasoning is closely linked with the physical body; Albert Einstein reported that he first got his special theory of relativity from a feeling in his muscles.

THE "NEW" MOVEMENT

Surely we are due for a reform in the education of body/mind/spirit. In doing the research for my new book, *The Ultimate Athlete,* I discovered that such a reform is not only possible but, in my view, inevitable. Away from the Super Bowl hullabaloo, away from the frantic cries of Number One, other games are being played and played very well. Another movement is now well underway, one that can transform our attitude toward sports, physical education, and the body.

This movement is exemplified by the growing army of joggers, hikers, swimmers, and cyclists, who are becoming increasingly knowledgeable about the benefits—and the long-term joys—of cardiovascular conditioning.

It is exemplified by ever-increasing legions of recreational athletes who turn from their television sets to the pleasures of the courts and of the lakes, streams, fields, and trails.

It is exemplified by experimenters who are now creating new games for the whole family, games with such unexpected and delightful names as Yogi Tag, New Frisbee, Infinity Volleyball, Boffing, the Mating Game, and Circle Football—games in which everyone is on the "varsity" and everyone plays.

It is exemplified by the booming interest in dance and the Eastern martial arts, yoga, and other disciplines, in which, at best, the body, mind, and spirit are seen as unified and in which the movements of the body are seen as joining us to the harmony of the universe itself.

It is exemplified by a new, holistic approach to medicine that views the conventional definition of health (absence of disease) as merely the starting point toward *good* health.

It is exemplified, perhaps most significantly of all, by the New Physical Education approach of the American Alliance for Health, Physical Education, Recreation, and Dance (AAPHERD). This approach, in brief, involves lifetime sports rather than the usual team sports in secondary school; movement education (the teaching of noncompetitive basic physical skills) in elementary school; and, in addition, individualized instruction and the inculcation of a strong self-concept at every grade level.

Physical education programs that use this approach have a quite novel look about them. At the high school level, visitors will note a deemphasis on dress regulations and showers and anything else that might get in the way of instruction and play. They will see more of the recreational sports such as tennis, archery, and golf, along with more exotic offerings, such as t'ai chi chu'an, body conditioning, yoga, scuba diving, and rock climbing.

At elementary schools, visitors will come upon even more unusual sights: for example, a large group of children learning ball handling, an operation in which every child has a ball and every child is moving. There is no sitting around waiting a turn in this mode of instruction, nor are there any losers.

The New Physical Education has not yet swept the field. The most optimistic estimate has less than a fourth of the nation's schools involved. But it enjoys the full support of AAPHERD's leadership and holds tremendous appeal for teachers and parents, once they become acquainted with it. Here, indeed, is an idea whose time has come.

The splitting off of the body from the mind and spirit constituted a major error in Western thought, one that must never be repeated. In returning the body to the educational enterprise, everyone involved stands to gain. Moreover, as I point out in *The Ultimate Athlete:* "We may well discover that sports and physical education, reformed and refurbished, may provide us the best possible path to personal enlightenment and social transformation in this age."

2

The Role of Physical Education in Health and Fitness

Delbert Oberteuffer

So far in the 20th century there have been four distinct periods of intensified interest in the role of physical education in fitness. We are today in the fourth

American Journal of Public Health, Vol. 52, No. 7 (July 1962), pp. 1155-62. Reprinted with permission of the American Public Health Association.

discernible period. Theodore Roosevelt started the first one when he publicly advocated the vigorous life as a way of making our nation strong. The second was caused by the revelations of the physical examinations in World War I, which shocked legislators to the point where some 27 states passed laws in the succeeding 10 years requiring that physical education be taught in schools as a way of improving the vigor of our youth. World War II brought the third national effort to improve the physical fitness of the general public as well as school children. Those of us who were tapped for this sort of civilian service will remember that we were directed to rope off streets and, by using available firemen and policemen, lead the public in a program of exercises aimed at improving the fiber of the embattled American. And now, for the fourth time in this century, a wave of interest is felt. It is marked by presidential citations of need and by extraordinary efforts from the Capitol to persuade communities to improve the fitness of youth by developing strong programs of health education and physical education, including a recommended daily 15-minute period of vigorous exercises.

Historically, such developments have occured before. At various times when nations have faced perils, either real or imaginary, efforts have been made to improve the fitness of youth as an important part of the solution to the problem. Programs of physical training in 19th-century Germany and Sweden and in 20th-century Italy, Germany, and Russia have been used for national purposes in support of political or social ideologies. Youth has been captured in every instance and drilled, exercised, and strengthened to support the beneficient system and, more importantly, to protect that system against its enemies.

So it is today. Undoubtedly, America needs a strong populace for either a warm peace or the cold war. To guard the health of the nation is a worthy ambition no matter what our destiny may be. To control disease, to improve nutrition, to prevent mental and nervous diseases, to seek emotional, social, and intellectual stability, and to secure appropriate growth and development of children and youth become almost an abiding national passion. We are committed to such effort and enthusiastically so. Our form of political life not only requires a nation of healthy citizens, but also guarantees them the right to be healthy.

But whenever we go through one of these periods of greater interest in fitness, we should at least be in possession of an accurate picture of need in order to develop a true program in response. We should be able to distinguish fact from fiction in both areas of need and program. How is it today?

A test of muscular strength and flexibility of the spine, given to several thousand children here and abroad, revealed that American youth compared unfavorably with Europeans, or Japanese, or whomever. The researchers concluded immediately: 1) that our children, in fact all of us, are weak and flabby, 2) that our technological culture is destructive of our capacity for survival, and 3) that if we do not do something about it we will lose the cold war. This position, widely advertised in the popular press, has created quite a national stir.

So once again, programs of physical education are asked to step up the intensity of their purpose and the vigor of their content in order to save youth, and thus our country, from desuetude, if not actual destruction! We have reemphasized an atrociously unscientific but popular term "physical fitness" and we are being told that our children are woefully deficient in it. It is alarming, in more ways than one, because it is not a situation marked by clear fact, clear need, and clear response. In fact, there is a great confusion in all three categories—of fact, of need, and of response or program.

For example, does one equate the sound advice and factual information of scientists in the area of child growth and development, or of pediatricians, with the television personality who advocates the criss-cross leg exercise for infants three months old? Does one equate the scientific papers appearing in the collection from the Institute of Normal Human Anatomy meeting in Rome in 1960, and bearing the imprint of such international names as Larson, Hollman, Simon, Wolffe, Jokl, Missiuro, and the others who contributed, with the prattle of those who run the exercise emporiums for money and who are advertised as our greatest physical educators? Does one equate the sound advice on exercise coming from exercise physiologists such as Karpovich, Steinhaus, or Mayer with opportunistic entrepreneurs who would not know the myocardium from oxygen debt?

But we wander. Our problem is: What is the role of physical education in health and fitness? Let me see if my version of the answer comes anywhere near your version.

THE MEANING OF FITNESS

In the first place, the need for activity on the part of the human organism has been well established. Documentation of this is unnecessary. The evidence is clear. Man is an active creature and activity is important to growth, development, and survival. The need for exercise is here to stay.

But, apparently, nature does not care a bit how one gets the activity needed. The "form" the activity takes is biologically unimportant as long as no harm is done. Run around the block, play football, dance a jig, or go climb a telephone pole. The heart does not care. Muscle does not care. The rectus abdominus, which is a pretty important muscle in maintaining visceral order against visceral chaos, does not care whether it is used in basketball, bowling, or burglary as long as it is used. If muscular strength is what we are after to correct the evil ways into which we have fallen, nature does not care how we get it—or at what price. Strength-building activities can be anything that builds strength—and thus they need to have no other purpose, no other meaning, no discernible relationship to anything significant except strength itself.

I am afraid this is the sort of thing that some are calling "physical" fitness — a sort of muscular development that comes from exercise and that can be used for any purpose at the discretion of the possessor.

In these terms, there would be relatively few problems involved in making the nation muscularly strong. Just set 40 million school children to exercising with sufficient vigor and keep them at it and we will accomplish our objective!

There are only two things wrong with this concept: Exercise is only partially responsible for fitness, and strength is only one of the concerns of physical education.

Our scientists, our philosophers, our educators, the better-informed physical educators, and even our poets have proclaimed that there is more to fitness than muscle strength. A conference of such people in 1956 described fitness as "that state which characterizes the degree to which the person is able to function" (AAPHER 1956). It implies the ability of each person to develop most effectively his or her potentialities. And the conference agreed that fitness is maintained at a high level only if motivation is present continuously. This requires an inner desire — an egogenic stimulation. The activities that produce fitness must have meaning! The conference listed seven components of fitness, all of which are related to each other and are mutually interdependent. These are:

1. Optimum organic health consistent with heredity and the application of present health knowledge.
2. Sufficient coordination, strength, and vitality to meet emergencies, as well as the requirements of daily living.
3. Emotional stability to meet the stresses and strains of modern life.
4. Social consciousness and adaptability with respect to the requirements of group living.
5. Sufficient knowledge and insight to make suitable decisions and arrive at feasible solutions to problems.
6. Attitudes, values, and skills that stimulate satisfactory participation in a full range of daily activities.
7. Spiritual and moral qualities that contribute to the fullest measure of living in a democratic society.

TRAINING VS. EDUCATING

Now what does physical education have to do with fitness as described in those terms? The relationship to all seven is the only thing that makes physical education "education." Otherwise it would be physical training — and there is a vast and uncomfortable difference between the two!

In the somewhat peculiar and not clearly understood combination of words "physical education," the noun "education" becomes of great importance. It is not the same thing as training. Physical training trains, just as you train a dog or a pony. Kelley and Rasey (1956, p. 106) say:

> Much of our education is designed to train people rather than to educate them. When one individual trains another, he delimits the variety of possible respones, making the desired responses automatic and eliminating the possibility of other responses. We can train lower animals, but we cannot educate them. Training, limiting possible responses, is enslaving, while educating is liberating. It is not that one is trained not to think but that the act of training by its very nature delimits thinking. In the degree that the individual thus trained does think, he has been robbed of confidence in his own thinking.

But physical education implies that someone, somehow, is being educated, through the games, sports, and dance culturally important to our race (and it is important to know the difference).

To educate means to enrich the capacities of human intelligence. It means to help individuals gain increasing possession of themselves and their powers; it means to recapitulate their culture, to deepen and widen its social content, to give them control over the methods of living within that culture. Some would say that the essence of education is the development of intelligence, of powers of thought, of the capacity for reflection, of human reason. The task of education is to develop the fullest capacity to take thought, to reflect, to weigh, to foresee, to consider consequences, and to choose among alternatives. There may be other descriptions of education, but in the main, they all describe a relationship between the learners and their environment, in which the former is assisted to gain some personal control over, and understanding of, the latter by the cultivation of powers inherent within people. This is to make people fit in the terms the conference described. They learn to do this. They cannot do it as children, and as life goes on, they develop their powers to the point where they can. Hullfish (1961) adds this thought: "The term learning may then be applied to any process within which potential stimuli become meaningful, change meaning, are discriminated with respect to possible meaning, and the like."

If we view meanings as the basic building blocks of learning, then any event that results in a reconstruction or reorganization of a meaning pattern may be called a learning experience. Any experience, then, that in consequence of its meaningfulness "increases ability to direct the course of subsequent experience" may be called an educative experience.

EDUCATING THROUGH THE PHYSICAL

Now if physical education means that someone is educated through or by the "physical" experience, or in a "physical" environment, then the experience

12

should be productive of the qualities described in the definitions. Can this happen? Does this happen? By accident, or by design? Maybe it is that no education at all takes place through the physical education experience, at least in these terms. Perhaps this is not what the term physical education is meant to imply. Perhaps the only relation physical education has to education is that experience in physical education so conditions the organism that it can receive the stimuli that permit the student to become educated! This is the idea of the sound body in which to house the sound "mind." This is the ancient dichotomous view. This belies man's unity. To many persons in physical education and to many from other fields, other values from the physical education experience all loom larger and more important than the educational ones. Physical values come first—educational values are a poor second, and only if something good happens to come along.

It should be clear, however, that if that point of view is held, then it is hypocritical to use the term physical education. The term should be physical training, or physical exercise, or some other term to describe what is happening. If "education" is the noun used, then a clear, reasonable, and demonstrable relationship to its substance must be developed in the physical education curricula. Someone must be educated. Educational outcomes must be sought, planned for, taught for, and obtained. They must be of prime concern, not secondary or incidental within a physical education program.

What kinds of outcomes could be considered educational? What experiences in physical education programs will be likely to cultivate this intelligence, develop this ability to think, to weigh, to reckon consequences, to assume possession of one's self and one's powers, and to become a rational person?

The answer is inherent in the questions. Only those experiences that demand thinking will produce thinking! Only the kind of participation that requires the student to weigh, to reflect, and to study will produce those qualities. It will not be likely that they will be produced by the kind of activity in which the participating individual does not become involved in some problem requiring solving, evaluating, and thinking. Can a team have the chance to solve some of its own problems or must the coach always direct the strategy and call the plays? Can a class become involved in seeking desirable outcomes from its work? Is social, religious, and racial integration of consequence to students? What responses can be developed to cheating, sportsmanship, values in athletics, and to appreciation of good play?

Experience in a well-conceived physical education program can aid in the solution of such problems. The understanding of integrative proceses and the relationship of the physiological, pscyhological, and other functional elements to development can be enhanced through physical education. Comprehension of strength, ability, courage, daring, and skill can be developed. One makes progress in the solution of such developmental tasks as achieving skill in motor control and coordination, independence in self-care, learning to live in groups, and in relation to competitors.

An analysis of the effects of these experiences from physical education relate directly to the stated components of fitness, and this kind of physical education has an important relation to fitness and health.

But, let us go one step further. There is, perhaps, no more compelling problem facing our educational system than that of deepening and widening our understanding of democracy. Presidents have said that our young people must be physically, mentally, and spiritually prepared for American citizenship. This seems to relate to components 4 and 7 from the conference report—social adaptability and qualities that make it possible to live in a democratic society.

How do you go about developing these qualities? By marching, drilling, exercising in groups and mobs under the impersonal supervision of an authoritarian drill master who counts the numbers while the victims pray they may be spared further boredom and, when released from it, vow never to have anything to do with physical exercise the rest of their lives? This is hardly a satisfying experience in adaptability to group living; hardly productive of the spiritual and moral qualities needed to live successfully in a democracy! This sort of thing may produce some muscular strength temporarily, but it is also very likely to produce emotional and perhaps even spiritual trauma.

POLITICAL IMPLICATIONS

To preserve the democratic way, to bring the oncoming generations into a clear understanding of its meaning, to develop a deep and unmistakable sensitivity to what democracy really is—this is a compelling challenge. The program of physical education cannot afford to be caught napping in this respect; nor can it be found guilty of teaching by precept or practice the ways of behaving and thinking that are characteristic of authoritarian regimes.

We have said that schols in general and physical education programs in particular have always been used as instruments of political and social power. One shudders at the memory of marching Hitler youth—fit, strong, singing their way through exercises and sports so they could better reflect the marching ruthlessness of the most inhuman regime the 20th century has known.

What social and political purpose, then, does 20th-century American physical education serve? It cannot be culturally neutral. Opportunities abound in the physical education program to provide experience with democratic processes. It should be said clearly and understood clearly that as long as physical education remains an element in the curriculum of a school or college dedicated to the perpetuation of the democratic way, no teaching or administrative practice may, with conscience, demonstrate other and contrary values. The autocratic empirical administrator is as bad as the authoritarian teacher or coach. Each is a menace, in his or her own way, to the planned intellectualized approach to the perpetuation of democracy through the schools.

In some programs, the students all wear the same kind of uniform, go through the same exercises, count the same cadence as they march, respond with the same imposed replies, and affect the same posturing as they go through their exercises. They conform. The standard is set. The motive comes from outside, from above. It takes no intellectual response to "count off" and to wave one's arms about in a calisthenic drill aimed at "physical condition."

It does, however, require self-initiated intellectual response to figure out the strategy of a game and execute it. Or to compose a dance, or to plot a course for an overnight hike. It requires self-initiated activity to practice what one has been shown on how to swim or how to kick a soccer ball. This type of activity must come from within, and be chosen willingly as a rewarding experience. This sort of activity is within the cultural tradition of a free people.

THE CHALLENGE

The opportunity is here. Modern physical education can serve as an educative experience or it can renounce its claims to education frankly and honorably and direct its energies to producing the sound body in which to house the sound mind. There is something pathetically unscientific about that effort, but there is nothing dishonorable in it—except that it must not use the term physical education.

But to seek the integrative development of the whole person, to be as concerned with one's ethics as with one's physiology, to be helpful in one's interpretations of motives, to aid people in understanding of human nature, to help explore those deep wells of yearning within oneself, to help people see that excellence is not measured wholly by scores—these are some of the other outcomes within the reach of a well-planned physical education curriculum.

And so we, at any rate, believe the role of physical education in health and fitness is clear and important. It is indispensable to both. Physical training, on the other hand, or merely muscle exercises for strength alone, may, paradoxically, be destructive of the many things they are designed to help. By their sheer meaninglessness and potential for boredom, and because they are almost invariably terminal experiences, and because they offer no intrinsic appeal, they may be so regarded by self-directing individuals as to drive them away from any desire to be fit or from any practice that may contribute to their fitness.

We must be careful, not merely, enthusiastic. Not just any activity as long as it produces sweat and strength is educative in the rational interpretation of that word. From modern physical education programs, we expect lasting values in continuous participation—an accumulation of "fitness scores" is not only insignificant compared to this but may actually be defeating this goal.

REFERENCES

AAHPER, 1956. Report on AAHPER fitness conference. *JOHPER* **27** (September) : 8.

Hullfish, H. G., and P. G. Smith, 1961. *Reflective thinking: the method of education.* New York: Dodd, Mead.

Kelley, E. C., and M. I. Rasey, 1956. *Education and the nature of man.* New York: Harper.

3

Modern Philosophy of Physical Education

Leona Holbrook

The old idea of philosophy as the "love of wisdom" has modern and expanded meanings. Wisdom through modern education and for life must be developed by reasoned thought, pursued by mentally capable persons, directed by personal and professional self-discipline, and predicated upon natural and social cause and effect relationships.

Philosophy can be related to the nature of man and the universe and can be based upon logical and empirical analysis. Philosophy can be critical and analytical of beliefs, concepts, and formulas prior to the action; and philosophy *must* be critical and analytical of action itself to determine the results of ideas, knowledge, motives, plan, and performance.

In life, in education, and in physical education, philosophy includes the motivating and evaluating concepts or principles that anticipate and guide the action; and the philosophy of physical education must be a synthesis of the results and the learned experience of the physical education action itself.

A philosophy for physical education may thus be a conceptualization and formulation for the teaching and learning process and may be an interpretation of favorable results of programs and activities in the field.

What may be taught and what has been learned in physical education may be identified, characterized, and perhaps classified. A modern definition of philosophy will clearly characterize physical education in which there is knowledge, plan, process, and appraisal. Philosophy is "the rational investigation of the facts and principles of being, knowledge, or conduct" (Random House Dictionary 1966, p. 1082). "Being," "knowledge," and "conduct" describe the concentration of the performer who is engaging in the major categories of activities that may be included in physical education: dance, gymnastics, team and individual sports, aquatics, intramural sports, interschool and intercollegiate athletics, and others.

DEFINITION OF PHYSICAL EDUCATION

Physical education is an instructional program of selected and planned activities in an educational setting employing knowledge and skill in physical or motor performance. Emphasis will be given to physical education as a program of planned activities for physical education objectives, coordinated with the aims of general education in its progress toward general and specific ends for life adjustment and life uses.

AIMS OF PHYSICAL EDUCATION

Those who philosophize within the field of physical education usually consider that "aims and objectives," though stated together, mean two different things. "Aims" constitute broad general classifications, or ways to go, and may not be unique to physical education at all. Aims may be broad concepts of human good or action along which all education is directed and toward which physical education can make its contributions in the same broad ways as do the other subject matter or laboratory courses. These aims may be found in statements of the National Education Association, the Cardinal Principles of Education (1918), the Educational Policies Statement (1944), the Statement of the Commission on Life Adjustment (1945), or the Imperatives in Education (1966). These aims do not call specifically upon any one of the fields, yet they depend for their realization upon all of the fields, including health, physical education, and recreation. Some of the oft-stated aims of education and the most frequently stated aims of physical education with an updating in current thinking may be summarized as: 1) to help each individual to come to an optimum performance within his or her capacity; 2) to give each person a sense of wholeness and completeness in existence and accomplishment; 3) to aid each individual in his or her self-development and sense of self-worth; 4) to help the individual to develop socially; 5) to help the individual in the development of standards and the establishment of needs and wants and their fulfillment; 6) to help the individual develop and maintain a sense of well-being, enjoyment, and participation; 7) to give the individual the skill, knowledge, and experience for creative, aesthetic, productive expression; 8) to prepare the individual for responsibility; and 9) to qualify the individual to meet change.

Cowell and Schwehn (1958) summarize the aims of education as seen through the eyes of physical education in the statement:

> Physical education activites have a real potential for contribution to general education . . . We have a special responsibility to contribute through physical education to . . . development . . . in the following: 1) to secure and maintain a condition of personal good health and fitness; 2) to develop effective ways of thinking; 3) to include desirable social attitudes; 4) to cultivate useful work habits and study skills; 5) to acquire a wide range of significant interests; 6) to develop an increase of appreciation of the dance, music, literature, art and other aesthetic experiences; 7) to develop social sensitivity and better personal-social relationships; 8) to use leisure in right ways; and 9) to acquire important information to develop a consistent philosophy of life.

The aims together may be briefed as: to develop the individual, to develop and sustain the society and democracy, and to prepare persons to live in a world of responsibility, concern, and ethical interdependence.

OBJECTIVES OF PHYSICAL EDUCATION

An objective is a goal to reach; an objective is intended attainment or accomplishment. Objectives are not aims or principles or guideposts. The words "objective" and "goal" may be used synonymously in discussing the teaching-learning acts in physical education. "Goal" is well understood by those who participate in or watch basketball and soccer-type games; a goal is an objective. Any currently stated, well-thought-out and presented statement of objectives for education can be developed and applied to objectives for physical education. Such a statement can be interpreted into structured situations for physical education teaching and learning.

General Objectives

Philosophic thinking that relates to physical education goes to the beginning of humans on the earth and their thinking in relation to their position as humans upon the earth. Part way along the continuum of time Plato said, "The results of a good physical education are not limited to the body alone, but may extend even to the soul itself." Plato as philosopher was stating the clear possibility of an objective for physical education.

Objectives within the profession for program offerings deal with the provision of facilities, the maintenance of equipment and service, the nature and quality of instruction, class size, the classification of students, the provision of auxiliary health services through examination and therapy, the intramural and extramural offerings, the intercollegiate program, the health instruction program, and the planned recreation programs.

The stated objectives for student attainment are conceived and planned by students and members of the profession. Professional views of quality have been evolved and philosophic backgrounds and program development presented in all of the areas of service within the larger discipline of physical education, which encompasses dance, school physical education, men's and boys' athletics, women's and girls' athletics, sports medicine, kinesiology, the professional education program for major students, graduate education, research, education of the mentally retarded, lifetime sports, and others.

The physical educator, in any and every assignment, must establish objectives with the participants. If the objectives are to be reached, participants must know of them, must share in setting the objectives, and must pursue the course of action and be committed to the progress that moves them toward the objectives.

Specific Objectives

In a democracy that allows for freedom and for individual, social, and professional responsibility, there are some varying interpretations of the stated objectives of physical education:

1. Organic power and vigor. Participants in a good physical education program should recognize in themselves organic power and vigor. They should realize that development has occurred through regular active participation in a planned program. They should be aware of good bodily function and an increase in energy with a decrease in fatigue even though they may perform more actively and meet more physical demands. They should be aware that they have more strength, greater endurance, and a heightened ability to resist fatigue. They should value power and vigor as sustaining qualities in life and to the contributions these qualities can make to others and to the country.

2. Neuromuscular skill. Skills should be improved in accuracy and increased in number as a result of a good physical education program. The learner must be taught by one who knows the correct skills for performance and who knows, in addition, how to teach those skills. Learning a skill is more than trial and error and imitation. A skill is learned by concept, correct techniques, and by trial and success. The rhythm, timing, reaction time, strength, speed, range of movement, flexibility, strategy, and learned skill of an activity are a gratification to the learner. Skills in sports and activity are of consequence in personal life and are of value for social entry into a society where sport is a dominating prestigious factor for most of life's activities of a social consequence. People will enjoy what they learn to do well. A specific objective of physical education is sufficient neuromuscular skill to prepare people to participate and to continue in activities they perform well and enjoy.

3. Knowledge and attitudes of personal and social consequence. Through a variety of well-conducted physical education activities participants gain some knowledge of themselves, their abilities, limitations, responsibility for their own progress and development, capacities compared with others, the need for independent action and relationships in cooperation, rivalry, interdependence, and competition. The well-planned and conducted program in physical education provides frequent and recurrent opportunities for individuals to develop self-confidence, to express sociability, to show initiative, to manifest self-direction, or to be sustained by a feeling of belonging.

4. Knowledge and attitudes of educative life worth. Individuals through a well-conceived, well-conducted program of physical education may develop interpretive ability and problem-solving powers. Situations that are governed by rules and choices and are directed by customs of rightness and interpretations of fairness or sportsmanship or loyalty, become part of the strong and positive educational force for good through the activities of physical education. A program of active participation should allow for and develop active imagination with originality and creativity.

5. Habits and attitudes toward endeavor and continuing participation. The learnings of physical education with its subdivisions and its related fields of health education and recreation education are for life applications. These applications make a persistent demand for immediate and continuous use. The lessons of the course are not ones to be stored up as money to be put into an annuity to be pulled out at retirement, nor are they insurance to be drawn on when normal functions have failed. The lessons of health education, physical education, and recreation education call for participants to be committed to the experience, to be self-directed toward the objective, to find a way to make a positive evaluation of the effort and the outcome, and to re-align themselves with a continuing direction and effort. Participants need to find their own satisfactions and joy in effort, in accomplishment, and in self. They need to live a little for leisure and to let leisure put some motivations and reasons for living into their lives.

STATEMENT OF THE SOCIETY OF STATE DIRECTORS OF HEALTH, PHYSICAL EDUCATION, AND RECREATION

1. *The Comprehensive School Health Program* (Society of State Directors, 1973)

Administration and Organization—The comprehensive school health education program should include a planned, sequential series of experiences in health and safety education at each grade level. . . . Health topics in other subject areas are desirable but should be correlated . . . and . . . never be substituted for direct health instruction.

Curriculum—The curriculum should be directly related to the needs, problems, and interests appropriate for the growth, development, and maturity level of each student involved.

School Health Services—It is essential, in meeting the educational and health needs of children and youth, to secure information through health appraisals of their physical, mental, and emotional status.

Healthful School Living—A properly equipped health service unit, with separate rest and isolation rooms for boys and girls, should be available. All school personnel should have periodic health examinations.

Personnel—Elementary teachers should have specific preparation . . . [for] competencies and understanding for effective health education . . . observing health status . . . referral . . . and follow-up. Teachers in the junior and senior high schools should be certified in health education.

2. *The Physical Education Program*

Class Instruction—Physical education is essential for all students from pre-kindergarten through grade 12. The daily instructional period for elementary school students (pre-K, K-6) should be at least 30 minutes in length, exclusive of time allotted for dressing, showering, recess, free and/or supervised play periods, and noon-hour activities.

The minimum instructional class period for middle schools and junior and senior high schools should be a standard class period daily, except where the length and frequency of the class periods are altered to offer students a more comprehensive program. Where modular or flexible scheduling is used, care should be taken to involve students in some combination of at least 300 minutes of physical education per week spread over three or more days.

All students in pre-kindergarten through twelfth grade should be scheduled for physical education according to physiological development, ability, interests, and individual needs.

Class size in physical education should be consistent with the activity being taught. Effective physical education instruction requires both large and small groups.

Program—Class instruction in physical education should provide a planned, balanced, varied progression of activities based upon needs, abilities, and interests of boys and girls at all developmental levels.

Evaluation of the curriculum by both students and teachers should be a continuous part of the program. Evaluation should be used to assess student progress toward stated goals, provide guidelines for adjusting current programs and planning new ones, and indicate needs for instructional improvement. Evaluation is an important means of interpreting the program to students and adults in order to improve community understanding of the values and outcomes of physical education.

Personnel—Certification standards for physical education personnel, consistent with general certification requirements, should be established and periodically reviewed by each State Department of Education. Increased interest and involvement in certification on the part of professional associations and teacher preparation institutions should be encouraged and welcomed.

Teacher aides, when utilized, should work under the direct supervision of a certificated physical education teacher and only in a supportive and supplementary capacity.

Elementary classroom teachers should have sufficient preparation and laboratory experiences in the basic skills, methods, and content to enable them to conduct an effective program under the guidance of a physical education specialist or supervisor and to relate the experiences in physical education to ongoing classroom instruction.

Extra-Class Activities—Extra-class activities should be provided for and financed by local boards of education. They should be administered by school officials, but community facilities and resource people should be utilized whenever the program can be improved through such measures. Extra-class competition should be as equal as possible based on the age, skill, size, and strength of participants. Education and development of the individual through satisfying and enjoyable participation in selected activities should be the primary objective of the program. Suitable activities should be conducted co-educationally for the development of wholesome boy-girl relationships.

The Interscholastic Athletic Program—The interscholastic athletic program should be provided for and financed by local boards of education with funds accountable through the general school budget. The program should be administered by school officials.

Interscholastic athletic leagues or conferences should be confined to pupils in grades 9-12. If middle school or junior high interscholastic sports programs are deemed necessary. AAHPERD guidelines for such programs should be followed closely. The interscholastic athletic program in all high schools should provide maximum opportunity for both boys and girls to participate in a variety of individual, dual, and team sports and should provide for different levels of size and ability. The high school athletic program for girls should be separate from the boys program and under the supervision of a woman physical education teacher.* Coaches should be certificated teachers, members of the school staff, and well-prepared for assuming their coaching responsibilities. Coaching certification is highly recommended.

3. *Recreation*

Administration and Organization—Schools have a basic responsibility to help the community develop awareness and understanding of the recreational

---

* *Editor's note:* This opinion may be at variance with recent Title IX requirements. Refer to Sections 3 and 7.

needs of its children, youth, and adults. The spirit of cooperation should pervade community relationships whether the schools are to be the central coordinating agency for recreation or whether they are to share responsibility with other legal jurisdictions in this enterprise. Schools should stimulate and effectuate teamwork and cooperation among the agencies and organizations concerned with developing community-wide recreation plans, in mobilizing existing school and community recreation facilities, and in the joint planning and financing of such facilities and programs in order to make efficient use of all available resources.

Program—The school curriculum should offer many opportunities for developing attitudes, understandings, knowledge, and skills that will lead to the wise use of off-the-job hours. Schools should provide planned experiences beyond the classroom, including outdoor education, in order to ensure maximum articulation between learning and recreational activities. Opportunities for children, youth, and adults to participate in a variety of the physical, aesthetic, cultural, and social aspects of recreation should be provided under school auspices.

Personnel—Continuing efforts should be made to convey to all teachers and administrators knowledge of the functional relationship between education and recreation through pre-service and in-service education. Schools should employ an adequate number of qualified recreation professionals, augmented by competent responsible paraprofessionals, aides, and volunteers, to conduct a broad program of recreation, including games and sports, aquatics, dance, music, art, crafts, dramatics, literary and other cultural pursuits, hobbies, camping and outing activities, and other forms of self-development and self-expression. Schools should provide continuing in-service education of such recreation personnel.

FAIR PLAY

Adrian C. Kanaar, M.D., explains that sport may serve well, or may be only a spectacle of questionable worth for the athlete (Kanaar 1971). Briefly paraphrased, he states that people love danger in sport but an acceptable sport should necessitate skill, require self-discipline, emphasize sportsmanship, and improve physical and mental development. Unacceptable sports brutalize physically or emotionally, endanger bystanders or imitators, and produce no mental or physical benefit.

Acceptable sports can be made unacceptable by foul play. amateur sport is that one participates for the love of the game and fair play, being judged on the basis of moral and ethical performance in human conduct and in the rule of the game.

Sport as activity and as competition calls for an attitude of mind marked by a spirit of truth and honesty with strict observance of all the rules, written and unwritten (French Committee for Fair Play 1972). Fair play begins with the strict observance of the written rule but carries respect for one's opponent and self-respect. It calls for measuring up to one's own moral standards. Fair play implies the sincere desire for one's opponent to be on equal terms with oneself, being scrupulous in regard to the means of winning, and resolutely and persistently refusing victory "at any price."

Fair play is individual or collective; it occurs before, during, or after the contest; it is matching comparable abilities; it is observance of the rule. Fair play can occur at any level of competition. It calls for the qualified and the champions to be good examples, anticipates that the loser should manifest high quality of conduct, expects that the disadvantaged will show themselves well as participants in fair play, considers that individuals or team members have equal responsibilities, asserts that "contact" sports are as subject to judgment as "distance" sports.

Responsibilities lie with players and athletes for self-respect, respect of the opponent, respect for the umpire or referee, respect for the public, and respect for the game. Responsibility for fair play lies with parents, teachers, sports leaders, referees and umpires, spectators and supporters, the press, radio and television, and lastly with public authorities.

For fair play to prevail, sport must be educational. Fair play is the very essence of sport.

REFERENCES

Cowell, C. C., and H. M. Schwehn, 1958. *Modern principles and methods in high school physical education,* pp. 15-16. Boston: Allyn and Bacon.

French Committee for Fair Play, 1972. Fair play. Paris: Place Fontenoy.

Kanaar, A. C., 1971. Sports: performance or spectacle. Unpublished paper.

Random House Dictionary of the English Language (unabridged edition), 1966, p. 1082. New York: Random House.

Society of State Directors, 1973. A statement of basic beliefs. *JOHPER* **44** (June) : 22-24.

4

Physical Education and Sport Philosophy: Foundations and Definitions

Earle F. Zeigler

Until most recently the term "physical education" was generally employed as a broad, inclusive term comprising the field of physical education, health education, safety education, athletics, recreation, and even dance education. In the early 1940s, after an extensive study of the literature, Cobb (1943, p. 6) stated that there were four basic beliefs about the place of physical education in education: 1) there is no place for physical education in education; 2) physical education is for the maintenance of health in order that students may carry on their intellectual work with the least strain; 3) physical education should develop students physically, mentally, and morally (mind-body dichotomy implied); and 4) physical education should contribute to the growth of the individual as an integrated personality by discovering the health, recreation, and personality needs of each student, and helping him or her to meet those needs through the program.

With beliefs 3 and 4 above, a "total fitness" concept is implied. It is true that modern man and woman have been much more successful than their uncivilized, prehistoric brothers and sisters in making an adjustment to their environment. They have had the experience of their forebears upon which to base their judgments underlying their actions. Their adjustment is dependent, however, upon complicated procedures. Their teeth depend upon the services of competent dentists. Often, their eyes must be aided through the competence of highly trained ophthalmologists, optometrists, and opticians. Highly

Some of this material has been taken from a paper entitled "Philosophical Perspective on the Future of Physical Education and Sport" in Raymond Welsh (ed.), *Physical Education: A View Toward the Future*. St. Louis: C. B. Mosby, 1977.

qualified medical doctors and surgeons preserve the health of their hearts, lungs, and other vital organs (even with transplants when necessary). Protruding neck, round shoulders, sagging abdomen, weakened back, pronated ankles, and foot problems are the results of modern society with its advanced technology. Muscles become weak, and the constant force of gravity exacts a toll upon the vertical human. Sedentary people's hearts pound wildly when they run 50 yards after a departing bus, or even when they climb a flight of stairs fairly rapidly.

Still further, modern men and women often have difficulty adjusting their elemental emotions to the habit patterns of "do's and don'ts" that represents today's civilization. When this occurs, and it seems to be happening with increased regularity, people crack under the strain and are referred to a physician, and perhaps a hospital, as victims of what has been designated as psychosomatic illness. The field of physical education, and those subfields related to it within the educational pattern, have an important role to fulfill. They can provide the health knowledge, the physical activity, and the recreational outlets whereby the boy and girl, and young man and woman, will learn how to take care of their bodies, how to use them effectively, and how to provide themselves with healthful recreational activities.

How, then, may physical education and sport be described from the standpoint of actual involvement? It can be exemplified by a child bouncing a ball on a school playground, an overweight adult doing a sit-up, or a high school girl taking part in educational dance. From another standpoint, sport and physical activity or education could be explained by a halfback scampering for the goal line in the Rose Bowl, boys and girls playing coeducational volleyball in a church recreation room, or a high school boy pinning his opponent in an interscholastic wrestling match. Even further, a doctor of philosophy candidate might be analyzing the contents of a Douglas gas bag full of a runner's expired air in an exercise physiology laboratory in a physical education department, or a housewife might be trying out rhythmic exercises —any or all of these activities described could well be designated as aspects of physical education and sport.

SIX MEANINGS OF PHYSICAL EDUCATION

The ambiguity of the term "physical education" may be clarified by approaching it from another direction (and the same could be done for the term "sport"). An extension of Frankena's categorization (1965, p. 6) transposed from an analysis of the meanings of the term "education" indicates that physical education may mean any one of six things:

1. The *subject-matter,* or a part of it (e.g., tennis or some other sport or active game; some type of physical activity involving exercise such as

jogging or push-ups; a type of dance movement or activity; movement with purpose relating to these three types of activities).

2. The *activity of physical education* carried on by teachers, schools, parents, or even by oneself.

3. The *process of being physically educated* (or learning) that goes on within the make-up of the pupil or child (or person of any age).

4. The *result,* actual or intended, of 2 and 3 taking place through the employment of that which comprises 1 above.

5. The *discipline,* or field of enquiry, in which people study and reflect on all aspects of 1, 2, 3, and 4 above; that which is taught (the "body-of-knowledge" emanating from scholarly investigation in the social science, humanities, and natural science aspects of physical education and sport) in departments, schools, and colleges of physical education.

6. The larger *profession* whose members employ 1 above; practice 2; try to observe 3 taking place; attempt to measure or evaluate whether 4 has taken place; and base their professional practice on the body of knowledge developed by those undertaking scholarly and research developed by those undertaking scholarly and research effort in the discipline 5.

(See Zeigler 1975, p. 425; this was adapted originally from Frankena 1965, p. 6, and extended from four to six definitions or meanings. The reader should also see Zeigler and VanderZwaag 1968, p. 8, for an earlier version.)

A PLETHORA OF OBJECTIVES

However the field is designated or defined, there can be no argument with the statement that its earlier twentieth-century leaders made a great many—often unverifiable—educational claims for it over the years. Notable among these leaders who defined a variety of objectives, starting in the early 1920s and extending into the 1950s, were Hetherington (1922), Bowen and Mitchell (1923), Wood and Cassidy (1927), Williams (1927), Hughes, with Williams (1930), Nash (1931), Sharman (1937), Wayman (1938), Esslinger (1938), Staley (1939), McCloy (1940), Clark (1943), Cobb (1943), Lynn (1944), Brownell and Hagman (1951), Scott (1951), Bucher (1952), and Oberteuffer (1951).

Hess (1959) assessed the objectives of American physical education from 1900 to 1957 in the light of certain historical events. These were: 1) the hygiene or health objectives (1900-1919); 2) the socio-educational objectives (1920-1928); 3) the socio-recreative objectives, including the worthy use of leisure (1929-1938); 4) the physical fitness and health objective (1939-1945); and 5) a total fitness objective, including the broader objectives of international understanding (1946-1957).

It seems logical that the profession should now plan for the possible achievement of a significant amount of consensus among the various philosophies of physical education and sport extant in the Western world. Further, continuing efforts should occur toward a similar type of consensus with countries of the Eastern world (as is occurring to a limited extent through the agency of the Philosophic Society for the Study of Sport and the International Council for Health, Physical Education, and Recreation, for example). Possible common denominators are as follows:

1. That regular physical education and sport periods should be required for all school children through 16 years of age.

2. That a young person should develop certain positive attitudes toward his or her own health in particular and toward community health in general. Basic health and safety knowledge should be taught in the school curriculum.

3. That physical education and competitive sport can make a contribution to the worthy use of leisure.

4. That physical vigor is important for people of all ages.

5. That boys and girls at some stage of their development should have an experience in competitive athletics.

6. That therapeutic exercise should be employed to correct remediable physical defects.

7. That character and/or personality development may be fostered through physical education and sport. (See Zeigler in Welsh 1977, pp. 59-60 for an elaboration of these proposed common denominators. The above are listed also in Zeigler 1977b, p. 4).

HISTORICAL BACKGROUND AND PERSPECTIVE

To achieve a better understanding of physical education and sport, we may gain truer perspective by viewing the question historically. There have been a number of attempts to define the nature of man and woman on a rough historical time scale. Van Cleve Morris (1956) presented a five-fold chronological series of definitions including analyses as: 1) a rational animal, 2) a spiritual being, 3) a receptacle of knowledge, 4) a mind that can be trained by exercise, and 5) a problem-solving organism. Within such a sequential pattern, the task of the field of physical education (and sport) could well be to help this problem-solving organism move efficiently and with purpose in such aspects of people's lives as sport, dance, play, and exercise. Such experience would, of course, occur within the context of people's socialization in an evolving world (Zeigler 1975, p. 405).

Then, in the mid-1960s, Berelson and Steiner (1964, pp. 662-667) traced six images of man and woman throughout recorded history, but more from the standpoint of behavioral science than Morris's philosophically oriented definitions. The first of these was the so-called *Philosophic Image,* in which men and women of the ancient world distinguished virtues through the employment of reason. This was followed by what was termed the *Christian Image,* which included the concept of "original sin" and possible redemption through the transfiguring love of God for those who controlled their sinful impulses. The third delineation was the *Political Image* of men and women during the Renaissance, in which they, through the introduction of their powers and wills, managed to take greater control of the social environment. In the process, sufficient energy was liberated to bring about numerous political changes, the end result being the creation of embryonic national ideals that co-existed with somewhat earlier religious ideals. During the eighteenth and nineteenth centuries, an *Economic Image* emerged that provided an underlying rationale for economic development in keeping with the possession of property and manufactured or crafted items along with improved monetary standards. There were early efforts to equate the concept of "individual good" with that of the "common good." At the same time, the third basic political division, class, was more sharply conceived.

The early twentieth century saw the development of a fifth *Psycho-analytic Image* that introduced another form of love—that for the ego (self). The instinctual impulses were being delineated more carefully than ever before. An effort was made to understand the role of childhood experiences in people's lives, and how these and other nonconscious controls often ruled actions because of the frequently incomplete gratification of basic human drives related to libido and sex. Finally, because of the rapid development of the behavioral sciences, Berelson and Steiner postulated the *Behavioral Science Image* of man and woman. This view characterizes the person as a creature who is continually and continuously adapting reality to his or her own ends. In this way, the individual is seeking to make reality more pleasant and congenial—to the greatest possible extent of the person's own reality.

PRIMITIVE PHYSICAL EDUCATION

It is true that physical activity has been a basic part of the fundamental pattern of living of every creature of any type that has ever lived on earth. Despite this fact, those who have written about history, including the history of education, appear to have slighted "physical culture" consistently (perhaps through bias). Woody (1949, p. vii) tells us that "lip-service has been paid increasingly to the dictum 'a sound mind in a sound body,' ever since western Europe began to revive the educational concepts of the Graeco-Roman world," but that "there is still a lack of balance between physical and mental culture."

The condition of their bodies must have always been of concern to men and women. In primitive society, there appears to have been very little organized, purposive instruction in physical education, although early men and women knew that a certain type of fitness was necessary for survival. The usual activities of labor, searching for food, dancing, and games were essential to the development of superior bodies. With physical efficiency as a basic survival need, people's muscles, including their hearts, had to be strong; their vision had to be keen; and they had to be able to lift heavy loads and occasionally to run fast.

Even if it were an objective, it would not have been possible to separate completely the physical and mental education of primitive youth. The boy and girl underwent informal apprenticeships that prepared them for life's various physical duties. A great deal of learning occurred through trial and error, and also through imitation. Tradition and custom were highly regarded, and the importance of precept and proper example were basic aspects of both physical and mental culture.

Testing in early societies was carried out through various initiatory ceremonies designed to given young men (and occasionally young women) the opportunity to evaluate themselves in the presence of their peers and elders. Almost all of the education was informal, and such an educational pattern followed typically the same traditions and customs from generation to generation. The practical aspects of life were learned by doing them repeatedly, and strict discipline was often employed if the child was lazy or recalcitrant.

There was, of course, very little knowledge about sound health practices. Vigorous exercise undoubtedly did much to help early people remain healthy until disease or an accident occurred. The health care in infancy and in early youth was probably even more deficient typically than health practice followed by adults in the society.

In preliterate societies, there does not appear to have been as sharp a division between work and play (or labor and leisure) as is found later in civilized societies. Children had many play activities because they simply were not fully ready for the serious business of living. Their parents had very little leisure in a subsistence economy.

PERSISTENT SOCIAL FORCES

There were at least five, and possibly six, social forces that have influenced the field during various periods of history, including the present time (Brubacher 1966; Zeigler 1977a, pp. 6, 20-21). These persistent historical problems (social forces) will be described briefly, as well as ten others that have emerged more recently as concerns of physical educators.

1. Values and norms. The persistent problem of values and norms seems to possess a "watershed quality" in that an understanding of those objects and/or qualities desired by people through the ages can evidently provide significant insight into this particular problem—and also into most, if not all, of the other recurring problems that will be discussed. (A problem is used in this sense, according to its Greek derivation, would be "something thrown forward" for people to understand or resolve.) Throughout history, there have been innumerable statements of educational aims or values and, almost invariably, there was a direct relationship with a hierarchy of such values present in the society under consideration. Physical education and sport have been viewed as curricular, co-curricular, or extracurricular.

2. Politics. The influence of politics, or the type of political state, has affected the kind and amount of education present in the society. Education has varied depending upon whether a particular country was a monarchy, an aristocratic oligarchy, or some form of democracy. A philosophically pro-gressivistic educational approach, applicable to the subjects of school health, physical education and sport, and recreation, can flourish only in a type of democratic society. Conversely, a philosophically essentialistic or tradition-alistic type of education, with its definite implications for physical education and sport, may be promoted successfully in any of the three types of political systems.

3. Nationalism. The influence of nationalism or patriotism on physical education and sport throughout history is obvious. If a strong state is desired, the need for a strong, healthy people is paramount. There have been many examples of this type of influence as far back as the Medes and Spartans, and as recently as some twentieth-century European and Asian powers.

4. Economics. The influence of economics has been most significant in that, throughout history, the field of education has prospered when there was a surplus economy and declined when the economic structure weakened. Educational aims have tended to vary depending upon how people made their money and created such surplus economies. Advancing industrial civili-zation has brought uneven distribution of wealth, which meant educational advantages of a superior quality to some. Education "of the physical" can be promoted under any type of economic system. In largely agrarian societies, much physical fitness can be gained simply through manual labor. In industrial societies, some means has to be developed whereby all will maintain a minimum level of physical fitness and health. The more individual freedom is encouraged in a society, the more difficult a government will find it to *demand* that all citizens be physically fit.

5. Religion. The influence of organized religion on education throughout history has been very strong, but there is evidence that the power of the church over the individual is continuing to decline in the twentieth century. In the Western world, the Christian religion should be recognized for the promulgation of principles in which men and women are considered valuable as individuals. Today a society needs to decide to what extent it can, or should, inculcate moral and/or religious values in its public schools. It seems reasonable to say that Christianity and Judaism have hampered the fullest development of physical education and sport, but it is true also that a number of religious leaders are at least partially revamping their earlier positions as they realize the potential of sport and physical activity as spiritual forces in people's lives.

6. Ecology. The influence of ecology has only been felt in a recognizable and significant way for the past five or ten years by North American society, so it is not unusual that very little attention has been paid to the environmental crisis by those in the field of sport and physical education. Although this problem has not been with us to a similar degree of intensity over the centuries as the five listed above, it now seems here to stay. Ecology is usually defined as the field of study that treats the relationships and interactions of human beings and other living organisms with each other and with the natural (or physical) environment in which they reside. Certainly all are aware of contradictory economic theories that appear daily in the press, but it is also obvious that very few people, relatively speaking, are aware of the collision course seemingly being taken if the ecological models have any validity at all. The physical educator/coach has a unique role to play in helping individuals to develop and maintain *physical* fitness within a concept of "total" fitness based on a goal of international understanding and brotherhood.

Whereas the persistent problems or social forces listed above influence all society, as well as the entire field of education, those included below have a much greater professional orientation for physical education and sport. Of course, these problems have also been influenced by various social forces.

1. Curriculum. A primary task in curriculum instruction is to determine which subjects should be included because of their *recurring* interest among educators and the public. Decisions must be made daily regarding the bases upon which a curriculum is selected. The curriculum has developed and expanded at a fantastic rate on this continent over the past two centuries, and many people now insist that this trend must be reversed so that the "essential" subjects can be taught adequately. The task of the physical educator/coach today is to ascertain the values that are uppermost in the society, and then to attempt to implement them to the greatest possible extent through the medium of sport and related physical activities.

2. Methods of instruction. We might argue that curriculum and method should go hand in hand if effective education is a desired end product. Initially, we should appreciate that effective methods of instruction involve more than merely what a teacher "does" to a subject matter. If we are talking about sport skills instruction in tennis, for example, the teacher needs to know how to teach tennis, what is taking place within the learner as he or she seeks to learn tennis from the instructor, and finally, what the end result is (i.e., what a learner does when he or she has learned to play the sport).

3. Professional preparation. Professional preparation of teachers to any considerable extent in the United States began in the late nineteenth century. Starting with the normal school, this educational unit has progressed in the twentieth century to college and/or university status. Throughout the world, generally speaking, professional preparation for physical education and sport is included at the normal and/or technical school level. University recognition was achieved first in the United States, and not until much later in Canada, where progress has been significant, however. More recently, Japan, England, and Germany have given the subject university status, and other countries in various parts of the world are following to a limited degree.

4. The healthy body. A study of past and present civilization indicates that the sociological states of war and peace produce quite different health emphases. When a country needs to win a war, freedom from disqualifying defects, strength, and endurance are important. During periods of peace, the emphasis in health can be placed on the related questions of longevity and environmental health. Much of the disagreement over the role that school health education should play in the educational pattern stems from differing educational philosophies and from the various concepts of health that prevail.

5. Women in physical education and sport. Throughout history, women's physical education and sport have been hampered, not only by the concept of the place of such activity in a society, but also by the place that women themselves held in most societies. It had been concluded erroneously that women simply did not possess the intellectual capacity to profit from the higher types of education. Certainly one of the significant trends of the twentieth century has been the social movement for women's liberation. The ultimate goal is, of course, an ideal program of physical education and sport at all levels for both males and females. The facts indicate that programs for both sexes of all ages should more nearly approximate each other in both scope and intensity.

6. Dance in physical education. In all ages, people have danced for personal pleasure, for religious purposes, for expression of the gamut of emotions, and for the pleasure of others. An analysis of the dance forms of a civilization can tell a qualified observer much about the total life of that society. The twentieth century has witnessed a truly remarkable development in the dance, as the body is being gradually rediscovered as a means of communication through the dance medium. As both an art and a social function, dance will probably always be with us, and will further reflect the dominant influence of the age in which it is taking place. In recent years on the North American continent, there have been varied opinions as to where a department or division of dance belongs on a campus. The usual place for dance instruction has been within the field of physical education, but there has been a move in some quarters to place dance under the aegis of the arts faculty.

7. Use of leisure. In primitive and preliterate societies, there probably was not so sharp a division between work and play as in civilized societies. Later, embryonic cultures developed certain folkways and ceremonials of a more controlled nature. Citizens in the industrialized world now have more leisure than ever before, although inflation is forcing many wives to seek work as well and husbands to take extra part-time jobs in addition to their regular employment. The promotion of the concept of "education for leisure" depends a great deal on whether the prevailing educational philosophy will allow sufficient support for the inclusion of such programs in the educational system. What we decide as professionals, and what others will accept, will exert a considerable influence on the place of physical activity and sport in our educational systems and, subsequently, in the leisure patterns of our communities at large for our mature citizens.

8. Amateur and professional sport. Sport (sometimes viewed as a pleasurable diversion) and athletics (a highly competitive activity) are both parts of the very lifeblood of our field and offer the possibility of great benefits and satisfaction to participant, spectator, and coach alike. Primitive and preliterate peoples undoubtedly felt the urge to play, and they often took part in games as part of religious observances. There is no denying that sport gave them the opportunity to practice skills upon which they relied for survival. Even in the earlier days, the aspect of overspecialization because of the desire to win has tended to tarnish the luster of the concept known as the "amateur ideal." There is an urgent need today for recognition of a semiprofessional category. There is a need further for professional athletes who will recognize the need to devote their lives to a social idea—to serve others through their contributions to the many phases of sport's development.

9. The role of administration (management). Social organizations of one type or another are inextricably related to men's and women's history as

human and social animals. Superior-subordinate relationships evolved according to the very nature of reality. We are now facing a situation in which a
steadily growing percentage of the personpower available has been necessary
to cope with the management of the efforts of the large majority of the people
in our society—a development that has been called the "Administrative
Revolution." Within this development, education has become a vast public
and private enterprise demanding wise management based upon administrative theory. In many educational institutions the administration of physical
education and athletics is now big business within big education, and the
same can be said for the management of professional athletics and professional
exercise establishments on a private basis. Unfortunately, there is practically
no theory that is tenable, and there is very little ongoing research about the
administrative task within this field.

10. The concept of "progress." This persistent problem can be viewed either
as a social force (influence) or as a professional concern, or as both! It relates
closely to the values that a society holds for itself. Any study of history
inevitably forces a person to conjecture about human progress. Certainly
there has been progression, but can this be called progress unless it is based
on an acceptable criterion? Further, it is doubtful whether we as humans can
be both judge and jury in this matter. In the field of physical education and
sport, we must search for agreement and the greatest possible consensus
among the conflicting positions or philosophical stances extant today. There
are certainly some common denominators that can be recommended at this
time based on the specialized fields of physical education and sport, health,
and safety education, and recreation education (i.e., the general education of
citizens for creative recreational participation).

THE REASONS FOR PHYSICAL EDUCATION AND SPORT PHILOSOPHY

No matter where you may travel on the North American continent, teachers
and parents, both individually and collectively, often express sharply divided
opinions as to what should be included in the curriculum. Health, physical
education, and recreation, not to mention competitive sports, are right in the
middle of this controversy. How should children and young people be
educated for the prevailing social conditions? Should education—and hence
physical education and sport—be "progressive," "somewhat progressive," or
should it deal exclusively with the "essential studies" that are time-proven?
Thus, physical education and sport may be viewed as curricular, co-curricular
(not a good term), or extracurricular. A possible desirable plan is to work for
an acceptable consensus that brings common sense and tradition into alignment with the results of available scientific knowledge. Then the philosophic
process, albeit a process that is defined in various ways, could be employed

by philosophers and those functioning within the departmental subdivisions of this discipline. In the final analysis, the people will make what they feel are the necessary decisions within a democratic society. These judgments will be based on the prevailing system of values and norms.

A RECOMMENDED PROGRAM PRIMARILY FOR JUNIOR AND SENIOR HIGH SCHOOLS

A person examining or evaluating the physical education and athletics program of a junior or senior high school might consider asking questions about the following categories or subdivisions:

1. Aims and objectives. Physical education and sport—a way of education through purposeful human movement in sport, dance, play, and exercise—often involving vigorous, muscular activities selected with concern for the students' growth and developmental patterns.

Health education—includes experiences that contribute to students' health knowledge, habits, and attitudes.

Recreation—all those activities students engage in for enjoyment during their leisure time; the activities should be reasonably consistent with socially accepted values.

2. The medical examination. Assignment for physical education and sport should be made on the basis of an initial medical examination.

3. The classification of students. Classification serves individual needs, promotes fair competition between individuals and groups, facilitates instruction, assembles students of like interests as well as like abilities, and helps insure program progression and continuity from year to year.

4. The individual (therapeutic) program. Those with remediable physical defects should receive help in improving their condition if possible; some form of interesting modified sport activity should be provided where possible.

5. Health instruction. Aside from specific classes designed for health instruction, indirect instruction through example and practice can do much to influence sound health practices.

6. The conditioning program. If a student has not met the minimum standards of a physical education classification test, the general level of physical conditioning should be raised and maintained.

7. The sports instructional program. Students who pass the various aspects of a classification test should be encouraged to elect some sports or physical recreation activity (of both an indoor and outdoor nature) in which they will receive instruction within the physical education and/or physical recreation and intramurals departments.

8. The elective program. Election of course experiences should, in all probability, be introduced at some point in the latter half of the high school (and/or college years) in keeping with the findings of earlier classification tests; there should be definite instruction, supervision, and guidance if credit is to be granted for courses taken contributing toward a high school diploma or college degree. The university experiences would presumably be of an advanced nature if university credit is desired.

9. Physical recreation and intramurals. The assumption here is that every student should have an opportunity to take part in competitive sport and physical recreation on a voluntary basis.

10. Interscholastic (intercollegiate) athletics. As many young men and women as possible should be included in this phase of the program; participation gives an opportunity for "physical, mental, and social" development; skilled coaches with a sound educational background are absolutely necessary.

11. Evaluation and measurement. Evaluation based on personal improvement primarily is highly important. Such measurement should be closely related to stated aims and objectives.

DISCIPLINARY STATUS FOR PHYSICAL EDUCATION AND SPORT

In the 1960s, physical educators realized the need for the development of a body of knowledge through a greatly expanded program of scholarly endeavor and research in a variety of subdisciplines (Zeigler and McCristal 1967). Some of the field's scientists had realized this earlier, especially in the physiological areas and certain aspects of psychology. Relationships are gradually being strengthened with such fields as history, philosophy, sociology, social psychology, management theory, physiology, psychomotor learning, biomechanics and kinesiology, anthropology, political science, comparative and international education, and the health aspects of exercise and sport.

The effort to define the field as a discipline by the provision of a body of knowledge upon which the profession may practice may well assist men and women substantially to realize a truly wondrous future both on this planet and in space. The kinesiologists, exercise physiologists, psychologists, and sociologists within physical education and sport are gradually discovering how people move, what happens to them when they move in certain ways, and how this influences their social relations. However, it will be in the province of those interested in the historical, philosophical, and international aspects of physical education and sport to assist the profession to "contemplate the trajectory" of this field in the twenty-first century.

As the body of knowledge within physical education and sport increases, and inventories of scientific findings from the various subdisciplinary areas—and the related disciplines themselves—improve in both quantity and quality, it will become increasingly possible to verify whether a planned program of physical education and sport does actually result in the achievement of the many objectives that have been claimed over the years. Maybe then the field will be able to achieve a consensus on certain "common denominators" in the "education of an amphibian" (Huxley 1964). The field of physical education may eventually be called human motor performance, human kinetics, kinesiology, human movement, sport, or what have you. The important point to remember is that this field is unique. It is that field of endeavor which concerns itself exclusively with the analysis of human movement in sport, dance, play, and exercise. Because of this, it should have a significant role to play in the education of males and females of all ages.

REFERENCES

Berelson, B., and G. A. Steiner, 1964. *Human behavior: an inventory of scientific findings.* New York: Harcourt, Brace and World.

Bowen, W. P., and E. D. Mitchell, 1923. *The theory of organized play.* New York: A. S. Barnes and Co.

Brownell, C. L., and E. P. Hagman, 1951. *Physical education—foundations and principles.* New York: McGraw-Hill.

Brubacher, J. S., 1966. *A history of the problems of education.* (2nd ed.) New York: McGraw-Hill.

Bucher, C. A., 1952. *Foundations of physical education.* St. Louis: C. V. Mosby.

Clark, M. C., 1943. A philosophical interpretation of a program of physical education in a state teachers college. Ph.D. dissertation. New York: New York University.

Cobb, L. S., 1943. A study of the functions of physical education in higher education. Ph.D. dissertation. New York: Teachers College, Columbia University.

Esslinger, A. A., 1938. A philosophical study of principles for selecting activities in physical education. Ph.D. dissertation. Ames: Iowa State University.

Frankena, W. L., 1965. *Three historical philosophies of education.* Chicago: Scott, Foresman.

Hess, F. A., 1959. American objectives of physical education from 1900-1957 assessed in the light of certain historical events. Ed.D. dissertation. New York: New York University.

Hetherington, C., 1922. *School programs in physical education.* New York: Harcourt, Brace and World.

Huxley, A., 1964. *Tomorrow and tomorrow and tomorrow.* New York: New American Library.

Lynn, M. L., 1944. Major emphases of physical education in the United States. Ph.D. dissertation. Pittsburgh: University of Pittsburgh.

McCloy, C. H., 1940. *Philosophical bases for physical education.* New York: Appleton-Century-Crofts.

Morris, V. C., 1956. Physical education and the philosophy of education. *JOHPER* **27** (March) : 21-22, 30-31.

Nash, J. B. (ed.), 1931. *Mind-body relationships.* (Vol. I) New York: A. S. Barnes and Co.

Oberteuffer, D., 1951. *Physical education.* New York: Harper & Row. (The 4th edition of this book was published in 1970 with Celeste Ulrich as co-author.)

Scott, H. A., 1951. *Competitive sports in schools and colleges.* New York: Harper & Row.

Sharman, J. R., 1937. *Modern principles of physical education.* New York: A. S. Barnes and Co.

Staley, S. C., 1939. *Sports education.* New York: A. S. Barnes and Co.

Wayman, A. R., 1938. *A modern philosophy of physical education.* Philadelphia: W. B. Saunders Co.

Williams, J. F., 1927. *The principles of physical education.* Philadelphia: W. B. Saunders Co. (The 8th edition of this book was published in 1964.)

————, and W. L. Hughes, 1930. *Athletics in education.* Philadelphia: W. B. Saunders Co.

Wood, T. D., and R. Cassidy, 1927. *The new physical education.* New York: Macmillan.

Woody, T., 1949. *Life and education in early societies.* New York: Macmillan.

Zeigler, E. F., 1975. *Personalizing physical education and sport philosophy.* Champaign, Ill.: Stipes.

————, 1977a. Philosophical perspective on the future of physical education and sport. In R. Welsh (ed.), *Physical education: a view toward the future.* St. Louis: C. V. Mosby.

————, 1977b. *Physical education and sport philosophy.* Englewood Cliffs, N.J.: Prentice-Hall.

————, and K. J. McCristal, 1967. A history of the Big Ten Body-of-Knowledge Project in Physical Education. *Quest,* Monograph 9 (December) : 79-84. NAPECW and NCPEAM.

————, and H. J. VanderZwaag, 1968. *Physical education: progressivism or essentialism?* (2nd ed.) Champaign, Ill.: Stipes.

SUGGESTED READINGS

Broekhoff, J., 1972. Physical education and the reification of the human body. In P. J. Galasso (ed.), *Proceedings, Second Canadian Symposium on the History of Sport and Physical Education.* Ottawa: Fitness and Amateur Sport Directorate.

Davis, E. C., and D. M. Miller, 1967. *The philosophic process in physical education.* (2nd ed.) Philadelphia: Lea & Febiger.

Felshin, J., 1967. *Perspectives and principles for physical education.* New York: Wiley. Gerber, E. W., 1966. Three interpretations of the role of physical education, 1930-1960: C. H. McCloy, J. B. Nash and J. F. Williams. Ph.D. dissertation. Los Angeles: University of Southern California.

Hellison, D. R., 1973. *Humanistic physical education.* Englewood Cliffs, N.J.: Prentice-Hall.

Metheny, E., 1965. *Connotations of movement in sport and dance.* Dubuque, Iowa: Wm. C. Brown.

Morland, R. B., 1958. A philosophical interpretation of the educational views held by leaders in American physical education. Ph.D. dissertation. New York: New York University.

Osterhoudt, R. G., 1971. A descriptive analysis of research concerning the philosophy of physical education and sport. Ph.D. dissertation. Urbana: University of Illinois.

Sanborn, M. A., and B. G. Hartman, 1970. *Issues in physical education.* (rev. ed.) Philadelphia: Lea & Febiger.

Shepard, N. M., 1960. *Foundations and principles of physical education.* New York: Ronald Press.

Steinhaus, A. H., 1963. *Toward an understanding of health and physical education.* Dubuque, Iowa: Wm. C. Brown.

VanderZwaag, H. J., 1962. Delineation of an essentialistic philosophy of physical education. Ph.D. dissertation. Ann Arbor: University of Michigan.

———, 1972. *Toward a philosophy of sport.* Reading, Mass.: Addison-Wesley.

Weiss, P., 1969. *Sport: a philosophic inquiry.* Carbondale, Ill.: Southern Illinois University Press.

Zeigler, E. F., 1964. *Philosophical foundations for physical, health, and recreation education.* Englewood Cliffs, N.J.: Prentice-Hall.

HISTORICAL
PERSPECTIVES

Introduction

Section 2 touches briefly on some historical aspects of physical education. The first chapter deals with history in general, while the remaining three chapters concentrate on selected areas of physical fitness, international relationships, and women in sport.

Moore and Trekell follow physical education in the United States from Colonial times to the present by delimiting time periods as follows: Colonial to 1900; 1900 to 1920; 1920 to 1940; and 1940 to the present. The advent of physical education in the public schools in placed in the 1900 to 1920 era. The period from 1920 to 1940 is identified as the era of great growth in sports competition. The period from 1940 to the present is, more or less, characterized as the "golden age" of physical education in the United States, not only from the point of view of greatly expanded school and community programs, but in teacher preparation as well. This period is characterized as one of application of the educational philosophy of physical education espoused by Oberteuffer in Chapter 2.

Cureton attributes much of the "modern" physical fitness movement in the United States to the needs of the military between 1940 and 1947. He chronicles the contributions of noted physical educators to the "war fitness movement." Interest in physical fitness waned for the next ten years but was rekindled with the publication of the Kraus-Weber report (see Section 5) and the reaction of President Eisenhower to it. The contributions that AAHPERD and the various Presidents' councils on physical fitness have made to the movement are discussed. Finally, the new national interest in physical fitness through participation in lifetime sports (discussed by Leonard in Chapter 1) is acknowledged.

Simri's main thesis is that the United States has been somewhat lacking in its interrelationships with other countries in the areas of physical education and sport. Until relatively recently, the United States, except for some women's organizations, has not participated actively in international physical education organizations and has tended to isolate itself in the area of sport. A major problem cited is the fact that the two major international sports—soccer and volleyball—are not among the three major American sports—football, basketball, and baseball. Although the chapter addresses itself mainly to the area of physical education and sports organizations, it does mention that in the historical "battle" among the physical education systems devised in Europe, the United States has tended to embrace the English system of sports rather than gymnastics as the basis for school physical education programs.

Cheska and Gerber trace women's entry into the sports world in the United States from about 1860 to the beginning of the twentieth century, and conclude that little activity of major consequence took place during that period. The women-in-sport movement really began to grow in the early twentieth century. However, serious sports competition for women was relegated largely to community organizations rather than the schools, since leading women physical educators had deemed intense athletic competition as inappropriate to the education of women in American society. The authors trace the gradual change in that philosophy, culminating in what might be called the present "revolution" in women's sports.

JSB

Section Editors

Dr. Asbury C. Moore, Jr., prior to his death in 1980, was a professor at the University of Illinois at Urbana-Champaign, where he also served as Associate Dean of Academic Affairs for the College of Applied Life Studies.

Dr. Moore was a leading scholar in the area of history and wrote numerous articles and has contributed to professional publications and books. He was a member of several organizations and served on NCPEAM and IAPER committees.

Dr. Marianna Trekell is an associate professor in the Department of Physical Education at the University of Illinois at Urbana-Champaign. She has also taught physical education in grades K-12 in public schools in Iowa and Ohio.

Dr. Trekell's primary area of interest is in the area of history, and she has written numerous articles and has contributed to professional publications and books. She is a member of several organizations and among other responsibilities has served as president of the NAPECW, co-president of the NAPEHE, president and treasurer of the MAPECW, and historian of the IAPER.

5

A Short History of American Physical Education

Asbury C. Moore and Marianna Trekell

THE COLONIAL PERIOD TO 1900

Immigrants to the New World (later to be called the United States of America) in the seventeenth century settled in the new land but held onto their "old" cultures. Their ways of living had been transmitted from one generation to the next and they carried these customs to their new homeland, establishing a pattern of living that maintained that a woman's place was in the home, that men toiled in conquering the land, and that children had some time to play. The agrarian, family-centered economic system of the times dictated the practicality of this pattern.

Most New Englanders, guided by their former customs, suppressed sports and frowned upon excessive merriment because the "law of God" would not support such a "wasting of time." In addition, in order to conquer the harsh frontier, there was little time for organized sports and leisure. Utilitarian objectives seemed to be the major reason for physical activity.

But as time passed and the wilderness was converted to villages, and as life became comparatively easy, the pioneers began to find time for some leisure activity. These activites centered around the work world and included barn and house raising, corn husking, log rolling, plowing bees, and so on. At the same time, some colonists engaged in recreational activities even though they were not related to the work code. Typical of these activities were amusement sports associated with inns and taverns. Although the tavern sports were forbidden by law, popular demand encouraged such activities as bear baiting, cockfighting, gander pulling, ratting, billiard games, card playing, quoits, bowls, and dancing. Children participating in recreational activities engaged in such games as kite flying, marbles, fives, rounders, hopscotch, running, and tag games. Sports of the day were very popular in the South, especially the English sport traditions that New England in general rejected.

Education in early Colonial America was left to parents and friends, but as the new landowners became better adjusted to life in the Colonies, efforts were put forth to build an educational program for the youth. Health and physical education were not included in the curriculum since the frontier society little understood their value. The idea of physical education as an essential part of American education was not considered until Noah Webster presented his views on the positive effects of physical education in 1790. From this beginning, some educators began to turn their attention to the importance of physical education in the schools.

From the War of 1812 to the Civil War, a variety of physical education programs were instituted in the schools. A significant first was the establishment of the Round Hill School in 1823 at Northampton, Massachusetts, which listed physical education as part of its curriculum. Its founders, Joseph Cogswill and George Bancroft, included "healthful sports and gymnastics" in the total school curriculum. In 1824, Dr. Charles Beck, a student of Jahn's German Gymnastic system, was hired as instructor of Latin and gymnastics at the school, thus becoming the first teacher of physical education in the United States (Van Dalen 1971, p. 378). Unfortunately, the school closed in 1834 due to financial difficulties.

During the period 1830 to 1860, enthusiastic advocates of various systems of physical education attempted to secure general adoption of their programs in the schools.

> The public schools showed little interest in physical education until the 1850's when some cities allowed a few minutes of calisthenics in the daily curriculum. In 1853, Boston became the first city to require daily exercise for school children. The Rincon School in San Francisco was notable not only for the time given to physical education, but also for the quality of the program conducted by its principal, John Swett, who came from New Hampshire in the Gold Rush. In 1860, Brooklyn, Hartford, and Cincinnati had school gymnasia in the high schools and pupils were given physical exercises (Van Dalen 1971, p. 378).

The types of gymnastics or physical training programs in the schools revolved more or less around the programs of the European systems. Concern for the specific needs of American youth, plus an evolving interest in the values of health and physical development, gave impetus to the early American programs. Prominent in this new movement were Catherine Beecher and Dio Lewis. In 1832 Beecher opened the Western Female Seminary in Cincinnati, offering calisthenics to her pupils, and published a book entitled *Course of Calisthenics for Young Ladies.* Lewis established a "new gymnastics" program that was incorporated in a number of schools, and in 1861 he opened in Boston the Normal Institute for Physical Education, the first teacher preparatory program of physical education. Supporting the need for the health and physical condition of college men, Amherst College employed Edward Hitchcock in 1861 as professor of hygiene and physical education and director of the first official department of physical education in an institution of higher education in the country. This program was established to correct the poor state of health and physical development of the students.

The passing of the Morrill Act of 1862, which required military instruction in all state colleges, affected physical education in the schools and colleges due to the inclusion of military drill as a form of physical activity. However, after the Civil War attention shifted to a strong emphasis toward physical exercise for the purpose of improving and maintaining a healthy body.

New systems of physical education were introduced with the programs of Dr. Edward Hitchcock at Amherst College and of Dr. Dudley A. Sargent at Harvard's Hemenway Gymnasium. These two programs were the principal American programs of physical education after the Civil War. The Sargent program placed special emphasis on educational, recreational, hygienic, and remedial values, while an interest in scientific measurement led to an anthropometric testing program (Weston 1962, p. 34). The Hitchcock program went far beyond exercising as he experimented with anthropometric testing to facilitate the development of a physical education program that would promote the physical development and health of the students (Weston 1962, p. 33).

With the growth of the several American systems of physical education during the last half of the nineteenth century and the widespread interest in German Gymnastics and Swedish Gymnastics, the latter being introduced in Washington, D.C., in 1883, leaders in physical education became concerned about the kinds of programs that should be incorporated into the school systems throughout the country. This led to what has been commonly referred to as the "battle of the systems." Arising out of the dilemma was the Boston Conference of 1889.

> [This conference] enabled the leaders in physical education to make comparison of the values of these systems to see if some agreement could be reached on the type of physical education program that would meet the needs and interests of the American people. At the conclusion of these meetings, it was the feeling by the more neutral leaders that each program had major weaknesses and that no one program was acceptable. The most valuable outcome of the Conference was a wholesome and enlightened attitude on the part of the leaders toward all the physical education programs considered important at that time (Weston 1962, p. 29).

As the battle of the systems was fermenting, many of the nation's leaders were becoming increasingly concerned about the poor health and fitness of

American youth. This led a number of states to pass laws requiring physical education in the schools. California in 1866 was the first state to pass legislation requiring physical education, followed by Ohio in 1892, Louisiana in 1894, Wisconsin in 1897, North Dakota in 1899, and Pennsylvania in 1901 (Van Dalen 1971, pp. 403-404).

Much of the credit for the successful enactment of this state legislation was due to the efforts of the American Association for the Advancement of Physical Education, the German Turnvereins in the United States, the proponents of the Swedish Gymnastic systems, and the Women's Christian Temperance Union.

As the leaders were discussing possible physical education programs that might be adopted for American youth, and the several states were attempting to enact state laws requiring physical education in the schools, William Gilbert Anderson, instructor at Adelphi Academy, was initiating the founding of the American Association for the Advancement of Physical Education. On November 27, 1885, he invited leaders of the profession to a meeting at Adelphi Academy to evelute physical education in order to determine its place as well as its value in the American educational system. The first association was known as the Association for the Advancement of Physical Education, with an original membership of 49. At the second meeting of the group, in 1886, a formal constitution was adopted and the name was changed to the American Association for the Advancement of Physical Education. "The objects of the Association shall be to disseminate knowledge concerning physical education, to improve the methods, and by meetings of the members to bring those interested in the subject into closer relation to each other" (Anderson 1941, p. 245).

Additional milestones during the latter part of the nineteenth century enhancing the growth of physical education were: Wellesley College in 1881 hired a fulltime teacher of physical education—a first for women's colleges (Lee 1971). A two-year course leading to a certificate was established at Oberlin college in 1892, and in the same year Indiana University established a short course in physical education leading to a certificate (Lee 1972). In 1893 Harvard College conferred the academic degree in physical education, the first school of collegiate rank to do so (Lee 1973).

While physical education was gaining a foothold in the educational system, other movements were developing that would add impetus to the progress of physical education. The YMCA program originated in England in 1841 and found its way to the United States in the middle of the nineteenth century. The purpose of the "Y" program was to contribute to the all-round development of man: physical, intellectual, and spiritual. Promoting the same objectives for women was the purpose of the YWCA when the first program started for women in Boston in 1866. Some of the outstanding early leaders and promoters of these programs were Robert J. Roberts, Luther Halsey

Gulick, James Huff McCurdy, and Mrs. Henry Durant. (For more information on "Y" programs, see Section 9.)

The playground and recreation movements developed as an outgrowth of the Industrial Revolution. Crowded conditions in the cities, slum areas, and unsanitary conditions resulting from the growth of industry stimulated the growth of playgrounds and recreation. There was a growing concern about the poor health of children and the lack of space in which they could play. The first organized playground in the United States began in Boston in 1885. This movement led to the enactment of state legislation when New York passed a bill in 1888 to provide organized play areas for children.

After the Civil War, with the advent of improved transportation, railroads, and automobiles, people become more interested in the camping movement. In 1881 the first private camp for boys was established in New Hampshire. Outdoor recreation of hiking and sports participation, away from the crowded city conditions, drew people to the mountains, wooded areas, and beaches.

Sports Increase with an Increase in Leisure Time

Sports and games became more popular as leisure time increased for the general population, particularly high school and college students. Sports and games were not considered a part of the physical education curriculum at this time, yet these activities provided a partial background for physical education and sports programs for the twentieth century. The most popular sport of the time was football, which aroused the greatest concern about the place of athletics in education. Other popular sports of the time were baseball, rowing, basketball, bicycling, bowling, and croquet.

As the interest and competitive spirit captured the attention of many people, especially college students, it was felt that an organization should be formed to regulate activities of the participants. The National Association of Amateur Athletics of America was formed in 1879 and evolved into the Amateur Athletic Union (AAU) in 1888. With the growth of athletics on college campuses, regulatory bodies needed to be established to superivse collegiate programs; thus, the Intercollegiate Association of Amateur Athletics of America was founded in 1885, the Intercollegiate Football Association was formed in 1876, and the Western Conference, later to be called the Big Ten, was organized in 1895-1896. High schools at this time did little to control athletic activities.

The year 1896 marked another important first that had implications for the world—the revival of the Olympic Games. The first modern Olympic games took place in Athens, Greece, due to the untiring efforts of Baron Pierre de Coubertin.

The nineteenth century set the stage for the growth of physical education, sports, and athletics for the twentieth century. However, the advancement of these activities was accompanied by changes in and growth of the United States—more industry with accompanying inventions, concerns for the economic situation, as well as society's concern for the value of life itself. These changes brought about a new philosophy of physical education based upon the idea that physical education was an avenue for promoting education.

1900 TO 1920

The period from 1900 to 1920 ushered in a "new physical education" that relied upon sports and games as a means of attaining educational goals to rival the formal gymnastics-dominated programs of physical education. Dr. Thomas D. Wood, Clark W. Hetherington, and Dr. Luther Halsey Gulick were the outstanding leaders in physical education who originated and fostered the movement that broke with formal gymnastics.

"Physical education" became the accepted term replacing the nineteenth century terminology of "physical culture, physical training, and gymnastics"; and attention was turned to preparing teachers.

Most of the early leaders were college personnel, of whom a considerable number were medically trained. Few full-time physical education positions existed. In 1885 there were no more than several hundred individuals teaching physical education in the entire United States. Some of these had formerly been weight-lifters, professional athletes, or circus performers. The professional preparation which was available in the several institutions which provided it varied from one to two years. One of the leading institutions prepared teachers for Turnverein, which probably employed more physical education teachers than the public schools (Esslinger 1959, p. 19).

The increasing demand for more physical education teachers and the need for more comprehensive academic preparation programs brought about a noteworthy change when private, noncollegiate normal schools that were preparing physical education teachers affiliated with some colleges and universities.

There was also a movement to establish departments of teacher education in physical education, and graduate instruction was introduced. Among the colleges and universities establishing departments of teacher education in physical education were Illinois in 1905, Oregon in 1907, Wisconsin in 1911, Missouri in 1914, Iowa in 1918, Indiana and Minnesota in 1919, and Michigan in 1921. Graduate instruction in physical education was begun in 1901 at Columbia University with the instituting of a program leading to the Master's degree. . . . By 1930 twenty-eight colleges and universitie were offering graduate preparation in physical education and with this development there came simultaneously a more pronounced emphasis on research, on tests and measurements, and on professional literature (Weston 1962, p. 55).

The emphasis in research changed during this period from anthropometric measurement and strength tests to physical achievement tests and cardiovascular research. Leaders in the research area were Dr. Edward Hitchcock, Dr. Dudley A. Sargent, Dr. Luther Halsey Gulick, Dr. George L. Meylan, Dr. James H. McCurdy, and Dr. Ward Crampton.

Interest developed in professional organizations with several associations being formed, while others changed their names. In 1904 Dr. Gulick organized an early Academy of Physical Education, which disbanded in 1918; however, a new group organized the present American Academy in 1926. The select professional physical educators who make up this Academy address themselves to major professional issues (see Section 9). In 1910 Amy Morris Homans invited directors of physical education in women's colleges of New England to meet and discuss their mutual problems. This eventually led to the formation of the National Association of Directors of Physical Education for College Women in 1924. The American Association for the Advancement of Physical Education changed its name to the American Physical Education Association in 1903. The Society of College Gymnasium Directors, became in 1908 the Society of Directors of Physical Education in Colleges.

Advancement of State Legislation

State legislation was again brought to the forefront when in 1918 the United States Commissioner of Education called 60 leaders of physical education to Atlantic City for a conference. As a result of this meeting, the National Committee on Physical Education was formed. It established the National Physical Education Service to promote state and federal legislation on physical education programs and playgrounds in all schools under their jurisdiction. From 1919 to 1921, seventeen states enacted physical education legislation and by 1930 the total was 39.

Sports were generally accepted in school programs during this period, especially the fast-growing activities of softball, badminton, football, basketball, handball, and lawn tennis. Dance gradually became a part of physical education programs with the most important forms being clog and tap, esthetic, folk, natural, modern, social, and square. In some public schools, however, emphasis was placed upon military drill when the United States became involved in World War I. The pros and cons of the values of military drill were argued until the close of the war, when programs reemphasized the needs of students, particularly the objectives of developing the children physically and intellectually, helping them become more social and stable individuals. These objectives would continue to undergird programs of physical education for a long time.

1920 TO 1940

The period from 1920 to 1940 was marked by an increase in the standard of living, technological advances, and a great increase in number of schools and students. School curricula were influenced by the social education movement and educational developmentalism promoted by John Dewey, a strong advocate of social education. "Learning by doing" was a phrase used in many educational settings and, indeed, in the area of physical education. Accompanying this movement was the increased interest in scientific work in physical education. The development of achievement tests, some cardiovascular tests, and some assessment for motor performance gave evidence of a concern for a scientific view of human performance. Public school programs began to offer a wider range of physical activities: dance, track and field, sports, and gymnastics. Between 1925 and 1930, Danish Gymnastics became popular for high school and college women (Van Dalen 1971, p. 461).

The continued support of physical education seen in the 1920s was dealt a misfortune as the United States experienced the Great Depression. The years 1931 to 1935 saw a sharp curtailment in school budgets, which affected all educational programs. Art, music, and physical education were either curtailed or eliminated during this time. However, during the latter half of the 1930s, physical education and health appeared once again as part of total school programs. An increase in money to hire special teachers of physical education, and access to facilities, enhanced the growth of the programs.

As legislation for required physical education in the schools became a reality, there was a demand for more physical education teachers. This demand was met as more institutions of higher learning developed four-year professional physical education programs with curricula to improve teacher preparation. In graduate programs, a stronger emphasis was placed on scholarly and scientific work. Aiding in the development of research in health and physical education was the *Research Quarterly*, first published by the American Physical Education Association (APEA) in 1930.

Growth of Sports Competition

In this same period, colleges and universities were expanding their sports programs. "Sports for the masses" appeared to be the phrase of the 1920s (Lewis 1973, p. 109). In 1922 Herbert Hoover, upon the proposal of Secretary of War John Weeks, established the National Amateur Athletic Federation (NAAF) (Van Dalen 1971, p. 448) to settle difficulties that arose over the selection of the representatives for the 1920 Olympic games. These troubles arose because the Amateur Athletic Union (AAU) dominated the American Olympic Committee, and this drew some criticism from the YMCA and the National Collegiate Athletic Association (NCAA). It was felt that such an organization would promote a greater interest in health and physical education. Through this action it was believed that a greater involvement in physical activity would increase the fitness of all.

The NAAF had two divisions, one for men and one for women. The men's division dissolved in the 1930s. The women's division continued its work in conjunction with the Women's Athletic Section of the American Physical Education Association. These two groups had tight control over the sports programs for college women. The concept of "sport for all" was emphasized. There was much concern about women entering the very competitive athletic games (see Chapter 8). "The deliberate sacrifice of the needs of the highly skilled few for specialized training, to the needs of the great majority for some type of experience with physical activity, was consistent with the prevalent educational philosophy of pragmatism and progressive education" (Gerber 1973, pp. 27-28).

Another innovation in athletics was the establishment of the National Federation of State High School Athletic Associations in 1922 (see Section 9). The purpose of this group was to establish standards for boys' athletics in high schools.

1940 TO THE PRESENT

The years from 1940 to the present witnessed many developments of unusual significance to physical education. During World War II improvements could not be made in facilities nor could new ones be constructed because of the demands of war production. Teachers entered the service and college enrollments decreased. Programs of physical education were dominated by military emphasis, with schools and colleges being encouraged to develop physical fitness (see Chapter 6) and at the same time retain physical education and athletics. Emphasis was placed on physical skills for military service and the development of strength and endurance. Physical educators were encouraged to specialize in research for the armed services in the areas of physical fitness, measurement, and rehabilitation techniques.

The scientific movement in physical education became established in college and university programs. Research laboratories were constructed and staff members were appointed as research professors. The most outstanding examples of these were Dr. Franklin M. Henry at the University of California, Dr. Thomas K. Cureton at the University of Illinois, and Dr. Charles H. McCloy at the University of Iowa.

Colleges and universities were demanding teachers with master's and doctor's degrees, and large secondary schools were requiring teachers to have a master's degree. This trend, along with increased research facilities, resulted in a significant increase in number of graduate programs and in publication of numerous research studies in physical education. In 1952 Dr. Cureton published the volume *Masters Theses in Health, Physical Education, and*

Recreation, in which he stated that 3878 master's theses had been reported between 1930 and 1946 (Cureton 1952, p. iii), and in 1947 he published his report on "Doctorate Theses Reported by Graduate Departments of Health, Physical Education, and Recreation, 1930-1946, inclusively," in which he reported that 420 doctoral theses had been completed (Cureton 1949, p. 1).

In the immediate postwar period physical education was faced with two serious problems: the building of facilities and desirable standards in undergraduate and graduate teacher education. To help solve the problem, three national conferences were sponsored by the AAHPER: a National Conference on Facilities held at Jackson's Mill, West Virginia, in 1946; a National Conference on Undergraduate Preparation in Health Education, Physical Education and Recreation at Jackson's Mill in 1948; and a National Conference on Graduate Study in Health Education, Physical Education and Recreation at Pere Marquette State Park, Illinois, in 1950 (Van Dalen 1971, p. 486).

Physical education programs offered a wide range of activities and encouraged students to learn and participate in sports they could enjoy. Interest also developed in programs for the handicapped, especially for those veterans returning to civilian life (see Section 6). Promotion and progress in elementary and secondary school physical education programs could be observed through an increase in time allotment for physical education, an increase in enrollment, granting of academic credit, and improved interest in physical education by school administrators.

Advances in Physical Education since 1950

A national survey by the National Education Association (NEA) for 1948-1949 revealed that organized programs in physical education were provided for 93 percent of elementary, 97 percent of junior high school, and 89 percent of senior high school students (NEA 1950). By 1949 state legislation regarding physical education had been passed in 41 states, and state directors were employed in most states. Their duties included the development of programs, facilities and equipment standards, teacher preparation and certification, in-service teacher education, and public and professional relations.

In the early 1950s a need for a physical fitness movement was apparent when figures were published on rejections of new military draftees and the results of the Kraus-Weber tests. Concern for the fitness of American youth brought about the establishment of a President's Council on Youth Fitness (see Section 9) and a President's Citizens Advisory Committee on the Fitness of American Youth. As a result of the suggestions made at the conferences held by these groups, most states established state fitness programs (see Chapter 6).

The advances in physical education since 1950 have won public acceptance and support even though there has been debate about how much emphasis should be placed on various aspects of the programs. Physical educators have been supported in their efforts by presidents, governors, and various scientific associations. Professional literature in the form of articles, pamphlets, and books is abundant. Research and test and measurement in physical education have reached a new high in scientific development, and a growing number of members of the profession are entering research work in the field. A new direction, "movement education," is being explored in physical education (Cassidy 1965, pp. 11-15). The AAHPERD is now in a strong position for action and leadership in the profession and publishes two official journals: *Journal of Physical Education and Recreation* (formerly *JOHPER*) and the *Research Quarterly*. The National College Physical Education Association for Men (NCPEAM) and the National Association of Physical Education for College Women (NAPECW) cooperate in publishing *Quest* (a creative literary journal for members of the profession). These two organizations combined in June 1978 to form the National Association for Physical Education in Higher Education (NAPEHE).

Magnificent gymnasiums have been built for both men and women. Graduate degrees are the rule today for physical education teachers in colleges and universities and are becoming more common for those in high schools. The number of colleges and universities offering major preparation programs in physical education had reached 615 undergraduate, 200 masters, and 46 doctoral programs by 1973 (HPER 1974, pp. 35-36). A physical education program for the general college student exists in practically all institutions (Oxendine 1972, pp. 26-28). In a comparison of surveys on state legal requirements for physical education made in 1964, 1969, and 1970, it was reported that there had been an overall increase in the physical requirements over the six-year period, the greatest increase being in the required elementary physical education (Grieve 1971, pp. 19-22). The founding of the National Intramural Association (see Section 9) in 1950 and the development of graduate programs in this area have been on the increase with the emphasis turning to lifetime sports such as archery, bowling, badminton, golf, tennis, and racquetball.

Notable Events in Sports

Notable events in sports during this time were: in 1952, for the first time, an American, Avery Brundage (now deceased), became president of the International Olympic Committee; the National Association of Intercollegiate Athletics (NAIA) was founded to give small colleges better representation in athletic competition (Lee 1972, p. 65); the Women's Advisory Board to the United States Olympic Development Committee was created in 1961 (Lee 1971); in 1962 the United States Track and Field Federation was born (Lee 1972, p. 65); the AAHPERD's Division for Girls' and Women's Sports (now NAGWS) sponsored its first sport institute in 1963 (Lee 1973, pp. 10, 11).

Courses in scuba diving, ice skating, figure skating, fencing, judo, karate, weight training, and ballet have been added to physical education programs. Sport clubs have been organized by students in tennis, sailing, judo, fencing, ice hockey, volleyball, rugby, and soccer.

The status of physical education in American society appears to be at its highest, and can be justified on educational grounds. "Our philosophy has gradually developed and matured and today we are educators rather than trainers. Instead of employing a borrowed program from Europe, we have developed a curriculum and methodology of our own—based upon the nature and needs of children growing up in a democratic society (Esslinger 1959, p. 19).

REFERENCES

Anderson, W. G., 1941. The early history of the Association (Part III). *JOHPER* **12** (April) : 244-245.

Cassidy, R., 1965. The cultural definition of physical education. *Quest,* Monograph **4** (April) : 11-15. NAPECW and NCPEAM.

Cureton, T. K., 1949. Doctorate theses reported by graduate departments of health, physical education, and recreation, 1930-1946, inclusively. *Research Quarterly* **20** (March) : 21-59.

———, 1952. *Masters theses in health, physical education and recreation.* Washington, D.C.: AAHPER.

Esslinger, A. A., 1959. Yesterday, today, and tomorrow. *JOHPER* **30** (September) : 19-20.

Gerber, E., 1973. The controlled development of collegiate sport for women, 1923-1936. *Proceedings,* North American Society for Sport History.

Grieve, A., 1971. State legal requirements for physical education. *JOHPER* **42** (April) : 19-23.

HPER directory of professional preparation institutions, 1974. *JOHPER* **45** (January) : 35-46.

Lee, M., and C. W. Hackensmith, 1971. Notable events in 150 years of physical education. *JOHPER* **42** (November-December) : 79.

———, 1972. Notable events in physical education: 1822-1972. *JOHPER* **43** (February) : 65.

———, 1973. Notable events in physical education: 1823-1973. *JOHPER* **44** (November-December) : 10.

Lewis, G., 1973. World War I and the emergence of sport for the masses. *Maryland Historian* **IV** (Fall) : 109-122.

National Education Association, 1950. Personnel and relationships in school health, physical education, and recreation. *Research Bulletin* **28** (October) : 90-92.

Oxendine, J. B., 1972. Status of general instruction programs of physical education in four-year colleges and universities: 1971-72. *JOHPER* **43** (March) : 26-28.

Van Dalen, D. B., and B. L. Bennett, 1971. *A world history of physical education.* Englewood Cliffs, N.J.: Prentice-Hall.

Weston, A., 1962. *The making of American physical education.* New York: Appleton-Century-Crofts.

6

Historical Development of the Physical Fitness Movement

Thomas K. Cureton, Jr.*

Since the beginning of human history, the practical experience of humanity has been to see that systematic, strenuous activity of a physical nature is developmental in its effect on the body; and people's natural activities of daily food gathering, cultivation of the fields, hunting and fishing, long migratory trips carrying loads and pulling drags or carts, and riding horses have brought about a gross type of physical conditioning. While all of this led to physical fitness, along with environmental acclimitization, civilized people developed ascetic segments of monastic confinement; the industrial civilization added to people's confinement in factories, offices, and automobiles—all tending to nullify the vigorous life of the agrarian and nomadic civilizations. Sport came to be looked upon as a diversion from toil and factory life for some and social-physical recreation for others in modern English-speaking

---

*   *Author's note:* No attempt has been made in this article to describe all of the specific activities related to fitness, stress testing in cardiac diagnosis, orthopedic manipulations and techniques, or medical treatment techniques. Refer to Volume II in this series for much more detail.

countries, but not as a principal means of cultivating physical fitness for the masses of people. When World War I burst forth, the flying machine was still rather primitive, and the great mass of fighting troops was land-trained, primarily by the officers in charge instituting mass calisthenics, combat games, forced marches, and the carrying of heavy equipment, guns, and ammunition. Full military participation in "field training" quite naturally developed physical fitness. Recreation was seen as contributing to "psychological attitude"—as an opportunity to play rather than work. It was offered by YMCA and Special Services personnel.

PERIOD OF WORLD WAR II

The newly formed military units found that three to six months of basic training, including "field service," was loaded heavily with conditioning activities, including an adjustment to outdoor life, marching, regularity of meals, and other living habits. Fitness advanced as well as technical proficiency. It was a great change from the industrial world of power machines, gadgets, and close confinement that had sapped the fitness of many men and women from the large industrial cities.

Even before World War II was declared in December 1941, members of the profession of health, physical education, and recreation, as well as its allied branches and affiliated organizations (see Section 9), realizing that the needs should be met, brought together the most pertinent materials and programs related to physical fitness. Leadership training in physical fitness accelerated (AAHPER 1935, 1941). Strong emphasis was placed upon safety precautions, civil defense work, and first-aid services.

Considerable expansion of ideas occurred about physical fitness of a more strenuous, even "survival" type. Walter Camp's Daily Dozen gave way to more strenuous programs for heretofore sedentary adults. Many types of "obstacle courses" appeared, and steeplechases and orienteering type courses became popular. The question was raised sharply about the fitness of college and senior high school students, although for some time the emphasis was questioned by educational leaders. But many new programs developed for students who were not drafted immediately.

While the Rogers Strength Index and Physical Fitness Index (P.F.I.) testing programs were used in many schools, as a carry-over from the 1930s, the military gave preference to the moving (running, dodging, climbing, jumping, swimming) programs and tests. Coaches preferred the Cozens type of athletic aptitude test, which involved running, dodging, jumping, throwing, and kicking a football. The trend continued toward the use of muscular endurance tests and programs (Cureton 1947; Federal Security Agency 1942; Larson 1946; McKenzie 1944) and upon strenuous "survival aquatics" courses and tests (Cureton 1943) although those groups of young people immediately facing induction were classified by more moderate tests that assessed basic physical fitness abilities (Cureton 1943a, 1947a, 1947b, 1951, 1972).

New Emphases

The wartime physical fitness programs brought many new emphases into the health, physical education, and recreation profession. There was constant interplay and sharing between the best military and civilian programs, each making major contributions to the other. Also, with so many of the best civilian physical educators in the armed forces, there was constant improvisation of methods by these leaders in the various branches of the armed forces as they attempted to adapt the best civilian programs of preconditioning to military needs and time constraints. The Navy Pre-Flight Schools, for instance, at the Universities of Iowa, Georgia, and North Carolina used athletic participation in a major way as part of their programs. After qualification of the candidate as a pilot with wings, combative programs were minimized to avoid injury. At the civilian high school level, a typical wartime program was the Victory Corps Program (Federal Security Agency 1942) produced under the auspices of the Federal Security Agency (advisor: Dr. Jackson M. Sharman) and the U.S. Office of Education.

To meet the need for easily administered tests with a very minimum of equipment, or none at all except an open space, the 18-Item Test was devised at the University of Illinois (Cureton 1947a) designed so that an entire physical education class could practice the test at once. The test correlated as high as 0.90 (N = 104) with a 14-Item Test, which required a six- to seven-pound medicine ball, chinning, and push-up bars. To predict all-around performance of the motor fitness type, these tests included emphasis on the motor ability components of balance, flexibility, agility, strength, power, and endurance. They were more diversified and more highly related to athletic ability than tests that emphasized one principal component, such as strength, power, or endurance (Cureton 1947a, p. 421). These tests are described in the *Physical Fitness Workbook* (Cureton 1947b) and were used to survey large numbers of students with respect to their ability to use their bodies in an all-around athletic way (Cureton 1943a). They were also used to test athletic abilities in champion athletes (Cureton 1951) and large numbers of adults (Cureton 1972).

Involvement of the AAPHER in Fitness Work, World War II

While physical fitness had been one of the objectives in health, physical education, and recreaion work for some time, and "Athletic Achievement Tests" were used commonly in gymnasiums and athletic and playground centers, focus on civilian wartime objectives dated from approximately the National Convention of 1942 in New Orleans, when President Nancy Schley

Duggan opened this convention with the theme "National Fitness Through Health, Physical Education and Recreation—Fitness for Victory." The entire issue of the *Journal of Health, Physical Education, and Recreation* of June 1942 was devoted to this theme, supported by Brigadier General Lewis B. Hershey, and aided by leaders from the country at large: Mayhew Derryberry (Education in Fitness), Henry P. Clapp (Crime Prevention), Robert L. Sutherland (Rehabilitation), Pauline M. Frederick (The Place of Physical Education), Edith M. Gates (Services of Private Agencies), Margaret Bell (Health (Guidance), George P. Stafford (Sports Program, Boys and Men), Ruth L. Atwell (Sports Program, Girls and Women), and Elizabeth Weems (Camping and Outdoor Programs). At this time, there was renewed emphasis on first-aid training, selection by body type, objective fitness-performance tests, and outdoor education. The Army's Special Services Branch began a special school to prepare recreational leaders for service in military camps and stations, both in the United States and abroad.

Dr. Jay B. Nash, in assuming the presidency of the then-named AAHPER, addressed a letter to the War Manpower Commission pointing out that: 1) high schools and colleges had a pool of many thousands of youths who needed fitness programs; 2) no one knew just how long the war would last; and 3) guidance was needed as to how much effort should be put into training such youth in physical fitness (Nash 1942). The reply indicated that everything possible should be done, thus leading President Nash to proclaim the War Fitness Conference, held in April 1943 (Nash 1943). This national conference identified special needs and outlined methods for achieving a high fitness level of youth in the United States. The AAHPER followed this meeting with many published articles and outlines of special programs. Commissioner of Education John W. Studebaker encouraged this movement and stimulated the production of a series of manuals published under the auspices of the U.S. Office of Education. These included *Physical Fitness Manual for High Schools* and *Physical Fitness Manual for Colleges and Universities.* During this same period, the National Civilian Office of Physical Fitness, with John B. Kelly as its executive, was opened under the authority of Congress in April 1943. The office was located at 601 Pennsylvania Avenue. It operated under the Federal Security Agency. Special attention was given to industrial fitness and swimming.

In the early period of World War II, and even before the war was anticipated, many articles attempting to define physical fitness began to appear in the literature. Although the emphasis came to focus strongly on the more *physical* objectives of physical education, authors were careful not to exclude objectives dealing with aesthetics, art forms, play, and sociability. Thus, educators emphasized "education *in* and *through* the physical" rather than *of* the physical. Since there were so many medical rejections from the draft, many for psychological reasons, emphasis was placed on programs known to achieve stabilization of the nervous system as well as the development of physical prowess. The keynote was "Physical Fitness is the Common Denominator." Education Week was devoted to emphasizing fitness, and the AAHPER used county fairs to demonstrate various aspects of fitness testing (Harris 1959; Hucklebridge 1959). George H. Grover (1959) summarized some of the trends resulting from programs adopted during the war period to improve the fitness of secondary school youth.

The war period was most interesting because it demonstrated the great range of adaptations and improvements in mental attitudes and fitnesses that could be made by the tests used. Requirements for fitness courses and the tests thereof were introduced into the high schools and colleges. Professionals and students alike responded with enthusiasm, vigor, and intelligent professional application. Examples of leadership given by educators to help the war fitness effort may be seen in the articles published in the *Journal of Health, Physical Education, and Recreation.*

Many new workbooks appeared, and survey reports on the fitness of students continued to be made for some years after the war ended in 1945. During the ten years following the war, an appreciable drop in mass fitness levels of college freshmen was demonstrated by the application of the same type of tests of physical ability used previously. While studies were made of cardiovascular tests, and norms for high school and college students were prepared (Cureton 1945), the overwhelming interest was in ability to demonstrate *basic physical ability.*

The wartime programs had added ingredients of marching and jogging, use of military commands, warfare aquatics and survival swimming, man-lifting and man-carrying (one-on-one, two-on-one, four-on-one, etc.), rough and tumble fighting and judo as self-defense, obstacle courses and steeple-chases, combat games (like pom-pom-pull-away), long hikes, sleeping out at night, first aid, and safety precautions and drills. Ability to drive cars, tractors, trucks, motorcycles, and jeeps became important for girls and boys and all adults. Rifle range courses provided some experience in the use of firearms. Camping activities became greatly expanded, as did orienteering and charting, knowledge of first aid and hospital services, and use of first-aid equipment. These activities merged into the Civil Defense program, which has continued ever since the war.

Further Role of the AAHPER

The AAHPER was very active in publishing a series of booklets aimed at the promotion of physical fitness as an ongoing part of American life for boys and girls in schools and colleges. These included: *Fitness for Leadership* (suggestions for colleges and universities), 1964, and *What the Coach Says about (Various Sports),* various dates. Many colleges, universities, and high schools developed programs and materials, and many of significance appeared in the literature. Institutes and clinics were conducted in connection with area and national meetings to stimulate interest and show the preferred techniques. A new section called the Aquatic Section, which has since become the Aquatic Council, appeared in the AAHPER organizational structure. Another new section was called Physical Fitness Programs. The Research Council (and Section) of AAHPER appointed various committees to undertake projects about physical fitness. These included "A National Fitness Test for Boys and Girls," "Objective Fitness Standards," and "Measurements and Evaluation of Value to School Administrators." A special project of the AAHPER consisted of a National Random Survey (made of large, medium, and small schools throughout the United States) supported by the U.S. Office of Education for the Federal Security Agency. The first survey was made in 1948 by Paul A. Hunsicker and Guy A. Rief (1964). It was repeated in 1965 and again in 1975. Results are summarized in Volume II of this series in the section on youth fitness. Also more fully documented in Volume II are many new booklets, textbooks, and workbooks appearing in connection with the physical education movement (Cureton 1943a, 1947a, 1947b, 1951, 1972).

Expansion of Programs and Complexity of Physical Fitness

Courses were developed in the colleges on the service (general education) and professional levels, and there was a great increase in research on the graduate level. Increased leadership resulted nationally from this expansion of programs at all levels. Physical fitness concepts became extremely complex and included aspects of physique, performance, and cardiovascular-respiratory components with obvious relationships to the social-nutritional environment, hereditary background, nervous tolerance, living habits, and many other factors. However, it had to be delimited for objective study. Multivariate methods of factor analysis and multiple factor prediction of performance produced such an array of interrelationships that no single view of physical fitness could be exclusive. Statistical analysis of physical fitness components, factors, and tests, and attempts to explain and predict selective performances, came into widespread use. An ever-growing list of research laboratories developed in the health, physical education, and recreation fields.

New types of tests appeared and others were refined, but the great majority of the schools and colleges were forced to work with rather simple equipment or none at all. Those with little equipment assessed physical fitness with motor-type tests, while those with adequate facilities (as in a few of the larger universities) tended to become laboratory-centered in their desire to probe the physiological systems more deeply or to contribute more fully to the disciplines of physiology and medicine. In the latter case medical help in the laboratory became a virtual necessity that only the larger university departments could provide. It is not now nor has it ever been the practice to require medical doctors to be present in gymnasiums, pools, workout rooms, field houses, and fields when physical education or athletic work is conducted; this also holds true for community playground areas.

POSTWAR EDUCATION AND IMPROVEMENT OF FITNESS

The extensive field of youth and adult health and fitness developed after World War II. Many new laboratories began to study fitness components of children and adults, without dealing directly with *disease* problems, but instead concentrating on the improvability of *normal* children and adults in a wide range of anatomical, physiological, and psychological characteristics. The University of Illinois College of Physical Education sponsored a symposium to interpret some of this work in 1960 (Staley et al. 1960) and again in 1969 (Franks 1969). There have been others, including the University of Oregon symposium in honor of Professor H. H. Clarke (Broekhoff 1976). In general, the conclusion was reached that much worthwhile work could be done simply as "fitness work" without involving the hospitals and their disease approach. Following medical examinations and employing reasonable precautions, professors and laboratory assistants conducted various types of courses (activities) to observe experimentally the effects of those activities on the human body. The results have flooded the literature and greatly advanced the scientific knowledge of the effects of exercise. Thus, many new courses of exercise physiology have been developed, both to prepare better leadership and to inculcate the new knowledge.

Fitness Studies of Youth

Attention turned about 1950 to laboratory and field studies aimed at developing the physical fitness of youth. These studies took place mainly in connection with Sports Fitness Day Schools attached to universities. These schools emphasized education *about* as well as development *of* fitness in youth. While all of the students in such schools were examined medically, the emphasis thereafter was on sports, developmental and training exercises, swimming, and improving nutrition. Testing was also directed at discovering "potential" athletes of several principal types, and many examples are now known of youth who have been helped from such studies made in the formative years of their lives. The schools were generally coeducational. While many such "recreational" schools existed previously, as did hundreds of private and institutional camps, all of which did some fitness work, the new emphasis was on "the scientific approach." Many professors, instructors, and graduate students now take part in this wholesome work. It represents a new dynamic-health-fitness approach.

63

LIFETIME SPORTS MOVEMENT

In the past few years, there has been a great surge of interest and participation in the sports of tennis, table tennis, paddle ball, racquetball, swimming, scuba diving, jogging, softball, golf, and "family fitness" activities such as camping. Such activities were formulated into a prgram of Lifetime Sports (AAHPER 1967) introduced through AAHPER as the "Lifetime Sports Project" by Charles H. "Bud" Wilkinson. The modern phenomenon of millions of viewers of television watching the best woman tennis player playing against and defeating a top-level male player has stimulated interest in women's sports. The large money prizes have whetted the interest. Snorkle swimming and scuba diviing have also been high in popularity, but some injuries and deaths have resulted in tighter regulations because of the need for specialized equipment. The YMCA National Aquatic Committee published the first book on this subject and was first to certify instructors for teaching scuba diving. This program involved "fitness" requirements and considerable knowledge of water exposure physiology. Many thousands of people of both sexes have been certified to use scuba diving equipment. Courses are now found in YMCAs, community recreational centers, and many colleges and universities.

Fitness has been a principal component in the educational work of Outward Bound schools and courses, long canoe trips, the training of male and female athletes, and specialized sport schools (i.e., football, swimming, baseball, basketball, track, etc.). Precompetitive training is now required in most sports.

Research Is Stimulated

With many colleges, universities, and social agencies, as well as the branches of the armed forces, showing strong interest in physical fitness, research was stimulated. Researchers focused their attention on the changes in fitness resulting from preconditioning programs, in-service programs, and special athletic training programs. Research showed that three months in basic military training resulted in marked fitness gains, due mainly to regularity, good eating habits, and moderate exercise. Vigorous field duty developed many fitnesses even further, reflecting an adaptation to the environment and ability to endure hard work for a longer time. The military, rather than the medical profession, controlled the medical standards; thus, many young men were rejected for psychological problems as well as for poor physical fitness or disease (Hershey 1952).

The profession of health, physical education, and recreation published several research monographs, but those produced by the State University of Iowa, Wellesley College, Boston University, and Springfield College as *Supplements to the Research Quarterly* focused on physical fitness tests, norms, and improvements (AAHPER 1935, 1941).

Research was provided by the military academics and all branches of the armed forces, thus placing many researchers and graduate students from physical education in such work. While each branch of the service had its own test, designed to meet its particular needs, a few of the tests used widely were the Brouha (Harvard) Step Test, Larson's Chinning Vertical Jump-Dipping Battery, muscular endurance tests and endurance runs, and forced marches (Larson 1946; Cureton 1943b, 1947a). Just as the war began in 1941, the AAHPER published the research monograph *Physical Fitness* (Springfield College Studies), dealing comprehensively with testing young men. Important elements of fitness were: 1) ability to bear stress (mental or physical, 2) ability to swim if thrown into deep water, 3) ability to run and dodge, 4) ability to carry loads, 5) ability to resist the weather, and 6) endurance on a forced march.

Research tends to put a legitimate check on the careless use of terms and phrases that purport to link sports and physical activity to health, such as "poor heart," "overweight and diabetes," "must have max VO_2 to be healthy," and so on. Professional workers realized that heredity, living habits, environment, nutrition, motivation, and many other factors were involved, not just exercise or "high max VO_2." Instead of placing the whole or main emphasis on any one component, there has been a gradual tendency to recognize the many factors involved and to use appropriately many-factored research methods to isolate the contributing factors and, if possible, give to each a relative quantitative value.

Multiple, matched standard score tables began to appear for the *separate* rating of test items known to be important: fat-folds, lean body mass (or density), weight, height, percent of weight for bone, muscle bulk and strength, and suitable body build index. Sheldon (1940) recommended the formula 1 divided by the cube root of w as a quantitative substitute for ectomorphy; strength is commonly substituted for mesomorphy and thickness through the abdomen in large, obese people for endomorphy. Each scale is made approximately equivalent to the spread of individual differences and scored 1 through 7.

The Research Council of the AAHPER has been very active in reviewing and formulating endorsements about test items of fitness. In 1951, the AAHPER published *Measurement and Evaluation in Health, Physical Education, and Recreation,* primarily to give some guidance to those who are not expert in such physical fitness measurements. Many analytical papers have been published in the *Research Quarterly* of AAHPER, 1930 to date, and also in other journals, such as *Medicine and Science in Sports, American Corrective Therapy Journal, Journal of Sports Medicine and Physical Fitness,* and many others currently available throughout the world.

Military Branches and the Academies

The military branches and academies, during both war and peace, have continued to make physical fitness "the common denominator" of effective service, along with technical military training. Sports and fitness make up an important segment of the life of all military personnel in service as it does in the academies. Since professional physical educators had much to do with the design and research of the military programs during the war, many articles descriptive of the programs they supervised were published in the *Research Quarterly* (1944, 1946). These studies showed considerable improvement in physical fitness over a one-year period of training with the AAF Physical Fitness Test. They also showed a deterioration of physical fitness of ground forces personnel from 21 to 46 years of age when training was discontinued.

PHYSICAL EDUCATION AND MEDICINE

A committee of physical educators and physicians was formed in 1943 to study the "Role of Exercise in Physical Fitness." Under the leadership of A. H. Steinhaus, chairman, and W. W. Bauer, F. A. Hellebrandt, Leon Kranz, Alice Miller, Henry A. Christian, A. C. Ivy, and Peter J. Steincrohn, a meeting was held in Chicago. This group accepted the idea that *exercise* in adequate amounts, and properly regulated, had most to do with the development of physical fitness; however, strong emphasis was also needed on personal habits, good choices in the use of leisure time, plus good air, water, food, and proper clothing. It was also pointed out that exercise did not in itself prevent or cure infectious diseases, but that medical science and public health services could be called upon to control and prevent epidemics and disasters (Bauer 1956).

The American Medical Association also became active on the civilian front, holding a conference at its headquarters in Chicago on April 28, 1945, under the leadership of Dr. Morris Fishbein, secretary of the A.M.A., and Aron Ward, writer for the *Chicago Tribune*. Representatives of the AAHPER were invited to this meeting. A small booklet entitled "Exercise and Health" was then published by the Health Education Section of the A.M.A. Physicians have since supported the use of "controlled exercise" for improving aspects of health.

Physical education researchers and physicians have conducted many cooperative meetings and projects related to health and physical fitness of humans. In 1964 two major meetings were held on "Preventive Cardiology and Exercise." One was organized in Burlington, Vermont, by Dr. Wilhelm Raab, cardiologist, and the other in Helsinki, Finland, by Dr. Marti Karvonen. A number of physical educators made contributions to the programs. Many such meetins have since been held, including those of a group known as the International Committee for Physical Fitness Research and Test Evaluation (organized by Professor Leonard A. Larson) that has met biennially for 12 years through 1976.

Organization of Sports Medicine

While sports medicine was well organized in continental Europe, it was not formally organized in the United States until 1948. A group consisting of Ernst Jokl, Adolf Henning, Frucht, Marti J. Karvonen, Don C. Seaton, Ernst Simon, and Peter Jokl had outlined its status and scope in 1946 in a presentation before the New York Academy of Sciences. The objective stated was "to advance the medical and other scientific studies dealing with the effect of sports and other physical activities of humans at various stages of life."

Physicians, mainly orthopedists, have shown interest in better diagnosis and treatment of athletic injuries, while physiologists have concentrated more on stress effects (exercise and temperature) and measuring and interpreting the various immediate effects of exercise and competition. Physical educators have shown more interest in classification of people for physical education classes and in the results of their programs on the participants. There are now many such studies on "Exercise and Health" and "Sport and Health."

The first National Convention of the American College of Sports Medicine was held in New Jersey in 1953, and annual meetings have been held ever since. The present programs are impressive and provide insight into the effects of exercise on training programs, injury prevention, and care and nutrition of athletes. The specialized journal is *Medicine and Science in Sports,* begun in 1968. Other similar journals are published in Czechoslovakia, Britain, Australia, Japan, and Italy.

THE U.S. GOVERNMENT, CONFERENCES, AND THE PRESIDENT'S COUNCIL

The U.S. government has taken an active role in physical fitness work through national fitness conferences and the President's Council. By following up the wartime work of the Federal Security Agency's Civilian Fitness Office, many clinics in regions and states of the country have been held, booklets printed, and industry awakened to make a more sincere effort to promote physical fitness.

The first major conference was held at Annapolis, Maryland, in 1956; nearly two years later, the second was held at West Point, New York, at the Military Academy. These two conferences made a forum for the president of the United States and top national experts to express their views. They helped to create a high level of interest in youth fitness. A summary is given in the June 1956 report of the meeting, pointing out that automation and mechanical gadgets have adversely affected the fitness of American youth, who were becoming more and more addicted to "soft living," while experiencing an increase in leisure time. President Eisenhower emphasized that the strength of the United States depended on the fitness of its youth, but this was remotely perceived, if at all, by the majority of the American adult population. He emphasized that fitness could not be taken for granted, and that methods should be found to reverse the trend in physical inactivity of Americans. He concluded that fitness of a physical nature went hand in hand with moral, mental, and emotional fitness.

The second National Conference on Youth Fitness was held at West Point in 1957 and was presided over by Richard Nixon, then vice-president of the United States. At this meeting he warned against a narrow, stereotyped program or the use of only a mass approach. He also stated that: 1) it was unlikely that federal funds would be forthcoming to support the program; 2) private organizations should carry most of the load; and 3) federal programs should be used mainly to "catalyze" interest in private programs. The conference itself recommended that backyard playground units be developed throughout the country for preschool children and parents. There was some disappointment that the conference produced so little. Other conferences were held but little progress was made.

President Eisenhower's Leadership

President Eisenhower, following his election in 1952, encouraged the continuation of some plan for motivating the fitness of Americans. The profession of health, physical education, and recreation had worked to develop a number of "physical fitness tests" during his administration. One of these tests was the Kraus-Weber Test (Kraus 1953) used in a study of 7134 boys and girls, in which American children were compared with European children. The test was based on a simple set of motor test items (refer to Section 5 on Therapeutic Physical Education) presented by Dr. Hans Kraus and Ruth Hirshland. While these tests were of "minimal" muscular ability, as is frequently encountered by medical doctors in their offices, the tests did not adequately measure the dynamic (athletic) characteristics of maximal strength, speed, power, or endurance. More adequate tests are now in use in the school systems, YMCAs, colleges, universities, and military forces. The report of the results of the test was given to President Eisenhower on March 19, 1954. The failure of 58 percent of American children compared to 9 percent of the European children "shocked the President." On July 11, 1955, John Kelly, formerly chairman of the Wartime Committee on Civilian Physical Fitness, discussed these results at a White House luncheon presided over by Vice-President Richard Nixon. The group attending the luncheon was composed of 20 leaders from education, sports, and youth fitness programs. They recommended holding a National Conference on Youth Fitness, to be held September 27-28, 1955, at Lowry Air Force Base. This meeting was postponed because of the President's heart attack and was rescheduled for June 18-19, 1956, at the Naval Academy, Annapolis, Maryland. Extensive recommendations were made to improve the fitness of youth.*

The appointment of the President's Commission and Citizen's Advisory Committee followed shortly after the Annapolis Conference, and Dr. Shane McCarthy was named executive director. In June 1957 Carter L. Burgess was named its chairman. The role of this national committee and its council was that of catalyst to the nation's fitness movement and to "alert" all related groups and organizations. The AAHPER became involved immediately and, after a conference, decided to develop the AAHPER Youth Fitness Test and booklet.

In 1948 joint committee conferences were begun between educators and physicians on the use of physicians in school physical education and health education (AAHPER 1948). These conferences have continued to the present, since physicians and dentists are involved in the examination of school children and adults. In this same year, the American College of Sports Medicine was organized (see Section 9).

President John F. Kennedy's Leadership

The strong moral support and personal enthusiasm for physical fitness given by President Kennedy, including his personal articles, appearances, and speeches in the interest of the nation's fitness, helped the AAHPER with its role. Charles H. "Bud" Wilkinson, football coach of Oklahoma University, was named "Physical Fitness Consultant to the President" and with a staff managed the Office of the President's Council on Physical Fitness of Youth. He issued a strong challenge to the profession of health, physical education, and recreation to take up more effective lines of physical fitness work. While athletic teams generally included physical conditioning work, each team having its own particular kind, Wilkinson advocated that "exercise" be taken by everyone. The aim was to "catalyze" the work in the schools and also to encourage all adult citizens to work to improve fitness status through industrial leagues, adult fitness classes, and more outdoor living.

In 1963 President Kennedy accepted a special award of the AAHPER for the support he gave to physical fitness programs and the AAHPER. He was a familiar figure at sporting events and on a cold day appeared on the field at the Army-Navy football game without his hat. Before his assassination, he changed the name of the council to the President's Physical Fitness Council to give it a wider range of activities with adults as well as youth. Interrelations

---

* Present at the Annapolis meeting were the following people representing the AAHPER and the U.S. Office of Education: Ruth Abernaty, Clifford Brownell, Charles Bucher, Ray O. Duncan, Hans Kraus, Mabel Locke, and Carl A. Troester, Jr.

were developed with civil defense organizations and fitness was encouraged with police, firemen, FBI, life guards, and public-park employees. Study was begun for higher fitness standards in all of these areas.

President Johnson's Leadership

Stan Musial became President Lyndon Johnson's consultant on physical fitness and demonstrated a high personal example. In his effort to carry forward the fitness work, he made a report on the "National Survey of Youth Fitness," a well-conducted random survey of public schools. This survey had been conducted by P. A. Hunsicker and G. A. Rief for the AAHPER and Federal Security Agency. The study showed evidence of some improvements in 10- to 17-year-old boys and girls (but less in girls) from 1958 to 1965. The AAHPER Youth Fitness Test was a rather simple motor test consisting of seven basic athletic abilities: pull-ups (modified for girls), sit-ups (feet held), shuttle run, standing broad jump, 50-yard dash, softball throw, and 600-yard run (AAHPER, 1976). In 1956 another random sample was taken using fewer numbers and controls. Little or no improvement was shown over the 1956 random sample. These studies were publicized widely throughout the nation.

President Nixon's Leadership

After Richard M. Nixon was elected president, there was a lull for two years in the activities of the council. Physical educators urged the continuation of the President's program and Office of the Council. A veteran physical educator and administrator, C.C. Conrad, was appointed to the post of executive director, and shortly afterward Glen Swengros, a physical educator and coach from Kansas City, was appointed program director. Captain James A. Lovell, a famous astronaut, was appointed consultant, and other appointments were made to assist in regional clinics and in writing program materials. The council was enlarged greatly and became the President's Council on Physical Fitness and Sports (see Section 9). Various heads of American sports were added to the council membership. Clinics were continued and Conrad began a vigorous program of Presidential Awards and other promotional work. The following took place in rapid succession: 1) the manual *Adult Fitness* was published; 2) other manuals were published, and reports of demonstration clinics were distributed widely; 3) a *Newsletter* was begun; 4) a *Research Digest* was begun; 5) support was given by the council to a plan for reorganization of Olympic sports administration; 6) the *Adult Fitness Survey* was conducted; 7) summer sports programs were projected in collaboration with the NCAA; and 8) strong support was planned for greater participation in Olympic sports. New bulletins included *Vigor* (a complete exercise plan for boys 12-18 years old) and *Vim* (a complete exercise plan for girls 12-18 years old).

The council sought support from major businesses with some success. Beginning in 1969 a series of National Institutes were held on "Executive and Employee Fitness" sponsored jointly by the President's Council and the National Industrial Recreation Association. These involved major speakers on related topics of health and fitness.

TRENDS AND NEEDS

The available time in the school curriculum for systematic physical education, including fitness and sports, has become a major issue. Physical educators and physicians have recommended a minimum average of one hour per school day and, part of this, a double period of at least once per week for play day and sports play for all. The California Association for Health, Physical Education, and Recreation has succeeded in obtaining legislative support for this time allotment,* and other state associations are campaigning for it.

Teachers prepared as *leaders* of fitness are also a major need. This requires better preparation of both the physical education specialists and the classroom teacher. The report of Elsa Schneider on elementary school physical education indicated that 50 percent of the elementary schools studied have no specialized physical education teachers. Considerable correlative instruction in health, tests and measurements, physiology of exercise, and body mechanics (biomechanics) is also needed. A series of national conferences has been conducted to help prepare a larger number of elementary teachers to do this work adequately.

Finally, an exciting new trend has developed in connection with the passing of new laws for the equalization of rights for women (see material on Title IX in Sections 3 and 7). Major adjustments have been made in the portioning of gymnasium and sports facilities and budgets. Coaches have been provided for women's teams, resulting in an upsurge of "athletic training" and fitness activities. Research on physical fitness of women has also been accelerated. But there is much to do in the future, since research on women has lagged behind that for men. The future history of the physical fitness movement in the United States will be enhanced and enriched when the full impact of the explosive increase in the involvement of women in physical fitness and sports activities is realized.

---

* *Editor's note:* Since this article was written, California legislation has passed making physical education optional in the twelfth grade.

REFERENCES

AAHPER, 1935. Physical fitness: Springfield College studies in physical education. Supplement to the *Research Quarterly* **6** (May) : 1-128.

——, 1941. Physical fitness: Springfield College studies in physical education. Supplement to the *Research Quarterly* **12** (May) : 298-493.

——, 1948. Physicians and schools, section III: the physician and physical education. *JOHPER* **19** (April) : 254-257, 304.

——, 1967. Report of the AAHPER Advisory Committee on the Lifetime Sports Education Project. *JOHPER* **38** (November-December) : 33-37.

——, 1976. Youth fitness test manual. (revised) Washington, D.C.: AAHPER.

Bauer, W. W., and F. W. Hein, 1956. *Exercise and health.* Chicago: American Medical Association.

Broekhoff, J., 1976. *Physical education, sports and the sciences.* Eugene, Oreg.: Microfilm Publications, University of Oregon, p. 406.

Cureton, T. K., Jr., 1943a. The physical unfitness of young men. *J. Am. Med. Assn.* **133** (September 11) : 69-74.

——, 1943b. *Warfare aquatics.* Champaign, Ill.: Stipes.

——, 1947a. *Physical fitness appraisal and guidance.* St. Louis: C. V. Mosby.

——, 1947b. *Physical fitness workbook.* (3rd ed.) St. Louis: C. V. Mosby.

——, 1951. *Physical fitness of champion athletes.* Urbana: University of Illinois Press.

——, 1972. *The physiological effects of exercise programs on adults.* Springfield, Ill.: C C Thomas.

Cureton, T. K., Jr., W. J. Huffman, L. Welser, R. W. Kireilis, and D. L. Latham, 1947. *Endurance of young men.* Monograph of the Society for Research in Child Development, Vol. X, Serial No. 40, No. 1, Washington, D.C.

Cureton, T. K., Jr., C. W. Turner, and E. M. Layman, 1943. Physical fitness—a selected bibliography. *Booklist* **39:** 231-240.

Federal Security Agency, 1942. *Physical fitness through physical education.* Pamphlet No. 2 of the Victory Corps Services. Washington, D.C.: U.S. Government Printing Office.

Franks, B. D. (ed.), 1969. *Exercise and fitness.* Chicago: The Athletic Institute.

Grover, G. H., 1959. Professional report from the National Conference on Fitness of Secondary School Youth. *JOHPER* **30** (April) : 47-48.

Harris, E. L., 1959. Fitness through fairs. *JOHPER* **30** (May-June) : 17.

Hershey, Mj. Gen. L. B., 1952. The inside story on rejection rates. *JOHPER* **24** (January) : 9, 26.

Hucklebridge, T. H., 1959. California's fair fitness program. *JOHPER* **30** (May-June) : 18-19.

Hunsicker, P. A., and G. A. Rief, 1964. *A survey and comparison of youth fitness, 1958-65.* Ann Arbor: University of Michigan, in cooperation with the U.S. Office of Education.

Kennedy, J. F., 1961. Keeping fit. *Commonwealth* **73** (June 6) : 377.

Kraus, H., and R. P. Hirshland, 1953. Muscular fitness and health. *JOHPER* **23** (December) : 17-19.

Larson, L. A., 1946. Some findings resulting from the Army Air Forces' physical training program. *Research Quarterly* **17** (March) : 144-164.

McKenzie, R. T., 1944. President of the American Academy of Physical Medicine. *JOHPER* **15** (February) : 76, 90.

Nash, J. B., 1942. Letter to the War Manpower Commission. *JOHPER* **13** (November) : 599.

Sheldon, W. H., S. Stevens, and W. B. Tucker, 1940. *The varieties of human physique.* New York: Harper.

Staley, S. C., T. K. Cureton, Jr., L. Huelster, and A. Barry, 1960. *Exercise and fitness.* Chicago: The Athletic Institute.

U.S. Army Air Force, 1944. The Army Air Forces' physical fitness research program. *Research Quarterly* **15** (March) : 12-15.

SUGGESTED READINGS

AAHPER, 1943. Editorial statement on physical fitness. *JOHPER* **14** (March) : 148-149.

Ainsworth, D., 1943. Our contribution to morale in times of war and peace. *JOHPER* **14** (February) : 57-59.

Cureton, T. K., Jr., 1943. Report on the aquatic standards. *JOHPER* **14** (February) : 86-87.

————, 1952. Survival aquatics for the emergency. *JOHPER* **23** (June) : 41.

Derryberry, M., 1942. The role of education in national fitness. *JOHPER* **13** (June) : 133-136.

Duer, A., 1958. Intercollegiate athletics and youth fitness. *JOHPER* **29** (May-June) : 23, 67.

Duncan, R. O., 1957. Forward with fitness. *JOHPER* **28** (October) : 17.

Friermood, H. T., 1944. Wartime physical education in the YMCA. *JOHPER* **15** (April) : 185-188.

Gardner, F. N., 1957. MCAA concerned with youth fitness. *JOHPER* **28** (April) : 20.

Grout, R. E., 1943. Fitness through health education. *JOHPER* **14** (October) : 429-450.

Halsey, E., and L. Huelster, 1942. The role of college women in war. *JOHPER* **13** (May) : 263-264.

Havel, R. G., 1959. Motivation for fitness. *JOHPER* **30** (October) : 18.

LaSalle, D., 1944. Fitness today on the home front. *JOHPER* **14** (December) : 535-536, 585.

Lawson, F., J. Lawyer, and L. Huelster, 1942. Some exercises for fitness. *JOHPER* **13:** 511-513.

McCloy, C. H., 1943. Militant physical education and physical fitness. *JOHPER* **14** (June) : 313-315, 340.

McCristal, K., 1943. Pre-military training. *JOHPER* (October) : 28-29, 38.

McNeely, S. A., 1951. Facilities, equipment and the emergency. *JOHPER* **22** (October) : 16.

Phillips, M., 1955. How fit are our American schoolchildren? *JOHPER* **26** (September) : 14-15.

Price, H. D., 1942. Tumbling and tumbling safety. *JOHPER* **13** (November) : 531-534.

Steinhaus, A. H., 1946. Contribution of sports to women's fitness. *JOHPER* **17** (October) : 468-506.

7

The Interrelationship of American and European Physical Education

Uriel Simri

The interrelationship of American and European physical education has undergone three major phases within the last two centuries. In the first phase, the import of European physical education to the United States prevailed; in the second, the United States tried to export its own physical education; in the third and present phase, there is a search for ways and means for a two-way interrelationship.

While the import of European physical education activities undoubtedly started with the settling of the United States, it should be pointed out that this phase reached its peak in the nineteenth century. At this time, the European settlers not only brought their systems of education to the United States, but also extended the so-called battle of the systems to American soil. In the long run, neither the German nor the Scandinavian gymnastic systems gained a strong foothold in the United States, and American physical education developed primarily in the footsteps of English physical education, namely, having sports and games as the foundation. It should be pointed out that a similar fate was also the destiny of an indigenous American system of gymnastics, Dio Lewis's "New Gymnastics" in the Civil War era.

The second phase of the interrelationship between American and European physical education began at the turn of the present century and the YMCA played a dominant part in it. At a YMCA affiliated school, Springfield College in Massachusetts, the game of basketball was originated in 1891. Volleyball was invented in 1895 at the Holyoke YMCA, also in Massachusetts. Subsequently, the YMCA undertook a successful attempt to spread these two sports all over the world. While it is true that the first attempts of this kind were made in Asia (basketball in 1898, volleyball in 1900), the games soon gained a foothold on the European continent. Paradoxically, it was the Eastern European countries that gave volleyball its greatest push as a competitive game between the two World Wars, and the United States has attempted ever since to catch up in a game invented within its own boundaries.

American attempts to export its major games of football and baseball, however, have been far less successful. American football is practically unknown outside the United States, with the exception of the Canadian version of the game. Baseball has caught on in Central America and in Japan, but has always remained a minor game in Europe, although 13 nations belonged to the European Baseball Union in 1953, under the influence of American troops stationed in Europe. Softball's fate has been similar, although over 20 nations are affiliated with the International Softball Federation, also founded in 1953 in Oklahoma City. The failure is even more emphasized due to the fact that in the last decade basketball and volleyball have begun to endanger the position of soccer as the most popular game in the world. It should be pointed out that two of the three most popular games of the world, soccer and volleyball, are not among the three most popular games in the United States. This has created an important obstacle to enhancing the interrelationship in the field of sports between the United States and the rest of the world. Another major obstacle has been the different attitude toward women's sports. The United States has always been more reluctant to develop these than Europe and has changed its attitude very slowly.

The third phase of the interrelationship between American and European physical education had its modest beginnings in the 1920s, but reached its peak in the present generation. This phase was symptomized primarily by the creation of international organizations that form a base for wide cooperation. The first important international organizations were the International Federation of Educational Gymnastics (1923), which was later to become (in 1953) the International Federation of Physical Education (FIEP), and the International Federation of Sport Medicine (FIMS), founded in 1928 during the Amsterdam Olympics by representatives from 21 nations. Although these organizations were primarily European, they undoubtedly laid the foundations for later international cooperation.

The female physical educators were among the first to organize internationally in the present generation when they created the International

Association of Physical Education and Sports for Girls and Women (IAPESGW) in 1953. Within a decade or so, this organization was followed by the International Council for Health, Physical Education, and Recreation (ICHPER, 1958), which is attached to the World Confederation of Organizations of the Teaching Profession, and the International Council for Sport and Physical Education (ICSPE, 1960), which is attached to UNESCO.

Contrary to the practice in earlier international organizations, American physical educators played an important role in the creation and operation of these organizations and cooperated closely with their colleagues from other continents, primarily with European physical educators. The frequent symposia, seminars, and professional meetings conducted by these organizations, their subcommittees, and other organizations have provided for a convenient exchange of ideas, knowledge, and information, thus contributing significantly to international cooperation.

The closer international cooperation within our generation has definitely enhanced the adaptation of physical education systems from one country to another. The best example of this phenomenon is the worldwide spread of English Movement Education (or "Educational Gymnastics," as it is known at present), which came into being in the 1940s and has since had a major influence on physical education programs around the world. It may well be that this European system of physical education has been more successful in penetrating the United States than earlier European systems because it was based on a pragmatic philosophy of education, whereas earlier systems had been based on an idealistic or realistic philosophy. It should also be noted that, seemingly, female American physical educators are more internationally minded, and as a result of this attitude, English Movement Education fell on a fruitful ground.

Undoubtedly, the Olympic movement has been a major contributor to international cooperation in sport and physical education. From a modest beginning with 311 athletes from 13 countries in 1896, the Olympic Games have flourished into an event in which well over 7000 athletes from 122 countries participated in 22 sports at Munich in 1972 (not counting the Winter Olympics) and a somewhat smaller number attended the 1976 games in Montreal. The Olympic movement was also instrumental in the creation of most international federations for sports, and the activities of these have spread so much that it was deemed necessary to create a special organization of International Sport Federations (AISF). In spite of many negative developments in the Olympic movement in recent years, it has played a major role in developing sports and in bringing together athletes, coaches, and functionaries from all over the world. One of these negative developments has been the overemphasis on competitive sports, which may have had its major beginning at the Nazi Olympics in Berlin in 1935 and which, until recently, played a major role in the Cold War.

The growing international cooperation of recent years does not necessarily mean that all differences in the outlook on physical education and sports between the United States and other countries have been settled; it means rather that the understanding and knowledge of the varying systems have grown. However, the differences definitely have not yet been bridged, and at present it seems that American physical educators are still less internationally minded than their compatriots in other countries. Only in recent years has the United States become aware of the immense developments in sport sciences in other countries led by the U.S.S.R., the German Democratic Republic, and the German Federal Republic. Although modest attempts, such as the pioneering Phi Epsilon Kappa project, have been made to gain knowledge from others, it seems that the United States still has a long way to go in order to overcome its traditional isolationism in sports.

The present differences in the outlook on physical education are perhaps best exemplified in the area of recreation, in which the United States has undoubtedlyh held the role of pioneer. Whereas the United States, both through the public and the private recreation services, catered more to the individual, the tendency in many European countries has been to emphasize more social and mass activities in this area of endeavor; only recently have these countries turned toward individualized recreation. Another major difference can be found in the attitude toward so-called minor sports. Whereas in the United States relatively little effort is being made to develop these sports, the European approach has been more one of equal rights of development of all sports. Needless to say, the differences of approach toward physical education have not been bridged. The differences can best be seen when we compare the approach of the Communist world to physical education, in which physical education is one of the means of achieving a political goal, with that of American physical education, which in recent years has emphasized such values as carry-over and lifetime activities. But in spite of the differences, it seems that the era of internationalism in physical education and its related areas is here to stay, as proven by the ever-growing cooperation among nations.

8

Women in Sport*
Alyce Cheska and Ellen W. Gerber

In 1972 the United States Olympic team marched into the stadium behind a flag carried by one of its women athletes, Olga Connolly. The honor of publicly reciting the Olympic oath, representing all the assembled athletes, also fell to a woman—a member of the West German team. By contrast, in the United States in 1801 a female teacher in Salem, Massachusetts, was almost ostracized when it was thought that she had instructed her female pupils in the techniques of skating; and in Germany in 1851 a woman was nearly stoned to death for daring to ice skate. These obvious changes in the status of women in sports represent distinct reversals of philosophical attitudes and opinions related to sports for women.

This essay attempts to explore these changes by reporting on the American woman in sport—her choice of activities, the attitudes and opinions that relate to her as a competitor, and the sportswoman herself in terms of what is known about her personality and motivation to participate and her physiological capacities as a female and athlete. Attention is focused on women in competitive sports, that is, organized and structured activities commonly accepted as sport, in which individuals and teams compete against one another for victory and/or records, and which takes place either within a school situation or in the larger social environment.

MORAL CONSIDERATIONS

Philosophically, women's participation in sport involved certain moral considerations. The largest issue stemmed from Puritanical conceptions of the immorality of using one's time unproductively, a major characteristic of sport and play. There also were certain activities deemed inherently immoral, such

---

* See Sections 3 and 7 for information on Title IX and other federal legislation concerning women's sports.

as those associated with cruelty to animals or physical harm to the participants, and those that violated sexual mores by placing men and women in a position to view parts of each other's bodies, as in bathing. The latter problem was especially related to women because participation in physical activity often required dress and positions that could lead to exposure of the ankles or legs, which were taboo body parts in Victorian America.

Another moral issue applied primarily to women was the problem of association. Such sport activities as there were often were accompanied by gambling and drinking; lower-class people were apt to be present as either participants or spectators. Obviously this was not a fit atmosphere for women, all of whom were regarded as "gentlewomen" when it came to such matters.

Finally, it was perceived as immoral to go against the *nature* of woman by encouraging or even permitting her to engage in activities that called for strenuous physical effort, a demonstration of physical prowess, or an overt attempt to compete against others. This belief, which pervaded American thinking until the latter part of the nineteenth century, helped set rigid boundaries to women's sport participation. The strength of the American attitude toward women was such that it overrode the "facts." For example, Colonial and frontier women and several generations of women workers demonstrated their capacity to engage in demanding physical labor. Certainly, their participation in sport activities proved that it was "in their nature" to derive enjoyment from competition and the demonstration of physical skills.

The change in public attitudes began with the understanding of the necessity of physical activity for health purposes. In the United States, for both men and women, the nineteenth century brought recognition of the relationship between physical activity and health. Numerous writers urged the undertaking of exercise, walking, horseback riding, skating, and other activities as appropriate for maintaining health. Catharine Beecher was an early advocate of physical activity for women, although today's liberated females would object to her rationale that it better enabled them to carry out the responsibilities of home and family. Beecher (1855, p. 122), who traveled widely, noted that "the more I traveled . . . the more the conviction was pressed upon my attention that there was a terrible decay of female health all over the land, and that this evil was bringing with it an incredible extent of individual, domestic, and social suffering."

Beecher also recognized that exercise would be more helpful and invigorating if it were amusing, and therefore she advised women to take up sports. Ultimately, this idea was accepted, and physical activity, even to the point of sports and games, was not only declared appropriate for women, but was also seen as a necessary adjunct to their role in society.

ENTRY INTO SPORT

Women's entry into sport was slow and gentle. It began with recreational physical activities such as horseback riding, fox hunting (largely in the South), bathing and later swimming, sleigh or carriage riding (usually driven by a male), ice skating (with a male partner to support and pull her around), roller skating, and bicycle riding.

Women's first real venture into competitive sport began with croquet in the early 1860s, America's first participation in mass sport. Croquet provided an opportunity for a respectable social encounter between men and women, did not demand vigorous or skillful effort, did not require indecorous costumes, and was not associated with gambling. It therefore provided a sport experience for women that did not violate philosophical attitudes toward their participation.

Women's sport activities expanded to archery, bowling, fencing, and, toward the end of the century, tennis and golf. The first tennis tournament for women took place in 1881, and the national women's singles championships, under the United States Lawn Tennis Association (USLTA), were established as early as 1887. The first golf championship, held under the auspices of the United States Golf Association, took place in 1895. In 1900 the first American women's gold medal in the Olympics was won by golfer Margaret Abbot.

Although a few women played baseball, the first team sport really organized for women was basketball, introduced into the colleges in the 1890s. Generally the game was played intramurally with interclass matches the favorite form of competition. The first intercollegiate basketball game took place in 1896 between the University of California, Berkeley, and Stanford University. Field hockey took its place in the Eastern colleges in 1901, followed during the next decade by soccer and volleyball; however, none of these sports ever approached the national popularity of basketball.

Development of sport in the colleges paralleled that of the larger social environment. Recreational clubs, organized by students, gave way to competitive events. In 1886 Vassar students held their first tennis tournament and in 1895 they held the first field day for women. Track and field must have been a specialty of Vassar, for *Spalding's Official Athletic Almanac for 1905* lists students at Vassar College as the holders of most of the women's track and field records of the day. In the 1890s the colleges started to organize athletic associations; the first one was founded at Bryn Mawr in 1891. These organizations, usually under the physical education department, helped to further the development of sport for women by providing a structure for collegiate sport participation.

THE NINETEENTH-CENTURY SCENE—A SUMMARY

Essentially, sport for women in nineteenth-century America can be characterized in the following ways. There were relatively few acceptable activities. Vigorous sports were not developed for either women or men. The costumes did not permit much movement, and those who engaged in sport were primarily gentlemen and gentlewomen who had no taste for hard effort. They were content to engage in that which was easily available and could be performed without working up in indelicate sweat. The activities were primarily of an outdoor nature. Indoor facilities, especially those available to women, had not been constructed on any large scale. Most activities were the individual sports until the colleges began to develop programs of physical activity for women, thus providing clusters of interested women gathered in one location.

Although health factors provided a convenient rationale for the participant, the primary purpose of sport seemed to be the opportunity for a respectable social encounter. Because sport gave men and women something to do together, the activities were often performed in a coeducational setting. Since for either sex the skill level and effort was not high, it was feasible for men and women to compete with one another or in couples. The change to separate sport activities for men and women was influenced by the colleges for women, which sponsored sport activities not involving men. The trend was further developed by the increasing levels of requisite skill and exertion that, in turn, demanded dress that at that time was not deemed suitable for corecreation.

A STEADY GROWTH

During the first two decades of the twentieth century, women's sports experienced a steady growth. In the schools, basketball and tennis were the most popular activities, with field hockey and baseball also favored by many colleges (Dudley 1909; Jacobs 1920). Outside the educational institutions, basketball, swimming, tennis, bowling, and track drew the most adherents and organized competition. The increase came on a variety of levels. In the colleges both intramural and extramural events were held. In the larger social environment competitions were held in conjunction with YWCAs, settlement houses, country clubs, and sports clubs organized for this purpose.

With the passage of the women's suffrage amendment, the 1920s ushered in a decade of new social freedom for women. The booming economy allowed more money and facilities to be provided for sport. The rise in power of organized labor ensured working people (many of whom were women) more leisure time. The jazz age was characterized by a growth of sport. Women especially experienced a great increase in the number and kind of available activities as well as the organization and level of competition. Participation levels were increased and, more important, extended to the middle and working classes on a new scale. Nonschool sport was especially affected.

New Activities

In addition to the more traditional activities, women took up surfing, sailboat racing, speedboating, aviation, curling, polo, fencing, table tennis, squash racquets, shuffleboard, skate-sailing, birling (log rolling), riflery, and even jai alai. The growth of winter sports was very much in evidence. Both men and women competed avidly in skiing, figure skating, speed skating, tobogganing, bobsledding, and dogsledding. Even when the colleges were deemphasizing competition, the Eastern college women retained their intercollegiate winter sports. However, the greatest number of sportswomen were taking part in bowling, softball, and basketball, which were generally under the auspices of the industrial leagues, municipal recreation departments, or colleges.

Organizations Develop

New organizations for women's sport were founded, such as the United States Field Hockey Association (1922) and the United States Women's Squash Racquets Association (1928). Special women's committees were established within older sport groups: for example, the Women's Committee of the Amateur Fencers' League of America (1927), whose avowed purposes were to stimulate interest and to help train women fencers for the Olympic team.

Three groups not associated with particular sports were the Committee on Women's Athletics of the American Physical Education Association (1917), which was changed to the National Section on Girls' and Women's Sports and in 1958 to the Division for Girls' and Women's Sports (DGWS); the Women's Division of the National Amateur Athletic Federation (1923); and the Athletic Conference of American College Women (1917), later known as Athletic Recreation Federation of College Women/College Women in Sport (ARFCW/CWS). The first was an outgrowth of the American Association of Physical Education's Women's Basketball Rules Committee founded in 1899. It gradually expanded its concerns to all of girls' and women's sports in educational institutions. The second group, established with the backing and collaboration of the women physical educators and other organizations, grew out of a national concern for the way in which sports for women were conducted (notably track and field after the AAU decided to sponsor it). It served as a potent force in girls' and women's sports, setting standards and serving as a clearinghouse for problems. In 1940 these two groups merged since their goals and personnel were more or less the same. The third group, which provided college women's athletic associations national, sectional, and state structure, became affiliated in 1961 with DGWS. Their united purpose was to foster the "play ideal" as opposed to the competitive attitude in sports.

High-Level Competition

Nevertheless, in the 1920s there was a growth of high-level competition, with national and international tournaments promoted for most sports. Women even entered previously all-male tournaments in sports such as speedboating, dogsledding, and aviation. National tournaments for women were organized in bowling (1917), basketball (1926), and softball (1933). The women also entered international competition and were in some cases phenomenally successful. The U.S. women swimmers in the 1920 Olympics swept the 100- and 400-meter freestyle events and the springboard diving competition, and also took a gold medal in the 400-meter relay. The first international tennis matches for the Wightman Cup began in 1923 and, thanks to Helen Wills, the American women won and continued to dominate international tennis.

However, when the American women entered international track and field competition in the so-called Women's Olympic Games held in Paris in 1922 and later in the 1928 Olympics, a great outcry arose in the United States. The Women's Division of the NAAF, with the endorsement of numerous concerned organizations, formulated an "Olympic protest" in which they not only sought to keep women from competing in track and field in the Olympics, but also generalized their opposition to high-level competition in all sports. Although they failed in their primary goal, they were very successful in their secondary one. At the very moment when highly competitive women's sport in the larger social scene was receiving unprecedented sponsorship, it was deliberately decided to eliminate it from the schools and colleges. This was the beginning of the "two-track" system in American women's sport—a system that continued for about 40 more years.

Professional Women Athletes

During this time, women not affiliated with educational institutions continued to engage in competition and, of course, in recreational-type activities as well. The variety and intensity as well as the participation levels did decline somewhat from the enthusiasm generated prior to 1935. In general, it was a quiet effort, virtually ignored by the media and the public at large.

One notable exception, however, was the discovery that women had spectator appeal. This led to the development of professional sport for women. In 1943 the All-American Girls Baseball League was organized; in the 1948 season it drew 910,000 paid admissions. The AAGBL folded in 1954, but in its heyday it had ten clubs, spring training camps and tours, postseason playoffs, and all-star appearances. Professional basketball began in 1936 and, despite a five-year time out during World War II, by 1947 over two million fans had paid to watch the women play. One group, the Red Heads, was still playing against men's teams in 1973.

Of course, the most popular and best known of the professional sportswomen are the tennis and golf players. Professional tennis was organized for both men and women in 1926, but it really was not popular until the 1940s when Alice Marble and Mary Hardwick played pro matches all over the country. In a parallel manner, the few professional women golfers playing for sporting goods companies were catalyzed into the National Women's Open Tournament in 1946, largely as a result of the public interest in Mildred (Babe) Didrikson Zaharias. The Ladies' Professional Golf Association, organized in 1950, still flourishes. A women's professional football league with four teams made its debut in 1972, and professional women jockeys have established their activities in recent years.

NONSCHOOL SPORTS ORGANIZATIONS

In this century extensive children and youth sports programs have been maintained by several nonschool organizations. The influential Amateur Athletic Union, founded in 1888, today maintains programmed activities for close to five million American youth. The AAU sponsors the annual Junior Olympics for boys and girls ages 7-17. The pre-Olympic trials for the selection of competitors representing the United States are conducted by the AAU. Currently the AAU promotes and governs amateur sports in 13 different activities from basketball to wrestling. It serves as the official representative of the United States in many international sports federations; however, this favored position is being eroded by other governing bodies such as the United States Collegiate Sports Council, which sends sports competitors to the biennial University World Games. Another example of a separate governing group for international competition, the National Archery Association, is the official representative to the Federation International Target Archery (FITA). The NAA governs target archery competition in the United States and selects members of the U.S. Olympic archery team. The U.S. Olympic Committee, with its 23 affiliate national sports governing groups, is the official U.S. voice in the International Olympic Committee, which sponsors the quadrennial Olympic Games.

The National Recreation Association has provided extensive services of planning, programming, personnel, publications, and research to community recreation programs. The Young Women's Christian Association (see Section 9) has traditionally offered physical activity programs to community youth and adults. Churches, political units, and labor unions have also offered sports programming for their constitutents. Sometimes, churches and political leaders have used sports for promotional purposes. Private youth agencies such as the Girl Scouts, the Campfire Girls, and 4H Clubs maintain viable sports programs for their members. Private commercial businesses successfully appeal to girls and women primarily in bowling, dance, golf, swimming, and tennis. Summer sports camps, particularly in the eastern part of the country, have enjoyed popularity for girls and boys alike.

A SPORT FOR EVERY GIRL

While highly skilled women and teams were flourishing, the school and college programs were focused instead on the masses of students. "A sport for every girl and every girl in a sport" was the motto of the leaders in educational sport, and they sought to implement their philosophy by providing full intramural programs. As various surveys (Levitt 1937; Scott 1945; White 1954) show, these were programs with a large number of participants competing for points or trophies in three to eight different sports per institution.

Such intercollegiate or interscholastic competition as there was took place primarily in the form of play days and sports days, events that minimized the competition and, therefore, the necessary level of skill. Telegraphic meets were favored in the Midwest where they proved a successful way to compete in sports such as bowling and archery. All girls and women who so desired were qualified for the programs offered.

DGWS ENCOURAGED EXTRAMURAL SPORT

In 1963 the Division for Girls' and Women's Sports (now NAGWS) of the AAHPER (now AAHPERD) modified its stand. It noted the value of competitive activities and their use in achieving desired educational objectives and therefore advocated a carefully planned program of extramural competition to meet the needs of the more highly skilled girl. The earlier DGWS slogan was replaced by "The one purpose of sports for girls and women is the good of those who play." From 1963 to 1970 the Women's Board of the U.S. Olympic Committee and the DGWS cosponsored five national institutes on girls' sports. The plan to increase the quality and quantity of sport programs for school and college girls had the effect, through cooperation with national sport groups, of opening the door to the approved extramural competition.

Prior to this date, the physical educators had chosen to isolate their work from the larger sport scene because of the incompatibility of the two philosophies of competition. By 1950 the first DGWS liaison personnel were designated to a major sport organization (the Council for National Cooperation in Aquatics). Since then, joint committees of DGWS and several national and international sports groups have worked toward standardizing playing rules and officials' ratings. Thus, for example, in 1964 the DGWS and the AAU agreed upon a common set of rules for basketball. Among others, the USLTA, the U.S. Field Hockey Association, and the U.S. Women's Lacrosse Association rules are shared by DGWS.

A National Joint Committee on Extramural Sports for College Women was formed by the ARFCW, NAPECW, and DGWS (1957) to aid the development of intercollegiate sports; it delegated its functions to the DGWS in 1965. In turn, the DGWS established the Commission on Intercollegiate Athletics for Women (1967) and charged it with being the controlling body for the schedule of national intercollegiate tournaments that it wished to establish. In 1972 this group became the Association for Intercollegiate Athletics for Women (AIAW). It establishes membership criteria, sets policies, sanctions events, and sponsors regional and national tournaments in seven sports: basketball, badminton, golf, gymnastics, swimming and diving, track and field, and volleyball. It also sanctions tournaments such as the Women's College World Series of Softball. Another important function is its cooperative work with, and voting rights in, important national and international sport governing bodies such as the United States Collegiate Sports Council. Through the NAGWS and AIAW, school and college sport for women, organized through physical education, is firmly connected to national and international sport taking place in the larger social environment. An interesting note is the local and state efforts of NAGWS to gain a more effective voice by women in the state high school athletics associations. Participation in interscholastic sports in the secondary schools has paralleled the expansion on the college level.

THE WOMEN ATHLETE—CONTEMPORARY ISSUES

When the physical educators chose to embrace the concept of intercollegiate sport, the two channels of development began to re-merge into a single concerted effort to promote girls' and women's sports. With this new focus came an interest in studying the female athlete both as a person per se and within the context of American social mores.

Physiological Aspects of Participants

Basic questions concerning the physiological aspects of female participation in sports are: 1) Does the female receive positive physiological benefits from sports participation? 2) What biological differences exist between the male and female that affect athletic performance? and 3) Should women's and men's sports activities have varied standards of excellence based on sex differences?

If one must be physically fit to participate in vigorous sports or if sports participation makes one fit, continues to be argued. Dr. Tenley Albright, Boston surgeon and former Olympic gold medal winner, maintains that to attain some degree of fitness one must perform the game or exercise at least 30 to 45 minutes, three times a week, for six weeks (Albright 1971). However, Dr. Kenneth Cooper (1970) points out that the vitally important cardiovascular aspects of physical fitness are only produced by rhythmical activities such as running, swimming, cycling, and brisk walking, and that brief intermittent activities, such as most ball games, have little effect in training. Research evidence indicates that men and women champion athletes, compared with nonathletes, have more highly efficient hemotological and cardiovascular systems (McArdle 1972). It can be concluded that physical training regimens are physiologically beneficial for both sexes (Brown et al. 1972), and that if these programs are abandoned, the benefits diminish (Drinkwater 1972; Michael et al. 1972).

From the moment of conception the female and the male organisms exhibit markedly different patterns of development. The normal female matures earlier than the male and produces a greater amount of estrogen and less androgen; the male produces significantly more androgen than estrogen; thus, each develops appropriate secondary sex characteristics (Wyrick 1971). The female anatomical structure is characterized by less bone and muscle mass, a lower center of gravity, and more fatty tissue as compared with the male's bone and muscle structure. Females have less genetic defectiveness in all "sex-linked" conditions and stronger overall resistance to most major diseases. With the advent of puberty, she will sequentially experience the specific female processes of ovulation, menstruation, pregnancy, and menopause (Scheinfeld 1965).

Menstrual cramps are common among adolescent girls; however, whether cause is anatomical-physiological change or related to psychological factors, physical activity almost always has a beneficial effect. Menstruation need not interrupt performance of most games and sports. Generally, female athletes are able to achieve their average sports performance throughout the entire menstrual cycle, including menses (Shaffer 1972). Research by Erdelyi (1961) and Gendel (1968) and others indicates no reason to restrict physical activity of women because of the reproductive organs and no need for concern about later effects of sports competition on pregnancy, labor, and later health.

The curve of development in vigorous athletic performance in the sexes is similar, with girls reaching their maximal stage between 12 and 13 years, while boys go on improving their performance until age 18-20 (Garai 1968). By the age of 20 the average male weighs 20 percent more than the female and is 10 percent taller (Anastasi 1958). The muscle mass of the male will exceed that of the female by 50 percent. The greater height and weight of the males appear to play and important role in the development of skills and interests in athletics and sport activities and the attainment of undisputed superiority by adult males in these physical skills (Garai 1968).

In comparing Olympic and world records in track and field and swimming, Van der Merwe (1972) noted a diminishing percentage difference of the records of men and women, but concluded that the males have anatomical and physiological advantages that will always favor them in these athletic events. Adrian (1972) states, "Where sports success is greatly related to or dependent upon strength and power, the average women cannot hope to achieve, much less surpass, the man's performance."

Psychological Aspects of Participants

Do women athletes have different personality characteristics than other groups of women? Can a woman be an athlete and still retain her femininity? How do parents, peers, and the participants themselves feel about high-level competition for women? What are the reasons motivating female athletes to commit themselves to intensive training and participation in sport? Are their motivations similar to or different from their male peers? These are some of the main questions that arose out of the new interest in girls' and women's sport.

Researchers sought answers to these questions, but it must be noted at this juncture that the research is scanty, fairly unsophisticated, and, in the case of some studies, done with instruments that are based on outmoded theories of femininity.

Personality profile. The personality of various populations of women athletes was studied by Ogilvie and Tutko (1967), Peterson, Weber, and Trousdale (1967), Ibrahim (1967), Malumphy (1968), Mushier (1970), Williams *et al.* (1970), Berkey (1972), Morris (1972), and Johnson (1972). These researchers each noted some significant differences in the women athletes as contrasted with the general female population. The athletes who were surveyed with a standard personality inventory (usually the Cattell 16 Personality Factor Inventory or the Edwards Personal Preference Schedule) were intercollegiate athletes or national or international class performers. The results generally showed that the women athletes were more achievement oriented, assertive or aggressive, autonomous, tough minded, conscientious, and expressed themselves freely. However, champion caliber sportswomen tended to be less social in that they were more cool, aloof, introverted, and reserved, with less need for affiliation or nurturance.

Most of the characteristics attributed to the women athletes are described in the pyschological literature as being more socially desirable than the more traditional traits assigned to the feminine stereotype. Thus, the athlete tends to be nonstereotypic but more socially desirable in terms of what is considered a healthy adult.

Attitudes toward competitors and their sports. The independence of the women athlete is further verified by her choice of sport as a mode of activity. Attitudes toward the sportswomen have been mixed but in recent years have become much more positive. The most recent surveys on attitudes toward women athletes (which are the only applicable to contemporary society) include studies by Harres (1968), Sherriff (1969), and DeBacy, Spaeth, and Busch (1970). Sampled were attitudes toward competition for girls and women held by college students in California, selected California parents and peers, and college men in New York State. They found attitudes to be moderately favorable, but, within the samples, wide ranges of opinions existed. In other words, there was still no general agreement on the favorableness of competition for women.

Perhaps more to the point, Brown (1965) and Griffin (1972) both studied the image of women athletes by having their subjects compare women in their roles as athletes with various other women's roles, including cheerleader, mother, sexy girl, housewife, girlfriend, and ideal woman. The results of both studies indicate that while college men and women viewed the women athlete as more active and potent than women in other roles, they also ranked them lower on the evaluative feminine image and role scales. In other words, the woman athlete is faced with the problem that her peer group is not yet ready to fully accept women in active and potent roles. The passive, impotent female is still preferred in today's society.

Furthermore, society has definite opinions as to which activities are appropriate for women and which are not. In general, activities that require an overt show of strength or endurance, that have the potential for body contact, or that have been played primarily by members of the working classes are on the nonapproved list. Rating high on the approved lists are activities that emphasize aesthetic appeal and activities that historically were popular with the wealthier classes. Thus, recent surveys by Harres (1968), Sherriff (1969), Garman (1969), and Petrie (1971), sampling California parents and peers, the general public and spectators at softball games, and college sport participants, showed that swimming and tennis were the top two activities, with gymnastics and bowling ranking third. At the bottom of each list were track and the team sports, including basketball, softball, and volleyball. The woman athlete, however, continues to exhibit the qualities noted earlier, asserting the right to make her own choices in accord with her personal preferences. Thus, surveys of participation in college and out, throughout the United States, indicate that the greatest number of women athletes are competing in the team sports as they have been for several decades.

Motivation of women athletes. It is difficult to account for women's athletic preferences because very little research has been done on the motivation of the woman athlete. Two studies by Petrie (1971) and by Berlin (1971) yield some insights. Petrie found that women emphasized companionship, fun and enjoyment, and social interaction as values for participation. Berlin found three pervasive motives: the contribution to a participant's self-regard, challenges for the attainment of mastery, and opportunity for expression and interaction. Morris (1972), in studying intercollegiate women swimmers, found their primary incentives were enjoyment of competitive team rather than club membership, parental encouragement, competition, and having their individual achievement recognized. Of course, each individual athlete participates for reasons of her own, which are usually complex and multifaceted. There is not yet sufficient data to ascertain whether these reasons differ in any significant manner from those of comparable male athletes. Certainly, autobiographical descriptions published by highly successful and obviously articulate athletes show remarkable similarity in their professed motivations and commitments to success (Neal 1972).

CULTURALLY ACCEPTABLE SPORT FORMS FOR WOMEN

A sport activity is amoral; it is only when interpretations are added by the participant and observer that value judgments of acceptability are born. The concept of "acceptable sport forms" is carried about in society's collective mind. Culturally, our society does not expect and certainly does not demand that women compete in sports.

Who the participant is affects the approval of the sport. Weisstein (1969) asks the question, "How are women characterized in our culture. . . ? They are inconsistent, emotionally unstable, lacking in a strong conscience or superego, weaker, nurturant rather than productive, intuitive rather than intelligent, and, if they are at all 'normal,' suited to the home and the family. In short, the list adds up to a typical minority-group stereotype of inferiority."

When the sport participant is a female, the image of inferiority affects her concept of self and that which others have of her and what she is doing. Traits considered undesirable in women include aggressiveness, independence, ambition, and devotion to some goal other than being a wife and mother. These are exactly the attributes young women must have to succeed in attaining a role different from the home orientation. Problems facing a young woman who wishes to pursue an interest in sports and athletic competition cluster in two areas: 1) conflicts that arise in choosing this role and 2) problems that are involved in achieving fulfillment in the chosen role. She is risking being different and therefore undesirable and unfeminine (Cheska 1970).

If the female engages in sport activities, then certain forms are generally more acceptable than others. Methany's list (1965) includes swimming, diving, skiing, figure skating, golf, archery, tennis, and bowling. She feels these forms are characterized by such principles as: 1) projection of the body into or through spaces in aesthetically pleasing patterns, as diving; 2) utilization of a manufactured device to facilitate bodily movements, as skiing; 3) application of force through a light implement, as golf; 4) overcoming the resistance of a light object, as archery; and 5) maintenance of a spatial barrier that prevents body contact with opponent, as tennis.

Methany further adds that it appears inappropriate for women to engage in contests in which: 1) the resistance of the opponent is overcome by bodily contact, as wrestling; 2) the resistance of a heavy object is overcome by direct application of bodily force, as shot put; 3) the body is projected into or through space over long distances or for extended periods of time, as marathon races.

Social expectations about women are difficult to change; however, some progress is being made in allowing the female to achieve in an achievement-oriented society, to be expressive and independent along with the male. As the female begins to understand what is fact, what is cultural, and what is myth, she will have a basis from which to understand and select the roles in life she would like to play (Zobie 1972).

Girls and women may have been led to a limited repertoire of roles from limited training in interaction situations: the present youthful generation appears to be more exposed to more possibilities for flexibility. Girls should understand that achieving in sport is a thing to do, or an interaction situation to be experienced, which does not have to change the girl's being or femininity outside of that situation, except perhaps to enrich it. The important goal is total involvement in the sport situation and then the ability to enter into other and different interaction situations after the game is over. A positive sense of self-esteem would enable them to elect their roles and enjoy their freedom of choice (Zoble 1972). One of these choices is the role of women in sports.

REFERENCES

Adrain, M., 1972. Sex differences in biomechanics. Paper presented at Women and Sport Conference, Pennsylvania State University, University Park, Pennsylvania, August 13-18.

Albright, T. E., 1971. Which sports for girls? in Dorothy Harris (ed.), *DGWS research reports: women in sports,* pp. 53-57. Washington, D.C.: AAHPER.

Anastasi, A., 1958. *Differential psychology: individual and group differences in behavior.* (3rd ed.) New York: Macmillan.

Beecher, C., 1855. *Letters to the people on health and happiness.* New York: Harper & Bros.

Berkey, R., 1972. Psychology of women who compete. *California Association for Health, Physical Education and Recreation Journal* **43** (January-February) : 6, 18.

Berlin, P., 1971. A theoretical explanation of the motives of college women to engage in competitive sport. Paper presented at the Third Canadian Psycho-Motor Learning and Sports Psychology Symposium, Vancouver, British Columbia, October 26.

Brown, H. C., J. R. Harrower, and M. F. Deeter, 1972. The effects of cross-country running on pre-adolescent girls. *Medicine and Science in Sports* **4** (Spring) : 1-5.

Brown, R. E., 1965. A use of the semantic differential to study the feminine image of girls who participate in competitive sports and certain other school-related activities. Unpublished doctoral dissertation. Tallahassee: Florida State University.

Cheska, A., 1970. Current developments in competitive sports for girls and women. *JOHPER* **41** (March) : 86-91.

Cooper, K. H., 1970. *The new aerobics.* New York: Bantam Books.

DeBacy, D. L., R. Spaeth, and R. Busch, 1970. What do men really think about athletic competition for women? *JOHPER* **41** (November-December) : 28-29, 70.

Drinkwater, B. L., and S. M. Horvath, 1972. Detraining effects on young women. *Medicine and Science in Sports* **4** (Summer) : 91-95.

Dudley, G., and F. A. Keller, 1909. *Athletic games in the education of women.* New York: Holt.

Erdelyi, G. J., 1961. Women in athletics. *Proceedings,* Second National Conference on Medical Aspects of Sports, American Medical Association, Chicago.

Garai, J. E., and A. Scheinfeld, 1968. Sex differences in mental and behavioral traits. *Genetic Psychology Monographs* **77**: 170-299.

Garman, J. F., 1969. A study of attitudes toward softball competition for women. M.S. thesis. Santa Barbara: University of California.

Gendel, E. S., 1968. Physicians, females, physical exertion, and sports. *Proceedings,* Fourth National Institute on Girls' Sports, pp. 9-12. Washington, D.C.: AAHPER.

Griffin, P. S., 1972. Perceptions of women's roles and female sport involvement among a selected sample of college students. M.S. thesis. Amherst: University of Massachusetts.

Harres, B., 1968. Attitudes of students toward women's athletic competition. *Research Quarterly* **39** (May) : 278-284.

Ibrahim, H., 1967. Comparison of temperament traits among intercollegiate athletes and physical education majors. *Research Quarterly* **38** (October) : 615-622.

Jacobs, E. E., 1920. *A study of the physical vigor of American women.* Boston: Marshall Jones.

Johnson, P. A., 1972. A comparison of personality traits of superior skilled women athletes in basketball, bowling, field hockey, and golf. *Research Quarterly* **43** (December) : 409-415.

Leavitt, N. M., and M. W. Duncan, 1937. The status of intramural programs for women. *Research Quarterly* **8** (March) : 68-69.

Malumphy, T. M., 1968. Personality of women athletes in intercollegiate competition. *Research Quarterly* **39** (October) : 610-620.

McArdle, W. D., *et al.*, 1972. Reliability and interrelationships between maximal oxygen intake, physical work capacity, and set-up test scores in college women. Medicine and Science in Sports **4** (Winter) : 182-186.

Metheny, E., 1965. *Connotations of movement in sport and dance.* Dubuque, Iowa: Wm. C. Brown.

Michael, E., *et al.*, 1972. Physiological changes of teenage girls during five months of detraining. *Medicine and Science in Sports* **4** (Winter) : 214-218.

Morris, B. J., 1972. College women swimmers' attitudes toward training and competing. M.S. thesis. Urbana-Champaign: University of Illinois.

Mushier, C., 1970. A cross-sectional study of the personality factors of girls and women in competitive lacrosse. Paper presented at AAHPER National Convention, Boston, Massachusetts, April 4.

Neal, P., 1972. *Sport and identity.* Philadelphia: Dorrance & Co.

Ogilvie, B., and T. Tutko, 1967. The unanswered question: competition, its effect upon femininity. Paper presented to the Olympic Development Committee, Santa Barbara, California, June 30.

Peterson, S., J. C. Weber, and W. W. Trousdale, 1967. Personality traits of women in team sports vs. women in individual sports. *Research Quarterly* **38** (December) : 689-690.

Petrie, B. M., 1971. Achievement orientations in adolescent attitudes toward play. *International Review of Sport Sociology* **6:** 89-98.

Scheinfeld, A., 1965. *Your heredity and environment.* Philadelphia: Lippincott.

Scott, G. M., 1945. Competition for women in American colleges and universities. *Research Quarterly* **16** (March) : 49-71.

Shaffer, T. E., 1972. Physiological considerations of the female participant. Paper presented at Women and Sport Conference, Pennsylvania State University, University Park, Pennsylvania, August 13-18.

Sherriff, M. C., 1969. The status of female athletes as viewed by selected peers and parents in certain high schools of central Callfornia. M.A. thesis. Chico: California State University.

Van der Merwe, G. W., 1972. The influence of anatomical and physiological differences between the two sexes on athletic achievement. Paper presented at International Olympic Academy, XII Session, Ancient Olympia, Greece, July 12-20.

Weisstein, M., 1968. *Kinder, kuche, kirche as scientific law: psychology constructs the female.* Boston: New England Free Press. (rev. ed., 1969)

White, C., 1954. Extramural competition and physical education activities for college women. *Research Quarterly* **25** (October) : 344-363.

Williams *et al.*, 1970. Personality traits of champion level fencers. *Research Quarterly* **41** (October) : 446-453.

Wyrick, W., 1971. How sex differences affect research in physical education. In Dorothy Harris (ed.), *DGWS research reports: women in sports,* pp. 21-30. Washington, D.C.: AAHPER.

Zoble, J., 1972. Femininity and achievement in sports. Paper presented at Women and Sport Conference, Pennsylvania State University, University Park, Pennsylvania, August 13-18.

SCHOOL PROGRAMS

Introduction

Section 3 presents acceptable physical education concepts and programs predominating currently in American schools. Due to its great length, the section was divided into five parts representing traditional school levels, and each part has a different editor. In deference to Title IX regulations and their potential effect on present programs in physical education, Chapters 19, 28, 35, and 43 focus on sex-integrated classes and/or programs.

The first five chapters of this section are on preschool physical education. Considerable attention to the status of research on the sequence and consistency of motor development is given by Doudlah and Rarick. Some controversy exists as to whether motor development follows an orderly sequence and proceeds at a consistent rate between and within individuals. There is general agreement that 1) adult motor skills are based on the reactions and reflexes of the prenatal period, 2) these reflexes are determined genetically, 3) the central nervous system integrates the processes inherent in motor development, and 4) the central nervous system needs environmental stimulation if the genetic potential of an individual is to be realized.

Most of the systems (discussed by Janus) used by therapists in treating delayed motor, personality, and learning development in preschool children are based on these four assumptions. The latter assumption is of paramount significance to the physical education of normal preschool children as well, in that it infers (Seefeldt and Eckert) the importance of parents, teachers, and therapists in providing early encouragement and practice in motor skills.

Chapters 14-19 focus on elementary school physical education. The main emphasis is on programs and curricula, including those for the physically handicapped (Hooley) and the mentally retarded (Kalakian). However, since many other facets are pertinent to the successful conduct of programs, chapters are included on organization (Zimmerman), assessment of program objectives (Espenschade), and facilities (Kerch). In addition, various authors touch on growth characteristics, traits, attitudes, and appropriate teaching methods.

Chapter 14 on curriculum is further divided into six parts based upon recommended main elements of an elementary phsyical education program. These include movement education (Zimmerman and Barrett), sports skills and games (Tanner), dance (Zimmerman), stunts and tumbling (Magida), problem-solving approaches (Barrett), and extraclass activities (Stafford).

Chapters 20-28, on junior high school physical education, cover many of he same topics as the previous chapters on younger children, but concentrate on the developing adolescent. For example, 1) Lockhart and Antonnaci outline the differences in growth and development between boys and girls aged 12 through 14; 2) Kilpatrick discusses various class-scheduling modules including flexible and ungraded scheduling techniques, and suggests specific activities that should be included in junior high school physical education programs; 3) Haas develops a rationale for participation in intramurals and expands his treatment of the subject to include utilization of facilities, types of activities, extent of participation, and awards; 4) Banjamin outlines the values of participation in athletics—interestingly, he reviews research on Little League players to substantiate beneficial effects of athletic participation in the junior high schools; and 5) Goldberger and Gober review the research on the "command" versus the discovery styles of teaching physical education and conclude that the individualized style of teaching should predominate in junior high school physical education.

Chapter 23 on the middle school was included because of the recent increase in the number of these schools nationally. Stafford offers a rationale for changing to the middle school concept—that is, a child-centered rather than a subject-centered emphasis—and points out that intramurals and recreation are to be stressed rather than interscholastic athletics.

Chapters 29-35, on high school physical education, begin with a comprehensive piece on major aspects of the more traditional high school physical education program and follow with more specific topics and innovative approaches. Wright discusses, in traditional language and terminology, aims and objectives, growth characteristics of high school students, the activity program, intramurals, and interscholastic activities. By contrast, Corbin uses the language of the business world when he speaks of students as consumers and suggests that schools should be held accountable for the "product" they turn out. He leans toward the integrated approach and the unit or modular approach. Kneer enlarges on the accountability theme and discusses the concept of competency-based physical education. She describes the physically educated high school student in terms of precise competencies in the psychomotor, cognitive, and affective domains.

Darst is critical of traditional physical education programs, suggesting that they have failed to create a learning environment conducive to lifelong enjoyment of physical activity. His solution, like Corbin's, is to subscribe to the Leonard philosophy (see Chapter 1) and stress a greater choice of activities, particularly of the lifelong type. Pate stresses the importance of a comprehensive testing program in physical or athletic fitness, motivation, cognitive information, and health-related fitness such as the amount of body fat, and so on. The inclusion of Wickens's chapter on the independent or private school recognizes the importance of this large segment of the physical education spectrum. With minor differences in emphasis, independent high school physical education programs tend to parallel those in public high schools.

The last part of Section 3, Chapters 36-43, covers college and university physical education, including each of the programs offered within the typical American college and university: basic instruction (activity), intramurals, intercollegiate athletics, and the undergraduate and graduate professional preparation programs. Most colleges and universities also include recreation programs and sports clubs, which are growing in popularity. However, the former is not discussed here, while the latter is mentioned only briefly in Price's article on intramurals.

The traditional basic instruction program is covered by Reuter, who discusses philosophy, statistics on number of schools with programs, the status of the physical education requirement for the general student, suggested programs, and commonly taught activities. A variation on the traditional theme is the foundation concept discussed by McCristal. In this program, all students are required to take a foundations course that includes lectures on exercise physiology and health-related topics, as well as to participate in physical fitness activities *prior* to selection of typical sports activities.

Description of the undergraduate and graduate preparation programs is left to Esslinger and LaSalle, and McCue and Esslinger. They discuss student origins, necessary faculty and resources, requirements for entry, and a recommended curriculum. These articles lack discussion on curricula leading to careers other than teaching; however, the vast majority of physical education majors still pursue teaching and coaching careers.

Price discusses the history of intramurals in higher education, the philosophy of intramurals, and administration of programs. He uses the table of contents of a proposed intramurals handbook to illustrate the large number of details that must be attended to in the proper administration of a comprehensive intramurals program.

Frost delivers a solid and impartial analysis of a most difficult and controversial subject — the relationship between physical education and intercollegiate athletics in higher education. He covers theoretical considerations, facilities, personnel, administrative structures, problems, and future prospects. He distinguishes between "smalltime" and "bigtime" athletics but insists that, regardless of the emphasis at a particular college or university, athletics must always be educationally defensible.

JSB

Warren Johnson   Helen Zimmerman   B. Don Franks

Lynn W. McCraw   Arthur A. Esslinger

Section Editors

Editor of Chapters 9-13, on preschool physical education, is Warren Johnson, professor of health education and physical education at the University of Maryland, where he is also director of the Children's Health and Developmental Clinic. A native of Denver, Dr. Johnson was educated at the University of Denver (Phi Beta Kappa), Boston University, and Harvard University. He served as a fighter pilot in the Marine Corps during World War II. He has received the Honor Awards of both the AAHPERD and the EDA and is a Fellow of the American Academy of Physical Education, the American College of Sports Medicine, the American School Health Association, and the Society for the Scientific Study of Sex. His book, *Science and Medicine of Exercise and Sport* (Harper 1960; 2nd edition, coedited with E. R. Buskirk 1974) is credited with having been a major factor in giving physical education scientific orientation. His clinic, launched in 1957, has become a model for clinical and humanistic physical education programs for children with developmental difficulties. Controlled research has given the clinic a scientific base that has helped numerous other clinics become established in this country and abroad.

Editor of Chapters 14-19, on elementary school physical education, is Helen M. Zimmerman, who taught general elementary school and physical education for the St. Louis Board of Education. She then moved to secondary school teaching upon completion of the master's degree at St. Louis University. She received M.S. and Ph.D. degrees from the University of Wisconsin. She was a consultant for elementary school physical education in the St. Louis schools at Harris Teachers College. In 1952 she joined the faculty at Southern Illinois University, Carbondale. She served in local and national offices and her publications include articles in the *Encyclopedia of Sports Medicine,* the *Research Quarterly, JOHPER,* and the *Illinois Journal of Education.*

Editor of Chapters 20-28, on junior high school physical education, is B. Don Franks, who received his education at the University of Arkansas (B.S.E., M.Ed., 1961) and the University of Illinois (Ph.D., 1967). He has experience in high school teaching and coaching (Arkansas), and college and university teaching and research at Pain College, the University of Illinois, Temple University, and the University of Tennessee. He has served as supervisor of the University of Illinois Physical Fitness Research Laboratory (under direction of Dr. T. K. Cureton and Dr. B. Massey), coordinator of Temple University Biokinetics Research Laboratory, and is currently chairperson of the University of Tennessee Physical Education Division. His major areas of interest are the evaluation of and recommendations for physical fitness. He has been involved with a moderate amount of research, writing, and professional activities in these areas. His research includes work (with others) on the acute and chronic effects of exercise on the time components of the left ventrical. His writing includes a book on evaluation (co-authored with Dr. H. Deutsch). He has also edited books of fitness and written chapters in books on erogenic aids (edited by W. P. Morgan) and stress testing (edited by Dr. E. Chung). He is past chairperson of the AAHPERD Physical Fitness Council and past secretary of the Research Council. He is a Fellow in the American College of Sports Medicine and has served on the Research Committee of NCPEAM. He has served on the president's advisory committee for NAPECW.

Editor of Chapters 29-35, on senior high school physical education, is Lynn Wade McCraw. He has been a graduate professor and former chairman of physical and health education at the University of Texas at Austin for over thirty years. He served five years in the U.S. Army and is a lieutenant colonel in the Army Reserves. He received the bachelor's degree from Austin College, Sherman, Texas, and holds the master's and doctorate from the University of Texas. He has contributed to the profession through research and publications, workshops and addresses for professional and lay groups, and service in numerous organizations. He is a past vice-president of the AAHPERD and has been a member of the AAHPERD Research Council since 1950. He served as president of the Texas AAHPERD and since 1954 has been executive-secretary and editor of the *Texas HPER Journal.* He was honored with membership in the American Academy of Physical Education and in Phi Delta Kappa and Phi Kappa Phi. He is included in several *Who's Who* publications and has received the Honor Awards from the AAHPERD, the Southern District of the HPERD, and the Texas HPERD.

Editor of Chapters 36-43, on college and university physical education, is Arthur A. Esslinger, now deceased. He was for many years a professor of physical education and dean of the school of health and physical education at the University of Oregon. He received the B.S. and M.S. degrees from the University of Illinois in 1931 and 1932, respectively, and the doctorate from the University of Iowa in 1938. He held positions at Bradley University and Stanford University and served as director of physical education at Springfield College from 1946 to 1953. He was active in many professional organizations such as the AAHPERD, having served as an officer in the Eastern District and the Southern District, and was president of the then AAHPER in 1959. He was a Fellow of both the AAHPERD and the American Academy of Physical Education. He had an illustrious career in the military, having held a number of prestigious positions such as chief, physical reconditioning branch, office of the Surgeon General, and director of physical training, Army Service Forces. He was the author of a number of military manuals and pamphlets on exercise, coauthor of a book on the organization and administration of physical education, and a regular contributor to *JOHPER,* the *Physical Educator,* and the annual *Proceedings* of the NCPEAM.

9

Genetic and Environmental Determinants of Movement Behavior

Vern Seefeldt

The motor development of infants and young children is currently the focus of renewed scientific investigation. Movement behavior of children occupied a prominent place in the research literature and clinical studies of several decades ago, but these reports were confined primarily to descriptive-experiential accounts of emerging skills on resident groups of children (Bayley 1935; Gesell 1940; Shirley 1931). Interest in motor development waned after the early 1940s as attention was diverted to the cognitive and social development of children. Recent evidence that associates cognitive skills with motor ability has been partially responsible for the resurgence of interest in this area (Ayres 1972; Frostig 1970; Hunt 1961; Piaget 1971). New efforts in movement behavior are characterized by the continued description of the stages, patterns, and sequences of movement in a physiologically changing individual (Milani-Comparetti 1967; Shambes 1973; Wickstrom 1970), but there are also the beginnings of theorizing about the reasons for change and why certain variables appear to be more important during certain periods than at others.

GENETIC DETERMINANTS

The genetic component of movement behavior is well defined in terms of the orderly sequence of reflexes and reactions that emerge from the maturing organism (Gesell 1941; McGraw 1943; Illingsworth 1967). Hooker's (1952) classical investigations on fetuses demonstrated the predictable nature of the human response as determined by maturation of the nervous system. Numerous developmental schedules that recorded the chronology of motor behavior of infancy and early childhood indicate that the orderly nature of motor behavior was not confined to intrauterine life (Bayley 1935; Frankenburg 1967; Hellebrandt 1961). The preoccupation of investigators with descriptive studies may have been responsible for the erroneous belief held by many that the emergence of motor skills was part of an inflexible series of events under the control of a maturing nervous system. The notion that motor development is governed by a predetermined force, unalterable by daily experiences, may have discouraged scholars from studying motor function as an independent or dependent variable in human behavior.

Current research evidence supports the view that the repertoire of movements common to human beings varies according to genetic constitution. Maturation is no longer regarded as an invariable condition for motor skill acquisition. Current concepts of "readiness" emphasize the role of previous experience in acquiring new skills. In essence, the previous dependence upon biological maturation as a prerequisite condition for learning has been replaced by considerations of how the environment can be modified to facilitate learning. Although it is impossible to distinguish the contributions made to motor development by genetics and environment, it is apparent that there is a compound influence in operation, with genetics determining the bounds of behavior and the environment modifying the expression of specific skills and attributes (Thompson 1970).

ENVIRONMENTAL DETERMINANTS

Manipulation of the environment to retard or facilitate the expression of motor skills is a time-honored practice in studies on infra-humans. Reports on numerous forms of lower life have demonstrated conclusively that restricted or inappropriate stimulation results in a reduced capacity of the organism to perform specific motor tasks. These results led to the definition of "critical periods" in the life of the organism, during which it apparently was more sensitive to certain stimuli that at other times in its life cycle.

The definition of a "critical" or "sensitive" period in its conventional usage involves a specific maturational period during which certain responses are acquired in a perhaps single opportunity process. It is now recognized that the limits of the critical period are not as narrow or rigid as they were previously believed to be. The concept of irreversibility, in conjunction with critical periods, has also undergone some modification because numerous reports have demonstrated that what was or was not learned at one period can be learned or unlearned at another time (Johnson and Cofor 1974, p. 392). The most recent concept of the "critical periods" hypothesis is that there are periods when the individual is especially sensitive to certain forms of stimulation. The permanence of the learning that takes place during these periods is determined in part by maturational age, previous experience, and the genotype. It should be noted that the reports of deviations from developmental pathways, which are the basis of experimentation on critical periods, have been conducted almost entirely on infra-human subjects. The involvement of human beings as subjects in "critical periods" research has generally resulted from retrospective study in which there has been little control of the sample or of the experiences encountered. Under these circumstances, it is impossible to tell when a particular stimulus was introduced or how mature the individual was at the time of optimum receptivity. It is evident that the critical periods for motor skills acquisition in human beings have been poorly defined.

Manipulation of the environment to facilitate the learning of motor skills is a relatively recent occurrence in childhood education. The recent emphasis on early experience as an essential part of education has a sound theoretical base, corroborated by reports of numerous experimental investigations. The rationale for early learning of motor skills is based on the plasticity of the nervous system in young individuals and hence its greater modifiability by environmental influences (Hebb 1949; Krech 1966). Hebb's theory of cell and phase assemblies, with its dependence upon specific experiences as a means of building the sensory-response system, calls for abundant stimulation at an early age. According to Hebb's theory, early experience provides a more complex and extensive sensory repertoire. This broad perceptual experience leads to the establishment of more complex motor responses, which in turn permit the individual to react with appropriate movements to a maximum number of tasks. Thus, early opportunities for sensation and movement provide a cycle of self-enriching experiences.

Recent attention to the remediation of gross motor disabilities has caused investigators to study the consequences of deprived environments on children and to discern what components are essential for the facilitation of motor development. In studies that span several decades, the recurring cause for delayed motor function in groups of children subjected to similar environmental conditions has been attributed to lack of appropriate sensory stimulation and the inability of the individuals to take advantage of whatever stimulation existed. Dennis's (1957) study of children in Iranian institutions, Spitz's (1946) comparison of the children in foundling homes and nurseries, and Goldfarb's (1945) account of institutionalized children all reported that the motor responses of children, who in their judgment had been deprived of essential sensory stimulation, were retarded, probably irreversibly, or inappropriate for their age level. In support of this theme, Geber (1957 and 1958) and Landauer (1963) attributed advanced motor development and increased stature to abundant stimulation during early childhood.

The least esoteric, but perhaps the most influential determinant of movement behavior in early and middle childhood, is the satisfaction that comes from moving skillfully. The joy of movement is an integral part of play, but awkward children are soon excluded from the play of their peers. Thus, those who encounter the variety of stimuli brought on by play also tend to learn to deal effectively with them, while those who are unskillful remain inactive and receive reduced stimulation.

REFERENCES

Ayres, A., 1972. Improving academic scores through sensory integration. *J. Learn. Dis.* **5:** 338-343.

Bayley, N., 1935. The development of motor abilities during the first three years. *Mono. Soc. Res. Child. Devel.,* No. 1, pp. 1-25.

Dennis, W., and P. Najarian, 1957. Infant development under environmental handicap. *Psychol. Monogr.* **71:** 1-13.

Frankenburg, W., and J. Dodds, 1967. The Denver Developmental Screening Test. *J. of Ped.* **71:** 181-191.

Frostig, M., and P. Maslow, 1970. *Movement education: theory and practice.* Chicago: Follett Ed. Corp.

Geber, M., 1958. The psychomotor development of African children in the first year and the influence of maternal behavior. *J. Soc. Psychol.* **47:** 185-195.

Geber, M., and R. Dean, 1957. Gesell tests on African children. *Pediatrics* **20:** 1055-1065.

Gesell, A., and C. Amatruda, 1941. *Developmental diagnosis.* New York: Hoeber.

Gesell, A., and L. Ames, 1940. The ontogenetic organization of prone behavior in human infancy. *J. Genet. Psychol.* **56:** 247-263.

Goldfarb, W., 1945. Effects of psychological deprivation in infancy and subsequent stimulation. *Amer. J. Psychiat.* **102:** 18-33.

Hebb, D., 1949. *Organization of behavior.* New York: Wiley.

Hellebrandt, F., et al., 1961. Physiological analysis of basic motor skills. *Amer. J. Phy. Med.* **40:** 14-25.

Hooker, D., 1952. *The prenatal origin of behavior.* Porter Lecture No. 18. Lawrence: University of Kansas Press.

Hunt, J., 1961. *Intelligence and experience.* New York: Ronald Press.

Illingsworth, R., 1967. *The development of the infant and young child.* London: E. and S. Livingstone.

Johnson, W. R., and C. Cofer, 1974. Personality dynamics: psychosocial implications. In W. Johnson and E. Buskirk (eds.), *Science and medicine and sport.* (2nd ed.) New York: Harper and Row.

Krech, D., M. Rosenzweig, and E. Bennett, 1966. Environmental impoverishment, social isolation and changes in chemistry and anatomy. *Physiol. Behav.* **1:** 99-109.

Landauer, T., and J. Whiting, 1963. Infantile stimulation and adult stature of human males. *Amer. Anthrop.* **66:** 1007-1028.

McGraw, M., 1943. *The neuromuscular maturation of the human infant.* New York: Columbia University Press.

Milani-Comparetti, A., and E. Gidoni, 1967. Routine developmental examination in normal and retarded children. *Devel. Med. Child. Neurol.* **9:** 631-638.

Piaget, J., 1971. *Biology and knowledge.* Chicago: University of Chicago Press.

Shambes, G., and S. Campbell, 1973. Inherent movement patterns in man. *Kinesiology* **3:** 50-58.

Shirley, M., 1931. *The first two years: a study of twenty-five babies. I. Postural and locomotor development.* Minneapolis: University of Minnesota Press.

Spitz, R., 1946. Hospitalism: an enquiry into the genesis of psychiatric conditions in early childhood: a follow-up report. *Psycho. Study Child.* **2:** 113-117.

Thompson, W., and J. Grusec, 1970. Studies of early experience. In Carmichael (ed.), *Manual of Child Psychology* **I:** 565-654.

Wickstrom, R., 1970. *Fundamental motor patterns.* Philadelphia: Lea and Febiger.

SUGGESTED READINGS

Dennis, W., 1960. Causes of retardation among institutionalized children: Iran. *J. Genet. Psychol.* **96:** 47-59.

Scott, J., 1962. Critical periods in behavioral development. *Science* **138:** 949-958.

10

Early Motor Developmental Sequences: Intrauterine through the First Year

Anna M. Doudlah

Early motor behavior in the human organism has been documented by cinematographic analysis of reactions to stimulation and spontaneous movement in fetuses secured by hysterectomy or hysterotomy. Localized muscular responses to electrical stimulation have been reported in six-week, menstrual age, fetuses; however, human fetuses were incapable of reflex activity in response to exteroceptive (tactile) stimulation until seven and a half weeks (Hooker 1952).

Responses to stroking around the mouth with a 25-mg pressure hair during the seventh through the eleventh week consisted of neck and upper trunk movement in a direction away from the source of stimulation. The evolving movement pattern included shoulder extension and pelvic rotation during the eighth week. By the ninth week pelvic rotation was marked and separate from the actions of the trunk and arms.

Spontaneous fetal movements first appeared during the ninth week. They consisted of stiff side-to-side movements of the body axis. This same response was observed in a fetus when it was inadvertently spun around. The consistency of response to different forms of input—stroking around the mouth (tactile) and spinning (vestibular), as well as observation of the same movement during spontaneous action—confirms the existence of this specific action pattern in nine-week fetuses.

The first reflex response to proprioceptive stimulation (stretch) occurred at nine and a half weeks. Passive extension of the fingers caused flexion of the wrist, elbow, and shoulder. Tactile stimulation of the palm at ten and a half weeks resulted in partial closure of the fingers without observable movement of the thumb.

During the 11th week, the face and sole of the foot became responsive to exteroceptive stimulation. Reflex responses to stimulation of these areas were localized, a developmental trend noted through the 12th week. The entire body, with the exception of the top and back of the head, became responsive to stroking by the 14th week.

Protrusion and closure of the lips, weak chest and abdominal contractions suggestive of respiration, and grasping were observed in 20-week fetuses. Tendon reflexes consisting of knee jerk and ankle clonus were noted in a 23.5-week fetus who was able to maintain self-sustained respiration for an extended period. This fetus was spontaneously active and moved the trunk and extremities in a variety of coordinated patterns.

Reflexes appearing later were the Moro at 25 weeks, grasp of sufficient strength to lift the fetus from the supporting surface at 27 weeks, sucking at 29 weeks, and discrete searching movements of the tongue on the lip after the lip was stimulated at 33 weeks. An excellent photographic display of early motor phenomena appears in Flanagan (1962) and Nilsson (1965).

The description of primarily reflex responses in the human fetus has served as one source of information from which principles of motor development have been formulated. These principles, used by many professionals who deal with infant development, are that motor development proceeds from head to toe (cephalo-caudal), central to peripheral (proximal-distal), and general to specific (gross-fine) (Gesell 1929). The theories that 1) development during gestation and 2) motor development within the time frame of birth to walking proceed in an orderly fashion are acceptable to professionals. However, the sequence of motor events as it appears in standardized tests of infant development (Bayley 1969; Cattell 1940), currently used screening instruments (Knobloch et al. 1966; Frankenburg and Dodds 1967; Giannini and Chusid 1972), and proposed methods of evaluating developmentally disabled infants and children (Hoskins and Squires 1973; Trombly and Scott 1977) varies considerably. The motor sequence depends on methods used to select test items, proposed use of the measurement tool, and the professional orientation of the researcher. The validity of most gross motor tests and assessment tools has not been established.

Developmental schedules published by Gesell (1929) and his co-workers at Yale serve as the main informational source on motor development for most professionals. The schedules are based on data gathered between 1927 and 1931. Gesell's pioneer effort in describing "patterns of mental growth" was mainly cross-sectional but sometimes longitudinal and cinematographic. It would not be considered systematic by modern standards.

Developmental tasks and means of eliciting desired motor behaviors were designed specifically by Dr. Gesell (1934). They were imposed on infants "to produce intentionally a normal process for our observation." Items relating to sitting, standing, and walking dominated the gross motor section of the Gesell schedules. Gesell's summary statement on the validity of the schedules was, "We are justified in claiming their general soundness and practical applicability until contrary evidence is revealed" (1938, p. 218). Photographs in Gesell's classic work, *An Atlas of Infant Behavior: Normative Series,* clearly demonstrate how the infants were manipulated in the laboratory to perform the tasks under study.

Most gross motor tests and assessment tools, as well as remediation strategies proposed for use in identifying, evaluating, and programming infants, especially those at risk, have been derived from the Gesell research. These tests and programs continue to perpetuate the bias toward motor items relating to positions such as sitting, standing, and walking. Manipulation of the child in the performance of motor tasks is an accepted procedure.

The idea that motor development, from birth to walking, might be a developmental process involving the interaction between an infant and his or her preprogrammed motor plan and the environment was advanced in 1971 by Pikler and in 1976 by Doudlah. Pikler limited observations of motor development in normal infants, temporarily housed in an orphanage, to ten motor items. Persons responsible for the daily care of the infants recorded the achievement of skill from their observations of self-induced (spontaneous) movements on the selected items. Pikler (1971, p. 57) did not allow anyone to manipulate the infant in positions or actions the child could not accomplish alone. Her position was:

> No "teaching" (direct help) by adults: The Institute withholds "teaching" in any form. Under "teaching" we understand systematic practice of certain motor-skills by holding or keeping the child in a certain position, whether by adult or by various equipment, or in any way helping him to make movements that he is not yet able to execute by himself in his daily life.

Motivated by variations in evaluation procedures and "developmental" approaches used with children having central nervous system dysfunction, Doudlah described the sequence of motor development in normal infants based on their spontaneous movement in a familiar environment (home). Spontaneous motor activity was recorded on film monthly for 20 infants over a 15-month period. Filmed data were subjected to inspectional analysis yielding lists of motor behaivors seen during the monthly filming session for each infant. Consistently appearing motor items were used to create a sequence of motor items grouped into movement phases and transitions descriptive of the attainment of skill leading to walking in the upright posture. This sequence, listed below, was found to be invariant as long as spontaneous movement was observed. There were individual differences in the performance of motor events and in rates of skill acquisition.

Phase 1. Movement in Place

Random movement: on back
Turns head
Lifts head in midline
Extension of body axis
Weight bearing: on elbows
Push/pull with legs/arms
Weight bearing: forearms/hands
Extension of body axis/push up

Transition 1. Rolling

Back to side
Belly to side
Back to belly
Belly to back

Phase 2. Movement through Space: Quadrupedal Position

Pivots
Pushes back
Weight bearing: hands/knees
Crawls
Oscillates: hands/knees
Creeps
Sits: unilaterally

Transition 2. Being Upright in Space

Kneels: both knees
Push/pull to standing
Stands on toes
Sits: upright independently
Kneels: knee/foot

Oscillates: kneeling both knees
Raise/lower body: kneeling
Oscillates: standing

Phase 3. Movement through Space in the Upright Position

Walks around objects
Stoops with assistance
Squats with assistance
Walks with assistance
Climbs
Walks independently
Stands up in space
Squats in space

Newly identified developmental phenomena in the spontaneous move-ment of infants using this cinematographic method were: 1) Definite forms of preparation prior to execution of motor tasks involving weight-bearing on arms and legs. This preparation in back, shoulder, and pelvic musculature before bearing weight on extended arms is illustrated in Figure 10.1, a photograph taken from the filming of a five-month-old girl. Note the complete-ness of the extension pattern in this infant (upper photograph) as she prepares for pushing up on hands (lower photograph). 2) The consistent appearance of oscillations following achievement of a new position such as extension of the body axis, weight bearing on hands and knees, etc. Oscillations occurred prior to movement in the newly achieved position, and consisted of repetitive, sometimes rhythmical movement in the direction of the future action. Rocking on hands and knees before crawling or creeping is a readily observed example in normal infants. 3) Standing, as it is executed spontaneously, occurs at arms length to the object used for support. The body is raised by extension of the weight-bearing leg in the knee/foot kneeling position. Initially, the body assumes a 60 to 70 degree angle to the supporting surface in the upright position. This position places a tremendous stretch on the muscles of the leg used in standing. 4) Standing on the toes appears to be a prerequisite to weight-bearing on the entire foot. 5) Squatting, initially using an object for support, is executed by bilateral weight-bearing on the entire foot while main-taining near 90 degree angles at the knee and ankle. It is an important part of the preparation for stability while walking in the upright position.

The two widely divergent approaches and their results in describing the sequence of motor development in normal infants indicate that the under-standing of this domain of human performance is far from complete. Compre-hensive information on early motor development awaits the systematic cinematographic investigation of spontaneously occurring motor phenomena as they are displayed in the movement of infants during the first year of life.

111

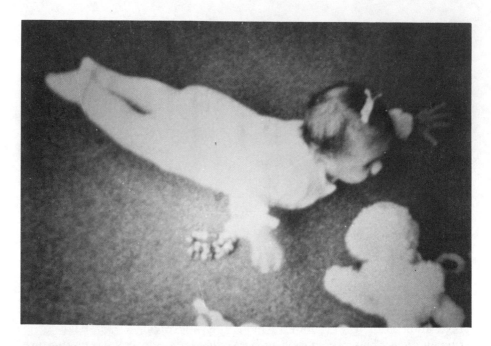

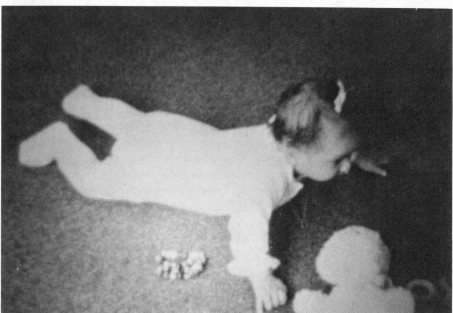

Fig. 10.1 A five-month-old girl demonstrating preparation of back, shoulder, and pelvic muscles (upper photograph) prior to bearing weight on hands (lower photograph).

REFERENCES

Bayley, N., 1969. *Bayley scales of infant development: motor scale.* New York: The Psychological Corporation.

Cattell, P., 1940. *Infant intelligence scale.* New York: The Psychological Corporation.

Doudlah, A., 1976. *A motor development checklist and motor development: birth to walking.* (18-minute videotape) Madison: Central Wisconsin Center.

Flanagan, G., 1962. *The first nine months of life.* New York: Simon and Schuster.

Frankenburg, W., and J. Dodds, 1967. *Denver Developmental Screening Test.*

Giannini, M., and E. Chusid, 1972. *Checklist: a simple screening device for developmental lags.* New York: American Academy of Pediatrics, Scientific Exhibit.

Gesell, A., 1929. Maturation and infant behavior pattern. *Psychol. Rev.* **36:** 307.

————, and C. Amatruda, 1974. *Developmental diagnosis.* (2nd ed.) New York: Paul B. Hoeber.

————, H. Thompson, and C. Amatruda, 1934. *An atlas of infant behavior: normative series.* New Haven, Conn.: Yale University Press.

————, 1938. *The psychology of early growth.* New York: The Macmillan Co.

Hooker, E., 1952. *The prenatal origin of behavior.* Lawrence: University of Kansas Press.

Hoskins, T., and J. Squires, 1973. Developmental assessment: a test for gross motor and reflex development. *Physical Therapy* **53:** 117.

Knobloch, H., B Pasamanick, and E. Sherard, Jr., 1966. A developmental screening inventory for infants. Supplement to *Pediatrics* **38.**

Nelson, W., V. Vaughan, III, and R. McKay, 1956. *Textbook of pediatrics.* (10th ed.) Philadelphia: W. B. Saunders Co.

Nilsson, L., 1965. Early scenes in a human life. In *Growth.* New York: Life Science Library.

Pikler, E., 1971. Learning of motor skills on the basis of self-induced movements. In J. Hellmuth (ed.), *Exceptional infant,* vol. 2. New York: Brunner/Mazel.

Trombly, C., and A. Scott, 1977. *Occupational therapy for physical dysfunction.* Baltimore: Williams and Wilkins.

SUGGESTED READINGS

Hoskins, T., and J. Squires, 1973. Developmental assessment: a test for gross motor and reflex development. *Physical Therapy* **53:** 117.

Super, C., 1976. Environmental effects on motor development: the case of "African infant precocity." *Developmental Medicine Child Neurology* **18.**

11
Development of Motor Skills, Two to Six Years

Helen M. Eckert

Motor development during the period of early childhood is characterized by a marked increase in facility and efficiency in the performance of phylogenetic motor skills and in the acquisition of a variety of ontogenetic activities. In general, the improvement in motor performance may be attributed to anatomical and body tissue increments that result in increased lever lengths and muscular strength and to neurological maturation that contributes to improvements in balance, coordination, and learning capacity.

Although a child usually utilized the heel-toe rocker action of the foot to transfer weight at two years of age, perfection of walking to the level of achievement of a smooth transfer of weight during the negotiation of a straight line or a sharp corner is not attained until around the age of four. The perfection of the locomotor skills of walking and running during this period may be attributed largely to improvements in balance rather than to increments in strength, lever length, or coordination of joint action. To illustrate, walking on tip-toe and ability to walk a straight line tend to coincide, and control in turning and stopping is not achieved until approximately three to four years, after the child has achieved the necessary strength and coordination of joint action to initiate and sustain movement. Variants of locomotor patterns such as galloping, skipping, and jumping, which require strength for the vertical projection of the body and/or the absorption of body momentum on landing, as well as the learning of neuromuscular patterns for joint action requirements, which differ from those in walking and running, are mastered by the majority of children shortly after control is achieved, by six years of age.

The changes that occur in the development of the overhand throw are indicative of the increased utilization of the body levers to increase the power of the throw. A stationary base, and movements in the anterioposterior plane with the arm and body, predominate in the throw of the two and three year old. The range of movement is increased when the arm and body movements are made in a horizontal plane during the next two years. Further leverage and hence greater range of movement and the potential for further distance is added when the previously stationary foot position is replaced by a step forward during the throw. This shift in the base of support, which generally occurs during the fifth and sixth years, involves a step forward on the unilateral foot to the throwing arm. This pattern persists into adulthood for a large percentage of girls. However, it does not produce the full range of leverage involvement and hence power potential of the contralateral step forward associated with the mature overhand throwing pattern achieved by the majority of boys at about six and a half years. In instances where a child is taught the mature throwing pattern at markedly earlier ages than those indicated, the appropriate pattern is achieved. But overt observation indicates that the coordination of joint actions is such that optimal power or accuracy of throw is not increased materially.

The changes that occur in positioning and action of the body levers in the development of two-handed catching illustrate adjustments in neuromuscular patterning conducive to greater precision of grasping and to absorption of momentum. The stationary body position and extension of the arms in front of the body when the child begins to play "catch," around two years of age, is gradually replaced during the next year by a scooping action of the arms and some adjustment of the body position with respect to the thrown ball. During the first attempts to catch the ball with the hands, their position is vice-like with the elbows continuing to remain in front of the body. Gradually, the positioning of the elbows shifts to the sides of the body to allow for give for the absorption of the momentum of the ball during the catch. Individuals who do not have many opportunities for two-handed catches often do not progress beyond the vise-grip in catching, whereas a mature pattern involves a change in position of the hands in relation to each other based upon the position of the ball; that is, thumbs together for high balls and little fingers together for low balls, resulting in the utilization of ball momentum to trigger the stretch reflex as an aid in grasping the ball and maximizing the arm position for absorption of momentum.

It should be noted that the size of the ball is an important factor in the facility with which a child catches and has some influence on the pattern used. For example, a large ball is much easier to catch with the arm-scooping pattern than is a small ball, and a small ball is much lighter and more easily controlled by the small hands of children. Similarly, the size and availability of equipment is an important factor in the learning of ontogenetic activities. For example, a five-year-old who has developed sufficient balance for sudden stops and changes in direction while running usually has little difficulty in learning to ride a two-wheeled bicycle, provided the bicycle is of appropriate size. In addition, two- and three-year-olds master such activities as skiing and skating, both roller and ice, provided equipment of suitable size is available.

The most important external factor in the development of motor skills is the degree to which the child's parents provide opportunities for, and encouragement of, such development. This is most clearly emphasized in the ontogenetic activities but is also reflected in the degree to which a child masters phylogenetic activities. For example, children who are not encouraged to throw and/or catch by either their parents or the culture will tend to terminate their development at immature levels in these activities. Parental encouragement of motor development is usually reflected by the type and amount of equipment made available to the child, but the actual presence and assistance of an adult is also crucial in the development of a number of ontogenetic activities. For example, children are able to swim for a duration of one breath within six months after birth, but the presence of an adult is necessary to lift the child's head out of the water at the crucial moment when the supply of air must be replenished. Similarly, a three- or four-year-old can learn gymnastics and work on apparatus, provided a knowledgeable adult is available for spotting purposes. Less dramatically, a five- or six-year-old can learn to play tennis with appropriately modified equipment if an adult is present to volley balls to the child.

In brief, the more opportunities and encouragement that children of two to six years have for the improvement of their motor skills, the greater will be the development of their motor skills.

SUGGESTED READINGS

Bayley, N., 1935. The development of motor abilities in the first three years. *Monogr. Soc. Res. Child Develpm.* **1:** 1-26.

Espenschade, A. S., and H. M. Eckert, 1967. *Motor development.* Columbus: Merrill Books.

Guttridge, M. V., 1939. A study of motor achievements of young children. *Arch. Psychol.* **244:** 1-178.

Hellebrandt, F. A., G. L. Rarick, R. Glassow, and M. L. Carns, 1961. Physiological analysis of basic motor skills. I. Growth and development of jumping. *Amer. J. Phys. Med.* **40:** 14-25.

Herkowitz, J., 1977. Movement experiences for preschool children. *JOHPER* **48** (March) : 15.

Siedentop, D. (ed.), 1976. Learning how to play. *Quest,* Monograph 26 (Summer). NAPECW and NCPEAM.

Wellman, B. L., 1937. Motor achievements of preschool children. *Child. Educ.* **13:** 311-316.

Whitehurst, K. E., 1971. What movement means to the young child. *JOHPER* **42** (May) : 34.

Wild, M. R., 1938. The behavior pattern of throwing and some observations concerning its course of development in children. *Research Quarterly* **9:** 20-24.

12

Stability of Growth in Motor Behavior in the Early Years of Life

G. Lawrence Rarick

Longitudinal observations (Gesell 1940; McGraw 1940; Shirley 1931, 1933) of the growth and development of children during the period of infancy have shown clearly that there is a sequential order in motor development. Certain reflexes such as the Moro response, the tonic neck reflex, the trotting reflex, and the grasping reflex, which are present at birth, gradually subside and ordinarily cannot be elicited after the twentieth week of life. The developmental sequences that lead up to bipedal locomotion follow a well-defined order. The infant gains strength and control of the muscles of the neck prior to acquiring sufficient muscular strength and control of the muscles of the torso for assuming sitting posture. Creeping and crawling behavior is a forerunner of walking, and children must master sufficient body control to stand unsupported before they attempt a first step. Similar orderly sequences are seen in the development of grasping behavior. The infant at approximately 24 to 28 weeks utilizes a "palm grasp" but does not acquire the mature pincher movement of the thumb and forefinger until near the end of the first year (Halverson 1931).

McGraw (1940) holds that behavioral development in infancy can be divided into four periods, each characterized by a progressive reduction in subcortical responses paralleled by an increase in cortical control of motor responses. The first four months see a gradual reduction in rhythmical movements and the loss of the reflexes present at birth. During the second period, the fourth to the ninth month, the infant gains voluntary control of the superior spinal region, and during the third period, from the ninth to the fourteenth month, there is increased control of the muscles in the inferior spinal region. The next ten months witness rapid development of the association centers of the brain.

It was first proposed that, in addition to following an orderly sequence, development is continuous rather than saltatory, and that it proceeds at the pace at which it starts (Hollingsworth 1928). Evidence from longitudinal studies gives only limited support to these hypotheses. While, in general,

117

development is continuous, behavioral changes in infancy are dependent to a large extent on related structural changes. Frequently the emergence of behavioral patterns lags well behind structural development, the magnitude of the lag and the subsequent rate of behavioral development often varying widely among children. For example, Shirley (1931) in her longitudinal observations of infants' behavioral changes in locomotor, vocalization, and manipulative abilities noted that, at some points in infancy, the developmental scores of the children under observation were well above the mean of the group on one or more of these traits, only to fall below the mean a few weeks later. The limited consistency of development among such abilities was indicated further by the relatively low intertrait correlation coefficients of developmental scores from one point in time to another. While the correlations across four-week intervals (ages 3 to 94 weeks) were substantial, all but a few being above .50, the coefficients between widely separated ages, up to the 49th week, were close to zero. There was, however, a greater tendency toward consistency of development during the second year. Thus, it was concluded that, while there was a well-defined order in the development of a particular trait in these children, there were periods when little progress was apparent, only to be followed by rapid gains within a brief period of time.

The recent research of Touwen (1971) bears out the earlier findings of Shirley (1933). Analysis of longitudinal data on the palmar grasp and the Moro response in 50 healthy low-risk infants indicated that there was no clear-cut relationship between the age of disappearance of the palmar grasp reflex and the age of first occurrence of the pincer grasp. Similarly, no relationship was found between the age of disappearance of the various components of the Moro response and the age of unsupported walking. Likewise, there was little relationship between the age of disappearance of the palmar grasp and the age of disappearance of the several components of the Moro response. Thus, there would seem to be little trait consistency within or between the disappearance of these subcortical responses, nor is the age of disappearance of these responses of value in predicting later motor development in infancy. It should be pointed out, however, that a correlation of .65 was found between the age of creeping unsupported and the age of walking.

In locomotor development, Shirley (1931) reported that the postural controls that lead up to walking showed considerable consistency in development. The correlation between the ages of standing with help and the ages of walking alone was .80±.06 and the correlation between the ages of creeping and the ages of walking alone was .84±.05. Using the age at which the infants first achieved a particular level of postural control, such as age of sitting alone momentarily, age of standing alone, age of creeping, or other similarly specified ages, the age of walking alone could, however, not be predicted within limits of less than four weeks. Thus, the evidence indicates that while there is little consistency in the rate of intertrait development, such as the development of manual and locomotor skills, the development of the postural controls that lead up to walking are, within limits, predictable.

There is considerable evidence to indicate that there is a "psychomotor constancy" in motor development that is sufficiently persistent to assure maintenance of the individuality of motor behavior early in life. The research of Gesell (1937), in which the motor behavior of children was assessed by means of cinematography, showed that six of the eight infants under observation for a period of three years retained the same relative rank in such behavioral traits as pellet placement, spoon control, and in the achievement of successive stages of prone progression and locomotion. Further support for the concept of "psychomotor constancy" comes from the longitudinal observations of Chess et al. (1959), who noted that the persistence of initially determined patterns of reactivity was retained throughout the first few years of life, and from the research of Birns (1965), who reported consistency of individual differences in the response intensity of the neonate in the first five days of life.

Shirley (1931), following her extensive study of the postural and locomotor controls of 25 babies, concluded that not only motor development but also motor interest and motor activity were persistent and could be predicted with considerable accuracy during this period. The evidence led her to hypothesize that motor aptitude or motor talent makes itself apparent early in life, a reflection of a neromuscular tendency that is seemingly a function of one's genetic endowment. The spontaneous practice noted in the more skillful infants was, in her judgment, a reflection of the maturation of the nervous system and an inborn disposition for physical activity.

The evidence, while at this point not conclusive, indicates that the development of motor behavior other than the time of disappearance of subcortical responses can be predicted within rather broad limits early in life. It is clear that in normal development innate forces at this age level are more potent in shaping the course of motor development of children than environmental.

REFERENCES

Birns, B. M., 1965. Individual differences in human neonates' responses to stimulation. *Child Develop.* **36:** 249-256.

Chess, S., A. Thomas, and H. Birch, 1959. Characteristics of the individual child's behavioral responses to the environment. *Amer. J. Orthopsychiat.* **29:** 791-802.

Gesell, A., 1937. Early evidences of individuality in the human infant. *J. Genet. Psychol.* **47:** 339-361.

————, and L. B. Ames, 1940. The ontogenetic organization of prone behavior in human infancy. *J. Genet. Psychol.* **56:** 247-263.

Halverson, H. M., 1931. An experimental study of prehension in infants by means of systematic cinema records. *Genetic Psychol. Monographs* **10:** 107-286.

Hollingsworth, H. L., 1928. *Mental growth and decline.* New York: Appleton.

McGraw, M. B., 1939. Behavior of the newborn infant and early neuromuscular development. *Res. Publ. Ass. Nerv. Ment. Dis.* **19:** 244-246.

————, 1940. Neuromuscular development of the human infant in the achievement of erect locomotion. *J. Pediat.* **17:** 747-771.

Shirley, M. M., 1931. *The first two years: a study of twenty-five babies. Volume I: Posture and locomotor development.* Minneapolis: University of Minnesota Press.

————, 1933. *The first two years: a study of twenty-five babies. Volume II: Intellectual development.* Minneapolis: University of Minnesota Press.

Touwen, B. C. L., 1971. A study on the development of some motor phenomena in infancy. *Develop. Med. Child. Neurol.* **13:** 435-446.

13

Motor Activity and Compensation for Delayed Developmental Progress in Preschool Children

Robert Janus

For many years systematic efforts to help children with various developmental disorders have suggested the crucial role of physical movement capability in the total developmental process—including the perceptual, cognitive, and social aspects. In recent years experimental and research programs conducted by persons representing various disciplines have produced objectives, including empirical evidence in support of earlier observations. That is, the "physical base" of total personality functioning has important implications for helping overcome or compensate for various developmental, including learning, disorders (Myklebust 1968; Oliver 1963).

Some of the representative theoretical formulations that are outgrowths of programs designed to compensate for developmental delays are identified here very briefly.

Ayres's (1972) work has led her to stress vestibular (rotating, spinning, rocking, and bouncing activities) and tactile experiences in the treatment of perceptual-motor dysfunction. Underlying the approach are the postulates that: 1) perceptual-motor functions develop through specific steps of sequential maturation; 2) there are specific central nervous system mechanisms that perform the integrative processes inherent in perception; and 3) both sequential maturation and the integrative mechanisms are dependent upon patterned stimulation and meaningful response.

Barsch (1968) uses the term "movigenics" to describe a program of activities aimed at achieving efficiency of movement in space. Increasing cognitive direction of movement is aimed at improving grace, ease, comfort, and efficiency of movement, and thereby enhancing image of self. The resulting enhanced confidence is seen as improving personality functioning generally.

Cratty (1971), who has acknowledged the pioneer research of Humphrey (1974) in this area, utilizes a program of movement activities designed to enhance cognitive learning. He has found "learning games" especially effective when accompanied by patient, motivating, and nonstressful help. He has stressed the need to teach for transfer of learning if what is learned in the "learning games" is to be perceived as being applicable to the specific "classroom" learning sought.

Getman (1971) has proposed a "visual-motor complex" theory as a basis for helping young children with developmental problems. Vision cannot develop its ultimate skill of performance without movement development and vice versa. These two systems are so inextricably interwoven that neither can operate effectively without the other. Vision is the guidance system for movement and movement the action system for vision in a continuous feedback process.

Frostig's (1969) approach to educational therapy for children with learning difficulties utilizes an interdisciplinary specialist team approach. Included in this approach is a program of movement education. Activities in the program are structured to develop sensory motor skills and self-awareness. Frostig believes that the ability of children to move influences (and in turn is influenced by) all their psychological abilities—their ability to communicate, to perceive, to solve problems, and the way they feel and interact with others.

Kephart (1968) considers a "perceptual-motor match" to be the goal of early development. That is, his program is aimed at achieving a matching of the perceived outer world with the child's inward awareness of it. He stresses the need to teach for generalization in movement, and a need to encourage movement discovery and problem-solving approaches to tasks. Four educationally significant motor patterns are offered for consideration in designing activities for a movement therapy program: 1) locomotion, 2) balance and maintenance of posture, 3) contact, and 4) reception and propulsion.

Johnson's (1972) "clinic" (Children's Health and Developmental Clinic) approach is concerned with improving the "neuromotor-perceptual organization and psycho-social skills" of children. Trained volunteer clinicians are utilized. The approach stresses individual attention (usually one "clinician" per child), esteem for fun, insistence upon respect for the child and his or her interests, and close communication with the parents. Children select their own activities from a wide range of possibilities, and these are used as the media for moving toward therapeutic and educational goals sought. Research has shown improvements in self-concept, perceptual motor skills, risk-taking behavior, and intellectual and perceptual performance (West et al. 1970; Fretz et al. 1969; Johnson et al. 1968).

There seems to be overwhelming evidence that children with varieties of developmental problems respond to planned movement-oriented programs both therapeutically and educationally. Perhaps it is time to think in terms of using such programs preventively early in the development of all children.

REFERENCES

Ayres, A. J., 1972. *Sensory integration and learning disorders.* Los Angeles: Western Psychological Service.

Barsch, R. H., 1968. *Enriching perception and cognition techniques for teachers.* Seattle: Special Child Publications.

Cratty, B. J., 1971. *Human behavior: exploring educational processes.* Wolfe City, Tex.: The University Press.

Fretz, B., W. Johnson, and J. Johnson, 1969. Intellectual and perceptual motor development as a function of therapeutic play. *Research Quarterly* **40** (December) : 687-691.

Frostig, M., 1969. *MGL: Move — Grow — Learn.* Chicago: Follett Educational Corporation.

Getman, G. N., 1971. Concerns of the optometrist for motor development. In *Foundations and practices in perceptional motor learning: a quest for understanding.* Washington, D.C.: AAHPER.

Humphrey, J. H., 1974. *Child learning through elementary school physical education.* (2nd ed.) Dubuque, Iowa: W. C. Brown.

Johnson, W., 1972. A humanistic dimension of physical education. *JOHPER* **43**: 21-35.

———, B. Fretz, and J. Johnson, 1968. Change in self-concept during a physical developmental program. *Research Quarterly* **39**: 560-565.

Kephart, N., M. Ebersole, and J. Ebersole, 1968. *Steps to achievement for the slow learner.* Columbus, Ohio: Charles E. Merrill.

Myklebust, H., and N. Wood, 1968. *Progress in learning disabilities.* Vol. I. New York: Grune and Stratton.

Oliver, H. N., 1963. The physical education of E.S.N. children. *Forward Trends* **7**: 87-90.

West, J., B. Fretz, and M. McDonald, 1970. Modifying risk-taking behavior. *Child Development* **41** (December) : 1083-1088.

SUGGESTED READINGS

Cratty, B. J., 1972. *Physical expression of intelligence.* Englewood Cliffs, N.J.: Prentice-Hall.

Fretz, B., and W. Johnson, 1973. Behavioral changes in mildly disturbed children following participation in a physical developmental clinic. *Psychological Reports* **36**: 855-862.

Johnson, W., and B. Fretz, 1967. Changes in perceptual-motor skills after a children's physical developmental program. *Perceptual Motor Skills* **24**: 610.

14

Curriculum

Movement Education

Helen M. Zimmerman

PURPOSES OF PHYSICAL EDUCATION

The goal of physical education is to help people meet the problems of living to the best of their ability. Good physical condition is sought, and perceptual motor abilities are developed. Children learn to perform psychomotor skills that are basic to physical movement, including activities for daily living, safety, occupational, and vocational needs. The goal of good physical condition includes the development of cardiorespiratory endurance, flexibility, agility, balance, and muscular strength adequate to meet the requirements of a normal life.

Physical education aims to assist the student in developing poise, self-confidence, and a realistic self-image. Children learn to use movement to express themselves creatively. Interaction with others and good social relationships are fostered. The development of favorable attitudes toward physical activity is important throughout the elementary school years.

Movement experiences are coordinated with classroom learning to clarify and increase understanding of concepts and vocabulary relative to space, time, direction, numbers, and proportions. Other cognitive learning in physical education includes the acquiring of basic concepts regarding the mechanics of movement, the factors that govern it, the physiological effects of exercise, and the need for continuing physical activity throughout life.

CHANGES IN ELEMENTARY SCHOOL PHYSICAL EDUCATION

In recent years physical education for children in elementary schools has undergone important changes relative to program and teaching methods. Increased emphasis on the process of learning has resulted in greater use of guided exploration, discovery, and the problem-solving method in physical education.* While the inclusion of a variety of activities is advocated for all elementary school years, wide scope of movement experiences is given major emphasis in the first three grades. Many schools have physical education programs designed to meet the needs of children with special problems—physical, mental, emotional, and social.

There is growing concern for the building of good attitudes toward physical activity early in life. A continuing desire to be physically active is seen as an important concomitant of the satisfaction associated with learning physical skills, the security of ready acceptance by peers, and the fun of using movement abilities in many ways.

ACTIVITIES INCLUDED IN THE PROGRAM

The activities in the elementary school program have been classified in several ways. The following categories are typical: 1) movement education,

---

* This part of the program is known by other titles such as "movement exploration" and "basic movement." The term "movement education" seems most appropriate because it indicates the wide area of movement, and also includes education. The material on "Changes in Elementary School Physical Education" and "Movement Education" are based on the work of Margie R. Hanson but were written by Helen Zimmerman.

2) sports skills and games, 3) dance, 4) stunts, tumbling, and apparatus activities, and 5) exercises.

MOVEMENT EDUCATION

The term "movement education" is applied to activities included in the program primarily to help children learn to manage their bodies efficiently in a wide variety of situations. Experiences to develop perceptual abilities and sensorimotor skills are begun in the first school year. The learning is personalized as a child discovers what the body can do and where and how it can move (see Figs. 14.1 through 14.4). Lessons focus on movements that occur in many daily life activities. Examples of these are twisting, bending, stretching, curling, throwing, and striking. After exploring the ways in which the body can execute specific movements, the child combines the actions with different forms of locomotion such as walking, running, or skipping. Children learn to use movement abilities for a variety of purposes ranging from self-expression and communication to creative endeavor.

Cognitive learning such as concepts of strong and weak, variations in shapes, judgments of time and space, and anticipation of actions of other people is enhanced.

Figure 14.1

Figure 14.2

Figure 14.3   **Figure 14.4**

In movement education lessons, children learn to evaluate their own efforts. Individual progress is emphasized rather than how one's performance compares with preset standards. Competition is kept at a minimum and used only when it is inherent in the activity.

Discovery and the problem-solving method of teaching are used extensively in these lessons. The teacher poses problems that allow the child to discover ways to use different movements. Information concerning problem solving is presented later in this chapter.

SUGGESTED READINGS

Barrett, K. R., 1965. *Exploration: a method for teaching movement.* Madison: College Printing.

Bilbrough, A., and P. Jones, 1964. *Physical education in the primary school.* London: University of London Press.

Diem, L., 1965. *Who can.* Frankfurt, Germany: Wilhelm Limpert.

Film loops for elementary school physical education, 1969. (A series of 8mm technicolor loop film cartridges on basic movement and fundamental skills.) New York: Holt, Rinehart and Winston. Produced in cooperation with AAHPER.

Gilliem, B. C., 1970. *Basic movement education for children: rationale and teaching units.* Reading, Mass.: Addison-Wesley.

Kirchner, G., J. Cunningham, and E. Warrell, 1970. *Introduction to movement education.* Dubuque, Iowa: William C. Brown.

National Instructional Television Center, 1970. *Ready-set-go.* (Television series and manual for K-3.) Field Services, Box A, Bloomington, Indiana. Produced in consultation with AAHPER.

Porter, L., 1969. *Movement education for children.* Washington, D.C.: EKNE and AAHPER publication.

Siedentop, D. (ed.), 1976. Learning how to play. *Quest,* Monograph 26 (Summer). NAPECW and NCPEAM.

Stanley, S., 1969. *Physical education: a movement orientation.* Toronto: McGraw-Hill of Canada Ltd.

Sports Skills and Games in the Elementary School

Patricia Tanner

In the increasingly sports-oriented culture of the United States, the development of children's sports skills and games-playing abilities has become important. Their acceptance in, as well as understanding and appreciation of, this culture is affected by their ability to perform in sports. However, the manner in which these abilities are developed is of primary importance in the total growth and development of each child. Usually educators now recognize the error in assuming that, given the space, equipment, and time, children will develop desirable skills, confidence, and knowledge sufficient to participate with competence in sports activities. Some children may do so, but many others, without guidance and encouragement, will remain inept and lacking in confidence. For them, an important avenue for learning and for personal development is reduced or converted to a negative experience. They find no satisfaction or enjoyment in what could be a most rewarding part of their ongoing life-style: participation in sports and leisure-time activities.

As an essential part of the physical education curriculum in the elementary school, very careful consideration is given to the developmental needs of young children in the acquisition of skills. Recognition is given to the different developmental stages that occur in these early years and to the effect of the introduction of appropriate sports-related activities at the various grade levels. It is obvious that primary grade children are in no way ready for the complex strategies and highly developed skill demands of the traditional sports. They are neither cognitively, physically, socially, nor emotionally ready. First, they need to acquire good control and coordination in the management of their own body movements and in the application of space, time, and force concepts in such basic skills as running, jumping, rolling, stopping, starting, twisting, turning, bending, and stretching. These simple skills are used continuously in most game situations. They must be explored before children can control equipment such as bats and balls with any degree of efficiency. This is why children find running, chasing, and tag games appropriate and a continual delight at this stage. They fully enjoy the opportunities for freedom of running combined with the excitement of the chase.

In these early years, the fundamental motor patterns underlying all throwing, catching, kicking, and striking skills follow a natural sequence of development. However, in order for the mature and more efficient forms of these skills to be achieved, children need not only practice, but also receive careful guidance and specific feedback before efficiency is acquired. Opportunities for activites providing the widest possible variety of experiences in manipulating objects of all kinds, shapes, and sizes become essential in planning the primary grade program. Yarnballs, hoops, ropes, tires, wands, rings, bats, paddles, and all kinds of balls are bounced, tossed, thrown, bowled, spun, caught, kicked, dribbled, struck, volleyed, aimed, and fielded, *ad infinitum.* Activities and environments are planned carefully so that they provide for a wide range of movement experiences for varying levels of ability. The progressively challenging situations used foster continuing advancement on the part of the most capable students. As children develop skills, they devise many simple games in which they progress from minimal involvement with others to more cooperative relationships with the group. The acquisition of greater skill and control stimulates interest in testing that skill in a variety of ways. Competition evolves in one-to-one, two-to-two, and increasingly expanding group situations. At this time, games appropriate to meet the child's developmental needs are introduced.

Swimming is an activity that has strong appeal for children of elementary and preschool ages. It can be learned readily by the young child and should be started as early as possible. Tiny Tot programs for preschool children are meeting with success and are increasing in number. Although most elementary schools do not have swimming pools, school authorities often collaborate with community organizations, park districts, YMCAs, and other groups in conducting "swimming campaigns" to involve children in the program.

As children progress through fourth, fifth, and sixth grades, many more specific skills required in the major or traditional sports are introduced. Emphasis continues to be placed on effective use of equipment. Space, time, and force concepts assume more importance in their application both to skills and strategies. Laws of motion and principles of movement are reinforced continually. Rules and strategies take on greater significance as both offensive and defensive play develops. Cooperation with teammates and

Fig. 14.5-14.8 A wide range of movement experiences.

awareness of opponents become more important. Scoring, safety, and sportsmanship take on new meanings. Attention is paid to speed, strength, flexibility, and endurance factors, since physical fitness affects performance. Much of the time is spent in improving skills already acquired, in adding new skills, and in applying them in adapted or modified games or game situations.

In upper elementary school special caution is needed to prevent emphasis on traditional forms of the sports in which larger numbers of participants lead to minimal participation on the part of many of the players. Since being vitally involved is so much a part of enjoyment, maximum participation on the part of each child must be safeguarded.

The elementary school program provides a continued, broad base of experiences from which future directions can be established. It is not the role of the school to encourage specialization to the detriment of total growth and development. In contrast, the physical education program provides a background of a wide variety of skills from which students may draw to particpate in any activities of their choice at a later date. An important goal of elementary school physical education is that each child develop confidence and sufficient success to assure enjoyment regardless of the acceptable activity.

SUGGESTED READINGS

Anderson, M. H., et al., 1972. *Play with a purpose.* New York: Harper & Row.

Blake, W. O., and A. M. Volpe, 1964. *Lead-up games to team sports.* Englewood Cliffs, N.J.: Prentice-Hall.

Christian, Q. A., 1977. *A beanbag curriculum: a homemade approach to physical activity for children.* (2nd ed.) Wolfe City, Tex.: University Press.

Cratty, B., 1970. *Active learning games.* Englewood Cliffs, N.J.: Prentice-Hall.

Mauldon, E., and H. B. Redfern, 1969. *Games teaching.* London: McDonald and Evans.

Moore, J. B., and A. W. Bond, 1975. Playgrounds. *JOHPER* **46** (January) : 21.

Schurr, E., 1967. *Movement experiences for children.* New York: Appleton-Century-Crofts.

Stanley, S., 1969. *Physical education: a movement orientation.* Toronto: McGraw-Hill of Canada Ltd.

Wickstrom, R. L., 1970. *Fundamental motor patterns.* Philadelphia: Lea and Febiger.

Dance*

Helen M. Zimmerman

Dance offers many opportunities for realization of educational goals. It provides means for creative expression involving the total individual and

---

* A major portion of the information here is based on "Guidelines for Children's Dance," a report of the Task Force of the Dance Division of the American Alliance for Health, Physical Education, Recreation, and Dance. Permission to use the information was obtained from Araminta Little, Vice-President of the Dance Division and Chairman for Dance, AAHPER, 1972-73; Ruth L. Murray, author of the Preamble to the "Guidelines for Children's Dance"; and Gladys Andrews Fleming, Chairman of the Task Force on Children's Dance. The report appeared in the June 1971 issue of *JOHPER,* published by the AAHPER. It was also reprinted and is available from the AAHPERD.

includes many opportunities for improving personal identity and self-concept. Stated below are the objectives of dance published by the Task Force on Children's Dance of the Division of Dance of the AAHPER in 1971. While most of the purposes are movement centered, others that are audience centered are intended to promote understanding and appreciation.

OBJECTIVES OF ELEMENTARY DANCE

To assist children through movement-centered dance activities and other movement experiences they may be having to:

Realize their biological urges to experience primal patterns of movement;

Develop an adequate degree of satisfaction in and mastery of their body movements for their own pleasure, confidence, and self-esteem;

Greatly expand their movement resources by offering them many opportunities to explore, discover, invent, and develop different ways of moving and to structure sequences;

Increase aesthetic sensitivity by emphasizing the expressive and imaginative potential of their movements, as well as the physical and athletic aspects;

Develop their appreciation of dance as art, by relating it to appropriate experiences in music, literature, painting, and sculpture;

Relate their movement effectively to accompanying sounds and to music;

Participate with others in recreational folk and ethnic dances by helping them learn traditional dance steps and understand the different ways they have been used through centuries of people dancing together;

Make dances for themselves and others and, when they seem ready for the experience, to perform them for peer audiences.

To assist the child through audience-centered dance activities to:

Understand the ancient and honorable tradition of dance as art and ritual;

Develop sensitivity to the essence of movement as communication as they
observe performances of their peers;

Appreciate the many forms of dance that have evolved in different cultures, all based on common movement resources from which people have drawn for their expressive purposes;

Understand, as they grow older, something of the demanding discipline and training of the body necessary for a professional dancer;

Enjoy viewing concert and theater dance, and develop a discriminating awareness of movement as an artistic medium.

Guidelines basic to dance for children and implications of the guidelines are presented by the Task Force of the Dance Division, AAHPER, in *Children's Dance*. The reader is referred to the latter publication as an excellent source of information and suggestions on this topic. The following brief summary of the guidelines and their implications indicates the nature and scope of children's dance.

1. Experiencing movement elements. The use of space, time, force, awareness of changes in body shape, and the relationship of self to others and to the environment; movement of various body parts, awarenes of body balance and shape, orientation to others and to the environment; use of contrasting or opposite words to achieve variety of movement (for example, heavy-light, tight-loose, and straight-curved); moving in their own space and then through space—alone, later with a partner, and in a small group; combinations of factors—heavy and loose, crooked, low and fast (see Figs. 14.9 through 14.12).

2. Providing for exploration. Investigating and inventing, using ideas from number 1 above, improvisation that encourages children to think and act; using imagery sources for movement such as walking and moving on ice or mud, different kinds of transportation, machines, literary sources, and properties such as paper, string, rope, cloth, feathers, and elastic.

3. Relating to rhythm. Gaining in sensitivity to musical sounds and ability to relate to them; synchronizing movement with musical structures such as pulse and accent and developing precision of movement; making rhythmic responses with the hands, feet, limbs, and total body; walking and jumping; moving in their own space and then through space; using and responding to drums, blocks, sticks, and gongs; moving in rhythm with others; using records, tapes, and other sources—the selections should be short and rhythmically stimulating with variations in tempo and with built-in imagery; following rhythmic patterns of the teacher or another child and also originating their own patterns; moving to nursery rhymes and songs, rounds, folk dances, singing games, the child's own name, television rhythms, and other sources.

4. Experimenting with basic movement, nonlocomotor and locomotor. Bending, twisting, stretching, spinning, reaching, falling—combining these with walking, jumping, and other forms of locomotion; learning traditional steps and combining them—step-hop, schottische, polka, waltz, mazurka.

Figs. 14.9-14.12 Children's dance in an elementary school.

5. Making dances. Originating sequences of movement having a beginning, middle, and end; expressing their own interests and communicating spirit; devising their own situations.

6. Relating to the other subjects in the curriculum. To music, language arts, science, and social studies.

7. Singing movement songs. The "togetherness" helps the shy child; using old movement songs ("Round and Round the Village") and more recent ones ("If You're Happy and You Know It, Clap Your Hands").

8. Traditional folk dances. Recommended for 8- to 12-year-olds; using short dances with easy steps they know or master first; simple song squares for middle grades; enjoy learning the interesting footwork of the horas and kolos.

9. Increasing physical power. Exploring movements involving various joint actions such as flexion, extension, rotation; use of gross muscle action and combined movements, and learning simple principles regarding them.

10. Relating to present culture. Experiences with ethnic and "fad" dance patterns, including those from the cultural background of the school community; building attitudes; developing fad dances through movement exploration, and later creating dances; viewing good concerts and theater dances.

11. Performing for others. Groups of children show their dances to classmates, schoolmates, and perhaps to parents; guard against exploiting children.*

SUGGESTED READINGS

AAHPER, 1973. *Children's dance* (September).

————, 1971. Guidelines for children's dance. *JOHPER* **42** (June) : 13-22.

Andrews, G., 1954. *Creative rhythmic movement for children.* Englewood Cliffs, N.J.: Prentice-Hall.

Hayes, E. R., 1964. *An introduction to the teaching of dance.* New York: Ronald Press.

Murray, R. L., 1963. *Dance in elementary education.* New York: Harper.

Russell, J., 1965. *Creative dance in the primary school.* London: MacDonald and Evans.

Stanley, S., 1969. *Physical education: a movement orientation.* Toronto: McGraw-Hill of Canada, Ltd.

Stunts, Tumbling, and Appartus Activities

Gilbert A. Magida

Stunts, tumbling, and apparatus activities offer elementary school students the opportunity to expand their movement abilities and experiences, broaden

---

* *Editor's note:* Refer to Volume II of the *Encyclopedia* for more information on dance. Also note that AAHPER at its annual conference in March 1979 added the word *Dance* to its title. The acronym is now AAHPERD.

their interests, and develop flexibility, agility, and good timing in body movement. These activities allow for individualization of instruction in that students work according to their own ability while measuring their progress as determined by individual goals. This allows for independence, which aids in self-decision and self-discipline. Courage, initiative, and a sense of accomplishment are outcomes of a well-planned program in stunts, tumbling, and appartus activities.

Stunts and tumbling offer the student challenging situations accomplished mainly on the ground. Twists, turns, rolls, stands, and balances offer variations in direction, plane, body position, and tempo of movement, allowing for opportunity to experiment and explore. Carefully planned progressions, introduced at the point of readiness of the student, allow for success and self-satisfaction. Such progressions also serve as a challenge toward further development and skill advancement. Appartus activities allow the student to increase muscular strength and body management by using equipment that takes the student off the floor. The need to support and balance one's weight on the various pieces of appartus available encourages muscular development and flexibility. A well-planned class will have students divided into small groups (four to six students), with each group working at a different piece of equipment. Sufficient time should be allowed for each student to participate at a given station before groups are asked to rotate to the next station.

Emphasis should be given to the various safety procedures when apparatus equipment is being used. A businesslike atmosphere must be established since accidents may be caused by irresponsibility. Proper spotting techniques must be emphasized as well as practices to insure the performer of assistance when necessary. Mats should be placed under all apparatus, especially at take-off and landing points. New skills should not be allowed until old skills have been accomplished in good form. New skills should be attempted only with the consent of the instructor, and in more complex moves the instructor should serve as the spotter.

Parallel bars, climbing ropes, rings, high bar, balance beam, vaulting box, horse, and an ample supply of mats are equipment necessary for a comprehensive program of gymnastics.

The development of strength and muscular and circulatory endurance is an important goal of physical education. Vigorous physical activity is necessary if the child's physical potential is to be realized. Research evidence indicates that heavy muscular activity in childhood tends to increase lateral growth and that vigorously active children tend to have sturdier bodies and to maintain more normal weight than do children who are generally sedentary. The goal of development of strength and of muscular and circulatory endurance can be accomplished by participation in a variety of activities that require regular use of muscles under conditions of increasing demands.

Physical exercises, defined here as calisthenics, are among the activities used for this purpose. They are also used as warm-up activities allowing for emphasis on specific body parts. Development of endurance of muscles as well as flexibility can be achieved through calisthenics.

Stunts, tumbling, and apparatus activities aid in muscular development in that the body weight must be balanced, supported, or lifted. A program of weight training emphasizing techniques and basic principles should be initiated in the upper elementary and junior high school grades. Self-testing activities are excellent for motivation, measurement of strength, and continued muscular effort calling for increasing demands.

Elementary school children react positively toward testing activities. They are not only eager to test their own abilities, but also curious to know how they compare with other boys and girls of their own age, height, and weight. The available literature contains adequate discussion of techniques and methods of attaining muscular strength and cardiovascular endurance.

A difficulty in the elementary school is the provision of time for specific exercises to develop strength and endurance. The major emphasis often is on other activities that will help boys and girls to more advanced and increasingly interesting uses of physical movements in dance, games, sports, gymnastics, and in daily life activities.*

SUGGESTED READINGS

DeCarlo, T., 1963. *Handbook of progressive gymnastics.* Englewood Cliffs, N.J.: Prentice-Hall.

Fogel, S., 1971. *Gymnastics handbook.* West Nyack, N.Y.: Parker Publishing Co.

Halsey, E., and L. Porter, 1963. *Physical education for children.* New York: Holt, Rinehart and Winston.

Mosston, M., 1965. *Developmental movement.* Columbus, Ohio: Charles E. Merrill.

O'Quinn, G., 1967. *Gymnastics for elementary school children.* Dubuque, Iowa: William C. Brown.

Vincent, W. J., 1972. *Gymnastic routines for men.* Philadelphia: W. B. Saunders.

---

* *Editor's note:* Refer to Volume III of this *Encyclopedia* for more information on gymnastics.

Problem-solving Approaches
Kate R. Barrett

A major characteristic evident in today's teaching of physical education is the variety of problem-solving approaches. The exciting effects that seem to result from allowing a student to find things out independently, or as Bruner (1971) stated, "to be his own discoverer," are being accepted more and more. As a result, methods distinguished by heuristic elements have increased steadily during the past decade.

In the late 1950s and early 1960s terms such as "exploration," "movement exploration," and "problem solving" were most commonly used to describe approaches used with children that had exploration and discovery as their major elements. As is often found with new ideas, confusion resulted as to the true meaning of these terms. Wide variation in interpretation became apparent. While interpretation varied, the focus of all the work was on helping children understand movement as it related to themselves, others, and the environment (see Figs. 14.13 through 14.17). In spite of the confusion, interest remained strong, and greater skill in using problem-solving approaches for teaching children resulted.

From these early attempts with heuristic approaches in elementary school education, the concept of "teaching strategies" gradually emerged. Strategy implies that there are different ways to design effective learning experiences that are predominantly heuristic in nature—a concept that was not present in the 1960s.

Barrett (1977), Bilbrough and Jones (1963), Mosston (1966, 1973), Tillotson (1969), and Shur (1975) have formulated different schemes for the sole purpose of helping teachers become more aware of the variation of strategies they might use while still giving children consistent opportunity to use their natural zest for self-discovery. This implies that giving children opportunity for self-discovery is a carefully thought-through process rather than random or disordered.

While there are specific differences between these schemes, all authors agree that the basis for teachers deciding what type of decisions to leave to the children, how many, and when, is dependent upon their own personal philosophies regarding children, physical education, and education. Because philosophical positions differ, teaching strategies will also differ. The comitment to exploration and discovery as a major style of learning for many children is strong, but it is now strengthened by greater insight into how to use it more effectively.

Figs. 14.13-14.17 Children participating in physical education games, dance, and gymnastics.

REFERENCES

Barrett, K. R., 1977. Studying teaching—a means for becoming a more effective teacher. In Bette J. Logsdon, *Physical education for children—a focus on the teaching-learning process*. Philadelphia: Lea and Febiger.

Bilbrough, A., and P. Jones, 1963. *Physical education in the primary school*. London: University of London Press.

Mosston, M., 1966. *Teaching physical education from command to discovery*. Columbus, Ohio: Charles E. Merrill.

————, 1973. *Teaching from command to discovery*. Belmont, Calif.: Wadsworth.

Schurr, E. L., 1976. *Movement experiences for children*. (2nd ed.) Englewood Cliffs, N.J.: Prentice-Hall.

Tillotson, J., et al., 1969. *A program of movement education for the Plattsburgh Elementary Public Schools*. The final report of a Title III Elementary and Secondary Program funded from September 1966 to August 1969, OEG 66-1934, SED 320.

SUGGESTED READINGS

AAHPER, 1977. *Annotated bibliography on movement education*. Washington, D.C.: AAHPER.

————, 1977. *Echos of influence for elementary school physical education*. Washington, D.C.: AAHPER.

Barrett, K. R., 1973. I wish I could fly—a philosophy in motion. In Paul M. Lepley and Robert Cobb (eds.), *Contemporary philosophies of physical education and athletics*. Columbus, Ohio: Charles E. Merrill.

Locke, L. F., and D. Lamdin, 1975. Teacher behavior. In D. Hellison (ed.), *Personalized learning in physical education*. Washington, D.C.: AAHPER.

Mauldon, E., and H. B. Redfern, 1969. *Games teaching—a new approach for the primary school*. London: MacDonald and Evans.

McKinney, D. E., 1977. But can game skills be taught? *JOHPER* **49** (September): 18-20.

Extraclass Activities
Elba Stafford

Elementary schools sponsor a variety of activities supervised by school personnel and conducted on school property or in school facilities immediately after the regular school day. The actual number or extent of these programs in the elementary schools of the United States is unknown because there is an absence in the current literature of articles describing this phase of the school physical education program. However, a general consensus drawn from discussions with physical education teachers from several states is that some type of after-school activity is conducted in the vast majority of elementary schools in this country. These activity programs usually include students in the fourth, fifth, and sixth grades but very rarely include students from grade three and lower. The programs are usually an outgrowth of, or a supplement to, the physical education period and are unique to each school situation. The content of the program could vary among schools from supervised recreation periods and special-interest club activities to competitive situations such as intramurals, playdays, and interschool competition. Each of these major areas of activity will be discussed separately.

The special-interest clubs are generally formed by groups of students who are interested in improving their own skills in a specific activity in a noncompetitive situation. The club participants work to develop individual and group routines in activities such as rope jumping, folk dancing, or balancing and gymnastic activities. Many times their concluding session is in the form of a performance for parents or a school group.

The most common form of competition found in the after-school activities program at the elementary school level is the playing of games between teams of students from within the school. The organizational structure of this intramural competition varies among schools. In some schools the basic units of competition are organized from permanent large groups such as the home room of the students or the physical education class they attend. In schools where larger organized units are used to designate eligibility for participation in intramurals, yearly records are kept and a winning unit is designated at the end of the school year. In other schools, the teams are selected from the students who report out for the first day of an activity, competition is conducted for this unit, and a winning team is designated. In these schools, the basic grouping changes with each activity and there is no continuity in records.

The team sports of touch football, soccer, basketball, and softball are the most popular activities for intramural competition. Some schools also include single-day events such as punting contests, basketball free-throw shooting contests, or special activities such as kite flying.

The organized play day at the elementary school level is usually in conjunction with an end of the school year celebration. Most play days are planned and organized for the students of one school, but in a few instances two elementary schools combine for the festivities of the day. The play days are planned for full participation of all the grade levels in the school in a variety of games, contests, and relays.

Considerable controversy has existed for many years regarding the appropriateness of interschool competition for the elementary school student. Attention has been focused on the aspects of injury to the immature growing body, and the emphasis placed on winning as well as on the fact that participation is limited to the few highly skilled students. Even though these arguments have been strong, interschool competition in physical activities is conducted by a limited number of elementary schools. The only definitive study in this area of activities was conducted in 1962 by a committee jointly sponsored by the AAHPER and the Society of State Directors of Health, Physical Education, and Recreation (AAHPER 1968). From a representative sample of elementary schools throughout the country, it was found that approximately 20 percent of the K-6 schools offered interschool competition in basketball. Lesser percentages of schools offered other activities such as touch football and softball. The decision each elementary school has had to make is whether an interschool competitive program can be conducted and still leave time, facilities, and competent staff to meet the psychomotor needs of all of the students in the school. Over three-fourths of the elementary schools evidently feel that other areas of physical education take precedence over the interschool phase.

After-school activities are prevalent in the elementary schools in this country and are used to provide opportunities for students to supplement the exercise and instruction received in the regular physical education class. The prevalent activities are, and should be, unique to each school setting.

REFERENCE

AAHPER, 1968. *Desirable athletic competition for children of elementary school age.* Washington, D.C.: AAHPER.

15

Leadership and Organization of Physical Education in Elementary Schools

Helen M. Zimmerman

TEACHING PERSONNEL

In many elementary schools physical education is taught by teachers who are especially prepared in physical education. However, there are also many schools in which the classroom teachers conduct the physical education classes. In the latter situations the school system frequently employs one or more specialists as supervisors or consultants to help the teachers. Assistance is given in various ways. The supervisors may visit the schools upon request, or they may be scheduled to teach each class once a week or more frequently. The classroom teacher does the teaching on the remaining days. Clinics and workshops are conducted to present new ideas and developments to teachers. The supervisor works with the teachers on curriculum development, identification of problems, and proposed solutions.

Recommendations concerning desirable professional preparation and qualifications of physical education teachers have been published by several professional groups. The Society of State Directors of Health, Physical Education, and Recreation (1973) issued a statement of beliefs. The report of the 1968 Conference for Teachers and Supervisors of Elementary School Physical Education also contains recommendations about this topic (AAHPER 1969). In a position paper on elementary physical education, the AAHPER (1969) advocated that qualified physical education teachers teach the elementary school classes. In addition it states:

> To assure that the most meaningful learning takes place, both the physical education teacher and the classroom teacher should work together to develop an understanding of the children and, through this understanding, should provide a program commensurate with the children's needs. Although the physical educator assumes the primary role in conducting the program, it is essential that he regard himself as one part of the total educational process. . . . When classroom teachers teach physical education, it is imperative that they be provided with regular leadership and guidance from resource people who are qualified by education and experience in elementary school physical education. In schools where differentiated staffing patterns are practiced, the value of auxiliary personnel to assist the physical education teacher should not be overlooked.

ORGANIZATION OF ELEMENTARY PHYSICAL EDUCATION

The length and frequency of physical education class sessions vary among the schools. Recommendations concerning time allotment, teaching loads, and other factors are presented in the AAHPER position paper (1969) in which the AAHPER advocated that 150 minutes a week should be devoted to instructional physical education, that this should be exclusive of time used in dressing and/or showering, and that the 150 minutes should be additional to time devoted to recess, noon-hour activity, and other free or supervised play.

Various states have passed laws requiring schools to provide physical education classes. These laws state minimal requirements intended to assure that at least the designated physical education classes are held. They are not intended to be regarded as recommended standards or goals. Interest in existing state laws and trends in laws has led to several surveys of legal requirements within the past 15 years. In a study by Grieve (1971) conducted in 1970, the results of his survey were compared with those of studies done in 1964 and 1969. The trends he noted in state laws that have relevance for elementary schools were that:

> there has been an overall increase in the physical education requirements over the six-year period (1964-1970). . . . The greatest increases have taken place in required elementary physical education. . . . At the elementary level there have been no reductions and eleven states have increased or added requirements. . . . All except five states have physical education requirements. Fourteen states have a daily period required in grades 1 through 6.

Many schools provide much more time for physical education than the laws stipulate, and as indicated above, many schools employ specially educated teachers of physical education.

REFERENCES

AAHPER, 1969. *Essentials of a quality elementary school physical education program.* Washington, D.C.: AAHPER.

————, 1969. *Promising practices in elementary school physical education.* Washington, D.C.: AAHPER.

Grieve, A., 1971. State legal requirements for physical education. *JOHPER* **42** (April): 19-23.

Society of State Directors of Health, Physical Education, and Recreation, 1973. A statement of basic beliefs about the school programs in health, physical education, and recreation. *JOHPER* **44** (June) : 22-24.

SUGGESTED READINGS

AAHPER, 1969. *Professional preparation of the elementary school physical education teacher.* Washington, D.C.: AAHPER.

McNeil, J. D., 1971. *Toward accountable teachers.* New York: Holt, Rinehart and Winston.

Melograno, V. J., 1973. Supervision by objectives. *JOHPER* **44** (March) : 27-28.

16

Assessment of Student Achievement

Anna S. Espenschade

Evaluation is an essential part of every instructional program. Only through systematic appraisal of pupil achievement and progress can it be determined to what extent objectives are being realized. Since it is the function of physical education to prepare pupils to meet the usual problems of living with a degree of success equal to their own ability, evaluations must be made on an individual basis and must be appropriate to that individual's stage of growth, development, and age-sex expectations. Opportunity should be provided for pupils to know how much progress they have made, what changes may be brought about through practice, and what goals they should reasonably expect to reach.

It is obviously impossible to evaluate all performances, so a representative sample relating to each objective must be selected. When a child first enters school or class and no previous record is available, initial observation should be made of the following: 1) handicapping conditions, poor balance, inadequate coordination, and control of movements; 2) poor reactions to vigorous activity such as unusual breathlessness, fatigue, or weakness; and 3) emotional problems, such as fear and withdrawal. If any of these are present, the child should be referred to a physician.

Performance objectives for pupils must relate to the attainment of their own optimum potential, and at no time should evaluation compare achievements of different pupils. It will be obvious, of course, to both teachers and pupils that some children perform better than others in a variety of activities. But it is important, especially with young children, that emphasis be placed upon individual progress and improvement, since capacities may differ markedly. Performance in running and jumping, for example, is related to age and sex as well as to height and weight. Overweight children are handicapped in climbing and hanging events. Strength, endurance, and special skills such as ball handling can be improved greatly by practice. Thus, pupils should learn their own particular abilities and limitations and be stimulated to improve.

PRIMARY GRADES

In the school situation in which one teacher alone is responsible for the group, all evaluation must be done through systematic observation. Thus, as children are participating in selected activities, the teacher notes and later records individual reactions and/or performances. By repeating this procedure several days, comprehensive records can be kept. These records may be anecdotal, ratings or checklists, the latter formulated by teacher or supervisor. Permanent cumulative records should be maintained and should accompany the children as they move to other classes. These should include information from initial observations as listed above concerning health and physical condition; ratings of posture and balance, standing and moving, and of management of their own bodies; notes on running and dodging, and moving over and around obstacles; and achievement in special skills included in the instructional program.

Knowledge and attitudes are demonstrated in behavior and performance in all aspects of the program. Leadership, cooperation, obeying the rules of games, and finding joy in movement all demonstrate potential outcomes of the program and should be noted on the record.

INTERMEDIATE GRADES

Program objectives for the intermediate grades emphasize physical fitness, special skills, knowledge, and attitudes. Some standardized tests are available for fitness and basic motor performances, such as those developed by the AAHPERD and by the states of California and New York. These provide norms by age and sex and permit children to find their relative position within the group. Since these norms are on a percentile basis, it is important for pupil and teacher both to realize that all children cannot be expected to be "average" (50 or above). Half of the children will fall below this figure and half above in any group approaching a normal distribution of scores.

Tests of this nature should be repeated late in the school year to permit comparison of results to determine normal progress or improvement. As the child's age changes, performance in test events must increase in order that position in the group be maintained. The child who continues to score 50, for example, will be progressing at an average rate.

Improvement in strength and endurance and in special skills may be expected with practice, and to a far greater extent than can be accomplished in the basic motor performances of running, jumping, and distance throwing. Early testing will establish status and repeated testing will show improvement.

A variety of test batteries of special skills have been devised but it would be inadvisable to attempt to give many of these as too much time will be taken from the instructional program. Selected tests may be used, however, to evaluate achievement of stated objectives. The results are useful to the teacher in planning instructional emphases and to the children in motivating practice.

It is inevitable that children will compare themselves with others and it is unrealistic to attempt to avoid this. Every effort must be made to show that improvement comes with practice of proper techniques and that individuals can expect to do very much better in some activities than in others. Thus, one may excel in ball games, another in swimming, another in gymnastics, tumbling, or dance.

Written tests may be given to the older children to ascertain knowledge about physical fitness and how to attain and maintain it; of game forms and rules; of desirable practices in athletics. These pupils may also establish personal goals and record progress toward reaching them.

REPORTING PUPIL PROGRESS

Parents should be informed concerning status and progress of their children. This may be done through report cards or conferences. Objectives should be stated clearly and individual progress toward these indicated. Reports may be in terms of ratings, scores, or comments. In all cases, the comparison should be between the child's current performance and previous records.

EVALUATION OF THE PROGRAM

The attainments of pupils in physical education are limited to some extent by competence of the teachers and resources provided them, by facilities and equipment available, by time allotment, and by curricular content. Several rating forms or score cards for appraisal of these factors have been developed by experts in the field. These may be used by a teacher to note desirable standards, or by a supervisor or administrator in status surveys.

17

Physical Education for Special Students

The Physically Handicapped

Agnes M. Hooley

Physically handicapped children are served best through "mainstreaming" or through adapted physical education, that form of the discipline that is planned specifically to meet the needs and potential of all who cannot take part in the usual program. This may include the blind and the deaf. Other categories involve children with skin disorders and allergies, as well as some with conditions that affect breathing, for example, asthmatics and some post-tuberculosis cases. Despite appearances of typicality, there are many children with cardiac disabilities and epilepsy. Cerebral palsy cases, often with multi-handicapping conditions, are numerous in most school systems.

The well-administered adapted physical education program can serve anyone who is seriously limited by a handicap. It is implemented primarily through modification in equipment, facilities, and rules, so that factors such as time, distance, and weight are brought within the use-realm of an individual. (Examples include shortened game periods, lessened track distances, and lightened projectiles such as shots or balls.) An aware and interested teacher and/or pupil can create dozens of activities that are achievable for a handicapped child; the clue is to understand what is possible. This kind of thinking has led to inclusion of swimming in programs for nearly all handicapped persons. It improves breathing efficiency, supports the body, and allows for various positionings of the body through a diversity of strokes.

The full roster of physical education activities is used whenever possible. These include movement education, dance, individual, dual, and team sports, acquatics, body mechanics, and gymanstics. Program individualization is used when it is more promising than group work. This may involve measures to teach habilitation, or "learning to live with a handicap," whereby students

147

adjust, yet demand as much of themselves as possible. Here, physical education becomes a matter of three types of sessions: cognition or knowledge-gaining sessions, behavioral or goal-reaching sessions, and production or "proof-of-the-pudding" sessions. It may involve working with stationary equipment or with a teacher or student-partner on a one-to-one basis or in a small group of handicapped persons. Gradually everyone who is seriously handicapped should be encouraged and helped to participate with normal persons so that physical education and recreation become normal experiences in a world of all persons, handicapped and nonhandicapped.*

This overall concept is utlized in physical education by making every effort to foster appropriate behavior and understanding, as well as use and appreciation of good movement, with the hope that learners will continue to enjoy movement as participants and spectators throughout life.

SUGGESTED READINGS

AAHPER. *Challenge.* Washington, D.C.: AAHPER.

Adams, R., and M. Putho, 1975. Physical activity for children with developmental hip disorders. *JOPER* **46** (February) : 69.

Cratty, B. J., 1973. *Movement behaviour and motor learning.* (3rd ed.) Philadelphia: Lea and Febiger.

Drowatsky, J., 1971. *Physical education for the mentally retarded.* Philadelphia: Lea and Febiger.

Francis, R., and G. L. Rarick, 1963. *Motor characteristics of the mentally retarded.* Washington, D.C.: U.S. Government Printing Office.

Geddes, D., 1974. *Physical activities for individuals with handicapping conditions.* St. Louis: C. V. Mosby.

Information Center on Recreation for the Handicapped. *ICRH newsletter.* Carbondale, Ill.: Southern Illinois University.

Kalakian, L., and J. Moran, 1973. *Movement experiences for the mentally retarded and emotionally disturbed.* Minneapolis: Burgess.

Pomerroy, J., 1964. *Recreation for the physically handicapped.* New York: Macmillan.

Rusk, H. A., 1964. *The handicapped and their rehabilitation.* St. Louis: C. V. Mosby.

Schleichkorn, J., 1977. Physical activity for the child with cystic fibrosis. *JOPER* **48** (January) : 50.

Short, F. X., 1975. Team teaching for developmentally disordered children. *JOPER* **46** (October) : 45.

Wheeler, R. H., and A. M. Hooley, 1969. *Physical education for the handicapped.* Philadelphia: Lea and Febiger.

---

* *Editor's note:* Refer to Section 6 for more information on programs for the handicapped and to Section 7 for the mandates of P.L. 94-142.

The Mentally Retarded and Emotionally Disturbed

Leonard Kalakian

Programming learning experiences for the mentally retarded and/or emotionally disturbed has only recently become a significant trend in physical education. Historically the profession's corrective and adaptive efforts have centered around individuals whose handicaps were primarily physical and/or orthopedic. Professional literature bears witness to these relative emphases and to the emerging trend.

Empirical evidence, if not controlled observations, would indicate that mentally retarded and/or emotionally disturbed children more closely resemble their normal peers physically and "motorically" than in any other single respect. Implicit in this similarity is that many children who have experienced frustration in classroom-oriented tasks may encounter welcome, unexpected success through movement experiences. A growing number of physical educators and, indeed, special educators have come to see physical education not in some ancillary role but as an integral contributor in the learning environment of the mentally retarded and/or emotionally disturbed child.

Physical and motor performance data indicate rather consistently that mentally retarded and/or emotionally disturbed children perform at varying levels below normal peers of the same chronological age. Poindexter has observed performance deficits among emotionally disturbed children in strength, power, agility, balance (dynamic and static), coordination, speed, and perceptual-motor awareness (AAHPER et al. 1969). Francis and Karick (1963) report that physical and motor performance norms for mentally retarded children fall two to four years below those of the normal chronological age peers of the retarded. Limited opportunities to realize physical and motor performance potential among these children must be considered a significant causative factor.

Effective programming for the mentally retarded and/or emotionally disturbed child, not unlike effective programming for normal children, epitomizes *education through the physical*. This concept recognizes the development of physical and motor attributes as one of the major thrusts of the profession. In addition, however, there emerges the premise that many concomitant values and learnings may be derived from physical education experiences including socialization, self-image enhancement, attention-spanning lengthening, and heightened perceptual awareness.

The socialization process may be enhanced as physical education experiences tend to bring the mentally retarded and/or emotionally disturbed child into direct contact with others. This consideration takes on increased importance with the awareness that social contacts of the handicapped tend to be inordinately limited by the handicapping condition.

Self-image may be enhanced through movement experiences. Being successful at something, especially something valued by oneself and one's peers, creates a potentially potent force in the enhancement of self-worth feelings.

Short attention spans are often apparent among mentally retarded and/or emotionally disturbed children. Movement experiences, with their concomitant tendencies toward concreteness, are among the few activities to which these children can relate readily. The relative comfort these children feel with movement experiences can result in the physical educator becoming an invaluable influence in attention-span maintenance and lengthening.

Heightened perceptual awareness is thought to be allied closely with movement experiences. Theories of perceptual-motor development suggest that all learning involves perception, and that initial perceptual abilities evolve from active ("motoric") exploration of the environment.

Author Pearl S. Buck has suggested ways that the quality of a civilization may be best judged by the ways in which it has treated its less fortunate members. In this respect, recent progress has been made in programming for the mentally retarded and/or emotionally disturbed, but even more apparent are efforts yet to be initiated.*

REFERENCES

AAHPER and NRPA in cooperation with the Bureau of Education for Handicapped Children, 1969. *Physical education and recreation for handicapped children.* (Proceedings of a Study Conference on Research and Demonstration Needs.) Washington, D.C.: U.S. Dept. of Health, Education, and Welfare.

Francis, R., and G. L. Rarick, 1963. *Motor characteristics of the mentally retarded.* Washington, D.C.: U.S. Government Printing Office.

SUGGESTED READINGS

AAHPER. *Challenge.* Washington, D.C.: AAHPER.

Cratty, B. J., 1969. *Motor activity and the education of retardates.* Philadelpia: Lea and Febiger.

Drowatsky, J., 1971. *Physical education for the mentally retarded.* Philadelphia: Lea and Febiger.

---

* *Editor's note:* Refer to P.L. 94-142 in Section 7 for recent federal legislation concerning the handicapped.

Geddes, D., 1974. Physical activity: a necessity for severely and profoundly retarded individuals. *JOHPER* **45** (March) : 73.

Information Center on Recreation for the Handicapped. *ICRH newsletter.* Carbondale, Ill.: Southern Illinois University.

Kalakian, L., and J. Moran, 1973. *Movement experiences for the mentally retarded and emotionally disturbed.* Minnepolis: Burgess.

18

Facilities and Equipment

Barbara Kerch

FACILITIES

A gymnasium or multipurpose room and an outdoor playground area comprise the teaching stations for elementary physical education. In some situations it is necessary to augment these facilities by using the classrooms. Outdoor playgrounds generally include an all-weather surfaced area (marked with circles, squares, and lines) to encourage self-directed play, an appartus area surfaced for safe landings, and a turf area for field games. Unless a building also houses middle or junior high school students, special facilities for dressing and showering ordinarily are not provided.

EQUIPMENT

Appartus of varying sizes and shapes and for various uses are installed on the playground and in the gymnasium to develop climbing, vaulting, hanging, and balancing skills. Targets, including basketball and softball backstops, soccer goals, net standards, hoops, tires, boxes, and painted circles and squares, are provided to enhance locomotor, manipulative, and sports skills. A record player with variable speed control is used for rhythmic and dance activities. Mats are essential for stunts, tumbling, gymnastics, and combative activities.

A ball pump, measuring tape, and a stopwatch are often available to teachers, the latter two for evaluation purposes. Indoor teaching areas are generally equipped with bulletin and chalk boards.

INSTRUCTIONAL SUPPLIES

Supplies for the younger children should include rubber utility balls of varying sizes and colors, a short jump rope, and a beanbag for each child's use in any given class. Hoops, long jump ropes, wands, plastic balls, yarn balls, long-handled wooden paddles, small bats, and bowling pins are usually available in lesser amounts. A record player, records, and percussion instruments are deemed essential for rhythmic activities. Plastic cones, field markers, bases, and chalk are used to identify goals and boundaries in games.

In the classes for children 10 to 12 years old, junior-sized soccer balls, footballs, basketballs, and volleyballs are used to develop the specialized skills of the popular team sports. Softball bats, batting tees, and bases are used extensively for both instructional and recreational purposes. Individual sports equipment includes tetherballs and poles, deck tennis rings, shuffleboard, and table tennis equipment, as well as standards, cross bars, and pits or mats to practice the high and long jumps. Records for dance are used extensively. Pinnies and scrimmage vests identify teams and officials. Appropriate reading and viewing materials concerning skills development and sports are provided in the materials center for study use.*

SUGGESTED READINGS

Aaron, D., and B. P. Winawer, 1965. *Child's play.* New York: Harper and Row.

Association for Childhood Education International, 1968. *Physical education for children's healthful living.* Washington, D.C.: The Association.

The Athletic Institute and AAHPER, 1965. *Planning areas and facilities for health, physical education and recreation.* Chicago: The Athletic Institute.

Haber, J., 1977. A recycled playground. *JOPER* **48** (January) : 30.

Thomas, N., and L. Robbins, 1976. An elementary school physical education complex. *JOPER* **47** (September) : 16.

---

*   *Editor's note:* See Section 7 for more information on facilities and equipment.

19

Sex-integrated Elementary Physical Education Classes, Grades K-4*

Marjorie Blaufarb

The requirement that physical education classes in elementary schools be integrated by the end of the first year after signing of the Title IX regulations of the Education Amendments of 1972 should present no difficulty in grades K-4. Primarily classes at this level have not been conducted separately for the sexes.

A comprehensive physical education program is founded on a common core of learning experiences concerned with efficient body management in a variety of movement situations. It serves the divergent needs of all pupils by providing a variety of learning experiences planned and carried out to emphasize the development of basic concepts, values, and behaviors associated with the ultimate goal for the physically educated person.

To meet the requirements of Title IX and to provide for the developmental needs of each girl and boy, it is only necessary to adopt the recommendations for instructional programs suggested in 1969 by the Elementary Physical Education Commission of the Physical Education Division of the AAHPER (1970). These recommendations read as follows. The instructional program should be designed to: 1) encourage vigorous physical activity and the attainment of physical fitness, 2) develop motor skills, 3) foster creativity, 4) emphasize safety practices, 5) motivate expression and communication, 6) promote self-understanding and acceptance, and 7) stimulate social development. It should include such experiences as basic movement, dance, games, practice in sports skills, stunts, and tumbling work with large and small appartus. When possible, the program should include aquatics. Each experience must be so structured that it is interrelated with the others, permitting children to generalize from one learning experience to the next.

---

* This material was extracted from a longer article written by the author entitled "Complying with Title IX of the Education Amendments of 1972 in Physical Education and High School Sports Programs" published by AAHPER in 1975.

Some of the experiences mentioned above will be only a very small part of the instruction in the K-4 program. As is already done by teachers individualizing instruction, sports skills and stunts and tumbling will be introduced gradually as boys and girls are ready for them. In some schools, even at grade 4, there has been some attempt to separate pupils by sex because some sports skills are introduced at that level. There is no sound educational basis for this separation; throwing skills, running skills, and dodging skills are necessary for all children to learn.

It is wise to look with suspicion on suggestions that some sports skills being introduced at this stage are too rough or dangerous for girls. It may be taken as a general rule of safety that activities too rough for one small child are too rough for all children of the same size and weight.

From the foregoing, and from what we know of the practices of most elementary physical education teachers, it seems safe to assume that there are few problems in complying with Title IX at this level. Teachers construct activities in keeping with the philosophy of the school in such a manner as to provide for the safety of the boys and girls. Many teachers will feel happy about what they are doing; some may be stimulated to be more adventurous in the choice of activities as a result of the self-evaluation that was required during the first year.*

REFERENCE

AAHPER, 1970. Essentials of a quality elementary school physical education program. A position paper of the Elementary School Physical Education Commission of the Physical Education Division of the American Association for Health, Physical Education, and Recreation. Washington, D.C.: AAHPER.

---

* *Editor's note:* For more specific information concerning complying with Title IX of the Education Amendments of 1972, see Section 7.

20

Characteristics of the Early Adolescent

Barbara Lockhart and Robert Antonnaci

Persons charged with the organization, administration, and teaching of physical education have recognized the necessity of understanding the growth and developmental patterns of children in order to have optimal programs in the schools. This realization of the importance of understanding not only physical growth, but also the emotional, mental, and social development of youth has resulted in improved programs of physical education that are making important contributions to the educational process.

The stage of development of youths from 12 through 14 years of age, who are in grades 7, 8, and 9 in school, is commonly referred to as early adolescence. The variation in physical development is more marked during this period than in any other. Jenkins et al. (1949, p. 198) stated that nearly two-thirds of the girls have matured by the eighth grade and may be called adolescents, but at this same time, nearly two-thirds of the boys are still pre-adolescents. By the ninth grade physical maturity will have been reached by nearly all the girls and a majority of the boys. The following physical, mental, emotional, and social traits characterize the growth and development of children in the junior high school years.

PHYSICAL CHARACTERISTICS

According to Jersild (1957, p. 28), physical changes are the most important single feature of adolescent development. The preadolescent, one who is beginning the cycle of puberty, experiences noticeable physical changes prior to puberty due to increased production of pituitary hormones and increased release of sex hormones. During this period there is rapid growth; some girls will attain 90 percent of their adult height, although a boy's growth usually extends over a longer period of time. Espenschade and Eckert (1967, p. 189) report that the spurt in growth occurs in girls between 11 and 13.5 years of age, with an average peak height gain of 3.25 inches per year; the growth spurt occurs in boys between 13 and 15.5 years of age with an average peak height gain of 4 inches per year. Accompanying this increase in height is the tendency to put on excess fat.

155

There is a great range in age as to when a child enters puberty. Girls may begin to menstruate between the ages of 10 and 16 and boys may mature between the ages of 12 and 16, with exceptions occurring either earlier or later. After puberty, sex differences in body build become apparent. Girls have a longer rate of gain in hip width and a lesser amount of gain in shoulder width than boys. Physiological changes, other than those directly associated with puberty, are also apparent in adolescence. As reported by Espenschade and Eckert (1967, p. 195-210), some of these changes are: 1) basal heart rate decreases and does so more markedly in boys than girls after 12 years; 2) basal body temperature is about one-half degree lower in boys than girls; 3) systolic blood pressure increases rapidly with a greater increase in boys than girls; 4) there is an increase in blood volume, more so in boys than in girls, with an accompanying increase in the number of red blood cells; 5) the resting respiratory volume, maximum breathing capacity, and vital capacity increase considerably in boys but not in girls; and 6) other respiratory changes occur in boys that allow their blood to absorb more lactic acid and other metabolites during exercise than can the blood of girls, without a change in the pH of their blood.

The motor abilities of the junior high school individual are reflective of these physical differences. The skill level increases at a much greater rate for boys than girls. Although both sexes enjoy better coordination, the girls tend to reach a plateau in skill development at this age. Muscular strength and endurance are more pronounced in boys than girls.

EMOTIONAL CHARACTERISTICS

As there is usually no specific age set by this society at which children become adults, adolescents become confused regarding the role they are expected to fulfill. At times they are treated as adults and at other times they are treated as mere children. They have misgivings about themselves and, at the same time, are developing pride in themselves. Adolescents have a need for receiving affection and support and are starting to realize their capacity for affection for others.

Although many anxieties and fears are revealed by adolescent behavior, by this time in their lives adolescents have learned to conceal many of their emotions. Great effort is employed in their struggle for independence and the development of a good rapport between themselves, their peers, and authority figures.

Insecurity may be so prevalent in the youngsters that they may not even try out for a team. Their self-critical attitude may keep them from meaningful experiences at this age level. Jenkins et al. (1949, p. 225) admonishes adults to aid adolescents in growing toward the realization that the kind of people they will become is determined by much more than good looks. Many youngsters are unhappy about their physical appearance and need help and guidance to accept it and make the best of themselves.

MENTAL CHARACTERISTICS

By the time children reach the seventh grade they are well aware of the importance of mental ability in our society. To gain the respect of parents, peers, and teachers, children work to develop their mental capacities. At this age, these capacities generally include: 1) ability to deal with the abstract, 2) growth in intellect and knowledge, 3) greater depth of understanding of self and others, 4) ability to solve complex problems, and 5) an increased amount of common sense.

Jersild (1957, p. 79) explains that 12- through 14-year-olds are gaining the ability to relate to ideas and things that will not affect them personally. Events, people, and places completely outside of the adolescent's own sphere of activity may be contemplated and discussed. Moral concepts that have been formulated are able to be internalized at this age.

Knowledge of the changing body is extremely important at this stage of growth. These young people are recognizing the inherent structure of their physical selves and are formulating their personal "body image." The ability to think objectively is increasing and will even allow them to take an objective view of themselves.

SOCIAL CHARACTERISTICS

Social acceptance in the junior high school years is quite often associated with physical prowess. Schurr (1967, p. 25) reports that boys are expected to be well skilled; however, girls may maintain their social status if their skill level stays the same or even regresses. At this age there is a tremendous desire on the part of both sexes to be a part of a group, and therefore, interest in participating in sports runs high. Approval and acceptance by peers often play a dominant role in structuring the behavior patterns of young people. Leaders among adolescent peers tend to have these qualities: 1) happy and cheerful, 2) able to take a joke, 3) fair, good sports, and 4) adept in physical activities.

Jersild (1957, p. 217) maintains that a competitive experience can be very beneficial to adolescents. It could provide them the opportunity to discover new potential within themselves, gain the attention that they deserve, and aid in developing a greater understanding and perception of themselves. Destructive competition may be as harmful as wholesome competition is beneficial. This is an age of increased conformity and awareness of social status.

The recognition of the physical, emotional, mental, and social characteristics of growth and development of the adolescent establishes a need for physical education to make as much of a contribution as possible to the individual's progress in each of these areas. Physical educators need considerable knowledge and understanding to be able to plan programs to benefit youngsters of the junior high school age level who, as a whole, have such a tremendous range in the various stages of growth and development.

REFERENCES

Espenschade, A. S., and H. M. Eckert, 1967. *Motor development.* Columbus, Ohio: Charles C. Merrill.

Jenkins, G., H. Shacter, and W. W. Bauer, 1949. *These are your children.* Chicago: Scott, Foresman and Co.

Jersild, A. T., 1957. *The psychology of adolescence.* New York: Macmillan.

Schurr, E. L., 1967. *Movement experiences for children.* New York: Appleton-Century-Crofts.

21

Aims and Objectives

Clyde Partin

The physical education program at the junior high school level should offer a wide variety of activities for boys and girls. The following aims and objectives should be included in a program of physical education at the junior high school level:

1. Provide a wide variety of physical education activities to all students.

2. Insure that the activities provided include games and sports of the individual, dual, and team type.

3. Offer a program that emphasizes physical fitness-type activities concerned with organic development, particularly those activities that lend themselves to the development of cardiovascular efficiency.

4. Offer a program that includes psychomotor skills and lifetime sports activities.

5. Develop a carefully designed program to provide the ultimate in health instruction, including not only health knowledge but also the development of proper attitudes and habits toward healthful living.

6. Place the proper emphasis on the social development of the individual through the medium of physical education activities, particularly through appropriate coeducational activities.

7. Develop a program that will allow individuals to appreciate the feelings of others through good sportsmanship.

8. Offer a program that allows individuals the opportunity to express themselves and be creative in their physical education activities.

9. Insure that the program offers the chance for individuals to become leaders through the democratic process.

10. Design the program to guide an individual in developing a philosophy of life that is consistent with all that is good in the field of physical education.

11. Include activities for *all* children, the normal as well as the exceptional child.*

22

Junior High School Physical Education
William Kilpatrick

Junior high school physical education exists to provide for the needs of a particular group of young people—those between 12 and 15 years of age. This age group includes both preadolescents and adolescents. During these years the physical growth is rapid, but the rate of growth varies by sex and for individuals within each sex group. In addition to growing physically, these

---

*   *Editor's note:* A more complete discussion of aims and objectives is included in Section 1.

159

young people are also maturing. The time of maturation varies by sex and individually within each sex group. These changes and variations in physical development and maturation create problems unique to the junior high school.

These problems are concerned with meeting the needs of these boys and girls—needs arising out of their physical growth and development, their social and emotional development, their intellectual development and intellectual cultural interest, and the demands of the society in which they live. To meet these needs, junior high school physical education must fulfill the functions of integration of learning experiences, discovery and exploration, guidance, differentiation, socialization and articulation with the elementary and senior high schools, and with related activities such as health, recreation, intramurals, and athletics. In fulfillment of these functions, undue emphasis should not be placed upon one or two at the expense of the others.

Required physical education instruction for this age level is more frequent than elementary or senior high school offerings. In many school districts, this is the only level that physical education is required.

Physical fitness is the primary contribution of physical education to the total educational program. Activities included in the instructional program should be very carefully selected on their total contribution for fulfilling student needs in relation to the aims and objectives of physical education. Class activities should provide a good balance with major emphasis placed on rigorous physical ativity and cooperative group activities. At each grade level, the program should include at least four team games, three individual sports, tumbling and gymnastics, acquatics, self-testing activities, dance, and rhythm.

The most traditional sports activities included in programs are:

archery	gymnastics, tumbling	table tennis
badminton	handball	tennis
basketball	shuffleboard	touch football
bowling	soccer	track & field
dance	softball	volleyball
field hockey	speedball	weight training
golf	swimming & diving	wrestling

Future consideration should be given to the elimination of the most repetitious activities in favor of new activities that might include:

cageball	flickerball	paddleball
cross country	gym hockey	rugby
European handball	lacrosse	snorkeling
field hockey (boys)	obstacle course	speedaway

Student assessment procedures should evaluate how well the activities and the teaching methods are helping students understand and achieve the aims and objectives of the physical education program.

Normal scheduling procedures have been by sex and grade level, usually including one-third or more students than assigned to other required classes. Title IX mandates that physical education class assignments may not be made on the basis of sex (see Chapter 28).

Flexible and ungraded scheduling techniques are now being developed to schedule students according to interest and ability. These techniques allow for large numbers of students to be scheduled into team sport activity classes such as soccer, field hockey, volleyball, and so on, and smaller numbers into individual instructional classes such as tennis, badminton, and special fitness developmental classes.

Classes are scheduled in a variety of methods. A daily instructional period is preferred. Every other day, odd or even days, or on an alternate block of time basis with either health or some other class is a common procedure. Daily classes are often scheduled to include a combination of two days of indoor or field activities, two days of aquatics, and one day of health or some similar combination. Another alternative might be by activities— team sports on two days, individual sports one day, and aquatics two days. The activity block schedule of a prescribed number of days for each activity is most common.

The class period usually consists of the same amount of time as other courses found in the curriculum. Flexible scheduling has created opportunities to increase the time allotment for certain offerings. Scheduling activity classes such as gymnastics for a period of one and a half to two hours provides more instructional and practice time, and reduces the percentage of time required to dress, shower, take attendance, set up equipment, and so forth.

Schedules should be developed to help students satisfy their own individual needs through the program aims and objectives within the existing facilities and competencies of the teachers.

Class organization should provide as much time as possible for instruction and participation, and only limited time for administrative details, roll call, selecting teams, and so on. Students should be provided opportunities to subordinate themselves to team requirements with nearly the same measure of discipline, control, and enthusiasm as that required of the school's varsity athletes. All students, rather than just the athlete, should be encouraged and given the opportunity to attain a high level of physical and skill development.

Each class period should include a series of exercises or activities designed to strengthen all parts of the body and to develop agility, balance, flexibility, power, and endurance, along with skill instruction, practice, and/or sport participation.

Class participation should provide students the opportunity to be brave, to develop a tolerance for discomfort, and a willingness to discipline one's own body and to develop a well-disciplined attitude toward the hard work principle in terms of heavy-energy-output-type activities. Possibilities for self-

Fig. 22.1 Girls' archery.

Fig. 22.2 Physical education coeducational activities.

evaluation, helping others, team play, sportsmanship, and leadership should be integrated into class organization.

Standards and grades should not be eliminated. Students want to keep records, they enjoy success, they want to win, but they do not want to be humiliated for losing. They need to maintain self-respect for making a good effort.

Numerous studies by Cureton (1964), Pollock (1968), Hambrough (1965), Elder (1967), Sherman (1967), and others indicate that the inclusion of heavy muscular and endurance-type activities along with a motivation variable will create desired physical changes in students that are not possible in the traditional recreation games and sports-type program.

Instruction in the various skills is provided to help motivate the student to enjoy participation in physical activities as well as develop a lifelong habit of regular physical exercise.

REFERENCES

Cureton, T. K., Jr., 1964. *Improving the physical fitness of youth.* Washington, D.C.: National Society for Research in Child Development.

Elder, H., 1967. The effects of the inclusion of endurance training on the physical fitness of eighth grade boys. Research report, Long Beach public schools, California.

Hembrough, G. D., 1965. The effects of a motivational variable on the performance of selected physical fitness items by selected junior high boys. M.S. thesis. Urbana: University of Illinois.

Pollock, M. L., B. L. Rothermel, and T. K. Cureton, Jr., 1968. AAHPER Physical Fitness Test score changes as a result of an eight-week sport and physical fitness program. *Research Quarterly* **39:** 1127-1129.

Sherman, M. A., 1967. Maximal oxygen intake changes in experimentally exercised junior high school boys. Doctoral dissertation. Urbana: University of Illinois.

SUGGESTED READING

The now P.E., 1973. *JOHPER* **44** (September) : 23.

23

Middle Schools and Physical Education

Elba Stafford

The basic concept of the emerging middle school provides for a reordering of the priorities of education for the age range from 10 to 14 years. It emphasizes a child-centered approach to education instead of the subject-oriented approach of the high school and, in many cases, the present junior high school. The importance of providing an atmosphere for positive physical, social, and emotional experiences is placed on the same priority level as developing intellectual capacities. With this new philosophical approach, many and varied instructional situations may be structured. A flexible approach to instruction is encouraged to provide better individualized instructional situations. A flexible schedule, which can vary daily, is planned by a team of teachers responsible for the educational experiences of a group of students. Innovative approaches to presenting learning situations are encouraged. Independent study programs are developed for individuals interested in pursuing a subject beyond the normal classroom situation. The middle school instructional concepts are probably best summarized by Grooms (1967), who states that the middle school is one of change, innovation, discovery, and inquiry, a place to develop skills and capabilities, a place of activity and reflections, a place for study, and a place for self-realization.

The change from the junior high school to the middle school organizational pattern is rapidly becoming the major change in this country's educational system in the last half century. The middle school as defined in the *National Educational Association Research Bulletin* of May 1969 is a school having a span of at least three grades, including grades 6 and 7, and having no grades below 5 or above 8. This concept of the middle school has been attractive to school administrators and school board members in the last 15 years. Data obtained by three separate surveys of middle schools indicate that there was a quadrupling of middle schools in the United States between the years 1965 and 1970. Cuff (1967) found that there were 499 operational middle schools during the 1965-66 school year; Alexander (1968) indicated that there were 1101 middle schools operating during the 1967-1968 school year. All indications are that this rate of growth or rate of change to the middle school concept is continuing to mushroom.

There seems to be widespread agreement that there are distinct advantages of having the pre- and early adolescent in a school situation separated from the older high school students as well as from the younger elementary school children. The middle school might do this to better advantage than the present junior high school because of the evidence of the earlier maturation of today's boys and girls. The majority of girls enter puberty between ages 10 and 12, and the boys between ages 12 and 13. On the other end of the middle school pattern, the ninth grade boys and girls are more physically mature and have attained a social maturity that will permit them to meet the objectives of a high school curriculum.

Another basic reason used in promoting the change to middle schools is that the junior high school has failed and is failing to meet the needs of the students at this age level. The junior high school has been classified traditionally as a part of secondary education and has generally taken on most of the characteristics of the high school. It is contended that this school is just what the name implies, a "junior" high school. This is in contrast to the name "middle school," which tends to give this separate organizational pattern a name of its own, and separates it from the image of the high school.

The purposes of educating pre-and early adolescents and of providing a bridging function between elementary school and high school have always been prime factors for a school in the middle. Perhaps the major reason for changing to the middle school can be that it provides an opportunity for schools to start over in planning the educational experiences for this age group and permits them to eliminate many of the built-in faults of the present junior high school.

This new organizational structure and philosophical approach has provided the physical education teacher with the opportunity to shed the unit or block teaching plan copied from the high school and to look for new approaches to teaching that will meet the specific needs of the growing and changing student they are responsible for educating. The emphasis is still being placed on teaching basic psychomotor skills and developing healthy and fit bodies, but the approaches used to accomplish these objectives are being changed or modified. Physical education teachers are participating members of teams responsible for planning the learning experiences of the students.

A variety of instructional approaches is appearing in middle schools in the United States. Some middle schools have developed individualized instructional packages that use written and audiovisual materials to present intructional situations to the students. Performance contracting is being used for individuals or groups who wish to perfect specific activity skills. Minicourses are being inserted into the program to meet specialized needs as well as to introduce students to unique activities not normally taught in physical education classes. Open laboratory sessions are becoming common in middle schools to permit students to work at activities of their own choice during un-scheduled time. Drop-in centers are being established in schools to provide students with the opportunity to gain knowledge and experience in recreational activities. Special interest activity clubs such as archery and cycling are being organized. Many coeducational classes are being taught in the individual and noncontact team activities. The physical and social needs and interests vary greatly during this transitional growth period. Therefore, the physical education teacher must be willing to plan the activity program to meet the varying needs of the middle school student.

An opportunity is also provided for a modification of the interscholastic program at this level to bring it into line with the educational objectives of the middle school concept. The emphasis is placed on mass participation of all of the students in a strong intramural and recreation program in every school. The time of the instructor and the use of the facilities are no longer dominated by the few exceptional students. All of the students attending the school are accorded the same right to the teacher's time and to the use of the facilities. Middle schools that do provide an experience of competing with another school provide the opportunity for every boy and girl in the school to participate in this experience.

It is no coincidence that this school level coincides with the pubescent growth range of most of our youngsters because it is hoped that, besides providing a bridging function for the educational structure, this separate level of education also provides an educational program focused on the spcial needs and interests of the pre- and early adolescent. The middle school, then, has the responsibility of helping the students make a satisfactory transition from the child-centered philosophy of the elementary school to the subject-centered high school curriculum, at the same time that they are growing physically and emotionally from childhood to adulthood.

REFERENCES

Alexander, W. M., 1968. A survey of organizational patterns of reorganized middle schools. U.S. Department of Health, Education, and Welfare, Office of Education, Cooperative Research Project 7-D-126. University of Florida.

Cuff, W. A., 1967. Middle schools on the march. *Bulletin of the National Association of Secondary School Principals* 51 (February) : 82-86.

Grooms, M.A., 1967. *Perspectives on the middle school.* Columbus, Ohio: Merrill.

National Education Association, 1969. Middle schools in theory and in fact. *National Education Association Research Bulletin* 47 (May) : 49-52.

SUGGESTED READING

Seefeldt, V., 1974. Middle schools. *JOHPER* 45 (February) : 32.

24

Intramurals

Richard A. Haas

Ideally, intramurals in the junior high school combine the best parts of a physical education program with recreational activities. Students who seek more opportunity to play or a higher degree of competition than offered in the regular physical education program can turn to intramurals to satisfy this desire. A complete intramural program will include a wide variety of competitive sports, both team and individual.

A skeptic might look at the rationale for an intramural program and state, "Why isn't that accomplished in physical education?" The best answer is that the intramural program allows the interested youngster additional time and opportunities for needed reinforcement to valuable principles taught in a regular physical education class. Some of the more important functions of a complete intramural program are:

1. The youngster may engage in competitive exercise and, in turn, relieve mental and emotional tension.
2. The student can realize beneficial use of leisure time.
3. Fitness habits learned in the regular program can be reinforced.
4. Through intramurals, the youngster can receive the rewards of group participation and cooperation. This can help the child in personality development and socialization.
5. Intramurals can help the student to discover skills, enhance coordination and muscular development, and to polish and sharpen the skills already possessed.

Most schools would find it quite difficult if not impossible to coordinate their physical education, athletics, and intramural programs in the time span of the "regular school day." It becomes necessary to utilize facilities before school, during noon hours, directly after school, in the evening, and sometimes even on Saturdays and vacation periods. An aggressive, enthusiastic director will use every available station as well as every available day each month in order to achieve a successful program.

The ideal program should include a balance between team and individual sports and between active and less active sports. The main thrust of the program should be directed toward fitness, perfecting skills taught in physical education classes, and recreational activities.

Ideally the intramural program should be designed to enable participation of the total student body. This means that such a wide range of sports and activities will be offered that each student will find at least one in which he or she is interested. There are arguments, both pro and con, as to whether varsity athletes should be allowed to compete in intramural sports. Those who advocate limiting their participation argue that youngsters with lesser ability would have more opportunity to compete. Others feel that barring varsity athletes would relegate the contests to an inferior status.

The greatest single award offered by the intramural program would be the enjoyment derived from play and healthy competition. In addition, awards or recognition of achievement can be given to the participants. These awards should never be so important that they overshadow the main purposes of fun, competition, physical fitness, and skill development.

SUGGESTED READINGS

AAHPER, 1975. Standards and guidelines for intramurals. *JOHPER* **46** (March) : 26.

Gilbo, J. R., 1976. Junior high intramurals: a positive approach. *JOPER* **47** (September) : 38.

Hyatt, R., 1974. The intramural story. *JOHPER* **45** (March) : 39.

25

Junior High School Athletics
Lawrence Benjamin

The junior high school athletics program is one that has been fraught with controversy over the years. Support for and against such a program can readily be found in the literature. Recently, however, this debate has abated considerably due to extensive research providing facts rather than feelings (Hale 1959 and 1971). The literature suggests what comprises a good junior high school program (Bucher 1965). The basic areas of controversy center around these aspects:

1. The outcomes to be derived from such competition at this level, vis-a-vis, winning teams or enjoyment.
2. The fact that athletic competition at this level is already a reality, like it or not.

3. The supervisor of competition.

4. The physiological, psychological, social, and emotional homogeneity of the competitors (Clark et al. 1961; Hale 1971).

There are other items that may be controversial but recently the question of such a program has come under scrutiny due to an evaluation of American education in general. With this evaluation the bases of justification for many educational programs were expenditures, racial balance, size of school plant, etc., and the educational relevance as compared with the total development of the child (Dannehl 1971). Another factor unrelated to aspects of the issue has evolved, that is, the participation of young women in junior high school athletic programs competing with and against young men of the same level. The New York State Education Department conducted research in order to supply itself with some answers to this dilemma (Grover 1970). Its findings concluded there was no evidence of physical, psychological, or social harm to the female participants or their male teammates. The only problems found were administrative; and it was therefore felt that all restrictions on the participation of girls on boys' teams in noncontact sports should be removed. Findings of other research tend to support the pros of the question (Albright 1964; Brown 1971; Hale 1971).

There have been numerous studies of the physiological adaptation of young children to exercise. The conclusion is that strenuous physical activity will not harm a normal child. Individuals who participate in competitive athletics exhibit greater popularity, social esteem, and social adjustment (Hale 1959).

Although there has been considerable research concerning Little League Baseball, Hale and others support the argument that, in terms of physiological, psychological, and sociological aspects, competitive participation for the most part was not harmful for young children (Hale 1959 and 1971).

Physicians who were also fathers of boys in Little League Baseball agreed generally that playing Little League was beneficial to their sons (Knowlton 1957). The American Medical Association Committee on the Medical Aspects of Sports has developed guidelines that concern junior high school athletes. The National Association of Girls' and Women's Sports has developed its own guidelines.

Research by Torg et al. (1972) reports that excessive competitive pitching by the preadolescent has produced a high incidence of shoulder and elbow abnormalities of Little League pitchers and that intensely competitive situations should be avoided. Competitive pressures and repetitious and demanding practice should be replaced by properly supervised games in which recreation and enjoyment are the objectives.

In order to prevent abusing the arms of the skeletally immature, Adams (1965 and 1968) suggests the following guidelines:

1. Discourage youngsters from practicing pitching at home before, during, and after the season.
2. Abolish curve ball throwing at this age (9-12).
3. Shorten the playing season, especially in Southern California, where it is overly prolonged.
4. Restrict pitchers to two innings per game until the epiphyses are completely closed.
5. Divide Little League into two groups—one for 9 and 10 year olds, the other for 11 and 12 year olds.

In view of these statements, one must realize that athletics are an important part of education. Not only are there competitive activities at the junior high level (some of which involve girls), but this competitiveness exists also at the pre-junior high level. Children will compete whether in school or out of school, with or without approval of school authority. Therefore, the question of allowing or forbidding athletic activities at this level is really a moot point (Bula 1971). The professional physical educator and the community must take steps to ensure that such activities encompass proper leadership and programs that fit the needs and developmental patterns of the students (Bucher 1965). If the proper safeguards are established and adhered to, as should be the case in all educational programs, athletics will have an excellent opportunity to elicit the desired social, physiological, and psychological outcomes.

Both educators and the general public accept the premise that a junior high school athletic program possesses educational values commensurate with the social, emotional, and physical development of young children. A few educational values generally associated with athletics in school activity programs are:

1. Athletics are fun and an acceptable and excellent form of energy release.
2. Athletics contribute to physical fitness.
3. Athletics teach self-discipline and sportsmanship.
4. Athletics has a unifying effort in terms of school spirit.
5. Athletics is a factor in keeping many students in school who might otherwise drop out (Dannehl 1971).

Predicated on these values, and in view of the findings that support the programs with carefully laid out guidelines, athletics are a vital and necessary part of the total junior high school program and therefore can be defended to the extent that they contribute to established educational goals.

REFERENCES

Adams, J.E. 1965. Injury to the throwing arm; A study of traumatic changes in the elbow joint of boy baseball players. *Calif. Med.* **102** (February): 127-132.

Grules, 1968. Bone injuries in very young athletes. *Clin. Orthopaedics* **58** (May-June): 129-140.

Albright, T. 1964. Sports for teenage girls. *Proceedings of the National Conference on Medical Aspects of Sports* **6:** 31-33.

Brown, C. H. 1971. New dimensions in physical activity and fitness for girls and women. *American Corrective Therapy Journal* **25** (May-June): 66-70.

Bucher, C. A., 1965. *Interscholastic athletics at the junior high school level.* New York: State Education Department.

Bula, M., 1971. Competition for children: The real issue. *JOHPER* **42** (September): 40.

Clarke, H. H., and K. H. Petersen, 1961. Contrast of maturational, structural, and strength characteristics of athletes and nonathletes 10 to 15 years of age. *Research Quarterly* **32** (May): 163-176.

Dannehl, W. E., and J. E. Razor, 1971. The values of athletics: a critical inquiry. *Bulletin of the National Association of Secondary School Principals* **55:** 59-65.

Grover, G. H. 1970. Girls on boys' athletics teams; report of an experiement by the New York State Education Department. Paper presented to the 12th National Conference on the Medical Aspects of Sports, November.

Hale, C. J., 1971. Athletic competition for young children. Paper presented to the conference on Sport and Social Deviancy, State University of New York, Brockport, December.

——. 1959. What research has to say about athletics for pre-high school age children. *JOHPER* **30** (December): 19-21, 43.

Knowlton, R. G., 1957. A muscular endurance study of preadolescent boys. M.S. thesis. Urbana: University of Illinois.

Torg, J. S. 1972. The little league pitcher. *Amer. Family Physician* **6** (August) 71-76.

——, H. Pollack, and P. Sweterlitsch, 1972. The effects of competitive pitching on the shoulders and elbows of preadolescent baseball players. *Pediatrics* **49:** 267-272.

26

Research on Teaching Physical Education

Michael Goldberger and Billy E. Gober

A review of the research on teaching physical education at the junior high school level would not seem to help teachers appreciably in deciding "how" to teach or how to actually control their behavior in the teaching-learning situation. There is a real paucity of research on teaching physical education in general, and particularly at the junior high school level. However, the most frustrating aspect of this research is the inconsistency in defining the teaching behavior, or treatment variable. Many of these studies use nonspecific terminology that does not communicate the nature of the behavior (e.g., traditional, informal, innovative). Others whose titles identify them as methodological quite often only manipulate subsidiary factors such as grouping, space, timing, audio-visual aids, or organization. Only studies that take into account the actual behavior of the teacher should be termed methodological. Specific styles of teaching do imply organization, grouping, timing, and the rest, but studying these subsidiary factors apart from the teacher's behavior has proven unproductive in helping the teacher decide "how" to behave in the gymnasium, the pool, or on the fields.

Mosston (1966) offers a paradigm that includes a "spectrum" of teaching styles, from "command" to "discovery." The spectrum presents teachers with an integrated series of alternative behavioral models, including the implications of each model on learning, from which they can make an intelligent decision as to the most appropriate style for their purposes. The spectrum is based on the axiomatic statement that "teaching behavior is a chain of decision making," decisions about what, where, whom, quality, quantity, and so on. In the first style on the spectrum, which is called "command," the teacher makes *all* the decisions and the students consequently play a subservient role. This teaching behavior is probably the most prevalent style found currently in the junior high school setting. As one proceeds along the spectrum from the "command" style, there are gradual shifts in who makes decisions from complete teacher decision making to complete student decision making. The spectrum now consists of seven identifiable styles.

Mariani (1970) compared two styles in teaching tennis and found the "task" style somewhat superior to the "command" style in achieving stroke proficiency. In another study, Dougherty (1971) found the "command" style superior to both the "task" and "individual programs" styles in developing physical fitness over a brief training period. Farrell (1970) found "programmed instruction" equally effective when compared to a "traditional teacher-directed method" in teaching tennis skills to university women. Mitchell (1970) found "programmed instruction" equally effective with high and low achieving junior high school students in health education. The liability of this approach appears to be a reduction in the opportunity for socialization between the students. No studies reporting the effects of the "cognitive" styles of teaching (guided discovery, problem solving, inquiry) on student achievement in physical education could be found.

Most of the studies reviewed reported nonsignificant or conflicting results. Logic would suggest that manipulating diverse teaching styles should produce changes in student achievement. Some of this inability to produce significant results can be traced to weaknesses in the research design and/or inappropriate instrumentation. There is a need for carefully controlled experimental studies designed to measure true differences in teacher behavior and the corresponding change in student achievement. To discriminate true differences in teaching style, objective measuring instruments such as the Flanders system of interaction analysis (Amidon and Hough 1967) should be employed. The Flanders system is an observational instrument that gives objective data about the "climate" of the classroom or gymnasium. It is based upon verbal interaction between teacher and students, but can be easily adapted to include the nonverbal interaction common to physical education classes. This system gives information concerning the amount of freedom the teacher gives students in the learning situation. It can be used as a tool for supervision, for evaluation, and for research.

Considering individual differences in physical growth alone would seem to indicate an "individualized" style of teaching should predominate at this school level. The vast differentiation in growth achievements (pre- and postpubescence) suggest a fallacy in stereotyping performance at this developmental level and indicates more individualized consideration of achievement. The assets of the "individual program" style—which consists of designing, prescribing, and conducting learning programs tailormade to fit the needs and characteristics of the junior high school student—would seem very appropriate for this level (Southworth 1968).

REFERENCES

Amidon, E., and J. Hough, 1967. *Interaction analysis: theory, research and application.* Reading, Mass.: Addison-Wesley.

Dougherty, N. J. 1971. A comparison of the effects of command, task and individual program styles of teaching in the development of physical fitness and motor skills.

Proceedings of the National College Physical Education Association for Men. **74:** 154-159.

Farrell, J. E., 1970. Programmed vs. teacher directed instruction in beginning tennis for women. *Research Quarterly* **41** (March): 51-58.

Mariani, T. 1970. A Comparison of the effectiveness of the command method and the task method of teaching the forehand and backhand tennis strokes. *Research Quarterly* **41** (May): 171-174.

Mitchell, W., 1972. A comparative study of effectiveness of programmed instruction in teaching health to low and high achieving junior high school students. Master's project. Philadelphia: Temple University.

Mosston, M., 1966. *Teaching physical education: from command to discovery.* Columbus, Ohio: Merrill.
Southworth, H., 1968. A model of teacher training for the individualization of instruction. U.S. Office of Education, Project No. 8-9020, University of Pittsburgh.

SUGGESTED READINGS

Anderson, W. G., 1971. Descriptive analytic research on teaching. *Quest.* Monograph 15. NACPEW and NCPEAM.

Locke, L. F., 1969. *Research on teaching physical education.* New York: Columbia University Press.

Nixon, J. E., and L. F. Locke, 1973. Research on teaching physical education. In R. Travers (ed.), *Second handbook of research on teaching.* Chicago: Rand McNally.

Schwartz, S. 1972. A learning-based system to categorize teacher behavior. *Quest,* Monograph 17. NACPEW and NCPEAM.

27

Physical Fitness
B. Don Franks

Regular vigorous physical activity causes desirable changes in youth and adults. These changes include improvements in: (1) body composition (e.g., reduction in fat (Mas 1957); (2) increased efficiency at rest (Cundiff 1966) and in response to submaximal exercise (Fardy 1961); (3) endurance, both muscular (Pollock et al. 1968) and cardiovascular (Sherman 1967); and (4) underlying skills such as agility, balance, flexibility, and strength (Knowlton 1957).

The importance of *regular* physical activity is illustrated in Johnson's study (1969), which showed daily physical education was better than two or three times per week on selected measures of body composition, muscular endurance, power, and skill.

The importance of *vigorous* physical activity is emphasized by Cureton (1964) and the joint statement by the AMA and AAHPER (1964). More vigorous programs cause greater changes than less vigorous programs (Holmes 1958; Knowlton 1957; Mas 1957). The recommendations concerning *minimum* time requirements for daily physical activity range from 30 minutes to an hour.

One sport or activity should not be emphasized to the exclusion of a variety of activities. No one activity can meet all of the physical education objectives. Overemphasis of one activity may prevent participation in a variety of activities. For example, Skubic (1955) found that boys participating in Little League Baseball spent a large percentage of their time in that one activity. Although Little League Baseball probably has little physiological benefits (Hanson 1967), it probably is not harmful per se. The main disadvantage would be that it might prevent participation in other activities that would be beneficial. The same point could be made about television. Markewicz and Graven (1966) found a "tired child syndrome" to be caused by excessive watching of television. One of the probable causes of this syndrome is lack of physical activity because of numerous hours sitting and watching. No one activity, regardless of its merit, should be emphasized to the extent that it excludes other valuable activities.

Important changes in physical fitness should be achieved through enjoyable activities. Either extreme of making fitness changes regardless of the interest of the participant, or having enjoyable activities that do not cause important changes, should be avoided. Above all, endurance activities such as running should never be used for punishment.

President Kennedy (1961) highlighted the importance of physical fitness instruction when he stated, "We must increase our facilities and the time devoted to physical activity; we must invigorate our curricula and give higher priority to a crusade for excellence in health and fitness."*

------

*Editor's Note: Volume II of this *Encyclopedia* is devoted to the topic of physical fitness.

REFERENCES

AAHPER, 1964. Exercises and fitness. A joint statement from AAHPER and AMA. *JOHPER* **35** (May): 42-44.

Cundiff, L. B., 1966. Effects of training and dietary supplements on selected cardiac intervals of young boys. M.S. thesis. Urbana. University of Illinois.

Cureton, T. K., Jr. 1964. *Improving the physical fitness of youth.* Washington, D.C.: National Society for Research in Child Development.

Fardy, P. S., 1961. The effect of general progressive strength activities on the upper body development of selected young boys. M.S. thesis. Urbana: University of Ilinois.

Hanson, D. L., 1967. Cardiac response to participation in little league baseball competition as determined by telemetry. *Research Quarterly* **38**: 384-388.

Holmes, R. A., 1958. The effects of various methods of training on endurance and cardiovascular tests. M.S. thesis. Urbana : University of Illinois.

Johnson, K.C., 1969. Effects of 5-day-a-week vs. 2- and 3-day-a-week physical education classes on fitness, skill, adipose tissue, and growth. *Research quarterly* **40** 93-98.

Kennedy, J. F., 1961 A presidential message to the schools on the physical fitness of youth. *JOHPER* **32** (September): Cover.

Knowlton, R.G., 1957. A muscular endurance study of preadolescent boys. M.S. thesis. Urbana : University of Illinois.

Markewicz, R. M., and S. N. Graven, 1966. When children complain of fatigue. *Child and Family* **5** (Summer) : 32-37.

Mas, J., 1957. The effect of physical activity on the adiposity of young boys. M.S. thesis, Urbana : University of Illinois.

Pollock, M. L., B. L. Rothermel, and T. K. Cureton, Jr. 1968. AAHPER physical fitness test score changes as a result of an eight-week sport and physical fitness program. *Research quarterly* **39**: 1127-1129.

Sherman, M. A., 1967. Maximal oxygen intake changes of experimentally exercised junior high school boys. Doctoral dissertation. Urbana : University of Illinois.

Skubic, E., 1955. Emotional response of boys to little league and middle league competitive baseball. *Research Quarterly* **26**: 342-352.

SUGGESTED READING

Hunsicker, P., and G. Reiff, 1977. Youth fitness report. *JOPER* **48** (January): 31.

28

Sex-Integrated Intermediate Physical Education Classes, Grades 5–8

Marjorie Blaufarb

It is in preparing lesson plans for grades 5 to 8 that more of the problems and anxieties of teachers begin to surface in connection with Title IX. It is at this level, beginning in grade 5, that traditionally there has been more emphasis on teaching sports skills for boys than for girls. This undoubtedly has been because male students had more sports opportunities in the higher grades and also because of that old "bugaboo" that some activities are not suitable for girls.

Boys and girls need to learn all types of skills so that they may realize their common abilities. The values of motor skills have equal importance to girls and boys and the instructional method is the same.

In grades 5 to 8, where children develop at very different rates depending on early or late puberty, teachers should be well aware of the need to keep track of the range of abilities of students, of their size and weight; teachers should select organizational patterns during lessons that take into account the socialization level of the children. It is especially needful in sex-integrated classes to be aware of these factors and to organize classes so that the same youngsters are not always opposed by each other. Pairing and grouping should not always be by skill or by size but sometimes at random and, on other occasions, for quite different reasons.

By grade 5, boys and girls who have been exposed to good physical education classes in grades K-4 are more skillful, have developed more control, and are ready to test themselves with mild competition and to begin to learn some sports. It is at this stage that the teacher will wish to guard

---

* This material was extracted from a longer article written by the author entitled, "Complying with Title IX of the Education Amendments of 1972 in Physical Education and High School Sports Programs," and published by AAHPER in 1975.

against the temptation to teach aggressive type activities to boys and non-aggressive activities to girls. Although the sexes may be segregated within the class when contact sports are being taught, it is recommended that some contact sports be modified a little so that they may be played together by all students.

Teachers who fear sex-integrated physical education sometimes fall into the trap of allowing the physical education class to become a "recreation" period. Traditional activities are discontinued in favor of more sedentary experiences with which the teacher feels more comfortable in the sex-integrated class. If this occurs, the boys and girls are being denied the vigorous physical activity they need to maintain good cardiovascular conditioning or physical fitness.

Almost all the activities that have been taught in segregated physical education classes are suitable for teaching in integrated classes. If there is only one physical education teacher in a school (which still happens in small junior high and middle schools) that person should look at his or her strengths and weaknesses realistically, lean heavily on the strengths revealed, and design programs within his or her capabilities that are known to be good for the boys and girls. More strengths than weaknesses may have been revealed by the self-evaluation, and the teacher may feel more comfortable in making the necessary changes and realize they are for the better.

In departments of two or more teachers, the administrator or department head will wish to look at the capabilities of all staff members and devise a program based on the strengths shown, at the same time allowing opportunity for individuals to learn other skills in team-teaching situations or in other forms of staff development.

Although not required by Title IX, opportunities should be provided at this level for participation in organized intramurals and other extramural programs such as sports days. Such intramural and other competitive opportunities should be available equally to both sexes. In some schools and school districts there has been an organized intramural and extramural program in grades 7 and 8, but the balance between girls and boys was inappropriate. In keeping with the requirements of Title IX, efforts will now need to be made to provide more participation for female pupils. In some school districts, invitational meets at a high school have been held, with all feeder junior high schools receiving invitations.

Title IX makes no curricular requirements except that physical education classes may not be conducted separately on the basis of sex. The courses may be oriented to an elective-selective process and include many single, dual, or carryover sports, or include more team sports depending on local practice. Students may be separated by sex within the physical education classes for participation in activities that involve bodily contact. These would include, according to Title IX, wrestling, basketball, boxing, rugby, ice hockey, and football, but not softball or baseball. Teachers aware of the needs of boys and girls may wish to modify these sports in such a way as to provide for the safety of the students so that they may be played in the sex-integrated situation. For example, international rules of basketball might be demonstrated and used in integrated classes.

Students may be scheduled into classes by skill level and this may sometimes result in a class being almost all one sex. This should not be viewed as an ideal solution or a way of avoiding integration. Where the use of a single standard for measuring skill adversely affects members of one sex, a different standard or standards that do not have such an effect must be used.* Such different standards could be age, size, weight, or strength, or a combination of these together with skill.

---

* Memorandum from the Director, Office of Civil Rights, Department of Health, Education and Welfare to Chief State School Officers, Superintendents of Local Education Agencies and College and University Presidents, September 1975.

29

Senior High School Physical Education

Rollin G. Wright

AIMS, OBJECTIVES, AND GUIDELINES

Just as at other levels of education, physical education in the senior high school is an indispensable segment of the total school program. Further, it is viewed as an integrating factor of school life, and as such it is a powerful socializing agent and promotes participation in a variety of school activities. The aims and objectives of physical education as discussed in Section 1 of this volume of the *Encyclopedia* apply to the senior high school just as to all other levels; however, there are differences in emphasis and application of these objectives. Normally, the emphasis at the elementary and junior high school levels is on developmental activities, whereas the senior high school physical education program should provide a learning-laboratory for maturing young adults.

Senior high schools are generally expected to develop and implement courses of study that lead to the general education of students in preparation for their future roles as productive members of society. The general aim of secondary education is to develop educated, healthy, well-adjusted, skilled, and productive citizens committed to a democratic society. Physical education contributes to this aim through its varied course offerings. The total physical education program should be planned in light of its unique contributions to the general objectives of secondary education. These objectives include intellectual, physical, social, and emotional factors.

All physical activities conducted or sponsored by the schools should contribute to the health and well-being of each individual. Each activity included in the program should be selected with full regard to values in human growth, development, and behavior and be designed to serve the interests, capacities, and maturation levels of the individuals or groups concerned (Cal. Dept. of Ed. 1950).

If the objectives of the program are to be meaningful to youth of this age, they must be stated in adult terms. Young adults are ready to discuss and experience exercise for the sake of maintaining a high level of physical fitness

181

throughout adult years. Most people have more leisure time today than ever before. Students at the senior high school age level are aware of the need for guidance in using their leisure hours constructively, both for the present and the future. Program developers should keep in mind that high school physical education is the capstone of a specific educational experience that started in the elementary school and progressed through 12 years of instruction and practice. They should plan and organize physical activities relative to traits, characteristics, and attitudes of senior high school students who are young adults ranging from 15 to 18 years of age. It is risky to generalize about age characteristics of school students since these characteristics vary significantly among individuals; however, some generalizations such as the following can be made:

Growth Characteristics and Needs for Grade 10 (Age 15 Years)

1. Has almost completely developed bone growth and sexual maturity
2. Vision well developed, but visual fatigue is common problem
3. Continues to evidence improvement in coordination and balance
4. Has adult eye-hand coordination
5. Shows marked fluctuation in levels of energy
6. Shows less tendency for fatigue than at age 14
7. Has noted sex differences in muscular development; boys' muscles become hard and increase in strength; girls' muscles remain softer than boys'
8. Is capable of longer spans of attention
9. Forms close attachments with adults and others
10. Uses reasoning on an emotional level; abstract reasoning is not fully developed.
11. Has high tension, which is evident in small mannerisms
12. Holds acceptance by peers as extremely important
13. Is concerned with social and ethical aspects of sexual behavior
14. Has a low threshhold for external stimuli
15. Views self as an emerging adult
16. Needs opportunity to learn efficient and effective movement patterns
17. Needs opportunity for participation in physical activities based on ability grouping
18. Needs opportunity to develop group associations and loyalties
19. Needs opportunity to develop a positive self-concept
20. Needs increasingly greater physical challenges

Growth Characteristics and Needs for
Grade 11 (Age 16 Years)

1. Demonstrates more stable physiological functions than at age 15
2. Has attained adult height
3. Experiences excellent health
4. Has adult eye-hand coordination
5. Demonstrates good motor coordination
6. Has continued interest in opposite sex
7. Expresses adult feelings toward biological functions
8. Has longer attention span than at age 15
9. Is capable of seeing relationships in abstract ideas
10. Reduces outlets of tension
11. Is more at ease with peers and adults
12. Has gained control over emotions
13. Is becoming more self-assured about handling personal problems
14. Boys demonstrate greater need for team sports than do girls who show increasingly less need
15. Needs opportunity to experience success in varied activities
16. Boys need opportunity to continue development in muscle strength
17. Needs opportunity to participate in activities that have carryover values.
18. Needs to participate in a program allowing for individual differences and interests
19. Needs to be able to select participation in both competitive and recreational-type activities

Growth Characteristics and Needs for
Grade 12 (Age 17 Years)

1. Exhibits more stable physical performance
2. Maintains adult level of eye-hand coordination
3. Has reached sexual maturity
4. Has maximized mental growth
5. Has stabilized, mature level attention span
6. Is beginning to relate present performance with future goals
7. Has continually improved reaction time that will tend to level off at about age 18 years
8. Has increased ability to concentrate, reason, and interpret

9. Is generally cheerful, friendly, out-going, and well-adjusted socially
10. Has acquired many friends of the same sex
11. Has learned to work together with members of the opposite sex
    12. Enjoys dating, dancing, and participation in club activities
13. Has established emotional independence from parents
14. Needs opportunity to practice leadership roles
15. Needs to assume some responsibility for selecting activities
16. Needs opportunity to participate in dance activities
17. Needs opportunity to participate in a variety of individual and dual type activities
18. Needs increased opportunity to participate in activities with members of the opposite sex

Irrespective of the school level, physical education shares with other educational experiences in striving to develop the character, personality, socialization, and appreciations of each individual. It should be stressed, however, that particularly in the senior high school there are three unique contributions that physical education can make independently to the educational process. First, specific activities can be offered that will provide the opportunity for each student to strive to reach optimum physical and physiological development. Second, physical education can lay the foundation of knowledge that will help each student to understand how much and what type of personal action must go into this development. Third, each student can gain a personal appreciation of the importance of obtaining and maintaining an optimum level of fitness. Thus, the primary objectives of physical education are expressed in terms of physical fitness, knowledge, and understanding rather than in terms of how many sports skills can be mastered. The degree to which sports skills are utilized, however, will indicate how successfully the primary objectives have been achieved.

THE PHYSICAL EDUCATION PROGRAM

The physical education program in the senior high school consists of two kinds of experiences: curricular and cocurricular. The former includes class instruction in varied activities and the adaptive or rehabilitative programs, whereas the latter consists of intramurals, interscholastic, and recreational programs. The various phases of the physical education program, divided into curricular and cocurricular experiences, are shown in Fig. 29.1 (Miller and Massey 1963).

"Core activites" are those course experiences in which instruction is required for all students.

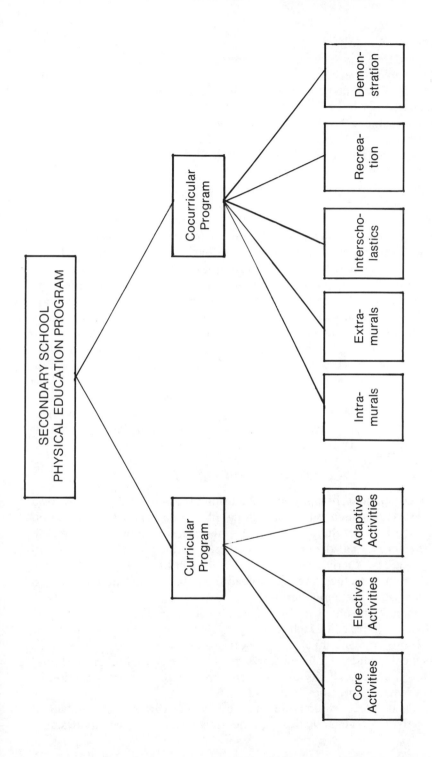

Fig. 29.1 Phases of the physical education program.

"Elective activities" are those course experiences offered on a regular basis, but students may select in which ones they will participate.

"Adaptive activities" are those course experiences designed to meet the specific needs of students who are physically handicapped, either temporarily or permanently.

"Intramurals" are those voluntary sport experiences planned for students within the same school.

"Extramurals" are those informal sport experiences between students of one or more schools.

"Interscholastics" are those competitive sport experiences between students from one or more schools.

"Recreation" are those experiences that provide an opportunity for students to participate in selected activities on a leisure-time basis.

"Demonstration" experiences are those engaged in by clubs or teams primarily to develop and demonstrate different sport skills.

The extensiveness of the physical education program will be governed, to a degree, by the size of the school. A "good" program is a "balanced" program no matter what the size of the school might be. A "balanced" program of physical education will include all of the components listed above if it is to meet the needs of all students. Each student should be able to select the appropriate actions necessary to reach and maintain his or her own optimum level of physical development. The task of physical education is not only to make the necessary physical action possible, but also to make the occurrence of that action probable and the need for it clearly understandable. No single aspect of the physical education program can accomplish this by itself as it takes a coordinated effort utilizing all phases of the program.

CURRICULAR PROGRAMS

The major components of a physical education program are determined by a number of variables, such as the educational philosophy of the school district, the expertise of the teaching staff, geographical factors, and climatic conditions. The references at the end of this chapter include several examples of curriculum guides. Nearly every school district will have developed its own curricular manual and these are available to the public, school administrators, teachers, and other concerned groups.

The junior high school program of activities was discussed in the preceding chapters. The senior high school program is built upon a sound junior high school program and involves instruction and practice in advanced skills as well as the introduction of new activities. The high school program should provide for greater flexibility and student involvement in the selection of activities, especially in grades 11 and 12.

"Core" and "elective" activities may be further divided into individual and dual activities, team activities, aquatic activities, rhythmic activities, and self-testing activities. A sampling of specific activities appropriate to young adults that might be included in a high school physical education program are:

1. Individual and dual activities—archery, badminton, bowling, fencing, golf, track and field, skiing, and gymnastics
2. Team activities—field hockey, speedball, touch (flag) football, soccer, lacrosse, and volleyball
3. Aquatic activities—swimming, diving, life-saving, smallcraft, synchronized swimming, and water polo
4. Rhythmic activities—square dance, folk dance, social dance, and modern dance
5. Self-testing activities—achievement tests in selected activities, standardized fitness tests such as the AAHPERD Youth Fitness Test and the Purdue Motor Fitness Tests

Adaptive activities may include therapeutic exercises, developmental exercises, selected activities such as archery, bowling, swimming, and others that can be modified to allow participation depending upon the severity of the disability.

Recreational activities may include fly and bait casting, mountaineering, campcrafter skills, equitation, horseshoe pitching, and cycling.

Only a selected few of the many possible activities have been listed above. It should be stressed that any activity selected for inclusion in the high school program should help the individual student progress toward the established five categories of physical education objectives: physiological, motor skill, intellectual, aesthetic, and social.

INNOVATIVE PROGRAMS

The 1960s and 1970s have been depicted as an era of change. Lippitt (1958) suggested that the modern world is, above everything else, a world of change. In fact, this is something upon which observers in nearly every field of thought and knowledge are agreed. All institutional segments of society are feeling the impact of the forces of change, and the schools, as a part of society, reflect such social needs and pressures. Balz (1940) recognized the problem of education in a changing society some years ago when he said: "The swirl of social change threatens to engulf mankind, and education must strive with double diligence to keep both its balance and its direction."

The concept of change is not new to our society; however, educators have been notoriously slow in introducing innovations and accepting new ideas. Paul Mort (1946) reported that when an educational innovation had been introduced in the 1930s approximately 15 years elapsed before even three percent of the nation's schools had instituted change. The rate of adopting innovation increased rapidly after the 10 percent point was reached, but complete diffusion in schools appeared to take as much as 50 years.

A number of leading schools throughout the nation have been brave enough to implement new patterns of organization aimed at providing better systems of educating secondary school youth. Innovations such as schools without walls, nongraded programs, team teaching, flexible scheduling, computer scheduling, computer assisted instruction and independent plans of study have exhibited great potential. The individuals and schools making an attempt to experiment with different modes of education are making a valuable contribution to the entire educational process; however, there are many unsolved problems in implementing educational innovations. Innovative programs may help to solve some existing problems, yet at the same time they create additional problems to be solved.

Current literature is replete with reference to innovative trends in education yet there is a marked lack of documentation concerning innovative physical education programs. Physical education specialists have not been involved extensively in experimentation and this has been a disadvantage to all programs. In fact, much of the related physical education literature deals with more traditional types of programs and, unfortunately, is not supported by research data. The physical education programs in the high schools vary quite markedly from a traditional "throw out the ball" variety to a program oriented primarily toward the development of physical fitness, such as the La Sierra High School program (LeProtti 1961).

In 1971 the Committee on Organizational Patterns, a unit of the AAHPER Committee for the Improvement of Instruction, submitted a report designed to apply theoretically the basic assumptions of flexible-modular scheduling to physical education. This is quite a time lag when compared to the 1956 action of the National Association of Secondary School Principals in appointing a Commission on Experimental Study of the Utilization of Staff in the Secondary Schools.

Selected examples of program experimentation in physical education are worth noting. Independent study programs have been adopted quite successfully in other subject matter fields and certainly hold significant potential for further development in physical education. In an attempt to appraise the utilization of independent study in physical education, Garcia (1965) reviewed physical education programs at 12 high schools utilizing the Stanford School Scheduling System and independent study. While independent study time seemed to be utilized effectively by most academic departments, the physical education department had not developed its independent study program to any extent.

The physical education program at Ridgewood High School in Illinois has been reported by Buikema and Smith (1963) and by Sadowski (1971). This program utilizes both independent plans of study and flexible-modular scheduling. Trump (1959) has been involved in designing new approaches to education since the early 1950s and has been responsible specifically for flexible-modular scheduling. In 1960 Lakeview High School in Decatur, Illinois, implemented Trump's recommendations for experimental flexible-modular scheduling. An outgrowth of this pilot program was an Independent Physical Education Program implemented by Flaugher in 1964. This program stressed physical fitness with students assuming the prime responsibility to assess their own levels of fitness, to plan and develop cooperatively individual programs of activity, to carry out their programs of activity, and to determine whether their goals had been reached through appropriate means of assessment. Flaugher's (1969) example of independent study in physical education was for the specific area of physical fitness. This is only one area of an innovative program of this type. It conceivably could be utilized in the areas of aquatics, gymnastics, or leisure-time sport skills, depending upon facilities, staff, and program emphasis. The fitness area was chosen because it seemed to be of the greatest need. The carryover possibilities of this program seem unique and worthy of further investigation.

Would independent physical education study, which attends to individual differences and interest, have any carry-over value? In a study conducted by Flaugher (1969), the students who were not enrolled in the Independent Physical Education Program were compared with those who elected to take it. Conclusive differences were shown. The students who took Independent Physical Education understood their own individual needs and demonstrated the ability to fulfill their personal fitness goals. These students were given the opportunity to engage daily in an individualized program, in a self-directed manner, during their high school career. The independent Physical Education study group remained more active and healthier following graduation from high school than did the control group who took regular physical education that had recreational activity as the primary goal. The Independent Physical Education graduate had the knowledge, purpose, understanding, and motivation to remain more active after high school graduation. It is clearly evident through success in other subject matter fields and success in experimental programs in physical education, such as the one at Lakeview High School, that innovative programs are of value and need to be implemented to a greater degree.

INTRAMURAL SPORTS

Mueller and Mitchell (1960) defined intramural sports as "the best title for recreational sports and activities promoted within the confines of an educational institution and under its jurisdiction." The purpose of the intramural program is to supplement the curricular activities offered in the physical education program so that the total objectives of physical education may be more fully realized. Intramural sports have formed a vital link in the pattern of aggregated educational experiences so necessary for all boys and girls in the modern American school. No student should be deprived of an opportunity to take part in a great variety of recreational experiences in a school program that may contribute to a long and happy life (Means 1963).

The objectives of the intramural program should be compatible and in harmony with the aims and objectives of physical education and of the entire educational program. The objectives are generally of two types: student and administrative objectives as stated by Voltmer, Lapp, and Scott (Evans 1960); or immediate and remote as classified by Mueller and Mitchell (1960). The immediate or student objectives deal with the habits, knowledges, and attitudes from the participant's point of view, while the remote or administrative objectives deal with the ideals toward which the intramural personnel strive.

Education is concerned with the total growth and development of the individual. Some of the specific goals of education that intramurals help to fulfill are: (1) respect for the worth and integrity of each individual; (2) consideration for the unique capacities, needs, and interests of the individual; (3) encouragement of the individual to develop to the fullest potential; (4) development of a strong sense of values; and (5) preparation of the individual for efficient, effective living.

A general consensus of the literature dealing with intramural sports programs reveals three major principles: (1) the aims and objectives of the intramural program should be compatible with the aims of physical education and education as a whole; (2) the program should be designed to reach the majority of the students it is attempting to serve; and (3) the overall objectives of the program should be interpreted to all of the teachers within the school so that the entire program can strive toward the development of the total individual.

Intramural sports on the senior high school level are highly desirable if the competitive needs of the majority of the students of the school are to be met. Interscholastic sports satisfy too small a percentage of the total student population to justify them as the only competitive phase of the physical education program. An intramural sports program, properly organized and administered, can make positive contributions to the social, mental, physical, and emotional development of the youth of senior high school age. Selected factors considered necessary to insure the development of a sound program include:

1. Support and encouragement of the program by the entire faculty and administrative staff.

2. Provision for leadership from the physical education staff and/or faculty members with an interest and expertise in this area

3. A varied program to meet the needs of all the students, with adequate facilities and equipment to permit the maximum number of students to participate in the program

4. Regularly scheduled activities

5. Adequate sources of publicity throughout the school year to maintain a high level of interest

6. Some form of homogeneous team selection to aid in obtaining equality of competition

7. An award system based on participation

8. An accurate and simplified method of recording participation and of earning credit toward awards

9. Some form of total school recognition for award winners

INTERSCHOLASTIC SPORTS

At the senior high school level interscholastic sports are considered to be an integral part of the overall physical education program as well as the total school program, and as such they are equally appropriate for both boys and girls. The physical education program is structured to meet the needs of the entire student population, whereas the interscholastic sports program is organized for those students possessing exceptional abilities and advanced-level skills in those sport activities comprising the program. To provide for the optimum development of the individual, competitive experiences are provided in relation to the level of maturation and skill development of individuals and/or groups in a given sports program. Competitive units should be organized and developed for those of lesser ability as well as the gifted, primarily on the basis of needs and interests. It is the responsibility of the school to provide the leadership, facilities, equipment, and administrative support necessary for the implementation of this program as for all other school-sponsored programs. The interscholastic sports program has unique contributions to make to the community, be it inner-city, urban, suburban, or rural, and the community should make maximum utilization of these contributions.

Activities generally included in the interscholastic sports program for boys are baseball, basketball, cross country, football, golf, gymnastics, swimming and diving, tennis, track and field, and wrestling. Those activities commonly included in the girls' program are archery, badminton, basketball, cross country, field hockey, golf, gymnastics, softball, swimming and diving, tennis, track and field, and volleyball. Unfortunately, some sports have become classified as "major" sports while the others are generally referred to as "minor" sports. The distinction is not based upon the value of one sport compared to another or to some preestablished goals, but rather upon how many spectators are attracted to the events, thereby providing greater revenue potential from the sale of tickets. Sport activities should be evaluated on the degree to which they meet the stated educational objectives and not upon gate receipts.

Following are guidelines for the development of an educationally sound interscholastic sports program:

1. Athletics should be considered an integral part of the school program, including physical education.
2. Teachers assigned to the athletic program should be as competent and as well prepared as other school personnel.
3. The athletic program should include a varied selection of activities based upon the needs and interests of the participants.
4. All aspects of fitness for effective living should be stressed throughout the athletic program.
5. The terms "major" and "minor" should be eliminated in describing sport activities. If such classification needs to be made, it should be in relation to the values and benefits to the individual participants.
6. Teachers, working with guidance personnel, should utilize the unique opportunities provided by athletics for the optimum development of the individual.
7. All aspects of the athletic program should be interpreted appropriately to the community so that a sound program can be developed without pressure from nonschool agencies.
8. Inservice education programs should be developed to aid participating personnel in developing and conducting sound programs.
9. All aspects of the athletic program should be considered as contributing to the total school curriculum, and therefore should be provided with the appropriate support of all the educational staff in relation to the values derived from the program.

The participation of girls in senior high school interscholastic sports programs has increased tremendously in recent years. Girls have become increasingly concerned about their role in sports programs. This concern is not confined solely to being able to compete in organized sports but also deals with equal funding and access to facilities. In essence, an increasing number of individuals are becoming more and more concerned about equal opportunity for total sports development, including both men and women, in all aspects of the sports program. Unfortunately many of the basic issues concerning equal opportunities in sports cannot be solved by the athletic association's administration of rules, the involved educators, or the participants, and therefore will be settled in the courts of this country. Several states' supreme courts have ruled that it is unconstitutional to ban women from men's noncontact sports in high schools; yet, this is merely an interpretation of the laws of this country and does not solve the problems of conducting such programs.* In the years ahead, we can look for many new creative and innovative programs to emerge that will vastly increase the opportunity for high school girls to engage in organized interscholastic sports programs.

REFERENCES

AAHPER Commission for the Improvement of Instruction, 1971. *Organizational patterns for instruction in physical education.* Washington, D.C. : AAHPER.

Balz, A. G. A. 1940. *The basis of social theory.* New York: Bureau of Publications, Teachers College, Columbia University.

Buikema, K. A., and J. E. Smith, Jr., 1963. Effective staff utilization. *JOHPER* **34** (March): 19-21.

California State Department of Education, 1950. A framework for public education in California. *Bulletin of the California State Department of Education* **19** : 13.

Cassidy, R. and C. Brown, 1963. Changes since Sputnik in programs of physical education. *JOHPER* **34** (April): 55-56.

Evans, W. R. 1960. Intramural athletics. *Bulletin of the National Association of Secondary School Principals* **44** (May): 114-117.

Flaugher, R., 1969. *Evaluation of independent physical education.* Unpublished instructional guide, Decatur, Illinois.

_____, 1964. *Progress through research and physical activity.* Unpublished instructional guide, Decatur, Illinois.

LeProtti, S., 1961. La Sierra's fitness program. *Scholastic Coach* **31** (September): 60-64.

_____, 1961. La Sierra's fitness program, part II. *Scholastic Coach* **31** (October): 26-30.

Lippitt, R., J. Watson, and B. Westly, 1958. *Dynamics of planned change.* New York: Harcourt, Brace.

Miller A. G., and M. D. Massey, 1963. *A dynamic concept of physical education for secondary schools.* Englewood Cliffs, N.J.: Prentice-Hall.

Mort, P. R., 1946. *Principles of school administration,* pp. 199-200. New York: McGraw-Hill.

---

* Editor's Note: Additional regulations and legal interpretations of the Title IX provisions discussed in Section 7 have since been handed down by HEW.

Mueller, P. and E. D. Mitchell, 1960. *Intramural sports.* New York: Ronald Press.

Sadowski, G. M. 1971. Flexible modular scheduling allows for student choice of independent study units. *JOHPER* **42** (September) : 25.

Trump, J. L. 1959. *Images of the future: a new approach to the secondary school.* Urbana, Ill.: Commission of the Experimental Study of the Utilization of the Staff in the Secondary School.

SUGGESTED READINGS

AAHPER, 1977. *Assessment guide for secondary school physical education programs.* Washington, D.C.: AAHPER.

Barry, P.E., 1976. *Ideas for secondary school physical education.* Washington, D.C.: AAHPER.

Bergen, E. V., and H. E. Pie, 1967. Flexible scheduling for physical education. *JOHPER* **38** (March): 29-31.

Beter, T. R. 1970. Attitudes of intellectually gifted twelfth grade girls toward physical education, and interest in physical activities and leisure time preference. *Physical Educator* **27** (March): 30-31.

Biggs, D. W., and E. G. Buffie, 1964. Invention, innovation and physical education. *JOHPER* **35** (October) : 19-20.

Cowell, C. C., and H. M. Schwehn, 1964. *Modern principles and methods in secondary school physical education.* Boston: Allyn and Bacon.

Daniel, A. N., 1969. An example of individual instruction in developmental physical education. *JOHPER* **40** (May) : 56.

Garcia, F. J. 1965. An investigation of the utilization of independent study time in physical education programs of selected high schools using flexible scheduling. Unpublished master's thesis. Sacramento: Sacramento State College.

Hermann, D., and W. Osness, 1966. Scientific curriculum design for high school physical education. *JOHPER* **37** (March) : 26-27.

Means, L. E., 1963. *Intramurals: Their organization and administration,* P. 7. Englewood Cliffs, N.J.: Prentice-Hall.

Saunders, R. J., 1969. Physical fitness of high school students and participation in physical education classes. *Research Quarterly* **40** (October): 552-560.

Teaching guide: senior high school physical education, 1960. Los Angeles City Schools, Division of Instructional Services, Publication No. SC-585.

Reams, D., and J. J. Bleier, 1969. Developing team teaching in physical education. *Bulletin of the National Association of Secondary School Principals.* **53** (November) : 8-18.

Roundy, E. A. 1966. Are our physical education programs meeting today's needs? *Journal of Secondary Education* **41** (May) : 221-224.

Wilkenson, D. B., 1968. Quality physical education; a school responsibility. *Education Digest* **33** (March) : 50-51.

30
Changing Consumers Mean New Concepts

Charles B. Corbin

In his book *The Ultimate Athlete,* George Leonard is not generous with his praise for physical education in American junior and senior high schools. He characterizes the high school physical education class as a place where uniform and shower inspections, regimented calisthenics, and teams sports participation are dominant. However, in addition to his criticism, Leonard suggests that the "next few years promise to be a period of unprecedented ferment and excitement in a field that has resisted substantial change for a long, long time."

The changes that took place in the 1970s and that will take place in the future are largely a result of changes in our consumers. For junior and senior high schools, the consumers are not only students but parents as well. More and more these consumers are reading what people like George Leonard are writing. Students, parents, and school officials are questioning the value of our programs. The results of recent studies have not helped us sell traditional physical education to our consumers. For example, one study showed that 63 percent of American adults interviewed felt that they learned in physical education as students in school was not applicable for use as adults. It was also found that 45 percent of adult Americans do not engage in physical activity for the purpose of exercise, and that those who do no regular exercise at all are the ones most likely to believe they get all the exercise they need.

In recent years many colleges and universities have taken notice of such findings and have started programs to better meet the needs of consumers. These programs are often called the "concepts" approach to physical education or "foundations" courses. They are organized around three basic objectives:

1. WHY—Helping students learn WHY physical activity is important to every person.
2. HOW—Helping students learn HOW to exercise properly given their own individual needs and interests.
3. WHAT—Helping students learn WHAT their needs really are—that there is some kind of physical activity for each person to enjoy, regardless of that person's physical abilities.

Reprinted from *JOPER* **49** (January 1978) : 43.

The success of the concepts approach at the college level is indicated by the fact that as many as 50 percent of American colleges now have programs of this type. Leonard suggests that this type of program is a necessary part of needed reform in physical education.

It is important that the concepts-type course not be limited to colleges and universities. In fact, if we are to be successful in selling our consumers on physical activity for a lifetime, the concepts approach must be started in junior and senior high schools at the very latest.

Some creative secondary school physical educators have recognized the criticisms of traditional programs and the needs of our modern consumers and have successfully implemented the concepts approach in their junior and senior high schools. These programs work! The students like them, and just as important is the fact that these programs are widely accepted by parents and school officials. Samples of how concepts programs have been implemented are illustrated below.

THE INTEGRATED APPROACH

In this approach special "concepts of physical education activities" are integrated with the more traditional physical education experiences into one combined program. At Topeka West High school in Kansas, a semester-long course includes lectures, class discussions, self-testing, sample exercise programs, and various laboratory experiences. Other activities such as volleyball, weight training, and basketball are also included in this integrated program. This same approach has been used effectively at the junior high school level at Ben Franklin Junior High School in New Jersey.

THE UNIT OR MODULAR APPROACH

The unit or modular approach can be fitted into any program. The concepts segment becomes one module or unit in the regular program. Warren Township High School in Illinois has incorporated a "concepts module" for grade 9 students. Various lectures, discussions, self-evaluations, and other activities are used to meet the course objectives. Scotia-Glenville High School in New York has instituted a similar, effective program.

THE MINI APPROACH

In the unit or modular approach a period of time from one to several weeks is devoted entirely to concepts-type activities; in the integrated approach entire class periods are devoted to these activities. In the "mini" approach small periods of five to 15 minutes within the regular class period are devoted to minilectures, minilabs, or minidiscussions. The mini approach can be incorporated easily into the regularly planned program. Grant High School in Oregon has used this approach successfully not only in physical education classes but with athletic teams.

CONSUMERS

Any of these three approaches can be used to teach the concepts of physical education in the secondary school. All have been tried and all are working. They are effective learning programs attractive to our consumers: the students, the parents, and school officials.

Students. Secondary school students appreciate the concepts approaches because they focus on the individual. Students who are normally not very good in physical education enjoy this approach. In addition, students enjoy concepts approaches because the students are learning something they can use for a lifetime.

Parent. In an age when parents are ever more critical of school offerings, the concepts approach has proved quite successful. Parents have been quick to accept the concepts approach because it, unlike the classes many of them took, will be useful for a lifetime. Many teachers find that parents learn right along with the students taking the course. Concord High School in Indiana reported that so many parents became interested in the program that an evening concepts class for parents was started. One of the greatest benefits of the concepts approach is the "strengthening of school/community relations."

School officials. Accountability is now a primary concern of school officials. The concepts approach has sound educational objectives and can help us show school officials what the community is getting for its money.

The concepts approach is not foolproof, nor is it a solution to all of our problems. However, properly conducted, these approaches can be used to make physical eduction an attractive and meaningful part of the school curriculum. As George Leonard has pointed out, we need to take a look at our physical education programs. His writings suggest that the concepts approach can be one of the exciting new developments in our field. These programs can become part of a good product our consumers are willing to buy.

31

Learning Environments to Create Lifelong Enjoyment of Physical Activity

Paul W. Darst

Programs of secondary school physical education have purported to accomplish a wide variety of goals throughout their history. Claims have usually been made in the areas of physical fitness, motor skills, mental abilities, and personal social-emotional adjustment. Curriculum development in most instances has occurred with these four goals in mind. Supposedly daily lessons have been organized so that all four goals would receive equal consideration. Unfortunately research strategies have not been very successful in proving the effectiveness of secondary school physical education programs in these goals or objectives (Siedentop 1976).

Programs of secondary school physical education may be attempting to accomplish too much for their participants. It seems feasible for physical educators to narrow the focus of their programs to a major goal of getting students to incorporate physical activities into their life-styles. Accomplishment of this goal would require teachers to have a positive effect upon students' attitudes toward participation in physical activities. Students may learn how to pass, dribble, and shoot a basketball and know when to pass, dribble, or shoot, but if they do not enjoy playing basketball, they will not incorporate basketball into their life-style.

Impact upon the affective dimension of learning is not an easy task for the physical educator compared with the ease of showing gains in the cognitive and psychomotor areas. The view taken here concurs with that expressed by Patt Dodds (1976): "I submit that physical educators have expended much effort on cognitive and psychomotor teaching tasks, but have only paid lip service to the affective domain."

---

* Reprinted from *JOPER*, **49**: 44 (January) 1978.

Secondary physical education curriculum planners need to become concerned with effective ways to create learning environments that will accomplish the goal of teaching students to enjoy physical activities for a lifetime. This is no easy task, particularly within the rigid authoritarian, negative atmosphere that many secondary teachers seem to find reinforcing for themselves and their administrators.

In many cases secondary physical educators have failed to plan systematically for the development of positive attitudes toward physical activities. If teachers do not plan for this type of learning, the chances are increased it will not occur. Much has been written about having a positive impact upon students' attitudes toward physical education (see "Suggested Readings").

Suggestions have been offered to make physical education programs more relaxed, spontaneous, enjoyable, and success-oriented. This chapter explores some specific suggestions for developing a secondary school physical education program that should help students to incorporate physical activity into their lifestyles.

CHOICE OF ACTIVITIES

Research indicates that secondary school students have already started to develop highly specialized interests. It is not necessary to force students into multiactivity programs, which often place them in certain activities that provide repeated failures. Students are much more motivated and will have a better chance for success in learning activities that they have chosen to learn.

Secondary programs should be as broadly based as possible within the given parameters. This broad base would increase the possibility that all students could find a type of physical activity that would provide them with some success. New, exciting forms of physical activity should be included in the program, for example, rock climbing, yoga, backpacking, skiing, and canoeing.

Students should be advised early in their secondary experiences in order to guide them into activities that will match their interests with selected activities and provide them with success. Low fitness students should be guided into special conditioning programs that will prepare them for future activities.

The curriculum should provide for intermediate and advanced levels of activities in order for students to develop their physical skills. Research indicates that students with a high level of skill tend to enjoy participation in the activity and will probably incorporate the activity into their life-style. In-depth instruction is different from a free-time, recreation period for an activity, and students need to be involved in an instructional environment.

TEACHER BEHAVIOR

Secondary school teachers need to provide their students with a visible model of a person who has incorporated physical activities into his or her own lifestyle. Teachers must take an active role in the teaching-learning process by demonstrating, participating, and encouraging. In addition teachers should try to develop a relaxed, positive, fun environment where students will leave with a good feeling toward physical activity.

Secondary teachers should help to develop the after-school programs for physical activities such as intramurals, sports clubs, and recreation programs. These activities will increase the opportunities for students to practice their skills and become more proficient. Students will also have an opportunity to meet other people with similar activity interests.

Secondary school physical educators need to direct their efforts influencing student attitudes toward active participation in physical activities. Physical education programs must accomplish more than psychomotor and cognitive learning. Students' attitudes must be affected in a positive manner so that a lifetime of active participation and learning of physical activities will occur. If secondary physical education teachers will accept and follow such an approach to organizing their teaching and learning environments, students should benefit for many years after they have left school.

REFERENCES

Dodds, P., 1976. Love and joy in the gymnasium. *Quest.* Monograph 26, pp. 109-116. NACPEW and NCPEAM.

Siedentop, D., 1976 . *Physical education: introductory analysis.* Dubuque, Iowa: Wm. C. Brown.

SUGGESTED READINGS

Dowell, L. J., 1975. *Strategies for teaching physical education.* Englewood Cliffs, N.J.: Prentice-Hall.

Heitmann, H. M. and M. E. Kneer, 1976. *Physical education instructional techniques: an individualized humanistic approach.* Englewood Cliffs, N.J.: Prentice-Hall.

Singer, R. N. (ed.), 1976. *Physical education: foundations.* New York: Holt, Rinehart and Winston.

Singer, R. N., and W. Dick, 1974. *Teaching physical education: a systems approach.* Boston: Houghton Mifflin.

32

Fitness Testing with a Realistic Purpose

Russell R. Pate

Fitness testing has become a traditional component of the secondary school physical education curriculum. Often, however, teachers have administered tests of fitness without giving ample consideration to the purposes of the testing process and the appropriateness of the test batteries selected. In many instances tests have been administered in a vacuum—that is, without telling students why they are taking the test and without making significant use of the test results. There are valid reasons for administering fitness tests in the secondary school, but implementation of a successful testing program requires a clear identification of the purposes for testing and the selection of specific tests that can best meet the goals of the testing program. This chapter is intended to stimulate readers to reassess their current beliefs regarding the proper role of fitness testing in the secondary school and to present some ideas to make the testing process more interesting and useful for both teachers and students.

Fitness testing as one segment of the curriculum should contribute in some way to accomplishing the overall goal of physical education. Each physical educator may have a somewhat different view of the goals of physical education, but we can agree that a major objective is to create an environment in which each student may acquire the skills, knowledges, and attitudes that encourage the adoption of a physically active life-style and maintenance of good physical fitness throughout adulthood. If this objective is accepted, it follows that our ultimate objective is adult fitness, not youth fitness. The physical fitness of children should not be overlooked, but ample evidence exists to demonstrate that physical fitness usually peaks during the early teen years and gradually declines throughout adulthood. Clearly, in most instances our problem is not development of fitness in children but maintenance of fitness as the individual moves into the years of early and middle adulthood.

---

*   Reprinted from *JOPER* **49** (January 1978) : 47-48.

OBJECTIVES OF THE TESTING PROCESS

In this context a relevant question is: Has our traditional approach to fitness testing contributed optimally to achieving the goal of lifetime fitness? Regrettably this question must be answered in the negative. Several problems have contributed to this failure, but one of the most prominent has been our tendency to use certain fitness tests out of habit, without thinking critically about the establishment of realistic and valuable goals for the testing process.

Following are some of the objectives that might be attained through fitness testing:

Objective 1. *Evaluation of the effects of a program on the fitness of the participants.* A commonly stated objective of secondary school physical education is the improvement of the students' physical fitness. While this objective may not always be realistic, pre- and posttesting does allow the teacher and administrator to evaluate precisely the effects of a program on fitness variables.

Objective 2. *Motivation of youngsters to improve their fitness.* Use of proper evaluation techniques and systems of tangible and intangible rewards can motivate students to work for improved fitness.

Objective 3. *Identification of low-fit youngsters.* Testing programs can provide objective means by which to identify students who fail to meet accepted fitness standards.

Objective 4. *Dissemination of cognitive information regarding fitness.* Fitness testing presents the student with an extremely tangible example of the teacher's idea of physical fitness. To a great extent, children's concepts of physical fitness are molded by the types of activities they perform while being tested. Also, testing can provide the springboard from which to launch discussions on the importance of fitness and the methods by which it can be improved.

Objective 5. *Identification of potential athletes.* Certain testing procedures allow the identification of youngsters who are likely to succeed in various types of athletic activities. For instance, speed, agility, power, and strength are important determinants of performance in our most common inter-scholastic sports.

SELECTING PROCEDURES

After identifying specific objectives, the teacher must proceed to select testing procedures that will be more likely to achieve those objectives. In the past this has been our greatest failure. We have assumed that a single test battery can serve to accomplish all our objectives. However, if the teacher hopes to deal effectively with the five objectives, a minimum of two test batteries will be needed.

In identifying objectives and selecting tests it is useful to think of two types of fitness: athletic fitness and health-related fitness. Athletic fitness depends on a broad range of motor performance abilities, from anaerobic power to cardiorespiratory endurance. In contrast, health-related fitness involves a range of components related to specific aspects of organic heatlh. While athletic fitness is of primary importance only to the minority of secondary school students who are athletes, health-related fitness is relevant to everyone throughout life. It is important to note that performance in several of the athletic fitness variables is determined largely by genetic endowment. On the other hand, nearly everyone is capable of attaining acceptable standards for the health-related fitness items. A logical conclusion is that tests of athletic fitness are useful only in the attainment of objective 5. However, objectives 1 through 4 can best be attained through use of a health-related fitness test.

The test most commonly employed in the schools today is the AAHPER Youth Fitness Test (AAHPER 1976). Although it has been described as providing an overall picture of the young person's general fitness, in fact the AAHPER Test evaluates athletic fitness primarily. With its emphasis on speed, agility, and power, the AAHPER test is far from an ideal measure of health-related fitness. Of the available test protocols, only the Texas Physical Fitness-Motor Test has provided two test batteries, one focusing on each of the two types of fitness. The South Carolina Physical Fitness Test (Pate 1977) concentrates entirely on health-related fitness. At the present time, the AAHPER leadership is considering a series of proposals that, if adopted, will significantly revise the AAHPER Youth Fitness Test. As proposed, the revised test would draw a clear distinction between athletic fitness (motor fitness) and health-related fitness.

Selecting a proper test is only one of several important steps. A serious weakness in many testing programs is the failure of teachers to use fitness testing as an educational experience for the students. Students react much more positively to a testing situation if the overall purpose of the test and objectives of each test item have been clearly explained. Having established specific objectives and selected an appropriate test, the teacher should be able to inform the students exactly why they are taking the test and what the test results mean.

For instance, the teacher may employ an athletic fitness test to attain objective 5. An appropriate introduction to the test would inform the youngsters that performance in certain test items may be indicative of their potential for success in certain athletic activities. On another occasion the same teacher could employ the skinfold test for estimation of body fatness. Such a session should be preceded by a discussion of the importance of body composition to lifelong health.

The point is that we should take advantage of testing situations to teach students about fitness. Furthermore, we must take precautions to ensure that children are not left with a confused or incorrect image of physical fitness as it pertains to adults. I fear that for years we have been telling youngsters that physical fitness is the ability, for example, to run a fast 50-yard dash. Lack of speed may limit one's performance in some athletic activities, but speed bears virtually no relevance to lifelong health. On the other hand, the child who is excessively fat ought to be aware of the health risks associated with such a condition. Take the time to tell students why a test is being given and what the results can mean to them as individuals, now and in the future.

If a program of fitness testing is to be meaningful for students and teachers, the test results must be used in significant ways. Test results should be forwarded to parents along with sufficient information to allow correct interpretation and follow-up. Youngsters who are found to score poorly on health-related fitness components should be provided with specialized intervention programs. Students who seem to show athletic potential should be so informed, though this should be done in such a way as to avoid discouraging others.

If testing is to be a motivator for improved fitness, each testing session should be followed by the establishment of realistic goals for improvement. In setting such goals consideration must be given to several factors. First, the trainability of the specific fitness component will determine to a large degree the improvement possible. For instance, cardiorespiratory endurance responds well to proper training. Second, the individual's current level of fitness affects improvement—the higher the fitness, the more difficult the improvement. Third, goals for improvement of a particular fitness component should reflect the emphasis to be placed on that component in subsequent programming. Often we assume that the mere presence of a youngster in physical education classes will automatically generate improved fitness. Such is far from the case.

Increased fitness will result only from exercise programs designed with specific fitness objectives in mind and that are consistent with our knowledge of exercise physiology. The teacher must recognize that the most important outcomes of the testing program will be those that affect the long-term attitudes toward fitness. Testing should be accomplished in a supportive, nonthreatening atmosphere such that the student exits the program encouraged and motivated, not discouraged and deflated. Individual improvement should be rewarded to the same extent as overall achievement.

Fitness testing can contribute to the attainment of several valuable objectives in physical education, but success will result only if specific objectives are identified and matched with proper test procedures. A clear distinction must be drawn between athletic fitness and health-related fitness. Health-related fitness is relevant to all students, and meaningful goals can be established for the improvement of each fitness component in this area. Current employment of fitness tests can help ensure that each student leaves the secondary school with an appreciation of lifetime fitness and an understanding of the means by which it can be maintained.

REFERENCES

AAHPER, 1976. *AAHPER youth fitness test manual.* Washington, D. C. : AAHPER.

Pate, R. R., 1977. South Carolina physical fitness test procedures. *S. C. Journal of HPER* **10:** 15-16.

Texas physical fitness-motor ability test. Governor's Commission on Physical Fitness, Austin, Texas.

33

Exit Competencies in Physical Education for the Secondary School Student

Marian E. Kneer

The public expects high school students to display a myriad of selected sophisticated tasks as a result of a secondary school education. These tasks range from foundational skills to build a college education to terminal skills to build occupational competence. What are the expectations for high school students as a result of physical education experiences?

A number of studies have been made to determine public and student expectations. Grebner (1971) found that the public expected physical education to achieve primarily fitness, safety, and emotional and character

---

* Reprinted from *JOPER* **49** (January 1978) : 46-47.

development objectives. Self-realization and enjoyment objectives were least valued. Kneer (1972) found that high school girls tended to seek sport skills and fitness but generally stated a preference for social outcomes. Realistic expectations must emanate from the profession, and secondary physical education curriculum guides generally reflect the purposes stated in the AAHPER position paper, *Guidelines for Secondary Physical Education* (AAHPER 1970). It describes physical education as:

> . . . a carefully planned sequence of learning experiences designed to fulfill the growth, development, and behavior needs of each student. It encourages and assists each student to:
>
> Develop the skills of movement, the knowledge of how and why one moves, and the ways in which movement may be organized.
>
> Learn to move skillfully and effectively through exercise, games, sports, dance, and aquatics.
>
> Enrich understanding of the concepts of space, time, and force related to movement.
>
> Express culturally approved patterns of personal behavior and interpersonal relationships in and through games, sports, and dance.
>
> Condition the heart, lungs, muscles, and other organic systems of the body to meet daily and emergency demands.
>
> Acquire an appreciation of and a respect for good physical condition (fitness), a functional posture, and a sense of personal well being.
>
> Develop an interest and a desire to participate in lifetime recreational sports.

High school educators generally have failed to translate these goals into specific terminal outcomes, which specify the quality and quantity to be expected. The tendency is to equate quality physical education with excellence in the athletic program. Frequently the expectations for gym class center on fun and sufficient activity to become physically fit. In some cases, the acquisition of a variety of sport-related movement skills appears to be the *only* outcome.

What should the physically educated high school student be able to perform to "win" in terms of the purposes of physical educational experiences? General agreement points to (1) developing physical competencies, (2) acquiring an understanding of the body as an instrument that has technical performance aspects and that is influenced by varied amounts of exercise, and (3) acquiring an appreciation of the value of physical activity as a possible worthwhile experience capable of enhancing physical and social well-being.

Winning and losing games is an easily understood outcome of athletic programs, but winning and losing in terms of the success or failure of students to achieve the stated objectives of a physical education program is more difficult. We have failed to clearly describe "winning" in terms of exit competencies that the student should achieve through the physical education experience or develop a "contest" to determine if the competencies have been achieved.

Writing terminal objectives that can be applied to all high school students is impossible—if not undesirable—because of students' varied entrance competencies in terms of physiological and psychological endowments. However, more specificity is needed. Better communication with students, administrators, parents, and the public in general as to the nature of these outcomes is as important as keeping score of games and revealing the "won-lost" record of teams. It is imperative that physical education programs seriously seek the several objectives that presently seem to be left to chance.

The tendency of high school physical educators to neglect specificity in describing the physically educated student is not only the recognition of individual differences but also the recognition of constraints of time, space, and other environmental influences on the teaching-learning experience. Nevertheless, it is time at least a baseline be set for all students. Certainly flexibility is desirable in applying the baseline expectations to provide for individual differences. The following are competencies recommended as possible and acceptable precise statements that describe the physically educated high school student.

PSYCHOMOTOR DOMAIN

Two major categories are identified in this domain: physical efficiency and psychomotor fluency. Physical efficiency refers to "conditioning the heart, lungs, muscles, and other organic systems of the body to meet daily demands" (Johnson 1977). Psychomotor fluency is described as the acquisition of basic movements and sport skills. Reasonable exit competencies for high school boys and girls in the psychomotor domain would be:

1. The ability to perform at least one sport activity, dance, aquatic, gymnastic, and self-testing activity at intermediate skill level.
2. The ability to perform the AAHPER Fitness Test at average levels.

COGNITIVE DOMAIN

This category is often referred to as activity concepts and includes knowledge of game rules and strategy, of the effects of exercise, and of the biomechanical principles of movement. Specifically a high school student should be able to:

1. Express an understanding of the rules and strategy of common sports such as football, basketball, baseball or softball, tennis, and golf.

2. Demonstrate understanding of the rules and strategy of the activities in which they have developed at least intermediate competence.

3. Demonstrate knowledge and understanding of the effects of exercise on the body and be able to prescribe exercise or physical activity to maintain or achieve future desired levels of physical well-being.

4. Demonstrate knowledge and understanding of biomechanical principles to efficiently use the body to generate force, support, and ability.

AFFECTIVE DOMAIN

This area is described as attitudes that guide social efficiency and personal enjoyment. Appropriate exit competencies should be:

1. Experience joy in using the body as an instrument for play and self-fulfillment.

2. Demonstrate fair play and concern for others through personal behavior and interpersonal relationships in games, sports, and other recreational activities.

3. Seek regular involvement in movement activities for psychological and/or physiological therapeutic purposes.

4. Accept consequences of competitive experiences as a meaningful and worthwhile expression that is not evaluated in terms of personal self-worth.

These exit competencies represent interpretations of commonly accepted goals of physical education. The description of the student's behavior as a result of physical education experiences may be adjusted. However, research has provided the high school physical education teacher with norms and standards that should guide the development of realistic and reasonable statements of expected outcomes. The curriculum will need to be shaped to attain these competencies, and procedures utilized that will evaluate the degree to which each student is physically educated.

Physical education must remain a part of the educational process. Paramount in that effort is the clear demonstration of the desirable student behavior that can be "won" through the physical education teaching-learning process.

REFERENCES

AAHPER, 1970. *Guidelines for secondary school physical education.* Washington, D.C.: AAHPER.

Grebner, F. D., 1971. Objective of physical education in elementary and secondary Illinois Public schools as perceived by certain societal publics. Doctoral dissertation. Urbana: University of Illinois.

Johnson, M. L., 1977. *Functional administration in physical and health education.* Boston, Houghton Mifflin.

Kneer, M. E., 1972. Influence of selected faction and techniques on student satisfaction with a physical education experience. Doctoral dissertation. Ann Arbor: University of Michigan.

34

Physical Education in the Independent School

J. Stuart Wickens

The first private school in the United States was founded in 1638. Slowly they increased in number ranging from boarding academies to country day schools, as well as military academies. While the early academies were considered institutions for the study of the arts and sciences, they were primarily college preparatory schools.

The present private schools are different from those of the past and are known as independent schools—independent in the sense that they are not dependent upon the financial and policy views of the public; and are operated along lines approved by the headmaster, faculty, parents, and students. They are not required to accept more students than the number for which they have faculty and teaching facilities; and they know the value of small classes and individualized instruction. Nearly all independent school graduates go on to college. There are approximately 3000 independent schools, day and boarding, which enroll a little over two percent of all elementary and high school students. The progress and contributions of the independent school are a matter of paramount national interest.

In 1850 Harvard, Yale, and Amherst erected the first gymnasiums in the United States, which were dedicated to the physical development of their students. Slowly the movement found its way to the private schools. The modern independent school feels it is vitally important that its students develop physically as well as mentally, and follows the philosophy of a sound mind in a sound body. All students are expected to participate in some form of physical activity throughout the school year. However, the independent school has its own approach as to what type of physical education program should be sponsored. To some extent this is influenced by the educational background, experience, and philosophy of the headmaster and faculty. Facilities and financial resources also affect to a great extent what can be accomplished.

It is recognized that to proceed efficiently toward any worth goal it is essential that the ultimate goal be known and that there be guidelines or worthwhile objectives. There is general agreement that the aim of physical education is to help in developing strong, healthy, vigorous students who have acquired certain knowledge and habits, attitudes and understandings, skills and abilities about health, body mechanics, sports, and recreation that are conducive to the following objectives:

1. To develop sound organic and functional powers and maintain a high degree of physical fitness
2. To develop lasting habits of personal hygiene and to render guidance in preventing, as well as assistance in recovering from, various types of illness or injury
3. To develop neuromuscular coordination
4. To develop interest and skill in play and recreation
5. To develop social and ethical standards

In most instances, a broad physical education program is offered in the independent school and is based on the known facts of growth and development of the student. Further, activities are graded and adapted to the age, size, ability, and experience of the individual to help achieve the objectives of the program. The organizational structure of the physical education program is similar to the public schools and generally consists of the following:

1. A required physical education class program
2. The intramural program
3. The interscholastic athletic program
4. A developmental and remedial program

In the physical education class, emphasis is placed on physical development and coordination; specific instruction is given in many of the fundamental skills and in sports with carryover value. Some emphasis is also placed on a preventive program of body mechanics education. A battery of physical fitness tests is administered to cover such components of fitness as muscular strength, endurance, speed, and agility and to make certain that a high degree of physical fitness is developed in each student. The findings and results of such tests are used to improve the instructional program, as well as to serve as a guide to certain types of activities that would be of greatest benefit to the individual.

The physical education program includes a comprehensive offering of intramural activities to suit the needs and interests of every student, and thus meet the demands of "sports for all." Facilities and opportunities are provided for instruction and participation in many carryover skills that may later form a basis for the maintenance of sound health and wholesome recreation.

Athletics have always formed a keystone in the private school structure—a keystone strictly subordinated to, yet welded into the whole to become an important phase of school life. Athletics are considered an integral part of the physical education program. The primary concern in the interscholastic athletic program is the health and well-being of each participant and the promotion of the satisfactions that one derives from taking part in any sport. At one time it was rather common practice to designate sports as major or minor; however, schools now recognize the many values inherent in both team and individual sports and there is a growing tendency in the independent school to treat all sports on an equal basis.

The physical education program in the independent school recognizes individual differences in inherited physical endowment, interest, and neuro-muscular skill potentialities. Its program is flexible enough to adapt to such differences, meet the individual needs and interests of each student, and be so taught that every activity becomes purposeful and useful.

The basic philosophy in the independent school is that physical education is not only for the athlete or the well and strong, but is also for the atypical, poorly developed, or physically deprived student who is in need of an individualized program to improve general strength, endurance, and appearance. Therefore, a developmental and remedial program is included as part of the physical education program throughout the school year for any student who, for medical reasons, is not allowed to participate in a particular sport. Such a program is concerned not only that each individual is conditioned properly before taking part in a sport, but also that those who lack proper physical development, who have remedial postural defects, or who are sub-par in strength and endurance, have a program to meet their needs. Special programs are available for medically referred, postoperative or postinjury students in order to ensure their safe return to normal activities, and prevent futher injury.

Indeed, physical education in the independent school is a continuous process with the ultimate aim of helping the student to maintain a healthful and useful life as an adult through continued use of the principles and skills learned in school. Increased individual competence, stemming from better

Fig. 34.1 Typical activities at Groton School, Groton, Massachusetts.

instruction and opportunities offered for participation in a broad physical education program, will lead to increased individual enjoyment from a particular activity.

35

Sex-integrated High School Physical Education Classes (Grades 9-12)

Marjorie Blaufarb

There are many views of what high school physical education is, but the National Association for Sport and Physical Education (NASPE/AAHPER), in its Secondary School Physical Education position statement, says that physical education is that integral part of total education contributing to the development of the individual through the natural medium of physical activity, which is human movement (AAHPER 1976). It is a carefully planned sequence of learning experiences designed to fulfill the growth, development, and behavior needs of each student. It encourages and assists each student to develop the skills of movement, the knowledge of how and why one moves, and the ways in which movement may be organized; to learn to move skillfully and effectively through exercise, games, sport activities, dance, and aquatics; to enrich the understanding of the concepts of space, time, and force related to movement; to express culturally approved patterns of personal behavior and interpersonal relationships in and through games, sport, and dance; to condition the heart, lungs, muscles, and other organic systems of the body to meet daily and emergency demands; to acquire an appreciation of, and a respect for, good physical condition (fitness), a functional posture, and a sense of personal well-being; and to develop an interest and a desire to participate in lifetime recreational sport activities.

---

*   This material was extracted from an article by the author entitled, Complying with Title IX of the Education Amendments of 1972 in Physical Education and High School Sports Programs," and published by AAHPER in 1975.

213

Although physical skills developed in physical education classes may be used in competitive athletics, and although a low level of competition may be appropriate at times in sports instruction, athletic programs are not a good model to use when considering steps to take to comply with the physical education clauses of 86.34 of the Title IX regulations. (See Section 7.)

In reading the position statement it appears that none of the desired outcomes of a good physical education program are inconsistent with sex-integrated physical education classes. But the fears of undesirable results arising from sex-integrated physical education classes are greater at the high school level than at any other.

If the intructional program is coordinated from K-12, by the time the student reaches grade 9, the skills taught in the primary grades can be directed into specific activities. The full range of activities taught in separate classes are suitable for integrated classes.

The NASPE Secondary School Council (1976) position paper calls for the secondary school instructional program to include a required core of experiences at progressive performance levels in the following activities; basic and creative movement, rhythm and dance, games, individual and team sports, gymnastics, aquatics where possible, and lifetime sports. In addition to core experiences, the selection of courses designed to produce advanced or specialized skills and knowledge should be available. The class should not be a "recreational"program in order to meet the requirements of Title IX.

Administrators and department heads are urged to build the curriculum around the known capabilities of the staff and the needs and interests of the boys and girls. Inservice education during the adjustment period will be necessary in many cases. Team teaching in which a confident, experienced teacher is teamed with a less experienced one, or a teacher is teamed with a colleague with skills and knowledges he or she does not have, could be viewed as a form of inservice education. If there is a demand for wrestling instruction, a sport in which women teachers might be less proficient, a male-female team would enable the less experienced woman to learn, by observation and practice, how to teach this activity. Some schools have introduced self-defense activities to both sexes with success, and these can appropriately be taught and learned in the sex-integrated setting.

The carry-over leisure sports lend themselves to sex integrated instruction, but care should be taken not to limit students to choices of only individual and dual sports in high school. Title IX does not require any particular kind of program or make specific requests about which activities should be included. Some students may still wish to have instruction in team sports they enjoy. Where a smorgasbord of activities is offered on an elective-selective basis, in courses such as square dancing, social dancing, or others in which couples are more appropriate, suitable registration procedures may be devised to achieve the desired result.

Course offerings must not be sex designated; that is, boys' basketball and girls' basketball. Courses are to be open to all, and it is only in the playing situation of contact sports that separation by sex may be made in an instructional situation. This is true at all levels of instruction.

REFERENCE

Secondary School Physical Education Council of the National Association for Sport and **Physical Education** of AAHPER, 1976. Secondary school physical education. Position statement. Washington, D.C.: AAHPER.

SUGGESTED READINGS

Arnold, D. E., 1977. Compliance with Title IX in secondary school physical education. *JOPER* **48** (January) : 19.

Blaufarb, M. 1977. Sex-integrated high school program that works. *AAHPER Update,* p. 3 (April).

Lumpkin, A. 1977. Let's set the record straight. *JOPER* **48** (March) : 40.

36

The Basic Instructional Program in Physical Education

Edward R. Reuter

The basic instruction program in physical education, frequently called the service program, is a curriculum of courses offering instruction in the physical activities of sport, exercise, and dance. The generally accepted objectives of this program are to promote the physical, mental, emotional, and social well-being of the individual by teaching skills and knowledges in physical activities.

The basic instruction program in physical education exists in over 95 percent of all four-year colleges and universities in the United States. Some form of physical education is mandatory for both male and female students in approximately 75 percent of these institutions as a part of the general education requirements for the bachelors degree. The usual requirement is completion of one year (32 percent of institutions) or two years (37 percent) with some schools requiring as little as one semester or more than five semesters.

There is a trend toward eliminating the physical education requirement that appears to be related to the pressure by students to eliminate all general requirements and to the current financial problems that exist in most state institutions. A total of 12 percent of the institutions have dropped their requirement in the past five years while a number have decreased the number of courses required. Private all-male institutions have increased their require-ment slightly, while 55 percent of all-female institutions have decreased their requirement during the past five years. In institutions where no requirement exists, about 25 percent (on the average) of the students take physical education on an elective basis.

Practically all institutions have policies that excuse certain students from the requirement. The most common is for medical reasons; others include prior military service, age, participation in varsity sports, enrollment in ROTC, marital status, and psychological problems. About 95 percent of all institutions report that less than 10 percent of the students are excused.

There is a trend, however, in the use of proficiency (competency) exami-nations in lieu of the requirements. Part, or the entire requirement, may be waived for students who can demonstrate skills and/or knowledge of certain activities at a passing level. While 30 percent of the institutions offer this alternative to the requirement, relatively few students exercise the option.

In some programs specific course requirements exist within the overall requirement. An attempt to educate students concerning the life-long benefits of physical activity has led to the development of "foundation" type courses utilizing lecture and activity/laboratory-type classes to provide experiences related to exercise physiology, principles of conditioning, relaxation, aerobics, and the dangers of sedentary living in modern society. Toledo University and the University of Illinois were among leaders in the foundation course movement. Student reaction to this course has been mixed.

Another requirement, aimed at providing a broad experience in activities, has dictated that students must have course backgrounds in different areas, such as team, individual, aquatic, combative, and recreational activities. Because of its special relationship to safety, some schools have a swimming requirement. Other institutions provide an "activity guidance program" where instructors recommend courses to students based on their individual needs and interests.

In over 80 percent of the programs, credit is allowed toward graduation, and in 70 percent of the institutions the grades earned in physical education count in the student's overall grade point average. While a large majority (85 percent) of the programs report grading systems that are consistent with academic courses, there is a trend toward allowing the student to take the option of a grade or a pass/fail mark. This option is also being used in nonprofessional academic courses to a greater degree. Grades in physical education courses are usually determined by an evaluation of skill, knowledge (through written examinations), physical fitness, and personal qualities of the student. A wide variety of grading procedures is used.

The time required by students in a basic instruction class is usually from 90 to 150 minutes per week, usually scheduled for two or three periods per week. Generally considered as laboratory hours, one credit is usually awarded for each activity course.

The most significant change in the basic instructional program has been the increase in the variety of courses. During the early years to 1930, the emphasis on physical fitness through calisthenic exercise, which was later expanded into an emphasis on team games, with some attention to swimming, combatives, and individual sports. In the past 10 years the greatest increases have been in the life-time sport area while the offerings in team activities have decreased. Another significant trend is the increase in coeducational classes. Over 65 percent of the programs have increased their offerings in coed courses during the past five years, and over 35 percent report that more than 75 percent of their courses are coed. In addition, many activity courses are now offered on beginning, intermediate, and advanced levels for students of various abilities.

The following activities are taught today at many colleges and universities, although probably no one institution offers all of them:

1. *Adapted Physical Activity Area* (for the handicapped)—corrective exercise, adapted sports, wheelchair sports
2. *Physical Fitness Area*—conditioning, circuit training, jogging, weight training, fartlek training, yoga, figure improvement, weight control, cross country
3. *Gymnastics Area*—competitive gymnastics, recreational gymnastics, tumbling, trampoline circus stunts
4. *Aquatics Area*—swimming, skin diving, scuba, water polo, synchronized swimming, springboard diving, surfing
5. *Team Area*—basketball, touch football, flag football, soccer, rugby, baseball, softball, volleyball, lacrosse, field hockey, ice hockey
6. *Combative Area*—boxing, wrestling, freestyle/Greco-Roman wrestling, self-defense, judo, karate, fencing
7. *Recreational Sports Area*—tennis, golf, handball, racquetball, squash, table tennis, badminton, archery, bowling

8. *Outdoor Area*—bait/fly/spin casting, mountaineering, winter mountaineering, hiking, downhill skiing, cross country skiing, ice skating, kayaking, canoeing, sailing, crew (rowing), camping, orienteering, sky diving, water skiing, horseback riding, bicycle touring.

9. *Dance Area*—Modern, jazz, folk, ballet, ballroom

A major factor in the large increase in the variety of activities is the desire by students to learn "lifetime" activities that may not have been offered in public school physical education. Institutions wishing to offer many of these activities are limited by their facilities, equipment, natural environment, and instructional staff. The shortage of prepared, qualified instructors in many of the most popular activities appears to be the major problem since professional physical education programs had not prepared prospective physical educators to teach yoga, karate, judo, fencing, racquetball, and outdoor activities. Some institutions providing courses in these activities have been forced to hire "nonprofessional" instructors who do not have physical education degrees, although they may be well prepared in their specialty.

SUGGESTED READINGS

Cogan, M. et al., 1973. Innovative ideas in college physical education. *JOHPER,* **44:** (February) 28.

Fresh ideas for college physical education, 1975. *JOPER* **46** (February) : 37.

Oxendine, J. B., and J. E. Roberts, 1978. The general instruction program in physical education at four-year colleges and universities: 1977. *JOPER* **49** (January) : 21-23.

Oxendine, J. B., 1972. Status of general instruction programs of physical education in four-year colleges and universities: 1971-72. *JOPER* **43** (March): 26.

37

The Foundation Concept in Physical Education

King McCristal

Many university basic instruction departments today have started foundations courses in physical education. The components of the foundation concept are not new. The principles involved predate the experience of most people in the profession. Good instruction in physical activity has always incorporated pertinent related health information and frequently the student has been instructed in the importance of exercise for all biological creatures. Unfortunately instruction of this type has been lacking, and few programs have explored widely the use of classroom instruction for contributing to knowledge in physical education.

The traditional physical education program has usually been centered almost entirely in skills. Occasionally some health knowledge and a bit of information on conditioning as well as safety precautions have been incorporated. Beyond this it was generally hoped that the degree of skill attained would attract a participant back to the sport in later years. It was also hoped that the physiological, psychological, and sociological outcomes of activity were so self-evident to the students that they would not fail to include swimming, badminton, or some other activity in their daily or tri-weekly exercise regimens after university days were finished.

Unfortunately, in this period of academic change, the old pattern is not sufficient. Well-skilled and active though undergraduates may be, they find it easy to slip into the ranks of the weekend athlete after leaving college. At age 35 or 40 they are relatively inactive and soon thereafter have fallen prey to the ways of our sedentary, technological society. The element missing from the traditional physical education course was the "know why" of exercise.

Students had never been impressed sufficiently with the basic physiological involvement because no one had ever bothered to intellectualize this information with them. They believed that exercise was good for the human creature. They knew, as most everyone does, that activity made them breathe faster and the blood run more rapidly through their circulatory systems, but they didn't understand it sufficiently well to make them want to build a daily exercise program into their schedule for living.

NEED FOR MOTIVATION

What this means in essence is that most university graduates have never been motivated. It is said that motivation is an internal or acquired determinant of behavior. Its place in the behavior cycle is between stimulus and response. Motivation is a process of arousing action, of sustaining activity once started, and of regulating the activity pattern. Some believe that knowledge and attitudes in themselves provide the base for motivation, but this can be a snare and delusion. How many people still smoke who know perfectly well the contents of the Surgeon General's report on smoking? Regrettably other procrastinators have sufficient knowledge about and proper attitude toward exercise but carefully manage to avoid it. Some authors believe that if the habits involved in exercise and sport are strong enough, any drive will cause one to participate even though the drive and reward lie outside the activities themselves.

The logic behind this concept supports the motivational mechanics of the foundations of physical activity courses offered for a number of years at the University of Illinois. A brief reference to the course's content and methodology is made here primarily to demonstrate the manner in which an attempt is made to change behavior patterns related to exercise. It is commonly thought that motivation is a primary outcome of the course and can influence the student's conduct beyond his or her freshman year.

The Aims of Foundations of Physical Activity

1. To develop an understanding of the role of physical education within our society
2. To acquaint the individual in relation to physical activity with the human organism
3. To acquaint the individual with some effects of physical activity on the growth and development of the human organism
4. To develop an adequate understanding of fatigue, relaxation, rest, sleep, diet, and aging as these factors relate to health and well-being throughout life
5. To conduct a testing program that includes classifying students' physiques and evaluating aspects of their organic and motor fitness
6. To provide a progressive conditioning program in which the student is exposed to several selected methods of conditioning
7. To provide counseling and guidance in the selection of activities gauged to meet immediate and future needs and which emphasize the values and limitations of various types of physical activity
8. To acquaint the student with several services offered within the university environment by the department of physical education

9. To make known facilities and methods from which a personal program can be designed and implemented.

HOW THE PROGRAM WORKS

The student attends one classroom lecture per week and two laboratory periods in the gymnasium. Typical of the classroom sessions are talks or films on human anatomy, physiology, kinesiology, the psychological and sociological aspects of exercise, obesity, arteriosclerosis, the bases of training overload, and modern concepts of health and fitness in later life. The student is assigned readings on these lecture topics in the foundations manual, which was written for this course.

The two laboratory periods per week are given over to testing and conditioning. Tests for strength, agility, and cardiovascular efficiency are administered. Somatotyping is explained and body typing done in order to arrive at a better estimate of individual exercise capacity. After the early laboratory meetings, the student takes a preliminary fitness test. Each test item is carefully recorded. The laboratory periods are then devoted to the learning and use of physical conditioning activities such as beginning interval training, weight training, and circuit training.

Dramatic changes are not likely to take place in students as a result of two half-hour lab sessions per week. It is important to remember, however, that every effort is made to correlate the lecture materials with laboratory activities. It is hoped this reinforces the formation of attitudes that will help influence behavior. Reported observations have indicated that at least 25 percent of students enrolled in foundations courses engage in conditioning sessions outside of physical education laboratory classes. After nine weeks of conditioning, the second fitness test is given. Students now have an opportunity to observe the gains they have made over the scores of the first test given. They are not graded on the improvement they make since this might eliminate most of the incentive to maximize the difference between the results of the tests. Generally a significant improvement between the two tests is noted.

More often than not, this is a new and pleasant experience for the student. Most of them have never participated in scientifically planned conditioning. Perhaps only 20 percent have participated in high school athletics and so are experiencing the changes that systematic exercise can develop for the first time in their lives. It is comforting to students who never could chin themselves to know that they now have the arm strength to pull up two or three times. They are also pleased with the realization that not only can they run a mile, but they can do so in less than seven minutes. Furthermore, in most cases, they are made to understand that they are still on the very lowest rungs of the ladder, the highest reaches of which represent their ultimate fitness potential.

The challenge this understanding excites in many first year students contains the seeds of motivation that will convince them of the desirability of a regular exercise program. This new experience is reinforced by a passable knowledge of what exercise is doing for them, and they have at their disposal a cardiovascular index they can use to help them determine the safe ranges of energy expenditure.

Another feature of the foundations course is the guidance procedure, which endeavors to aid the student in making wiser choices of other physical education courses. This technique considers one's present needs, the carry-over value of various activities, their possible family use, as well as one's present level of skill and interest in the activity. No effort is made to insist that students enroll in specific courses indicated by their guidance profile sheet. It is found, however, by spot checking that students are influenced strongly by the guidance procedure.

SUGGESTED READINGS

Adams, W. C., et al., 1965. *Foundations of physical activity*, ed. by K. J. McCristal. Champaign, Ill.: Stipes.

Cofer, C. N., and W. R. Johnson, 1960. Personality dynamics in relation to exercise in sports. In W. R. Johnson, *Science and medicine of exercise in sports*, pp. 525-559. New York: Harper and Brothers.

Cogan, M. 1970. Creative approaches to physical education. *Proceedings of the National College Physical Education Association for Men.*

Hunsicker, P. A. 1954. A survey of service physical education programs in American colleges and universities. *Proceedings of the College Physical Education Association for Men.*

Oxendine, J. B., 1972. The status of general instruction programs of physical education in four-year colleges and universities: 1971-72. *JOPER* **43** (March) : 26.

Young, P. T., 1961. *Motivation and emotion*, pp. 22-23. New York: John Wiley and Sons.

38

The Community Dimension of College Physical Education

William P. Johnson and Richard P. Kleva

The community college, by definition dedicated to its community, accepts responsibility for equalizing post-high school educational opportunities for all who seek them. In fulfilling its mission of bringing higher education within geographic and financial reach of all citizens, the college must regard the entire area it serves as its campus and all citizens within that area as its student body.

This is a large order, but the competent community college is prepared to fulfill it. That college is concerned not only with the totality of its constituencey, it also considers the individual as well, recognizing that the viability of the community depends on the quality of life engendered in its individual citizens. It is in the enrichment of these lives that the college makes one of its greatest contributions.

But no individual fulfillment can occur unless all individuals have the greatest possible opportunity to develop themselves, physically as well as mentally. The community, therefore, cannot permit its educational institutions merely to stuff students' heads with facts in the notion that to do so it to educate; it cannot tolerate skill training that makes an illusory contribution to well-being while leaving its trainees unable to cope with a world in which their physical skills will soon be obsolete.

Thus, physical education departments in community colleges have both the opportunity and the obligation to develop exciting program approaches to teaching the discipline—unless of course they agree with the handful of gloom peddlers who suggest that the profession has reached an hour of *crisis*.

Four specific areas for development are: (1) a fitness learning laboratory (profile), (2) community athletics programs, (3) walk-in recreation opportunities, and (4) adult life fitness enhancing courses.

FITNESS LEARNING LABORATORY

The development of a fitness learning laboratory, complete with a fitness profile available to all, may be the key to new programs in physical education.

---

*   Reprinted from *JOHPER* **44** (April 1973) : 40-41.

Good exercise habits and proper attitudes toward activity, adopted early in life, may offer the best likelihood of a high degree of physical fitness, optimal health, and the prevention of disease throughout life. Program expansion to include all members of the community, on a credit or noncredit basis, may be just the boost some tired programs need.

At a time when physical education is undergoing severe scrutiny, a fitness profile that identifies individual interests and physiological needs accurately, combined with a laboratory that provides monitored individual programs to meet these needs, is an educational necessity.

A spin-off program might easily be a mobile testing laboratory that considers the potential value of profiling all members of the community. Emerging preliminary evidence suggests that routine physicals prolong life. Clearly these remain beyond the reach of many citizens; the persons who most need examinations are often the least able to pay for them. The fitness profile serves as a health screening test and a source of information that physical education departments can use to counsel community members into meaningful adult life activities. Profiling can be done on site at local industries, in shopping centers, at schools, and in recreation and adult education programs.

An extension of the fitness learning laboratory is the cardiac work evaluation referral center. In its practical aspects, the principle of rehabilitation is applied most extensively and systematically to restoring the earning power of the cardiac patient who has had to reduce activity in or abandon a gainful occupation. However, such an approach implies a physical education program that provides an outstanding social, economic, and humanitarian service to the community. One of the chief achievements of cardiac rehabilitation activities has been their clear demonstration to the public at large that permanent invalidism, traditionally expected of most cardiac patients, is a serious injustice to the patient.

The development of a preventive medicine program for an entire community, based upon exercise stress testing, is another area that college physical education should explore. The monitoring of one or more physiological functions during the performance of a specific amount of exercise is an available procedure for the comprehensive medical evaluation of an individual. Such an evaluation provides unique information about an individual's cardiorespiratory status and dynamic functioning that cannot be obtained or estimated accurately from measurements under rest conditions. Most communities do not have this service available at a cost that the majority of its citizens can afford. Since most college physical education departments are in a position to do so, they have an obligation to become involved with their communities by making available exercise stress testing, including such elements as preclinical or silent heart disease detection, prediction of the risk of disabling coronary heart disease, individual physical fitness assessment, determination of an individual's physical working capacity for an occupational task, and evaluation of the effectiveness of various therapeutic programs (surgery, drugs, diet, exercise, etc.).

COMMUNITY ATHLETICS PROGRAMS

Physical educators who are sincerely interested in reemphasizing the educational values of athletics activities might consider the community athletics programs approach—providing a broadened athletic experience to all interested members of the college community. The value of athletics programs should not be limited to the gifted two to ten percent who make up the traditional athletic community. Rather, we propose a fellowship of community residents who have a mutual interest in athletic activity. All post-high school community residents should be allowed to compete, provided they have medical clearance to do so and membership fee to cover insurance costs.

We are dealing here with two classifications of community residents—fulltime students and others with a need for athletic expression. The college would provide facilities, coaching, and competition for fulltime students in these areas: intramurals, intercollegiate and club athletics, AAU and related opportunities, and intergroup competition. Other members would have the following competitive outlets available: club, AAU, and intergroup competition. In other words, we propose the provision of an athletics program that doesn't say "No" to anyone but instead says, "If you want to play, we have something for you."

The program, operating basically like other traditional athletics teams, nevertheless is characterized by a major difference—the inclusion of any community resident, regardless of age, sex, or skill level. Obviously all sports and all programs do not need this approach. But struggling programs can use it to expand their athletics offerings and bolster sagging athletics interests. The wrestling program at Brookdale Community College, for example, used the community athletics program approach for the 1972-1973 season.

WALK-IN RECREATION

A most important student concern that the physical education profession must recognize is that physical education facilities frequently are tied up by varsity teams so that nonteam members never, or only on rare occasions, find the gymnasium available for their use. Walk-in recreation is one answer to this student complaint.

At Brookdale we are opening the gymnasium and all our auxiliary facilities whenever possible for student and community use under the supervision/instruction of the physical education department. Walk-in recreation is scheduled for the lunch hour, early afternoons, evenings, weekends, and summer. Moreover, the fitness learning laboratory is available to all on a drop-in basis 60 hours per week.

Paraprofessionals or faculty members, as part of their assigned teaching loads, are always present to provide equipment, basic instruction, and organizational and supervisory services. Some recreational activities (e.g., tennis) are handled on a court appointment basis; others such as cycling and archery merely require equipment checkout.

Physical education's most salient asset is probably the variety of recreational activities it can make available. Not to exploit that asset is a severe self-handicap, which the profession can ill afford to impose at this time.

ADULT LIFE FITNESS-ENHANCING COURSES

One way to align physical education with all other aspects of college life is to develop course offerings that meet the needs of any individual in today's world. The professed values of physical education are valid only if we provide opportunities for all members of the community to experience them. Thus, physical education courses must be developed that will include personal fitness performance objectives as well as skill and knowledge objectives (both cognitive and affective). Correlations between individual courses and elements of the fitness profile must also be established whenever possible; otherwise, course prescription cannot occur.

Unless it is to become obsolete, a danger that seems imminent from current trends, physical education must adopt modern approaches to its offerings such as contract teaching, continuous progress registration, independent study projects, minicourses, opportunities for course challenge, and involvement in community service programs. Offerings must be of the highest quality, the most interesting, the most readily accessible, and the best dollar value in our communities. Brookdale Community College already is implementing this concept, with highly gratifying results.

39

The Undergraduate Professional Program in Physical Education

Arthur A. Esslinger and Dorothy La Salle

Professional preparation in physical education in the United States originated in Boston, Massachusetts, in 1861. Dio Lewis initiated this program in his Normal Institute for Physical Education. The course ran for 10 weeks. Instruction was provided in anatomy, physiology, hygiene, and gymnastics. Special work on Per Henrick Ling's Swedish methods for treating chronic diseases was offered. This school continued for seven years, and 421 men and women graduated from the course. These people met much of the demand for instructors in the new gymnastics, which came first from New England cities and later from all over the country.

The German Turner movement was responsible for the second professional program in physical education. Their Normal School opened in New York City on November 22, 1866. The first class included 19 men. The school was subsequently moved to Chicago, Milwaukee, and Indianapolis. It is still in operation today as a division of Indiana University. It originally was designed as a one-year curriculum. This included the history and aims of the German Turner movement, anatomy, first aid, and gymnastics.

It was from these beginnings that our present undergraduate physical education programs have evolved. The length of the course was gradually extended from one to two years and eventually to three and four years. It was not until the early 1930s that the four-year program became the accepted standard.

In over a century the number of institutions offering the undergraduate major program and the numbers of students enrolled in these programs have increased enormously. The bachelors' degrees granted with a major in physical education in 1968-69 were men, 10,646; women, 7,351; total 17,997. In 1969-70 the numbers were men, 12,675; women, 8,220; total 20,895.

The major elements involved in an undergraduate professional program in physical education include students, faculty, adequate resources, and curriculum.

STUDENTS

Since the quality of the program depends appreciably upon the quality of the physical education majors, the selection and retention of students for the program merit serious consideration. Many colleges and universities have developed an elaborate program for this purpose while other institutions take almost any candidates who apply for admission. In fact some schools engage in an active recruitment program in order to obtain superior candidates. Recommended admission standards include:

1. Good health, above-average physical development, special skill attainments, and desirable personality attributes.

2. A previous academic record that promises successful performance in an institution of higher education. This may involve a satisfactory grade point average in all high school subjects taken for graduation or a satisfactory score on the College Entrance Examination Board Scholastic Aptitude Test.

The retention of students in the program should be based upon the maintenance of a desirable academic record, satisfactory performance of skill requirements, continued evidences of good health practices, and demonstration of a pattern of conduct desirable for a teacher and leader of youth.

FACULTY

The number and quality of the faculty is the most important element in an undergraduate professional physical education program. The number should be sufficient to handle all the necessary assignments within the department without incurring a teaching load in excess of that of faculty members in other departments within the institution.

The faculty should have made excellent academic records and should hold graduate degrees from accredited institutions. Faculty members should have a breadth of experience and ability in their professional fields and should be especially competent in their areas of assignment. Previous teaching experience in the public schools is mandatory for those who supervise student teaching and teach courses in methods and materials of physical education. A desirable goal is to determine that every course taught in the department is handled by a faculty member who is highly specialized in that area.

ADEQUATE RESOURCES

The major resources include facilities, equipment, supplies, and library materials. The facilities, equipment, and supplies should be adequate for the basic instructional program, the intramural sports program, and the intercollegiate athletic program, as well as the program of professional preparation. The facilities should be sufficient in number, adequacy, and quality to provide for all physical education activities. In addition, well-designed and well-equipped classrooms and seminar/lecture rooms are necessary for instructional use. Special demonstration and research laboratories are needed for instruction in kinesiology, physiology of exercise, evaluation, and adapted physical education.

The annual library budget should be adequate to purchase the books, periodicals, pamphlets, and audio-visual materials that are required.

CURRICULUM

State departments of public instruction in the United States require those desiring to teach physical education to complete a four-year college course leading to either a baccalaureate degree in science (B.S.) in arts (B.A.), or in education (B.Ed.). In addition they must meet certain other requirements to be certified by the state for teaching in the public schools.

In some states students must be prepared to teach a second subject in addition to their major.

A total of 120-124 semester hours usually is required with specific hours in various categories as follows:

Academic Foundations	60
Physical Education Foundations	36
Teaching Foundations	18
Electives	6-9

A typical curriculum for teaching of physical education follows:*

I. ACADEMIC FOUNDATIONS
   A. English
   B. Social sciences
   C. Natural sciences & mathematics
   D. Electives

Courses in humanities, speech, psychology, anthropology, and fine arts are especially recommended.

---

* *Editor's note:* Many undergraduate major curricula exist today besides the kind focusing on teaching.

II. PHYSICAL EDUCATION FOUNDATIONS

A. Skills

1. Games and sports
2. Rhythmic and dance activities
   a. Folk and national dance
   b. Modern dance
   c. Creative dance for children
3. Swimming and water safety
4. Stunts and gymnastics

B. Physical Education Theory*

1. Anatomy
2. Kinesiology
3. Physiology and physiology of exercise
4. History of physical education
5. Principles of physical education
6. Sports in American culture
7. Analysis of expressive movement
8. Measurement and evaluation
9. Administration of physical education

C. Related Courses in Health

1. Health instruction (hygiene)
2. Community health
3. Safety education
4. First aid
5. Conditioning & Care of athletic injuries

D. Related Courses in Recreation Leadership

1. Community recreation
2. Playground organization & management

III. Teaching Foundations

A. History of education
B. Organization of the public school in the U.S.
C. Methods of teaching physical education in the elementary school
D. Methods of teaching physical education in the secondary school

---

* An increasing number of institutions are offering courses preparing the student to teach physical education to the physically and/or mentally handicapped.

E. Athletic coaching
F. Curriculum development in physical education
G. Supervised student teaching†

SUGGESTED READINGS

AAHPER, 1974. *Professional preparation in dance, physical education, recreation education, safety education, and school health education.* Washington, D.C.: AAHPER

Careers in Physical Education, 1975. *Briefings* **3.** NAPECW and NCPEAM.

Competency-based teacher education, 1975. *Briefings* **2.** NAPECW and NCPEAM.

Herndon, M. E., et al., 1976. Professional preparation: an international relations approach. *JOHPER* **47** (October) : 19.

40

The Graduate Program in Physical Education

Betty McCue and Arthur A. Esslinger

ORIGINS OF GRADUATE WORK IN PHYSICAL EDUCATION

Columbia University is credited with offering in 1901 the first master's degree program in physical education. Oberlin College conferred its first such degree in 1904. The first programs in physical education leading to the Ph.D. degree were offered in 1924 by Teachers College, Columbia University and by the School of Education, New York University; the first such programs leading to the Ed.D. degree were offered by Stanford University and by the University of Pittsburgh in 1929.

The first graduate programs in physical education emerged generally as a part of the graduate offerings of schools and colleges of education. Often the

---

† 2.5 grade point average required on a 4-point scale.

degrees granted were in reality graduate degrees in education with various amounts of specialization in physical education and health education. As late as 1942 schools of education offered 85 percent of all doctor's degrees and 51 percent of all master's degrees available for the graduate major in physical education. In recent years, due primarily to expanded knowledge and the attendant increased need for specialization, there has been a trend in the universities toward the establishment of distinct and separate graduate programs in physical education, either in autonomous departments or, more frequently, in separate schools or colleges of physical education.

In 1943, 56 institutions offered master's degrees in physical education and 20 institutions offered such programs leading to the doctorate. In 1970, 214 institutions offered master's degrees in physical education and 37 offered doctoral programs. Many master's and doctoral candidates earn their degrees in another field but take considerable course work in physical education in the form of a minor or a supporting area. There is no way to obtain reliable statistics in regard to the amount of such graduate study.

The number of physical education graduate students varies widely from institution to institution. A considerable number of colleges and universities grant less than five graduate degrees per year. On the other hand, some of the larger universities grant between 75 and 100 master's and doctor's degrees every year. In reality most of the doctoral work in physical education is accomplished in 30 colleges and universities.

PURPOSES AND STRUCTURE OF GRADUATE STUDY

The aim in graduate study in physical education is to extend the individual's capacity for scholarly endeavor, research, and creativity. Recognition of the need for scientific research workers and humanistic scholars in physical education is increasingly acknowledged and reflected in the variety of programs of study offered throughout the country. The purposes of graduate study, reflected in school curricula in varying degrees, include: basic research, the preparation of researchers and scholars, advanced preparation of practitioners (teachers, supervisors, activity specialists, and administrators), extension of the range of nonverbal expression (dance, games, sports, etc.) through encouragement of human invention and imagination, and the development of leaders who have the ability to employ their rational powers with sensitivity, aesthetic appreciation, and moral responsibility.

For the most part graduate courses are based upon undergraduate prerequisites and represent a continuum in depth of basic areas of physical education. Graduate courses are more concerned with principles, philosophy, history, and research than with skills, techniques and factual information. Graduate study must involve original and mature thinking; thus, graduate education should be designed to develop the ability of students to read widely and rapidly with comprhension; to find and use available source materials in the solution of problems; to produce work of an original nature; to do independent and critical thinking; to find, organize and evaluate evidence; and to formulate and defend conclusions.

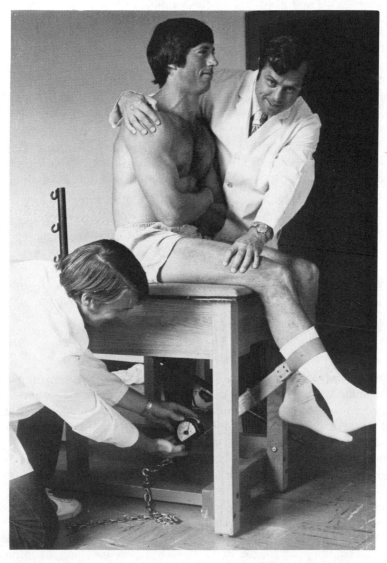

Fig. 40.1 A research experience. Courtesy of the University of Oregon, Eugene, Ore.

It is generally agreed that a quality graduate program must involve a majority of the following experiences for the master's program: some course offerings open to graduate students only, a research experience or production, comprehensive knowledge as well as a major area of concentration, and opportunity for intensive specialization in related basic disciplines. The doctoral program requires scholarship and proficiency in the area of specialization, flexibility to accomodate the student's interests and desired professional goals, a formal dissertation, scholarly study or creative project, and residency requirements of at least one year.

Typical patterns of graduate study and their purposes have been outlined as follows:

1. A five-year articulated program of undergraduate and graduate work culminating in a professional teacher degree that may or may not be a master's degree

2. A one-year graduate program designed primarily for elementary and secondary school teachers or other professional personnel and culminating in a terminal master's degree, usually without thesis

3. A one-year master's program, research oriented, designed as the first step in a graduate program leading to the doctorate — a thesis is required

4. A three-year graduate program, often without foreign language and the formal dissertation requirements, terminating in a doctorate, most frequently the Ed.D. degree

5. A three-year graduate program, with foreign language and formal dissertation requirements, terminating in the Ph.D. (AAHPER 1967).

CURRICULUM

The core body of knowledge of physical education concerns human motor performance. The following areas of scholarly study relate to and should be studied as part of physical education: (1) motor learning and motor development. (2) biomechanics, (3) exercise physiology, (4) behavioral aspects of physical education. (5) social, cultural, and aesthetic aspects of physical education, (6) meaning and significance of physical education including philosophical and historical considerations, (7) evaluation, (8) administration, and (9) curricular aspects of physical education including supervision, instruction, and curricular development. Current practice in many institutions is that not *all* graduate students study *all* of the listed areas.

An in-depth knowledge of one or more foreign languages has been required traditionally for the Ph.D. degree. In recent years this requirement has been broadened, sometimes for the Ed.D. as well, to require "demonstration of competence in scholarly tools appropriate to the particular degree, such as foreign language, statistics, and research methodology" (AAHPER 1969).

Graduate study should be planned to offer breadth of learning in the field of physical education as well as leading toward specialization and competence in research or other scholarly pursuits. Within the sequence of learning experiences the substantive content of physical education and related scientific principles should be the foundation for all course development. The areas of study are not mutually exclusive, and as a student pursues an area of concentration, this study may follow one of the several categories within the profession such as physical education for the atypical, physical education in the elementary school, or the administration of athletics.

GRADUATE FACULTY

The strength of an undergraduate and graduate program in physical education depends more on the faculty than any other factor. An adequate number of highly qualified faculty members is indispensable to a quality program.

For the undergraduate professional program all faculty members should possess graduate degrees from accredited institutions. The doctorate is preferred, but in certain areas individuals with master's degrees who have extensive experience, a national reputation in a professional specialty, and authoritative status would be acceptable. For graduate work faculty members should hold doctor's degrees except in very unusual circumstances.

Since the scope of physical education has been broadened in recent years, it is expected that faculty members will be highly specialized in one or two areas. The time when a faculty member was qualified to teach in four or five different areas of physical education is past. The depth of preparation of a teacher is a major consideration today.

Experience in the public schools is invaluable for physical education faculty members. This experience should be at the level for which the students are preparing. Certain courses such as statistics, research methods, anatomy, physiology, kinesiology, and physiology of exercise do not require teachers who have taught in public schools. These are exceptions, however. There is little question that faculty members teaching students who are preparing to teach in public schools would find it advantageous to have had teaching experience in public schools.

It is highly desirable for a department to have faculty members who have obtained their various degrees from a variety of institutions. The temptation to employ graduates of one's own department should be resisted. A small number of such faculty members is acceptable particularly if they have obtained their other degrees from different institutions.

The number of faculty members is a vitally important consideration. The work load of physical education graduate faculty members should be commensurate with that in other schools and departments within the institution. For doctoral programs the Council of Graduate Schools in the United States recommends: "Four or five graduate faculty professors in the subject field, at least, should be the participants in the doctoral program, and a minimum of up to ten may be necessary for the larger, more subdivided fields."

ENTRANCE REQUIREMENTS AND STUDENT ADVISEMENT

Colleges and universities have established standards for admission of their students. These are generally minimum standards. Scholarly competence, usually measured by grade point average, has been the primary requirement for admission. Schools in which criteria in addition to the grade point average are assessed may include a considered judgment of the quality of the school from which the grades were earned. Some graduate faculty believe that grade point average related to the quality of the school attended, and the scores on standardized tests, are the most important predictors of success used in the admission of graduate students.

The following policies for admitting and advising graduate students are recommended (AAHPER 1967):

> Admission should be based on a number of selection factors rather than on a single absolute standard. This is especially true in "marginal" cases. The following criteria are suggested for consideration: (1) an applicant's profesional preparation, (2) previous experience, (3) intelligence and knowledge, (4) communications skills, (5) personal integrity, and (6) professional interest and willingness to work. Due to the nature and specificity of certain advanced study programs, audition and/or personal interviews may be required.
>
> Admission standards for the doctoral degree should be more selective than those established for the master's degree.
>
> A portion of the graduate students should be from out-of-state and foreign countries.
>
> Advisement of students should be realistic in terms of their background and their professional goals. Admission to graduate study should not be interpreted as a guarantee of successful completion of degree requirements; however, advisors should be sensitive to the nature and scope of the programs of study that will best fulfill the student's goals.
>
> Personnel records that are helpful in the advising of students include:
>
> Application form — provides background information on experience in the profession.
>
> Transcript of all academic work — provides academic background.
>
> Evidence of aptitude — from Graduate Record Examination, Millers Analogy Test or other appropriate tests.

References—provide relevant information concerning personal and professional qualities.

Communications skills—a writing sample, scores on reading and/or comprehension tests."

REFERENCES

AAHPER, 1967. *Graduate education in health education, physical education, recreation education, safety education and dance.* Washington, D.C.: AAHPER.

_____, 1969. *Self-evaluation check list for graduate programs in health education, physical education, recreation education, safety education, and dance.* Washington, D.C.: AAHPER.

U.S. Department of Health, Education, and Welfare, 1967-68, 1968-69, 1969-70. *Earned degrees conferred: institutional data.*

SUGGESTED READINGS

Lawson, H. A., 1976. Professional studies program in graduate physical education. *Quest,* Monograph 25, pp. 67-75. NAPECW and NCPEAM.

Siedentop, D., ed., 1976. Graduate study in physical education. *Quest,* Monograph 25 (Winter). NACPEW and NCPEAM.

41

The Intramural Athletics Program

Hartley Price

HISTORY

Significant historical events for intramurals in the United States include: In 1913 departments of intramural athletics were established at the University of Michigan and The Ohio State University under the supervision of a faculty member. In 1917 The National Athletic Conference of American College

Women opposed varsity athletics for women and favored the promotion of intramurals. In 1920 the directors of intramural athletics of the Western Intercollegiate Athletic Conference began holding annual meetings—intramural athletics had boomed due to the influence of World War I. In 1928 the University of Michigan built the first intramural sports building. In 1932 the Committee on Women's Athletics was recognized as an official section of the American Physical Education Association and stressed standards for intramural activities. In 1933 a section for intramural athletics was established within the College Physical Education Association. In 1938 a section on intramural athletics was begun within the Division of Men's Athletics of the AAHPER.

Additional historical developments are: Following World War II there was a great increase in the popularity of intramural athletic programs throughout the country. In 1950 the National Intramural Association was organized. In 1957 the National Section for Girl's and Women's Sports was changed to Division for Girl's and Women's Sports (DGWS). In 1957 Purdue University built a corecreation gymnasium—since then, outstanding intramural facilities have been constructed at Michigan State University, University of Illinois, Oklahoma State University, and University of Washington. In 1966 the National Intramural Sports Council was organized jointly by the Division of Men's Athletics (DMA) and the Division for Girl's and Women's Sports (DGWS) of the AAHPER, and graduate work with a specialization in intramurals is now offered at the University of Illinois and the University of Minnesota.

Extramural or intermural activities are an outgrowth of intramurals. They take place outside rather than inside the walls of the school and represent an intermediate phase between intramurals and intercollegiate athletics. Different names have been given to the program at different times. The first title was intramural athletics. Then followed intramural sports (I-M), intramural and recreational sports (IMREC), intramural activities, intramurals and recreation, and intramurals per se. The change to "sports" rather than "athletics" was to indicate an emphasis upon sports for recreation rather than the stress of varsity athletics. "Sports for All" became the goal of the program. Also, intramurals have been included in department titles such as Department of Health, Physical Education, and Intramurals; or Division of Intercollegiate and Intramural Athletics.

More and more there seems to be a movement toward sport clubs. During the late 1920s and 1930s a sport usually became varsity by first proving itself popular in the intramural program. Then a widespread interest in intramural programs appeared in the 1940s. Later this was frowned on by athletic directors because they thought an outstanding varsity football player might lose a year of eligibility by representing his school in a sport such as table tennis as an I-M champion in extramural competition with the I-M champion of another school. After World WAR II in the 1940s and 1950s, recreational sports and corecreational activities became more and more popular.

PHILOSOPHY

Physical education should endeavor to contribute to the effective integration and to the joyous development of the individual physically, mentally, morally, and socially. Big muscle play activities should be presented according to the needs, capacities, and interests of the developing individual in a genetic sequence so that the problem-solving patterns of conduct on the one hand, and the development of a self-disciplined, integrated personality on the other hand, may be effected in a forward-moving social setting.

Physical education in a university may be concerned with the following objectives in the service curriculum: the development of fitness, both physical and mental; the development of certain social and ethical qualities that characterize good citizenship in a democracy; and the development of skills and interest for leisure both now and for the future long after the student has left school.

The effectively balanced program of physical education should include the following types of activities: team sports, individual sports, rhythms, aquatics, gymnastics and tumbling, combatives, and open country sports such as canoeing, hiking, mountain climbing, ice skating, skiing, water skiing, and other activities pertinent to the locality.

Likewise, intramurals should include all the above-mentioned categories. Popular team sports include basketball, volleyball, softball, flag football, touch football, soccer, speedball, waterpolo, ice hockey, and lacrosse. Individual sports include archery, tennis, table tennis, badminton, bowling, gymnastics, fencing, golf, swimming, basketball free throw, horseshoes, handball, paddleball, weight-lifting, crosscountryf, rifleshooting. Sigma Delta Psi (all-around athletic honorary): archery, indoor track, outdoor track, wrestling, squash, fencing, codeball, and skish. Most of the above activities are conducted separately by men and women, although some activities like volleyball, softball, archery, tennis, table tennis, badminton, bowling, gymnastics, fencing, golf, swimming, physical conditioning, scuba, sailing, roller skating, shuffleboard, kiteflying, and bicycle festival are conducted on a coeducational basis. Thus, an excellent university program should offer intramural sports (competitive) during the fall, winter, and spring; recreational sports such as tennis, basketball, billiards, and golf; corecreational sports like volleyball, bowling, tennis, softball, and gymnastics; sport clubs that might compete on an extramural basis or be purely recreational; and faculty-staff sports including square dancing, volleyball, badminton, golf, and horseshoes.

The intramural program should relate both to the physical education curriculum and the intercollegiate sports program. Skills, knowledge, attitudes, and appreciations should be taught in physical education that may be put into practice effectively in intramurals by the students in their own leisure time. The student will become involved if given the opportunity.

Likewise, the sports on the intercollegiate roster should be offered in intramurals and during the same season if the facilities permit. Thus, touch football should be scheduled in the fall; basketball, gymnastics, swimming, and wrestling in the winter; and baseball or softball, and track in the spring. The other activities should also be offered during their seasons as much as possible.

ADMINISTRATIVE PROBLEMS AND RESPONSIBILITIES

The intramural program should be organized, supervised, and administered as much as possible by the students themselves. If it is dominated by faculty it becomes a voluntary physical education program rather than an intramural program, which should be truly recreational. An effective managerial system must evolve through the students themselves if the program is to reach its full potentiality.

Proper orientation should be made in the fall to clarify the program. Also, at the end of the year, closing meetings should be held to finalize all proposed changes for the coming year.

Adequate publicity is imperative. Posters showing the calendar of events should be posted. Also, the calendar of events should be included in the intramural handbook as well as daily, weekly, and monthly items in the student newspaper.

Full details of administration cannot be covered in this short chapter on intramurals as they vary in different locations. The items mentioned below must be developed carefully to produce an effective program.

The health and welfare of the student should be considered constantly. Participation in the competitive program should be based on a medical examination. There should also be a re-check before very strenuous activities. Conditioning activities should be required before arduous activities in order to avoid excessive fatigue. The environment should be safe and sanitary to encourage proper health habits. A sound program must operate with full attention to finances, facilities, and equipment. Activities should be based on needs, interests, and capacities of the individual. They should be selected both for their in-school value and their carry-over to later adult life. Other considerations should be given to the number and age of participants as well as climatic conditions and available facilities, equipment, and supervisory staff. Effective supervision should be provided for all activities to ensure favorable conditions for the development of sociability and good will among the students. Qualified officials should be provided for all contests. Competition should be so organized that the units of competition are equalized as much as possible. Democratic procedures should be practiced so that effective leadership may be developed in all phases of the program, especially in the managerial system. Provision should be made for inservice preparation for leadership.

Game rules, eligibility rules, and program regulations must be established. Activities should be scheduled for the convenience and satisfaction of all. The best type of tournament should be selected to obtain the most participation in terms of the facilities, equipment, and time available.

A simple, efficient, and fair point system has to be devised and administered properly. The striving for the winning of awards should be kept to a minimum. The student should be concerned with achieving the inherent values of engaging in physical recreation without regard to the award that might be won.

Financial support should be provided by the institution as much as possible without depending on entry fees. Both the men's program and the women's program should be given equal recognition. Corecreational activities should be encouraged as much as possible.

Workshops should be held regularly in order to introduce new ideas and innovations into the program. Such items could include new activities, eligibility rules, awards, equipment, facilities, financing, rules and regulations, officiating, scheduling, and tournaments. An effective program of publicity and public relations is essential. Continued communication with the student body must be maintained all year. The publishing of all mimeographed material and an intramural handbook are important. The intramural office must be operated in a competent way to organize, supervise, and promote all activities properly. All business details must be carried out efficiently.

In summary, administrative details must be worked out for the items listed below to be included in a proposed intramural handbook. These details are not given as they would vary in each program.

An intramural handbook is of value for an extensive intramural program. A suggested table of contents might include the following:

1. Calendar of intramural activities: approximate dates for starting various tournaments or for starting open or scheduled practice sessions for particular sports.
2. Series of articles by people important to the proper coordination and support of the program.
3. Description of intramural organization: names of personnel important to the conduct of the program: namely, advisor or director of intramural activities, activity advisors or field supervisor, officiating advisor, coordi-

nators, and secretary. The names of personnel on the intramural board would be listed, including intramural chairman, treasurer, secretary, club president(s), publicity manager, unit representative(s), corecreation chairman, and sport manager(s). In addition, the names of personnel on the protest or mediation board should be listed, and also the names of student managers—senior, junior, and sophomore managers as well as sport managers.

4. Suggestions to unit representatives including house managers, class manager(s), and club representative(s).

5. List of names of all unit managers.

6. Names of members of intramural officials club.

7. Zones of independent participation—division of the campus into zones of equal strength.

8. Independent rules of eligibility.

9. Map of the independent district and zone system.

10. Directions to independent district and zone managers.

11. Participation rules: eligibility rules, classification of students for competition, entry fees, protests, deadlines, forfeits, postponements, health examination, injuries, facilities and equipment, practice sessions, officials, and sportsmanship.

12. Location of fields and facilities.

13. Intramural sports services: list of all activities in the intramural program showing local modifications of rules, hints about playing the game, entry fee, points that will be awarded, and winners from the previous years.

14. Announcements for the current year pointing out the possibility of starting new activities if sufficient interest is shown.

15. Officials' club.

16. Participation point system: allotment of participation points for all intramural activities, to the organization and to the individual.

17. Comparison of entries for the past three or four years, number of teams and individuals in each sport and in the entire year's program.

18. Intramural side lights: material of interest to the student body such as the corecreation program and other special occurrences of the past year and plans for the year ahead.

19. Awards and names of all winners for the all-year trophy, each tournament, sportsmanship, and best official.

20. Special events such as turkey run, sports festivals, sport days, play days.

21. Recreational activities service: explanation of the program of recreational activities largely of a noncompetitive nature.

22. Corecreation program indicating the calendar of special corecreational events.

23. Intramural rankings throughout the past years.

24. Code of sportsmanship or ethics. (This material may appear on the back cover of the handbook.)

SPORTS CLUBS

The sports club movement is becoming more popular every year. Every endeavor should be made to form new sports clubs with individuals who have similar interests. Some of the most popular sport clubs are karate, judo, gymnastics, fencing, soccer, wrestling, sailing, weightlifting, skiing, badminton, volleyball, scuba, and skin diving. This type of sports organization has been prevalent in Europe for a long time. The activities are often administered by voluntary coaches, officers, and managers. The trend tends to exemplify the amateur philosophy of "sports for sports' sake." In the United States it might be of great significance where varsity sports are becoming more and more expensive, thereby curtailing other sports.

REFERENCES

Kleindienst, V. and A. Weston, 1964. *Intramural and recreation programs for schools and colleges.* New York: Appleton-Century-Crofts.

Leavitt, N., and H. D. Price, 1958. *Intramural and recreational sports for high school and college.* New York: Ronald Press.

Means, L. 1963. *Intramurals: their organization and administration.* Englewood Cliffs, N. J.: Prentice-Hall.

Mueller, P., 1971. *Intramurals: programming and administration.* New York: Ronald Press.

SUGGESTED READINGS

Brumbach, W. B., 1974. Sports clubs—physical education's new partner. *Proceedings of the 77th Annual Meeting of the NCPEAM,* December 26-29, 1973, Kansas City, Missouri.

McGuire, R., 1977. *Bibliography of references for intramural and recreational sports.* Cornwall, N.Y.: Leisure Press.

Moyer, D. H., 1977. Increasing participation. *JOPER* **48** (February) : 36.

Standards and Guidelines for intramurals, 1975. *JOPER* **46** (March) : 27.

42

The Relationship of Physical Education and Athletics

Reuben B. Frost

Athletics and physical education are in many ways intimately related. They include many of the same activities in their programs, they are generally conducted under the direction of people with similar interests and educational backgrounds, they utilize essentially the same kind of facilities, and they are often parts of the same or related organizational units. There are, however, some differences.

The participants in varsity athletics are usually those with special talents and endowments. Those less gifted in athletic ability have little or no opportunity to participate at the varsity level, regardless of their desires and needs. While the goals and objectives of athletics and physical education are in some instances the same, they are not always identical and the emphases may differ considerably.

The need to satisfy the many publics, the regularly scheduled public demonstrations of the athletes' ability, the extreme emphasis on winning, and the apparent need for expert and sophisticated coaching are not present to any appreciable degree in physical education but are very visible parts of intercollegiate athletics. On the other hand, the emphasis on organic development, the goal of personal fitness, the teaching and learning of motor skills, and other educational objectives are usually more apparent and more precisely articulated in physical education.

It is apparant that this relationship needs further analysis and elaboration. It will be considered under the headings: theoretical considerations, facilities, personnel, organizational relationships, and problems and prospects.

THEORETICAL CONSIDERATIONS

Athletics consist of feats of speed and strength, contests between teams of athletes, meets in which individuals and/or teams compete with each other, and programs of such activities in schools, colleges, social agencies, and clubs. Examples of athletics are track and field meets,* rowing regattas,

---

* In many countries of the world the term "athletics" refers to track and field only and does not include other sports.

basketball games, tennis matches, championship swimming meets, wrestling tournaments, and gymnastics meets.

Physical education consists of the modifications and adjustments that occur in an individual through the medium of physical activity. Such physical activity may include athletics but may also be in the form of calisthenics, movement exploration, isometric training, dance, jogging, circuit training, canoeing, orienteering, or rhythmic exercises.

The overall purposes of physical education, as of all education, are the improvement of society and the development and self-realization of the individual. The goals are: (1) normal growth and maturation, (2) the development of organic vigor, (3) neuromuscular development, (4) social adjustment, (5) mental, emotional and physical health, (6) self-expression, (7) the satisfaction of psychological needs, and (8) self-fulfillment.

When athletics are designed and conducted to serve these purposes and achieve these goals, they *are* physical education. When athletic programs have as their priorities the glorification of the athletes, the publicizing of the institution, satisfying the alumni, making money, and building prestige, they are neither physical education nor education.

Most colleges and universities have established aims and objectives for their athletic programs that are in harmony with the educational goals of the institution, emphasize the development of the individual, and strive to improve society. Philosophically therefore, and by definition, athletics *are* physical education.

Walter Schwank (1971) in his perceptive article entitled "The Role of Athletics in Education," sums it up this way:

> The objectives of intercollegiate athletics should, according to some college authorities, be identical with those of physical education. In certain educational groups the only justification for intercollegiate athletics is its contribution to educational and physical education objectives. On the other hand, there are programs in some schools conducted for reasons which cannot legitimately be defined as educational.

FACILITIES

Very few institutions have adequate facilities for physical education and athletics. To meet the needs of large numbers of students with varied interests and capabilities, an institution should sponsor and fully support: (1) a basic instruction program, (2) a program for the handicapped, (3) an intramural program, and (4) an intercollegiate athletic program (men and women).

In most instances men and women require separate facilities for the men's and women's programs. There are situations and certain types of activities where coeducational programs are to be preferred. Dance, archery, badminton, tennis, aquatics, golf, and orienteering are examples.

Unless facilities are reasonably adequate the director is apt to encounter conflicts between: (1) the men's and women's intercollegiate programs, (2) the intramural and intercollegiate programs. Occasionally there may also be problems in the scheduling of basic instruction courses.

There can be no exact guide to the size and number of the physical education and athletic facilities. Their size, shape, and character today are so varied and so innovative that they cannot be described generally. The purposes for which they are used are equally diverse.

In large institutions where thousands of spectators throng to see intercollegiate contests, there is a vast difference between the facilities provided for athletics and those needed for physical education. The considerations when planning athletic facilities include seating space for spectators, parking space for cars, rest room and cloak room services, ticket booths and turnstiles, traffic planning both within the building and without, entrance and egress provisions, press box and other news media facilities, telephone systems, and the many other details so important when presenting spectacles and performances for the general public.

When planning facilities for physical education, attention must be given to teaching stations for 20 to 30 different activities, research laboratories for the several sciences, lecture rooms, audiovisual aids, and offices for faculty.

There are a number of institutions where athletics programs, professional preparation programs, basic instruction programs, and intramural programs, all for both men and women, are conducted in the same facilities and by the same staff. This requires special attention to facility planning and scheduling. Coordinating committees, a specific staff member in charge of facility maintenance and scheduling, and buildings and fields planned for the programs conducted, can solve many of the facility problems that may develop. Appropriate representation of all facets of the program in planning and administering facilities is essential.

Fortunately new and innovative architectural plans, moveable equipment, adjustable partitions, and synthetic surfaces have increased the flexibility of facilities to the point where they will accomodate many more activities and more extensive programs than was previously the case. Adequacy of facilities will, however, continue to play an important role in the harmonious operation of combined departments. (See Section 7.)

PERSONNEL

In smaller colleges it is common practice to employ individuals who will have both coaching duties and teaching assignments. Coaches teach and teachers coach. This makes for an excellent relationship where the duties are not too demanding. The coaches understand and appreciate the task of the physical education teacher and the physical education teachers have a better perspective of the problems facing those who deal with the imponderables of intercollegiate athletics.

In institutions where athletics are conducted on a "big time" basis, the demands on the coaches are so great that they have neither the energy nor the right frame of mind to give to the teaching of physical education classes the kind of attention and the degree of commitment that make it effective and worthwhile. The pressures of operating in the white glare of publicity cause even the most idealistic coaches to give priority to the coaching duties. The fascination of preparing teams for the highly publicized contests and the continuous emphasis on conference standing and "won-lost records" cannot be denied.

Likewise, the individual who is committed to research, to the teaching of philosophical subjects, to keeping abreast of the latest developments in motor learning and curriculum planning, cannot give the necessary time and energy to these responsibilities if he is also expected to attend "chalk talks," participate in motion picture analysis sessions, recruit athletes, and coach teams.

A compromise between the theoretical and the ideal approach on the one hand and a pragmatic approach on the other seems to be the best answer. Individuals must analyze the situations in which they find themselves, review their responsibilities, and establish priorities. Whether they are administrators, coaches, physical education teachers or a combination of these, they must work out a solution and choose the best course. If change is necessary they must work patiently and intelligently to bring about change. Educational goals should point the direction.

Of considerable interest and importance is the development in the last decade of special programs (and in some states special certification requirements) for coaches and athletic administrators. While this trend is at present confined mostly to the secondary level, it will very probably affect college coaches in the near future. It may presage a greater distinction between the educational background of coaches and physical education teachers than that which has prevailed.

ORGANIZATIONAL STRUCTURE

Most of the many different organizational structures for physical education and athletics that exist in the educational institutions of the United States may be placed in three categories:

1. A department or division that includes both the athletic program and all facets of the physical education program. The same individual serves as director of both physical education and athletics. He or she reports to an

academic dean for physical education purposes and the president's office for athletics.

2. Completely separate and autonomous organizational units, one for athletics and one for physical education. Very often there is a dean of the school of health, physical education, and recreation reporting to the vice-president for academic affairs, and a director of athletics reporting directly to the president or one of his top assistants.

3. A division, school or college of health, physical education, and recreation with sub-units for athletics, health education, recreation, intramurals, physical education. The director or chairman of each sub-unit reports directly to the dean of the school or college, who is responsible for both athletics and physical education.

The larger institutions are most apt to have completely autonomous and separate organizational units for athletics and physical education. In these institutions instructors and teachers are more apt to be specialists with fulltime duties in their respective areas. Athletics are more responsive to the demands of alumni, news media, and fans, and the athletic director and coaches spend most of their time recruiting, reviewing films, planning practices, administering budgets, dealing with the public, and coaching their teams. They have little or no time to teach physical education, although a few of them are employed on a parttime basis to teach in their specialty. The physical education teachers in such an institution are free to teach, research, write, and carry on extra duties required of the profession. They generally have no coaching responsibilities.

In small institutions coaches teach and do the best they can with their multitudinous coaching responsibilities. In most schools they are given a reasonable amount of credit toward their teaching load for coaching.

In general it may be said that the more it is necessary to share facilities, personnel, equipment, and financial resources, the sounder is the rationale for combined departments. Coordination is more easily effected and harmonious relationships maintained if one administrator is responsible for administering budgets, activity areas, and equipment that must be used for both physical education and athletics.

PROBLEMS AND PROSPECTS

Philosophically athletics are a phase of physical education and physical education is a phase of education. Both should make their maximal and optimal contribution to the goals of education.

Practically, in institutions where the emphasis is on "big time athletics," it is better to separate athletics and physical education, or else the curricular and scholarly aspects are apt to suffer. Much depends, however, on the leadership and the commitment of the individuals concerned. Many coaches are excellent physical education teachers and many physical education teachers are excellent coaches. Some individuals are able to carry more and greater responsibilities than others. Some situations are more demanding of coaches than others. Some circumstances make for more difficulty coordinating activities and programs than do others. Good interpersonal relationships are more easily maintained in some institutions than in others.

It is impossible to predict what the future holds. One hopes all institutions will insist that athletics and physical education keep educational objectives as their goal, that each institution will seek, earnestly and sincerely, the type of organizational structure, the kind of facilities, the quality of personnel, and the philosophy of education and sport that will make athletics and physical education at their institution as wholesome and educational as possible. This will require a commitment to youth, insistence on following the spirit and the intent of rules, and administrators and coaches who have sound educational philosophies. It will also necessitate continuous education of school personnel and the general public.

REFERENCE

Schwank, W. C., 1971. The role of athletics in education. In E. S. Steitz (ed.), *Administration of athletics in colleges and universities.* Washington, D.C.: AAHPER.

SUGGESTED READINGS

AAHPER, 1968. *Proceedings of the first national conference of college and university administrators.* Washington, D.C.: AAHPER.

————, 1963. *Athletics in education: a platform statement by the division of men's athletics.* Washington, D.C.:, AAHPER.

Baley, J. A., 1966. Physical education and athletics belong together. *The Physical Educator* **23** (May) : 77-78.

Barnes, S. E., 1965. Criteria for evaluating the administration of intercollegiate athletics. Doctoral dissertation. Columbus: Ohio State University.

Blaufarb, M., 1977. Sex-integrated programs that work. *Up-Date* (November-December). Washington, D.C.: AAHPER.

Dodson, C. 1974. How to comply with Title IX. In *Proceedings of the national federation's fifth annual national conference of high school directors of athletics.* Elgin, Illinois, December.

Donnelly, R., 1963. Summary of recent trends in organizational structure of college physical education programs for men. Minneapolis: University of Minnesota.

Esslinger, A. A., 1968. Certification for high school coaches. *JOHPER* **39** (October) : 42-45.

Frost, R. B., 1971. The director and the staff. In E. S. Steitz (ed). *Administration of athletics in colleges and universities.* Washington, D.C.: AAHPER.

————, 1975. *Physical education: foundations, practices, principles.* Reading, Mass: Addison Wesley.

————, and S. J. Marshall, 1977. *Administration of physical education and athletics: concepts and practices.* Dubuque, Iowa: William C. Brown Company.

Kimball, E.R. 1955. Current practices in the control of intercollegiate athletics Doctoral dissertation. Eugene, Ore.: University of Oregon.

Marshall, S. J. , 1969. The organizational relationship between physical education and intercollegiate athletics in American colleges and universities. Doctoral dissertation. Springfield, Mass.: Springfield College.

NCAA manual, 1976-77, 1977. Shawnee Mission, Kan.: NCAA Publishing Service.

Resick, M. C., and C. E. Erickson, 1975. *Intercollegiate and interscholastic athletics for men and women.* Reading, Mass.: Addison-Wesley.

Scott, H. A., 1951. *Competitive sports in schools and colleges.* New York: Harper and Brothers.

Shea, E. J., and E. E. Wieman, 1976. *Administrative policies for intercollegiate athletics.* Springfield, Ill.: Charles C. Thomas.

Sports programs for girls and women: A DGWS position paper, 1974. *JOHPER* **45** (April): 12.

43

Sex-Integrated College Physical Education Programs

Marjorie Blaufarb

At all other levels of education, course offerings in the general physical education program at the university level may not be provided separately on the basis of sex, nor may participation therein be refused on such basis. In

---

*   This material was extracted from an article entitled, "Complying with Title IX of the Education Amendments of 1972 in Physical Education and High School Sports Programs," and published by AAHPER in 1975.

practice this means that curriculum offerings may not be sex-designated, and a more recent ruling by the Director of the Office of Civil Rights/HEW, in answer to an inquiry, stated that physical education departments should not be sex-designated even though courses are open to both sexes, because such designations have a chilling effect on students.

The regulations to effectuate Title IX make no curriculum requirements except with regard to open access. The College and University Physical Education Council of the National Association for Sport and Physical Education (Task Force 1975) recommended curriculum standards for the general program as follows:

A broad range of course experiences should constitute a reservoir from which students may select activities designed to meet their needs and interests, and at times and of duration compatible with other university pursuits. While faculty qualifications, space, and facilities may influence course offerings, a quality program should provide a knowledge and understanding of the discipline of physical education through experiences in the following areas: individual, dual, and team sports; rhythms, aquatics, combatives, conditioning, sports appreciation, and recreational carry-over skills. Emphasis should be given to the less traditional areas of survival skills, movement repertoire, and communicative skills, as well as movement for the pure joy of movement.

Survival skills can be classified as either physiological or safety related. Physiological survival involves nutrition and exercise levels adequate to maintain the muscular system, organs, and body structure at an efficient level of health. Safety survival skills are usually related to quick reactions and the capacity to use available strength effectively in an emergency. Techniques designed to avoid bodily injury during participation in sports are part of this instruction.

It will be seen that within the range of offerings suggested there is none that is impossible to present on a sex-integrated basis within the limits set by the federal regulations, which are that in activities that include bodily contact the sexes may be separated within the class. In a report on the status of general instruction programs of physical education in four-year colleges and universities during 1971-72, Joseph B. Oxendine of Temple University stated that "coeducational courses continue to grow to the extent that the majority of physical education courses are now coeducational." This indicates that by this time there is wide experience at the college level in sex-integrated programs.

Most problems reported seem to be concerned with evaluation and grading. It is important to use a grading system consistent with the objectives of the course and the policies of the school as a whole. These policies should be stated clearly and understood by all students prior to the beginning of the instructional phase of the course. One should bear in mind that, where use of a single standard for measuring skill or progress in a physical education class has an adverse impact on members of one sex, a different standard or standards that do not have such an effect must be used. The use of different standards for measuring progress would take care of situations where grades are given based, among other criteria, on strength factors. In a bowling class, for example, where experience has shown that a sufficient number of male students can achieve an average of 200 but females for the most part can only achieve 180, it would be permissible to adopt those different average scores as grading standards. Faculty members will naturally be observant of changes in the skill levels of students since, with greater opportunities, these will undoubtedly change.

Another situation that would call for variations in class organization and good judgment in deciding how students would oppose one another would be in a self-defense class. If the men in such a class were always teamed with women of the same size or smaller than themselves, they would never gain experience in defending themselves against another man or a bigger person. This type of activity would call for variations in organization to allow for this problem.

Where there is some doubt about a reasonable standard to use in assessing progress or competence, teachers can appeal to the governing body of the sport involved for information on the standards it uses for mixed participation.

Offering courses at the beginning, intermediate, and advanced levels may improve the learning situation when courses are being integrated, and it may be that four or five levels could be made available in some cases. Foundations of physical education courses, which combine intellectual content with laboratory experiences, have been sex-integrated frequently and fit well into the philosophy of Title IX. Such courses try to assist students in gaining enough information about the value of fitness and the nature of their personal needs that they can make intelligent decisions concerning the role of physical activity throughout life (Task Force 1975).

This chapter was not designed to look at professional preparation programs for physical education teachers and coaches. However, one area in professional preparation should be addressed—different requirements for graduation of male and female students are not only violations of the Title IX regulations but would make it more difficult for beginning teachers to teach effectively in the sex-integrated situations they will find in schools.

REFERENCE

Task force of the College and University Physical Education Council of the National Association for Sport and Physical Education of the AAHPER, 1975. *JOHPER.* **46** (September) : 24-28.

PHYSICAL EDUCATION, FITNESS, AND SPORTS IN THE ARMED FORCES

Introduction

This Section points out the extent of involvement and the kinds of programs of physical education/athletics included in the military establishments of the United States. Statements are included for all five of the armed forces, all four of the military academies, but only two of the military institutes/colleges.

Three major types of programs appear to prevail in the armed forces:

1. Physical readiness training programs, mandatory for those undergoing recruit training or training for specific tasks, such as paratrooper
2. General physical fitness programs of self-conditioning and weight control, recommended but not required for all personnel
3. Sports programs, including recreational, intramural, and interpost contests.

All of the Military Services employ some type of periodic physical fitness testing with slightly different requirements for male and female personnel. The regularity with which the tests are employed and the importance given them varies from service to service and from unit to unit, depending upon the attitudes of local commanders who are ultimately responsible for the physical well-being of their personnel. The requirements of the United States Marine Corps appear to be the most demanding. All of the services have athletics organizations that make it possible for their outstanding athletes to compete in national (AAU) and international (Pan American and Olympic Games) contests.

The military academies place a great deal of importance on the physical education of their personnel. Typical is the United States Military Academy, which requires participation in (1) an extensive physical fitness and sports activities program, (2) attendance in lectures on physiology of exercise and health-related topics, and (3) proficiency in physical training leadership including coaching, officiating, and administrating of sports programs.

All of the academies employ periodic physical fitness testing with standards differing slightly for men and women. Results and follow-up on these tests are treated much more seriously than in the military services.

The academies are probably best known for their extensive intramurals and athletics programs in which large percentages of their students participate. Some academies require participation in one or the other. All of the academies are members of the NCAA, and the athletic exploits of "Army," "Navy," and "Air Force" are well known to the American public.

The military institutes and colleges appear to function somewhat like typical American colleges but with a military emphasis.

The physical education program at the Virginia Military Institute includes lectures in the psychological and physiological aspects of exercise, instruction in developmental activities (weight training, physical fitness, etc.), as well as extensive intramurals and athletics programs. All students are given the Cooper Aerobic Test.

The physical education program at The Citadel contains many of the above features. In addition, it is unusual among establishments with a military emphasis in that it offers an undergraduate degree in physical education.

Section Editors

Marvin H. Eyler is professor and dean of the college of physical education, recreation, and health at the University of Maryland. He obtained the A.B. degree from Houghten College and the M.S. and Ph.D. degrees from the University of Illinois, Champaign. His primary interest areas are history of sport, social science of sport, and physical education. He has served as president of the North American Society of Sport History. He is a Fellow of the American Academy of Physical Education, and the American College of Sports Medicine. He has been very active in AAHPERD, the National College Physical Education Association for Men, the Eastern District of the AAHPERD, and the National Christian Physical Education Association. He has published extensively in his areas of primary interest and has served as associate editor and editor of *Quest*.

Benjamin H. Massey is professor of physical education at the University of Illinois, Urbana. He received the B.A. degree from Erskine College. He taught and coached at the secondary and junior college level and entered military service where he served as a physical training officer in the Army Air Force. The M.S. and Ph.D. degrees, with a major in physical education, were received from the University of Illinois. At the University of Maryland, 1950-1964, he directed the exercise research laboratory, coordinated graduate studies in the College of Physical Education, Health, and Recreation, and taught in the areas of exercise physiology, kinesiology, and measurement. From 1964 to 1969 he was a professor at the Pennsylvania State University, returning to the University of Illinois in 1969 to assume directorship of the Physical Fitness Research Laboratory upon retirement of Dr. T.K. Cureton. He relinquished his administrative responsibilities in 1977 and now devotes full time to advising graduate students and researching and teaching in the area of human performance and exercise. He has authored and coauthored numerous research articles and a number of books.

44

The United States Army

Paul Hunsicker and James Dawson

The United States Army dates to June 14, 1775, when the Second Continental Congress authorized the creation of the Continental Army. From colonial days to 1947 the army organization and title changed to meet the defense needs of a growing and expanding nation.

In 1947 the title of the Department of the Army was established and the department was a separate service of the Department of Defense by the National Security Act of that same year. The Department of the Army consists of the executive part of the department and all field headquarters forces, reserve components, installations, activities, and functions under the control or supervision of the Secretary of the Army.

The overall function of the Department of the Army is the preparation of land forces necessary for the effective prosecution of war except as otherwise assigned and, in accordance with integrated mobilization plans, for the expansion of the peacetime components of the army to meet the needs of war.

PHYSICAL FITNESS

The army physical fitness program, a function of the Deputy Chief of Staff of Operations, Department of the Army, is specified by Army Regulation 600-9. This regulation divides the program into four parts: (1) a personal fitness program for individuals who do not benefit from a unit-level program; (2) unit-level physical readiness training conducted at the company, troop, or battery levels as part of the overall training program; (3) army sports program for those personnel who desire to participate in sports competition; and (4) weight control program for those overweight and underweight personnel needing to attain an optimum weight.

Individual Physical Fitness Program

All male and female personnel who are not engaged actively in a unit-level program are encouraged to develop and follow a personal program of physical fitness. The purpose of the individual program is to develop a high level of physical fitness in personnel of all ages through such activities as calisthenics, weight training, jogging, and life-time sports.

Physical Readiness Training

This part of the fitness program is mandatory for cadets, trainees, students undergoing instruction in service schools, in special courses such as officer candidate, ranger, and airborne training, and as part of the training programs of combat, combat service, and combat service support units. Both men and women of all ranks are required to participate. These programs emphasize vigorous activity for both men and women. Activities consist of conditioning exercises, strength circuits, jogging, cross-country running, relays, team contests, team sports, water survival (drown proofing) training, and swimming. In addition, men participate in obstacle and confidence courses, grass drills, and combatives. The purpose of this program is to develop a high level of fitness and prepare the individual to meet the physical demands of the job for which he or she is being trained.

The frequency of physical fitness testing is determined by field commanders. The type of tests for various categories of personnel are prescribed by the Department of the Army. Male personnel take the following tests: (1) trainees undergoing basic combat training (first seven weeks) are tested using the basic physical fitness test; (2) trainees undergoing advanced individual training during the second period of individual training, and also all unit personnel, undergo the advanced physical fitness test; (3) students and faculty of service schools, and unit personnel who maintain responsibility for their own physical fitness program, undergo the staff and specialist physical fitness test; (4) ranger, special forces, and airborne students are given special qualifying physical fitness tests; and (5) personnel over 40 years of age who volunteer to be tested are given the army minimum physical fitness tests. Female personnel undergoing basic training and advanced individual training are tested on the basic training and advanced individual physical fitness test; female personnel assigned to field units are administered the permanent party physical fitness test.

Research and development of individual physical fitness and physical readiness training programs are the responsibility of the United States Army Infantry School, Fort Benning, Georgia. Training programs, literature, training media, equipment and facility requirements, and physical fitness tests are developed by the school and approved by the Training and Doctrine Command at Fort Monroe, Virginia and by the Department of the Army prior to adoption.

Army Sports Program

This phase of the physical fitness program is conducted at the following four levels: (1) unit level recreational sports, (2) intramural sport competition, (3) varsity or interpost sports competition, and (4) All-Army and All-Service Championship competition. As an extension of the all-Service championships, individuals or teams are selected to compete in the Conseil International du Sports Militaire, the Pan American Games, and the Olympic Games.

The purposes of these programs are manifold and include: (1) introducing personnel to sports, (2) improving physical fitness, (3) providing wholesome leisure-time activities, (4) encouraging social contacts, (5) contributing to unit, base, and service morale, and (6) improving interservice relations.

Weight Control

Weight control is part of the physical fitness program and consists of a cooperative effort by the local commander and the surgeon at each installation. The purpose is to maintain control of body weight throughout the command as prescribed by Army Regulation 632-1. The program consists of prescribed diet and exercise as appropriate to the individual. Commanders refer overweight or underweight personnel to medical officers who in turn prescribe remedial programs. Individuals may volunteer to undergo the program. Remedial action is carried out under the supervision of medical personnel to include reconditioning specialists, who generally have had professional schooling in physical therapy, or by the individual under the supervision of command personnel. The proponent for this part of the program is the Surgeon General, Department of the Army, Washington, D.C.

LEADERSHIP

The majority of leadership for the physical fitness program is provided by military personnel. Civilian sports specialists are employed at the special service level at each post or installation to assist the special services officer to organize, direct and supervise the intramural and interpost sports. A civilian physical education specialist is part of the staff at the infantry school to assist with the assigned mission of research and development. Generally, noncommissioned officers serve as instructors, although officers are utilized in that capacity also. Officers serve as supervisors of physical readiness training and as unit special service officers to manage the sports participation of teams or individuals representing that particular unit.

Military personnel are trained in organization and administration of physical readiness training and sports. Noncommissioned officers receive instruction at the noncommissioned officers academies, at drill sergeant schools, and as students at branch service schools such as armor school, signal school, infantry school, etc. Officer candidates, basic officer students (usually second lieutenants), and advanced officer students (usually captains) receive instruction at branch service schools as part of their course of study.

45

The United States Navy

Philip J. Rasch and David A. Garcia

The commanding officer of each U.S. Navy unit is charged with the responsibility for the maintenance of adequate levels of physical fitness by the personnel under his command. Voluntary participation in sports programs is considered the best means of achieving and maintaining the desired level of physical fitness. Under certain conditions obesity may be considered grounds for separation from the service.

Any male who has not reached his 40th birthday is expected to be able at any time to demonstrate the minimum physical achievements set forth in the Table 45.1. Failure to perform at the required level in any one of the events constitutes a failure for the entire test. Minimum requirements are not prescribed for males over 40, but they are expected to maintin a level of fitness sufficiently high to insure efficient performance of assigned duties.

Women members of the navy must maintain a level of physical fitness that will develop proper health, physical poise, and good personal appearance. The importance of proper weight control is emphasized. At least once each quarter, they must meet the minimum performance requirements in a total time of 15 minutes, as shown in Table 45.2.

Table 45.1

Minimum Performance Standards for Navy Male Personnel

Category	Minimum performance		
	Ages 17-25	Ages 26-33	Ages 34-39
I. Arm and shoulder strength			
Push ups	20	18	15
or			
Pull ups	4	4	4
II. Abdominal and trunk strength			
Sit ups	30	27	25
III. Explosive leg power			
Jump and reach	15″	14″	13″
or			
Standing broad jump	6′8″	6′6″	6′4″
IV. Endurance			
300 yard shuttle run	60 secs	62 secs	64 secs
or			
Stationary run	200 counts in 3 mins	200 counts in 3 mins	200 counts in 3 mins

Table 45.2

Minimum Physical Performance Standards for
Navy Female Personnel

Category	Minimum performance
Bend and bob	16 repetitions
Standing two-way stretch	16 repetitions
Supine body lifter	16 repetitions
Supine body curl	8 repetitions
Swan exercise	12 repetitions
Knee pushups	12 repetitions
Supine body twister	12 repetitions
Jog and jump	4 repetitions

REFERENCE

Department of the Navy, 1974, BuPers Instruction 6100.2B (November).

46

The United States Air Force

Marvin H. Eyler

The Department of the Air Force was established and made a separate service of the Department of Defense by the National Security Act of 1947. The Department of the Air Force includes the executive branch and all field headquarters forces, reserve components, installations, activities, and functions under the supervision of the Secretary of the Air Force. The United States Air Force, as such, is within the Department of the Air Force. The air force consists of (1) the regular air force, the Air National Guard of the United States, the Air National Guard while in the service of the United States, and the Air Force Reserve; (2) all persons appointed or enlisted in, or conscripted into, the air force without component; (3) all air force organizations, with their installations and supporting and auxiliary combat, training, administrative, and logistic elements; and (4) all members of the air force, including those not assigned to units, necessary to form the basis for a complete and immediate mobilization for the national defense in the event of a national emergency. The air force includes aviation forces, both combat and service.

The overall function of the United States Air Force is the preparation of air forces necessary for effective prosecution of war and participation in the defense of the United States as occasion requires. Specific functions include: organizing, training, and equipping air force forces for the conduct of prompt and sustained combat operations in the air—to defend the United States air attack in accordance with doctrines established by the Joint Chiefs of Staff, to gain and maintain general air supremacy, to defeat enemy air forces, to control vital air areas, and to establish local air superiority except as otherwise assigned. The air force coordinates its efforts with the other services through strategic air warfare, joint amphibious and airborne operations, and logistical air support of the army, including air lift of supplies and men, aerial photography, tactical reconnaissance, and interdiction of enemy land power and communications.

The command organizational structure of the air force is designed around a functional and geographical pattern. Functionally the USAF organization may be classified as: offensive, defensive, supporting, training, and researching. In some instances a single command may be responsible for two or more functional elements. For example, USAFE and PACAF have both an offensive and defensive responsibility. The simplicity of this organizational arrangement facilitates administration and expedites action in the performance of assigned functions. The Chief of Staff, directly responsible to the Secretary of the Air Force, has several necessary personal staff members and six deputy chiefs. The major commands, some 17 in number, are responsible directly to the Chief of Staff.

PHYSICAL TRAINING AND FITNESS PROGRAMS

The air force physical fitness program, a function of general military training, is required in basic training centers and at cadet centers. Each male military person under 50 years of age is required to have a copy of AFP 50-56, the USAF aerobics program. The purpose of this program and that of the women's XBX plan (AFP 50-5-2) is to develop a high level of fitness among airmen and airwomen of all ages by providing an easily followed, interesting, and increasingly demanding program. The exercises include only those that stress the heart and lungs.

The physical fitness programs for men allow the choice of any one of six different options: walking, running, cycling, swimming, stationary running, and a handball, basketball, or squash program. Each of these programs has norms based upon ages 29 and under, 30-39, 40-49, and over 50 years of age.

The XBX plan of physical fitness for airwomen is taken from the Royal Canadian Air Force 5BX program. The program is recommended, not required. The exercises are designed to improve the general condition by increasing muscle tone, muscular strength, muscular endurance and flexibility, and the efficiency of the cardiorespiratory functions.

INTRAMURAL SPORTS

The intramural sports program supplements the base instructional program and has as its objectives: to provide for the wholesome use of leisure time, to provide opportunities for social contacts, to contribute to the development of squadron and unit spirit, to create interest in sports participation, and to provide a variety of sports activities that will provide opportunities for year-round participation for all base personnel.

All air bases have voluntary programs in intramurals. Usually league competition is encouraged for points toward the annual Base Commander's Trophy. Although varying from base to base, the intramural program is usually the responsibility of the sports training officer or the special service officer.

INTERSERVICE ATHLETICS

The USAF sports program is authorized by AF Regulation 215-6. The program covers not only interbase competition but USAF worldwide championships.

It also includes interservice competition, national championships, AAU events, Olympic, and Pan American games. The air force encourages men and women to participate extensively in organized competitive sports.

The program is the responsibility of the Assistant Deputy Chief of Staff for Military Personnel, whose office provides policy and staff supervision. More specifically, the functions include:

1. Planning and supervising a full and diversified sports program to meet leisure-time needs of air force personnel

2. Supervising preparation of directives to further air force sports activities

3. Maintaining liaison with other military and civilian groups engaged in promoting sports activities, such as the United States Olympic Committee, Amateur Athletics Union of the United States, Amateur Softball Association and other similar national and international groups

4. Designating an air force representative on the Interservice Sports Council. (This council consists of one officer each from the air force, army, navy, and marine corps.)

5. Assisting in preparing budget estimates, allocating funds and equipment, and planning sports facilities

6. Initiating and coordinating plans for air force participation in high-level air force and interservice competition, and in authorized regional, national, and international nonservice competition.

Each major command establishes and supervises a comprehensive sports program and encourages, within limitation of time and funds, worldwide competition. The specific responsibility for this program at the base level has been given to the base personnel services officer.

Interbase competition is presently limited to baseball, basketball, football, and boxing. Varsity sports for women, following the rules of the National Association of Girl's and Women's Sports, include volleyball, golf, bowling, tennis, and swimming.

Members of the air force are authorized by law and by Department of Defense directives to train for, attend, and participate in the Counseil International du Sport Militaire (CISM), Pan American, and Olympic Games, and any other international amateur sports events when the Secretary of State determines that the interest of the United States will be served by such participation. Authority is also extended to administer personnel for planning, observing, or coordinating matters pertaining to authorized international amateur sports competitions.

Normally the air force sports program will be supported with appropriated funds. When these funds are not available, nonappropriated funds may be used to procure additional quantities of authorized table-of-allowances items and certain other items not on TA, as well as essential services required to conduct or support programmed activities at all levels of competition.

Appropriated funds will be used to construct, improve, rehabilitate, relocate, maintain, and operate facilities for sports participation. Normally nonappropriated funds will not be used to procure land or for construction.

The major responsibility for organizing and holding USAF worldwide championships is assigned to Hq USAF. USAF worldwide championships are opened to all MAJCOMs. However, certain smaller commands are grouped together in an organization designated as UNICOM. Member commands of UNICOM select one representative team among them to participate in each worldwide team championship. Oversea bases will participate with the major oversea commands having jurisdiction over such bases.

The responsibilities of Hq USAF in worldwide competition are:

1. Designate a host base that will appoint a qualified project officer to supervise the conduct of the championship

2. Brief the host-base project officer on the responsibilities and on the development of plans for conducting the championship

3. Approve tournament brackets or competitive schedules, selection of officials, and expenditure of funds for the championship

4. Arrange for continued participation, if any, of USAF representatives in higher level competition

5. Provide appropriate awards

6. Announce as far in advance as is consistent with proper planning:
   a) address of the host base
   b) dates for the competition
   c) deadlines for submission of entries to the host base
   d) special instructions pertaining to personal and team equipment

47

The United States Marine Corps

Philip J. Rasch and David A. Garcia

The United States Marine Corps physical education program for men is designed to improve the trooper's physical fitness for combat, regardless of his age, grade, or duties. Its objective is to develop the man's ability to march a long distance carrying a heavy pack and still have the physical resources necessary to close with and destroy the enemy. Consequently, the emphasis is on stamina, that is, muscular and cardiovascular endurance and strength.

Marines are required to engage in a continuing and progressively strenuous physical conditioning program for a minimum of three hours per week, with five hours recommended. It should consist of at least three exercise periods a week of not less than 60 minutes each. The responsibility for meeting this requirement is shared by the individual marine and his commanding officer. In addition, the marine must present a trim military appearance; obesity is considered grounds for hospitalization and/or discharge.

A physical fitness test is administered twice a year. Successful completion requires that the marine demonstrate acceptable performance in each test event and achieve at least the minimum passing score for his age group. Scoring is based on a maximum of 300 points, 100 for each of the three events. Five points are awarded for each pullup, to a maximum of 20 repetitions. One point is awarded for each situp up to 60 repetitions; all additional repetitions are given two points each. To earn 100 points in the three-mile run, participants must cover the distance in 18 minutes. Six points are subtracted for each additional minute required. Standards established for marines 45 years of age and under are shown in Table 47.1. Failure to meet the minimum standards in any one event constitutes failure of the entire test. Men who fail the test are placed on a supervised development program.

Marines over 46 years of age are encouraged to take the test if medically capable. If they do not, they must engage in some form of physical conditioning program commensurate with their age and physical ability. In addition, all members of combat units must demonstrate their ability to march 25 miles in eight hours while carrying packs, helments, and weapons (unit endurance test).

The goals of the program for women marines are the development of levels of physical fitness that will enable them to accomplish their duties with

Table 47.1

Minimum Physical Performance Standards for Marines 45 and Under

Age	Pullups	Bent knee situps	3-mile run (minutes)	Subtotal points	Required additional points	Passing score
17-26	3	40	28	95	40	135
27-39	3	35	29	84	26	110
40-45	3	35	30	78	7	85

energy and dispatch, control weight, and maintain a satisfactory physical appearance. Women marines are expected to engage in a minimum of three hours of physical conditioning each week, consisting of not less than three exercise periods of a minimum of 30 minutes each. Minimal physical performance standards for women marines are shown in Table 47.2. Failure in any one event constitutes failure in the entire test.

Women marines over 36 years of age are not required to take the physical performance test but must maintain their personal appearance, weight, and physical fitness at levels that will permit their assignment to any billet appropriate to their age and grade.

Historically the marine corps has supported intramural and varsity athletics strongly. Their success in the boxing competition of the Conseil International du Sport Militaire has been particularly noteworthy.

Of historical interest is the fact that in 1967 the marine corps established a Physical Fitness Academy at Quantico, Virginia, as part of an effort to reorganize and revitalize the physical training program in the corps. Courses were instituted for physical training instructors, close combat instructors, water safety and survival instructors, and physical fitness coordinators

Table 47.2

Minimum Physical Performance Standards
for Female Marines 35 and Under

Event	Passing score	
	Ages 18-25	Ages 26-35
Four-block shuttle run	27 seconds	27 seconds
Knee pushups	30	25
Bent knee situps	28	23
Jump and reach	11 inches	11 inches
600-yard run-walk	2 min 42 sec	3 min

(officers). A research facility was included. Professional guidance was provided by an advisory council composed of distinguished scientists and educators throughout the country. The academy was abolished in 1973, an apparent casualty of President Nixon's economy program.

REFERENCE

Marine Corps, 1971. Order 6100.3F (December 17).

48

The United States Coast Guard

Benjamin H. Massey, Louis C. Steele, Berry L. Meaux, and R. A. Schultz

The U.S. Coast Guard, smallest of the armed forces, was founded in 1790 when the first United States Congress authorized 10 small boats to protect the nation's coast against smugglers and enforce custom laws. From this small beginning, the coast guard grew in strength to a peak force in World War II of 171,000 men spread in units throughout the world. In the early 1970s there were a little more than 37,000 officers and enlisted men on active duty, with an equal number on reserve status.

The coast guard, as the principal maritime law enforcement agency of the federal government, has the mission of enforcing or assisting in the enforcement of all applicable federal laws upon the high seas and waters subject to the jurisdiction of the United States, and of maintaining at all times a state of readiness for military service.

Specific functions of the coast guard include: (1) enforcing maritime law, (2) saving and protecting life and property, (3) providing navigational aid to maritime commerce and to transoceanic air commerce, (4) promoting the efficiency and safety of the U.S. Merchant Marine, and (5) readiness at all times for military operations.

The coast guard, in fulfilling its function, consists of many units constituting a network extending from the arctic to the antarctic, and from Asia to the Mediterranean. The units include lighthouses, long range aid to navigation

(LORAN) stations, search and rescue stations, cutters, icebreakers, and air stations equipped with helicopters and fixed wing search planes.

Administratively, the U.S. Coast Guard is housed under the Department of Transportation, becoming in time of war, and at the discretion of the President, an arm of the navy. Organized into 12 districts, each with its district commander, the coast guard has fewer large bases than the other services. Two of the coast guard's larger installations are the recruit-training bases situated at Cape May, New Jersey, and Alameda, California. The coast guard maintains technical schools, an officer candidate school at Yorktown, Virginia, and the Coast Guard Academy at New London, Connecticut, which has the mission of training cadets for positions of leadership as officers. Organizationally, with respect to such things as officer ranks, uniform regulations, pay scale, and general codes, the coast guard is similar to the navy.

Physical education in the coast guard is focused primarily on the development and maintenance of physical fitness. Regulations mandate the following with respect to physical education (Coast Guard Personnel Manual).

Objectives

The general objective of this program is to maintain that level of physical fitness among male coast guard military personnel that is necessary for efficient and alert execution of assigned military tasks without undue fatigue and with ample energy to meet unforeseen emergencies. The specific objectives of this program are:

1. To present standards of physical fitness for all male coast guard military personnel graduated according to age
2. To establish requirements for testing and reporting the physical fitness of male coast guard military personnel
3. To provide guidance for unit and individual programs of physical education and weight control
4. To prescribe policy regarding the disposition of male coast guard military personnel who cannot meet the minimum physical fitness standards of this program.

Responsibilites

The commanding officer of a Coast Guard unit is responsible for the health and welfare of his crew, including its physical fitness. Maintaining physical fitness of assigned personnel includes:

1. Evaluating personnel physical fitness
2. Comparing this evaluation with prescribed standards

3. Enabling personnel to meet, or exceed, these standards through:
   a) voluntary sports programs
   b) unit physical education exercises
   c) individual programs of self-conditioning and weight control
4. Recording the physical fitness of personnel in terms of prescribed standards.

All male military personnel under 40 years of age and on active duty, including initial active duty for training, are required to participate in this program. Personnel over 40 years of age are encouraged to maintain standards of physical fitness through voluntary participation in the program, but are required to control their weight following the standards in Article 3-C-23, Medical Manual (CG-294).

Physical Fitness Standards

Table 48.1 contains the minimum physical achievements required for all male coast guard military personnel under 40 years of age on active duty, including

Table 48.1
Minimum Physical Performance Standards for Coast Guard Male Personnel*

Category	Minimum performance		
	Ages 17-25	Ages 26-33	Ages 34-39
I. Arm and shoulder strength (one event only required)			
Push ups	20	18	15
or			
Pull ups	4	4	3
II. Abdominal and trunk strength			
Sit ups	30	27	25
III. Explosive leg power (one event only required)			
Jump and reach	15"	14"	13"
or			
Standing broad jump	6'8"	6'6"	6'4"
IV. Endurance (one event only required)			
300 yard shuttle run	60 secs	62 secs	64 secs
or			
Stationary run	200 counts in 3 mins.	200 counts in 3 mins.	200 counts in 3 mins.

* Failure to perform any one of the minimum requirements constitutes an unsatisfactory performance for the entire test.

initial active duty for training. Commands with the responsibility for training of newly procured personnel including cadets, officer candidates, and recruits are authorized to establish for these personnel higher minimum standards of physical fitness subject to approval by the commandant. In order that newly procured personnel develop a proficiency in swimming, specific commands shall include in their programs minimum standards of swimming and lifesaving; therefore, the Superintendent, Coast Guard Academy, shall require all cadets to: (1) swim at least 100 yards unassisted; and (2) pass the *intermediate* swimming requirements of the American National Red Cross.

The Commanding Officer, Reserve Training Center, Yorktown, shall require all officer candidates to: (1) swim at least 50 meters unassisted; and (2) pass the *beginner* swimming requirements of the American National Red Cross.

The Commanding Officers Training Center, Cape May, and Training/ Supply Center, Alameda, shall require all recruits, both regular and reserve, to: (1) swim at least 50 yards unassisted; and (2) pass the *beginner* swimming requirements of the American National Red Cross.

All male personnel who have not reached their 40th birthday will be subject to meeting these minimum requirements at any time. Personnel may be excused from testing for medical reasons. However, they should be reinstated in the normal testing schedule as soon as they return to unrestricted duty. Overweight in itself is not considered adequate medical excuse from testing. However, when conditions resulting from overweight are such as to incur possible harm as a result of attempted performance, excuse can be given.

Periodic testing of personnel should be scheduled by commanding officers to insure that the minimum requirements are being maintained. All required personnel should be tested at least once each quarter, and are subject to testing by inspection parties at any time.

Commands at sea are not required to administer this prescribed testing during periods in which adverse weather conditions prevail. However, this is not intended to imply that personnel so involved in operations at sea under these conditions are exempt from the minimum requirements of these prescribed tests.

Commanding officers should insure that all affected personnel have undergone adequate preparation prior to scheduling of the test. Attempted performances by personnel not prepared adequately could result in unwarranted injuries. Personnel considered to be physically incapable of attempting performance of minimum requirements should be referred to the nearest medical facility for examination.

The regulations also specify that an unsatisfactory performance may be attributed to several causes including excess body weight, lack of coordination, and organic deficiencies; and that commanding officers are to take appropriate measures to correct the situation. The measures to be taken may incorporate a medical examination, prescribed therapeutic programs, and conditioning activities including vigorous sports, group calisthenics, weight training, walking, running, and swimming. Consistent failure to meet minimal physical fitness standards can lead to stringent action including disenrollment from officer candidate school or retention at a base until a minimal level of fitness is achieved.

Overweight is of special concern. "Overweight personnel of the coast guard are a threat to themselves because of the effect upon their health; they are a threat to others who depend upon them for effective leadership. They cannot properly represent the coast guard; and they do not set the required leadership example" (Coast Guard Personnel Manual).

Overweight individuals are subject to a medical evaluation, mandatory therapeutic regimens to reduce weight, and in extreme cases, medical board and command action including separation from the service.

At Cape May, New Jersey, and Alameda, California, the eastern and western division recruit training bases respectively, recruits are subjected to a well-structured program of physical training and athletics designed to develop an acceptable level of physical fitness. Structured programs, but not as extensive, except for the Coast Guard Academy, may be found at other bases. Following completion of recruit training or officer school, maintenance of an acceptable level of physical fitness is primarily an individual matter. A check is made quarterly, however, in the form of the prescribed physical fitness test.

The program for recruits at the two training bases consists of daily periods of calisthenics plus approximately 30 hours over the eight-week training period devoted to scheduled instruction in basic sports, swimming, drown-proofing, intramural sports, and special remedial classes for those recruits who fail to fulfill the minimum physical fitness test requirements or swimming requirements.

At the two recruit bases, and at the Coast Guard Academy, New London, Connecticut, facilities are adequate and a well-rounded program of intramural and varsity athletics is maintained. Other bases of lesser size have relatively limited intramural and varsity sports programs, depending upon size and the persuasion of the commanding officer. Many stations and units are too small to support any type of structured program.

Physical education leadership rests with officers and enlisted men with other duty classifications, and a limited number of civilians hired as physical education and recreation specialists. The coast guard does not have a physical training MOS as such, but officers and enlisted men may devote full time to their physical training and sports assignments.

REFERENCE

Coast Guard personnel manual. Section J—Physical Fitness Program. Section 3-j-1 through 3-j-6.

SUGGESTED READINGS

Pictorial report, C. 1969. Alameda, Calif.: U.S. Guard and Supply Center.

U.S. Department of Transportation, 1972. *United States Coast Guard, ships, planes, and stations.* Washington, D.C.: U.S. Governfment Printing Office, CG-214.

49

The United States Military Academy

Paul Hunsicker and Frank Kobes

The United States Military Academy was founded in 1802 as an all-male institution. The institution is now coeducational with the first class of 10 women admitted in summer 1976.

Pierre Thomas was appointed on March 1, 1814, as civilian instructor of fencing with the title of Sword Master. As such he was probably one of the first fulltime physical educators in any educational institution in America. The title was changed to Master of the Sword in 1881 and Director of Physical Education in 1949.

The current physical education program has as its aim to graduate men and women who are physically prepared to meet the performance challenges of a military career. The specific objectives are:

A. Physical ability

1. To develop optimum body strength, endurance, coordination, and similar physical characteristics that contribute to the development and maintenance of physical and organic efficiency
2. To develop skills which aid in efficient performance
3. To provide broad experience and develop sufficient skill in sports and activities that will enable the cadet to remain physically active throughout his or her military career

B. Applied Physiology

1. To gain basic knowledge of anatomy, physiology of exercise, and mechanics of movement

273

2. To understand and appreciate nutrition and weight control
3. To know the modern concepts of personal health

C. Physical Training Leadership

1. To understand the organization and conduct of military physical training
2. To be able to coach, officiate, and administer an army sports program

D. Concomitant learning

1. To develop personal pride in maintaining good physical condition, that is, "staying in shape"
2. To develop the following desirable character traits and emotional and social qualities: sportsmanship, teamwork (of vital concern in all phases of the program), aggressiveness, self-confidence, determination, and the ability to think and act quickly and effectively under pressure

The program recognizes individual differences and is sufficiently flexible to the extent that cadets have the opportunity to advance according to their own capabilities rather than according to the average of their particular activity class. The following achievements are offered as a guideline:

A. Required. Each cadet must:

1. Complete the standard course by demonstrating adequate skill in basic elements of physical performance as measured by boxing, wrestling, and gymnastics (self-defense for women in place of boxing and wrestling), water survival techniques, carry-over sports, and leadership of military physical training
2. Participate in the elective course—a variety of elective carry-over sports and activities
3. Maintain standards of physical condition
4. Understand the continuing requirement for physical fitness

B. Desired. Each cadet should:

1. Coach an athletic team, officiate, or serve as a member in the athletic chain of responsibility
2. Participate as a team member in at least one contact sport

The four-year program has a heavy emphasis on physical development at the fourth class (freshman) level. This is phased into more individual sports activities and leadership experiences so that by the time the cadet reaches first class (senior) level, the purpose of the program is to provide leadership experience along with the development of carry-over sports.

The cadet's level of fitness is monitored throughout his four years via an army physical fitness exam, physical ability tests, an indoor obstacle course and a two-mile run. A special feature includes a guidance program, which provides assistance to any cadet needing or desiring help in physical education.

An extensive intramural program (see Table 49.1) provides broad sports experience, physical activity, and leadership experience in athletics. The program is administered by the cadets through the Cadet Brigade Commander and subordinate staff officers under the supervision of the associate professor for intramural athletics.

The Military Academy is a member of the National Collegiate Athletic Association and the Eastern Collegiate Athletic Conference, as well as other sports associations. Competition is carried on in approximately 18 sports.

The administrative organization is shown in Fig. 49.5. The physical education faculty consists of a permanent professor who serves as director, 11 army uniformed civilian physical education specialists who are permanently appointed, 25 rotating army officers, and 10 enlisted personnel/civilian instructors who must be college graduates with a major in physical education.

The officers assigned to this office are predominantly West Point graduates who have had six or more years prior service in the army. Assignments are usually for three years and in most cases are preceded by one year of graduate study at a civilian university. The director is a Military Academy graduate with broad study in the field of physical education, as well as

Table 49.1
A Typical Intramural Schedule at the U.S. Military Academy

Fall	Winter	Spring
Company competition in flickerball	Company competition in basketball	Company competition in boat racing
Tackle football	Boxing	Cross country
Orienteering	Handball	Lacrosse
Soccer	Squash	Touch football
Tennis	Swimming	Water polo
Track	Volleyball	Brigade open tennis tournament
	Wrestling	Variety of individual and dual sports activities
	Brigade open competition in boxing, wrestling, handball, and squash	

275

Figs. 49.1-49.4 Men and women participate in sports activities. Courtesy of the U.S. Army.

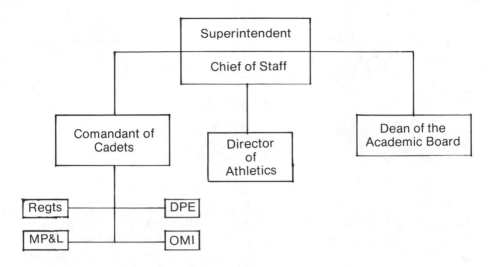

OMI—Office of Military Instruction
MP&L—Military Psychology and Leadership
Regts—Four Regiments of Cadets
DPE—Dept. of Physical Education

Fig. 49.5.

extensive experience in the army. The permanent personnel are graduates of civilian colleges or universities with advanced study in at least one area of specialization.

SUGGESTED READING

So far, so good: a report card on coed military academies, 1977. *U.S. News & World Report,* July 11, pp. 26-31.

50

The United States Naval Academy

Marvin Eyler and L.B. Thalman

The purpose of the United States Naval Academy is to prepare young men and women morally, mentally, and physically to be professional officers in the naval service. Since its founding by George Bancroft in 1845 as the Naval School, it has provided high quality education and training leadership to hundreds of thousands of young men. Women for the first time were admitted as students to the Naval Academy in summer 1975, with the first class consisting of 81 cadets. The bedrock of today's academy education is in the professional, sea going, and shipboard subjects required of each graduate. The cadet may choose from any one of 26 major fields of study.

An equally important part of a cadet's experience at the academy is leadership training, which includes, among other elements, required physical education classes with stress on physical fitness, and required participation in either an intramural sport (there are 24) or in one of the 21 varsity sports.

PHYSICAL EDUCATION

The department of physical education, which functions directly under the commandant, has primary responsibility for the development of physical fitness and sport skills. Major emphasis is placed upon fitness: physical, mental, emotional, and spiritual. The overall objective of physical education, therefore, is to develop the skill, strength, endurance, agility, and competitive spirit of midshipmen in order that they may be capable of enduring severe physical hardships, be proficient in training and instructing others, and acquire useful habits of physical fitness.

Parameters that determine the content of the physical education curriculum are: the readiness level of the entering fourth class, staff knowledge of the needs for physical education and athletics in military life, needs revealed through questionnaires and experiences of officers currently engaged in sea and shore duty, and athletic activities conducted by the Intra-Brigade Sports Program.

The more specific objectives of the department include the development of the following: endurance, strength, agility, and aquatic proficiency to overcome severe physical hardships on sea, in the air, and on land; skills and attitudes in carry-over sports to insure a continuing maximum level of physical fitness; an understanding of principles and methods employed in organizing, supervising, and conducting physical education and athletic programs, and training and instructing others; and strong qualities of moral and physical courage, group loyalty, sense of fairness, leadership ability, and mental alertness while participating in highly competitive situations.

The program, which is required for four years, consists of 160 drills (hours), 68 of which are devoted to the fourth class (first year), 34 hours to the third class (second year), 33 hours to the second class (third year), and 25 hours to the first class (fourth year). Of the 160 hours, seven are devoted to four working subjects; swimming, boxing, wrestling, and gymnastics. Midshipmen are also graded on four physical fitness tests measuring speed, agility, strength, and endurance.

The physical fitness test includes chins, leg raises, dips, and running tests. The mile run is graded from 5:38 or faster as an 'A' and 6:31 or slower as an 'F.'

The department of physical education is organized as follows:

1. The head of the department is responsible directly to the commandant of midshipmen to assure that the physical education curriculum is in support of and in accordance with the mission of the Naval Academy.

2. The organization of the physical education department is built around an allowed staff of eight naval and two marine officers consisting of the head of department, executive officer/physical education officer, first lieutenant, intramural sports program officer, marking officer, and two instructors. The key civilians are the deputy physical education officer, and scheduling supervisor. In addition to the officers and civilians assigned by billet, there are officers and civilians assigned as coaches and instructors.

3. Operation of the physical education program requires 24 civilian instructors and a number of nonacademic employees. The civilian instructors carry the major part of the teaching load in the drill program. These instructors generally are physical education specialists selected on the basis of their professional training, character, and teaching ability. Other civilian employees are requir ' for maintaining storerooms and necessary equipment and facilities.

INTRAMURAL SPORTS

The intramural program is designed to accomodate those midshipmen who do not participate in the varsity sport program. The program, while administered and supervised by the department of physical education, depends largely upon the cooperation of company and battalion officers who assume considerable responsibility in organizing teams, supervising practice, and selecting officials.

The specific objectives of the program are:

1. To provide experiences in athletic competition so that qualities of military leadership such as confidence, aggressiveness, determination, and the will-to-win may be practiced and developed.

2. To enhance the development of physical and mental dexterity so as to increase one's chances of survival.

3. To relieve the nervous tensions that develop from academic pressures and rigorous military training.

4. To introduce a wide variety of sports for carry-over value following graduation.

5. To afford first classmen (seniors) opportunities for coaching, managing, and officiating various sports. These experiences require a midshipman to exercise leadership qualities, organizational ability, a sense of responsibility, and self-composure.

6. To develop "esprit de corps." As members of company or battalion teams, midshipmen are provided with the opportunity for group membership with a common goal of competing and winning within a given framework of rules.

7. To provide an opportunity to utilize athletic knowledge and skills gained through the required physical education curriculum.

8. To develop an appreciation of the worthy use of leisure time.

9. To cultivate a more wholesome attitude toward top physical fitness, participation, keen competition, and good sportsmanship.

Competition in 22 sports is conducted at the company and battalion level during three separate periods each year. Contests between regiments are permitted for brigade championships only. Midshipmen are not permitted to participate for points in a particular sport in more than one session during the academic year.

VARSITY SPORTS

Intercollegiate athletics form an important part of the overall Naval Academy program. Navy fields varsity teams in 21 intercollegiate sports. It has been estimated that during the last few years, over 80 percent of the brigade has participated at one time or another in some form of intercollegiate sport.

The Naval Academy Athletic Association (NAAA) is a nonprofit organization charged by the superintendent with the responsibility for providing and administering the intercollegiate sports program for the midshipmen. The association discharges its responsibility without the use of appropriated funds. The NAAA personnel are responsible for arranging the varsity schedules, providing coaching staffs and equipment, and maintaining a central office to handle the administrative details of the athletic program.

The association's affairs are conducted by an athletic board of control, composed of six members and chaired by the commandant of midshipmen. In addition to the president (director of athletics) and vice president (assistant director of athletics) of the NAAA, one member of the board is appointed by the superintendent, another elected by the athletic council, and a third elected by the board of control.

The Naval Academy is a member of the Eastern College Athletic Conference (ECAC) and the National Collegiate Athletic Association (NCAA). It is represented and conforms to the regulations of these organizations through the offices of the Naval Academy Athletic Association.

The coaching staff is composed of head coaches, a large staff of highly qualified assistants, a professional medical staff, and an administrative staff that handles the supervision of the entire sports program that sends midshipmen into over 200 contests each year.

The facilities for athletics include a modern 28,000-seat Navy-Marine Corps Memorial football stadium; a 5000-seat field house surfaced throughout with tartan multipurpose floor covering; 100 acres of lighted playing fields; an indoor swimming pool; a 5000-seat baseball stadium; a 6217-yard championship golf course; facilities for the rowing and sailing programs; and a number of squash, handball, and tennis courts.

SUGGESTED READING

So far, so good: a report card on coed military academies, *U.S. News & World Report,* July 11, pp. 26-31.

51

The United States Air Force Academy

Paul Hunsicker and Charles Oliver

President Eisenhower signed legislation establishing the Air Force Academy on April 1, 1954. The first class arrived at Lowry Air Force Base, Colorado, in the fall of 1955. Three years later the academy was moved to its permanent base on the eastern slopes of the Rampart Range north of Colorado Springs. The academy initially was all male, but in the summer of 1976 the first class of 157 women was enrolled.

The head of the department of physical education is responsible directly to the director of athletics. The staff of the head of the department of physical education consists of the deputy heads, chiefs of the instruction division, intramural division, and research and evaluation division, and the executive officer.

The objectives of the physical education program include the following:

1. Body development
2. Development of interest and skill in carry-over skills
3. Development of leadership skills
4. Development of positive attitudes toward personal and air force-wide physical fitness
5. Development of knowledge and understanding of the fundamentals of physical fitness, rules, and strategy of sports.

Each cadet takes part in the instructional program that includes approximately 20 courses over the four-year span. Courses are offered in aquatics, combatives, carry-over activities, physical development activities, and remedial activities.

Testing and evaluation is carried out prior to the candidates' appointment to the academy and during their four years there. All cadets are required to take the USAFA Physical Fitness Test (PFT) each semester. During their final year, the cadets take the Air Force Aerobics Test, which involves a one and a half mile run against time. The physical fitness test minimums are shown in Table 51.1.

Table 51.1
Physical Fitness Test Minimums at the U.S. Air Force Academy

Class	Semester	Test items				
		Pull-ups Pull-ups	Standing broad jump	Push-ups	Sit-ups	600-yd run 1/12 mile track
4th	1st	None established				
4th	2nd	3	6'6''	24	40	2 min 7 sec
3rd	1st	5	6'9''	27	45	2 min 0 sec

1st Cl—Aerobics—1½ mile run. Times convert to standard PFT score. 11:45 minimum passing time. 9:45 converts to standard score of 400.

The intramural sports program is extensive and has as its objectives:

1. To give each cadet an opportunity to develop a competitive, aggressive attitude through participation in contact sports
2. To give each cadet an opportunity to practice athletic techniques taught in the physical education program
3. To familiarize each cadet with the administration of an intramural program.
4. To provide leadership experience by giving each cadet the opportunity to coach, manage, officiate, and train squadron intramural teams

The sports are conducted during the fall, winter, and spring. A typical schedule is shown in Table 51.2. Although there is an officer in charge of intramurals, the program is cadet-oriented in that the cadet group operations officers direct intramurals for their respective groups. All teams are coached and managed, and all contests are officiated by cadet upper classmen.

Table 51.2
Intramural Program at the U.S. Air Force Academy

Fall	Winter	Spring
Football	Boxing	Soccer
Lacrosse	Wrestling	Swimming
Cross country	Squash racquets	Basketball
Flickerball	Handball	Rugby
Tennis	Water polo	Fieldball
	Volleyball	

The Air Force Academy is a member of the National Collegiate Athletic Association and teams compete independent of any conference. The program is extensive and includes some 15 sports.

The physical education program is authorized 40 positions with about half of the instructors doubling as coaches. All officers for assignment in the department are selected on the basis of their educational and military records, their experience in physical education teaching and coaching, and their personal appearance and bearing. Advanced educational opportunities are offered those instructors who have demonstrated initiative in pursuit of advanced degrees.

SUGGESTED READINGS

So far, so good: a report card on coed military academies, 1977. Project 'Blue Eyes': *Report*, July 11, pp. 26-31.

Thomas. J.C., 1977. Project 'Blue Eyes': the integration of women into the U.S. Air Force Academy. Paper presented at the joint NAPECW-NCPEAM Conference, Orlando, Florida, January 7-8.

52

The United States Coast Guard Academy

Benjamin H. Massey and Carl W. Selin

The United States Coast Guard Academy, New London, Connecticut, is an accredited four-year college maintained by the federal government for the purpose of training commissioned officers for the coast guard. The enrollment in the early 1970s was about 1100 cadets. The objectives of the institution are to provide: (1) an environment that encourages a high sense of honor, loyalty, and obedience; (2) a sound undergraduate education; and (3) training that enables graduates to assume duties as officers.

Physical education plays an important role in the education of the cadet. "Realizing that extensive physical education and recreational sports programs are essential to the fulfillment of its educational philosophy, the academy insists upon a cadet's participation in some aspect of the athletic program during each of his four years." (*Catalog of Courses* 1972-73).

The physical education program falls into three areas: instruction, intramural athletics, and intercollegiate athletics. Cadets are required to enroll in the instructional program throughout their entire four years at the academy and also to participate in competitive athletics at the intramural or intercollegiate level. About 70 percent of the cadets participate in the intercollegiate program. Facilities for physical education are outstanding. A five-level field house constructed in 1967 provides abundant indoor space, including a 1.1-acre tartan-surfaced field, tennis courts, three basketball courts, handball courts, and a swimming pool. There is also a second gymnasium and some outdoor areas.

INSTRUCTIONAL PROGRAM

The instructional program, staffed by more than a dozen faculty, is housed administratively in the academic division. Physical education is required three hours per week each semester of the first three years and one hour per week the senior year. The mark for the year's work represents an average of the first semester mark, second semester mark, and score made on the biannual physical fitness test, which consists of five items: pull-ups, two-minute sit-ups, standing long jump, 300-yard shuttle run, and two-mile run.

The curriculum includes: First year—foundations of physical activity, survival swimming, gymnastics, wrestling. Second year—beginning tennis, handball, volleyball, advanced swimming. Third year—golf, personal defense, badminton, life saving. Fourth year—electives from scuba diving, tennis, leadership, weight training, handball, badminton, water safety, golf, and skiing.

The mission of the instructional program is the development of basic physical fitness, skill in selected carry-over sports, and qualities of leadership necessary to military service. Research and development are important, with each faculty member encouraged to participate in research projects significant to the program. Faculty members participate in an academy research council comprised of representatives from the four service academies.

INTRAMURAL ATHLETICS

An intramural program is conducted based on intercompany competition, which includes an extensive array of competitive sports. A typical annual program might encompass 18 sports with both a varsity and junior varsity team being fielded by each company in basketball, volleyball, and soccer. The sports are those included typically in intramural programs in colleges and universities plus a few rather unusual sports such as sailing, pistol competition, aerial tennis, flicker ball, and claw ball. Flicker ball combines the elements of basketball and football, and claw ball is related to lacrosse.

Each session a cadet must select a sport in which to compete. Each company has a cadet athletic officer who, along with the cadet regimental officers, handles some of the administrative responsibilities under the director of intramurals, who is a faculty member. Team coaches and captains are assigned to the company by cadet athletic officers. An athletic commission, comprised of cadet company athletic officers, maintains records, handles protests, and recommends policy and rule changes to be incorporated into the *Intramural Athletics Handbook*.

INTERCOLLEGIATE ATHLETICS

The intercollegiate athletic program is headed by an athletic director who is responsible administratively to the assistant superintendent of the academy. The program is staffed with about 40 coaches. A typical annual program might include 16 varsity sports: football, soccer, cross country, sailing, basketball, wrestling, swimming, rifle, pistol, gymnastics, indoor track, baseball, track, tennis, golf, and crew. Junior varsity and/or freshman teams are fielded in 12 of the sports. Opponents are schools of similar enrollment in the New England and New York area, such as Trinity, Amherst, Williams, Brown, Dartmouth, Harvard, and Yale. The Coast Guard Academy is a member of the National Collegiate Athletic Association (NCAA) and the Eastern Athletic Conference (ECAC).

REFERENCE

Catalogue of courses, 1972-73. New London, Conn.: United States Coast Guard Academy.

SUGGESTED READINGS

So far, so good: a report card on coed military academies, 1977. *U.S. News & World Report,* July 11, pp. 26-31.

Bulletin of information, 1971/1972. New London, Conn.: United states Coast Guard Academy.

53

The Virginia Military Institute

Clark King and Benjamin H. Massey

The Virginia Military Institute (VMI), founded at Lexington, Virginia, in 1839 as the first state military college, is a state-supported undergraduate college for men with an enrollment of about 1300 cadets. The mission of VMI is to educate citizen-soldiers. The student is offered a choice of majors from the general fields of engineering, liberal arts, and the sciences. The chief executive officer is the superintendent, who is assisted in administering the affairs of the institute by his staff, the academic dean, and the faculty.

At VMI physical education, a nondegree program, is considered an important aspect of the training of men destined to become citizen-soldiers. The mission of the program is to provide each cadet with experience whereby he may gain insight into his own capabilities and realize that the body is able to overcome fatigue and endure far beyond the limitations suggested by the mind. The program is broadly based, encompassing classroom instruction, developmental activities, fitness testing, intramural sports, and intercollegiate athletics. The following are specific objectives of the program:

1. To provide an introduction to human anatomy, exercise physiology, and the role of nutrition in human health
2. To demonstrate the effectiveness of exercise in relieving psychological tensions, maintaining weight control , maintaining physical condition, and ameliorating of the aging process
3. To improve strength, coordination, and endurance
4. To develop skill in selected lifetime sports
5. To develop self-confidence
6. To provide opportunities for recreation

All cadets must earn four credits in physical education to qualify for graduation. The program includes classroom lectures on the psychological and physiological benefits of exercise, developmental activities such as weight training and fitness exercises, and sports participation, both in the intramural and intercollegiate programs. Freshman classes meet once per week, and participation in a special training course is required two days per week during the first semester for all freshmen not engaged in intercollegiate athletics. After the first semester, freshmen join all other cadets who are not engaged in intercollegiate athletics in an intramural sports program.

An important aspect of physical education at VMI is the Cooper aerobic testing and conditioning program. All cadets during the sophomore and junior years are measured three times each year on Cooper's aerobic test. Further, those cadets not engaged in intercollegiate athletics during the third and second class years participate in Cooper's aerobic conditioning program. Those in athletics earn their aerobic points by engaging in a sport.

Organizationally, the instructional and intramural sports programs are housed within the physical education department, which is an academic department, with a department head responsible to the academic dean of the institute. The intercollegiate athletic program, headed by an athletic director responsible solely to a faculty athletic committee, is a nonacademic department.

The intramural director, a physical education department member, organizes and administers, with student help, a year-round sports program. The program consists of 17 different activities, including such diverse activities as handball, cross-country running, weight training, boxing, softball, aquatics, and orienteering. Approximately 75 percent of the cadets participate in the program during any given season: fall, winter, or spring.

The intercollegiate athletic program is similar to that of other colleges of similar size. The activities include football, cross country, and soccer in the fall; wrestling, swimming, basketball, indoor track, and rifle in the winter; and baseball, track, golf, and tennis in the spring. The program is open to all cadets who have passed 24 semester hourse of course work in the preceding year of attendance. About 30 percent of the corps of cadets participate in the intercollegiate athletic program. VMI is a member of the Southern Conference of the NCAA.

Facilities at VMI are relatively extensive for an institution of its size and include a baseball diamond with additional practice spaces, four indoor and six outdoor basketball courts, two tackle and four flag-football fields, a soccer field, eight handball courts, two swimming pools, artificially surfaced indoor and outdoor running tracks, fully-padded wrestling room, weight training room, two playing fields of about 10 acres for intramural club and free recreational sports, and free use by cadets of a local community 18-hole golf course.

54

The Citadel, The Military College of South Carolina

Charles J. Dillman, J. William Dellastatious, and John P. Smyth

The Citadel, the Military College of South Carolina, is a small liberal arts college with an enrollment of about 2000 men. Various professional educational programs are offered from 16 underaduate curricula within the college. In addition, extensive programs of military studies are provided by the air force, army, and navy. Students must select a program of military preparation and a major area of professional study. These educational programs are carried out within the framework of strict military training and regulations.

The department of physical education is responsible for programs of undergraduate professional preparation, intramurals, required physical education and sports clubs. The undergraduate professional preparation program prepares physical education majors for secondary-school teaching in the fields of physical education, athletics, and a selected minor. The undergraduate curriculum provides for a well-balanced education requiring students to elect courses from the physical, biological, and social sciences as well as from the humanities. An extensive program of professional courses and independent study is offered within the department to meet the needs and interests of each student. A relatively small student-faculty ratio permits the faculty to give each undergraduate major personal attention and guidance.

The highly structured intramural program provides extensive opportunities for students to participate in a variety of competitive activities. Competition is always keen in a military environment. Consequently, participation in the intramural program is extremely enthusiastic. The intramural sports are: badminton, three-man basketball, basketball free-throw, basketball golf, bowling, fencing, flag football, golf, gymnastics, handball, innertube water polo, jogging, paddle rackets, Sigma Delta Psi, skish, softball, steeplechase, swimming, table tennis, tennis, track, volleyball, weight lifting, wrestling, and team handball.

Freshmen and sophomore students are required to take physical education. During the first semester all freshmen are required to take a foundation course in adult fitness. This course focuses on programs, assessment, and maintenance of physical fitness. Students complete the rest of the physical education requirement by electing activities from a program consisting mainly of individual and dual sports. No academic credit is given for required physical education.

The sports clubs program provides opportunities for students to participate on an intercollegiate level with other college clubs in popular sport activities not sponsored by the respective athletic departments. The activities sponsored under the sports clubs program include gymnastics, bowling, crew, sailing, judo, fencing, scuba, and parachuting.

Intercollegiate competition in 11 sports is administered by the athletic department. The sports are: football, cross country, soccer, basketball, indoor track, wrestling, rifle, tennis, golf, track, and baseball. The Citadel is a member of the Southern Conference and the NCAA and has a distinguished record of athletic competition.

SUGGESTED READING

Department of physical education, ten year self-study, 1962-1972. Department of Physical Education, The Citadel.

THERAPEUTIC EXERCISE AND PROGRAMS

Introduction

In the preceding two sections dealing with physical education programs in the schools and in the military, the words "adapted," "therapeutic," and "rehabilitation" have appeared on a regular basis. Every well-rounded physical education program boasts a component that services the physically and/or mentally atypical.

In the past few years, due largely to the passage of Public Law 94-142 (see Section 7), the adapted phase of the physical education program has received national focus. This section and the following one will demonstrate that the physical education profession has indeed been concerned and involved with the needs of the physically and mentally handicapped, although admittedly comprehensive programs on a national scale have been lacking.

Author Ryan sets the tone by challenging physical educators to share their expertise with medical and other professions interested in exercise as a therapeutic modality. Kendall and Kendall follow with a liberally-illustrated chapter on good and faulty posture, and correction of the latter. Many of the principles and recommended practices are corroborated in the article by Cureton.

The reader may note at this point that, for the first time in this volume, considerable space is devoted to the "how-to." Specific exercises are recommended in detail for ameliorating specific debilitating conditions. Typical of this kind of format is the chapter by Klein in which he describes specific exercises for the treatment and prevention of the "low-back syndrome" discussed at length in the article by Kraus. The chapter on controversial exercises then reminds us that considerable controversy exists among exercise therapists, kinesiologists, and physicians concerning some exercises used traditionally in most physical fitness programs.

The role of exercise in the prevention of, and rehabilitation from, cardio-vascular disease is addressed in chapters 61-64. Considerable positive scientific evidence is offered by Wilson and Boyer and corroborated in the rather technical literature cited by Landry. For those who would believe that the present nationwide interest in the use of exercise for rehabilitation of cardiac patients is a relatively new concept, the article by McCloy demonstrates that, at least as early as 1943, some physical educators were actively involved in such programs.

The potential uses and values of specialized modes of therapeutic exercise are discussed in the chapters by Gruber (aquatics), Ryan (yoga), and Perrine (isokinetic exercise).

Normally athletics trainers are not included in discussions about adapted physical education and therapeutic exercise. This is probably due to the fact that they service a presumably highly fit group. However, Reid and Oxley remind us that logically, by temperament, attitude, and professional expertise, the athletics trainer is very much a part of the "therapeutic exercise team." Klein substantiates this claim by providing an example of specialized equipment (the bench technique) and specific exercises the athletics trainer might use in the rehabilitation of an injured knee.

Section Editor

Allan J. Ryan was a scholastic and collegiate middle distance runner and these experiences created his interest in physical education and sports. As a practicing general surgeon for 18 years, he was active in treating athletes and produced a book, *Medical Care of the Athlete,* in 1961. He served as a member and chairman of the American Medical Association Committees on Medical Aspects of Sports (13 years) and Physical Activity and Physical Fitness (10 years). In 1965 he began service at the University of Wisconsin-Madison as athletic teams physician and in the university health service. He was also a member of the departments of physical education for men and rehabilitation medicine, achieving the rank of professor. He retired from the university June 30, 1976, to become editor-in-chief of the *Physician and Sports Medicine* and *Postgraduate Medicine* both monthly publications of the McGraw-Hill Company. Dr. Ryan is a Fellow and past president of the American College of Sports Medicine and an Honorary Fellow of the British Association for Sports Medicine. He was coeditor of *Sports Medicine* with Fred L. Allman, Jr., MD.

55

Physical Education and Therapeutic Exercise

Allan J. Ryan

Where the goals of movement are primarily therapeutic, closely coordinated teamwork of the physical educator, exercise physiologist, physical therapist, psychiatrist, physiatrist, psychologist, occupational therapist, recreational therapist, and corrective therapist is essential to a successful result.

The role of the physical educator in therapeutic exercise is to call on knowledge derived from the basic studies of anatomy, physiology, kinesiology, motor learning, and the technology of games and sports skills, and to identify and teach the patterns of body movement that will be most suitable to apply to the therapeutic problem presented by the individual subject. This may involve an entirely new learning experience for the individual who requires therapy or a relearning of movement patterns previously acquired but lost as the result of illness or injury. It may be necessary because of irreparable losses to learn to achieve the same objective through slightly different skills or reproduce the same pattern in a mirror image in an opposite extremity.

Therapeutic exercise may be conceived of in two quite different ways: exercise that allows handicapped persons participation in games or sports activity to help them achieve emotional and social objectives and a degree of physical fitness, but exercise that does not necessarily exert any favorable effect on their handicapping conditions; and exercise that has as its primary objective improving physical or mental function following illness or injury, but in which social and emotional objectives may be achieved incidentally. The former is generally referred to as adapted physical education and the latter as rehabilitative or corrective exercise therapy. The role of physical educators in the first is primary, and they may be the only therapists working directly with the subject. In the second instance they may play more of a secondary or supporting role, or perhaps influence therapy even more indirectly through the instruction of other therapists.

The characteristic setting for adapted physical education is institutional, whether it is in a school, college, or camp environment. Although we have made great advances in developing the theory of this form of education, and many training courses are offered in this specialty with degrees granted at the undergraduate and graduate levels, the practice has fallen far behind that of many other countries. Only one state had a requirement that special classes in adapted physical education must be offered in every school prior to the passage of P.L. 94-142 required such programs in all schools accepting federal funds (see Section 7). Probably there was no single reason for this failure to meet such an important challenge to our educational system. The somewhat less than enthusiastic support of physical education requirements generally and increasing educational costs proportionate to shrinking revenues, must share the major portion of the blame equally, however.

Adapted physical education programs that concentrate chiefly on the development of skills for sports and games are doing only part of the job. All handicapped persons should have the opportunity to develop their physical fitness within the limits of what is possible. Every program should offer activities demanding enough to produce a training effect. When the desired level of physical fitness is reached, and indeed during the process of reaching it, serious efforts should be made to motivate the individual to continue to be physically active on a regular basis in order to maintain the level that has been reached.

Unfortunately, there is a dearth of organizations and facilities that will allow and encourage the handicapped to continue vigorous physical activity once they have left the institutions where they were training. We do have special camps, but these are chiefly seasonal and only short stays are possible because of the large numbers seeking admission. Physical educators and recreation leaders should be making greater efforts to open existing institutional facilities to those handicapped persons who are isolated in their homes.

The question of whether those requiring adapted physical education should be segregated completely from those in regular physical education classes cannot be decided arbitrarily, since there are both advantages and disadvantages of segregation as well as integration. The decision has to be made on the individual level without applying any arbitrary restrictions. Under the right circumstances handicapped persons draw inspiration and support from those who are not handicapped. They may have a better opportunity for more equal interchange among their own group, however. The nonhandicapped learn from their association with the handicapped to be patient, and the necessity of understanding the problems of those less fortunate in adjusting to the real world through the model of a world at play.

The application of therapeutic exercise to convalescence from acute illness and trauma has been generally neglected in favor of rest. The physical educator has the knowledge to join the physician in the prescription of

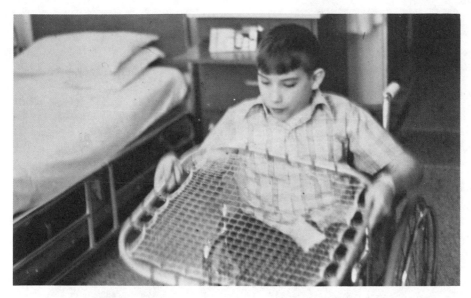

Fig. 55.1 Boy with congenital spinal defect bouncing an object on a net to improve coordination and perception.

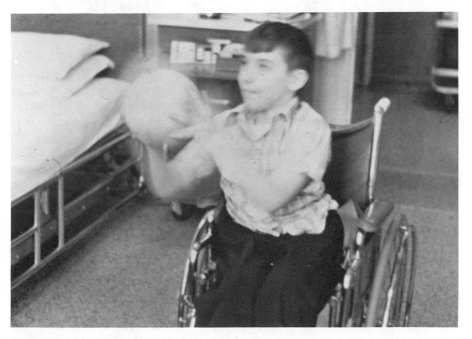

Fig. 55.2 Boy with congenital spinal defect shooting a basketball to develop upper extremity strength and coordination.

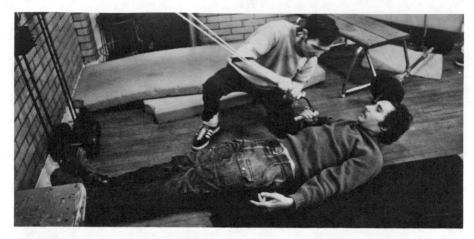

Fig. 55.3 Trainer instructing patient with post-operative shoulder with use of pulley weights to restore strength and normal range of motion.

Fig. 55.4 Post-coronary attack patient exercising by jogging. Courtesy Jules Alexander.

Fig. 55.5 Patient who had a coronary artery occlusion taking rehabilitative exercise on bicycle ergometer.

graded and modified sports and game activities for such convalescents. This has been left largely to the corrective therapists, many of whom are also trained in physical education—the occupational, physical, and recreational therapists. Present programs, where they exist, can be criticized on the grounds of being too restricted in scope and not using outdoors activities sufficiently.

Greater strides in bringing therapeutic exercise to those suffering chronic diseases and their acute components are now being made more than ever before. Chronic obstructive lung disease, arteriosclerotic heart disease, obesity, and paraplegia have received the most attention so far. Physical educators have become involved in many of these programs as members of the therapeutic team. They are called on not only for their knowledge of the necessary games skills and their ability to teach them, but for their experience in measuring and evaluating the physical effects of exercise. They are also even more involved in so-called intervention programs where persons who have been identified as having a high number of risk factors, but do not have frank clinical symptoms, are given exercise programs to prevent the emergence of the full-blown clinical state. This may also be therapeutic, but at a subclinical level.

Therapeutic exercise for the mentally retarded and emotionally debilitated is now only at the beginning of what should be a much greater development in future years. Dance as well as sports and games is playing an important part in this phase of rehabilitation. Interest is stimulated in the support of these activities by the introduction of competitive elements, and participation also is increased substantially. The physical educators and others who are involved in the supervision of such programs must be very cautious not to let the competitive situation dominate the practice, as it has in interscholastic and intercollegiate education to the extent that elitism pushes aside participation for all.

We should be able to look forward to a time when physical educators generally are as much involved in the various aspects of therapeutic exercise as they are now in the teaching and supervision of exercise, sports, and games as a means for healthy persons to enjoy recreation while maintaining and increasing personal levels of physical fitness. The impetus for continued progress in this area must come from physical educators themselves, but must be strongly encouraged and supported by the medical profession.

SUGGESTED READINGS

Adams, R. C., A. N. Daniel, and L. Rulhman, 1972. *Games, sports and exercises for the physically handicapped.* Philadelphia: Lea and Febiger.

Arnheim, D. C., D. Auxter, and w. C. Frowe, 1969. *Principles and methods of adapted physical education.* Saint Louis: C.V. Mosby.

Daniels, A. S., and E. A. Davies, 1965. *Adapted physical education.* (2nd ed.) New York: Harper and Row.

Drowatzky, J. N., 1971. *Physical education for the mentally retarded.* Philadelphia: Lea and Febiger.

Engerbretson, D. L., 1977. The diabetic in physical education, recreation, and athletics. *JOPER* **48** (March) : 18.

Fait, H. F., 1972. *Special physical education—adapted, corrective, developmental.* (3rd ed.) Philadelphia: W.B. Saunders.

Frye, V., and M. Peters, 1972. *Therapeutic recreation: its theory, philosophy and practice.* Harrisburg, Pa.: Stackpole Books.

Logan, G. A., 1972, *Adapted physical education.* Dubuque, Iowa: William C. Brown.

Vodola, T. M., 1972. *Individualized physical education program for the handicapped child.* Englewood Cliffs, N.J.: Prentice-Hall.

Wheeler, R. H., and A. M. Hooley, 1969. *Physical education for the handicapped.* Philadelphia: Lea and Febiger.

_____, 1968. *Guide for programs in recreation and physical education for the mentally retarded.* Washington, D.C.: AAHPER.

_____, 1968. *Physical activities for the mentally retarded (ideas for instruction).* Washington, D.C.: AAHPER.

_____, 1969. *Practical guide for teaching the mentally retarded to swim.* Washington, D.C.: AAHPER.

_____, 1968. *Programming for the mentally retarded in physical education and recreation.* Washington, D.C.: AAHPER.

_____, 1966. *Recreation and physical activity for the mentally retarded.* Washington, D.C.: AAHPER.

_____, 1970. *Sports as a means of rehabilitation—proceedings of an international seminar at Wingate Institute for Physical Education and Sport in September 1970.* Israel: Wingate Institute.

56

Developing and Maintaining Good Posture

Henry O. Kendall and Florence P. Kendall

Good posture is important for proper functioning of the body and contributes to good appearance. Proper alignment of the body parts promotes efficiency of movement and endurance. The person who has good posture and who moves gracefully projects poise, confidence, and dignity.

From a mechanical standpoint, in good posture the bones and joints are in position to take the stress of weight and movement, and the musculature is firmly balanced to hold the body organs in place. In poor posture, the bones are out of line and the muscles and ligaments take more strain than nature intended. Besides being unattractive, faulty posture may cause fatigue, muscular strain, and, in later stages, pain. In some cases poor posture affects the position and functioning of vital organs, particularly those of the abdominal region.

STRENGTH, FLEXIBILITY, AND MUSCULAR BALANCE

Muscular strength is essential to good posture, and it is important that such strength be well balanced. Developing strength in certain muscles, without also strengthening the opposite muscles, will tend to distort alignment rather than promote good posture.

Flexibility depends on free joint motion and muscle length. Children tend to be very flexible, and it is natural that they lose some of this flexibility along with developing more strength as they grow older. It is not advantageous for the average young person or adult to have excessive flexibility.

To strengthen muscles, the muscles must contract. In so doing, they move the bones to which they attach closer together. For the muscles to lengthen, they must relax, allowing the bones to which they attach to move away from each other.

While it is important to be able to shorten or to stretch muscles through a good range of motion, it is also very important that they not remain in shortened or stretched positions continuously for long periods of time.

Basic to an understanding of muscular balance is the fact that muscles that remain in a somewhat stretched position tend to weaken, while those that remain in a somewhat shortened position tend to become tight and stronger than their opponents. Even if muscles are only slightly stretched or shortened, muscular balance can be upset if they remain in this position for long periods of time.

HABITUAL POOR POSTURE

Habitual faulty posture means being in a position of poor alignment continually. The result of an habitual faulty position is that an adaptive stretching or shortening of muscles takes place. These changes can be overcome by properly directed exercise and by practicing good posture.

Webster says "practice is the active doing of something in a systematic way," and that is exactly what is needed to restore good alignment.

It is important that postural exercises be done slowly and held for several seconds. They are designed not only to strengthen certain muscle groups, but also to help develop the "feel" of good posture. When this "feel" has been mastered, it should be practiced often until it becomes a habit.

Along with exercises to strengthen some muscle groups, it is important to temporarily omit certain exercises that would tend to increase the faulty alignment. After the weak muscles have been strengthened and have enough endurance to help maintain good position, the exercises that have been temporarily omitted may be resumed but should not be done to excess.

In the selection of all exercises and activities, care should be taken to maintain a balance in strength of all muscle groups so as to keep the body in good alignment.

THE SCHOOL'S RESPONSIBILITY

The school's responsibility for promoting good posture is twofold: inspection and instruction.

The *inspection of* pupils' posture should be included routinely in the health appraisal. Children should be checked individually while wearing suitable attire—shorts for boys and shorts and halters for girls. Cooperation of school and parents is important to thorough posture inspection.

In the series of illustrations that follows, individuals show both good alignment and characteristic postural faults in front, back, and side views.

The school and the teacher also should be concerned with *instruction* of pupils in the elements of good posture. If children are taught to maintain correct alignment at an early age, it is possible to avoid many of the faults and their resultant problems that tend to occur as children grow older.

Most school-age children are capable of assuming good posture. Whether they maintain it most of the time depends on motivation, proper muscular balance, and the development of good postural habits. Motivation must be accompanied by guidance in the right direction. Overzealous or misdirected effort on the part of the teacher or the subject may result in exaggerated posture or negative attitudes.

Suggestions for the Teacher

1. Know the reasons for good posture and be able to describe the elements of good posture in simple terms (see accompanying illustrations and descriptions).
2. Set an example by practicing good posture.
3. Learn to recognize the common faulty postural tendencies (see illustrations).
4. Avoid exaggeration of postural positions that cause distortion of good alignment.
5. Recognize the fact that posture is flexible. While it is desirable to maintain a good position of the body most of the time, it is not harmful to assume relaxed positions at times.

GOOD POSTURE: FRONT VIEW

Head is held erect, not turned or tilted to one side. Shoulders are level. Arms hang easily at the sides with the palms of the hands toward the body. Hips are level, with the weight of the body borne equally by both legs. Kneecaps face straight ahead. Feet point straight ahead or toe out slightly. In other words, they may be parallel, or the feet may be about one inch farther apart in front than at the heels. The weight of the body is carried toward the outer sides of the feet, and evenly balanced between the heel and the forefoot. Evidences of good posture are illustrated in Fig. 56.1.

Stand in front of a mirror and check to see that feet and knees are in good position, and that hips and shoulders are level. Make a habit of standing in a good position, with weight borne evenly on both feet.

Good posture must be built from the feet up. If the feet and knees are in good position, there is a better chance that the rest of the body will line up properly.

Faulty Posture—Feet and Knees

Problem: In Fig. 56.2, the feet are pronated, that is, ankles are rolled inward and weight is borne on inner sides of feet. Arches tend to flatten. Kneecaps face somewhat inward because of inward rotation of legs at hip joint.

Figure 56.1   **Figure 56.2**

To help restore good alignment: Roll weight toward outer sides of the feet by pulling up with the muscles that lift the arches. At the same time, rotate the legs outward until kneecaps face straight ahead by making firm the muscles over the back of the hips.

When sitting on the floor, sit in a cross-legged position (tailor fashion or Indian fashion).

Do exercise as shown in Fig. 56.3. Positions shown in Fig. 56.4 and 56.5 are to be avoided.

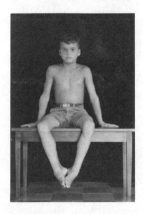

Figure 56.3   **Figure 56.4**   **Figure 56.5**

Problem: In addition to pronation of the feet and inward rotation of the legs, knees that are pushed into back-knee position, causing an apparent bowing of the legs, are referred to as "postural bowlegs."

To help restore good alignment: Correct the pronation of the feet and the rotation of the legs as shown in Fig. 56.2, and bring the knees slightly forward into an "eased" position (see Fig. 56.6).

Break the habit of standing with knees pushed back.

Practice standing in the corrected position often, until it becomes a habit.

Do exercise as shown in Fig. 56.3.

Problem: In Fig. 56.7 feet are pointed outward (out-toeing or slue-foot position). Kneecaps face somewhat outward because of outward rotation of the legs at the hip joints.

Too often it is assumed that any knock-knees or bowing of the legs is a structural (bony) abnormality that cannot be altered by a program of postural exercises. Fig. 56.2, 56.7, and 56.8 are significant in that they show how an individual with good alignment of the bones of the legs (Fig. 56.1) can assume a variety of faulty positions at will. Also implicit in this demonstration should be the fact that properly directed exercise and instruction can help restore good alignment if the condition has not existed for so long that structural changes have occurred.

To help restore good alignment: Practice standing with feet and knees facing straight ahead. Practice walking along a straight line.

Do exercise as shown in Fig. 56.9. Avoid position shown in Fig. 56.10.

Note: If feet toe out but kneecaps face straight ahead, it is not advisable to try to correct the position of the feet if, by so doing, the knees are made to rotate inward.

Problem: Postural knock-knees resulting from a combination of outward rotation and back-knee position (Fig. 56.8).

To help restore good alignment: Correct the outward rotation of the legs by turning the legs inward until the kneecaps face straight ahead, and correct the back-knees by bringing the knees slightly forward into an "eased" position (see Fig. 56.6).

Practice standing in the corrected position often until it feels natural and becomes a habit.

Do exercise as shown in Fig. 56.9.

Shoes

The wearing of proper shoes is a most important consideration in maintaining good posture of the feet and knees. Improper shoes tend to distort a normal foot or "run over" in the direction that a weak foot tends to roll.

Most shoes have some stiffness (support) around the back of the heel. When feet have a tendency to roll inward or outward, the wearing of shoes

   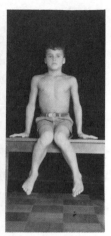

Figure 56.6   **Figure 56.7**   **Figure 56.8**   **Figure 56.9**

Figure 56.10

such as loafers, which have no stiffness (support) around the heel, should be avoided.

As a part of physical activity programs, standing, walking, running, and jumping often are done on hard surfaces and may result in strain of the arches of the feet. A small arch support incorporated in tennis shoes helps to minimize the strain.

Feet withstand a great deal of stress. In running, the weight is almost constantly on the toes and the balls of the feet, but the forepart of the foot was not designed to take the stress of continous standing or walking in high-heeled shoes. Gradually over a period of years the metatarsal arch (across the front of the foot) weakens and the foot may become painful in that area.

The normal foot is not pointed at the toes, but some shoes are pointed in the direction of reshaping the foot. When high heels are added to pointed toes, there is a tendency for the foot to slide forward into the space that is intended only as an airspace. When the front of a high-heeled shoe is cut out (as in toe-out shoes), the foot rides forward and the toes squeeze together.

If the feet are kept in good shape, a person can wear almost any fashionable shoe at times, but should avoid the continual use of shoes that distort the normal shape of the foot.

With proper walking, shoes will show fairly even wear over the heel and sole, except at the back of the heel where there will be more wear because this part of the shoe strikes the surface first.

Sometimes shoes wear out along the outer side of the heel toward the back. This is often taken to mean that the ankles roll outward, and parents or shoemakers will often decide to put a metal tap on the heel in that area. This metal piece makes the shoe roll inward. Generally this is not the thing to do. The heel wears out in this area because this part of the shoe strikes the surface first when a person walks with too much out-toeing. Very often the person who toes outward, rolls the feet inward as the weight is transferred to the front of the feet, and the metal on the shoe increases this rolling-in of the ankles. To save the shoe from wear, but also to save the foot from further trouble, the metal tap may be put on but must be set down into the heel (countersunk) level with the rest of the heel. If out-toeing is corrected, the transfer of weight from heel to toe will be more normal, and the shoe will show more even wear.

GOOD POSTURE: BACK VIEW

In Fig. 56.11, illustrating good posture, the head is straight, not turned or tilted to one side. Shoulders are level. Shoulder blades are flat against upper back, not protruding or winged, not far apart or squeezed close together, and not hiked upward. Arms hang easily at sides, palms of hands toward body. Spine is straight. Hips are level, weight even on both legs. Legs are straight. Heel cords are straight.

Stability of the hips from side to side requires good strength of the muscles over the outside of the hips. These muscles are strengthened by leg-raising sideways from lying or standing positions.

Exercises to Help Maintain Good Strength of the
Lateral (Outside) Hip Muscles

1. Leg raise sideways, one side and then the other. Do *not* attempt to raise leg higher than 18 to 24 inches, but hold the position several seconds. Keep body and leg in straight line. Do not swing the leg forward at the hip joint (see Fig. 56.12).

Figure 56.11

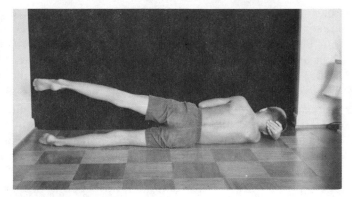

Figure 56.12

2. With body erect, step sideways with wide steps, in one direction and then in opposite direction.

3. For a strong test and exercise of these lateral hip muscles, try standing on one foot as in Fig. 56.13 and 56.14. Reverse and stand on the other foot. If muscles are not strong, the hips will move toward the table as an effort is made to balance on one foot at a time.

Faulty Posture

Problem: In Fig. 56.15 illustrating faulty posture, the head is forward and is tilted toward left shoulder. (Neck muscles are prominent, especially on the left.) Shoulders droop forward, right lower than left. Shoulder blades are wide

Figure 56.13

Figure 56.14

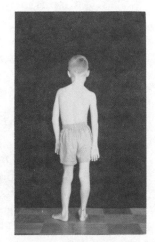

Figure 56.15

apart. Hands face backward, indicating arms are rotated inward at shoulder joints. Spine is curved toward the left. Hips are not level, right higher than left. The right leg is pushed back at the knee, and more weight is carried on it than on the left. The left leg is bent at the knee and rolled inward at the ankle. Feet toe out. This description tends to be characteristic of right-handed persons who stand in faulty positions. Left-handed individuals tend to deviate in the opposite direction.

To help to restore good alignment: When this type of posture becomes habitual, and not just an occasional slumped position, an effort should be made to restore good alignment before adaptive changes take place in the muscles.

Limit this effort to instruction and practice in proper standing, showing subject how to get hips level and shoulders level. A shoulder will usually be low on the side of a high hip and, if the hips are brought into level position, the shoulders will tend to become level. The exception will be in the case of an S-curve of the spine (sideways curve) in which the shoulder will be low on the side of the low hip.

Work for symmetry but avoid the use of symmetrical exercises because they may increase, rather than decrease, the faulty tendencies.

Descriptive Comments That May Be Used to Help Restore Good Alignment

1. "Stand tall."
2. "Place weight evenly on both feet."
3. "Keep both knees straight, not bent or pushed back."
4. "Stand in front of a mirror and try to make hips level and shoulders level."
5. "If right hip is more prominent, try to push left hip slightly toward left until hips are level (or vice versa)."
6. "Standing in a slouched manner with the hip protruding sideways gets you off to an early start on a 'middle-aged spread,' so start avoiding it now."

STANDING, SITTING, LYING

Everyone stands more on one foot than the other at times, but such a position should not become habitual.

Right-handed persons frequently stand on the right foot, lie on the left side, and sit on the left side. Taking these positions throws the spine toward the left and, if done a great deal, may cause the spine to stay curved in that direction. Left-handed persons frequently show the opposite tendencies.

Avoid making a habit of standing, lying, or sitting in positions shown in Figs. 56.16, 56.17, and 56.18.

Proper exercises to correct round shoulders are very important (Fig. 56.19). With arms at sides, palms of hand forward, draw shoulder blades back and slightly downward, flat against the upper back. (Also see exercises for good body alignment, later in this chapter.) Do *not* push elbows back beyond the side line of the body, or squeeze shoulder blades too close together. Also, avoid arching the low back while doing the exercise.

Pushing the elbows back does pull the shoulder blades together, but should be avoided in cases of round shoulders. The shoulder blades are pulled upward and squeezed too close together in an unnatural position, and the head tends to be pushed forward (Fig. 56.20).

Figure 56.16

Figure 56.17

Figure 56.18

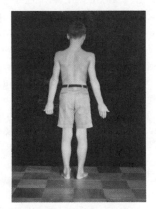

Figure 56.19

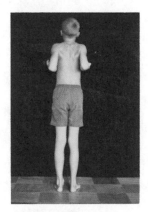

Figure 56.20

GOOD POSTURE: SIDE VIEW

In Fig. 56.6 illustrating good posture, head is erect and back, chin above the notch betwen the collar bones, with a slight forward curve in the neck. Shoulders are in line with the ear. Arm hangs easily at the side. Upper back is erect. Chest is held moderately elevated by holding the upper back erect. Abdominal wall is flat. The low back is held in good position (curved slightly forward). Hips are midway between forward and backward tilt. Knees are straight but "easy," not bent, pushed back, or stiff. Feet are pointed straight ahead or toed-out slightly. Weight is carried over the arch, evenly balanced between the heel and forefoot.

Descriptive Comments to Help Promote and Maintain Good Posture

1. "Stand tall. Remember that the tallest distance between your head and your hips is a straight spine, but slight curves are normal. To check for normal curves of the spine, stand with your back to a wall, heels about two inches from the wall. Place one hand behind your neck with the back of the hand against the wall, and the other hand behind your low back with the palm against the wall. Now your entire back should touch either your hands or the wall."

2. "Let your arms hang easily at your sides as you draw your shoulder blades back. Do not push your elbows back beyond the side line of the body."

3. "The position of your hips controls the position of the low back. Keep the hips midway between forward tilt and backward tilt to maintain the normal curve in the low back. Belts on trousers or skirts should be parallel with the ground."

4. "The position of your upper back controls the position of your neck. The head tends to stay level (because eyes seek eye-level), but if the upper back slumps the neck curves forward. If the upper back is straightened, the curve in the neck tends to return to normal."

5. "The position of your upper back also controls the position of the chest. As you straighten your upper back, your chest is raised into good position. Do *not* try to bring your chest up by arching your lower back. It *must* be done by your upper back."

   Problem: Fig. 56.21 exemplifies poor posture of the hips and lower back. The hips are tilted forward and the lower back is arched (lordosis).

   To help restore good alignment: Hold a good position of the head and upper back while pulling up and in with "lower" abdominal muscles and down in back with the hip muscles to reduce the curve in the low back. The motion should be that of flattening the lower abdomen and "tucking the hips under."

   If hip flexors are shortened, stretch hip flexors daily until normal length is restored (see Fig. 56.22).

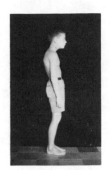

Figure 56.21   **Figure 56.22**   **Figure 56.23**

Avoid strong hip flexor exercises such as single or double leg-raising until lordosis is corrected.

Problem: Fig. 56.23 exemplifies a "slumped" posture in which the upper trunk sways back and the head and pelvis sway forward out of good alignment. The head is forward. Shoulders slump forward. Upper back is rounded (kyphosis). Chest is depressed. Abdomen protrudes. Hips sway forward. Knees are bent. (Frequently knees are pushed back, instead of bent, with this type of faulty posture.)

To help restore good alignment: Standing with back to a wall, correct the position of the head, shoulders, upper back, and low back, all at the same time.

In this slumped-type of posture, no effort should be made to tilt the pelvis back because it is already tilted back slightly. Instead the overall body alignment should be corrected by bringing the pelvis back and the upper trunk forward at the same time.

Hip flexor muscles may be somewhat weak in this type posture with hips swayed forward. Alternate leg-raising, with back kept flat, can be used to advantage to strengthen both the abdominal and hip flexor muscles when both are weak.

In both types of faulty posture shown in Figs. 56.21 and 56.23 there is generally a weakness of the lower external oblique abdominal muscles. In the lordosis posture the weakness has allowed a *tilt* of the hips forward; in the other, it has allowed the hips to *sway* forward. In both instances pulling the hips back to good alignment is done by the upward and inward pull of these oblique muscles.

Descriptive Comments to Help Restore Good Alignment

1. "To help get the 'feel' of tilting the hips and pulling up and in with the lower abdominal muscles, pretend you are stepping sideways through a

313

narrow space and you have to make yourself as thin as possible from front to back."

2. "The correct position of the hips and abdomen makes you look more slender than when you protrude front and rear."

3. "Your belt should be parallel with the ground, not slanted forward (as in Fig. 56.21, or back (as in Fig. 56.23)."

Exercises to Strengthen Muscles That Hold Body in Good Alignment, Side View

Starting position. In wall-Standing (Figs. 56.24 and 56.25), stand with back to wall, heels two inches or three inches from wall, with feet and knees in good alignment:

1. Feet pointing straight ahead, or slightly outward, with weight toward outer side of feet

2. Kneecaps facing straight ahead

3. Knees straight, not bent or stiff

In wall-sitting exercises (Figs. 56.26, 56.27, and 56.28, sit with back to wall (or in modification, sit back-to-back with partner). Legs may be in any one of the following positions:

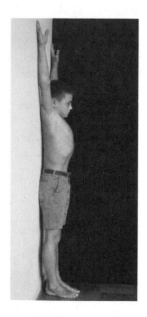
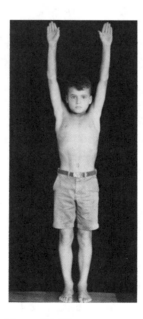

Figure 56.24   **Figure 56.25**   **Figure 56.26**

314

Figure 56.27   **Figure 56.28**

1. Cross-legged
2. Knees bent and feet flat on floor
3. Legs out straight

Movement. After assuming the starting position, then do the following:

1. Straighten upper back and hold upper back and head against the wall (or against partner's back and head).
2. Pull up and in with the muscles of the lower abdomen, bringing lower back close to the wall (or to partner's lower back).
3. Hold the good position of the trunk as arms do one of the following: (a) raise arms forward to horizontal, then out to side to touch wall, turning palms upward; (b) raise arms forward to overhead; (c) raise arms sideways to horizontal, turning palms upward; (d) raise arms sideways to diagonally overhead, palms upward; (e) raise arms sideways to full overhead, palms facing each other.

TO HELP MAINTAIN OR RESTORE NORMAL FLEXIBILITY

Figure 56.29 demonstrates forward-bending to stretch back and hamstring muscles. Touching the toes is normal for any age group except the ages 10 to 14 when it is normal for many children to be limited a few inches. Often the limitation is not a result of shortened (tight) muscles, but results from the fact that the legs are long in relation to the trunk. When this is the case, do not force the child to touch toes. Doing so may cause too much stretching of the back.

When forward-bending to touch the toes is done as an exercise, it is better to do it in the sitting position than in the standing. In sitting the knees will not go into back-knee position and the hips will not twist to one side or the other.

Fig. 56.30 shows forward-bending as it appears if back has normal flexibility and the hamstrings are tight. When this is the case, use alternate leg-raising (see Fig. 56.31) instead of forward-bending to stretch the hamstrings. In forward-bending the back may "give" more than the hamstrings.

Alternate leg-raising to slightly below right angle is normal range of motion for the hamstring muscles (Fig. 56.31).

With one knee bent up to the chest to *keep the back flat,* press the other leg down toward the floor, pulling with the muscles over the back of the hips to stretch the hip flexor muscles over the front of the hips. Do not let back arch (Fig. 56.22).

Exercises shown in Figs. 56.32, 56.33, and 56.34 increase flexibility but should be avoided if the upper back is round and the shoulders and head are

Figure 56.29

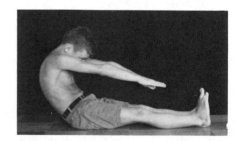

Figure 56.30

Figure 56.31

Figure 56.32

Figure 56.33

Figure 56.34

forward. After the strength of the upper back muscles has been restored, and the person can maintain good alignment, these exercises may be resumed but should *not* be done to excess.

"Upper" Abdominal Muscles

The term "upper" is used in connection with the abdominal muscles for convenience in referring to those muscles that act to flex the upper trunk toward the pelvis, bringing the trunk into a curled position. The term is not based on an anatomical division of the muscles.

Analysis of the trunk-raising exercise in relation to upper abdominal muscles. Curling the trunk is done by the "upper" abdominal muscles (Fig. 56.35). The feet should *not* be held down during this phase of the exercise.

After the trunk is curled as far as the back will bend, the hips and upper trunk are lifted up by the hip flexors (Fig. 56.36). If needed to counterbalance body weight, feet may be held down during this phase.

Avoid the type of sit-up shown in Fig. 56.37. When abdominal muscles are too weak to curl the trunk, a sit-up can be done with an arched back by the action of the hip flexors. But this exercise tends to weaken rather than strengthen the abdominal muscles. (See below for proper exercises to strengthen "upper" abdominals.)

The sit-up *always* requires hip flexor action for *completion,* and is a good abdominal exercise *only* if the trunk is curled.

Leg position during the sit-up. With the *legs out straight* the hip flexors do not contract until the pelvis starts to come up from the floor.

317

With the *knees bent* the hip flexors come into action immediately with the trunk-curl. Avoid the knees-bent sit-up if hip flexor exercises are to be avoided.

Good abdominal strength is important to body function in general. The ability to do a curled-trunk sit-up with hands clasped behind the head, or at least with the arms folded across the chest, should be an accomplishment of the average individual above age six or eight.

Exercises to help restore strength in "upper" abdominal muscles. When weakness exists, the situp with feet held down should be avoided. Raising only the head and shoulders into a trunk-curled position (Fig. 56.35) should be used, beginning with modifications of the arm positions: *Start* with arms extended forward, *progress* to arms folded on chest, *later* clasp hands behind the neck.

Avoid overdoing sit-ups. There is marked overemphasis on the sit-up exercise with the result that round shoulder tendencies increase. Since the second phase of sit-ups is a strong hip flexor exercise, there is also the danger that lordosis tendencies increase. Wall-sitting or wall-standing exercises that emphasize straightening the back should be considered equally important.

From the standpoint of good posture the strength of the "upper" abdominals is not as important as that of the "lower."

"Lower" Abdominal Muscles

The term "lower" is used in connection with the abdominal muscles for convenience in referring to those that act to tilt the pelvis backward and flatten the low back. It is not based on an anatomical division of the muscles.

Analysis of the double leg-raising exercise in relation to "lower" abdominal muscles. Raising the legs is done by the hip flexors. Holding the pelvis tilted back and the low back flat is done by the abdominals (Fig. 56.38). This exercise may be used to help maintain good abdominal muscle strength, provided the back can be kept flat as the legs are lifted and provided hip flexor muscles are not tight.

Avoid double leg-raising exercise when abdominal muscles are weak. With weak abdominal muscles the back cannot be held falt as in Fig. 56.38 but arches as the legs. Doing this exercise may cause strain and further weakness of the abdominals. (See below for proper exercises to strengthen "lower" abdominals.)

Because double leg-raising is always a strong hip flexor exercise, there should be frequent checks on the length of these muscles (see Fig. 56.22). If shortness develops, daily stretching of the hip flexors should be done until normal length has been restored.

Figure 56.35

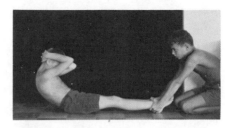

Figure 56.36

Figure 56.37

Figure 56.38

Exercises to help restore good strength in "lower" abdominal muscles.   Start with leg-sliding exercise (Fig. 56.39) and wall-sitting and wall-standing exercises.

The starting position for the leg-sliding exercise is shown in Fig. 56.39; completed position is shown in Fig. 56.40.

Lie on back, knees bent, feet flat on floor, arms up beside head. Flatten lower back by pulling up and in with the "lower" abdominal muscles, making them *firm*. Keep these muscles firm and the back flat while sliding the feet along the floor until the legs are straight. Return to knee-bent position, sliding one foot back at a time. Chest should not be raised high, nor pulled down

Figure 56.39

Figure 56.40

while doing this exercise, but subject should hold lower abdominals firm, and breathe in and out normally.

Progress to: back-lying, alternate leg-raising, keeping the lower back flat on the floor.

Later: back-lying, knees bent, straighten both legs upward (close to 90 degree angle) and lower slowly, but only as far down as subject can go with the back flat. When the back starts to arch, bend the knees and lower the legs.

As the abdominal muscles get stronger, the back can be kept flat as legs lower all the way.

POSTURE IN SITTING

To sit erect, but also to be at ease, the type and size of the chair must be suited to the individual (Fig. 56.41). A person can rest back against a straight-back chair and be in good posture.

Sitting "slumped" puts a strain on many parts of the body, especially the back (Fig. 56.42). (Besides, it puts a strain on the people who have to look at you!)

Sitting up too straight, as in Fig. 56.43 arches the low back too much. A person cannot sit at ease in this position.

Let your posture in sitting be graceful, never disgraceful!

Sit with knees together and feet flat on the floor, or with feet crossed, or at times with knees crossed. If the knees are crossed, one over the other, they should be alternated so they are not always crossed in the same manner.

While some people, especially those with problems of poor circulation in the legs, should avoid sitting with knees crossed, there is good reason why so many people sit this way. Unless people are sitting in chairs that give adequate support to the low back, there is a tendency, when they try to sit erect, for their hips to tilt forward to the point of arching the low back. If the

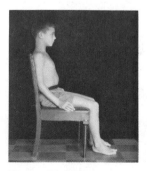

Figure 56.41

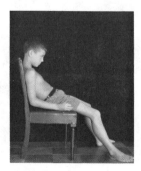

Figure 56.42

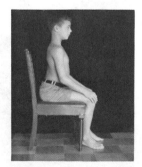

Figure 56.43

knees are crossed, the hips cannot tilt as far forward, and the hips and low back are in a more stable position.

Perhaps the social disapproval of ladies sitting with the legs crossed stems from the era when it was considered unladylike to show the ankles.

MISCELLANEOUS

In restoring or maintaining good posture, certain idiomatic phrases may be used to describe required activity (see Table 56.1). Specific description in these instances is preferred to a "catch-all" phrase.

A posture chart should be used to record postural faults so that proper corrective measures may be taken.

Table 56.1
Description of Activity

Avoid these phrases	*Use* these instead
Press your chin back!	Head back, but no double chin! Get your chin above the notch between your collar bones.
Throw your chest out!	Raise your chest by straightening your upper back.
Throw your shoulders back! Push your elbows back!	Draw your shoulder blades back *without* pushing your elbows back!
Squeeze your shoulder blades together!	Get your shoulder blades flat against your upper back.
Lock your knees!	Stand with knees straight but not stiff.
Stand with weight on the balls of your feet.	Balance your weight between the heels and balls of your feet.

SUGGESTED READING

Clarke, H. H. (ed.) 1979. Posture. *Physical Fitness Research Digest*, Series 9, No. 1 (January). Washington, D.C.: President's Council on Physical Fitness and Sports.

57

Principles of Posture and Body Mechanics Conditioning

Thomas K. Cureton, Jr.

GOOD POSTURE

Good posture is an expression of physical fitness, a barometer of feeling tone and health, and a reflection of a good mental attitude. Postures may be tense or relaxed, attentive or disinterested, buoyant or dejected, vigorously alert and ready for action, or slovenly indisposed toward action. Posture is one form of personality expression, and good posture usually reflects strength and energy reserve.

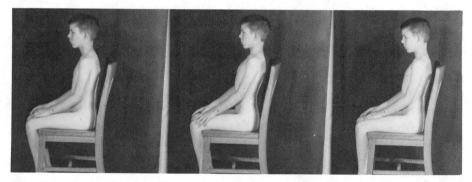

Fig. 57.1 Good sitting posture.

Poor posture may be due to poor nutrition, poor muscular tone or imbalance of muscles acting upon a segment. It may reflect poor physical condition, low strength for the weight of the segments, or poor circulation resulting in fatigue of the affected muscles. In this sense, posture is related to health.

Posture is functionally good when the circulation is good. Poor head, neck, and chest posture may cause poor circulation to the pancreas; that is, when the suspensory ligament is relaxed, allowing a slump of the organs in the chest, a retarded diaphragmatic action and shallow respiration can result. If long continued the effect may impair health. Tenseness retards or hampers circulation. Corsets, belts and tight shoes may hurt normal posture and circulation.

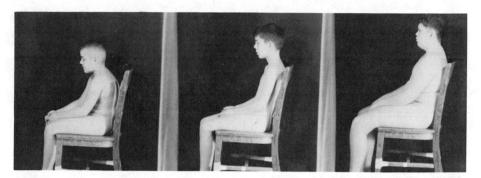

Fig. 57.2 Poor sitting posture.

Protuberant abdomen.   A protuberant abdomen may reflect weak abdominal muscles, engorged viscera, a thick mass of mesentery, and fat. It may also reflect the dominant endomorphic characteristic—a long and bulging intestine, and a lack of desire to look fit. Extreme endomorphs may have intestines over 40 feet long, whereas, extreme ectomorphs may have a length less than 20 feet. Proper conditioning of the abdominal muscles will usually produce a flatter, stronger abdominal wall with greater habitual tone, which causes the curved muscle bands to flatten.

Alternate bending and squeezing the abdominal region, as in trunk bending forward to the full limit, will squeeze the abdominal contents. Repeated alternation of squeezing and relaxing movements produces changing abdominal pressures, which acts as massage to stimulate the cellular activity in the intestines, improve the blood flow in the area, accelerate evacuation, and in due time may tend to reduce the fat.

Head position. Good head position, moderately upright and poised, is helpful to breathing and economy of effort, and helps to keep the organs of the chest elevated by means of the suspensory ligament. This ligament attaches to the cervical spine and acts to support the diaphragm, lungs, and liver. The burden of such support falls upon the posterior neck muscles and, for this reason, they should be especially well conditioned by means of neck retractive exercises: resisting pressure to pull or push the neck forward as in the "stick body" exercise in which the sloped body is supported from the back of the head and from the heels. Of course, standing with the head very erect, hyperextended backward or forced fully backward is a good exercise in itself.

Chest position. Good chest position is also based upon the training of the chest elevator muscles, the upper posterior thoracic muscles and a sense of feel (kinesthetic sense) of a desirable position. Chest expansion and elevation exercises are usually beneficial. Flexibility of the whole thoracic cage is highly desirable and exercises that promote the full breathing capacity (sometimes called "vital capacity") are indicated, such as vertical bobbing with full inspiration above the water and full expiration in 7 to 10 feet of water in the pool, along with full stretching of the chest underwater. Deep breathing exercises with full thoracic excursion are excellent to condition the respiratory muscles and promote the circulation through the heart and lungs. Such exercises cause hypoventilation, raise the pH of the blood, and exercise the muscles of the chest and diaphragm.

Shoulder position. Good shoulder position is based upon a proper feel (kinesthetic sense of position), structural length of clavicles, and good tone of the shoulder retractor muscles. The rhomboids especially should be alternately contracted and stretched; the shoulders should be held in the retracted position and the muscles tensed for periods of time in the shortened position. Exercises or work that pull the shoulders forward should be followed by compensatory stretching exercises.

Pelvic position. Good pelvic position, that is, not slumped in the extreme forward-tilted position, is dependent upon a good sense of proper stance with weight somewhat forward over the balls of the feet and good tone of the hamstring and glutei muscle groups. These muscles serve to control the position of the pelvis, whereas the support is commonly attributed mistakenly to the rectus abdominis muscles running lengthwise up the front of the abdomen. The pelvis can be held fully retracted, as the lumbar spine is flattened against a wall, by the posterior retractors while the abdominals are relaxed in full inspiration. From the prone lying position these muscles can be strengthened and shortened by chest-raising or leg-raising exercises, flutter kicks on the front, and all forceful hyperextension exercises. A well-conditioned pelvic region resists the tendency of the pelvis to drop forward in the "slouch" position. Furthermore, a firm, balanced pelvis is essential to good upper trunk posture as excessive spinal curves are associated with pelvic slump and forward hips.

BALANCE AND CONTROL

Firm balance and control in walking and running are dependent upon condition of the deep lateral muscles of the trunk and the legs more than is generally recognized. As the body weight is placed upon one foot, the center of gravity comes gradually over the contact surface of the foot on the ground, but the action of the lateral muscles is definitely involved to push the body over the base of support, and also the lateral muscles on the unsupported side act strongly to resist the tendency for the weight to stay over the pushing foot.

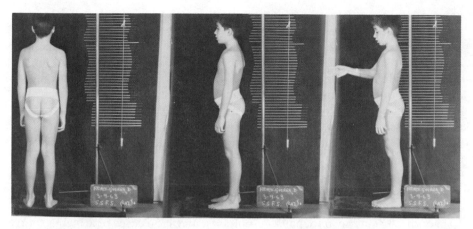

Fig. 57.3 Good standing posture.

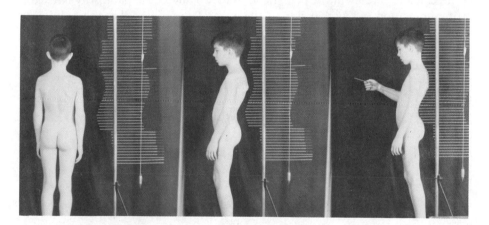

Fig. 57.4 Poor standing posture.

Such interplay of the lateral muscles, especially the quadratus lumborum, asymetrical action of the sacrospinalis muscles, the lateral leg rotators of the hip, and the abdominal transversus and obliquus, take the burden of maintaining dynamic balance on the feet in walking, running, hurdling, and jumping. Balance tests are used to indicate the degree of body control and endurance developed in the lateral muscles.

FOOT FITNESS

Support of the body weight on the feet for long periods of time, as well as forceful elastic rebound of the foot arch and "leg spring" action, are dependent upon the extent to which the foot, leg and lower back muscles are conditioned. Soft muscles with poor tone usually result in lower arches of the feet, greater pronation (bulging and lowering of the feet on the medial border), and quick fatigue and pain. The foot is held up and supported on its strong outside border by the leg muscles (tibialis posterior, peroneus longus, tibialis anterior) and the lateral longitudinal arch on the medial side of the foot. Few people can continue to hop more than two minutes in succession. By training people in hopping exercises such as: (1) vertical rise on toes of both feet, (2) side-straddle hops, (3) alternate stride hops, (4) hops on one foot, alternately, and (5) deep knee-bend (squat) jumps, the feet and legs may be strengthened and great resistance to foot fatigue developed.

The care of the feet is a problem not to be underestimated. In a report of draftees 70 percent had some trouble with the feet. In 6710 cases there were 1073 corns, 300 ingrown toenails, 82 bunions, and 1256 cases of athlete's foot. Weakness of the muscles of the arch and of the long arch-supporting muscles in the calf and foreleg may cause the arch to fall and cause pain. Any unusual protuberance on the medial side of the arch may indicate that the scaphoid bone has slipped out of place, resulting in pain and a flat foot. If a big toe is

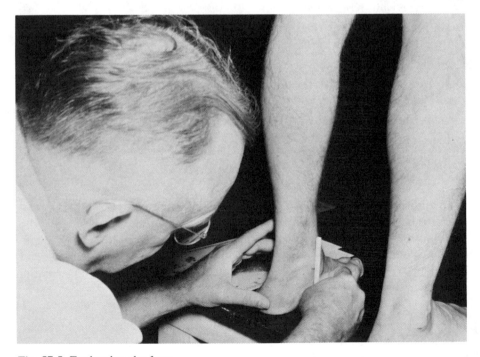

Fig. 57.5 Evaluating the foot.

bent out of line by a pointed shoe, it will ache, and a bunion will probably develop at the end of the first metatarsal phalanx. Wearing shoes that shut off all air, and sometimes circulation too, will cause the foot to deteriorate, the skin to become weak and smelly, and ultimately lead to problems. High heels on shoes worn by women may lead to undue shortening of the achilles tendon and a flattening of the anterior arch. Running too much on the toes will cause cramps in the calf, or shin splints. Shoes should fit with plenty of room for the toes, be wide enough, and be ventilated to some extent. Toenails should be cut square and not too short.

Preventive Exercises

There are 10 exercises that if done persistently will help keep the feet in condition:

1. Stretch and flex the toes two or three times per day with the shoes off.
2. Grip a pencil from the floor by flexion of the toes.
3. Walk on the outside edges of the feet.
4. Push-up to toes while leaning against wall with feet about four feet from the wall; hands on the wall—do until tired.
5. Half-knee-bend-squats leaning against a wall, with feet about two feet from the wall, hands on the wall; do until tired.
6. Heel-toe walk, progressing from 100 yards to one mile.
7. Hops: (1) up and down, (2) straddle jump, (3) scissors in place, (4) hop on right foot, then left foot (kick the opposite leg).
8. Walk and jog repeatedly.
9. Lie on back with feet against wall.
10. Roll back onto shoulders, with feet against wall or free of support to back, and flex the knee fully—one at a time, alternately.

In addition to these exercises, foot care should include: (1) massaging the toes for a few minutes while washing the feet, (2) using good foot powder to dry the feet after showering, and (3) treating mild cases of athlete's foot with ointments and referring severe cases to a medical doctor.

ANATOMIC MISALIGNMENT

There is a distinct relation between abnormal anatomic arrangement and physiologic functions. For example, pronated and flat feet result in pain and interference with the function of the ankles, knees, and hips, and frequently cause backache. Misalignment of the joining surface causes increased strain upon the supporting muscles and ligaments, interference with blood and lymph supply, and improper use of articular cartilages. These abnormal relations frequently give rise to joint inflammation.

SUGGESTED READING

Clarke, H. H., (ed.), 1979. *Physical Fitness Research Digest,* Series 9, No. 1 (January). Washington, D.C.: President's Council on Physical Fitness and Sports.

58

Back Pain: Rehabilitation Through Exercise
Hans Kraus

MUSCLE FUNCTION AND USE

The development and maintenance of a muscle function is closely correlated to its use. In order to produce work, a muscle contracts; its ability to contract and its strength are largely dependent on the amount of work it habitually has to perform. If a muscle is prevented from working, be it by injury, immobilization or disease, atrophy and weakness follow. In order to increase its strength, an overload of work has to be given. The ability of a muscle to relax depends on continued use of this quality as well. It is this ability of the muscle to relax that is so frequently found impaired by our sedentary lives, by maintaining the muscle in shortened position and under tension in excess to that necessary to maintain requirements of position and posture (Buchthal et al. 1944: Buchthal and Kaiser 1944; Clemmesen 1951; Fulton 1926). This constant tension and shortening of muscle may lead to contracture (Hajeck et al. 1947; MacKenzie 1940; Tiegel 1876).

If we remember that constant adequate use is a prerequisite for maintaining all the elements of muscle function, it becomes understandable why under-exercise may result in weakness, tightness, and undue increase of tension, if this lack of movement is accompanied by the continued influx of unreleased stimuli causing tension syndrome.

LOW BACK SYNDROME

The most frequently seen orthopedic problem in which weakness of muscles plays as important a part as tension and tightness is the "low back syndrome." The big muscle groups used in managing the body in various positions and movements are rarely used adequately by the sedentary person. The abdominal muscles are kept slack; the back muscles, while used to keep the body erect, are used in a static rather than dynamic fashion. The muscles of the lower extremities are not given any strengthening exercises at all and are usually held in positions producing shortening of the hamstrings. It is this static and unbalanced use of the body that plays an important role in the etiology of the increasingly frequent "low back pain."

In the past, childbirth and various gynecological difficulties were blamed as the cause of this pain. More recently, incidents of it in men rose remarkably, and in the last World War back pain was one of the most important causes for disability of servicemen. Disc disease and anomalies of lumbosacral spine were held responsible for a large number of these cases but many of them remained without well defined and diagnosed pathology. Backache frequently occurs after seemingly trivial trauma such as bending for a pencil, opening a window, or a weekend round of golf. After an initial episode, recurrences come with increasing frequency until a patient becomes a chronic backache sufferer.

The idea that poor posture and muscle insufficiency may cause backache has been understood for a long time (Goldswaith et al. 1945; Taylor 1868). It is only lately that more authors have been aware of the muscular origin of many back complaints (Gaston 1951, 1959; Goldswaith et al. 1945; Johnson 1958; Kendall 1952; Kraus 1952, 1952; Steindler 1935; Stimson 1947). On the other hand, the fact that X-ray changes are frequently not correlated with the presence of pain is increasingly emphasized (Gaston 1959; Ghormley 1958; Hussar 1956; Kendall 1952; Williams 1955).

Especially outspoken on the topic are Hussar and Guller (1956) who come to the conclusion that "as a rule pain is not associated with roentgenographic findings."

MUSCLE TESTING

With the etiology of muscular deficiency in mind, routine muscle testing was made part of the examinations of a group clinic to investigate the cause of low back pain. This was organized in 1944 at Columbia Presbyterian Medical Center by Dr. Barbara Stimson under the auspices of Dr. Clay Ray Murray and Dr. Darrach. This clinic, consisting of a number of specialists (orthopedic surgeons, neurosurgeons, neurologists, internists, specialists of physical medicine, and other specialists) evaluated some 3000 patients. An additional 2000 were studied by a similar group clinic at the Institute of Physical Medicine and Rehabilitation, New York University. Besides a thorough conventional examination, all these patients were subjected to muscle tests to determine relative strength and flexibility of their key posture muscles. It was the idea of the investigating team that underexercise might result in relative muscle deficiency and thereby cause chronic and acute back pain. The Kraus-Weber tests (1945-1954) for minimum muscular fitness (Fig. 58.1) were used as follows:

Position 1: Lying supine, hands behind neck. Examiner holds feet down on table. Command: "Keep hands behind neck, roll up into a sitting position."

Position 2: Lying supine, hands behind neck and knees bent. Examiner holds feet down on table. Command: "Keep hands behind neck and roll up into a sitting position."

Position 3: Supine with hands behind neck and legs extended. Command: "Keep your knees straight and lift feet 10 inches off the table for 10 seconds."

Position 4: Lying prone with pillow under abdomen, hands behind neck. Examiner holds feet and hips down. Command: "Raise trunk and hold for 10 seconds."

Position 5: Prone over pillow. Examiner holds back and hips. Command: "Lift legs up, hold for 10 seconds."

Position 6: Standing erect in stocking or bare feet, hands at sides. Command: "Put your feet together, keep knees straight, lean down slowly, see how close you can come to touching the floor with your finger tips."

These movements test the ability of large trunk and hip muscles to lift the patient's own weight. They are therefore self-correlating since one should have enough strength to manage one's own body weight. The flexibility test measures length and flexibility of muscles against the size of the patient. This again is a self-correlating test not requiring standardization.

It was shown by various authors (Matthews 1957; Sleight 1956) as well as by our own computations that this flexibility test (floor touch test) depends not on the size of the examined person since relative arm-trunk-leg length is near constant. Failure of this test therefore indicates muscle stiffness and lack of flexibility.

The test battery was originally part of a 16-point examination used in the evaluation of posture of school children and had been employed and validated on several hundred patients. The original evaluations were made in the posture clinic, founded by Dr. Sonya Weber at Columbia Presbyterian Hospital, in an effort to correlate structural and functional measurements. The test was applied to all back sufferers. Over 80 percent of these patients (Fig. 58.2) examined at the clinic belonged in the category of muscle weakness or stiffness and did not show any specific disease, lesion, or anomaly that could be blamed for their afflication (Gaston 1959; Kraus 1945; Stimson 1947).

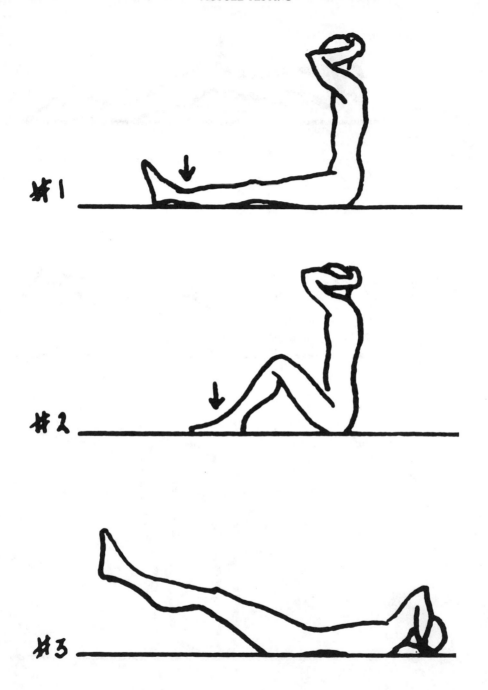

Fig. 58.1 Kraus-Weber tests for minimal muscular fitness (phases 1-3).

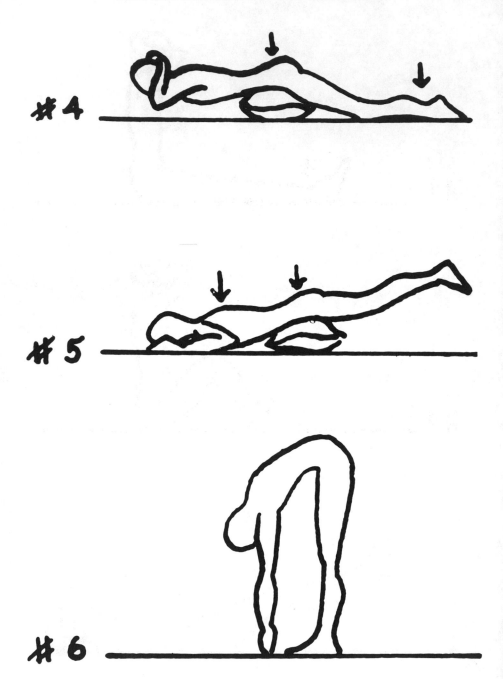

Fig. 58.1 (continued)

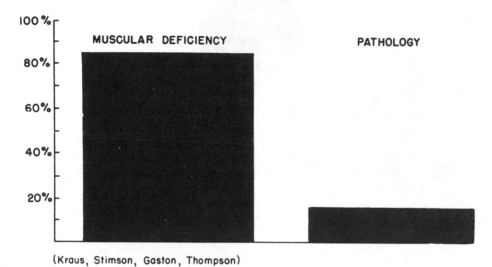

LOW BACK PAIN
OVER 80% OF LOW BACK PAIN IS DUE TO MUSCULAR DEFICIENCY

(Kraus, Stimson, Gaston, Thompson)

Fig. 58.2 Eighty percent of low back pain is due to lack of adequate physical activity.

THERAPEUTIC EXERCISES

These muscular deficient patients were treated with gradually increasing therapeutic exercises. The exercises were prescribed to improve strength or flexibility of muscle groups found wanting in the tests. A total of 233 of the cases were followed for about eight years (Fig. 58.3). It was found that the symptoms of these patients improved with improving muscle strength and flexibility, and that they regressed when their therapeutic exercises or physical activities dropped off and their weaknesses reappeared. Generally speaking, a very strong parallel existed and continued between poor muscle status on one hand, and pain and disability on the other. Tightness and stiffness of back muscles responded to a program of exercises aimed at limbering and stretching affected muscles. It was interesting to observe how the response varied, depending on tensions. While strengthening the muscles could be counted upon to progress in a rather regular and systematic fashion, flexibility showed great dependence on tensions, whether caused by psychological problems or outside irritations. The interrelation between the poor flexibility of a muscle and the tension status of the patient was quite evident, and where it existed it had to be observed and cared for adequately. We encounter here an example of the "tension syndrome," a syndrome produced by suppression of motor response to nervous stimuli.

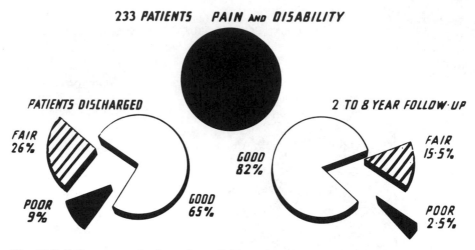

Fig. 58.3 Follow-up study showed parallel between poor muscle status and pain and disability.

EXERCISE IMPORTANT IN RELIEVING BACK PAIN

Observations made for years led to our firm conviction that underexercise was an important factor in back pain. Exercise has a "protective value" in prevention of back pain—directly by keeping posture muscles flexible and strong and indirectly by serving as an outlet for nervous irritations (Kraus 1964, 1962, 1961, 1959, 1956).

In our civilized cities we lead the lives of caged animals. We have little opportunity to move and little chance to respond to outside irritations. Besides, most of us are burdened by emotional problems, adding to the need for release. Since our civilization does not permit the natural response of fight or flight and since we do not have vicarious outlets by heavy exercise, tension is stored up in our muscles. This constant tension shortens muscles and deprives them of elasticity. Once this muscle tightness has reached a sufficiently high level, and lack of physical activity has weakened our tense muscles, the stage is set for the first episode of back pain. Picking up a paper or pencil may precipitate the first attack. It leaves the muscles weakened and more stiffened—ready for the next episode of pain that in turn will compound the symptoms.

Once minor episodes of back pain have accumulated, the muscle imbalance is increased and frequently local disturbances in the muscle itself occur. Tenderness of the constantly tightened muscle, and localized painful areas (Fig. 58.4), termed triggerpoints (Mayer 1956; Morris 1958; Sainsbury 1954; Scapinelli 1967), will appear and the episodes will increase, both in intensity and frequency. Triggerpoints have been biopsied by Glogowsky and Wallraff (1951) and found microscopically to be degenerated areas of muscle tissue. Further analysis of these areas shows a conglomeration of nuclei and the shrinking and homogenization of muscle fibers. There is invasion of fibrous tissue and fatty tissue into the nodule. The cause of the muscle pain is probably prolonged muscle spasm or muscle tension interfering with circulation and producing anoxia of the respective areas in the muscles, which in turn, leads to degeneration. Triggerpoints cause radiating pain, both in upper and lower back, with radiation patterns to the extremities. Such back pain

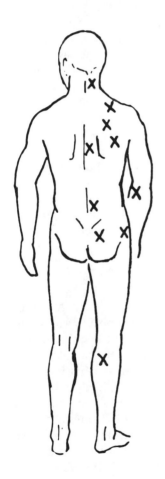 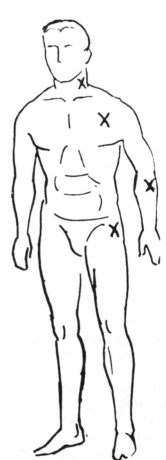

Fig. 58.4 Locations of triggerpoints.

sufferers will frequently be diagnosed as having "discs" even though there are no neurological signs or symptoms and no positive X-ray findings to bear out this diagnosis. From that moment on patients, seeing future surgery as an increasing possibility and frequently being asked to "live with" their discomfort and to refrain from "excessive motion," become more and more sedentary. Occasional minor spurts of activity inflict major punishment on their constantly deteriorating muscle potential. At this stage it is much harder to reverse the trend. It requires not only a planned retraining program, which may extend over months, but also local treatment of tender areas, with local injection of triggerpoints, followed by spasm-relieving therapy. We use sinusoidal current, ethyl chloride spray, and muscle relaxing movements.

Complications, due to the additional nervous tension caused by the patient's anxieties, fear of diability, and discomfort, have to be faced. The "low back syndrome" has now reached the stage where the treatment is difficult, time-consuming, and often hopeless. At this stage habit formation has made it much harder for patients to resume, or even more difficult to begin, an active life for the first time. It is equally difficult for them to tolerate muscular discomfort associated with exercise, and it is an added hardship for them to devote time and concentration to the task of retraining not only their muscles but their whole attitude. When patients have reached this stage, and frequently much sooner, they have lost the sense of active well-being that should be present in healthy individuals, and they are reconciled to physical inactivity that might at first have seemed limited and unpleasant to them.

MINIMUM OF STRENGTH AND FLEXIBILITY NECESSARY FOR A HEALTHY BACK

Earlier we mentioned a battery of muscle tests we have used to gauge strength and flexibility of posture muscles. We have seen time and again how dropping below requirements of these tests coincided with back pain, and how returning to this level of muscle efficiency coincides with relief. We have therefore come to accept our tests as a borderline criterion, that it, as the *minimum* of strength and flexibility desirable to maintain a healthy back. It has to be kept in mind that these minimum requirements for "muscular fitness" designate a level that is far from the optimum. It indicates a danger zone. It should make us aware that once we are unable to manage our own weight and our own length efficiently, we are more likely to suffer muscular disabilities such as lower back pain. Not meeting this level indicates that our physical activities have dropped to the point where they may not suffice to maintain the balance between intake and outlet; intake of stimuli on one hand and outlet by motor action on the other.

We must keep in mind that we examine key posture muscles from a relative viewpoint. Their deficiency as tested against one's own body has to be looked at in light of the person's requirements and physical activity. Heavy weight lifters may be exceedingly strong and able to meet much more than all the requirements of the strength test, but poor training may have neglected their flexibility and may have made them a poor risk when they make sudden movements. Sedentary workers may be both weakened in some of their trunk muscles and tight in back and hamstring muscles. A woman may have been perfectly balanced until childbirth strained her abdominal muscles, and until increased demand of lifting a child exceeds her ability to restore trunk muscle power quickly enough to live up to the task.

Examples could be added *ad infinitum*. They illustrate that any evaluation of relative muscle deficiency has to be contemplated from the point of view of the individual. Looked at in this way, it will give a valuable clue when examining the balance of the person, a balance brought about by proper interaction of physical as well as emotional factors. It is in this light that we should look at the back pain sufferer as a person whose condition is caused by physical inactivity under circumstances that combine lack of exercise with emotional stresses and nervous strain.

CONCLUSION

The physical educator can play a most important role in the prevention of backache. In the light of the fact that a high percentage of our children between ages 6 and 16 fail the simple muscular fitness tests (57.9 percent in our original study), the establishing of fitness programs starting in elementary school and continuing throughout the school years, including college, is an essential public health need. The prevention of back pain as well as other orthopedic disabilities would therefore be another important task for the physical educator and the public health service. Unfortunately, at present little effort is being made in this area due to stress on games and contact sports.

As in Swiss schools where one hour of physical fitness work is obligatory from elementary throughout the whole school experience, we too must establish similar programs. They should first attempt to attain the minimum muscular fitness of our children and then attempt to preserve it. Games, as in Switzerland, should be open to anyone who wishes to participate on an optional basis. This would eliminate the many unhappy, sidelined, and left-out children who do not make the teams, or are relegated to unprestigious positions on lower level teams.

Similarly, physical fitness classes for reconditioning sedentary adults, restoring their muscular strength, flexibility, and ability to relax, are equally important. This would provide a tremendous opportunity for physical educators in the area of preventive medicine. Unfortunately the potential has hardly been tapped compared to the situation abroad where there are thousands of such reconditioning places in Russia and hundreds in the Germanys, Switzerland, and Austria. Even though in recent years there has been a great increase in physical fitness programs for adults in the United States, the trend has far from reached its peak.

REFERENCES

Buchthal, F., and E. Kaiser, 1944. Factors Determining tension development in skeletal muscle. *Acta Physiol. Scand.* **8:** 38-74.

———, and G.G. Knappirs, 1944. Elasticity, viscosity and plasticity. *Acta Physiol. Scand.* **8:** 16-37.

Clemmesen, S., 1951. Some studies on muscle tone. *Proceedings of the Royal Society of Medicine* **44** (August) : 637-646.

Fulton, J. F. 1926. *Muscular contraction and the reflex control of movement.* Baltimore: Williams & Wilkins.

Gaston, S. R. *Preliminary report of a group study of the painful back.* New York: Low Back Clinic, Columbia Presbyterian Medical Center.

———, 1959. *Low back pain due to other than intervertebral disc injuries, in trauma.* Philadelphia: W.B. Saunders and London: Harrison L. McLaughlin.

———, and E. B. Schlesinger, 1951. The low back syndrome. *Surgical Clinics of No. Am.* **31** (April).

Ghormley R. K., 1958. Etiologic study of back pain. *Radiology* **70** (May) : 649-653.

Glogowski, G., and J. Wallraff, 1951. Ein Beitrag zur Klinik und Histologie der Muskelharten (Myogelosen). *Z. Orthop. Grenzgeb.* **80:** (238-268).

Goldswaith, J. E., L. T. Brown, and L. T. Swaim, 1945. *Essentials of body mechanics in health and diseases.* Philadelphia: J.B. Lippincott.

Hajek, N. M., M. E. Godby, and H. M. Hines, 1947. Functional changes in muscle and nerve resulting from prolonged states of shortening. *Arch. Phys. Med.* **28** (November) : 690-695.

Hussar, A. E., and E. J. Guller, 1956. Correlation of pain and the roentgenographic findings of spondylosis of the cervical and lumbar spine. *Am J. Med. Sc.* **232** (November) : 518-527.

Johnson, D. A. 1958. Diagnosis of postural myoneuralgia. *Modern Medicine,* (April 15).

Kendall, H. O., F. P. Kendall, and D. A. Boynton, 1952. *Posture and pain.* Baltimore: Williams & Wilkins.

Kraus, H., 1952. Diagnosis and treatment of low back pain. *G. P.* **5** (April) : 55-60.

_____,1952. Prevention of low back pain. *J. Ass. Phys. and Ment. Rehab.* **6** (September-October) : 12-15.

_____, 1964. Preventive aspects of physical fitness. *N.Y.J. Med.* **63** (May) : 1182-1185.

_____, and S. Eisenmenger-Weber, 1945. Evaluation of posture based on structural and functional measurements. *Physiotherapy Rev.* **25** (November-December) : 267-271.

_____, and R. P. Hirschland, 1954. Muscular fitness and orthopedic disability. *N. Y. J. Med.* **54** (January 15) : 212-215.

_____, and S. Weber 1962. Back pain and tension syndromes in a sedentary profession. *Arch. Environ. Health* **4** (April) : 408-414.

_____, and W. Raab, 1961. *Jypokinetic disease—diseases produced by lack of exercise,* Springfiled. Ill.: Charles C. Thomas.

_____, W. Nagler, and S. Weber, 1959. Role of exercise in the prevention of disease. *G. P.* **20** (September) : 121-126.

_____, B. Prudden, and K. Hirschhorn, 1956. Role of inactivity in production of disease—hypokinetic disease. *J. Am. Geriat. Soc* **4** (May) : 463-471.

MacKenzie, C. 1940. *The action of muscles.* Paul E. Hoeber, Inc.

Matthews, D. K., et al. 1957. Hip flexibility of college women as related to length of body segments. *Research Quarterly* **28** (December) : 352-356.

Mayer, J., et al. 1956. Relation between calorie intake, body weight, and physical work. *Amer. J. Clin. Nutr.* **4** (March-April) : 169-175.

Morris, J. N., and M. D. Crawford, 1958. Coronary heart disease and physical activity of work: Evidence of a national necropsy survey. *Brit. Med. J.* **5111** (December 20) : 1485-1496.

Sainsbury, P. and T. G. Gibson, 1954. Symptoms of anxiety and tension and the accompanying physiological changes in the muscular system. *J. Neurol. Neurosurg. & Psychiat.* **17** (August) : 216-224.

Scapinelli, R., and Ortolani, M., 1967. Preponderanza dei fattori dinamici su quelli statici nella patogenesi dell'artrosi vertebrale e dell'ernia del disco. *La Clinica Ortop.* **19** (July-August).

Sleight, R. B., 1956. Human Engineering. *Research and Engineering* **2** (February) : 30-34.

Steindler, A. 1935. *Mechanics of normal and pathological locomotion in man.* Springfield, Ill.: Charles C. Thomas.

Stimson, B., 1947. The low back problem. *Psychosom. Med.* **9** (May-June) : 210-212.

Taylor, G. H., 1868. *An exposition of the swedish movement cure.* New York: Samuel R. Wells.

Tiegel, E., 1876. "Ueber Muskelcontractur im Gegensatz zu Contraction. *Pfluger's Arch. fur die Gesammte Physiol.* **13:** 71-83.

Williams, A. J., and T. Fullenlove, 1955. Herniation of intervertebral discs: An evaluation of the indirect signs. *California Med.* **83** (December) : 433-434.

59

Back Exercises

Karl K. Klein

Chronic low back pain is, by and large, the major physical stress problem in adult society today. The vast majority of these problems are idiopathic in nature and are of a nonpathologic origin. If medical evaluation rules out a pathological involvement, then the stress mechanism is more than likely related to mechanical and muscular imbalance within the structure. Two major areas of the body structure that are commonly found to be related to the symptoms are: (1) muscle imbalance in the hip flexor-extensor mechanisms resulting in postural imbalance, and (2) lateral asymmetry of the pelvis, or the short-leg syndrome.

Of major influence in postural imbalance are the iliopsoas (Michel 1971), the major hip flexor, and the rectus femoris, which tends to increase a forward tipping of the pelvis. Their constant use in movement tend to shorten them and overcome their antagonists, the abdominals and the gluteals, which are responsible for pulling the pelvis up in the front (abdominals) and down in the back (gluteals). Other muscles involved secondarily in the forward tilting of the pelvis are the low back erector spinal muscles, which increase the lumbar curve, and the hamstrings, which actually may be stretched and weakened due to the forward tilting of the pelvis. The tendency to believe that the hamstrings are tight—when forward bending is used as a testing procedure for flexibility—may well be questioned! If the pelvis is pulled upward by the abdominals before forward bending, more flexibility can be demonstrated in the action, but due to the characteristics of the hamstring muscles, lack of flexibility is often associated with the problems of low back stress.

In lateral asymmetry of the pelvis, if no pathology to cause directly a major unilateral limb shortening is involved, there are numerous idiopathic anatomical causes for lateral tipping of the pelvis. Such factors can be a minor shortness of one leg, a decreased angle of the neck of one femur, one low arch or flat foot, unilateral ankle pronation, unilateral malpositioning of the acetabulum and/or unilateral valgus, or knock knee. Any one or a combination of any of these factors can be responsible for the short-leg syndrome. Standing X-ray studies by Pearson (1954) of 831 school children, taken every two years during their school years, indicated that 93.7 percent of the children demonstrated varying degrees of lateral asymmetry. Standing lateral postural measurement studies conducted by Klein (1969), of 585 elementary, junior, and senior high school boys indicated 74, 85, and 92 percent of these groups respectively showed evidence of measurable lateral asymmetry of the pelvis. In a similar measurement study of over 500 chronic low back cases in college-age students and faculty, Klein (1970) found 100 percent demonstrated measurable lateral asymmetry as being significantly related to the problem. Studies by Beal (1950) and others have stressed the point that unilateral leg length discrepancies appear in a high incidence of the population and are related significantly to the problem of low back stress. Since there is evidence that lateral asymmetries are highly related to the incidence of low back stress, examination for such possibilities should be an integral part of the total muscular and postural evaluation process when studying the problem.

It is also important to recognize that there are other factors involved, especially among the adult population. Kraus (1965) has made significant contributions to understanding and problem solution in this area. His work has dealt with the causes and effects of low back pain from childhood to adulthood. He has stressed the mechanisms of underexercise and muscle tension as being related significantly to the adult problem. His basic tests for physical fitness (Kraus 1971), as described in the first AAHPER fitness tests for children, were fundamentally designed to test for low back stress. Physical inadequacies in the child were predictable of future stress in the adult society. The same tests have also been utilized in evaluation of adult problems.

The works of Lowman (1937), Kendall et al. (1952), Redler (1952), Green (1951), Nicholas (1960), and Lovett (1912) also have to be recognized in this area of low back stress. They have through their work and writings, made major contributions to understanding of cause and effect in the relationships of muscular weakness, postural defects and minor asymmetries of growth in the pelvis and legs as interrelated factors.

There are several ways in which an individual can be tested for muscular imbalance and lateral postural asymmetry. For our purpose in physical education it would be impractical to attempt to illustrate all of the techniques that can be utilized to test effectively for muscular imbalance. The major areas of concern are muscular tension expressed as shortening of the iliopsoas, rectus femoris, paraspinal and hamstring muscles, general weakness of the abdominals, and lack of a good postural concept. The simplest evaluating tests are those of Kraus (1965). Other sources for tension testing of the involved muscles are found in Kendall (1952).

Once the tension and weaknesses are determined, exercises to develop muscle flexibility can be initiated on a daily basis. An example of a successful series of flexibility and strengthening exercises is found in Fig. 59.1, with further explanation below. These exercises should be done daily. They are recommended for continued use even beyond the time when the low back stress has been ameliorated.

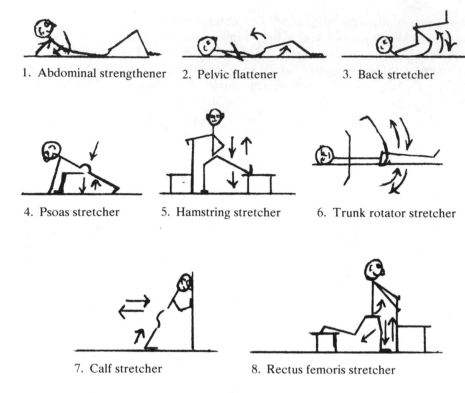

1. Abdominal strengthener   2. Pelvic flattener   3. Back stretcher

4. Psoas stretcher   5. Hamstring stretcher   6. Trunk rotator stretcher

7. Calf stretcher   8. Rectus femoris stretcher

Fig. 59.1 Special exercises for low back and flexibility (partial William's series).

Exercise Instruction

1. Precede exercise program with an evaluation for muscle tension and lateral postural evaluation. Record findings.
2. Teach exact exercise technique. *Emphasize moderate, sustained stretching only to a point of comfort.*
3. Do all exercises four to five times in series. Alternate sides where indicated.

Exercise Explanations

1. *Abdominal Strengthener:* roll up head, neck and shoulders, keep low back on floor, hold 8-10 counts, relax, repeat.
2. *PelvicFlattener:* contract abdominals and gluteal muscles, force low back to floor, hold 8-10 counts, relax, repeat.
3. *Back Stretcher:* pull knees to chest and squeeze, 8-10 counts, relax, repeat. On relaxation, hold on to knees but extend arms.

4. *Psoas Stretcher:* have foot in front of knee on forward leg, rear leg straight, keep hips level, push hips downward to *point of tension* in groin area of rear leg, hold, release (hips up), repeat. Do same procedure other side, 8-10 counts for each stretch.

5. Hamstring stretch: stand with one leg extended sideward, heel on bench, press hip downward on elevated leg side to point of mild stretch of hamstrings and leg adductors, hold 30-40 seconds, release, repeat. Do same procedure for other side.

6. *Single Leg Cross-Overs:* on back with arms sideward on mat and legs straight, swing right leg across toward left hand, *keep knee straight,* roll at hips. The ultimate objective is to reach the foot to the opposite hand but this will take some time to gain the necessary flexibility.

7. *Gastrocnemius and Plantaris Stretcher:* stand near wall, toes slightly inward, weight on outer borders of feet, reach forward to wall, bend arms, lean forward, *keep heels on floor* to a *mild stretch* of calf muscle, hold 50-60 seconds, release, repeat 4-5 times, 2-3 times daily.

8. *Rectus Femoris Stretcher:* top of one foot on low stand, hands grasp back of chair, *trunk erect,* pull abdominals up, back flat, push hips forward to stretch rectus, bend forward knee to increase tension, mild stretch only, hold 50-60 seconds, release, repeat. Same to opposite side. Repeat 2-3 times each leg.

DETERMINING LATERAL PELVIS ASYMMETRY

The basic procedures for evaluation of lateral pelvis tipping are made from the posterior iliac spines. The technique is described as follows:

> The subject stands on a low table with feet slightly apart, legs parallel and knees straight ahead with the arms hanging naturally at the sides. The investigator stands (or may be seated) directly behind the subject, with the eyes at the level of the subject's posterior iliac spines. The investigator palpates the posterior spines (most posterior point) with the thumbs. The initial palpation is made with the eyes closed, then the points are marked. The amount of imbalance is esti- mated initially by observation. The calibrated blocks are placed beneath the heel of the low side so as to level the points of the pelvis. Repeated palpations are made during the leveling process. The imbalance is taken as the thickness of the lift needed to level the posterior iliac spines. The imbalance is recorded in inches and converted to centimeters. A diagram is drawn on the record card to indicate the direction of the slope of the base before adjustment. The base difference represents the thickness of the lift placed on the heel of the subject's shoe of the low pelvis side. If the deviation is over a half inch, an adjustment is placed on the sole of the shoe about one-half the heel thickness. Any side sway of the subject will cause a mininterpretation of the measurement, so it is

necessary to have the legs parallel and directly beneath the hips to insure accuracy of measurement.

Reliability coefficients of .94-.97 and objectivity coefficients of .94-.96 have been obtained by experienced testers.

This technique of measurement is recommended by Dr. C.L. Lowman, Dr. I. Redler and Dr. W.A. Schwab. The test checks about 94 percent with standing X-ray studies of leg imbalance when the imbalance is one-fourth inch or more.

Recommended procedures in working with those with low back stress are:

1. Administer the standing lateral postural test to determine if lateral pelvis asymmetry is present. Record the findings as suggested in the measurement procedures above.

2. Administer the basic exercise tests as suggested by Kraus (1965). In addition, specific tests for iliopsoas, gastrocnemius, and rectus femoris tension should be administered and recorded.

   a. For iliopsoas tension, have subject lie supine on the table, knees hanging free over the edge. Have the person flex one knee and leg pulling it down to the chest with the hands. If the opposite leg lifts off the table it indicates iliopsoas tightness on that side. Repeat to opposite side. Make note of the psoas tension.

   b. For gastrocnemius tension, have subject long-sitting on table with heels on the table. With feet at 90 degrees with lower leg, have person dorsiflex the foot by contracting the anterior tibialis muscle. Free dorsiflexion of the foot to 15-20 degrees will demonstrate no gastrocnemius tension. Failure indicates tension. Record results.

   c. For tension in the rectus femoris, have person lie prone on table and flex one knee to place rectus femoris on tension. The instructor then places one hand on the subject's hips and the other under the bent knee lifting or extending the leg upward. If the subject experiences tension on the rectus femoris of the extended leg, rectus tension is indicated. Record results.

After the postural evaluation and muscle testing is completed, teach the person stretching and strengthening exercises. Along with the exercises, teach the person the fundamentals of good body mechanics, and pelvic control in standing, movement, and sitting. Stress the importance of mental practice in order to obtain results.

After three to four weeks again check the standing lateral posture as well as for increases in muscle flexibility. Record your findings. At this point, if the lateral asymmetry still exists, and more than likely it will not change from the original measurements, even though the low back stress may be completely eliminated, advise the use of a heel lift on the shoe to balance the pelvis and lateral posture mechanically. This is recommended as a preventive measure. Also, emphasize the importance of continuation of the exercises on a daily basis. Once flexibility is obtained, it will only be maintained with continued exercise effort. As a closing suggestion, emphasize the importance of the exercise series before as well as following activity.

REFERENCES

Beal, M. C. 1950. A review of the short leg problem. *Journal of American Osteopathic* **Association 50** (October) : 109-121.

Green, W. T., 1951. Discrepancy in leg length of the lower extremities. *American Academy of Orthopaedic Surgery, Institutional Course Lectures (VIII)* Ann Arbor: J.W. Edwards Company.

Kendall, H. O., F. P. Kendall, and D. A. Boyton, 1952. *Posture and pain.* Baltimore: Williams & Wilkins.

Klein, K. K., 1969 A study of the progression of lateral pelvis asymmetry in 585 elementary, junior and senior high school boys. *American Corrective Therapy Journal* **23** (November-December): 171-173.

_____, 1970. Progression of lateral asymmetries of growth: comparison of boys in elementary and high school with adults with chronic back symptoms. *D.O.* **11** (October) : 107.

Kraus, H., 1965. *The cause, prevention and treatment of backache, stress, and tension.* New York: Simon and Schuster.

_____, and W. Raab, 1961. *Hypokinetic disease.* Springfield, Ill.: Charles C. Thomas.

Lovett, R. W., 1912. *Lateral curvature of the spine and round shoulders.* P. Blakiston's Son and Company.

Lowman, C. L., C. Colestock, and H. Cooper, 1937. *Corrective physical education for groups.* New York: A. S. Barnes.

Michel, A. A., *Orthotherapy.* 1971. New York: Mr. Evans and Company.

Nicholas, P. R. 1960. Short leg syndrome. *Brit. Medical Journal* **5189** (June 18) : 1863-1865.

Pearson, W. M., 1954. Early and high incidence of mechanical faults. *J. Osteopathy* **61:** 18.

Redler, I., 1952. Chemical significance of minor inequalities in leg length. *New Orleans Med. Surg. Journal* **104** (February) : 308-312.

60

Controversial Exercises

Philip J. Rasch and Fred L. Allman, Jr.

At the 1971 meeting of the advisory board of the U.S. Marine Corps Physical Fitness Academy, the physical fitness training program of the corps was reviewed at some length. During the discussion one of the board members, an orthopedic physician, remarked, "At least 90 percent of the exercise programs include exercises as detrimental as they are valuable." To the corrective therapist in the field, such a statement may come as a shock. It is the purpose of this chapter to present the reasons why some standard calisthenics have come under fire from physicians, physical educators, and kinesiologists.

The Full Squat

Perhaps the best known example is the *full squat,* which here is to be understood as including the full deep knee bend, quick waddle, "Russian bounce," and similar movements. So far as the writers are aware, this exercise was first subjected to published criticism by O'Keefe (1946), who based his objections on the teaching of the late Leon Kranz, a kinesiologist at Northwestern University. It was later condemned by Lowman (1975), the National Federation of State High School Athletic Associations, the Committee on the Medical Aspects of Sports of the American Medical Association (1962), and others, and has been attacked in a long series of papers by Klein (1961). Opposition to the exercise is based largely on the fact that during the final phase of nonweight-bearing flexion of the knee there is a small amount of inward rotation of the femur at the tibia. The final seating of the femoral condyles into the contours of the menisci is sometimes called the "screw-home movement" of the knee. This axial rotation of the femur is necessary to complete the locking of the knee joint.

It is Klein's contention that when the feet are anchored to the ground by the body weight, and perhaps by a barbell on the shoulders, the normal rotation of the femur cannot take place. Consequently the femur forces the tibia into an abnormal external rotation, thereby stretching the anterior fibers of the medial and lateral ligaments. Further, the anterior cruciate ligaments

---

* Reprinted from *American Corrective Therapy Journal,* **16** : 95-98 (July-August) 1972.

are stretched by the "jacking apart" of the knee joint that occurs during full flexion as a result of the femur acting as a lever pivoting on the bunched calf muscles. Klein holds that the ligaments are the first line of defense in knee stability; once they become loose the knee is predisposed to injury, particularly when struck from the side.

The journals devoted to weight training argue that Klein's thesis is negated by the fact weight trainers seldom suffer knee injuries. This argument overlooks the fact that nothing in weight training results in the lifter's knees being struck from the side, as is a common occurrence in football. Consequently they are not really talking to the point. It has also been argued that the additional strength developed in the muscles by the practice of full squats more than compensates for any possible weakening of the ligaments. However, Lowman (1960) alleges that the exercises may produce chronic synovitis of the knee joint, regardless of its effects on the ligaments or muscles.

It is evident that this problem requires further study. In the meantime, the safest procedure would seem to be to squat only to the point that the thighs are parallel with the floor, and to eliminate completely the duck waddle and all bouncing squat movements from any exercise regimen.

The Straight-Leg Sit-Up

The straight-leg sit-up is often prescribed to "strengthen the abdominals." Anatomically the rectus abdominus (D in Fig. 60.1) originates on the crest of the pubis and inserts on the cartilages of the fifth, sixth, and seventh ribs. It is a prime mover for spinal flexion; consequently its range of movement is limited by the cumulative movement possible in the intervertebral joints. During straight-leg sit-ups it acts primarily to stabilize the pelvis, while the actual movement is accomplished largely by the contraction of the hip flexors, principally the iliopsoas (C in Fig. 60.1). It has been estimated that these muscles may develop a tensile pull of approximately 1360 pounds in full contraction in the average adult (Michele 1962). Since the femur provides a solid base of insertion, increased tonus in the psoas may result in pulling its origin—the last thoracic and all lumbar vertebrae—forward, thus increasing the lordotic curve of the back.

Some years ago it was rumored that certain Mr. America competitors had suffered from this problem due to their practicing thousands of sit-ups to achieve abdominal definition. This is also particularly common in women, many of whom suffer from weak abdominals and an exaggerated lumbar curve. For this reason the exercise has been roundly condemned by many of the writers in the field (Flint 1964; Kendall 1965; Nelson 1964; Soderberg 1966).

There is no perfect answer to the problem in the sense that it is possible to exercise the abdominals without involving the iliopsoas, but the use of bent knees and a trunk curl is advisable. In the bent knee position the tension on

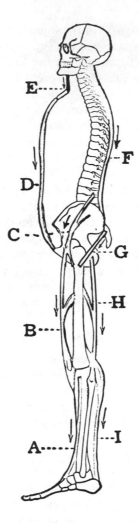

Fig. 60.1 Antagonistic muscle groups responsible for erect posture. A—tibialis anterior; B—quadriceps femoris; C—iliopsoas; D—abdominals; E—neck flexors; F—spinal extensors; G—gluteus maximus; H—hamstrings; I—triceps surae. (Reprinted from Philip J. Rasch and Roger K. Burke, *Kinesiology and Applied Anatomy,* 4th ed., Philadelphia: Lea and Febiger, 1971.)

the iliopsoas is somewhat slackened and the pelvis can be tilted to allow the back to be rounded. A truck curl commencing at the upper levels of the spine will carry the trunk about one-third of the way toward the sitting position, but completion of the movement is largely dependent on the hip flexors. Whether the knees are extended or flexed appears to have little effect on the magnitude of the muscle potential for the abdominals as recorded on the electromyograph (Flint 1965).

The Leg Lift

Objections to the practice of the leg lift in the supine position are basically the same as those to the sit-up. Here again the actual lifting of the legs is accomplished by the iliopsoas, while the abdominals act to stabilize the pelvis and keep the lower part of the back flat. Obviously, an isometric contraction of the abdominal muscles is required to accomplish this, but the exercise provided is principally for the hip flexors (Flint 1964). Kinesiological considerations and electromyographic studies (Flint 1965) suggest that the best exercise for developing the abdominals would be the "Vee-up," but this requires an amount of strength and balance that places it in the category of advanced exercises.

Perhaps it should also be mentioned here that Michele (1962) recommends practice of the lunge when it is desirable to stretch the iliopsoas. During the movement, pressure is applied over the rear buttock by the ipsilateral hand.

Toe Touching

Toe touching from the standing position is sometimes advocated as an abdominal exercise. Actually, it has no value for this purpose. The individual's trunk is drawn forward by gravity and resisted by the controlled relaxation of the spinal extensors (F, Fig. 60.1). It is returned to the upright position by contraction of these same muscles. The abdominals remain relaxed throughout. Probably the main effect of the exercise is to stretch the hamstrings (H, Fig. 60.1). These comprise half of the force couple that keeps the pelvis at a proper angle of tilt. Stretching them increases the likelihood of an undesirable forward tilt. The knees are forced into hyperextension and the extensors of the back are elongated.

Some kinesiologists believe that many of the back troubles experienced by housewives are caused by the continued mild overstretch of the spinal extensors, resulting from their assumption of a modified toe-touch stance while making beds, dusting, picking up objects from the floor, etc. If a bouncing movement must be added to the exercise in order to touch the fingers to the toes, the insult to the joints of the lumbar spine is compounded.

Back Hyperextension or Swan Exercise

The opposite of toe touching is back hyperextension from the prone position, sometimes called the swan exercise. In a more extreme form this may be done on a bench or platform so that the trunk is flexed to approximately 90 degrees before extension is initiated. When properly performed the movement terminates when the body is in the prone position, but vigorous young subjects have a tendency to go into full hyperextension. The latter position has a serious disadvantage: If the abdominals are weak and a "sway back" condition exists, practice of this exercise will further accentuate the condition. At least one kinesiologist (Flint 1964) has recommended elimination of the common standing backbend exercise for this reason.

Bent-Over Rowing

The bent-over rowing motion is an exercise used by weight trainers. Some kinesiologists believe that this position should never be assumed because the long lever of the spine and head, and the weight of the trunk, head, arms, and resistance, place a great strain on the lower trunk extensors. Morris et al. (1961) have calculated that lifting 200 pounds places a force of 1483 pounds on the lumbrosacral disc. Unquestionably it is safer if the exercise be performed with the forehead resting on some sort of support in order to remove any possibility of lower back strain.

Heel Raises

Heel raises may be done to strengthen the triceps surae or "to strengthen the longitudinal arch" of the foot. With the former, there is no quarrel. The latter, however, is another matter. The triceps surae insert into the posterior aspect of the calcaneus. As contraction of these muscles raises the back part of this bone, it tends to depress the front part. This action stretches the plantar muscles, ligaments, and fasciae, weakening the arch.

Obviously the corrective therapist should give careful consideration to these points before including any of the foregoing exercises in a conditioning program. This is not altered by the fact that most of them are more or less "standard" and may have long been familiar to the therapist from a military or athletic experience.

REFERENCES

AMA Committee on Medical Aspects of Sports, 1962. *Tips on athletic training* **IV**: 11-12.

Flint, M. M., 1964. Selecting exercises. *JOHPER* **35** (February) : 19-23, 74.

————,1965. An electromyographic comparison of the function of the iliacus and the rectus abdominus muscles. *Physical Therapy* **45:** 248-253.

————, and J. Gudgell, 1965. Electromyographic study of abdominal muscular activity during exercise. *Research Quarterly* **36:** 29-37.

————, 1965. Abdominal muscle involvement during the performance of various forms of sit-up exercise. *Am. J. Phys. Med.* **44:** 224-234.

Kendall, F. P. 1965. A criticism of current tests and exercises for physical fitness. *J. Am. Phys. Therapy Assoc.* **45:** 187-197.

Klein, K. K., 1961. The deep squat exercise as utilized in weight training for athletics and its effects on the ligaments of the knee. *J. Assoc. Phys. and Mental Rehab.* **15:** 6-11, 23.

Lowman, C. L., 1975. Mimeographed release (January).

————, and C. H. Young, 1960. *Postural fitness,* p. 173. Philadelphia: Lea and Febiger.

Michele, A. A., 1962. *Iliopsoas,* p. 123. Springfield, Ill.: Charles C. Thomas.

Morris, J. M., et al., 1961. Role of the trunk in stability of the spine. *J. Bone and Joint Surg.* **43-A:** 327-351.

Nelson, D. O., 1964. Focus on two fitness exercises. *JOHPER* **35:** 22-23.

O'Keefe, F.L., 1946. Early conditioning for football. *Athletic Journal* **26** (June) : 24ff.

Soderberg, G. L., 1966. Exercises for the abdominal muscles. *JOHPER* **37:** 67-70.

61

Physical Education in the Prevention of Coronary Heart Disease

Philip K. Wilson and John L. Boyer

The heart is truly a magnificent machine. Daily within the human being the heart pumps over 8000 gallons of blood through 12,000 miles of vessels. As fuel the pumped blood would run an automobile for 12 to 15 years, or keep a plane in air for 40 hours. The heart is a muscular pump weighing less than 350 grams and is about the size of a person's fist. It is amazing in its functional efficiency. A person has yet to develop a machine even 10 times the size or weight of the heart that is nearly as efficient for even half the life expectancy of the average American.

However, even with its great efficiency, diseases related to the heart and the entire cardiovascular system kill more Americans yearly than the next five causes of death by disease combined. Claiming over 700,000 persons annually, coronary heart disease is America's greatest single killer. Coronary heart disease accounts for 40 percent of all deaths of men aged 40 through 59. In addition to the great number of Americans who die annually from coronary heart disease, 200,000 die of a stroke, 25,000 die from hypertension, and 15,000 from rheumatic fever and related rheumatic heart disease. The estimated annual cost within the United States of coronary heart disease and related cardiovascular abnormalities is 52 million days of productivity and $19.5 billion ("Heart Facts 1973").

EXERCISE AND CORONARY HEART DISEASE

When considering the magnitude of the cardiovascular disease epidemic, it comes as no surprise that a great amount of research has been conducted concerning the topic. A major portion of the research effort has been directed toward the identification of "risk factors" that appear to predispose an individual to coronary heart disease. Fletcher and Cantwell have identified the following as possibly being "risk factors" for coronary heart disease: blood lipid abnormalities, hypertension, cigarette smoking, carbohydrate intolerance, physical inactivity, overweight, diet, heredity, personality and behavior patterns, electrocardiographic abnormalities, disorders in blood coagulation, elevation in blood uric acid, and pulmonary function abnormalities (Fletcher 1971). However, with current advances in medicine and medical research a number of "risk factors" are losing status and eventually may be considered no longer valid indicators of the likelihood of presence or of future development of coronary heart disease.

Where some coronary heart disease "risk factors" are likely to be discounted, the relationship between physical activity and the presence or degree of coronary heart disease is becoming widely accepted. Dr. Wilhelm Raab, director of cardiovascular research at the University of Vermont, indicates that "lack of exercise is the major cause of coronary heart disease" (Raab 1967). The American Medical Association supports the value of exercise by stating, "Proper exercise as a way of life helps keep healthy hearts healthy, and prevent the onset of cardiovascular disease." Dr. Edward L. Bortz, former president of the American Medical Association, says, "If American men would accept an exercise program as a regular part of their lives, in three to five years we would cut the coronary death rate in half" (Meness 1969).

Apparently involvement in regular, vigorous exercise is an important factor in the prevention of coronary heart disease. However, what is the explanation for the relationship? What is the explanation for the possibility that an individual who regularly partakes in vigorous exercise is less likely to suffer a myocardial infarction, and if a heart attack does occur, is more likely to survive the attack?

Research Relative to Exercise and Cardiovascular Function

A great amount of research has been conducted concerning the improvement of cardiovascular parameters through physical work. Cureton alone has published over a hundred articles and numerous books, related to the topic of cardiovascular improvement through exercise (Cureton 1970, 1969; Raab 1967). Valuable exercise physiology research relative to cardiovascular function has also been conducted and reported by Astrand, Balke, Buskirk, Cooper, Falkner, Haskell, Jokl, Karronen, Mathews, Morehouse, Mortone, Pollack, Skinner, Stoedefalke, and Wilmore. Through the work of such investigators the improvement of cardiovascular parameters through exercise is presently a fairly accepted concept.

Research Relative to Physical Activity and the
Incidence of Coronary Heart Disease

The relationship between physical activity and coronary heart disease has been the subject of numerous studies within the United States and throughout the world. The majority of the studies indicate that physically active individuals are less likely to develop coronary heart disease as compared to physically inactive persons. Studies conducted within the United States have dealt with blue collar workers compared to professional men (Fox 1972), railroad personnel (Brozek 1963, Taylor 1962), farmers compared to professional men (Am. Heart Assn. 1972; Morris 1957, Wilhelmsen 1971), and sedentary compared to active individuals (Breslow 1960; Frank 1968; Kannel 1971; Paffenbarger 1970; Spain 1961; Taylor 1962). Outside of the United States, studies have been conducted on busmen (Morris 1954: Shaper 1971), and sedentary compared to nonsedentary individuals (Brunner 1971; Kraus 1961; Morris 1957; Oslo Life 1956; Pedley 1942; Ryle 1949). All of the cited studies support the position that those individuals who are physically active are less likely to develop coronary heart disease as compared to those individuals who are relatively inactive. Though there is a small number of studies that have not supported this hypothesis, the relationship appears to exist (Chapman 1957; Kahn 1963; Keys 1970; Stamler 1960).

Physiological Mechanisms

Obviously exercise is an important factor in the prevention of coronary heart disease. However, what is the explanation of the hypothesized relationship? What is the possible explanation for the strong possibility that the individual who regularly partakes in vigorous exercise is less likely to suffer a myocardial infarction, and if a heart attack does occur, is possibly more likely to survive the attack? Fox, Naughton, and Gorman have identified those factors that may be affected by physical activity and, therefore, may reduce the occurrence or severity of coronary heart disease (Fox 1972). See Table 61.1. It is important to realize that concrete research only partly supports the development of these mechanisms through exercise. Future research will sustain or refute the validity of the hypothesized relationship.

PHYSICAL EDUCATION AND ITS RELATIONSHIP TO CORONARY HEART DISEASE

What is the relationship of the profession of physical education to coronary heart disease? Physical education may very likely be the key to reversing the epidemic of coronary heart disease within the United States. What is more basic to the profession of physical education than physical activity? If one accepts the relationship of physical activity to coronary heart disease, the place of the physical education profession in the prevention of coronary heart disease is apparent. It is even likely that a portion of our students in physical education classes are already in advanced stages of coronary heart disease. Autopsy studies on American men killed in Korea and Viet Nam, British

Table 61.1
Effects of Physical Activity

Increase	Decrease
Coronary collateral vascularization	Serum levels of triglycerides and cholesterol
Vessel size	Glucose intolerance
Myocardial efficiency	Obesity-adiposity
Efficiency of peripheral blood distribution and return	Platelet stickiness
Electron transport capacity	Arterial blood pressure
Fibrinolytic capability	Heart rate
Arterial oxygen content	Vulnerability to dysrhythmias
Red blood cell mass and blood volume	Neurohormonal overreaction
Thyroid function	Strain associated with psychic "stress"
Growth hormone production	
Tolerance to stress	
Prudent living habits	
Joie de vivre	

pilots killed in air crashes, and Chilean men and women dying from automobile accidents, revealed that within a significant percentage of relatively young men and women, coronary heart disease is present (Pres. Council 1972).

However, involvement of elementary, junior high school, high school, college, and university students in exercise through our physical education classes is hardly a realistic and satisfactory solution to the problem. In contrast, education of our students in regard to the value of physical activity, in regard to the effect of exercise on the human body, and in regard to the relationship of physical activity to coronary heart disease, may contribute to the development of desirable attitudes within our students toward exercise, and a personal commitment to partake in vigorous physical activity on a regular basis. In addition to the development of an attitude toward exercise, physical educators must develop within the student the necessary neuro-muscular skill to derive satisfaction from participation in the selected activity.

The ingredients to the prevention of coronary heart disease by the profession of physical education involves education of the student in regard to the effects of smoking, the value of regular vigorous exercise, and the benefit of proper nutritional practices. The physical educators must also develop within the student the necessary neuromuscular skills in those vigorous activites so as to result in continued participation by the student beyond the school years. The measure of success of the physical education profession is whether the individual participates regularly in vigorous physical activity throughout life, and not simply through the school years.

Physical Education and Cardiac Rehabilitation

Rehabilitation of the medically classified cardiac patient through physical activity should also be a major concern of the physical education profession. No longer does the medical profession adhere to the concept that the post infarct patient should not exercise. A past president of the American Heart Association, Dr. Irvin Page, says, "It's foolish to suggest that because a person has suffered an injury to his heart, he should not exercise. The heart is a muscle, and like any other muscle, it is meant to be used. No muscle should be permitted to become soft and flabby" (Chapman 1957). Numerous books and articles have been written on the topic of rehabilitation of the cardiac patient through exercise, as well as the physiological effect of regular, vigorous exercise to the cardiac patient (Acker, 1971; Chapman, 1957; Gottheiner, 1968; Hellerstein, 1969, 1965, 1966; Intrntl. Symp. 1967; Jokl 1971; Kasch 1969, 1970; Karvonen 1967; Larsen 1971; Maistelman 1969; Morse 1972; Proc. Natl. Workshop 1969; Raab 1967; Redwood 1972; Int. Soc. Card. 1970; Stone 1972). What then is the place of physical education within the concept of cardiac rehabilitation? The organization and operation of cardiac rehabilitation programs should be the responsibility of the physical education profession. Properly prepared physical educators should be experts in the application of exercise, whether it be to a grade school student or a middle-aged post infarct patient. However, the development and operation of cardiac rehabilitation programs must be a shared concern of members of both the physical education profession and the medical profession. A quality cardiac rehabilitation program involves physician referral of patients, medical examinations, graded exercise testing of the patient, exercise prescription, diet regulation, emergency techniques, and in some cases actual physician attendance for exercise sessions. The task of developing exercise programs for cardiac patients is a great one. However, can the profession of physical education be concerned with the physiological well being of only student-age individuals? The profession also has a very definite obligation to devote its expertise toward the physiological well-being of all individuals.

CONCLUSION

An attempt has been made to inform the reader of the status of coronary heart disease within the United States, and the relationship of physical activity to the development of coronary heart disease. The physical education profession must assume responsibility for developing proper attitudes toward exercise, diet, and smoking, as well as teaching the necessary neuromuscular skills, so that students might benefit from desirable daily practices concerning health and exercise. In addition, the physical education profession must assume a leadership position in the physiological rehabilitation of cardiac patients. However, the rehabilitation of cardiac patients through exercise must be a combined effort of both the medical profession and the physical education profession. The benefit of such combined efforts of the two professions would be of great magnitude to not only the involved patients, but also to the involved community.

REFERENCES

Acker, J.A., Jr., 1971. The cardiac rehabilitation unit: experiences with a program of early activation, *Circulation,* **44** (October) (suppl. II) : 119 (Abstract).

American Heart Association, 1972. *Exercise testing and training of apparently healthy individuals: a handbook for physicians.*

Breslow, L., and Buell, P., 1960. Mortality from coronary heart disease and physical activity of work in California, *J. Chron. Dis.,* **11** (April) : 421-444.

Brozek, J. et al., 1963. Skinfold distribution in middle-aged American men, *Annals of New York Academy of Science,* **110** (September 26 : 492-502.

Brunner, D., and Manelis, G., 1971. Physical activity at work and ischemic heart disease. In: Larsen, O. A., and Malborg, R. O. (eds.), *Coronary heart disease and physical fitness.* Baltimore: University Park Press.

Chapman, J. M., et al., 1957. The clinical status of a population group under observations for two or three years. *Am J. Pub. Health,* **47** (April) (4, Pt. II) : 33-42.

Cureton, T. K., 1970 1970. *Physical fitness workbook for adults.* Champaign, Ill.: Stipes Publishing Co.

_____, 1969. *The physiological effects of exercise programs on adults.* Springfield, Ill.: Charles C. Thomas.

Fletcher, G. F. and Cantwell J. D., 1971. *Exercise in the management of coronary heart disease: a guide for the practicing physician.* Springfield, Ill.: Charles C. Thomas.

Fox, S. M., Naughton, J. P. and Gormen, P. A., 1972. Physical activity and cardiovascular health, *Modern Concepts of Cardiovascular Disease,* **41** : 17-20.

Fox, S.M., and Skinner, J. S., 1964. Physical Activity and cardiovascular health, *Am. J. Cardiol.,* **14** : 731-746.

Frank, C. W., 1968. The course of coronary heart disease: factors relating to prognosis, *Bull. N. Y. Acad. Med.,* **44** (August) : 900-915.

Gottheiner, V., 1968. Long range strenuous sports training for cardiac reconditioning and rehabilitation, *Am. J. Cardiol.,* **22** (September) : 426-435.

Heart Facts, 1973, 1972. American Heart Association.

Hellerstein, H. K., Burlando, A., Hirsch, E. Z., Plotkin, F. H., Feil, G. H., Winkler, O., Marik, S., and Margolis N., 1965. Active physical reconditioning of coronary patients, (suppl. IV) : 124-129.

Hellerstein, H. K., 1969. Relation of exercise to acute myocardial infarction: therapeutic, restorative, preventive, and etiological aspects, *Circulation,* **40** (November) (suppl. IV) : 124-129.

Hellerstein, H. K., and Hornsten, T. H., 1966. Assessing and preparing the patient for return to a meaningful and productive life, *J. Rehab.,* **32** (March-April) : 48-52.

International Society of Cardiology, 1970. Symposium: Rehabilitation of a non-coronary heart disease.

International symposium on physical activity and cardiovascular health, 1967. *Canad. Med. Ass. J.,* **96** : 695-915.

Jokl E., and McClellan, J. T., 1971. *Exercise and cardiac death.* Baltimore: University Park Press.

Kahn, H., 1963. The relationship of reported coronary heart disease mortality to physical activity of work. *Am. J. Pub. Health* 53(July) : 1058-1067.

Kannel, W. B., Sorlie, P., and McNamara, P., 1971. The relation of physical activity to risk of coronary heart disease: the framingham study. In: Larsen, O. A. and Malmborg, R. O. (eds.), *Coronary heart disease and physical fitness.* Baltimore: University Park Press.

Kasch, F. W., and Boyer, J. L., 1969. Changes in masimum work capacity resulting from six months training in patients with ischemic heart disease, *Medicine in Science and Sports,* **1** (September) : 156-159.

_____, 1970. Exercise therapy in hypertensive men, *JAMA,* **211** (March 9) : 1668-1671.

Karvonen, M. J., and Barry, A. J., 1967. *Physical activity and the heart.* Springfield, Ill.: Charles C. Thomas.

Keys, A. (ed.) 1970. Coronary heart disease in seven countries. *Circulation* **41** (Suppl. I, : 1-211.

Kraus, H., and Raab, W., 1961. *Hypokinetic disease.* Springfield, Ill.: Charles C. Thomas.

Larsen, O., and Malmborg, R. O., 1971. *Coronary heart disease and physical fitness.* Baltimore: University Park Press.

Maistelman, H. M., 1969. An exercise program for the cardiac patient. Presented at a symposium in continuing medical education on rehabilitation of the cardiac patient, School of Medicine, State University of New York at Buffalo (May 26-27).

Meness, W., 1969. *Exercise your heart.* London: Collier Books, Collier-McMillan Ltd.

Morris, J. N., and Raffle, P. A. B., 1954. Coronary heart disease in transport workers, *Brit. J. Ind. Med.* **11** (October) : 260-264.

Morris, W. H. M., 1957. Heart disease in Indiana farmers. In: Rosenbaum and Belknap, *Work and the heart.* New York: Paul B. Hoeber.

Morse, R. L., 1972. *Exercise and the heart: guidelines for exercise programs.* Springfield, Ill.: Charles C. Thomas.

Oslo Life Insurance Companies' Institute of Medical Statistics, 1956. Myocardial infarction: an epidemiologic and prognostic study of patients from five departments of internal medicine in Oslo, 1935-49, *Acta Medica Scand.,* **154** (Suppl. 315) : 1-58.

Paffenbarger, R. S., et al., 1970. Work activity of longshoremen as related to death from coronary heart disease and stroke, *New England J. Med.,* **20** : 1109-1114.

Pedley, F. G., 1942. Coronary disease and occupation, *Can. Med. Ass. J.,* **46** (February) : 147-151.

President's Council on Physical Fitnes and Sports, 1972. Physical fitness research digest. Washington, D.C. Series 2, Nos. 2, 3 and 4.

Proceedings of the National Workshop on Exercise in the Prevention and Treatment of Heart Disease, 1969. *J. S. Car. Med. Assoc.,* **65** (December) (Suppl. 1 to No. 12).

Raab, W., 1967. *Prevention of ischemic heart disease.* Springfield, Ill.: Charles C. Thomas.

Redwood, D. R., Dosing, D. R., and Epstein, S. E., 1972. Circulatory and symptomatic effects of physical training in patients with coronary-artery disease and angina pectoris, *New England J. Med.,* 286 : 959-965.

Ryle, J. A., and Russell, W. T., 1949. The natural history of coronary disease, *Brit. Heart J.,* **11** (October) : 370-389.

Shaper, A. B., Morris, J. N., and Meade, T. W., 1971. The London busmen. In: Larsen O. A., and Malmborg, R. O., (eds.), *Coronary heart disease and physical fitness.* Baltimore: University Park Press.

Spain, D., 1961. Heart disease and employment. Occupational physical exertion and coronary atherosclerotic heart disease, *J. Occup. Med.,* **3** (February) : 54-58.

Stone, W. J., 1972. The effects of physical training on post coronary patients, *Abstracts*. AAHPER National Convention.

Taylor, H. L., 1962. Coronary heart disease in physically active and sedentary population, *J. Sports Med. and Phys. Fitness,* **2** (June) : 73-82.

Stamler, J., et al., 1960. Prevalence and incidence of coronary heart disease in strata of the labor force of a Chicago industrial corporation, *J. Chron. Dis.,* **11** (April) : 405-520.

Wilhelmsen, L., and Tibblin, G., 1971. Physical inactivity and risk of myocardial infarction: the men born in 1913 study. In: Larsen, O. A. and Malmborg, R. O. (eds.), *Coronary heart disease and physical fitness.* Baltimore: University Park Press.

SUGGESTED READINGS

Encyclopedia of Sport Sciences and Medicine. 1971. New York and London: The MacMillan Company.

Morrison, S. L., 1957. Occupational Mortality in Scotland, *Brit. J. Ind. Med.,* **14** (April) : 130-132.

62

Physical Activity and Occlusive Arterial Disease
Fernand Landry

The progressive obliteration of the arteries of the heart and of the peripheral blood vessels, especially those of the lower extremity, are well known to be associated with aging, malnutrition, habitual physical inactivity, and other poor health habits. Myocardial infarctions (heart attacks) and severe limitations in walking ability are expected outcomes in these two instances. In North America coronary heart disease and diseases of the arteries, arterioles, and capillaries ranked in 1973 as the first and the sixth causes of death in men and as the first and fourth causes in women, all ages combined.

Contemporary research has shown that training can induce significant changes in fitness. Endurance as a function of the cardio-circulatory-respiratory system can be influenced by proper training methods (Edblom 1968). This is manifested normally in various combinations and to varying degrees by the following: decreases in resting heart rate and systolic blood pressure at rest; increases in heart volume (especially during the growth years); decreases in heart rate, arterial blood pressure, pulmonary ventilation, and blood lactate and pyruvate during a submaximal effort; lengthening of the distolic phase of the heart cycle; decreases in the daily work of the heart; improvement of oxygen utilization at the tissue levels; and significant increases in physical working capacity.

Tissue changes are also known to occur as a result of adaptation to training, although unanimity at this point is not present among scientists. These include increases in muscular capillarization and improvement of capillarization in the heart tissue or, at least, development of collateral vessels.

The outcomes of training programs depend upon a number of factors in which the type, intensity, and frequency of exercise are at least as important as the general cardiovascular condition of the patients participating in them. Local vascular changes elicited in exercising muscles and the general circulatory adjustments resulting from increased physical activity obviously reflect in a number of ways the functional state of the cardiovascular system. As such they are known to be of considerable help in diagnosis and treatment of peripheral and coronary obliterative disease.

There is evidence that the stimulus of increased blood flow associated with, or resulting from physical exercise, has significant training effects in patients with the effect of such therapy, found by experience, is now understood sufficiently in terms of the mechanisms of its action to warrant recommendation of its use, if age and other impairments to health do not constitute contraindications.

Physical exercise and physical therapy have long been utilized in the treatment of obstructive arterial disease. Schoop (1973) has found evidence that as early as 1898 forced walking up to the threshold of pain was commonly recommended for patients with intermittent claudication.

Recent research reports confirm the increased walking tolerance of patients with arteriosclerosis obliterans (ASO) Alpert 1966; Baitsch 1968; The effect of such therapy, found by experience, is now understood sufficiently in terms of the mechanisms of its action to warrant recommendation of its use, if age and other impairments to health do not constitute contraindications.

Variables such as "maximal walking distance" (MWD) and "Maximal walking time" (MWT), although relatively subjective estimates, are nonetheless easily applicable to a wide spectrum of situations ranging from controlled laboratory investigations to individualized home training programs.

The beneficial aspects of walking and mechanisms of action in occlusive arterial disease are:

1. Increases in walking ability generally occur with training in patients with intermittent claudication.

2. The threshold of intermittent claudication (muscular pain after muscular contractions of the legs with chronic arterial circulatory disturbances) is generally retarded as a result of training.

3. Increases in walking ability can be expected to correlate better with blood flow changes when patients have single segmental occlusions.

4. Increases in walking ability can occur early, late, or continuously over a training period.

5. Maximal walking distance alone does not appear to be a valid parameter for assessing blood flow in muscles.

6. Increases in muscular blood flow during exercise in occlusive arterial disease is associated with a decrease in blood supply to the skin and to the nonexercising muscles (Koppelmann 1973).

7. During exercise venous flow may be consistently higher than arterial, particularly at higher work loads, suggesting that during exercise about 35 percent of the leg blood flow may be supplied via collateral arterial pathways (Cronestrand 1973).

8. Dilation of the collateral arteries as a reason for the improved claudication distance during and after training are now believed to be well established according to (Schoop 1973).

9. Rapid regression of the effects of training after discontinuation of exercises suggests that collateral dilatation occurs only as long as exercise is continued (Larsen 1966).

10. The mechanisms involved in increased walking tolerance of patients with intermittent claudication have been shown to be a reduced flow to the trained proximal muscles, enzymatic adaptation at the cellular level, and improved walking technique.

11. A pace of 120 steps a minute seems conducive to learning a favorable walking technique (Schoop 1973).

REFERENCES

Alpert, J., Garcia, H., and Lassen, N. A., 1966. Diagnostic use of radioactive xenon clearance and a standardized walking test in obliterative arterial disease of the legs. *Circulation,* **34** : 849-855.

Baitsch, G., and Baitsch, R., 1968. Kombinationstherapie peripherer durchblutungs-strorungen mit vasodilatantien und bewegungstherapie. *Munch. med. Wschr.* **42** : 2456- 2463.

Blumchen, G., Landry, F., Kiefer, H., and Schlosser, V., 1970. Hemodynamic responses of claudicating extremities. *Cardiology,* **55** : 114-127.

Cronestrand, R., Juhlin-Dannfeldt, A., and Wahren, J., 1973. Simultaneous measurements of external iliac artery and vein blood flow after reconstructive vascular surgery: Evidence of increased collateral circulation during exercise. *Scand. J. Clin. Lab. Invest.,* (suppl. 128) : 167-172.

Edblom, B., Astrand, P. O., Saltin, B., Stenberg, J., and Wallstrom, B. M., 1968. Effect of training on circulatory response to exercise. *J. Appl. Physiol.,* **24** : 518-528.

Fitzgerald, D. E., Keates, J. S., and Macmillan, D., 1971. Angiographic and plethysmographic assessment of graduated physical exercise in the treatment of chronic occlusive arterial disease of the leg. *Angiology,* **22** : 99-106.

Holm J., Pahllof, A. C., Bjorntorp, P., and Schersten, T., 1973. Enzyme studies in muscles of patients with intermittent claudication. Effect of training. *Scand. J. Clin. Lab. Invest.,* (suppl. 128) : 201-205.

Koppelmann, J., 1973. Skin and muscle flow during exercise in intermittent claudication. *Scand. J. Clin. Lab. Invest.* (suppl. 128 : 93-96.

Larsen O. A., and Lassen, N. A., 1966. Effect of daily muscular exercise in patients with intermittent claudication. *The Lancet,* **2** : 1093-1096.

Schoop, W., 1963. Grundlagen der konservatieven therapie arterieller verschlusskrankheiten. *Verh. dtsch. Ges. KreisForsch.,* **29** : 118-129.

————, 1964. Bewegungstherapie bei periphern durchblutungstorungen. *Med. Welt.* **10** : 502-506.

————, 1965. Leibesubungen in der prophylaxe under therapie von peripheren durchblutungsstorungen. *Therapiewoche,* **15** : 725-730.

————, 1966. Auswirkungen gesteigeter koperlicher aktivatat auf gesunde und krankhaft veranderte extremitatenarterien. In: *Koperliche Aktivatat und Herz und Kreislauferkrankungen,* Munchen.

————, 1973. Mechanism of beneficial action of daily walking training of patients with intermittent claudication. *Scand. J. Clin. Lab. Invest.,* (suppl. 128) : 197-199.

Skinner, J. S. and Strandness, D. E., 1967, Exercise and intermittent claudication. I. Effect of repetition and intensity of exercise. *Circulation,* **36** : 15-22.

————, 1967. Exercise and intermittent claudication. II. Effect of physical training. Circulation, **36** : 23-29.

Thulesius, O., Cjores, J. E., and Mandaus, L., 1973. Distal blood flow and blood pressure in vascular occlusion; Influence of sympathetic nerves on collateral blood flow. *Scand. J. Clin. Lab. Invest.* (suppl. 128 : 53-57.

Zetterquist, S. 1970. The effect of active training on the nutritive blood flow in exercising ischemic legs. *Scand. J. Clin. Lab. Invest.,* **25** : 101-111.

SUGGESTED READINGS

Barbey, K., and Barbey, P., 1963. Ein neuer plethysmograph zur messung des extremitatenduchblutung. *Z. KreislForsch,* **52** : 1129-1140.

Bollinger, A., Schlumph, M., Butti, P., and Gruntzig, A., 1973 Measurement of systolic ankle blood pressure with doppler untrasound at rest and after exercise in patients with leg artery occlusions. *Scand. J. Clin. Lab. Invest.* (suppl. 128) : 123-128.

Elsner, R. W., and Carlson, L. D., 1962. Postexercise hyperemia in trained and untrained subjects. *J. Apply Physiol.,* **17** : 436-440.

Lezack, J. D., and Carter, S. A., 1973. The relationship of distal systolic pressures to the clinical and angiographic findings in limbs with arterial occlusive disease. *Scand. J. Clin. Lab. Invest.* (suppl. 128) : 97-101.

Lundberg, A., and Pernow, B., 1970. The effect of physical training on oxygen utilization and lactate formation in the exercising muscle of adolescents with motor handicaps. *Scand. J. Clin. Lab. Invest.,* **26** : 89-96.

Sanne, H., and Sivertsson, R., 1967. Effect of physical training on collateral growth. Experimental study on the cat. Cited from B. Folkow, *Scand. J. Clin. Lab. Invest.* **19,** (suppl. 128) : 211-218.

Tonnesen, K. H., and Uhrenholdt, A., 1973. Skin vasomotor response to exercise in normal subjects and patients with valvular heart disease. *Scand. J. Clin. Lab. Invest.* (suppl. 128) : 51-52.

Sumner, D. S., and Strandness, D. E., 1970. The effect of exercise on resistance to blood flow in limbs with an occluded superficial femoral artery. *Vascular Surgery,* **4** : 22-237.

63

Home Exercises for Convalescing Cardiac Patients

Charles H. McCloy

PART I*

Progressive cardiologists are increasingly prescribing exercise reconditioning programs for patients who have made significant progress in recuperating from cardiac accidents. The general trend of the advice given is frequently to tell the patient to begin to take walks, first walking slowly (about two to two-and-a-half miles per hour), and walking only a short distance (usually at the beginning, about a quarter of a mile), and gradually to increase the distance up to about a mile twice a day; and then gradually to increase the pace, eventually from about two-and-a-half miles per hour to about three-and-a-half

* Reprinted from the *Journal of the Association for Physical and Mental Rehabilitation,* **11** (November-December) : 181-185, 1957.

miles per hour. After that patients are told that, if they suffer no angina or other untoward effects, they may increase the distance gradually to about two miles a day. All too frequently, this is the only advice given relative to exercise.

There are two difficulties with such advice. First, it is not appropriate in cold weather. Few cardiologists would care to advise a patient to walk in this manner when the temperature is very far below 40° F. Breathing the cold air can cause anginal complications. Hence, if this is the sole exercise program, the patient exercises little during the cold weather and usually gets out of condition during the winter. The second difficulty is that walking, while a fairly effective exercise for stimulating the heart muscles to develop, is very inferior exercise for general muscular develoment, and patients are apt to remain muscularly soft, and muscularly below par for reconditioning for resuming their normal jobs.

Two things can be done to meet these objections. In 1943 when the writer was working in the reconditioning consultant division of the office of the surgeon general of the army, one of his major assignments was to prepare the exercise formulary for physical reconditioning, later known as *TM 8-292, Physical Reconditioning* (and eventually divided into two manuals, *TM-2892, Physical Reconditioning,* and *TM-2892, Advanced Physical Reconditioning).* In the preparation of these manuals, everything prepared was first cleared with the appropriate medical officers in the office of the surgeon general. For example, exercises for cardiac patients were first cleared with the cardiologists in the office of the surgeon general and later with cardiologists at Walter Reed Hospital. Corrective exercise programs were cleared with the chief of orthopedics at the office of the surgeon general, etc. Everything prepared was then tried out in different army hospitals.

Two exercise programs, both of a calisthenic nature, were prepared for cardiacs by Dr. George T. Stafford of the University of Illinois (then working with the army school for enlisted reconditioning personnel) and the present writer. The first program was conducted entirely while the patient was reclining so that the weight of the body would not be added to each exercise thus reducing the amount of general exercise dosage. When the cardiologist approved, the patients were moved to an intermediate program where many of the exercises were engaged in while standing. This program was considerably more strenuous than the beginning program. These programs were then experimented with under the eye of the cardiologist at England General Hospital in Atlantic City, were modified and later standardized. The point is, they were found to be satisfactory and resulted from adequate experimentation with cardiac patients (these patients were largely post-rheumatic fever patients).

These programs can be used by recuperating cardiac patients at home, in any kind of weather. The intelligent patient can provide a self-check by counting the 15-second pulse rate after each exercise, and where indicated can rest for some time between exercises. Much more of the body's musculature is stimulated to development by such a program than is true of a walking program. In good weather, it is recommended that the subject "work out" by a walk once a day, and work out once by using the home calisthenics exercise program. One workout should be done in the morning and one in the afternoon.

The two exercise routines are shown in Fig. 63.1. The beginning exercise routine for convalescent cardiac patients is, of course, to be begun only when indicated by the physician in charge. In no case is the patient to close the glottis and "bear down." He should continue to breathe easily and regularly, thus avoiding any significant increase in either intrathoracic or intraabdominal pressures.

The dosages of each of these routines should begin with about four movements for each exercise (complete movements), and should increase the number gradually from week to week as it is found that the patient can increase the numbers of executions of each exercise without any discomfort. In other words, the patient continues to increase the work load as long as tolerance is within limits of complete comfort.

Beginning Conditioning Exercises for Cardiac Patients

All exercises for this group will be done on the bed or mat.

1. Exhale and contract abdomen
   Cadence: slow
   Starting position: on back, knees partially drawn up, arms by side.
   Movement:
   (1) Exhale slowly and fully and draw the abdomen inward as far as possible.
   (2) Recover to starting position.
   (3) Inhale slowly raising chest as high as possible, pressing downward slightly with the arms against the mat.
   (4) Recover to starting position.

2. Arms forward to sideward
   Cadence: moderate to slow.
   Starting position: on back, arms forward.
   Movement:
   (1) Move arms sideward to side shoulder level position, at the same time inhale deeply.
   (2) Recover to original position and exhale deeply.
   (3) Repeat count (1).
   (4) Repeat count (2).
   Four to six executions.

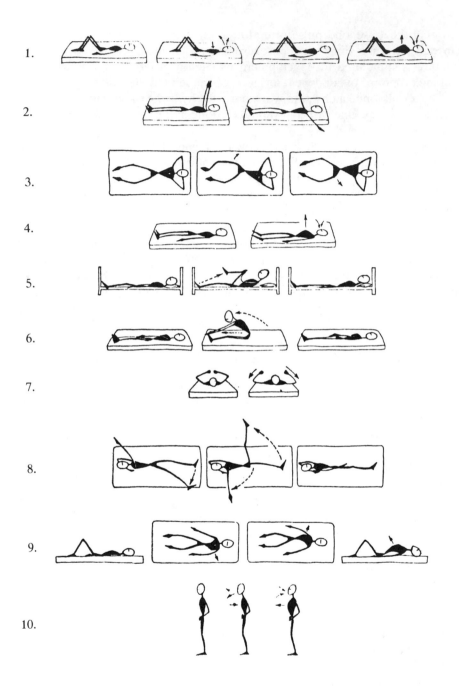

Fig. 63.1 Beginning (1-17) and intermediate (11-19) exercises for cardiac patients.

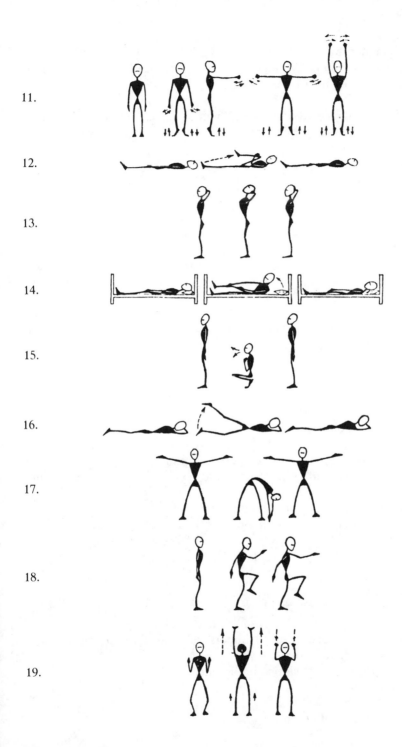

11.

12.

13.

14.

15.

16.

17.

18.

19.

3. Hip swinger

Cadence: moderate.

Starting position: on back, fingers laced behind head, feet about 1 foot apart and drawn up near hips.

Movements:

(1) Lift hips clear of bed and swing them as far as possible to the left.

(2) Lift hips again and swing them as far as possible to the right.

(3) Repeat count (1).

(4) Repeat count (2).

Four to six executions.

4. Cat stretch

Cadence: moderate.

Starting position: on back, palms on mat.

Movement:

(1) Stretch the legs, tightening muscles on both sides of the leg (quadriceps and hamstrings), and stretch toes downward hard. Learn to make muscles hard like trying to "make a muscle" on upper arm. Inhale with this count.

(2) Relax the leg muscles generally but raise the toes upward, and exhale.

(3) Repeat count (1).

(4) Repeat count (2).

Four to six executions.

5. Knee puller

Cadence: moderate to slow.

Starting position: on back, at attention.

Movement:

(1) Raise left knee up toward the chest, grasping the leg below the knee with both hands and pulling knee hard up to chest. At the same time exhale deeply.

(2) Recover to starting position and inhale.

(3) Repeat count (1) with opposite leg.

(4) Repeat count (2).

Same, arms forward, and arms sideward, four to six times in each position.

6. Sit-up

Cadence: slow.

Starting position: on back, hands on thighs, feet under covers, if in bed.

Movement:

(1) Sit up, moving forward until fingers can touch lower leg between knees and feet, and exhale.

(2) Recover to starting position, and inhale.

(3) Repeat count (1).

(4) Repeat count (2).

Six to eight four-count executions.

7. Breaking chains

Cadence: slow.

Starting position: on back, elbows raised sideward, slightly off the mat, fists clenched in front of shoulders.

Movement:

(1) Pull elbows back hard as if trying to break a chain held in the two hands. Press elbows hard against the bed, then relax.

(2) Pull again, then relax.

(3) Repeat count (2).

(4) Recover to starting position.

Four to six executions.

8. Swing and kick

Cadence: moderate to slow.

Starting position: lying on the left side with left side of head resting upon left forearm.

Movement:

(1) Swing right leg straight forward along the mat and at the same time swing right arm to the rear. Exhale with this movement.

(2) Swing right leg downward and backward behind left leg, and swing arm forward and up above head in line with body. Inhale with this movement.

(3) Repeat count (1).

(4) Repeat count (2).

Do three to four executions lying on left side, then turn over and repeat on opposite side.

9. Rib stretcher

Cadence: slow.

Starting position: on back, knees fully bent, hands about one foot from side of the body.

Movement: (Do each movement three to six times before proceeding to the next. This is not a four-count exercise.)

(1) Lift chest and stretch to left as far as possible, then return to position.

(2) Repeat movement (1) to right.

(3) Arch back and raise chest as high as possible.

(4) Combine the first three movements. Do first execution left, upward, right; do second execution right, upward, left: continue reversing the direction for each execution.

Progression in the drill for beginning cardiac patients should be about one repetition each day up to the time when the individual can take about 20 minutes of exercise. As the patient progresses in strength there should be fewer rests between each different exercise.

Intermediate Conditioning Exercises for Cardiac Patients

The intermediate exercise   program for convalescing cardiac patients, to begin when approved by the physician, is somewhat more strenuous than the exercises given above. Again, the beginner can start with about four executions of each exercise and work up as tolerance becomes adequate. In every case progress should be relatively slow. In no case should the increase be more than one execution per day in each exercise, and if the slightest chest discomfort is experienced the patient should probably go back one or two executions from that used currently.

10. Breathe and contract
Cadence: slow
Starting position: standing, hands on abdomen.
Movement:
(1-2-3-4)Exhale in four counts, drawing out more each time. (5-6-7-8) Inhale on four counts, attempting to inhale more on each count.
Repeat 10 times.

11. Grip and stretch
Cadence: moderate to fast.
Starting position: attention.
Movement:
(1) With arms downward, clench fists tightly, and rise high on toes.
(2) While extending fingers, lower heels to the floor.
(3) Repeat count (1).
(4) Recover to starting position.
Same, arms forward arms sideward, and arms upward. Four to six executions in each position. Cadence is counted in each position.

12. Knee puller
Cadence: moderate to slow.
Starting position: on back at attention.
Movement:
(1) Raise left knee up toward the chest, grasping the knee with both hands and pulling knee hard up to chest, at the same time exhaling deeply.
(2) Recover to starting position and inhale.
(3) Repeat count(1) with opposite leg.
(4) Recover to starting position and inhale. From 10 to 15 executions.

13. Neck firm
Cadence: moderate to slow.
Starting position: erect, fingers laced behind head.
Movement:
(1) Raise chest high, pulling head backward against resistance of hands,

keeping elbows back, bending upper back backward slightly, inhaling.

(2) Recover to starting position and exhale.

(3) Repeat count (1).

(4) Repeat count (2).

From 10 to 15 executions.

14. Curl and twist

Cadence: moderate to slow.

Starting position: on back, arms by side, feet separated about two feet.

Movement:

(1) Raise head and shoulders only from the bed, raising right shoulder the higher. Touch left knee with right hand. At the same time, raise left leg off bed about six inches.

(2) Recover to starting position.

(3) Repeat count (1) to other side.

(4) Recover to starting position.

From six to ten executions.

15. Knee bend and curl

Cadence: slow.

Starting position: attention.

Movement:

(1) Bend knees to full knee position and at the same time flex forearms forward. Hands are just in front of shoulders. Exhale on downward movement.

(2) Recover to starting position and exhale.

(3) Repeat count (1).

(4) Repeat count (2).

From six to ten executions.

16. Prone leg raising

Cadence: slow.

Starting position: prone, head supported on hands, and forearms flexed.

Movement:

(1) Raise left leg backward with knee straight.

(2) Recover to starting position.

(3) Raise right leg backward.

(4) Recover to starting position.

From eight to ten executions.

17. Turn and bend

Cadence: moderate.

Starting position: side-straddle, arms sideward.

Movement:

(1) Turn trunk to left, lowering both hands to ground beside left foot, and exhale.

(2) Recover to original position, and inhale.
(3) Repeat count (1) to opposite side.
(4) Repeat count (2).
Three to four executions on each side.

18. Stair climb

Cadence: moderate to fast.
Starting position: attention.
Movement:
For about 30 seconds. By the end of the third week, the patient should be able to do a slow jog of not more than one minute. The patient will do well to inhale on two steps and exhale on two steps. For the first few days, the patient does a stationary jog and by the end of the first week regular jogging is started.

19. Air push

Cademce: very slow.
Starting position: feet apart, knees slightly bent, arms forward and palms up as though holding a heavy weight on the hands.
Movement:
(1) Extending knees, go through the motion of pushing a heavy weight above the head. Inhale at the same time.
(2) Reverse position of palms and do an imaginary pull-down, finishing with legs bent and fists clenched in front of chest.
(3) Repeat count (1).
(4) Repeat count (2).
From six to ten executions.

After patients can work up in this intermediate program to the place where they are doing at least 12 executions of each exercise, and without more than about a half minute between exercises, a more strenuous program, designed for normal people, can be found in the army manual *TM 8-292*, beginning with page 118.

PART II*

A third type of program is based upon research published in Germany in 1953. Hettinger and Muller (1953) found that if a muscle is put on an isometric tension equal to two-thirds of its maximum tension and kept at this degree of tension *just once a day*, the muscle will increase in strength from

---

* Reprinted from the *Journal of the Association for Physical and Mental Rehabilitation* **12** (January-February 1958) : 5-7.

two to five percent per week up to the individual's physiological limit. To make this principle clear, suppose a normal subject is able to flex the forearm carrying a 30-pound dumbbell in the hand. If the same individual then were to grasp a weight of 20 pounds and hold a semiflexed position (with the elbow at 90 degrees, *just once a day,* a development stimulus would result that would cause that muscle to develop in strength quite rapidly up to, as stated above, from two to five percent per week. This result is attributed by the authors of the research to be the result of the anoxia in the muscle being brought about by the cutting-off of the capillary blood supply by the muscular effort. A later study by Muller (1957) seems to show that if the contraction is held only momentarily, it achieves the same result.

Working on this principle, the present author has prepared a series of 17 exercises in which subjects may offer isometric resistance to their own movements using only a small part of the body at one time, thus not raising the blood pressure significantly. The subjects, again, should under no circumstances close the glottis, but should breathe easily and continuously. There is *only one* contraction for each muscle group to be executed each day. The outline follows:

Isometric Tension Exercises

In these exercises (see Fig. 63.2) the principal muscles exercised by each movement are indicated for the information of the physician.

1. Subject stands or sits with arms elevated, forearms half-flexed, and one fist pressing against the palm of the opposite hand, hands immediately above the top of the head. Subject presses both hands together against each other over the head. (Deltoid and trapezius).

2. Subject stands or sits with hands pressing together (one fist in the palm of the opposite hand) with hands immediately in front of chest, elbows at shoulder height. Subject presses hands together hard in front of chest. (Pectoralis major group).

3. Subject stands or sits with hands clasped in front of chest, elbows at shoulder height. Subject pulls hands apart vigorously. (Shoulder retractors—trapezius, rhomboids, posterior deltoid).

4. Subject either stands or lies on back on floor, with arms straight and hands resting on front of thighs. Subject presses against thighs hard, keeping elbows straight. (Latissimus and teres major group, and long head of triceps).

5. Subject standing or sitting, hands clasped behind occiput, elbows forward. Subject pulls head backward hard against resistance offered by hands and arms. (Flexors of head and neck).

Fig. 63.2 Isometric tension exercises for cardiac patients.

Fig. 63.2 *(continued)*

14

15

16

6. Subject stands or sits with heels of hands against forehead, elbows forward. Subject presses head forward against resistance of hands. (Flexors of head and neck).

7. Subject sitting, with forearms half flexed and hands underneath thighs just behind the knees. Subject pulls upward with hands, as though attempting to flex forearms. (Biceps and other forearm flexor muscles). If physician feels that this exercise should be "diluted" a bit, it can be done one hand at a time with rests in between.

8. Subject seated, bending slightly forward, with hands pressing downward on fronts of thighs just behind knees. Subject attempts to flex the trunk, above the small of the back, forward as far as possible (as though trying to press the chin against the umbilicus). Subject holds this position for the required six seconds. (All abdominal muscles).

9. Subject lying supine on floor or bed, keeping small of back on the surface upon which he is lying. Subject attempts to flex his trunk, above the small of the back, forward as far as possible. ("As though he were trying to press his chin against his umbilicus,") Subject holds this position for the required six seconds. (All abdominal muscles)

10. Subject standing, with feet wide apart sideways. Subject takes a sideward lunge position to the left and presses down hard against the left (bent) knee with left hand (elbow straight). Later the same exercise is done to the opposite side. (The oblique muscles of the abdomen).

11. Subject reclines supine on floor or bed, with legs almost straight. Two fists are placed against the supporting surface, one fist opposite each ear. Elbows are upward toward the ceiling. An attempt is made to raise the body from head to heels (with knees as straight as possible) from the surface, and holds this position for the required six seconds. (All erector spinae muscles, and all extensors of thighs).

If patients are too weak to bridge with knees straight, they may at the beginning bend the knees slightly, pulling the feet upward from six inches to one foot up toward the hips. As they become stronger, they should straighten out more.

12. Standing on one foot, subjects do a partial squat (from half to a three-fourths squat) on one leg and hold it for the required six seconds. As they get stronger, they will squat slightly farther down. Subjects then repeat the exercise with the opposite leg.

13. Subjects stand close to some heavy object such as a table, or dresser, or foot of the bed, hold onto this object with hands, pulling upward on the object. They then rise on the ball of one foot, with the other foot off the floor and hold it for the required time. (Triceps surae).

14. Subjects recline supine and press the two legs together, one over the other at the knees, and attempt to pull legs apart. (Thigh abductors).

15. Subjects recline supine with legs straight, hook feet together, one over the other at the ankles, and attempt to pull feet apart. (Thigh abductors).

16. Subjects lying supine, with left thigh rotated laterally and with lower leg flexed about 60 degrees. The heel of right leg, also flexed, is pressed backward against the instep of the left foot and subjects attempt to flex the right lower leg. (Gastrocnemius and hamstrings). The subjects then repeat the exercise with the other leg.

17. (Not found in Fig. 63.2.) Subjects stand and raise chest as high as possible, taking a deep breath and holding the inhalation (glottis open) for six seconds. They then exhale and hold it in as much of an exhalation position as possible for the six seconds. (The exercise is planned to exercise the respiratory muscles of the chest and diaphragm primarily to prevent the not-uncommon deterioration of respiratory muscles and the ligaments of the thorax that will eventually reduce the vital capacity of the lungs.)

Note that these exercises (including those done first on one side and then on the other), if there were no pauses between exercises, could be gone through in a little over two minutes. This of course is not desirable. The patient should rest as much as necessary between exercises, possibly checking progress by noting pulse rate, and discontinuing the routine any time any suspicion of anginal symptoms appears.

The advantage of this type of routine is two-fold. First, it is quick and easy to perform and results in a steady increase in muscular strength, thus preparing the patient muscularly for return to active work. Second—and this sounds fantastic, but there is some evidence that it is true—after the first year one execution a month will maintain it! During the first year the strength will have been increased probably at least 50 percent, usually more than that. This leaves the individual ordinarily strong enough to engage in any form of activity appropriate for an excardiac.

These three exercise routines are offered for experimentation with convalescent cardiac patients. It should be noted that such experimentation with the first two exercise outlines (Part I) has already been conducted (in the army's reconditioning program) and found successful. However, most of this experimentation was done with patients recovering from rheumatic fever, and very little of it was done with patients who had had coronary occlusions. The isometric tension program was, of course, not available in 1943 as it was not published until 10 years later. Experimentation with the isometric tension exercises has been conducted with one experimenter (the present author) and has been found to be effective.

REFERENCES

Hettinger, T. and E.A. Muller, 1953. Muskelleistung und muskeltraining, *Arbeitsphysiologie* **15** (October) : 116-126.

Muller, E. A., 1957. The regulation of muscular strength. *J. Assoc. Phys. Ment. Rehab.* **11** (March) : 5, 44-47.

64

Isometric Exercise and the Cardiovascular System

Donald O. Nutter, Robert C. Schlant, and
J. Willis Hurst

Muscular contractions may be classified into two general types. When a muscle varies its length during contraction, its contraction is referred to as *dynamic or rhythmic*. (Although it is sometimes also referred to as *isotonic* [constant tension], this term is seldom applicable in human motion, since tension usually varies during contraction.) Examples of this form of exercise are walking, running, swimming, throwing, scrubbing, lifting, sawing, nailing, screwing, and hammering. When both ends of the muscle are fixed so that no significant shortening can occur, the contraction is referred to as *isometric* or *static*. Although isometric exercise accomplishes no external work, it requires significant energy and produces profound effects upon the cardiovascular system. Isometric contractions occur in innumerable normal activities, including holding, carrying, or attempting to push objects, as well as in maintaining the upright body posture. The purpose of this chapter is to review the effects of isometric exercise upon the cardiovascular system, including its potential hazards as well as its value as a test of cardiovascular function.

CARDIOVASCULAR ADJUSTMENTS TO ISOMETRIC EXERCISE

In 1938 Asmussen and Hansen demonstrated an increase in heart rate, blood pressure, cardiac output, and oxygen consumption during sustained, "static" muscular effort. Tuttle and Horvath confirmed these findings in 1957 and emphasized the rapidity of the changes as well as the elevation of diastolic blood pressure during static exercise, in contrast to dynamic exercise, which usually causes either no change or a slight decrease in diastolic pressure. Subsequent studies have demonstrated the following characteristics of sustained, static isometric exercise:

Heart rate. The pulse rate begins to increase within seconds after the onset of isometric contraction (Freyschuss 1970; Petro 1970). The increase in heart rate is predominantly the result of a rapid withdrawal of vagal influence on the heart (Freyschuss 1970, 1970; MacDonald 1966). Atropine significantly inhibits the tachycardia, but propanolol has little effect upon this response (Freyschuss 1970). The increase in heart rate also occurs in subjects who have had succinycholine injected into the brachial artery to produce total neuromuscular paralysis of the muscle groups activated during handgrip (Freyschuss 1970). In these circumstances the *intention* to perform a handgrip in the paralyzed forearm produces increments in heart rate and aortic pressure that average 64 and 55 percent, respectively, of those produced by control handgrips. Thus at least part of the pulse rate response at the initiation of isometric exercise may be related to autonomic nervous system influences of central origin (Freyschuss 1970). Other investigators have suggested that the initial heart rate response under normal circumstances of isometric exercise may result from reflexes originating in muscle spindle mechanoreceptors (Petro 1970).

Blood pressure. Within a few seconds after the onset of a sustained isometric exercise, the arterial systolic, diastolic, and mean blood pressures begin to increase even when the relative tension or strength of contraction is relatively low: 10 to 15 percent of a maximal voluntary contraction (MVC) (Donald 1967; Freyschuss 1970, 1970; Humphreys 1963; Lind 1967, 1967, 1966, 1964; MacDonald 1966; Tuttle 1957). The blood pressure elevation is associated with abrupt increases in cardiac output and heart rate. Stroke volume does not change systematically during 10 or 20 percent MVC, but it often decreases during 50 percent MVC when heart rate acceleration is pronounced. Total systemic vascular resistance does not usually change during isometric exercise, although it may increase in some older subjects. In these older individuals isometric exercise results in a small increase in cardiac output, but also in high blood pressure response due to more intense vasoconstriction and a raised total systemic vascular resistance (MacDonald, 1966). During isometric exercise there is a redistribution of the increased cardiac output that is produced by regional increases or decreases in vascular resistance (see below).

Blood pressure elevation is more marked and occurs more rapidly with stronger isometric contractions, that is, as the strength of contraction is increased from 5 to 20 to 50 percent MVC (Humphreys 1963; Lind 1964). Both the blood pressure elevation and the heart rate elevation are proportional to the *relative* force of the sustained contraction and the intensity of motor innervation and to the *duration* of the contraction, but *not* to the absolute tension produced or to the bulk or mass of the activated muscles (Donald 1967; Humphreys 1963; Lind 1967, 1967, 1966, 1964). Furthermore, when two muscle groups contract at the same relative MVC or tension, there is no additive effect upon the circulatory response (Lind 1967). If two or more muscle groups contract simultaneously at different relative MVCs or tension, the increments in heart rate and blood pressure are the same as when the group at the higher relative tension contracts separately at that tension (Lind 1967).

The blood pressure elevation is of functional importance because it helps to maintain the blood flow to the contracting muscles, which tend to compress or throttle the intramuscular vessels (Donald 1967; Gaskell 1877; Gray 1967; Hirche 1970; Humphreys 1963). Isometric contractions of 15 percent MVC or lower, the blood pressure elevation, in combination with the normal vasodilitation of contracting muscle, are able to increase blood flow to the muscle adequately to meet metabolic needs and to avoid fatigue. As a result contractions of this intensity can usually be maintained indefinitely. With contractions stronger than 15 percent MVC, however, the blood flow to the muscles cannot satisfy the metabolic demands of the contracting muscle even though the flow is greater than at rest. Under these circumstances, the muscles acquire a metabolic "debt," which is repaid during the hyperemic recovery phase after release of the contraction. Blood flow to muscles contracting isometrically appears to be completely stopped when the MVC is in excess of 70 percent (Freyschuss 1970; Humphreys 1963; Lind 1964). The marked decrease in blood flow that occurs as the intensity of contraction progressively increases is reflected in the rapidly decreasing duration of contraction that can be sustained with increasing strength of contraction. Despite the significant increases in arterial blood pressure during sustained isometric contraction, the blood flow to *inactive* muscle groups and to skin does not increase. These findings are compatible with vasoconstriction in these areas.

The increase in blood pressure and in cardiac output may be produced in part by the tachycardia and in part by a reflex from the contracting muscle (Alam 1937; Humphreys 1963; Lind 1964) that results in both vasoconstriction of inactive vascular beds and inhibition of the normal baroreceptor reflexes. The belief that a reflex contributes to the pressor response is supported by the observation that if the circulation to the exercising arm is occluded, the blood pressure does not return to control values until the tourniquet is released (Lind 1968). It seems likely that the reflex originates from chemical stimulus in the contracting muscles, and it has been suggested that the potassium ion concentration is the chemical stimulus for this reflex (Donald 1967; Lind 1966). The concentration of potassium ion in the venous effluent from contracting muscles follows a pattern similar to the central cardiovascular responses to isometric contractions (Donald 1967) and the arterial infusion of potassium into the isolated hindlimb of dogs has been shown to elicit similar reflexes (Wildenthal 1968).

Cardiac output. During sustained isometric exercise, the cardiac output is increased in excess of the metabolic demands of the contracting muscles and in excess of the increase in total oxygen consumption (Lind 1964). The distribution of the increased cardiac output during isometric or static exercise is not fully resolved. Some of the increased flow goes to the contracting muscles themselves if the strength of contraction does not exceed 70 percent MVC. Myocardial blood flow probably increases secondary to the markedly increased demands for oxygen associated with the tachycardia, arterial hypertension, and probable increased myocardial contractility. The increased flow to these areas, however, is inadequate to account for the increased cardiac output. Other vascular beds, including muscles, skin, and splanchnic areas, have shown either no increases or increases inadequate to account for the remaining increased cardiac output (Lind 1964).

COMBINED ISOMETRIC (STATIC)
AND DYNAMIC (RHYTHMIC) EXERCISE

When isometric exercise is superimposed upon dynamic exercise, the cardiovascular effects tend to be additive. Thus, when sustained handgrip contraction is performed by subjects walking on a treadmill, at an oxygen consumption of 1.1 L/min, the increase in blood pressure is the same as that produced by an equivalent handgrip alone, despite the marked lowering of systemic vascular resistance produced by the dynamic exercise (Astrand 1968). On the other hand, during an extreme combination of isometric and dynamic exercise (for example, treadmill walking at an oxygen consumption of 2.8 L/min and handgrip of 50 percent MVC), the pressor response is less than that produced during less strenuous walking, possibly because of the extreme muscular vasodilatation produced by the vigorous walking and the absolute capacity of the cardiovascular system (Lind 1967).

Interestingly it appears that performing an isometric exercise can improve the performance of those muscles undergoing dynamic, rhythmic exercise (Lind 1967). This improved function presumably results from an increased blood flow to these muscles as a consequence of the higher arterial blood pressure and cardiac output in combination with further vasoconstriction of noncontracting muscles.

Clinically, brief periods of combined dynamic and isometric exercise are frequent during normal activities. More extended periods are encountered during such activities as walking while carrying a heavy object such as a suitcase or a parcel. Carrying objects is a form of isometric exercise whether the forearm muscles are used to grip the handle of the object or the weight is allowed to rest in the crook of the fingers (Donald 1967). The combined exercises involved in stretcher-bearing have been studied in detail by Lind and McNicol (1968). When the subjects carried a loaded stretcher by its handles, their blood pressure rapidly increased and fatigue set in after three minutes. If the stretcher was supported by a shoulder harness, however, the men could carry the stretcher for prolonged periods with little change in blood pressure or other circulatory changes.

COMPARISON OF ISOMETRIC EXERCISE
WITH DYNAMIC EXERCISE

The hemodynamic response to isometric or static exercise differs in several important aspects from the response to dynamic or rhythmic exercise. Dynamic exercise is associated with relatively marked increases in heart rate, and cardiac output, and a moderate increase in arterial systolic blood pressure, while diastolic blood pressure increases little if at all, and may decrease due to the marked vasodilatation of the contracting muscles. The mean pressure usually increases only slightly or moderately, while the total systemic vascular resistance decreases markedly due to the vasodilatation of the active muscles. In contrast to these responses, sustained isometric or static contractions produce a more moderate increase in heart rate and cardiac output, but vigorous increases in both systolic and diastolic arterial pressures. Total systemic vascular resistance changes little or not at all, except in some older subjects in whom it may increase.

Muscles undergoing isometric contraction of more than 15 percent MVC are unable to increase blood flow enough to avoid fatigue, despite the induced vasodilatation and the increased arterial blood pressure. This limitation of muscular blood flow and the complete stoppage of flow at MVC in excess of 70 percent are due to the throttling of blood vessels produced by the high intramuscular pressure (Donald 1967; Gaskell 1877; Humphreys 1963). In contrast, during dynamic muscular contractions blood flow to the muscles is markedly increased, even during maximal exercise, and is even assisted by the rhythmic contraction and relaxation.

ISOMETRIC EXERCISE IN PATIENTS WITH HEART DISEASE

Patients with heart disease respond to isometric exercise with the same hemodynamic response pattern as subjects without heart disease. Since the initial suggestion (Hurst 1969) for using standardized isometric exercise as a useful stress test in the evaluation of patients (Atkins 1971; Fisher 1971; Helfant 1971; Kivowitz 1971; McCraw 1972; Mullins 1970; Saltz 1971; Siegel 1970) have confirmed its usefulness. Thus, isometric handgrip exercise (the "grip test") may help detect latent left ventricular dysfunction by inducing the development of an abnormally elevated left ventricular end-diastolic pressure (Atkins 1971; Fisher 1971; Helfant 1971; Kivowitz 1971; Mullins 1970; Saltz 1971; Siegel 1970). In patients in whom this pressure is already abnormally elevated, the stress of isometric exercise induces further, more marked, elevation. Handgrip exercise can also be utilized as a cardiovascular stress during more sophisticated estimates of ventricular function and contractility. Such studies of ventricular function in patients have suggested that the normal response to isometric exercise is associated with an increase in myocardial contractility.

In addition to its usefulness in the assessment of ventricular function, isometric exercise is a simple, reproducible, noninvasive stress test to elicit or intensify cardiac pulsations, sounds, and murmurs. Thus, ventricular gallop (S_4) or atrial gallop (S_3) sounds (and corresponding atrial diastolic pulsations) are frequently accentuated or elicited in patients with left ventricular dysfunction during a sustained grip test (Siegel 1970). Similarly, the murmurs of aortic and mitral regurgitation and of mitral stenosis are accentuated (Lind, 1968). Isometric exercise or a grip test can be performed simply, without elaborate equipment, by a supine patient without interfering with physical examination or other special tests that are being obtained simultaneously. Patient cooperation is obviously necessary during either dynamic or isometric exercise testing in the evaluation of cardiac performance or findings. In particular, the Valsalva maneuver must be avoided during isometric exercise testing.

As a stress test, isometric handgrip produces less tachycardia but greater elevation of mean systemic arterial pressure than does moderate dynamic (treadmill) exercise. In our experience, patients with coronary atherosclerotic heart disease have a higher incidence of angina pectoris during maximal treadmill exercise than during maximal isometric handgrip exercise (Siegel 1970).

Although brief episodes of moderate isometric or static exercise occur throughout normal activity, it is seldom sustained and the hemodynamic changes are seldom adequate to induce symptoms, even in patients with coronary artery disease. When such exercise is more sustained and more intense, however, it does result in a marked increase in myocardial oxygen requirements and can induce angina pectoris. Severe isometric exercise can be particularly dangerous, since the subject may not have the dyspnea or the tachycardia usually associated with other forms of exercise. In addition, the fatigue symptoms from the muscles undergoing static contraction may divert the patient's attention. A particularly vigorous circulatory response to com-bined static and dynamic exercise occurs during overhead work while standing with arms raised above the head (Astrand 1971, 1968). In patients with preexisting hypertension, static exercise produces about the same absolute increments in systolic, diastolic, and mean arterial pressures as in normal subjects, and the blood pressure may reach extremely high levels (Hoel 1970).

Although a high incidence of dangerous cardiac dysrhythmias during or after handgrip exercise was reported in one study (Atkins 1971), this has not been our experience in several hundred handgrip tests in patients with a wide variety of cardiac diseases. Ventricular ectopic rhythms occured in only three of our patients, and these reverted spontaneously in all. On the other hand, premature ventricular beats have occasionally been noted, and the handgrip test is a moderately potent stress test for inducing angina pectoris. Continuous electrocardiographic monitoring should be employed when isometric testing is used in patients with known coronary artery disease or rhythm disorders. Contraindications to isometric exercise testing include myocardial infarction within three months, severe arterial hypertension, symptomatic cerebro-vascular disease or cerebrovascular malformations, and serious rhythm dis-orders.

In general, isometric exercises of moderate severity and duration are not advisable for the aging subject or the patient with known heart disease. In such circumstances dynamic exercises, which have a more beneficial effect upon physical endurance than do static exercises, are preferable.

REFERENCES

Alam, M., and Smirk, F. H., 1937. Observations in man on a blood pressure raising reflex arising from the voluntary muscles, *J. Physiol.* (London), **89** : 372-383.

Asmussen, E., and Hansen, E., 1938. Uber den einfluss statischer muskelarbeit auf atmung und kreislauf, *Skand. Arch. Physiol.*, **78** :283-303.

Astrand, I., 1971. Circulatory responses to arm exercise in different work positions, *Scand. J. Clin. Lab. Invest.*, **27** : 293-297.

Astrand, I., Guharay, A., and Wahren, J., 1968. Circulatory responses to arm exercise with different arm positions. *J. Appl. Physiol.*, **25** : 528-532.

Astrand, P. O. and Rodahl, K., 1970. *Textbook of work physiology.* New York: McGraw-Hill Book Co.

Atkins, J. M., Matthews, O. A., Houston, J. D., Blomqvist, G., and Mullins, C. B., 1971. Arrhythmias induced by isometric (handgrip) exercise and dynamic exercise (Abstract), *Clin. Res.,* **19** : 303.

Donald, K. W., Lind, A. R., McNichol, G. W., Humphreys,f P. W., Taylor, S. H., and Staunton, H. P., 1967. Cardiovascular responses to sustained (static) contractions, *Circ. Res.,* **20** and **21** (suppl. I) : I-15—I-32.

Fisher, M., Nutter, D., and Schlant, R., 1971. Hemodynamic evaluation of isometric exercise testing in cardiac patients (Abstract), *Circulation,* **43** and **44** (suppl. II) : II-50.

Freyschuss, U., 1970. Cardiovascular adjustment to somatomotor activation: elicitation of increments in heart rate, aortic pressure and venomotor tone with the initation of muscle contraction, *Acta Physiol. Scand.,* Suppl. **342** : 1-63.

———, 1970. Elicitation of heart rate and blood pressure increase on muscle contraction, *J. Appl. Physiol.,* **28** : 788-761.

Gaskell, W.H., 1877. On the changes of the blood stream in muscles through stimulation of their nerves, *J. Anat. Physiol.* (London) **11** : 360-402.

———. (1876), Uber die aenderungen des blutstroms in den muskeln durch die reizung ihrer nerven, *Arb. Physiol. Leipzig,* **11** : 45-88.

Gray, S. D., Carlsson, E., and Staub, N. C., 1967. Site of increased vascular resistance during isometric muscle contraction, *Amer. J. Physiol.,* **213** : 683-689.

Helfant, R. H., deVilla, M. A., and Meister, S. G., 1971. Effect of sustained isometric handgrip exercise on left ventricular performance, *Circulation,* **44** : 982-993.

Hirche, H., Raff, W. K., and Grun, D., 1970. Resistance to blood flow in the gastrocnemius of the dog during sustained and rhythmical isometric and isotonic contractions, *Pflueger Arch.,* **314** : 97-112.

Hoel, B. L., Lorentsen, E., and Lund-Larsen, P. G., 1970. Haemodynamic responses to sustained handgrip in patients with hypertension, *Acta Med. Scand.* **188** : 491-495.

Humphreys, P. W., and Lind, A. R., 1963. Blood flow through active and inactive muscles of the forearm during sustained handgrip contractions, *J. Physiol.* (London) **166** : 120-135.

Hurst, J.W., Schlant, R.C., Siegel, W., Nutter, D. O., Jacobs, W., and Stonecipher, H. K., 1969. Indirect evaluation of cardiac function. Presented at the 42nd Annual Scientific Sessions of the American Heart Association, Dallas, Texas (November 15).

Kivowitz, C., Parmley, W. W., Donoso, R., Marcus, H., Ganz, W., and Swan, H.J. C., 1971. Effects of isometric exercise on cardiac performance: the grip test, *Circulation,* **44** : 994-1002.

Lind, A. R., and McNicol, G. W., 1968. Cardiovascular responses to holding and carrying weights by hand and by shoulder harness, *J. Appl. Physiol,* **25** : 261-267.

————, 1967. Circulatory responses to sustained handgrip contractions performed during other exercise, both rhythmic and static, *J. Physiol.* (London) **192** 595-607.

————, 1967. Local and central circulatory responses to sustained contractions and the effect of free or restricted arterial inflow on post-exercise hyperaemia, *J. Physiol.* (London) **192** : 575-593.

Lind, A. R., McNicol, G. W., and Donald, K. W., 1966. Circulatory adjustments to sustained (static) muscular activity. In: Evang, K. and Andersen, K. L. (eds.), *Physical activity in health and disease: proceedings of the Beitostolen symposium* (Norway, 1966). Oslo: Universitetsforlaget.

Lind, A. R., Taylor, S. H., Humphreys, P. W., Kennelly, B. M., and Donald, K. W., 1964. Circulatory effects of sustained voluntary muscle contraction, *Clin. Sci.*, **27** : 229-244.

MacDonald, H. R., Sapru, R. P., Taylor, S. H., and Donald, K. W., 1966. Effects of intravenous propanolol on the systemic circulatory response to sustained handgrip, *Amer. J. Cardiol.* **18** : 333-344.

McCraw, D. B., Siegel, W., Stonecipher, H. K., Nutter, D. O., Schlant, R. C., and Hurst, J. W., 1972. Response of heart murmur intensity to isometric (handgrip) exercise, *British Heart J.,* **34** (June) : 605-610.

Mullins, C. B., Leshin, S. J., Mierzwiak, D. S., Matthews, O. A., and Blomqvist, G., 1970. Sustained forearm contraction (handgrip) as a stress test for evaluation of left ventricular function (Abstract), *Clin. Res.,* **18** :322.

Petro, J. K., Hollander, A. P., and Bouman, L. N., 1970. Instantaneous cardiac acceleration in man induced by a voluntary muscle contraction, *J. Appl. Physiol.,* **29** : 794-798.

Saltz, S., Grossman, W., Paraskos, J., Segal, H., Dalen, J., and Dexter, L., 1971. Left ventricular function: response to sustained isometric handgrip (abstract), *Circulation,* **43** and **44** (suppl. II) : II-34.

Siegel, W., Gilbert, C., Stonecipher, H. K., Nutter, D., Schlant, R., and Hurst, J. W., 1970. Isometric handgrip and treadmill exercise in atherosclerotic heart disease (Abstract), *Circulation,* **41** and **42** (suppl. III) : III-98.

Tuttle, W. W., and Horvath, S. M., 1957. Comparison of effects of static and dynamic work on blood pressure and heart rate, *J. Appl. Physiol.,* **10** : 294-296.

Wildenthal, K., Mierzwiak, D. S., Skinner, N. S., Jr., and Mitchell, J. H., 1968. Potassium-induced cardiovascular and ventilatory reflexes from the dog hindlimb, *Amer. J. Physiol.* **215** : 542-548.

65

Aquatic Instruction as Exercise Therapy

Joseph J. Gruber

Programs of therapeutic aquatic instruction and recreation should make a number of contributions to the education of the handicapped. Specifically swimming as both exercise and therapy can improve the level of physical fitness, emotional security, and social adjustment of the individual (Daniels, 1965). The development of recreational skills in swimming, boating, canoeing, sailing, and fishing will contribute to the adaptive functioning of the handicapped in society (Lynch 1972).

SPECIAL VALUES OF AQUATIC THERAPY

Handicapped people are usually far more inactive than normal individuals. Quite often they are isolated from society and have few opportunities to participate in physical activity designed to help them approach an adequate functional level in their daily living. As a result the handicapped exhibit a lag in motor skill development usually accompanied by a low level of physical fitness, inadequate personal-social adjustments and a restricted choice of leisure activities (Gruber 1969).

Some of the special values of participating in aquatic therapy would include the following:

1. Movements that cannot be done on land due to the pull of gravity on the body can be performed in water. Bodily support and the movements of weak muscles are aided by the buoyancy of the body in water. Many who cannot walk without prosthetic devices or who are confined to wheelchairs can walk and swim when in water (Arnheim 1969). Water provides a mild resistance to muscle action in proportion to force applied. The jerky and uncertain movements of the spastic child or the uncontrolled pendular movements resulting from tremor are reduced as a result of the fluid resistance of water. This can assist in the development of muscular control, coordination, range of motion, and an improvement in the strength and endurance of working muscles (Arnheim 1969; Lowman 1937).

2. Movements result in a general massaging action of water on the body. This promotes both local muscular relaxation and a general release of tension throughout the body (Arnheim 1969; Daniels 1965). This soothing effect should facilitate instruction and assist in treating the hypertensive and emotionally disturbed patient (Lowman 1937).

3. Swimming provides good all-around exercise for the musculature of the body, the lungs, and the cardiovascular system. As a result, one's physical fitness can be improved and maintained, which should delay the development of degenerative cardiovascular disease. Regular aquatic exercise can also contribute to weight reduction and control. These improvements in fitness should provide the handicapped with the stamina necessary to engage in water sports and in other daily activities (Daniels 1965; Gruber 1969; Newman 1970).

4. The psychological and social outcomes are as important as the acquisition of swimming skills and the elevation of one's physical fitness level. When the handicapped learn to swim, feelings of fear, inadequacy, and inferiority are greatly reduced (Daniels 1965). They realize that they have achieved a skill that many "normals" have not yet mastered. The feelings of success at having accomplished what many people thought unattainable for the handicapped should develop self-confidence and serve as a motivational base as the handicapped person explores new activities (Daniels 1965; Fait 1972; Grove 1970). Achievers in aquatics are now able to project themselves from a position of relative social isolation to one of increased social contacts and acceptance by their peers as well as normal individuals (Daniels 1965).

5. When aquatic activities are conducted properly they are usually fun for most people. The handicapped recognize an opportunity to learn an aquatic skill that can make them more like "normal" persons. The acquisition of swimming skills provides the handicapped with opportunities for a lifetime of aquatic recreation with their family and friends at rivers, lakes, beaches, and pools (AAHPER 1971; Arnheim 1969; Council: Aquatics-AAHPER 1969; Daniels 1965; Fait 1972; Lynch 1972).

6. An additional dividend is the excellent education that the general public receives every time a wheelchair patient rolls up to the edge of a community pool, falls into deep water and comes up swimming unassisted.

TYPES OF DISABILITIES BENEFITTING FROM AQUATIC THERAPY

The aquatic therapist must know the nature and limiting adaptive resources present in each person's disability as well as the implications for rehabilitation

(Council: Aquatics—AAHPER 1969). The natural movements of the various swimming skills and strokes (floating, dog paddle, elementary back stroke, back crawl, breast stroke, side stroke, front crawl, and diving) are used as therapeutic exercises while learning to swim the stroke (Daniels 1965). Patients requiring flexion and extension of the hips and knees as corrective exercises can accomplish this as they learn to do the flutter kick on their front or back, the dolphin kick, or the scissors kick. The aquatic specialist must work as a team with the patient's physician and physical therapist in planning the program of aquatic therapy. Each person's disability will require an individually planned program of swimming instruction (Grove 1970). Motor function testing will determine the type of stroke or survival skill to be taught in the initial stages of learning.

Some of the more common disabilities that can be ameliorated through swimming programs are: postural and body mechanics defects; orthopedic problems resulting from accidents, sports injuries, and birth defects; rheumatic fever and certain types of cardiac conditions; stroke effects; neurological disorders such as epilepsy, cerebral palsy, spina bifida, and poliomyelitis; muscular dystrophy; visual and auditory problems; mental retardation; emotional disorders; and other medical problems such as diabetes, obesity, hypertension, thyroid difficulties, arthritis, anemia, dysmehorrhea, certain allergies, and asthma (AAHPER 1971; Anderson 1968; Arnheim 1969; Council: Aquatics—AAHPER 1969; Daniels 1965; Fait 1972; Lowman 1937; Lynch 1972; Newman 1970; Wright 1970). Some persons may never master actual swimming skills due to the nature and/or degree of infirmity. However, they should be encouraged to participate as much as possible to reap the benefits of socialization through peer and adult interaction (Daniels 1965; Grove 1970).

POOL EQUIPMENT AND FACILITIES

Whenever possible the pool facilities should be modified so that architectural barriers to the mobility of the handicapped may be eliminated. Ramps should be built into stairways, and doorways should be widened whenever possible so that those who arrive in wheelchairs, with walkers, or on crutches can move about with a minimum of difficulty. Rest rooms must be modified so that people in wheelchairs have easy access to the facilities. Dressing cabinets with adequate storage space for braces, artificial limbs, crutches, and clothing should be provided ("City Equips . . ." 1970; Daniels 1965; Lowman 1952; Wright 1970).

The swimming pool itself should be equipped properly with a hoist so that heavy individuals can be lowered into the water. Underwater stairs, parallel bars, and handrails should be provided for gait training as well as providing a hand-hold for those engaging in various types of swimming drills.

Other useful equipment for certain forms of therapy would include under-water chairs, portable whirlpool devices, and rescue boards. Aids for swimming instruction and recreational games would include air mattresses, water polo balls, inflated rings that fit snugly under the armpits, life belts, styrofoam floats that can be attached to the arms and legs, inflatable neck collars, and arm or leg fins that can replace the artificial limbs of amputees (Anderson 1968; Arnheim 1969; "City Equips . . ." 1970; Jokl 1965; Jokl 1958; Lowman 1952; Wright 1970).

The principal goal of therapeutic swimming instruction programs would be to have each person move about in the water with a minimum of the instructional devices just mentioned or with none at all.

PROGRAM SUPERVISION

The aquatic program must be organized and administered by a team of experts who pool their knowledge of swimming instruction, physical medicine, sanitation, therapeutic exercises, safety, and drug administration (Council: Aquatics—AAHPER 1969). The physician, nurse, physical therapist, aquatic specialist, locker room attendant, and life guards should meet regularly to review policies, discuss case histories, and plan the most effective program of instruction for each individual. If certain pupils require frequent medication and/or specialized hydrotherapy, a registered nurse and physical therapist should be in attendance during instructional periods to implement the prescription of the physician. When necessary the physical therapist can assist the swimming instructor by preparing the student for instruction using certain exercises designed to promote strength, relaxation, and flexibility. Implementation of the program is enhanced by using volunteer helpers from the Boy Scouts, Girl Scouts, Explorer Scouts, college students, and other community social service groups (Council: Aquatics—AAHPER 1969; Wright 1970). These people meet the handicapped when they arrive at the pool, assist them in and out of the pool facilities, help them dress and undress, escort them to the rest room when needed, and serve as a swimming companion when the subject is in the water. It should be emphasized that the aquatics expert is in charge when the rehabilitation team and the students enter the pool facilities.

Health and safety are promoted when the aquatic specialist conducts an orientation program for parents, relatives, volunteer helpers, physicians, nurses, therapists, life guards, and the handicapped. All are taken on a tour of the pool facilities. Purposes of the program are explained and each person's responsibilities are outlined. Brief sessions covering elementary forms of rescue and artificial respiration are held for the therapists and volunteer helpers. At least two life guards should observe all pool activity. The guards are not to take part in the instructional or recreational phases of the swimming period (Am. Red Cross 1955; Council: Aquatics—AAHPER 1969; Meehan 1970).

Air and water temperatures must be kept at comfortable levels. The best therapy will occur when the water temperature is between 86 and 92 degrees. Cooler water results in chilling, elevated muscle tension, and a psychological aversion to water. Robes and large bath towels should be available so that the swimmers can "wrap-up" during rest periods when they are not in the water (Council: Aquatics—AAHPER 1969; Fait 1972).

TYPES OF AQUATIC PROGRAMS

A planned program of progression in swimming skills should be adapted to the individual needs of each learner. Some may not progress far but the majority of handicapped people can achieve at least an intermediate level. Some could attain advanced levels of skill (Newman 1970; Wright 1970). Basic survival skills such as floating with or without the aid of floats, breath control, water entries, and recovery to the surface unassisted, plus resting back stroke and the dog paddle, can be learned by most (Council: Aquatics—AAHPER 1969). Those who can should be advanced to instruction in the other strokes—the side stroke, breast stroke, and back and front crawl. Elementary diving from the side of the pool or from the low and high board can be taught to many of the handicapped. The handicapped are also capable of organizing their own water shows, swim meets, modified water polo, and forms of synchronized swimming. They tend to make unique contributors to the events within their swimming abilities (Council: Aquatics—AAHPER 1969; Daniels 1965; Newman 1970; Wright 1970).

Progression can advance to learning the basic skills needed to enter a boat or canoe in the swimming pool. Paddling and rowing skills can be developed at the same time muscles are being exercised (Lynch 1972). Some of the bait and fly-casting skills can also be taught in the pool.

It seems appropriate to mention that handicapped children could achieve quite well in some of the national agency aquatics programs such as those promoted by the Young Men's Christian Association, American Red Cross, Boy Scouts, and Girls Scouts (Am. Red Cross 1955; Grove 1970; Newman 1970). Most of these agency programs provide instruction in swimming, diving, boating, canoeing, and sailing. Some handicapped may eventually qualify for life-saving and water-safety instruction.

A successful swimming program can open the doors to other areas of success and is a big step toward as complete a rehabilitation as possible within the limitations of each individual (Newman 1970).

REFERENCES

AAHPER, 1971. *The best of challenge,* pp. 89-95. Washington, D.C.: AAHPER.

American National Red Cross, 1955. *Swimming for the handicapped* (instructors manual). Washington, D.C.: American National Red Cross.

Anderson, William, 1968. *Teaching the physically handicapped to swim.* New York: Transatlantic Arts, Inc.

Arnheim, D., Auxter, D., and Crow, W., 1969. *Principles and methods of adapted physical education,* pp. 134, 318. St. Louis: C.V. Mosby Co.

City equips swim center for the handicapped, 1970. *Swimming Pool Weekly,* **44** (March 23) : 36-38.

Council for National Cooperation in Aquatics and the AAHPER, 1969. *A practical guide for teaching the mentally retarded to swim.* Washington, D.C.

Daniels, A. S., and Davies, E., 1965. *Adapted physical education (2nd ed.), New York: Harper and Row.*

Fait, H. F. 1972. *Special physical education, adapted, corrective, developmental (3rd ed.).* Philadelphia: W.B. Saunders Co.

Grove, F., and Weber, Y., 1970. Aquatic therapy: a real first step to rehabilitation. JOHPER. **41** (October) : 65-66.

Gruber, J. J., 1969. Implications of physical education programs for children with learning disabilities, *Journal of Learning Disabilities,* **2** (November) : 44-50.

Jokl, E., 1964. *The scope of exercise in rehabilitation.* Springfield, Ill.: Charles C. Thomas.

————, 1958. *The clinical physiology of physical fitness and rehabilitation.* Springfield, Ill.: Charles C. Thomas.

Lowman, C. L., and Roen, S. G., 1952. *Therapeutic use of pools and tanks.* Philadelphia: W.B. Saunders Co.

Lowman, C. L., 1937. *Technique of underwater gymnastics.* Los Angeles: American Publications, Inc.

Lynch, W. J., 1972. Canoeing for recreation and rehabilitation, *Parks and Recreation,* **7** (July) : 20-21, 46.

Meehan, D. S., 1970. Handicapped swim clinic, *JOHPER,* **41** (October) : 66-67.

Newman, J. 1970. Swimming for the spina bifida, *JOHPER,* **41** (October) : 67-68.

Wright, B. 1970. The wedde handiswimmers, *JOHPER,* **41** (October) : 69-70.

66

Yoga and Fitness

Allan J. Ryan

Interest in the practice of yoga has been recurrent in the United States since the last century, when it was introduced as part of the cult of theosophy. The current upsurge of interest has been stimulated largely by Western study and practice of Oriental philosophy and of the martial arts such as karate and judo. Currently there is less interest in the doctrinal aspects of yoga as a philosophy than in certain of its physical practices. These are now being taught and recommended as a means of achieving and maintaining physical fitness.

Yoga is one of the six classic systems of Hindu philosophy. It is characterized chiefly by its emphasis on the importance of body control in achieving union (which is what the word "yoga" means) with the object of all knowledge. In the case of those who practice yoga as a religious way of life, this object is Brahma, the universal spirit. In the case of atheists, it becomes a deeper knowledge of self.

There are eight stages of yoga practice that make a ladder leading to this perfect knowledge. The first stage is self-control (yama); second, religious observance (niyama); third, postures (asana); fourth, the regulation of breathing (pranayama); fifth, restraint of the senses (pratyahara); sixth, steadying of the mind (dharana); seventh, meditation (dhyama); and eighth, profound contemplation (samadhi). Having passed through these eight stages, the adept is supposed to have achieved the final liberation of the spirit from matter (kaivalya), attaining the ecstasy of the knowledge of reality.

One school of this philosophy has grouped the eight stages into four groups of two each, describing them as the four paths to union with divine perfection. These paths, which are complementary, are said to be suited to certain temperaments. The first, raja yoga, comprises the sixth and seventh stages, and emphasizes the action of the mind. The second, karma yoga, comprises the first and fifth stages, and stresses the will. The third, bhakti yoga, includes the second and eighth stages, and concerns itself with devotion. The fourth, hatha yoga, takes in the third and fourth stages, and deals with the body and the life force.

HATHA (PHYSICAL) YOGA

The results of the practice of hatha, or physical, yoga are equated by its proponents with what are supposed to be the characteristics of youth:

flexibility, grace, serenity, relaxation, ability to sleep restfully, vitality, endurance, maintenance of proper circulation, strength of vital organs and glands, firmness and strength of muscles, taut and smooth skin, normal weight, quick recovery, alertness, and clarity of mind. Since these are all characteristics that are highly desired, it is quite natural that any system promising such assets would be eagerly welcomed. Yoga does not promise to prolong life, only to forestall the appearance of aging, which is identified particularly with loss of flexibility.

Reasonable mastery of the postural and breathing techniques taught to beginners is usually promised if performance is regular for periods of from 6 to 12 weeks. Ability to perform correctly the more difficult postures may take as long as three years. The postural activities are not supposed to be exercises in the ordinary sense, since their purpose is to stretch the body and relax tension, not to build muscle size or strength. The values of calisthenics and sports in this regard are indeed derided by serious practitioners of yoga.

As a practical matter, muscle strength may be somewhat increased in certain groups due to the dynamic tension brought about in maintaining some of the postures for extended periods of time. These are not necessarily muscle groups that would be used much in work or sports activities, and therefore overall strength may not be increased as measured by conventional estimates of this aspect of general physical fitness. Because there is some relationship between weight and strength, and because the diet of the orthodox yoga practitioners is lactovegetarian, disposing them to be lean and not well-muscled, strength seems to be below the average for persons otherwise similar in age and height.

RHYTHMIC DEEP BREATHING

The main principle of breath control in yoga is the practice of deep breathing on a rhythmical basis, with emphasis on complete relaxation and absence of strain. Breathing should be done as during a deep sleep. Eight different varieties of yogic breathing have been described. Perhaps the three most imporant are bhastrika, sitali, and ujjai. Bhastrika alternates quick, shallow, forcible inhahalations and exhalations through the nostrils with a deep inhalation, held as long as possible, then exhaled completely. In sitali, the tongue is protruded and curled, as breath is inhaled and exhaled through the tube so formed between the pursed lips. Ujjai is a series of deep, long breaths through the nostrils with the abdominal muscles slightly contracted.

Rhythmic breathing is practiced by attempting to correlate the rate of breathing with the pulse rate. The idea is to breathe in steadily for a period of four pulse beats, hold the breath for two beats and then breathe out for four beats. The "cleansing breath" is carried out by taking a deep inspiration and than exhaling forcefully with the lips pursed. In the "walking breathing" exercise, emphasis is placed on maintaining a continous flow of air in and out, avoiding the period of breath-holding. The "recharging breath" is carried out in the same manner as any other deep breath, except that the palms are pressed together during both inspiration and expiration. The "mountain pose" is carried out by doing rhythmic breathing in the lotus position. The "breathing exercise for good posture" is carried out by making a deep forward bend while exhaling after a deep inhalation.

The maximum consumption of oxygen with a minimum amount of effort, rather than the improvement of maximum breathing capacity for sustained effort, appears to be the objective of yogic breathing. The few functional tests that have been performed on practitioners of yoga indicate relatively poor function, certainly below any level consistent with what we define as physical fitness.

YOGA AND THE HEART

Control of the heart rate, which is said to be an accomplishment of the more experienced practitioners, can be established for brief periods by performing the valsalva maneuver, attempting to exhale forcefully against a closed glottis. This may cause an apparent arrest of the heart by diminishing the peripheral pulses to the point where they cannot be detected by palpation, although their presence has been ascertained in such situations by the use of a very sensitive plethysmograph. This is apparently the result of reduced venous return to the heart. The heart sounds may be so diminished and masked by muscular sounds that it is difficult to pick them up with a stethoscope. Nevertheless, an electrocardiogram taken at this time will show a regular but reduced heart rate, perhaps with an increase of the P-R interval or decrease or disappearance of the P wave.

The only evidence relating to change in cardiac function as the result of the practice of yoga is meager and partially contradictory. There is no reason to believe from a conceptual analysis of yoga practices that the ability of the heart to increase the efficiency of the circulation or to recover from strenuous exercise is improved. Indeed, many yoga practitioners feel that each person's heart is allotted only a certain number of beats for a lifetime and that speeding of the heart by vigorous exercise may only hasten that person's death.

In summary, the available evidence relating to the theory and practice of yoga does not indicate that it makes any positive contribution to the development of physical fitness as we understand it, with the possible exception of the improvement in flexibility that results. Unsupervised attempts to emulate some of the more demanding feats of breath holding or to assume some of the more difficult postures might result in some harm to the untrained individual.

ANNOTATIONS ON YOGA*

The ancient Yoga takes many forms in which physical and mental doctrines are followed separately and together. Yogis have claimed ability to control certain involuntary bodily functions, to survive live burial, and to control heart beat.

Survival after live burial implies voluntary control over metabolic activity and oxygen consumption. Shri Ramanand Yogi of Andhra claimed to have been sealed in a dugout underground pit for 28 days. Anand et al. enclosed him in an airtight metallic and glass box, with an effective capacity of 2,263 liters, for eight hours on one occasion and ten hours on another. Two other individuals were studied as controls; one stayed in the box for four hours and the other for seven hours.

The basal oxygen utilization of Shri Ramanand, determined with a Benedict-Roth b.m.r. apparatus, was calculated to be 19.5 liters per hour, which was within the normal range for his surface-area. During his eight-hour confinement an average of 26.9 liters per hour was used in the first three hours, while a candle was burning in the box, and 12.2 liters per hour after the candle went out. In the second experiment, the oxygen consumption averaged 13.5 liters per hour— 21.3 liters in the first hour and 10 liters per hour in the middle part of the experiment; his carbon dioxide output followed the oxygen uptake reciprocally. One control showed no change in basal oxygen requirement in each of the two four-hour experiments, while the other control showed an oxygen consumption above basal requirement in the seven-hour experiment. Respiratory and cardiac rates increased in both controls as the oxygen concentration fell and the carbon dioxide concentration rose. Shri Ramanand, on the other hand, had an initial heart-rate of 85 per minute and, in the greater part of the experiment, it ranged between 60 and 72 even though the oxygen concentration fell from 19.33 to 15.86 percent. In the last hour, when the oxygen concentration fell from 15.86 to 14.64 percent the pulse-rate rose to 80-90. Simultaneously, the carbon-dioxide concentration rose from one to five percent and then, at the end of the last hour, to 5.6 percent. Meanwhile, his respiratory rate remained at 20 per minute during the first eight hours and rose to 26 in the last two hours. An electroencephalogram during the experiment showed low-voltage fast activity and other changes associated with the drowsy state of sleep replacing the basal dominant alpha rhythm. Delta rhythm, associated with deep sleep, was not recorded. Two or three hours after the end of the experiment Shri Ramanand developed a pyrexia of 101.5°F, which lasted six to seven hours. He stated that this happened after each live burial.

---

* *J. Sports Med. and Phys. Fitness* **2** (March 1962) : 50.

Anand et al. interpret these results as indicating a voluntary reduction of basal metabolism, possibly mediated through the autonomic nervous system, which this man could induce by his yogic practices.

Three Yogi who claimed to be able to stop their hearts beating were studied during several attempts, each lasting 10-20 seconds. At each attempt the subjects voluntarily increased their intrathoracic pressure by holding their breath in inspiration and expiration with a closed glottis and forcibly contracting the abdominal and chest muscles. Anand et al. found that heart-sounds became inaudible to auscultation and that pulsation in the radial artery and in a finger plethysmograph disappeared during these attempts, but no electrocardiographic or radiographic arrest of the heart was demonstrable.

67

Isokinetic Exercise and the Mechanical Energy Potentials of Muscle

James. J. Perrine

The basic function of muscle is to convert electrochemical energy into mechanical energy. The electrochemical energy transformations in this conversion process have been described in great detail by the biochemists. However, it is only by delving into the mechanics of how mechanical energy develops and is consolidated by and transmitted from the elastic component, that the mechanical energy potentials of muscle can be fully understood.

It is not easy to visualize the mechanics of a complex mechanical energy system in which mechanical events take place within fractions of a second. The same difficulty has existed for identifying or quantifying the types and amounts of mechanical energy that are needed for different functional activities. The terms ordinarily used for describing muscular potentials— "strength" and "endurance"—would seem to be incomplete in this respect.

*   Reprinted from the *Journal of Health, Physical Education, Recreation,* May 1968. Copyright, 1968, by the American Association for Health, Physical Education, and Recreation, National Education Association, 1201 - 16th Street, N.W., Washington, D.C. 20036.

For the purpose of developing muscular potentials, only two basic possibilities in exercise mechanics have been generally recognized and implemented: isotonic and isometric exercise. To be sure, many variations in technique and equipment have been devised for their implementation.

It is advantageous to consider muscular contractions and their functional applications as processes of mechanical energy production and consumption. It becomes natural then to consider directly measuring and developing neuromuscular systems for specific types of mechanical energy output.

Both of these operations have become a practicality with the formulation and recent implementation of a third basic method of muscular exercise: isokinetic exercise. Isokinetic exercising, a new approach to muscle training, provides for the development of human neuromuscular systems for all critical types of muscular energy output.

Isokinetic exercise employs a simple but unfamiliar physical principle for loading a dynamically contracting muscle: positively controlling the speed of the motion produced by the contraction. To put into perspective the potential advantages of this type of loading for accomplishing specific mechanical energy training objectives, an hypothesis of the probable mechanics behind the development and transmission of mechanical energy by muscles will be offered.

BASIC PHYSICS OF MECHANICAL ENERGY

Mechanical energy is, strictly speaking, the intangible "faculty" possessed by a mechanical system for doing physical work; it is what diminishes when work is done. In actual practice, however, available mechanical energy will always manifest itself by physical force developed in some form, such as the pressure of a compressed gas, the weight of a suspended body, the tension of a stretched spring, the inertial force (resistance to being slowed or stopped) of a rotating flywheel.

A physical force may have a direct application for some stationary activity such as supporting a load, or it may be used to accomplish physical work. Physical work is the term given the result when any force acts through some distance in space, i.e., the force overcomes some resistance and moves its point of application. Consistent with its derived definition, the mechanical energy that is possessed by a system is always quantified in terms of the physical work it could accomplish.

A distinction is made as to whether a system has energy to do work by virtue of its advantageous configuration or position (e.g., the stretched spring or the suspended weight) in which case it is termed as possessing potential energy, or whether it has energy to do work by virtue of its being in motion and therefore possessing momentum (e.g., the rotating flywheel) in which case it is termed as possessing kinetic energy. To avoid confusion it should be noted that both potential and kinetic forms of energy *could* be considered "potential" from the standpoint of being able to do work at a future time, and both *could* be considered "kinetic" from the standpoint of being able to accomplish work dynamically.

When a system is *storing* mechanical energy in any form and therefore is *not* accomplishing physical work, it may be possible to measure the amount of force it is developing. However, its "energy" (work performing) potential cannot be measured directly but only extrapolated, either from the known work that was done on the system to bring it to its existing level of stored energy, or from a calculation of, or if possible a measurement of, the work accomplishable by the system in some typical work performance test made of the system.

When a system is *transmitting* mechanical energy in any form and therefore *is* accomplishing physical work, the energy transfer can be quantified by considering the work from three possible standpoints, as follows:

1. The parameter of work: The *amount* of physical work accomplished in some constituent bout, or in total, but irrespective of how much time it takes to accomplish the work. Units of work consist of an integration of any applicable units of distance and force, such as foot-pounds.

2. The parameter of power: The *rate* at which the work is being accomplished at each instant. Units of power consist of an integration of the work units divided by an applicable unit of time, such as foot-pounds per second.

3. The parameter of energy: The *amount* of energy that is conceptually lost by a system when it performs an amount of work. It is worthy of note that since the term energy refers strictly to the *faculty* for doing work, it should not be expressed in *absolute* work units even though its full work producing potential is clearly apparent. Rather, energy is more meaningfully expressed in *relative* work units, such as foot-pound-seconds, indicating that the actual amount of work it does effect is always relative to the specific rate and time duration circumstances under which it is utilized.

All processes involving energy transfer will obey one supreme rule: the total energy output from a system can never exceed the total energy that is put into the system. This principle, it will be seen, has special significance for the energy developing potentials of muscle.

Every muscle fiber is a complete mechanical energy system in itself. It contains both components to produce mechanical energy and components to absorb and temporarily store the energy.

The actual sources of mechanical energy in this system are the sarcomeres. Sarcomeres are extremely tiny structures that work against a viscoelastic load in repetitive firings. The mechanical energy developed in one sarcomere firing is much too small in force and too brief in time to be directly useful for any gross muscular activity. Therefore, a multiple elastic component in each muscle fiber first is stretched by, and thereby absorbs all the bits of energy that are transmitted by the sarcomeres attached to it. In this way, their energy is consolidated within the elastic component as a store of "potential" energy (as in the stretched spring) with considerably greater force and work capabilities. It takes only a fraction of a second for the full elastic component of a typical muscle fiber to be saturated with stored energy by the millions of sarcomeres located within a fiber, each firing several times in that brief period.

Once an elastic component has acquired potential energy, it continuously tries to dissipate the energy either by reshortening itself in between sarcomere firings, or by shortening the sarcomeres and, correspondingly, the overall fiber length. Thus, when a muscle fiber must maintain tension in even a simple static contraction, its sarcomeres must continue to fire repetitively to maintain a continous rate of energy input to the elastic component, and thereby offset the continous rate of energy dissipation that would otherwise permit the tension to decay.

If a muscle fiber is to both maintain tension and shorten at the same time, so as to accomplish physical work, its sarcomeres would have to provide input energy to the elastic component at a *rate* sufficient to offset both the rate that energy is being lost through the inherent dissipation, plus the rate that energy is being expended for the physical work. The higher the tension maintained in the elastic component during shortening, or the higher the shortening speed attained with the same tension, either representing a higher *rate* of working (power developed) by the fiber, the greater would be the *rate* at which mechanical energy is needed by the elastic component from the sarcomeres. In other words, the mechanical power output of an elastic component cannot exceed its mechanical power input.

Since the mechanical power input to a fiber's elastic component would be a function of the frequency at which the sarcomeres fire, the maximum possible power input is probably determined by the maximum frequency at which the sarcomeres can be fired. This maximum frequency/power-developing potential of a fiber would theoretically establish its tension-velocity curve, that is, how much tension the fiber could develop at all possible shortening speeds. In the body, however, a fiber's tension-supporting capacity may be inhibited at some level substantially below its projected power developing potential *at the lower speeds* because its efficiency and safety factors fall off at high tensions.

A fiber's power-developing potential, however, probably is the limiting factor for how much tension it can develop at any shortening speed on its tension-velocity curve beyond the point where a tension supporting limit would affect the theoretical power curve. Similarly, the power-developing potential of a fiber probably determines how fast the fiber can shorten against any submaximal load.

It is probable that the longer the total time a fiber generates tension, either statically or dynamically, the greater will be the *total amount* of chemical input energy its sarcomeres consume. Similarly, the higher the *rate* of energy (power) developed and transmitted by a fiber, the greater will be the total amount of energy its sarcomeres consume in an equal amount of time.

A muscle apparently stores locally a quantity of the chemical energy it consumes and can utilize this energy at high rates for short periods of time. For longer duration activites it would be more dependent on the chemical energy released into the bloodstream at a relatively slower rate by the intermediate metabolic systems.

Keeping in mind the foregoing hypotheses relating to how mechanical energy is developed in individual muscle fibers, the mechanical energy output of whole muscles may now be considered.

MECHANICAL ENERGY OUTPUT OF WHOLE MUSCLES

A whole muscle is simply an assemblage of many separate energy-producing fibers. Therefore its mechanical energy capabilities would be derived from summations of the energy outputs of some number of its component fibers acting together.

It appears that different sets of a muscle's fibers may be responsible for the energy developed at different shortening lengths of the muscle as a whole, possibly due to their relative physical placement within the muscle. It also appears that the central nervous system may control the relative number of fibers active within a muscle and the frequency at which they fire. Thus, by some efficient manipulation of these two variables, the central nervous system can adjust the energy developed by the whole muscle to suit any type of submaximal mechanical demands presented by a functional activity. As for a muscle's absolute capacities, it is clear that once the maximum possible number of its fibers have been activated, the muscle's output would be restricted by the tension-supporting and power-developing limitations of its individual fibers, as previously reviewed.

Since all skeletal muscles are attached to and work through limbs and other body segments, the external mechanical output capacity of a muscle must be measured at, and expressed in terms of the energy it develops at, or transmits from, some skeletal point.

For static activities, a muscle's capacity is represented simply by the maximum amount of force it can develop statically in specific joint positions and, possibly, by the amount of time it can maintain a static contraction.

For dynamic activities a muscle's capacity would be quantified in terms of any one or a combination of the following aspects of the mechanical energy it can transmit:

1. The maximum amount of force it can develop at all points in a range of joint movement. This represents the maximum amount of physical work the muscle can accomplish in one contraction through a given shortening range.
2. The maximum amount of force it can develop at different speeds of joint movement. This represents the maximum work rate or power the muscle can develop at specific speeds of shortening.
3. The maximum number of repetitions or total time-duration the muscle can repetitively accomplish a given amount of work (maintain a given average power output). This represents the maximum amount of energy the muscle can transmit in a given time period.

The mechanical demands imposed on a muscle by any functional activity can be understood best in terms of these definitive parameters of muscular energy output. Similarly, a muscle's performance limitations might be dealt with best by training approaches that correctly diagnose and treat these parameters as specific training objectives.

If the terms "strength" and "endurance" are to be useful, they must be assigned clear meaning within the framework of the mechanical energy potentials of muscle. If "strength" is to represent the tension capacity of muscle, it must be expressed relative to some speed of shortening (isometric being zero speed). If "endurance" is to represent the working-time capacities of muscle, it must be expressed relative to some average work rate.

MUSCLE TRAINING

It has long been observed that muscles somehow improve adaptively in response to regular, mechanically-demanding usage. All regimens of muscle training are designed to stimulate, as efficiently as possible, this process of adaptation. In recent years scientists realized that this adaptation process follows the principle of specificity, that is, that muscles tend to improve their capacity for the specific type of mechanical demand imposed upon them, rather than in any generalized way. The problem has been to diagnose and define correctly the critical muscular output potential(s) needed for some physical activity and to impose those demands in regular training, within the limitations of the mechanics of available exercise systems.

It would appear now that the energy requirements of the vast majority of functional activities fall within four basic types of mechanical demand from the standpoint of the probable mechanics underlying muscular energy output:

1. A demand on the muscle's strength capacity either statically or at the slower shortening speeds of the tension-velocity curve where tension would be limited primarily by fiber tension-supporting capacity.

2. A demand on the muscle's strength capacity at the higher shortening speeds of the tension-velocity curve where tension would be limited by fiber power-developing capacity.

3. A demand on the muscle's endurance capacity for relatively high rate/short duration power outputs.

4. A demand on the body's endurance capacity for relatively low rate/extended-duration power outputs.

With untrained muscles the probable first response to an intensive loading by any exercise method would be the activation of previously dormant fibers. This would explain the rapid gains commonly observed during early training stages. Following this, progress in the development of any specific energy potential would depend on whether the mechanical conditions of the exercise were sufficiently demanding to stimulate physiological changes in the specific energy mechanisms. It is difficult to verify precisely what physiological changes do occur in human muscles with specific types of activity. Certainly, the potential changes to be considered include (1) the number of fibers or myofibrils becoming active at various shortening lengths and/or the amount of contractile protein developed; (2) the fiber's actual *in situ* capacity for frequency of firing; (3) the amount of sarcoplasmic protein stored by the muscle; and (4) the energy-storing capacities and energy-converting efficiencies of the intermediate metabolic systems.

Regardless of how they occur physiologically, muscular adaptations can and do occur specifically to the different energy output demands imposed. The important difference between various exercise methods is how efficiently they obtain the desired improvements or how far they can carry the improvement of a specific energy output potential.

Exercise Mechanics

All isometric or isotonic exercise systems have certain inherent mechanical limitations that leave them actually unable to impose a maximal mechanical demand on a muscle with respect to some of the often critical energy output potentials.

Isometric exercise. Isometric exercise occurs against a load that prevents external movement and offers resistance inherently proportional to the muscle's static tension-developing capacity at one shortening length. However, there is no external dynamic work accomplished at all, so that the intrafiber power developed is inherently limited. Evidence indicates that the resulting improvement is in the low-speed strength category and primarily affects only the fibers active at the one shortening length exercised.

Isotonic exercise. Isotonic exercise occurs, by definition, against a load that allows movement but offers basically a constant resistance through a range of movement. In actual practice the term "isotonic" exercise is usually construed as applying to any form of dynamic exercise where the resistance is not proportionate to the muscle's actual dynamic force curve, such as exercise with springs, weights, friction devices, etc. Therefore, (1) the magnitude of an isotonic resistance normally must be limited to the largest load that can be moved at the weakest point in some range of movement (this resistance will be less than maximal during the rest of the range and thus will not load the muscle to its full tension-developing capacity in much of its shortening range; and (2) the exercise speed is subject to considerable acceleration, and because it is unstable and unpredictable, it is difficult in practice for a muscle to develop its maximum power output.

ISOKINETIC EXERCISE

Isokinetic exercise occurs against a load that allows movement at a mechanically fixed rate of speed and offers resistance inherently proportional to the muscle's dynamic tension-developing capacity at every point in its shortening range and at some optimal shortening speed.

To load a muscle by the isokinetic principle, a special mechanical device is required. An isokinetic exerciser consists of a unique speed-controlling mechanism that operates as a speed-governor on a dynamic exercise motion. It has suitable input attachments for positioning and holding at fixed, preset speeds and various functional exercise patterns. The attachment or grip always remains at rest except when it is being moved by an individual, and it can be moved with the slightest effort at or below the set speed, through any range of movement desired.

However, when an individual applies maximum effort to an isokinetic exerciser, it will instantly accelerate to its set speed, and then by preventing any further acceleration above that speed, it will load the dynamically "harnessed" muscle exactly proportionate to its maximum dynamic tension capacity, through a full range at that speed. As the muscle's tension capacity and skeletal advantage varies through the range of movement, the resistance caused by the speed-governing action of the device will fluctuate accordingly and naturally accommodate to the muscle's force-transmitting capacity at every point in the range. In this way, the device consistently loads the muscle for maximum work accomplishment with each repetition and does so without overstressing it at any point. As the muscle's tension-developing capacity improves, the loading automatically keeps perfect pace with the improvement.

In isokinetic loading, the desired exercise speed always occurs immediately, with resistance then developing as a function of the amount of tension the muscle can develop at that speed and not the reverse—resistance first, speed secondarily—as it is in isotonic exercises.

By determining an appropriate exercise speed and presetting it on the isokinetic exerciser (thereby fixing the shortening speed at which the muscle will be loaded), it is possible to allow a muscle to contract at the specific shortening speeds on the tension-velocity curve where it can develop either its (1) maximum peak tension, (2) most work per repetition, (3) highest power output, or (4) some submaximal average power output per repetition for a maximum time duration. Or it can be loaded at a specific joint speed corresponding to some special physical activity. Thus, isokinetic exercise is uniquely suited to training muscles for all critical types of mechanical energy output.

In performing isokinetic exercises individuals simply concentrate on generating greater and greater contractile force through a range at the fixed speed. They can rely on the fact that the isokinetic device will safely and surely control the resultant motion at the preset speed and along the desired exercise pattern.

It is very difficult to contemplate the feel of an isokinetic muscle contraction or to anticipate the high amount of dynamic muscular tension that can be attained by this method of muscle loading. It is not likely that an individual has experienced any other mechanical situation, either in functional activities or in exercising, in which a *maximum* effort, exerted dynamically, did not result in considerable acceleration of the load. For slow speed isokinetic efforts, the closest familiar counterpart would be pedaling a bicycle uphill or putting maximum effort into rowing a heavy boat. As for high speed isokinetic efforts, it is especially difficult to imagine delivering a maximum effort at a high speed while that speed remains advantageously steady. The isokinetic exerciser is especially designed so that it cannot be accelerated from any preset speed within its control range.

An isokinetic exerciser does not cause a muscle to contract eccentrically following a concentric contraction; in fact, the opposite muscle group can be loaded to its relative maximum on the return movement of a full repetition. Thus, a muscle can always relax briefly and receive circulation between every contraction. This may even produce a pumping effect on circulation and experience indicates that it provides freedom from the muscular ache and lingering weakness commonly developed in uninterrupted contraction exercises. Thus, in addition to the potential physiological and metabolic benefits with intermittent contractions, the freedom from discomfort may be important to an incentive for exercising regularly.

Isokinetic Muscle Dynamometry

While allowing a muscle group to develop maximum dynamic tension over a shortening range and at a specific performance speed, an isokinetic device can measure the muscle's external output under these fixed dynamic conditions by means of an internal load-cell. Thus, it can be considered as a true muscle dynamometer because it can directly and accurately measure the muscle's maximum force curve, work, power, and endurance capacities—at all performance speeds.

Cardiovascular and Metabolic Fitness

The potential advantages of isokinetic exercising are not necessarily restricted to its applications in regard to developing the neuromuscular system itself. It is not yet clear what intensities of physical activity are best for conditioning the cardiovascular system, developing pulmonary capacity and efficiency, losing weight, etc. But, since isokinetic exercises can be set up indoors to achieve anything from low power output from small muscle groups to ultra-high concurrent power outputs from several large muscle groups (potentially equal to or even exceeding strenuous running or swimming), it may have practical advantages in these other areas important in overall physical fitness.

Research will need to be done to determine how isokinetic exercising would be best used in the pursuit of each of the various fitness objectives. Special consideration should be given to the unique opportunity it presents by offering any desired level of power output, natural circulation contractions, and indoor accessibility.

Joint Strengthening

The potential advantages of isokinetic exercise for joint strengthening should be mentioned in view of the increasing problem of joint injuries in sports. A joint is a torque-transmitting mechanism. It can suffer damage if it is called upon to transmit a torque force exceeding its capacity.

Like muscles, joints apparently will also respond to repetitive training and develop greater capacity. However, in isotonic training, the mechanical advantage factor allows a potentially dangerous differential to exist between muscle and joint capacities. As was mentioned, any isotonic training load must be limited to a fraction of the muscle's actual torque-developing capacity at the optimum point in its shortening range. This isotonic load, however, is all that the joint must carry in any position. Consequently the joint is trained to handle only a fraction of the peak torque that the muscle can, and does frequently, develop at optimum positions during intense sports activity.

Isometric exercise can load a joint repetitively with a high static torque, but this repetitively focuses all the load on a few points of a joint's bearing surface. If this method is not eventually irritating in itself, it nonetheless poses the logistical problem of strengthening the many possible joint positions.

Isokinetic exercise of joints is optimal, loading the joint with all the torque the muscle can develop at every point in a dynamic range of movement. Thus, the joint's training in isokinetic exercise should progress commensurate with the muscle's developing torque capacity.

SUMMARY

The basic theory of isokinetic exercise has been presented with an explanation of its potential advantages for developing the different mechanical energy potentials of muscle. A hypothesis of the probable mechanics of muscular energy production and transmission has been offered.

Isokinetic exercise does not represent any one type of exercise, but is actually a new training modality that, through the control of exercise speed, makes possible and practical many different types of muscle training. It may serve as its own best means of illustrating the different types of mechanical energy output of which muscle is capable.

Discussion of the potentials of isokinetic exercise has been limited to its immediate application in conventional exercise situations, where the straight mechanical energy potentials of muscle are to be developed. No attempt has been made to delineate its significant application potentials for training neuromuscular coordination and control, or for motor learning and skills.

As the versatility and effectiveness of this new method of neuromuscular loading are demonstrated in relation to present muscle training objectives, its advantages for training other aspects of human performance will become evident.

68

The Role of Athletics Trainers in the Prevention and Care of Injuries

S.E. Reid and T.E. Oxley

Athletics trainers have a very responsible position in the care of the athlete. They must view sports participation with understanding and enthusiasm. They must be loyal to the coach and fair to the athlete. It is mandatory for the trainer to gain the respect and confidence of the players and at the same time to be sympathetic to their problems. The trainer must be cognizant of athletes who minimize their injuries and aware of players who magnify their ailments.

It is necessary that trainers align themselves with physicians who are sympathetic to the cause of sports. It is incumbent upon trainers to develop such a rapport through easy communication with these doctors that they will have confidence in the trainer's ability to care for the injured athlete and be assured that they will be consulted about injuries that require care beyond the capability of the trainer or where medico-legal problems are likely to ensue. Trainers must not dispense drugs without the approval of the team physician. The doctor, on the other hand, must not undermine the confidence that has been developed in the players for their trainer but must conform to an established chain of command from the player to the trainer to the team doctor.

Unique in the medical and paramedical fields is the fact that quite often the trainer sees the injury as it is happening and is ready to examine the player before swelling and pain obscure the physical findings. Athletes who compete in contact sports, for example, subject themselves to many types of violence, and close observation by the trainer will avoid catastrophies. It is imperative that trainers be able to recognize injury and, more importantly, the severity of injury since many times they must determine whether an athlete should continue to compete in a contest. Therefore, it is necessary for the coaches to have the highest confidence in the trainer's judgment. The trainer must, however, realize his limitations and seek medical advice from the team physician for all injuries requiring medical attention.

A large percentage of injuries incurred even in contact sports are minor and many of these require only first-aid type of care. The obvious injuries can be readily diagnosed and treatment instituted. There are, however, several serious injuries, especially involving the head and neck and intra-abdominal contents, that may not produce obvious symptoms. When neglected, serious consequences may result. The trainer must realize that even a physician cannot diagnose some of these problems without careful observation in a hospital facility. How then can the trainer be expected to make such vital decisions on the spur of the moment? The trainer cannot afford to take risks in such situations and must remove the athlete from play regardless of the effect on the outcome of the game. The trainer cannot be influenced by the pressures of the crowd or the delay of the game in assessing the extent of injury in an unconscious player. Except for carefully establishing an airway, the player should not be moved until he has regained consciousness and is able to help in localizing the site of the injury.

Trainers play a large role in the prevention of injury, and in some respects in preventing causes of injuries. They may, for example, recommend that an athlete do special exercises in order to strengthen a weak area of the body. They make recommendations to the coaches to include drills and warm up exercises designed to reduce injury. Adequate and proper-fitting equipment is also a vital concern of the trainer for the prevention of injury. Athletics trainers are also concerned with the rules of the game and often recommend changes that reduce incidence of injury. Safety in athletics is foremost on the mind of the trainer.

Athletics trainers have many roles to play. They may be required to educate the physician concerning the specific requirements of sports medicine that exist because of the motivation and physical fitness of the athlete and the urgency to restore the injured player to as nearly complete recovery as possible. The trainer must be a psychologist, a nurse, a physical therapist, a dietitian, a diplomat in his dealings with coaches, parents, and players, but most of all must have good common sense. Trainers must be knowledgeable in the care and fitting of athletic equipment and be experts in the rehabilitation of the injured athlete. They must be willing to learn and anxious to improve their own capabilities. They must not, however, exceed their realm of responsibility. It is indeed a complex role that they must play.

SUGGESTED READINGS

Bowlus, W. C., 1979. First priority: certified trainers. *JOPER* **50** (June) : 71-72.

Kegerreis, S. 1979. Health care for student athletes. *JOPER* **50** (June) : 78-79.

Wilmore, J., 1977. *Athletic training and physical fitness: physiological principles and practices of the conditioning process.* Boston: Allyn and Bacon.

69

The Bench Technique: Knee Exercises

Karl K. Klein

This exercise technique has exceptional value for use in the reconditioning program. Extensive research has been done in comparing results with the "single boot technique" as well as comparing the strength gains made with the involved and uninvolved leg in reconditioning programs. For all practical purposes the bench exercise is capable of developing bilateral strength in both the quadriceps and hamstring muscles during the same exercise and has produced bilateral strength gains equal to or higher than those produced by other systems of progressive exercise (Klein 1963, 1962, 1963, 1971).

The bench technique utilizes an increase in repetitions of exercise weekly, with the body weight being held fairly constant throughout the exercise period. During the bilateral exercise periods the person should concentrate on the functioning of the muscle groups of the weak or involved leg. The physiological response has shown that the weak musculature gains strength and bulk more rapidly than the stronger musculature so bilateral strength balance will result.

The process of establishing the initial repetitions of exercise will be described under Functional Operation. Due to the existing muscular weakness in the postoperative or injury situation, it may be advisable to have the subject use the extended arms with fingers on the bench to give some support during the initial knee-extension movements. The back should be kept straight and perpendicular to the floor during the exercise.

Subjects should be encouraged to do the exercise without hand assistance as soon as possible. They are likely to feel that the uninvolved leg is doing most of the work during the first few days, but with the bench the weak musculature will begin to respond to the exercise action.

Terminal extension emphasis is under constant stress in this exercise technique. Cruciate ligament instability does not necessitate any specific change in the technique. Fig. 69.1 illustrates the functional use of this system in postoperative treatment. When reconditioning is started within 10 to 14

---

* Reprinted from *The Knee in Sports,* Austin, Texas: Jenkins Publishing Co., The Pemberton Press, 1971.

days following surgery, the loading effect can be changed slightly so as to reduce the exercise stress. This is easily accomplished by moving the foot-stabilizing bar out an extra notch or two so that the fulcrum behind the thigh is four to six inches above the knee instead of the two to three inches originally recommended. As soon as possible and as soon as it is comfortable for the subject, move the foot bar back to the recommended position. If chondromalcia is present, this technique should be modified. In such cases the program outlined for this condition should be utilized, as will be described later.

FUNCTIONAL OPERATION

The step-by-step execution of the bench exercise is described here. Fig. 69.1 shows the steps of the exercise from the starting position, as shown by the student on the left, to full-knee extension shown by the student on the right. Once full extension is reached (two seconds), a controlled return to the starting position is made (two seconds). In this complete single-exercise movement both the quadriceps and hamstring muscles are used; the quadriceps perform in their normal extension function, and the hamstrings act as extensors in the terminal 15 to 20 degrees of extension when the foot is in contact with the floor, as used in this exercise technique (Bowen 1949).

The front edge of the bench is two to three inches above the knee joint when the leg is in full extension. If the distance is increased to change the position of the fulcrum, the leverage factor will reduce the amount of body weight against the muscle work.

After the exercise cadence has been learned, a maximum set should be attempted. This amounts to all the repetitions that can be done before fatigue forces a stop. After a few minutes rest, the process should be repeated. A third set should follow a second rest period. The largest number of repetitions accomplished should be used as the starting loading for the first week of exercise. Progressive increments of the exercise loading can be taken from Table 69.1, the sample exercise chart. A six- to eight-week program should be followed.

The work load may be increased by two modifications: (1) using an increased lean-back of the body, and/or (2) strapping 20 to 30 pounds of weight over the shoulders and keeping the body erect.

The progressive nature of the bench technique is indicated by the rapid increase in measured strength development. This fact has been demonstrated in the original experimental research with this technique by comparing it with the traditional single-boot technique.

A tensiometer strength increment of 100 or more pounds can be anticipated in the total score for the quadriceps and hamstring muscles. Measured results compare favorably with those of other exercise systems. Muscular endurance is also influenced.

Fig. 69-1. The bench technique of exercise

BENCH CONSTRUCTION

Fig. 69.2 shows the construction design of the exercise bench. The frame may be built of wood or steel. The original bench built at the University of Texas at Austin was constructed in 1954 and is still used daily.

The foot bar is adjustable to fit the varying leg length. In construction, the forward arms that hold the foot bar might be extended six to eight inches. Instead of the 24 inches shown the forward extension should be 30 to 32 inches. This will give the bench added utility for use by the taller person.

The bench is also usable as a leg conditioning procedure for many sports: football, basketball, swimming (especially the butterfly), track, wrestling, handball, squash, badminton, and other individual sports.

STRENGTH DEVELOPMENT

Just what ultimate strength development might be obtained through various forms of exercise is difficult to determine. When we discover what causes one subject (males in this case) to develop a 50 percent increase in strength capacity, while another subject of the same sex, age, and physique, on the

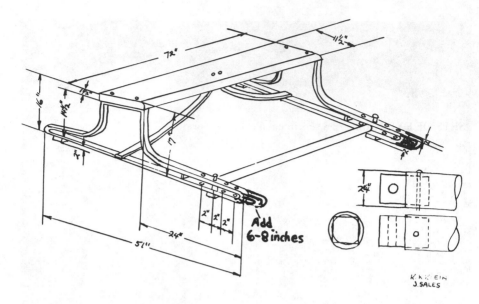

Fig. 69-2. Bench construction.

same exercise program, develops only a 30 percent increase, we may be able to determine the ultimate in strength development. It would be safe to say, however, that the goal to achieve for optimal muscular protection is bilateral as well as antagonistic muscular balance.

THE BENCH TECHNIQUE FOR CHONDROMALCIA

Although early functional activity recommends the boot and straight-leg lifting technique to protect the posterior patellar surface, the emphasis on the vastus medialis muscle development for joint stability is generally inadequate. Remember that when this condition is present very limited movement of the patella through its range of motion across the joint (femoral condyles) is important for protection of the total joint surface.

The bench technique, through a decreased range of movement, is usable for specific emphasis on the vastus medialis. The concept of limiting range of movement was suggested by Dr. John B. Gunn, an orthopedist from Dallas, Texas, and discussed with Dr. Thomas I. Lowry, an orthopedist from Austin, Texas, before it was placed in research and in functional operation in the rehabilitation laboratory.

The exercise demonstrated in phase 3 of Fig. 69.1 illustrates the functional concept of this procedure. With the use of pads or a designed box on

Table 69.1: Exercise Chart (Sample Program)

RM—	Repetitions of Motion
CADENCE—	4 seconds per single movement of exercise—2 seconds to leg extension and 2 seconds to starting position
REST PERIOD—	1-2 minutes between exercise sets may be active by movement.
SETS OF EXERCISE	2-3 sets in each exercise period.

1st Week

2-3 sets

1st day—	(1st set) learn technique	10-15RM
	(2nd set) number of repetitions possible until fatigue i.e.	25RM
	(3rd set) same as 2nd	25RM
2nd Day—	(1st set) same number as 2nd set of 1st day	25RM
	(2nd & 3rd set) same as 1st set	25RM
3rd and 4th Day—	(2-3 sets) increase repetitions by 5	30-30RM

2nd week

1st day—	increase repetitions by 5	35-35-35RM
2nd Day—	same as 1st day	35-35-35RM
3d and 4th Day—	increase repetitions by 5	40-40-40 RM

3rd week

1st day—	increase repetitions by 5	45-45-45RM*
2nd Day—	same as 1st day	45-45-45 RM
3rd and 4th Day—	increase repetitions by 5	50-50-50RM

* note-45RM X 4 sec. each = 3 min. per set 3 sets = 9 min. of exercise 1 min., rest between sets = 2 minutes minus 2 min. of rest. Total exercise period 3 sets = 11 minutes.

4th week

1st Day—	increase repetitions by 5	55-55-55RM
2nd Day—	same as 1st day	55-55-55RM
3rd and 4th day—	increase repetitions by 5	60-60-60RM

Each exercise program should be followed by a short period of hamstring as well as quadriceps stretching.

the bench, the starting position of the exercise permits only 10 to 15 degrees of knee flexion. As the knees are straightened, the major action of the patella is upward in line with the quadriceps mechanism, and very minimal pressure is placed on the patella against the femoral condyles at this terminal phase. Although the entire quadriceps and hamstring muscle groups are functional in this action, the major emphasis is on the vastus medialis, and at full extension the vastus action is complete (Fig. 69.2). Concentration on vastus medialis action of the involved musculature should be stressed.

REFERENCES

Bowen, W. P., and H. A. Stone, 1949. *Applied anatomy and kinesiology.* Philadelphia: Lea and Febiger.

Klein, K. K., 1962. A preliminary study of the bench and boot technique of progressive resistive exercise in rehabilitation." *Journal Assoc. Phys. and Mental Rehab.* **16** (March-April) : 49-51, 59.

————, 1963. A comparison study of the boot and bench technique of progressive exercise in rehabilitation. *Journal Assoc. Phys. and Mental Rehab.* **17** (September-October) : 138-141, 147.

————, 1963. Strength maintenance following specific rehabilitation, validation of a rehabilitation apparatus. (Mimeographed). Research Grant RD446, Vocational Rehabilitation Administration, Dept. H.E.W., The University of Texas and Eastern Washington State college.

————, and F. L. Allman, Jr., 1971. *The knee in sports-conditioning injury prevention, rehabilitation and studies related to the knee.* Austin, Tex.: The Jenkins Publishing Co., The Pemberton Press.

PROGRAMS FOR THE HANDICAPPED

Introduction

In this section Julian Stein sets the tone when he challenges professionals to desist from conducting programs that categorize impaired persons by condition, and to strive instead to individualize and humanize programs. The need to "mainstream" individuals whenever possible (presently required by federal law) is also stressed. He also attempts to untangle the present confusion in terminology by making careful distinctions among the terms "impaired," "disabled," and "handicapped," and by clarifying the differences between corrective exercise, developmental exercise, therapeutic exercise, and adapted physical education.

Wessel reiterates the challenges of Stein, then proceeds to outline what is needed to improve programs for children in terms of attitudes, staff, and other resources. She also presents organizational models for delivering services to the handicapped.

The next two chapters deal predominantly with programs at the college/ university level. In the first, Nugent presents an impassioned expression of his personal feelings and philosophy concerning the handicapped. The remainder of the article is devoted to a description of the program at the University of Illinois—a pioneering and tremendously comprehensive program serving virtually all aspects of the lives of handicapped students. This program, originated and nurtured by author Nugent, might well serve as a national model. The next chapter discusses the origins and purposes of a surprisingly large number of national and international sports organizations through which the handicapped may demonstrate their athletic abilities. Of particular interest are the classification schemes developed for handicapped athletes.

In the final chapter, Hayden presents a comprehensive summary of what is known about the mentally retarded in the areas of physical fitness, gross motor ability, physical development, and the effects of physical education and sports programs upon the mentally retarded. In connection with the latter, positive effects have been clearly established, though not absolutely quantified, through research. The potential of physical education in concomitant areas such as intelligence, self-concept, body-image, school performance and others has not been established scientifically.

Section Editor

Timothy J. Nugent received degrees from Tarleton State College, Texas, and the University of Wisconsin, Madison. He is professor and director of the Rehabilitation Education Center, University of Illinois, Champaign-Urbana. He was the founder of the first comprehensive program of higher education for the severely physically disabled and founder of Delta Sigma Omicron, national rehabilitation service fraternity. He sponsored and directed the first national wheelchair basketball tournament in 1949, and was founder of the National Wheelchair Basketball Association. He is also a major contributor to the United States Wheelchair Sports Fund and its activities.

Among his many awards are election to the Hall of Fame of both the NWBA and the National Wheelchair Association, and the AAHPER William G. Anderson Award. He is regarded as one of the pioneers in the area of physical activity, sports and recreation for physically disabled persons. He has contributed to this area both as a practitioner and educator, as well as a researcher. He has served as a consultant to many state legislatures and government agencies. He has also lectured at universities both in the United States and abroad.

70

A Clarification of Terms

Julian Stein

WHO ARE THE HANDICAPPED?

The terms impaired, disabled, and handicapped are often used synonymously and interchangeably. Afflicted with hardening of the categories, society imposes labels, particularly upon individuals with various physical, mental, emotional, and social conditions. This is a paradox when one considers that we live in an era in which emphasis is upon the individual and what he or she can do. Lip service is given to an individual's potential while too many programs, activities, and efforts focus on disability and deficiency. The paradox is even more confusing and incomprehensible when one realizes that this is not the way in which many individuals with various conditions look upon themselves. There are important differences among impaired, disabled, and handicapped persons. Involved professionals must promote appropriate definitions, and the exact use of each. These terms should be differentiated in the way individuals with the various conditions look upon themselves, not in ways that have been culturally imposed by society and by persons not afflicted with these conditions.

Impaired individuals have identifiable organic or functional conditions; some part of the body is actually missing, a portion of the anatomical structure is gone, or one or more parts of the body do not function properly or adequately. The condition may be permanent and unchangeable as in the case of amputation, congenital defect, cerebral palsy, other brain damage, or fibroplasia. It may be temporary or correctable, such as functional speech defects, some learning disabilities, various emotional problems, certain social maladjustments, or specific movement deficiencies.

Disabled individuals are limited or restricted because of impairments in executing some skills, doing specific jobs or tasks, or performing certain activities. Individuals with certain impairments should not be automatically excluded from activities simply because the condition makes it appear that they cannot participate safely, successfully, or with satisfaction. Some impaired persons attain high levels of excellence in activities in which they are not supposed to be able to perform or participate. Is this success in spite of or

* Reprinted from *JOPER* **42** (September 1971) : 63-68.

because of us, or because of their disabilities? Despite numbers of success stories of persons who have overcome severe physical handicaps to become champions such as Glenn Cunningham, Bobby Morrow, Wilma Rudolph, Shelly Mann, Pete Gray, and Tom Dempsey, not all individuals are highly motivated and willing to go the extra mile for such progress and achievement. We must also recognize potential relationships and effects of various activities upon different impairments, and how undue pressue and unwise use can complicate certain conditions and actually cause harm to some individuals.

Handicapped individuals, because of impairment and disability, are those who are adversely affected psychologically, emotionally, or socially. Handicapped persons reflect an attitude of self-pity. Some individuals with impairments and disabilities adjust extremely well to their conditions and live happy and productive lives. In their eyes they are not handicapped, even though society continues to label them handicapped. Undoubtedly many persons in society with neither an impairment nor a disability are handicapped emotionally.

A major contribution of physical education and recreation programs is providing the impaired and disabled with challenging opportunities, meaningful experiences, and functional activities that accent positive achievement so that negative feelings do not develop or become so pronounced. Activities and approaches need to concentrate upon peoples' abilities, not their impairments, emphasize potential not deficiency, and encourage rather than discourage so that impairments and disabilities are less likely to become handicaps.

ADAPTED PHYSICAL EDUCATION

Historically various terms, each with its own accepted connotation, have been used to describe specialized programs of physical activities for the impaired, disabled, and handicapped. Corrective exercise is supposed to remedy postural divergencies through individually planned exercise programs. Developmental exercise is planned to increase exercise tolerance of the weak and ill through individually planned and progressively vigorous programs. Therapeutic exercise provides individual prescriptions of movement activity for the impaired, disabled, and handicapped. Adapted physical education seeks to modify sports and games so that the impaired, disabled, and handicapped can participate.

The Committee on Adapted Physical Education of AAHPER defines adapted physical education as

> a diversified program of developmental activities, games, sports, and rhythms suited to the interests, capacities, and limitations of students with disabilities who may not safely or successfully engage in unrestric-

ted participation in the vigorous activities of the general physical education program.

This 1952 statement was prepared for general use in schools and colleges rather than for special schools, residential facilities, and day-care centers. However, this definition can and should apply to any motor activity or movement program designed specifically for the impaired, disabled, and handicapped in any setting with an educational focus or purpose. By definition, adapted physical education includes physical activities:

1. planned for individuals with learning problems resulting from motor, mental, or emotional impairments, disabilities, or dysfunctions
2. planned for the purposes of rehabilitation, habilitation, remediation, prevention, or physical development
3. modified so the impaired, disabled, and handicapped can participate
4. designed for modifying movement capabilities
5. planned to promote maximum/optimum motor development
6. occurring in a school setting or within a clinic, hospital, residential facility, day-care center, or other setting where the primary intent is to influence learning and/or movement potential through motor activity

THERAPEUTIC RECREATION

Therapeutic recreation is based on the humanistic view that impaired, disabled, and handicapped persons are entitled to personal fulfillment through recreation and leisure-time activities in the same way as those without handicapping conditions. Adaptations and services necessary to make such personal fulfillment possible are the responsibilities of society. Therapeutic recreation service is designed to help ill, impaired, disabled, or handicapped persons meet their own basic needs for recreation and to enhance the rehabilitation and convalescence of individuals with varying types and degrees of illnesses, impairments, disabilities, handicaps, and social problems.

Therapeutic recreation, as defined by the National Therapeutic Recreation Society, is

. . . a special service within the broad area of recreation services. It is a process which utilizes recreation services for purposive intervention in some physical, emotional, and/or social behavior to bring about a desired change in that behavior and to promote the growth and development of the individual.

This definition reflects broadening realms of therapeutic recreation service that apply to recreation services for special groups in the community, and in other types of agencies as well as in hospitals and medically oriented facilities.

**Differentiated Characteristics of Physical Education and
Therapeutic Recreation Services**

Tables 70.1 and 70.2 show that physical education and therapeutic recreation services differ very little. While terminology and semantic differences are obvious as processes, both are concerned with providing:

1. Special services for individuals with severe, profound or multiple conditions that necessitate intensive, special individual attention, often on a one-to-one or small group basis, with special facilities, equipment, supplies, and methods. Participants can feel greater security in these programs, identify more readily with the teacher or leader working with them, and have opportunities to respond positively to the concentrated efforts.

2. Half-way services for individuals with the potential to participate in one or more activities in regular programs but at the moment lack sufficient characteristics and traits to be able to participate safely, successfully, and with satisfaction. Poise, self-confidence, emotional stability, social awareness, intelligence, common sense ability or skill, experience, or opportunity may influence and contribute to this situation. Concentrated small and/or large-group approaches in which sheltered opportunities, adaptations, and increasing opportunities to participate more independently enable individuals to progress from this stage into one or more aspects of regular programs.

3. Regular services for individuals who can safely, successfully, and with satisfaction participate in one or more activities in a regular program, whether it be school-centered physical education or community-based recreation. The ultimate goal through either physical education or therapeutic recreation is self-actualizing behavior in which an individual functions as independently as possible and, to as large a degree as possible, integrated with his nonimpaired, nondisabled, and nonhandicapped contemporaries.

Integration can be achieved by including the disabled individual in the same activity as his able-bodied counterparts, or by recognizing his participation in well-defined activities. It is important that such participation not result from, or result in, unwarranted solicitousness. There should never need to be two sets of standards for evaluation (or satisfaction), whether by self or by others. In almost all instances it is insulting or degrading to make the evaluation, "You do so well for the condition you are in."

There are many activities wherein the disabled can participate and even compete on equal terms with their able-bodied counterparts. There are many other activities wherein they cannot and wherein considerable physical, emotional, mental and/or social harm might result. We must avoid "trumped-

Table 70.1
Differentiated Characteristics of Physical Education Services

Type/level service	Desired outcomes
Regular Services	
Extra-school activities	Totally integrated program of physical
Interschool activities	activities
Regular physical education activities	
Half-way Services	
Partially integrated school programs	Maximum physical, mental function
Developmental activities	Physical movement skill
Modified sports and games	Social adjustment
Specialized exercise programs	Emotional adaptability
Special Services	
Segregated school programs	Physical, social, and emotional changes
Clinical programs	through:
Hospital programs	Rehabilitation process
Institutional programs	Counseling
	Treatment, corrective, and
	therapeutic approaches
	Diagnostic/prescriptive
	procedures

up" situations. Dispersion is not integration and accommodation is not segregation.

In many ways physical education and recreation services provided at the special and half-way levels are more similar to one another than therapeutic recreation services are to standard recreation programs and to leisure activities, and than special physical education services are to regular physical education services. Similarly, regular physical education and standard recreation programs and leisure activities have many points, directions, and objectives that make them closely related.

While these are important similarities that closely ally physical education and recreation, each has its own characteristics and traits that must be considered.

Physical education is primarily school-centered, while recreation is oriented to community and institutional settings. Physical education programs are usually conducted between 8 a.m. and 4 p.m.; recreation programs usually take place during the out-of-school hours.

Recreation programs encompass a gamut of activities such as arts and crafts, music, dramatics, camping, physical activities, community service,

Table 70.2

Differentiated Characteristics in Therapeutic Recreation Service

Type and level of service	Basic goals of the service and participation	Relationship of TR specialist with the client or patient
Therapeutic recreation service	*Therapeutic Goals* Contribute to treatment Contribute to rehabilitation Behavior change Social adjustment Therapeutic recreation procedures	*Intensive* One-to-one Small group
Recreation for ill and handicapped	*Participation Goals* Sheltered opportunity Adaptation Remedial teaching Counseling	*Concentrated* Small group Large group
Standard recreation program	*General Recreation Goals* Physical conditioning Mental well being Personal growth and development Creative fulfillment Individual expression	*Active* Large group Mass participation
Leisure activity	*Individual Goals* Amusement Diversion Relaxation	*Implied* Residual role through attitudes, skills, habits imparted to clients

Reproduced from *Therapeutic Recreation Journal* (Fourth Quarter, 1970; Vol. IV, No. 4) with permission of John Nesbitt, President, National Therapeutic Recreation Society.

collections and hobbies, and service projects, while physical education focuses on activities involving physical fitness, motor skills, movement, and physical prowess. While many recreational activities revolve about physical and motor abilities, the total spectrum of offerings is much broader than in physical education.

Physical education by and large is a means to an end, whereas recreation often is considered an end in itself. While some skill teaching takes place in recreation programs, skill teaching is the hallmark of physical education. Conversely, preparing an individual to use his leisure time in more constructive and wholesome ways is a basic goal of all physical education.

NONCATEGORICAL APPROACH

Traditionally impaired, disabled, and handicapped individuals have been classified, categorized, and programmed according to specific physical, mental, emotional, or social conditions. Basic to a categorical approach is the false assumption that all persons with the same condition have identical needs, interests, and abilities; they are looked upon as mechanized robots from an assembly line. Failure to recognize the uniqueness of each person negates the concept of individual differences. In fact many persons find as much difference among those with the same condition as between these individuals as a group and those with other conditions or those with no impairment, disability, or handicap. To plan and program for all visually impaired, orthopedically involved, cerebrally palsied, or cardiac patients in the same way is not more valid and justified than planning and programming in the same way for all children of the same chronological age, sex, or home state.

A close parallel exists between the false dichotomy of mind and body and the false assumption that all individuals with the same handicapping condition fit a standard mold. Differentiations of mind and body and labeling conditions are necessary for discussion purposes, as learning experiences for students, and for developing certain understanding, appreciation, and knowledge. However, when programming for and dealing with real people, the wholeness of individuals and the totality of their functions and being are obvious; segregating according to isolated parts is at best an academic exercise. Specifically applied to physical education and recreation programs, a noncategorical approach focuses on individuals as they function in various types and levels of programs and activities. All their physical, mental, emotional, and social characteristics influence involvement, success, achievement, and satisfactions from physical education and recreation activities. A noncategorical approach deals with real, live, functioning people, not a condition that may or may not affect ability to perform certain movements, skills, and activities.

Categories and conditions per se should not be the major criteria when grouping for physical education and recreation activities; these are concerns for methods and approaches but not necessarily for grouping.

Many impaired, disabled, and handicapped youngsters who can participate and compete with their classmates are still kept in special programs for these activities. Special programs cannot become one-way streets; every effort must be made to get youngsters back into the mainstream in those things in which they can participate and compete. Three groups should be considered whatever the activity:

1. Those who have the ability, confidence, experience, awareness, stability, understanding, background, interest, and motivation to participate safely,

successfully, and with satisfaction in one or more activities on an integrated basis.

2. Those who have the potential in all the traits listed above but for the present are lacking some element that will enable them to participate safely, successfully, and with satisfaction in one or more activities. They need a half-way physical education-recreation program to gain the needed characteristics before they can enter the regular program.

3. Those who need long-range opportunities in special sheltered programs because of the severity and complexity of their conditions. A great deal of talk goes on about getting youngsters back into the mainstream of society, but in too many cases it is not reflected in programs and activities. Much more attention needs to be given in this area, especially in physical education and recreation programs.

Within this framework youngsters are guided and placed in situations in which they can compete and participate. Physical and motor activities are not considered as entities but in terms of each specific area so that individuals who are outstanding in one area but weak in another are programmed according to their specific abilities, limitations, and needs. The major criteria are not their physical, mental, emotional, or social deficiencies for placement in physical education or recreation activities, but their total ability to function in the activities of immediate concern. Sufficient flexibility to individualize activities, methods, and procedures is a fundamental administrative consideration in noncategorical programming.

One of the greatest challenges facing us today is to find ways of putting aside our provincialisms, whatever our responsibility and wherever we serve, in order to interact meaningfully with others, regardless of their disciplinary affiliation or specialization, so as to build programs, activities, methods, approaches, procedures, and techniques based on the characteristics, traits, interests, and abilities of those we serve. The time to start is now; let us show the way. Working together in the tradition of our disciplines, physical education, health education, and recreation can be great forces in unlocking the future for all impaired, disabled, and handicapped persons. Competing rather than cooperating hinders the programs and progress for the children, adolescents, and adults in our communities, schools, centers, and homes.

71

Improvement of Programs for Handicapped Children

Janet A. Wessel

Many new developments in educational programs and services have emerged since the mid-1960s for those in our society whom we call handicapped. One of the most significant developments in the area of education has been in special education. The major purpose of special education is to provide and maintain the kinds of programs that are conducive to the growth and learning of children with special needs. Children for whom special provisions need to be made in order to achieve optimum development in the educational program are usually identified by the term atypical or exceptional, namely those children who deviate from what is supposed to be "normal" in physical, mental, emotional, or social characteristics to such an extent that they require special education services in order to develop to their maximum capacity. In keeping with this dynamic concept of special education it seems appropriate that physical education programs in special education embrace what has been and is known as adapted, corrective, remedial, therapeutic, special, and developmental physical education activities.

P.L. 94-142 and Section 504 of the Vocational Rehabilitation Act mandate education in the public schools for all handicapped children and youth. Such legislation is based on the principle that the right to equal educational opportunity implies the obligation to provide free public education for all children. To achieve this end, three major goals in special education for organizing services include: (1) comprehensive educational services appropriate to the psychomotor, affective, and cognitive needs of all handicapped children and youth; (2) organizational structure and personnel for delivery of educational services to meet the needs of each handicapped child and youth, and (3) acceptance of handicapped children and youth within the mainstream of educational planning and placement and within the community settings (CEC 1973).

With this thrust in special education, there has been a dramatic increase in the physical educational services for handicapped children. Progress has been made in implementing physical education programs in our schools and institutions for children with special needs and in the professional preparation of physical eduction teachers and recreational leaders for the handicapped (Guidelines 1973; P.E. and Rec. for Handicapped 1970). The delivery of physical education services for the handicapped has been located primarily in special classes or in special schools and institutions for the handicapped, namely physically or otherwise health-impaired, emotionally disturbed, blind and the blind-deaf, the mentally retarded, and those children with learning disabilities.

The rapid growth of physical education programs for the handicapped makes it virtually impossible to begin to name all of the various program activities for the handicapped that have been developed recently throughout the country.

Formal recognition of the need for physical education programming for the retarded was not made until 1965. The Joseph P. Kennedy, Jr., Foundation, with the leadership of the AAHPER, appointed a Task Force on

Fig. 71-1. "Handicapped Students may gain competence in home and neighborhood activities as a result of learning primary motor skills." Courtesy: I CAN Field Unit.

Programs for the Mentally Retarded. This coalition brought about the creation of the Project on Recreation and Fitness for the Mentally Retarded. This title was changed in 1968 to Project on Recreation and Fitness for the Handicapped.

The objectives of current programs of physical education for the handicapped usually include improving physical fitness, performance in motor skills, and in desired personal and social traits (Cratty 1969; Fait 1972; Getman 1966; Godfrey 1969; *Handicapped* 1965). Some programs have focused on only one of the above objectives, namely, physical fitness or motor performance. In recent years motor performance programs have been implemented to develop body awareness, spatial relationships, balance, hand-eye coordination, and basic mobility or locomotor skills (Cratty 1969; Delacato 1963; Fait 1972; Kephart 1960; Seefeldt 1973).

Program development has been so rapid that many current programs are based on very thin research evidence (P.E. and Rec. for Handicapped 1970; Deno 1971). In many instances programs have been selected for desired outcomes and children fitted to programs regardless of their needs, interests, and learning characteristics. Other programs "just grow" based on the philosophy that virtually no programs exist and anything done is an improvement.

The present era of "accountability" might raise the question about the effectiveness of our program efforts for the handicapped. What should be taught? Under which administrative organizational plan or delivery system can it be taught most effectively? In what setting should it be taught? What are the personal and educational characteristics of the effective physical educator or recreator for the handicapped? Accountability involves continuous evaluations and reevaluations of our existing programs in physical education and recreation for the handicapped as well as the development and implementation of alternative programs. What is it we are trying to accomplish in our programs? What is of most value? What ought we to be doing? How should we be doing it? Who should teach it?

Because the current goal of special education is keeping handicapped learners in the educational environments, the development of strategies for improvement of physical education delivery systems and programs in mainstreaming clearly are apparent. Not only must we find new ways to deliver physical education services to the handicapped in public school systems, but we must also take a new look at teacher education—the validity of our current preparatory practices—if we are to improve the physical education opportunities for all handicapped children and youth (Getman 1966).

Two crucial issues in the improvement of physical education programs in special education for handicapped children exist:

Appropriateness of physical education delivery systems to the handicapped.
The effectiveness of current physical education programs for the handi-

capped must be validated. Alternatives to current physical education practices must be found. The role of the physical educator in the planning of a support system for integrating handicapped children into the mainstream must be refined. The special needs of the handicapped must be identified and the learning program situation components analyzed. Strategies for collecting data to generate alternative program solutions must be developed, and teacher education must be reexamined in light of competencies needed for new role expectancies.

Systematizing approaches for designing instructional models for teaching and programming for children with special needs. The effectiveness of physical education programming needs to be verified. Objectives must be refined, a model must be developed for a more scientific and systematic approach to programming for the handicapped, and programs must be constructed accordingly. Physical education in special education must concern itself with cost and methods of presenting the curriculum.

In order to answer the what, how, and how much of physical education programs, more descriptive and experimental evidence is a necessity.

SUGGESTIONS FOR A MODEL DELIVERY SYSTEM

If physical education is to have a role in special education it must become that branch of education concerned with the development and delivery of physical education technology for children who suffer from impairments in their abilities to learn and perform in the regular physical education school program. While these impairments may occur in a variety of functions relevant to learning and motor performance, and may spring from a variety of causes, the emphasis of physical education in special education is not on causes in the "chronic disease" model sense, but on the development of skills necessary for independent functioning within the community.

Physical education for all children is based on several underlying assumptions:

1. That there are basic skills that students should be able to perform in order to function effectively in socio-leisure activities, to maintain health and fitness and to function independently. These basic skills are objectives for all students—handicapped or nonhandicapped.

2. That there is a body of literature that indicates that most individuals learn motor, communicative, and social behaviors in approximately the same order.

3. That instructional objectives may be sequenced according to the "normal" developmental order or on the basis of some empirically verified training sequence.

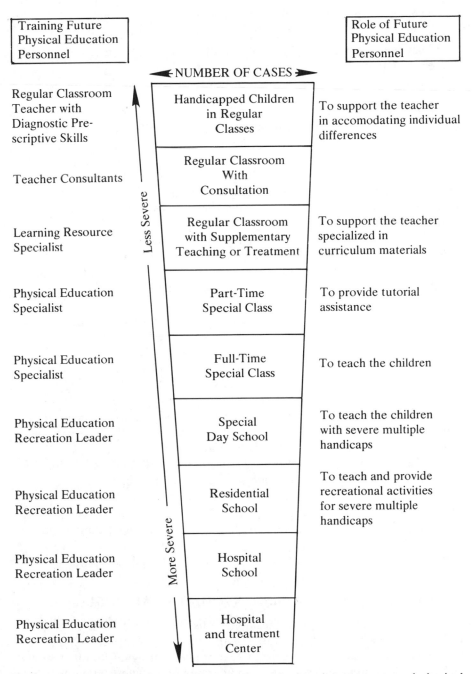

Fig. 71.2 A cascade model of services for special education programs and physical education personnel. (Adapated from M.C. Reynolds, A framework for considering some issues in special education. *Exceptional Children*, 1962, **F** : 367-370).

4. That the sequence of objectives provides the basic framework for relating educational assessment to instructional planning and evaluation.

5. That the instructional objectives should be adaptable to various handicapped populations by modifying the sequence into greater or fewer steps.

Fig. 71.2 provides the organizational model for the continuum of physical education services in special education (Reynolds 1962). Such a model allows for a variety of ways of servicing handicapped children, extending from placement in a regular physical education class, to special physical education that is provided in institutional settings. The number of children who will need special physical education beyond the range of mainstream accommodations in the regular physical education classes will be dictated by the nature of mainstream provisions.

The Cascade Model is used in Fig. 71.2 to indicate the considerable differences in the numbers of children likely to be involved at the different levels of services. The specialized facilities are seen to be needed by the least number of children. This model is applicable to the organization of physical education for children with various kinds of special needs. It does not presume that traditional categorical-labeling descriptions of children in special education are essential to the provision of effective learning opportunities in physical education.

This concept may be applied to the numbers of physical education teachers likely to be involved at the different levels of services. It suggests the teaching competencies needed for sequential programming and directed teaching at the different levels. Resource teacher programs are developed along four important dimensions: (1) identified criterion performance, (2) daily instruction and assessment, (3) individual instruction, and (4) management of individual programs. Resource programs are designed to explore and incorporate alternative means, such as preparing and supervising peer and cross-age tutors, that allow for expanded services while maintaining quality instruction and curricular experiences. Physical education teacher preparation programs for the handicapped are being redesigned according to teacher roles (Tyler 1950). These guidelines are in keeping with the trend toward keeping handicapped children in the regular educational environments.

SUGGESTIONS FOR DESIGNING INSTRUCTIONAL MODELS

Physical education programs are established so that the student may learn a desired set of behaviors deemed most important. The instructional model is an empirically derived set of learning experiences designed to elicit valued behaviors or competencies for the handicapped child with a given degree of reliability. An individualized instructional model requires a prescription of learning experiences selected and sequenced to complement the behaviors in which the student is deficient.

In short, a quality instructional model is organized around a specified and measurable physical education outcome. It is designed to provide data continuously on the effectiveness with which it meets its objectives. It is designed to be flexible or corrective in light of evidence made available through an evaluative feedback loop. Also, as a means to the personalization of instructional experiences, an instructional model is designed with multiple entry points and multiple paths to pursue, thus permitting a student to enter at levels commensurate with his or her skills, and allowing the student to progress through the levels at a rate commensurate with his or her learning style.

In recent years, curriculum development and research has made tremendous strides in utilizing a systems approach to designing, implementing, and evaluating curricula designed for target populations (Boekel 1971; Goldstein 1969; Typer 1950; Wessel 1973).

Based on this work, Fig. 71.4 presents a flow chart with corrective feedback for all the components influencing the form and content of any instructional model. The flow chart represents a process that is required by developers or teachers to: (1) know what it is that they want to accomplish;

Fig. 71-3. "Recognition of individual differences means instructing the student in those skills deemed most essential to maximize potential." Courtesy: I CAN Field Unit.

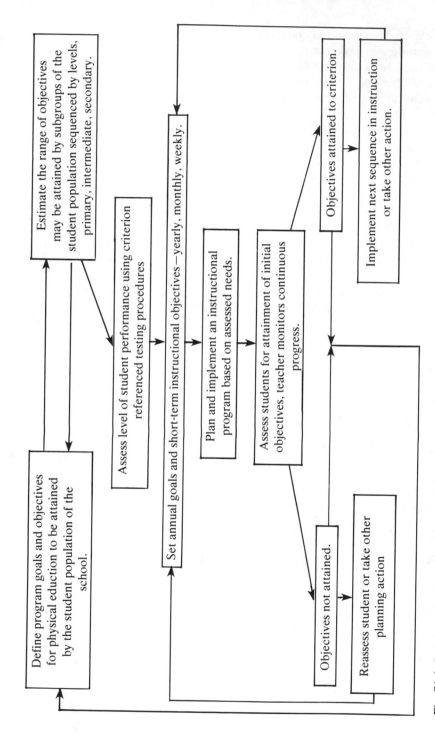

Fig. 71.4 Continous Instructional Plan for Implementing, Monitoring and Evaluating IEPs in Physical Eucation.

(2) order the events in such a way that they can be accomplished; (3) assess whether these events do in fact accomplish what they are intending to accomplish; and (4) modify the program so it does result in accomplishing goals.

A large-scale application of this systems approach using the flow chart shown in Fig. 71.2 has been used for designing instructional programs in the I CAN Programmatic Research Project in Physical Education for the Mentally Retarded, funded by U.S.O.E. Bureau of Education for the Handicapped. This project has been undertaken by the Field Service Unit in Physical Education and Recreation at Michigan State University. The objectives of the project have been to develop individualized physical education curriculum materials, implement the curriculum materials in physical education programs, evaluate program effectiveness in producing desired outcomes, and disseminate the I CAN materials.

Using a systems approach, the I CAN Curriculum is designed not only with the student, but also with the teacher, in mind. The best teachers are those able to develop a curriculum to meet the needs of children in their own classes. The I CAN materials format was developed to facilitate this instructional task through the components shown in Table 71.1.

Fig. 71-5. "With I CAN, educational adaptations can be made for individual differences." Courtesy; I CAN Field Service Unit.

Fig. 71-6. "The primary motor skills found in I CAN include objectives from aquatics, body management, fundamental skills, and health/fitness." Courtesy: I CAN Field Service Unit.

THE FUTURE: A PERSPECTIVE

The I CAN materials present a carefully structured physical education curriculum to facilitate adapting programs according to the needs of each handicapped child. There are unique features built into the program that provide this flexibility:

1. It offers an individually prescribed program and at the same time is easily adapted to group instruction.
2. It contains diagnostic tools tied to the instructional objectives. Thus, the teacher can use the tools to assess student strengths and needs and prescribe teaching-learning activities relevant to the learner's level of instruction.

Table 71.1
The I CAN Materials Format

Teacher task components	Description
Planning	Selection of content performance objectives
Assessing	Determination of learner's baseline performance level of instruction
Prescribing	Selection of teaching-learning activities based on need
Teaching	Selection of relevant teaching style and implementing the learning activity
Evaluating	Post-hoc assessment of learner
Recommending	Recycle, terminate, remediate

3. It can interrelate all major skills of the classroom and the activity program.
4. It manifests total program flexibility so that its components may be integrated into an ongoing curricular project or locally developed curricular programs based on need assessment: school, community, teacher, child.
5. It meets the requirements for individual education programs.
6. It can be translated into a form that interfaces with computer-based individualized objective data banks.

There is little doubt that the influence of systems approaches to curriculum development and new directions in evaluative research techniques will bring about a wholesome and invigorating effect upon instructional programs for special target populations. Undoubtedly one of the most significant advances in physical education during the 1970s is the emphasis that has been placed on developing and implementing relevant and appropriate instructional materials for target populations of handicapped children in our schools and communities. The focus of this effort will continue to be directed toward the instructional materials themselves, as well as the professional community involved in professional preparation and the delivery of services to the handicapped. The professional community will give serious consideration to the development of accountability models in physical education for the handicapped. To meet this challenge, increased emphasis and funds will be given to three interrelated activities: (1) the preparation of competent regular and special education teachers with (2) relevant and appropriate instructional materials for target populations that result in (3) student progress toward desired goals.

The goal for improvement of physical education programs for the handicapped is to establish models and translate them into practice. Only in this way will the field of physical education contribute valid, relevant, and appropriate instructional programs and materials for target populations of handicapped children in their most appropriate educational environments.

REFERENCES

Boekel, N., and J. Steele, 1971. Science education for the exceptional child, *Focus on exceptional children*, **4** : 1-16.

CEC policy statements approved by delegate assembly, 1973. *Exceptional children*, **40** : 70-73 (September).

Cratty, B., 1969. *Perceptual-motor behavior and educational processes.* Springfield, Ill.: Charles C. Thomas.

Delcato, C., 1963. *The diagnosis and treatment of speech and reaching problems.* Springfield, Ill.: Charles C. Thomas.

Deno, E., 1971. Strategies for improvement of educational opportunities for handicapped children: suggestions for exploitation of EPDA potential. In: M. C. Reynolds and M. D. Davis (eds.) *Exceptional regular classroom.* Minneapolis: University of Minnesota.

Fait, H., 1972. *Special physical education* (3rd ed.). Philadelphia: W.B. Saunders Co.

Gallegher, J., 1976. New directions in special education, *Exceptional children,* **33** : 441-447.

Getman, G., 1966. *Physiological readiness.* Minneapolis: Pass Publishing Co.

Godfrey, B., and Kephart, N., 1969. *Movement patterns and motor education.* New York: Appleton-Century-Crofts.

Goldstein, H., 1969. Construction of a social learning curriculum, *Focus on Exceptional Children,* **1** : 210-225.

Guidelines for Professional Preparation Programs for Personnel Involved in Physical Education and Recreation for the Handicapped, 1973. AAHPER (February).

Handicapped, 1965. East Lansing, Mich.: Workshop Proceedings, Bureau of Publications, College of Education, Michigan State University.

Kephart, N., 1960. *The slow learner in the classroom.* Columbus, Ohio: Charles Merrill.

Physical education and recreation for handicapped children, proceedings of a study conference on research and demonstration needs, 1970. Bureau of Education for the Handicapped, DHEW.

Reynolds, M. C., 1962. Framework for considering some issues in special education. *Exceptional children,* **7** : 367-370.

Seefeldt, D., 1973. Substantive issues in perceptual motor development. Presented at the Symposium on Research Methodology in Perceptual-Motor Development, Springfield College, Mass. (May 12-13).

Tyler, R., 1950. *Basic principles of curriculum development.* Chicago: University of Chicago Press.

Wessel, J., 1973. *I CAN Programmatic Research Project in Physical Education: A Special Education Program.* Michigan State University.

438

72

Beyond the Secondary Years

Timothy J. Nugent

The individual with a disability has the same inherent right to all avenues of pursuit in his or her community, state, and nation as do all others. These should include the pursuit of one's aspirations, interests, talents, and skills in all areas of endeavor, and should certainly include physical activities, physical well-being, and meaningful leisure experiences.

These may take place in such definitive settings as a community college, a junior college, vocational training institute, or major university. However, many individuals, whether able bodied or disabled, do not pursue objectives through these well-defined, somewhat well-structured avenues or institutions—some by choice and some because of circumstances beyond their control. This in no way lessens our responsibility to them.

We must look beyond the institutions in which we work, our professional disciplines, our categorical concepts, and our limitations on disability if we are truly to fulfill our professional responsibilities to the special populations whom we boast to serve. Much of this should have had, but unfortunately has not had, its beginning in the elementary and secondary schools.

Fig. 72-1. Preschool child.

Such neglect creates great voids in the lives of individuals as they enter into the postsecondary years, and more particularly, if they enter into the highly competitive situations that are a part of colleges and universities. It is the absence of normal growth and development opportunities and experiences, in any and all avenues of the individual's life, that may be the basis for adulthood problems, and with which we must be concerned, including the areas of physical skills, strength, tolerance, and leisure pursuits.

DIFFERENTIATING FACTORS

There are many differences in the postsecondary years of which we must be cognizant. The first of these is that there is no singular pathway from which we shall receive those with whom we are called upon to work, as is most often true in the elementary and secondary years where, even with some educational setbacks, we are dealing with specific age groups in well-defined situations. As an example, at the University of Illinois entering freshmen with severe permanent physical disabilities have ranged in age from 14 to 40 years. Those entering above the freshman level have ranged from 18 to 59 years. Many of these were disabled for many years before they knew of an opportunity to pursue higher education or before they believed enough in themselves to make the effort. Initially others had pursued other vocational endeavors and only upon the advent of a severe permanent physical disability were they forced to restructure their lives completely and choose completely different avenues for the pursuit of socio-economic independence and satisfaction. Still others had been disabled very early in life but had been denied the opportunities for normal elementary and secondary schooling and normal growth experiences even in a superficial manner. Subsequently they began their higher education later than normal, having to make up their prior deficiencies. Those who, by perserverance or by third-party influence, began their higher education at a normal or near-normal age level, may have significant problems that relate directly to the voids in their earlier life.

With the exception of the community college and many of the junior colleges that are community-oriented, the program content, program responsibilities, and program scope are vastly different at the college and university than at the elementary and secondary levels. The elementary and secondary schools, as does the community college, have very specific and limited responsibilities as they relate to the individual for a period of five to seven hours daily, sometimes less. The parents or the family assume responsibility for the individual and for those things that would normally accrue to the individual both prior to and after school and on weekends. The parents and family share other responsibilities with the faculties of the schools.

At the university or college level most institutions assume responsibility for 24 hours each day the year around. This demands a genuine concern for the accessibility and usability of all facilities by individuals with severe permanent physical disabilities, housing arrangements, food services, mobility and/or transportation, leisure time, and the development of well-conceived, well-administered, and well-coordinated supportive services. These services include medical services, including various definitive medical specialties (e.g., urology), physical therapy, functional training, physical education, recreation, and athletics, occupational therapy, prosthetics and adaptive equipment, counseling, facilities—equipment and transportation, and a definite plan for the coordination of all facilities and services existing on the campus. In addition, specific services for the blind and the deaf should include: orientation and mobility training, Braille and tape transcription, direct reader services, tactile aides, Braille calculators and other specific equipment, and interpreters. A large corps of select, qualified volunteers may be necessary in support of each of these services.

In the general planning of facilities and programs, we must concern ourselves with six functional groups:

1. Non ambulatory disabilities—impairments that, regardless of cause or manifestation, for all practical purposes confine individuals to wheelchairs.

2. Semiambulatory disabilities—impairments that cause individuals to walk with difficulty or insecurity. Individuals using braces or crutches, amputees, arthritics, spastics, and those with pulmonary and cardiac ills may be semiambulatory.

3. Sight disabilities—total blindness or impairments affecting sight to the extent that the individual functioning in public areas may be insecure or exposed to danger.

4. Hearing disabilities—deafness or hearing handicaps that might make individuals insecure in public areas because they are unable to communicate or hear warning signals.

5. Disabilities of incoordination—faulty coordination or palsy from brain, spinal, or peripheral nerve injury.

6. Aging—those manifestations of the aging processes that significantly reduce mobility, flexibility, coordination, and perceptiveness but are not accounted for in the aforementioned categories.

In specific professional or supportive services there must be a greater delineation as to the cause and *specific* manifestations of each disability, with greater emphasis focused on individuals as they relate to their particular goals and the environment. We should never categorically identify or program for individuals by the name of the disability.

In each instance we should deviate as little as possible from that which is considered "normal." There should be no exceptions to curricular requirements, although innovative means that are not commonly practiced on campuses may be used to fulfill those requirements. For example, individuals with severe manifestations of cerebral palsy, including speech involvement, might not be able to participate, realistically, in a spoken foreign language course but might fulfill the knowledge requirement of the foreign language by reducing their academic loads on campus and taking the foreign language via correspondence, in most instances from the same university. The knowledge of the language is achieved without penalizing or handicapping the individual because of unavoidable verbal communication problems.

Beyond the institutional settings of the community college, junior colleges, vocational training institute, or university, there should be a far greater emphasis on including the severe, permanent, physically disabled and the aging in all those things that are a part of the community and taken for granted by all other people. In short, whether within a given institution or on a community-wide basis, we must plan both programs and facilities for the inclusion of all people, including the disabled and the aging, and not just the "average" person. We must begin to design programs and facilities for the way in which all people might choose or need to function, rather than force them to function within the limits of inadequate design.

The specialties and subspecialties of professional disciplines play different roles in the lives of different individuals at different times. We must recognize our responsibilities to all people, including the disabled and aging, and commit ourselves wholeheartedly to the development of programs on their behalf.

There is no common denominator to disability. A disability can occur any time from the prenatal period to the very moment that precedes death. Disability can result from countless causes and result in countless manifestations. Even in a given cause of disability there can be countless manifestations. The age of onset of disability, the time in one's life when it occurs (situationally, not chronologically), the initial treatment programs, the duration of a disability, and the environment in which individuals with a disability find themselves, particularly the home, the school, and the community, all affect the individual and all affect the role that we might possibly play in the life of that individual at any given time.

A BRIEF PHILOSOPHICAL STATEMENT

All individuals, regardless of nationality, race, religion, economic status, or physical status, have five basic social-psychological needs, although these might manifest themselves in different ways. These are identified readily as: (1) the need to belong or to be accepted for one's self, not categorically; (2) the need for recognition, again individually and not categorically; (3) the need for the opportunity to pursue one's aspirations, develop one's interests and talents, and to exercise one's skills in any and all endeavors of life; (4) the

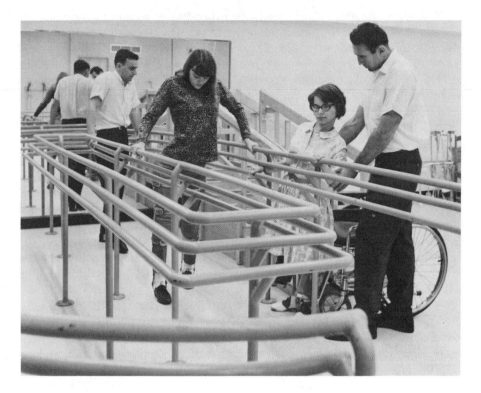

Fig. 72-2. Special railing.

need for security, this is, not financial security but the security that one feels within himself or herself; and (5) faith. This faith is manifest in a Supreme Being in which some of us might choose to believe, in the faith that we have in those about us, in the faith manifested by others, and in the faith that one has in oneself.

Each of us has been privileged to travel five avenues of life in order to arrive at our present stations. These might be identified as: (1) the avenue of *self*-exploration; (2) the avenue of *self*-identification, to identify oneself as a part of and apart from the rest of the world; (3) the avenue of *self*-expression; (4) the avenue of *self*-administration; and (5) the avenue of *self*-discipline.

We are inclined to take these things for granted, but a closer look will identify that in the past, and still too prevalent in the present, these very fundamental things have been denied individuals with a disability and are often denied the aging, although in different ways.

Individuals with disabilities must be projected into situations that are challenging in all areas of personal endeavor because the potential of people tends to develop to the degree to which it is challenged.

Whatever our particular specialty or subspecialty, we must always recognize the wholeness of people, as people, and the wholeness of the situation in which people find themselves.

With complete confidence in our own endeavors, we must recognize the contributions of all of the other professional disciplines and work in concert with them. We must earn and demand the respect of the other disciplines and we must accord them respect because each will play a different role in the lives of different individuals at different times. No single discipline is going to be the sole salvation of, or answer to, individuals with severe permanent disabilities, nor can any one discipline command the action singularly.

We must find the means by which they can realistically and effectively be included in all of our programs and facilities wherein the reciprocities of people with people and people with things can have their appropriate effect. Imposed isolation is degrading and results in degenerative processes in most aspects of an individual's life.

All of the forementioned are essential in order that an individual can develop an appropriate concept of self without which none of us can hope to make our way.

There are hundreds of thousands of individuals with a disability but very few disabled individuals. Although this is a play on words, it carries a meaningful message. The first is a description, focusing on the individual with unique individual differences; the second is often a judgment. A disability, even the most severe, is usually quite specific in nature and does not necessarily have to be a "handicap" in the life of the individual, although it can be a genuine inconvenience. The things that make a specific disability into a major handicap are the apathy that exists toward individuals with disabilities, the lack of accessible facilities and programs, the lack of public transportation, the lack of normal reciprocities, and the resultant concept of self.

As empathetic professionals we can do a great deal to take the handicap or the inconvenience out of most specific physical disabilities.

THE ROLES OF HEALTH, PHYSICAL EDUCATION, AND RECREATION

If health, physical education, and recreation play an important role in the life of anyone then they should play a more important role in the life of an individual with a severe permanent physical disability.

Individuals who have lost a part of their bodies or have lost the function of a part of their bodies, particularly such fundamental things as bowel and bladder function, skin tolerance, and even such vital organs as the kidneys, have need for a sound basic knowledge in health, in personal hygiene of a more definitive nature than is true in the lives of most individuals, and in well-substantiated attitudes toward health care and maintenance.

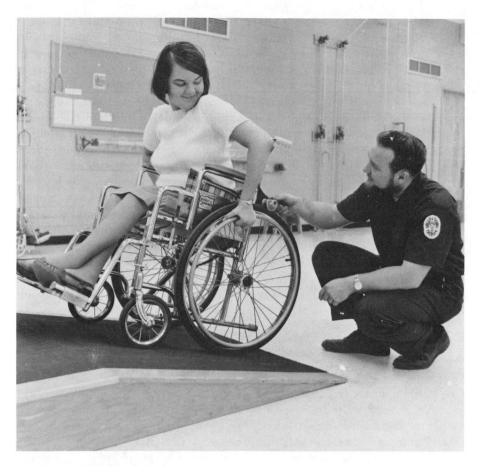

Fig. 72-3. Anti-rollback device.

If physical fitness is important to anyone, it is proportionally more important to a person with an illness or a physical disability. This is particularly true of certain physical disabilities wherein physical maintenance is a major objective, the lack of which is a major threat to the individual.

Recreation, or the wise use of leisure, has played and shall continue to play an ever increasing role of importance in the lives of all people. Its importance increases in magnitude and significance when related to individuals who are ill or who have a disability: those who, because of unfortunate circumstances beyond their control and because of society's apathy more than by personal desire, have had an excess of leisure and have been prone to inactivity; those who, because of people-created physical and attitudinal barriers, have often been denied the opportunity to participate and thereby have been denied experiences in growth and development that greatly enrich life.

In the past we have had considerable experience with and have made considerable progress in ameliorative programs of functional disabilities and lesser permanent disabilities. We have made considerable inroads in general reeducation and strengthening programs and have made notable progress in adaptive physical education among individuals with these lesser conditions.

The individuals with which we are presently concerned are those with gross involvements such as: (1) those paralyzed from the region of the neck down as a result of a cervical lesion of the spinal cord or lesser levels of paralysis resulting from a lesion of the spinal cord at a lower level; (2) those with gross paralysis resulting from bulbar polio and similar conditions wherein most of the physical resources have been taken away from the individual; (3) those with such compounded disabilities as total blindness with both arms amputated, hemiplegia with perhaps the good leg or the good arm amputated, paraplegia resulting from spinal bifida with subsequent disarticulation of one leg including the hip socket and partial nephrectomy, paraplegia accompanied with blindness or deafness, multiple manifestations of cerebral palsy; and (4) those with such progressive disabilities as dystonia, muscular dystrophy, multiple sclerosis, and countless other causes and manifestations of severe disability.

THE UNIVERSITY OF ILLINOIS PROGRAM

The first university to make an all-out effort to make all of its buildings and facilities accessible to and usable by everyone, including the severely permanently physically disabled, and to develop appropriate supportive services and programs on their behalf in all areas of personal endeavor, was the University of Illinois, which initiated these efforts in the mid and late forties.

In relatively recent years several other universities have developed comparable programs. Each of these had its beginning upon the initiative of different professional disciplines on the various campuses, from varied perspectives and for varied reasons. Although there are great variances in the nature of the beginnings of these programs, it is hoped that they will eventually, each in its own way, fulfill the total needs of all individuals with disabilities in all endeavors of life in meaningful ways.

Much of which follows is based on the more than a quarter of a century of experiences on the University of Illinois campus, the many multidisciplinary and interdisciplinary researches conducted as an integral part of the program's development, and the many projects and programs that have grown out of the university's initial efforts.

Because of the great demands made upon the University of Illinois' pioneering program after it once had proven itself, a quota was placed upon the program as early as 1952.

Fig. 72-4. Special seating.

For many years an average of 225 to 250 severe, permanent, physically disabled students have been in attendance at the University of Illinois as fulltime residential students each year. Of these, 130 to 150 were confined to wheelchairs all of the time, 35 to 40 were totally blind, legally blind, or severely visually impaired, and the remainder represented many ambulatory and semiambulatory manifestations of disability as previously identified, including lesser numbers of deaf. Many of these students had compounded disabilities such as those identified earlier.

From the very beginning these students lived in regular university residence halls, attended all regular classes and continued to pursue over 75 curricula in 15 colleges and schools of the university.

They participated in almost every phase of extracurricular activity— newspapers, radio, television, bands, orchestras, choruses, fraternities, sororities, activity clubs, and various campus governing groups, often excelling and assuming leadership. They also participated in wheelchair football, wheelchair basketball, wheelchair baseball, wheelchair track and field, wheelchair archery, wheelchair square dancing, wheelchair fencing, wheelchair bowling, and many other wheelchair activities including golf and tennis. Blind students participated regularly in bowling, cycling, horseback riding, ice skating, swimming, camping, judo, wrestling, and many other activities. All, of course, participated in many activities of lesser organization and many social recreational activities of an individual or unstructured nature.

Fig. 72-5. Orientation session.

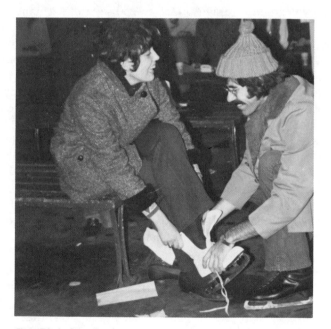

Fig. 72-6. Ice skating.

Fig. 72-7. Square dancing.

Fig. 72-8. Judo.

Halfway House Program

In 1962 the university's Division of Rehabilitation-Education Services developed a halfway house program at the university. This is where the most severely disabled, such as C-3 and C-4 traumatic quadriplegics, severe manifestations of bulbar polio, and comparable disabilities, are housed if they show the potential to benefit from a college education but are not able to enter into the regular residence hall programs. The staff of the halfway house is instructed what to do and what not to do, and how to work with the individuals with disabilities so as to lessen the degree of dependence on the part of the individual on a day-to-day basis.

Many individuals who entered the university via the halfway house program were later able to enter into the residence halls. Some eventually moved into apartments and lived quite independently and self-sufficiently.

Others remained in the project house throughout the entirety of their schooling. Upon graduation, however, they were in a position to assume responsibility for themselves such that they could accept an appropriate position knowing that they could instruct individuals how to assist them, get by with minimal assistance in the morning and the evening, and program themselves throughout the day. This has been the difference between making their way or not making their way.

The concern of individuals with severe, permanent, physical disabilities is not whether they are dependent or independent, but the degree of independence that each can achieve and the ability of the individual to assume responsibility for self and not be dependent upon the thinking and decisions of others.

On the Campus

On campus the students are not accorded any form of attendant help. Facilities have been designed and constructed for their independent function. Old buildings have been remodeled and modified. For many years all new buildings were designed and built so as to be equally accessible to, and usable by, the "able" and "disabled." These include buildings of all types and dedicated to many different uses. Entrances, public telephones, water coolers, residence hall desks and beds, showers, toilets, cafeteria service, dining areas, even library and laboratory facilities, have been so designed. The communities have entered into the program enthusiastically and, throughout the surrounding communities, building and facilities (including churches on the one hand and taverns on the other) have been made accessible to, and usable by the severely physically disabled, including those confined to wheelchairs. Throughout the campus and communities curbs are cut and ramped in business districts, residential districts, and recreational areas.

Individuals with physical disabilities are right at home on campus or in the communities of Champaign and Urbana. They are not "a sight to behold." They attract little attention and do just about what they please.

Accessible facilities and programs are of little value if an individual with a disability cannot get to them. Therefore, the university developed a transportation system that accommodates the individual in a wheelchair, the individual with an ambulatory disability and able-bodied persons alike. An able-bodied individual can enter the bus via the front door and a person in a wheelchair can either follow or precede (see Fig. 72.9). Four buses run on regular but different routes and schedules, each making two complete runs each hour and operating between 10 and 14 hours each day.

Fig. 72-9. Bus transportation.

Developing Individual Responsibilities

The disabled students are very much responsible for their own destinies in most everything. Space does not permit the description of all of the methods employed in all aspects of the program, but an example in the area of recreation might be significant.

Every fall each wheelchair football team receives 100 points for each player lost from the previous season, 100 points for each game lost during the previous season, 100 points for each newly eligible player, and certain specified bonus points. These are used in bidding on new players.

Twice a week for the first two weeks of each season, all teams and all new players practice together under the guidance and supervision of staff personnel. Fundamentals are taught and reviewed along with safety measures, rules, specific skills, and techniques. Players on each team, of course, are scouting the new players during this time.

At the end of the second week the teams hold a draft meeting. The players themselves make the decisions. A team can bid almost all of its points on one player if it concludes that particular player is the one it needs. Once on a team, a player remains on that team permanently, even if the team loses every game in a season or for three seasons. Team members must look ahead, organize and work to improve themselves. This has worked exceedingly well for years. The bidding is exciting fun. The esprit de corps on teams is tremendous. Everyone plays. Everyone works to improve as an individual and as a team. At no time is there intervention from faculty and staff.

It is particularly noteworthy that all social, recreational, and athletic activities, an annual publication, a biweekly newsletter, achievement awards, etc., are managed and financed by the disabled students themselves through their rehabilitation service fraternity, Delta Sigma Omicron. In addition, these "handicapped" students contribute close to $3,000 each year to benevolent causes, thereby demonstrating their concern for others. There was no state-appropriated funds in any of these activities for 26 years, and no "soft" federal money.

Of equal importance is the fact that there have been no injuries of consequence in all of the activities participated in by the severely disabled at the University of Illinois. However, the university has experienced 30 fractured legs among wheelchair students, all in normal campus situations, and all but three as a result of the "help" given them by well-meaning, able-bodied people.

There has been an insignificant number of pressure sores and no significant instances of kidney, bladder, or bowel problems among the severely disabled, including those with spinal cord injuries, including cervical level, who are vigorously active. Many of them may also spend more than eight hours a day in academic laboratories or at an engineering or architectural drawing board.

Rehabilitation-Education Services

The Rehabilitation-Education Center provides professional services unique to individuals with physical disabilities, particularly severe disabilities such as spinal injuries, blindness, deafness, cerebral palsy, and all others. Medical treatment is supported by consultation and specialized care from a certified urologist, neurologist, neuro-surgeon, orthopedic surgeon, physiatrist, plastic surgeon, dermatologist, ophthalmologist, oculist, otologist, and dentist. The center offers physical therapy, occupational therapy, functional therapy, counseling, special testing, recreation and athletics, driver education, transportation, and the coordination of federal-state agency services. Services for the blind and deaf include, among other things, orientation and mobility, Braille and tape transcription, direct reader service, tactile aids, and interpreters. The center maintains a large corps of select, qualified volunteers under professional supervision in support of each of the services.

The center also has specialized equipment in support of student needs, such as a one-hand typewriter, selectric typewriters with special interchangeable type heads (mathematics, physics, chemistry, etc.), typewriters with special shields for use by quadriplegics, cerebral palsied and others, Braille writers, Braille calculaters, Braille duplication, tape recorders, prosthetic, orthotic and adaptive devices, unique medical supplies, wheelchairs, Long Canes (for the blind), and maintenance and repair services.

The center has established cooperative academic examinations procedures, which are now well proven, for those students whose disabilities include communicative problems such as the blind, the deaf, the cerebral palsied, and the quadriplegic. This has the effect of decreasing disruption of classes, not requiring extra time on the part of the classroom teachers, not giving them advantages over other students, not being penalized academically for a communicative problem over which they have no control, and maintaining standards of academic performance and objectivity.

Consultation is available to faculty and administrators on the handling of specific problems of specific individuals with disabilities. Over the years many departments have established and maintained sound cooperative programs with the division and the center on behalf of students with disabilities.

Consultation is also available on the planning and building of new facilities and the remodeling of existing facilities to assure maximum accessibility and usability to individuals with all causes and manifestations of disability. Policies require the approval or concurrence of the center on all building and remodeling projects.

The center includes many specialized laboratories in direct support of teaching, research, and service. The center offers professional internships and professional workshops in many disciplines, and conducts research of multidisciplinary scope. Some interns come from universities other than the University of Illinois. The faculty of the center teaches or shares in the teaching of several undergraduate and graduate courses in several other colleges and departments. Faculty and staff of the center work closely with, and coordinate services of, related units on campus and in the communities.

The Rehabilitation-Education Center is truly a center. It houses the Division of Rehabilitation-Education Services and also houses faculty from other departments and colleges within the university whose teaching or research responsibilities relate directly to the services and laboratories found within the Rehabilitation-Education Center. It brings together all core disciplines that relate directly to supportive services to the severely physically disabled, and also many other disciplines that relate directly and indirectly to research and preparation of specialists in areas of consequence in the ultimate delivery of services to those with physical disabilities. There is a continuum of interdisciplinary and multidisciplinary research. Several departments within other colleges of the university utilize the center's laboratories, clinics, and other facilities for teaching of specific courses and for research. Students with disabilities served by the center are also unique resources to these departments and curricula.

Students with physical disabilities receive full credit in physical education for their participation in physical therapy and functional training. Others have received full credit for participation in recreational and sports activities.

Figure 72.10 identifies those other departments and curricula that feed continually into the various services of the division and the center. This is reciprocal in nature. In addition, many others are involved similarly, but do not maintain such a continuum.

Graduates and Former Students

The university has graduated hundreds of individuals with severe permanent physical disabilities and countless others with lesser disabilities. They are doctors of medicine, engineers, architects, lawyers, elementary and secondary teachers, professors at major universities across the nation, businessmen, and leaders in municipal, state, and federal government. They can be found in many foreign lands. Those who attended the university and did not graduate for one reason or another have good positions commensurate with their schooling.

SUGGESTED READINGS

American National Standards Association, 1961. *American standard specifications for making buildings and facilities accessible to, and usable by, the physically handicapped.* New York. ANSI A117.1.

Athletic Institute, 1968. *Planning college facilities for health, physical education, and recreation* (2nd ed.). Chicago: The Athletic Institute.

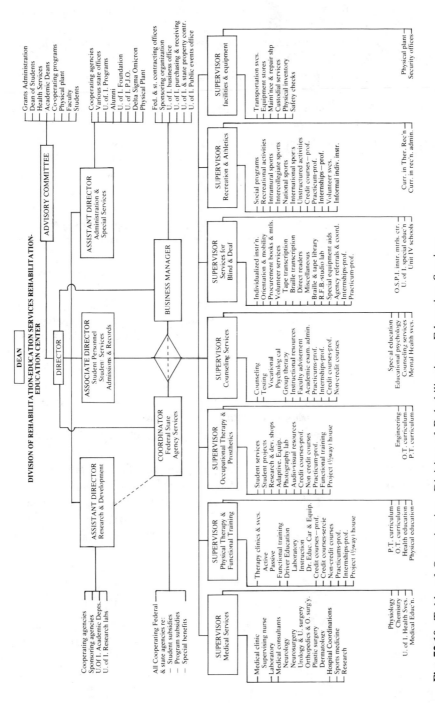

Fig. 72-10. Table of Organization, Division of Rehabilitation — Education Services, Rehabilitation — Education Center, University of Illinois, Urbana, Illinois.

Athletic Institute, 1965. *Planning facilities for health, physical education, and recreation* (3rd ed.). Chicago: The Athletic Institute.

Daniel, A. N., 1969. An example of individual instruction in developmental physical education. *JOHPER,* **40** : 56 (May).

Flanagan, M.E., 1969. Expanding adapted physical education programs on a state wide basis. *JOHPER,* **40** : 52-55 (May).

Gart, W. 1969. An adapted physical education program in a new senior high school. *JOHPER,* **40** : 49-51 (May).

Nugent, T. J., 1960. The design of buildings to permit their use by the physically disabled. *New building research.* National Research Council, Publication # 910.

_____, 1956. Development of services for the disabled student. *The academic advisement of disabled students, institute proceedings,* Syracuse University School of Social Work (June).

_____, 1969. Dilemma of public transportation for the handicapped—for everyone— and what can be done about it. *Community responsibilities for rehabilitation,* Rehabilitation International.

_____, 1971. Expanding horizons in recreation. *Proceedings of the 1971 mid-west regional therapeutic recreation symposium* (September).

_____, 1969. Precepts and concepts on research and demonstration needs in physical education and recreation for the physically handicapped. *Physical education and recreation for handicapped children.* Proceedings of U.S. Office of Education National Conference.

_____, 1966. Problems and solutions. *Mobilizing community resources for mental health through recreation.* Illinois Department of Mental Health (May).

_____, 1972. Recreation as a force in rehabilitation. *Proceedings of the U.S. regional workshop on spinal cord injuries.* Charleston, West Virginia.

_____, 1969. Research and demonstration needs for the physically handicapped. *JOHPER,* **40** :47-48 (May).

State University of New York, 1967. *Making facilities accessible to the physically handicapped—performance criteria.* State Construction Fund.

Tipton, C. M., and D. M. Hall, 1960. The rotometer and its use by disabled students. *The journ. of assoc. for phys. and mental rehab.,* **14** : 72-73 (May-June).

U.S. Department of Health, Education, and Welfare, 1972. The creation in recreation. *Rehabilitation record* (May-June).

73

Outstanding, Ongoing Sports Programs for Those with Physical Disabilities

Timothy J. Nugent

THE NATIONAL WHEELCHAIR BASKETBALL ASSOCIATION

The association, conceived in 1948, held it first national tournament and was organized officially at the Galesburg campus of the University of Illinois in April 1949. The six teams in the original tournament were the Chicago (Illinois) Cats, Evansville (Indiana) Rockets, Hannibal (Missouri) Rolling Rockets, Kansas City (Missouri) Rolling Pioneers, Minneapolis (Minnesota) Rolling Gophers, and the University of Illinois Gizz Kids. The first national champions were the Kansas City Rolling Pioneers. The NWBA celebrated its 25th anniversary with its 25th Annual National Tournament in March 1973 on the campus of the University of Illinois in Champaign, Illinois. The NWBA has grown to 16 well-established conferences and over 100 teams, including independent teams whose remote geographical location precludes conference play. Presently 32 teams enter into postseason tournament play at eight regional tournaments scattered throughout the United States. Two teams from each region advance to the four sectional tournaments, and the winner of each sectional tournament advances to the national championships. Active players range in age from 12 to 60 years, with one of the nation's outstanding players making All American at the age of 50.

No one individual can take credit for having invented wheelchair basketball. It began almost simultaneously in varied form at several of the Veterans Administration hospitals immediately following World War II because of the determination and unharnessed energy of many veterans who were not to be denied. Yet the Veterans Administration hospitals forbid participation in such vigorous wheelchair sports by its spinal cord injured patients. It is a credit to the Paralyzed Veterans of America at many places, particularly California and New England, that play was sustained.

---

* These programs and the personnel involved can be a source of information and guidance to professionals, and a great source of inspiration and motivation to individuals with comparable disabilities.

The National Wheelchair Basketball Association and the national tournament were founded by Timothy J. Nugent, professor and director of the Rehabilitation-Education Services, University of Illinois. He subsequently served as commissioner for the first 25 years, helped to bring about standardization of rules and procedures, helped develop a workable organization, and directed and/or cosponsored 20 national tournaments.

Although many women in wheelchairs expressed interest in participating in wheelchair basketball and several efforts were made, it was only in the 1970s that the effort met with a measure of success. The first regularly scheduled wheelchair basketball game between two recognized women's wheelchair basketball teams took place February 1974 on the campus of the University of Illinois. It was also the first intercollegiate women's wheelchair basketball game since the teams involved were the Southern Illinois University Squidettes and the University of Illinois Ms. Kids.

For further information write to: Office of the Commissioner, Box 100, Rehabilitation-Education Center, Oak street at Stadium Drive, Champaign, IL, 61820. (See also Physical Classification of Competitors for Wheelchair Sports, later in this chapter.)

THE UNITED STATES BLIND GOLFERS ASSOCIATION

The organization was founded during the first National Blind Golfers Tournament at the Dearborn Country Club in Michigan July 1948. Seven blind golfers participated in the first tournament.

It all really began when Bob Anderson of Los Angeles, California, invited Charlie Boswell of Birmingham, Alabama, Clint Russell of Fort Worth, Texas, and Marvin Shannon of Duluth, Minnesota, to participate with him in a blind golf match at the Inglewood Country Club in California in 1946. This was a special promotional event with the funds being given to charity.

Since 1948 the USBGA has held an annual tournament with the exception of 1953 and 1964. Presently the USBGA and its annual national tournament include men only. The annual tournament is a 36-hole medal play tournament preceeded by a one-day informal Pro-Am tournament for fun. Participants must have medical certification that they are totally blind in order to participate and must qualify with an 18-hole score of 135. Deliberations to lower the qualifying score are under way. In competition the coaches or instructors are allowed to accompany players to identify distances, directions, and positioning.

The USBGA encourages blind individuals to play golf and assists them with the purchase of clubs and initial professional lessons. Members of the USBGA have also played in several tournaments against blind golfers in Canada and have included Canadian blind golfers in their annual tournaments.

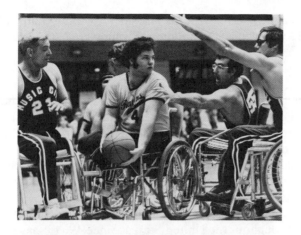

Fig. 73-1. Basketball.

For further information write to: President, United States Blind Golfers Association, 220 Brown Marks Building, Birmingham, AL, 35203.

THE AMPUTEE GOLFERS ASSOCIATION

The AGA was founded in 1949 by Dale Bourisseau and a handful of "golf-minded" members from Possibilities Unlimited in Cleveland, Ohio. They were soon to receive help from such outstanding golf personalities as Henry Picard, Bob Harlow, Herb and Joe Graffis, and Horton Smith.

The first National Amputee Golf Tournament was held in 1949 at Chagrin Valley Country Club in Ohio with only 12 competitors. It was an 18-hole tournament won by John Cipriani of Buffalo, New York.

A national tournament has been held every year since then at various country clubs throughout the United States. Since 1964 it has been a 72-hole tournament regularly drawing well over 100 qualified competitors. Competition is made equitable by dividing competitors into eight divisions based on their score on their first 36 holes of qualification. The Amputee Golfers Association includes women. The women's national tournament is held concurrently with the men's but as a separate tournament. To date there have been fewer women competing than men.

For additional information write to: The Amputee Golfers Association, 24 Lakeview Terrace, Watchung, NJ, 07060.

THE AMERICAN BLIND BOWLING ASSOCIATION

The organization was founded in 1951 by a few bowlers from Philadelphia, Pennsylvania, and New York City. From that humble beginning, state, regional, and national tournaments are now held annually. The ABBA sponsors bowling in various ways throughout the season, giving awards to bowlers who match or exceed published target scores and by presenting other awards to bowlers who attain the highest scores in particular categories throughout the entire season. The association also conducts a national mail-o-graphic tournament and has helped to develop blind bowling associations in various areas throughout the United States. It now boasts over 3,000 members and 100 sanctioned leagues in the United States and Canada. The national tournaments attract more than 1000 blind bowlers annually. They include both men and women.

During the 1950s Martin Mahler, a blind bowler who also manufactured precision equipment, designed and developed a lightweight, collapsible, portable, easily-stored, easily-erected "rail" for blind bowlers. It is simple for a blind person to carry the rail from home or school to a bowling alley in a small, lightweight, duffle-type bag. The rail can be set up, appropriate to the needs of the individual, alongside the approach to the lane. It is stabilized by placing two bowling balls on the specially designed base at each end. Subsequently Mahler developed another larger and stronger rail to be used in tournament play. Several schools, such as the University of Illinois, make these rails available to blind students.

No one knows precisely when bowling programs for the blind were first employed or what some blind individuals may have done on their own initiative, but evidence is available that substantiates that the Overbrook School for the Blind in Philadelphia encouraged bowling by its blind as early as 1910.

For additional information write to: The American Blind Bowlers Association, 3701 Connecticut Avenue, N.W., Suite 220, Washington, D.C. 20008.

Fig. 73-2. Bowling.

THE AMERICAN WHEELCHAIR BOWLING ASSOCIATION

The AWBA was founded in 1962 in Louisville, Kentucky, by Richard Carlson, who also served as its first president. The first tournament was held at Joe Dries' Parkmoor Lanes in Louisville, Kentucky. Anticipating only a few competitors, Dries and Carlson were surprised to have 30 wheelchair entrants from 13 states. The first AWBA Tournament Champion was Douglas Keaton of Raytown, Missouri, who also was a member of the first national wheelchair basketball championship team. Since then the tournament has been held annually in 11 cities in 10 states throughout the United States.

The AWBA has helped develop local and state wheelchair bowling leagues and wheelchair bowling associations. It has stimulated many special tournaments throughout the nation. The AWBA is sanctioned by the American Bowling Congress and as such includes only male bowlers. However, the AWBA is helping to establish a national women's bowling association. Throughout the year it is not uncommon to see a wheelchair bowler on a regularly sanctioned able-bodied ABC team in a winter league or to see a wheelchair bowler with his able-bodied wife competing in sanctioned mixed league competition. The majority of its members bowl in ABC-AWABA sanctioned wheelchair leagues in their home towns. Various types of competition and awards have developed throughout the years.

For further information write to: Executive Office, American Wheelchair Bowling Association, 2635 N.E. 19th St., Pompano Beach, FL, 33062.

For information on national wheelchair women's bowling competition, write to: Mrs. Alma Ladwig, 6418 W. Bennet Avenue, Milwaukee, WI, 53219.

NATIONAL AMPUTEE SKIERS ASSOCIATION

This association was organized officially and incorporated in 1967 under the leadership of Jim Winthers of Sacramento, California, although several smaller groups had begun activities for amputee skiers beginning in the early 1950s. Two groups stand out as having begun definitive programs in amputee skiing about the same time — a group in Oregon under the leadership of Dick Martin and the group in California under the leadership of Jim Winthers. The National Amputee Skiers Association had developed six chapters throughout the United States when it decided to merge with other groups of similar interest and enlarge the scope of its activities. In June 1972 it became the National Inconvenienced Sportsman's Association under the joint initiative of Doug Pringle and Jim Winthers. It now has 12 chapters that devote a great deal of time to teaching skiing to the blind, the deaf, postpolio, and other handicapped individuals. Leadership on the East Coast is credited to Ben Allen of Boston, Massachusetts. Both men and women have always been included in both the old and new organizations.

The association held its first national championship races in Oregon in 1963. It presently conducts regional races in the East, the Midwest, the Rocky Mountain area, and the Far West, followed by national championship competition each year.

For more information write to: Executive Offices, National Inconvenienced Sportsmans Association, 3738 Walnut Avenue, Carmichael, CA 95608.

THE SPECIAL OLYMPICS

This event, consisting of appropriately planned and supervised sports competition for the mentally retarded, had its beginning under the sponsorship and support of the Joseph P. Kennedy, Jr., Foundation. The first Special Olympics were held in Chicago, Illinois, in 1968. Since then under the guidance of the National Special Olympics Program, similar competitions have been developed at the community and state levels. The National Special Olympics are held biennially. Other competitions are held more frequently.

The Special Olympics include both girls and boys of varied ages, with events and groupings planned for equitable competition.

For additional information write to: Special Olympics, Joseph P. Kennedy, Jr., Foundation, 1701 K Street, Washington, D.C. 20000.

THE NATIONAL WHEELCHAIR GAMES AND THE NATIONAL WHEELCHAIR ATHLETIC ASSOCIATION

The games and the NWAA both had their beginning in 1957. The games include competition in wheelchair track and field, fencing, archery, table tennis, swimming, and weight lifting. For a short time they included some other activities such as wheelchair bowling, but have dropped these because of the development of specific programs in wheelchair bowling and because of difficulties in sponsoring all of these activities simultaneously.

The games and the NWAA were founded by Benjamin H. Lipton, director of the Joseph Bulova School of Watchmaking. They have been held in New York City under his direction and under the cosponsorship of the Paralyzed Veterans of America, the National Paraplegia Foundation, and occasionally other interested organizations, each year since their beginning. The national games committee hopes that the national games might be held in various cities throughout the nation.

From rather humble beginnings wherein anyone so motivated could participate in the national games, they have evolved into highly skilled and competitive games with a very definitive organization and procedure while increasing participation many-fold. Individuals must now qualify for the national games through regional games sponsored throughout the United States. Only those individuals who meet specific times, distances, or scores,

Fig. 73-3. Discus.

Fig. 73-4. Javelin.

Fig. 73-5. 60-yard dash.

or place first and second in specific events, qualify for the national championships. The games include events at all levels for both men and women. Team championships were awarded until 1972 when it was decided that the activities and individuals would best be served if team championships were eliminated.

For further information on the National Wheelchair Games and the National Wheelchair Athletic Association, write to: Chairman, N.W.A.A., Bulova School of Watchmaking, 40-24 62nd Street, Woodside, L.I., NY, 11377. (See also Physical Classification on Competitors for Wheelchair Sports, later in this chapter.)

THE NATIONAL INTERCOLLEGIATE WHEELCHAIR GAMES

These games were first held at the University of Illinois in Champaign, Illinois, March 1968, and featured only two established university teams, the University of Illinois and Southern Illinois University, and several independent competitors. Since then other colleges such as Wayne State University and Southwest Minnesota State College, have sent representative teams, and small groups of individuals from other schools have participated as individuals. The Intercollegiate Wheelchair Games are not yet firmly established because it has only been in recent years that other colleges and universities have become involved in facilitating the higher education of the severely permanently disabled, and they are widespread geographically. It is known that nucleus groups just beginning at other colleges have organized for

Fig. 73-6. Archery.

various forms of competition. Future growth is quite evident. The Intercollegiate Games have always been held at the University of Illinois in Champaign, Illinois.

For further information write to: Supervisor, Recreation and Athletics, Rehabilitation-Education Center, Oak Street at Stadium Drive, Champaign, IL, 61820.

WHEELCHAIR FOOTBALL AND WHEELCHAIR BASEBALL

Wheelchair football had its beginning at the University of Illinois in 1949. Three regularly organized teams have played a double round-robin schedule each football season since then. The season also includes an annual All Star Game against the alumni. Groups from other parts of the United States have sought and accepted invitations to play from time to time but, for want of proper facilities elsewhere, the sport has not grown. The same may be said for wheelchair baseball, which is played at the University of Illinois.

THE U.S. WHEELCHAIR SPORTS FUND, INC.

The fund was established in 1961 to take the initiative and assume the major responsibility for raising funds to send our most achieved disabled athletes to international competition when and where appropriate.

The National Wheelchair Basketball Association selects, through season-long competitions, those outstanding wheelchair basketball players who will represent the United States in international competition, and helps to support their participation financially.

Selections for international competition in all other sports is achieved through competition in the Annual National Wheelchair Games, by the National Wheelchair Athletic Association, which also helps to support financially the participation of the selected athletes, both men and women.

The two groups merge into one representative team. Many from each group will participate in the events of the other.

For further information write to: Chairman, U.S. Wheelchair Sports Fund, Joseph Bulova School of Watchmaking, 40-24 62nd Street, Woodside, L.I., NY, 11377.

INTERNATIONAL COMPETITION

International competition is extensive, well-defined and growing. Recreational and sports activities were recognized as an essential and integral part of the rehabilitation scheme in 1948 at the Stoke-Mandeville Spinal Cord Injury Center in England under its director, Dr. Ludwig Guttman. In 1952 the Stoke-Mandeville Center invited a group of wheelchair athletes from Holland to

Fig. 73-7. Football.

Fig. 73-8. Baseball.

participate with them in those events that had already been developed. This constituted the first major international competition in wheelchair athletics. Since then the Stoke-Mandeville Games have been held annually at Stoke-Mandeville with the exception of the regular Olympic years, at which time they become a sanctioned and added part of the regular Olympic Games, and are known as the Paralympics. The Stoke-Mandeville Games and the Paralympics have grown to include participants from more than 35 nations around the world and continue to grow each year. The games have contributed greatly to progress in the rehabilitation of the severely disabled in all countries throughout the world, and have helped enrich the understanding between nations since disabilities are in no way selective or discriminatory. Some nations subsidize, partially or fully, the wheelchair athletes; some the year round. Sir Dr. Ludwig Guttman continues to chair the International Wheelchair Sports Committee.

In 1954 the National Wheelchair Basketball Association invited a Canadian team from Quebec to participate in its sixth Annual National Tournament. Now several Canadian teams are members of the National Wheelchair Basketball Association. These same Canadian teams also foster regularly scheduled competition between teams in Canada.

Fig. 73-9. Fencing.

The Pan-American Wheelchair Games are held bienially during odd-numbered years featuring select teams from Canada, the United States, Central America, and South America. They were first held in Winnepeg, Canada, in 1967.

The British Commonwealth Games foster competition among the nations that make up the British Commonwealth. Every fourth year they are held at various places within the British Commonwealth. The first British Commonwealth Games were held in 1962.

THE PHYSICAL CLASSIFICATION OF INDIVIDUALS FOR WHEELCHAIR SPORTS COMPETITION

Classification of individuals is essential and well-defined so as to make competition equitable and inclusive of the greatest numbers.

Wheelchair basketball, a team sport, has a relatively simple classification system.

Class I: Complete spinal paraplegia at T-9 or above or comparable disability where there is a total loss of muscular function originating at T-9 or above.

Class II: Complete spinal paraplegia at T-10 or below or comparable disability where there is significant loss of muscular function of hips and thighs.

Class III: All other leg disabilities.

A Class I player is assessed one physical classification point, a Class II player is assessed two physical classification points, and a Class III player is assessed three physical classification points.

At no time may a team have more than 12 physical classification points on the floor at one time. The classification of a player must be written into the scorebook at the same time and in the same manner as is the line-up. Failure to do so properly results in various penalities. It then becomes the responsibility of the official scorer to see to it that at no time in the game does a team, by substitution, exceed its physical classification point limit. Violation results in specific penalties. Many teams have been most successful playing far below this limit.

In individual competitions such as track and field, swimming, table tennis, etc., the classification system needs to be much more definitive to bring about equitable competition. The National Wheelchair Athletic Association Classification System is as follows:

Class IA: All cervical lesions with complete or incomplete quadriplegia who have involvement of both hands, weakness of triceps (up to including grade 3 of the testing scale) and with severe weakness of the trunk

469

and lower extremities interfering significantly with trunk balance and the ability to walk.

Class IB: All cervical lesions with complete or incomplete quadriplegia who have some involvement of upper extremities but less than IA with preservation of normal or subnormal triceps (4 or 5 on the testing scale) and with a generalized weakness of the trunk and lower extremities interfering significantly with trunk balance and the ability to walk. Class IB will include to the first dorsal segment (T1).

Class II: Complete or incomplete paraplegia below T1 down to and including T5 or comparable disability with total paralysis or poor abdominal muscle strength (02 on testing scale).

Class III: Complete or incomplete paraplegia or comparable disability below T5 down to and including T10 with abdominal and spinal extensor musculature sufficient to provide some element of trunk sitting balance, but not normal.

Class IV: Complete or incomplete paraplegia or comparable disability below T10 down to and including L3, without quadriceps or very weak quadriceps with a value up to and including 3 on the testing scale, and gluteal paralysis.

Class V: Complete or incomplete paraplegia or comparable disability below L3 down to and including S5 with Quadriceps in grades 4 or 5.

THE INTERNATIONAL SYSTEM OF PHYSICAL CLASSIFICATION

Cervical Level

Class IA: Upper cervical lesions with triceps not functional against gravity (i.e., below Grade 3 MRC Scale).

Class IB: Lower cervical lesions with good triceps, wrist extensors, and flexors, having no finger flexors or extensors of functional value (i.e., below 3 MRC Scale).

Class IC: Lower cervical lesions with good triceps and strong finger flexors and extensors to power 4 MRC Scale, but having no interossei or lumbrical musculature of functional value. (T1)

Thoracic (or torso) Level

Class 2: *T1 to T5 inclusive*—having no balance when sitting.

Class 3: *T6 to T10 inclusive*—with ability to keep balance when sitting, ignoring nonfunctional (MRC Grade 1 and 2) lower abdominal muscles.

Class 4:   *T11 to L3 inclusive*—provided that quadriceps power is nonfunctional (MRC Grade 1 and 2).
Point Score for lower limbs: 1-20 Traumatic
1-15 Polio

Class 5:   *L3 to S2 inclusive*—provided that quadriceps function is MRC Grade 3 and above.
Point score for lower limbs: 21-40 Traumatic
16-35 Polio

Class 6:   Point score for lower limbs: 41-60 Traumatic
36-50 Polio

Not Eligible for Entry into Competition

Traumatic points score 61 and above.
Poliomyelitics point score 51 and above.

The International Recognized Muscle Testing Point system

This system ranges from 0-5 as follows:

0= A total lack of voluntary muscle contraction (i.e., complete paralysis).

1= Contraction without any mobility (trace or flicker).

2= Contraction with very weak movement when gravity is eliminated (poor).

3= Contraction allowing full range against gravity (fair).

4 = Contraction allowing movement against resistance and gravity (good).

5 = Contraction allowing movement against strong resistance or normal strength (normal).

SUGGESTED READINGS

Cerveny, G. R., 1962. An analysis of values derived from sports and physical recreation by severely physically disabled college students. Unpublished master's thesis, University of Illinois, Urbana, Illinois.

Elliot, R. D., 1967. A descriptive analysis of the cooperative swimming program for selected permanently severely physically disabled male and female young adults at the university of illinois. Unpublished master's thesis, University of Illinois, Urbana, Illinois.

Kuwada, G. Y., 1959. A manual for players and coaches of wheelchair basketball. Unpublished master's thesis, University of Illinois, Urbana, Illinois.

Lipton, B. H., 1970. The role of wheelchair sports in rehabilitation. *International rehabilitation review*, Volume 21, Number 2, New York: Rehabilitation International.

Nugent, T. J., 1964. Let's look beyond—to add meaning to recreation in rehabilitation. *Recreation in treatment centers.* U.S. Department of Health, Education, and Welfare.

Sports alive, 1960. Chicago: Spencer Press. Library of Congress Catalog Card #60-13708.

74

The Mentally Retarded

Frank J. Hayden

The importance of exercise, play, and sport in the lives of both children and adults has been fairly well established in North American society for many years. Strangely enough the extension of this belief to children and adults who are mentally retarded, and its expression in practice, is a relatively recent phenomenon.

In 1966 a national survey by Brace (1968) indicated that nearly one-third of the mentally retarded in elementary schools of the United States received no physical education instruction whatsoever. A more rigorous survey by Rarick et al. (1970) suggested an even more serious situation. Data from 335 schools in 21 states revealed that 45 percent of the educable retarded received no instruction in physical education while only 25 percent received an hour or more per week.

There are many indications of substantial increases in the quantity and quality of physical activity programs for the retarded since 1967. One of the major forces in this area has been the Joseph P. Kennedy, Jr., Foundation, which initiated much of the early work in training, demonstration, and research (Lapriola 1972). In 1967, Title V of Public Law 90-170, an amendment introduced by Senator Edward Kennedy, authorized $10 million for programs in physical education and recreation for the retarded and handicapped—the first federal funds specifically earmarked for this purpose. The Bureau of Education for the Handicapped program initiated by these funds provided $1 million a year for training and $350,000 for research.

Since the 1960s there has been concerted effort within the physical education profession to establish research and demonstration needs in regard to the retarded. There has also been a strong concern for increasing and improving the training of physical educators of the mentally retarded, usually within the context of "adapted physical education." There are at least 50 colleges and universities currently offering specialized degree programs that combine preparation in physical education and special education.

RESEARCH IN PHYSICAL EDUCATION FOR THE RETARDED

One reason for inadequacy in this part of physical education is the limited amount of research on factors related to the content and conduct of activity programs and on the effects of physical activity on the retarded. The available literature was reviewed by Stein in 1963 and again in 1968 and by Hayden in 1974. The pertinent studies are largely descriptive and comparative. Of the few experimental studies published almost all suffer from inadequate controls and samples. There is a large amount of information available on activities and programs, most of which is put forward on face validity and personal experience.

The research that is available verifies common observation: average retarded children are slower, weaker, fatigue faster, and are less skillful than their nonretarded counterparts. However, there is also evidence that they can make great physical improvement and that when they do they may benefit in several ways other than physical.

PHYSICAL FITNESS OF THE RETARDED

If a child lacks the strength and endurance to perform and practice, development of gross motor behavior and athletic skill can be seriously retarded, resulting in progressive restriction in play and recreational activity. For many of the retarded this seems to be the case. While there are great individual differences, the generally lower levels of physical fitness among both educable and trainable children have been documented by almost every investigator who has measured them.

Rarick et al. (1970) measured a carefully selected sample of educable boys and girls and reported a mean difference of two to four years between their basic fitness performance and that of normal children. Hayden (1965) made a similar comparison with a restricted sample of trainable children in Toronto and found an average difference of four to six years with the difference widening as the children got older. One result of these studies has been the publication of standardized fitness tests and normative tables for educable (AAHPER 1968) and trainable (Hayden 1965) children.

As we would expect, poor fitness and restricted activity are accompanied by increased fat. Rarick and Dobbins (1972) report educable children to be 30 percent fatter than normal. Hayden (1965) found that trainable males carry 25 percent and females 46 percent more fat than nonretarded children of the same age. Once again these are mean comparisons.

While the low fitness levels of the retarded are well documented, there is considerable evidence that they can be changed. Studies involving vigorous exercise invariably report significant improvement on fitness test items.

Gross Motor Skill of the Retarded

There is a considerable body of knowledge regarding discrete, fine motor learning and performance in retarded children but relatively little regarding gross motor skills such as running, hopping, jumping, skipping, throwing, catching, and climbing, which are of more immediate concern to the physical educator. The tests utilized in this area usually include, singly or in some combination, elements of speed, reaction time, flexibility, power, balance, coordination, and perhaps strength and endurance. The evidence that is available indicates a motor retardation of considerable magnitude, although not as severe as the intellectual one. This deficiency increases as the complexity and precision requirements of the task increase.

Comparing educable and normal children, Rarick and Dobbins (1972) found a difference of one standard deviation for boys and one and a half standard deviations for girls. Hayden (1968) suggests an even greater motor lag in trainable children. However, these and other investigators have pointed out a wider degree of variance in the retarded. While the mean scores compare very unfavorably, it is not unusual to find even trainable youngsters scoring in the upper quartile for normals. There is also evidence that on less complex motor tasks, some retarded children can perform as well as *any* children, given adequate training and motivation. Table 74.1 is a sampling of national records in the Special Olympics for the mentally retarded (L.A. County 1972). There are extremely few people at any level of intelligence who could match these performances.

Table 74.1
National Records in the Special Olympics

Sex	Age	Event	Performance
Boys	15	50 yd. dash	5.7 secs.
Boys	open	300 yd. run	31.8 secs.
Boys	18	Softball throw	289'7''
Girls	18	50 yd. dash	6.2 secs.
Girls	12	Standing long jump	7'5½''
Girls	15	50 yd. freestyle swim	30.1 secs.
Boys	open	440 yd. relay	46.4 secs.

Despite the discrepancies in performance level, the organization of gross motor abilities and their patterns of development in the retarded are quite similar to those of nonretarded youngsters, but at a younger age. Rarick and Dobbins (1972) in factor analysis of motor data from 145 normal and 261 educable boys and girls, discovered a fairly well-defined factor structure in the retarded that was very similar to that of the normals. There was indication of less specificity, with some factors appearing as composites of hypothesized basic components. (It is probable that this tendency would be more evident in trainable-level subjects.) From these results, the investigators suggested that the form and content of physical education programs for educable children need not vary greatly from that utilized for the nonretarded.

One major problem for research in this area has been to establish satisfactory performance tests. The results of motor performance testing may well be contaminated by cognitive elements. Even after the subject understands the test requirements, there may be a problem in eliciting the attention and effort that it requires. The attitude, skill, and experience of the tester are at least as important to validity as the test itself. Hayden (1968) has reported very high test-retest correlation coefficients for tests of strength, speed, power, flexibility, and endurance with trainable children, but only after considerable orientation, instruction, and careful application. The quest for adequate tests has involved a great variety of motor tasks: locomotor, playground skills, simple exercises, stabilometer, general physical functioning, fitness-performance, and throwing at targets.

There is no question that significant improvements in the gross motor skills of the retarded can be effected through well-planned programs of physical education. As would be expected, the learning takes longer than with normal children, and there are indications that some degree of overlearning improves performance and retention of that performance, although some evidence on overlearning or relearning contradicts this. It may be that the retarded learn and retain these skills quite differently from the nonretarded. It is important for physical education to determine strategies employed by the retarded in learning gross motor skills and to translate these into effective teaching practice.

Nature and Nurture in Physical Development

It appears that until relatively recently the poor physical fitness and motor ability of the intellectually handicapped were accepted as an unavoidable concomitant of their retardation—at least for the lower I.Q. levels. To a certain extent this was probably justified since their growth and development, which are closely related to physical performance, lag significantly behind those of normal children. The more severe the retardation the greater the delay in growth.

Maturation also comes later to the retarded. Delays in both skeletal and sexual maturation have been documented. These delays are also related to the degree of retardation. Institutionalized children appear to be more retarded in growth and development than those who are not.

If children are smaller, lighter, and reach puberty later, it is hardly surprising that their physical performance is poorer. If in addition these children have a greater prevalence of physical handicaps, are more prone to injury, and have possible brain damage, we would certainly expect them to be slower, weaker, more easily fatigued, and more poorly coordinated. It seems quite natural to accept the awkward and clumsy movements so apparent in many of the retarded as automatic "side effects" of mental deficiency. But how much of this motor retardation is really inescapable for a specific individual and how much is the product of a sedentary life style that starts early in childhood and progresses throughout the lives of most retarded persons?

There is ample evidence that significant restriction of anyone's physical activity can lead to most of the physical fitness and motor problems characteristic of the retarded. It is also evident that for a variety of reasons most of the retarded are severely underexercised. Most physical education and recreation activities are not suitable for them: the rules are too complex, the skills required are too demanding, and the activity is too strenuous for their low levels of fitness. Out-of-school play opportunities are extremely restricted for the retarded because: they often need close supervision and cannot be sent alone to the playground or pool; it takes them a long time to master skills such as swimming, bicycle riding, and skating, which can provide good vigorous play; often they miss out on neighborhood play because they cannot "keep up" physically or mentally; their parents and teachers may overprotect (and overfeed) them; they are not as spontaneously active in their play as the normal child (Horne 1942); and the recreational activities most popular with them are often sedentary ones such as TV watching and movies (Heinmark 1971). Comparison of the typical daily regimens of retarded children and their nonretarded counterparts suggests quite strongly that restriction of physical activity may be the major cause of their physical inadequacies rather than something inherent in their retardation.

Correlations obtained between motor-fitness test items and various environmental factors tend to confirm this (Rarick 1967). Data obtained from a national sample of 4235 educable children showed no significant correlation between performance and parent occupation or parent education level. Significantly better performances were obtained from those who received one hour or more of physical education per week than from those who did not. Further, the results showed better performances from children of larger families and those who had more older siblings. One explanation for this is that participation in a normally active environment and the provision of normally active models may stimulate the retarded to increased physical activity resulting in better physical ability.

There is good reason to believe that the physical fitness and motor retardation of the mentally retarded is produced at least as much by *nurture* as it is by *nature,* and therefore can be significantly changed. The measured results of carefully planned physical education programs support this.

EFFECTS OF PHYSICAL EDUCATION AND SPORT PROGRAMS

Exercise, sport, and games can make remarkable changes in the physical condition and physical performance of the retarded and can do so in a relatively short period of time. Significant improvement in gross motor behavior has been achieved within eight weeks (Chasey 1970) and in physical fitness within six weeks (Brown 1968) through school programs. Significant reductions in weight and fat have been made within two weeks in a residential camp setting (Drowatzky 1968). Hayden (1965) reported closing one-half of the "fitness gap" between trainable and normal children in seven months with no decline in the rate of improvement at the end of this period. The program consisted of three half-hour periods of instructional physical education per week.

The best controlled experimental study of the effects of physical education on retarded children was conducted in Texas in 1968 by Rarick and Broadhead. Their sample consisted of 275 educable mentally retarded and 205 minimally brain-injured children who were divided into four groups: individualized physical education, group physical education, art (Hawthorne).* and control. The programs were continued daily for a period of 20 weeks. The experimental group showed significant gains over those of the controls in six of seven fitness tests administered. The improvements were made by both boys and girls with the individualized instruction producing more than the group program.

Physical education programs have been designed to achieve a great variety of objectives and the results are closely related to the designs. A program of coordination exercises has produced improvement in the fine motor skills of children with minimal brain dysfunction (DeHaven 1970). Structured physical education and psychoeducation therapy has improved the psychomotor function, physical condition, and social behavior of mildly retarded boys (Giles 1968). Resistance and weight training have increased the

---

* Refers to the Hawthorne effect, i.e., controlling for the fact that some groups improve simply because of the esprit de corps that develops when a group knows it is being studied.

grip strength and arm and shoulder strength of trainable-level boys and girls (Hayden 1965). A program of interval running and running games has increased the running endurance and stamina of trainable children (Hayden 1965).

Further evidence of the "specificity of effects" was obtained from a study in Boston in which 100 educable retarded boys were assigned to one of three programs: "free play," "play," and "skill." The greatest gains in physical fitness and motor ability were produced by the latter program, which was the most vigorous (Boston Univ. 1967).

While improving their physical abilities the retarded may benefit in other ways. A good many secondary benefits have been claimed or assumed for physical activity programs, but very few have been measured. One investigator (Knowles 1970) has reported a decline in illnesses in an activity group although there was an increased incidence of accidents among the boys. Children of low motor ability were more subject to accidents. Hayden (1965) measured the effects of a physical training program on the ability of trainable children to perform a low-skill work task that incorporated the basic motor elements of most sheltered workshop and industrial jobs assigned to the retarded. He found that after 13 weeks the task performance of a training group was comparable to that of a group that practiced the specific task regularly. A group trained *and* practiced was significantly better than either of the other two. All three performed better than a control group, which neither trained nor practiced.

Personality changes in the retarded through sport and physical education have been suggested by many authors. Furthermore, it is the impression of many teachers and parents of the retarded that the self-concept and general motivation levels of their children have been changed as a result of such programs. Although this assumption seems logical, and there is some research information to support it (Oliver 1958; Rarick 1968), the direct, objective evidence has yet to be established.

PHYSICAL ACTIVITY AND INTELLECTUAL DEVELOPMENT OF THE RETARDED

With any program for the mentally retarded it is natural to question its effect on their intellectual functioning, although that may not be a primary or even secondary goal of the program. A number of physical education studies of retarded populations have included measures of intelligence. However, the relationship between physical activity and intellectual functioning in the retarded is far from clear. Research information of this nature on the retarded is of two types: (1) correlational data on gross motor performance and intellectual functioning—which do not indicate a relationship (Fait 1959;

Francis 1959; Hayden 1968; Rarick 1972) and (2) experimental data on changes in intellectual functioning after participation in activity programs—which do suggest a relationship (Beter 1973; Corder 1966; Oliver 1958).

Although the correlations with gross motor performance are low and nonsignificant they increase significantly as the motor task becomes more complex and the perceptual-motor requirements more demanding. Significant correlations have been found using simple and complex motor proficiency tasks as well as tests of reaction time, agility, equilibrium, and kinesio-perceptual matching. It appears that these correlations may be higher within particular I.Q. ranges and with specific rather than general academic skills.

After a 10-week period of training, during which they spent about half of the school day in physical education and games, 25 percent of a group of "educationally subnormal" boys showed significant increases in I.Q. (Oliver 1958). When this study was replicated by another investigator the results were similar; however, the changes in a Hawthorne group that was added to the research design were not significantly different from those of the experimental group (Corder 1966). If activity programs do result in better intellectual performance it may be through a factor not specific to physical activity. Some factors suggested are relaxation, arousal, attention span, and sociometric status.

Since the general expectation for failure is high in the retarded, reduction of that expectation through success in physical education may result in better academic performance. Both Rarick (1968) and Oliver (1958) have reported indications of higher levels of aspiration and motivation among retarded children following experimental activity programs.

Ismail (1969) states that attention to motor responses can lead to improvements in learning achievement not necessarily reflected in increases in I.Q. Other investigators have also concluded that motor proficiency is related in varying degrees to classroom behavior and school performance. This also appears to be the subjective experience of many classroom teachers of the retarded. Although considerable research is required before the contribution of physical education to intellectual development of the retarded can be established, the increasing concern since the 1960s to include more exercise, play, and sport in their lives has been stimulated, in large part, by a belief that such a relationship does exist.

SPORT, GAMES, AND PLAY PROGRAMS

The reports on activities that have been used successfully in programs for the retarded have run the gamut from baseball batting to cross-country skiing. It would be difficult to name a game or sport that has not been adopted or adapted in some form for both trainable and educable children. All recent texts on adapted physical education contain a section on activities for the retarded. Manuals have been published specifically on physical fitness, beginning swimming, and sports training for the retarded, as well as texts on motor activity, learning games, and physical education.

Camping programs for the retarded have operated for many years, and a bibliography of materials in this area was published (Freeberg 1969). Many articles have appeared since that time including reports on day, residential, and integrated camps. One of the most impressive camp programs is operated by Temple University. Its program has been considered significant enough for research and demonstration support from the National Institutes of Mental Health.

A number of recreation and education agencies have been interested in playground design and equipment for the handicapped. Reports have been published on playgrounds for severely retarded, physically handicapped, and for both. A "Learn to Play Center" was designed by the Kennedy Foundation to provide an environment in which children could learn recreational skills (Hurtwood 1968).

Gymnastics has been used in many forms including therapeutic exercise, trampoline, rhythmics, and even competitive free exercise and tumbling. Because of its potential contribution not only to physical fitness but also to motor-perceptual development and self-image, gymnastics may be the most valuable form of activity for the retarded.

If gymnastics is number one, then swimming is a close second and for the same reasons. A great variety of material has been written on swimming for the retarded: how to organize programs, instructional methods, aquatic therapy, fitness benefits, and training for competition. In 1971 an informational sheet was published showing 123 references in this area (AAHPER 1971).

There seems to be little question that most retarded youngsters can participate in the same exercises, games, and sports as the nonretarded. They may have to be a little older, or the activity may have to be adapted slightly—but they can do it if given time and patient instruction. If they are able to develop these proficiencies it seems reasonable that, like normal children, they should have an opportunity to demonstrate and test them in athletic competition.

Sports Competition for the Retarded

Local and state-level competition has existed in some sports such as basketball and bowling for many years, but in 1968 the Kennedy Foundation launched a national program that had as its goal the provision of opportunities for sports training and competition for retarded persons at all levels of ability. In its first five years the Special Olympics had attracted 300,000 participants to local, area, regional, state, and national games in the United

States, Canada, and France. Its announced goal was one million athletes by 1975 (Hayden 1972). Although a systematic evaluation of the psychomedical effects of Special Olympics has yet to be done, preliminary surveys indicate that parents, teachers, and coaches of participants feel that the experience is beneficial and in no way harmful (Cratty 1970). They support continuation of the games even at the national level (Rarick 1971). They see the primary aims of the program as being: (1) physical fitness, (2) self-concept, and (3) social interaction. They feel that it has secondary benefits in increasing pride, peer acceptance, interest in physical activity, and attitude and performance in school.

The medical problems at the games have not been major ones. For example, in 1972, 43,000 athletes participated in 40 statewide games. A total of 619 were treated for minor ailments such as sunburn, abrasions, headaches, and nausea (Hayden 1972). Seizures have not been a significant problem, reflecting the fact that medication allows for increased participation of epileptics in athletics (Comm. on Children 1968).

A survey of teachers and volunteers at one state games revealed that 91 percent had no real difficulty in interesting the children in the program. Ninety percent saw "some improvement" and 40 percent "much improvement" as a result of participation (Brower 1969). The same study included interviews with 228 participants. They were almost unanimous in saying they enjoyed the training and practice and wanted to return another year.

The range of performances in the Special Olympics is most interesting. In most meets the competitors are assigned to one of four divisions according to ability. At the 1970 National Special Olympics all of the Division IV competitors could have been bested by approximately 95 percent of normal children. However, 10 percent of Division I competitors could have competed satisfactorily against the better athletes in the Junior Olympics (Hayden 1970).

Special Olympics currently includes track and field, swimming, basketball, volleyball, soccer, gymnastics, bowling, and floor hockey. Materials are available from the Kennedy Foundation on how to organize a local program, how to train for the various events as well as technical information on organization and rules. In both the United States and Canada the Special Olympic concept has been applied to Winter Games, including tobogganing, speed skating, figure skating, broomball, snow shoeing, and cross-country and downhill skiing.

CONCLUSION

Physical education is provided first of all for physical benefits. Its potential for improving the physical condition and physical performance of the retarded has been clearly identified, although not clearly quantified.

Fig. 74-1. Special Olympics—Floor hockey.

Fig. 74-2. Special Olympics—swimming.

It appears that aside from a lower performance level, the educable retarded are very similar to normal children in their learning and performance of gross motor tasks and therefore would benefit from programs similar to those of proven benefit for "normals." The picture regarding the trainable retarded is much less clear and requires considerably more investigation. For example, it is interesting to note that a profession so concerned with *muscle* has yet to produce a careful evaluation of the trainability of the hypotonic, flaccid muscle of children with Down's Disease.

It is possible for physical education to influence a great many secondary, nonphysical characteristics. Among those that have been postulated are pride, self-concept, body image, confidence, school performance, peer acceptance, perception, intelligence, and specific cognitive performances. Its effectiveness in these areas is going to be very closely related to how activities are taught and the environments in which they are performed. At the same time many physical and nonphysical benefits are highly specific to the activity. In other words, program outcomes are going to be a direct reflection of what the physical educator decides to do and how he decides to do it.

The role of physical education in the intellectual development of the retarded has probably been overemphasized. The logic is sound but the evidence is weak. This is not to say that we do not recognize the potential value of certain types of activities on cognitive performance. There is a whole area of research in perceptual-motor activity that this paper has not discussed (Beter 1973; Cratty 1969, 1971; Ismail 1969; Kephart 1960, 1964). However, physical education for the retarded should not be evaluated or promoted primarily on its ability to raise their I.Q. scores.

It seems evident that many retarded children are doubly handicapped because of restrictions in their physical activity. The major reason for this has been an acceptance of their poor levels of performance. However, performance in play and sport as in other areas is related to expectation, and with the retarded we have expected too little.

REFERENCES

AAHPER, 1968. *Special Fitness Test Manual for the Mentally Retarded.* Washington, D.C., AAHPER.

————, 1971. *Aquatics for the impaired, disabled, and handicapped.* Information gathered and organized by participants at the 1971 special workshop sponsored by the National Council for Cooperation in Aquatics. Washington, D.C., AAHPER.

Beter, T. R., 1973. Effects of concentrated physical education and auditory/visual perceptual reading programs upon three variables of EMR children. *The physical educator,* **30** : 130-131.

Boston University, 1967. *A final report: the development and evaluation of three types of physical education programs for EMR boys.* Boston: Boston University, School of Education.

Brace, D. K., 1968. Physical education and recreation for mentally retarded pupils in public schools. *Research quarterly,* **39** : 779-782.

Brower, M.J., 1969. The Michigan special olympics: 1969. Unpublished study, Kalamazoo, Michigan: Western Michigan University.

Brown, J., 1968. The effect of a physical education program on the muscular fitness of TMR boys. *Am. correct. ther. j.* **22** : 80-81.

Chasey, W. C., 1970. The effects of clinical physical education on the motor fitness of educable mentally retarded boys. *Am. correct. ther. j.* 24 : 74-75.

Committee on Children with Handicaps, 1968. The epileptic child and competitive school athletics. *Pediatrics,* **42** : 700-702.

Corder, O. W., 1966. Effects of physical education on the intelligence, physical, and social development of educable mentally retarded boys. *Except. Child.* **32** : 357-364.

Cratty, B. J., 1969. *Motor Activity and the Education of Retardates.* Philadelphia: Lea and Febiger.

————, 1970. A survey of attitudes toward and observations of the Special Olympics for retarded children: a pilot study. Unpublished study, Los Angeles: University of California.

————, 1971. *Active Learning.* Englewood Cliffs, N.J.: Prentice-Hall.

De Haven, G., and J. Murdock, 1970. Coordination exercises for children with minimal brain dysfunction. *Phys. ther.* **50** : 337-342.

Drowatzky, J.N., 1968. Effects of a two-week residential camp program upon selected skinfold measures, body weight and physical fitness of TMR children. *Am. correct. ther. j.* **22** : 87-91.

Fait, H. F., and H. J., Kupferer, 1959. A study of two motor achievement tests and its implications in planning physical education activities for the mentally retarded. *Am. j. ment. defic.* **63** : 292-311.

Francis, R. J., and G. L. Rarick, 1959. Motor charactersitics of the mentally retarded. *Am. j. ment. defic.* **63** : 792-811.

Freeberg, W. M. 1969. Camping for the handicapped: a selected bibliography. *Therapeutic recreation journal,* 3 : 38-41.

Giles, M., 1968. Classroom research leads to physical fitness for retarded youth. *Education and training of the mentally retarded,* 3 : 67-74.

Hayden, F. J., 1965. The influence of exercise and sport programs on children with severe mental deficiency (I.Q.$<$50). In Antonelli, F. (ed.). *Sports psychology,* Rome: International Society for Sports Psychology.

————, 1965. *Physical fitness for the mentally retarded.* Toronto: Metropolitan Toronto Association for Retarded Children.

————, 1968. The nature of physical performance in the trainable retarded. In Jervis, G. A. (ed.) : *Expanding concepts in mental retardation:* A symposium. Springfield: Charles C. Thomas.

_____, 1970. 1970 International Special Olympics—evaluation of division I performances. Unpublished report for the Joseph P. Kennedy, Jr., Foundation.

_____, 1972. The nature and number of medical problems experienced at Special Olympic games in the United States. Unpublished report prepared for the Joseph P. Kennedy, Jr., Foundation.

_____, 1972. Building olympic champions—sports training and sport competition for the mentally handicapped. Paper presented at the 5th International Congress on Mental Retardation. Montreal (October).

_____, 1974, Physical education, sport, and the mentally retarded. In Wortis, J. (cd.): *Mental retardation and developmental disabilities—an annual review,* Vol. VI. New York: Brunner Mazel Inc.

Heinmark, R., and R. McKinnon, 1971. Leisure preferences of mentally retarded graduates of a residential training program. *Therapeutic recreation journal,* 5 : 67-68, 93-94.

Horne, B., and C. Philleo, 1942. A comparative study of spontaneous play activities of normal and mentally defective children. *J. genet. psychol.* 61 : 43.

Hurtwood, Lady Allen, 1968. *Planning for play.,* London: Thames and Hudson.

Ismail, A. H., 1969. The relationship between motor and intellectual development. In Brown, R. C., and B. J. Cratty (eds.) : *New perspectives of man in action.* Englewood Cliffs, N.J.: Prentice-Hall.

Kephart, N. C., 1960. *The slow learner in the classroom.* Columbus, Ohio: Charles E. Merrill.

_____, 1964. Perceptual-motor aspects of learning disabilities. *Except. child.* 30 : 201-206.

Knowles, C. J., 1970. The influence of a physical education program on the illnesses and accidents of mentally retarded students. *Am. correct. ther. j.* 24 : 164-168.

Lapriola, E. M., 1972. The Joseph P. Kennedy, Jr. Foundation and its role in physical education and recreation for the mentally retarded. Unpublished M.A. thesis, University of Maryland.

Los Angeles County, Dept. of Parks and Recreation, 1972. 1972 International Special Olympics—Final Results. Los Angeles: Department of Parks and Recreation.

Oliver, J. N., 1958. The effects of physical conditioning exercises and activities on the mental characteristics of educationally sub-normal boys. *Br. j. educ. psychol.* 28 155-165.

Rarick, G. L., 1967. *Environmental factors associated with the motor performance and physical fitness of educable mentally retarded children.* Madison, Wisc: University of Wisconsin (Dept. of Physical Education).

Rarick, G. L., and G. D. Broadhead, 1968. *Effects of individualized versus group instruction on selected parameters in the development of educable mentally retarded and minimally brain injured children.* Washington, D.C.: U.S. Office of Education.

Rarick, G. L., 1968. The factor structure of motor abilities of EMR children. In Jervis, G. A. (ed.) : *Expanding concepts in mental retardation: A symposium.* Springfield: Charles C. Thomas.

Rarick, G. L., J. H. Widdop, and G. D. Broadhead, 1970. The physical fitness and motor performance of educable mentally retarded children. *Except. child.* **36** : 509-514.

Rarick, G. L. 1971. Evaluation of local Special Olympics programs. Unpublished study, Berkeley, University of California.

Rarick, G. L., and D. A. Dobbins, 1972. *Basic components in the motor performance of educable mentally retarded children.* Berkley California: University of California (Department of Physical Education).

Stein, J., 1963. Motor function and physical fitness of the mentally retarded. *Rehabil. lit.* **24** : 230-242.

————, 1968. Current status of research on physical activity for the retarded. In Jervis, G. A. (ed.): *Expanding concepts in mental retardation: a symposium.* Springfield: Charles C. Thomas.

ADMINISTRATIVE ASPECTS

Introduction

The previous four sections have discussed various types of physical education programs found in the schools and the military with some peripheral mention of programs found in the community at large. On occasion, intentionally or inadvertently, various authors touched on various components that would normally be included in a discussion of program administration. The purpose of Section 7 is to identify more comprehensively these components, and present selected examples of their application in physical education.

Author Spaeth offers a brief outline of the amounts and types of traditional administrative research conducted in physical education. She summarizes the results of a number of research studies, in the administration of physical education and athletics, that have used the methods of social science research. New directions in administrative research are also discussed, including: (1) research on the scientific knowledge that might serve as the basis for professional practice; and (2) a concerted effort to study the dynamics of administration from a theoretical perspective to supplement the traditional information-gathering approch is the chapter by Bookwalter, who used score cards and rating scales to evaluate the undergraduate professional physical education programs of a large number of universities.

Spaeth also identifies the two major areas of administration: (1) program aspects including curriculum development and evaluation; and (2) technical-managerial aspects including personnel administration, finance and business management, facilities and equipment, and public relations. The topic of facilities and equipment is singled out for emphasis in this section by Keller, who outlines procedures and references to be used in obtaining information on facilities, equipment, and supplies, and by Orban, who describes an "ideal" physical education facility in a higher education setting.

This section would not be complete without a chapter on the administration of athletics. Shea reviews and analyzes the literature culled from research, athletics organizations, professional education groups, investigations and surveys, texts on administration in physical education and athletics in particular, and higher education in general. Underlying his presentation is the theme of the continual struggle to keep athletics (and its administration) free from exploitation and consistent with educational principles. He closes with the prophetic statement that the 1980s will present the administration of physical education and athletics with a new set of economic, political, and social problems.

The final two chapters lend validity to Shea's prophecy. It is probably safe to say that compliance with the mandates of Title IX and P.L. 94-142 will "test the mettle" of physical education and athletics administrators for many years to come.

Section Editor

Roy Jacob Keller received a B.S. degree from Winona State College, the M.S. degree from Washington State University, and a doctorate from the University of Illinois. He has taught at both the high school and university levels. He was an associate and then full professor and chairman of the department of health, physical education and recreation, St. Cloud State College (Minnesota) from 1965 through 1967. Since 1967 he has held various positions at the University of Illinois, Urbana, and presently serves as director of the physical education department coeducational activity program.

He has written a textbook, *Modern Management of Physical Facilities,* contributed to several books, and written numerous articles published in professional journals.

75

Some Examples of Administrative Research

Marcia J. Spaeth

Administration has been an area of research in physical education and athletics for more than three quarters of a century. Most early investigations were by administrators themselves and concerned facilities or departmental organization and staffing. As graduate programs developed in the universities, the topics of administrative research broadened and master's theses and doctoral dissertations became the primary source of administrative research.

Administrative research has generally been treated as a subtopic within more general reviews of physical education research. The most comprehensive review of early research was a doctoral dissertation based on the files of the National Research Committee, a predecessor of the AAHPER Research Council (Trethaway 1953). Trethaway collected the titles of 3083 research reports in physical education, interschool athletics, and school recreation completed between 1895 and 1940; he then analyzed a sampling of 789 of the abstracts and summarized the major developments in each area.

A summary of research for 1930 through 1946 appeared in the *Research Quarterly* (Cureton 1949). The article included the complete listing of the 420 doctoral dissertations in the review.

Summaries of physical education research have appeared in each edition of the *Encyclopedia of Educational Research* (Esslinger 1941, 1950; Rarick 1960; Montoye and Cunningham 1969). Within these reviews are brief summaries of administrative research under such headings as Status of Physical Education, Organization and Administration, and Administrative Practices. These reviews have been concerned primarily with policies, procedures, practices, and regulations—the more technical aspects of administration.

Administrative research for 1940 to 1967 was reviewed in a doctoral dissertation by Spaeth (1967). A bibliography of research on administrative topics was compiled from published research reports, and 35 of these were selected for analysis in relation to a research paradigm from the field of educational administration.

Reviews of administrative research are also found in the related literature chapters of theses and dissertations on specific administrative topics. These chapters provide references to related research and reviews of previous methodology and findings.

Based on a review of doctoral dissertations reported in the literature from 1940 to 1973, the following provides a broad overview of recent administrative research:

Administrative research studies may be classified according to task areas. Task areas may be grouped under two major headings—*program aspects* (including curriculum development and evaluation and relating the students to the program, and *technical-managerial aspects* (including personnel administration, finance and business management, facilities and equipment, and public relations). The administrator must have factual information and knowledge of administrative processes in relation to each task area. Program aspects in order of frequency studied were: intercollegiate athletic programs for men, college physical education programs, secondary physical education programs, interscholastic athletics for boys, intramural programs in colleges, elementary school programs, intercollegiate athletics for women, interscholastic programs for girls, and intramural programs in public schools. Technical-managerial aspects in order of frequency studied were: (1) personnel (including, in order of frequency, characteristics of men and women faculty members; job analysis of administrators, supervisors, and directors; characteristics, qualifications, and attitudes of administrators; job analysis of faculty, teachers, and coaches; department chairmen at the college and university level; administrative or leadership behavior; and selection of faculty); (2) facilities and equipment; (3) finance, insurance, and liability; and (4) public relations.

Many of the above topics were studied more intensively in certain decades than in others in the period reviewed. None of these topics was studied more intensively in the 1940s than in later decades. Topics studied more intensively during the 1950s were: secondary programs, elementary programs, selection of faculty, and insurance. Topics studied more intensively during the 1960s were: college physical education programs, facilities, job analyses, equipment, finance, and intramural school programs. Topics studied more intensively during the 1970s (representing only the first quarter of the decade) were: all aspects of personnel other than job analyses and selection of faculty, and athletic programs of all kinds and at all levels except public school intramural programs.

Topics not classified by task areas in order of frequency studied were: administrative policies, practices, and procedures; evaluation of faculty, teachers, and coaches; organizational structure; aims and objectives; evaluation of administrators; and role studies.

Much of the research referred to above falls within the traditional framework of task areas and, to a much lesser extent, of administrative processes. The need for research that would contribute more significantly to administrative thought and practice was emphasized by Zeigler (1959). During the late 1960s and early 1970s a whole new focus of research on the dynamics of the organization evolved.

NEW DIRECTIONS IN RESEARCH

There is a new emphasis in administrative research upon the development of a body of scientific knowledge that will serve as a basis for professional practice. The importance of administrative theory and administrative concepts has been recognized, leading to the use of theoretical models in the design of research, theoretical propositions to be tested, and theoretical interpretation of the findings.

The relationship of administrative theory to administrative research was explored in a study by Spaeth (1967). An analysis of administrative research in physical education and athletics prior to 1967 revealed an almost total lack of theoretical orientation in the design of research and interpretation of the findings in the sample of administrative research studied. Several recommendations were made for the redirection of administrative research in physical education and athletics.

The meanings of selected concepts in administrative theory as perceived in the fields of educational administration in general, and of physical education administration in particular, were the focus of a study using a form of the Osgood Semantic Differential (Penny 1968). Penny found that there were significant differences in the meanings attributed to these concepts by administrators and by graduate professors teaching administration courses in these two fields. In a later study the same research design was replicated with athletic administrators (Hunter 1971).

Paton (1970) analyzed administrative theory as presented in graduate administration courses in physical education. He found that in only a few instances were significant sections of administrative theory included. Paton also emphasized the need for a redirection of research emphasis to include the use of theory and models developed in related administrative fields.

Attention has recently been focused on administration as a process. There has been a concerted attempt to study the dynamics of administration from a theoretical perspective to supplement the familiar information-gathering approach to administrative research. In particular, administration has been viewed as a social process. The behavioral approach, using the concepts, theories, and methodologies of the social sciences, has supple-

493

mented the traditional approach. The behavioral approach focuses on the interactions between people rather than on the technical aspects of administration. Much of this research depends upon the use of computer technology due to the complexity of the variables and the large quantities of data frequently associated with social science research.

Studies involving fundamental administrative processes such as planning and evaluating appear rather frequently in the literature. Studies of the more basic processes of decision making and communication represent a new direction in research. Beeman (1960) studied the decision-making processes involved in the control area of administering university intramural programs. He used the case problem and critical incident techniques to develop generalizations applicable to administrative problems in this area.

Douglas (1969) studied the decision-making processes used by physical education departments in colleges and universities using a modified form of Likert's *Profile of Organizational Characteristics.* He concluded that most department chairmen involved their faculty members in a participative form of governance, though not to the extent both groups indicated they desired.

Swerkes (1972) developed a conceptual model based on systems theory for the development of physical education curriculum. The model conceptualizes curriculum development as a decision-making system involving many of the sub-processes (e.g., planning, operationalizing, and evaluating) that comprise what is known as the administrative process. This study illustrates clearly the use of the administrative process in a specific task area, namely curriculum development.

Several studies have focused on the important process of communication. Small's study (1955) of staff relationships in 122 college and university physical education departments included communication as one of seven areas of investigation. Based on data from the above groups, Small concluded that there were few or no problems with communication between staff members and their chairmen or directors, but that communication with related groups such as the health service and custodial staff was frequently better than between men's and women's departments.

Case (1969) studied the communication structure of a college of physical education consisting of six subunits in a large state university by analyzing actual regular contacts between persons in the college. His findings showed that individuals in positions of authority in the organization structure were also the key communicators and liaison persons in the communication structure. The factors highly significant in determining communication patterns within the college were sex, departmental affiliation, and office location.

Steele (1971) also studied the communication patterns of a school of health, physical education, and recreation consisting of four subunits in a large state university. He obtained data by questionnaire from each faculty member about 17 items of information being communicated within the school. Steele's findings that the administrators were the key communicators, and that sex, division affiliation, and office location were highly significant factors in the communication structure, support the findings reported earlier by Case.

Yeager (1971) studied the interpersonal communication patterns in a women's physical education department consisting of 22 faculty and administrative personnel. Yeager's research was based on a social-psychological theory of communication known as symbolic interactionism. Yeager concluded that contacts between persons, even though reciprocated, do not necessarily involve all the elements necessary for communication to occur. Yeager also identified substantial differences between the actual communication contacts and the contacts desired by the participants. The differences were in the direction of a stronger sender role in the desired setting with the receiver role ascribed to other persons.

The study of leadership has developed from the trait approach through the situational approach to the behavioral approach. Most early studies of leadership involved small, unstructured groups. More field studies of organizational leadership are needed.

Small's study (1955), reported above in relation to communication, was one of the earliest studies of staff relationships in physical education that used social science concepts and theories in the design of the research instrument. Areas of investigation included group structure, group feeling, goal direction, participation, productivity, communication, and administrative leadership. Small concluded that directors of departments tended to assume major responsibilites for group action and pointed to the need for more experience among staff members and their leaders in meeting and solving problems as a group.

Beeman's study (1960), reported above in relation to the decision-making process, also revealed director attitudes toward participative group management in the administration of university intramural programs. Beeman concluded that in the majority of cases the directors favored including student participants in the decision-making process.

Douglas (1969) studied the administrative leadership of college and university undergraduate physical education departments using a modified form of Likert's *Profile of Organizational Characteristics.* Douglas concluded that many of the departments studied were administered by chairmen who involved their faculty members in a participative form of governance. In relating administrator variables to style of leadership, significant differences toward more participative governance were found for department chairwomen and for chairmen devoting one-quarter to one-half of their time to administrative duties. The administrative behavior of department chairmen having served six to ten years revealed a significant difference toward less participative governance. Both faculty and chairmen observed the present status as being somewhat participative, but both groups would like it to have been more participative than it was.

Olafson (1969) studied perceptions of leader behavior and departmental characteristics in 22 university and junior college physical education departments using the *Leadership Behavior Description Questionnaire XII* by Stogdill and a *Departmental Dimensions Questionnaire*. He concluded that the perceived departmental characteristics and the perceived leader behavior differed significantly at the two levels. The findings also showed that leader behavior of the department chairmen was perceived similarly by the faculty and the department chairmen, but in significantly different ways by the deans.

Allen studied perceived leader behavior, leadership style, group atmosphere, and position authority in departments of physical education for women in 27 colleges and universities, using four subscales of the *Leader Behavior Description Questionnaire XII,* the *Least-preferred Coworker* and *Group Atmosphere* scales by Fiedler, and a *Leader Authority* scale based on Hunt. The findings revealed significant differences in the perception of leader behavior between the faculty members and department chairmen. Department chairmen perceived their own behavior as being more considerate and allowing more scope for initiative, decision, and action than was perceived by their faculty members. All 27 departments were determined as having a favorable group atmosphere. However, faculty members as a total group, and in 10 institutions in particular, indicated a less favorable estimate of group atmosphere than did their leaders. Leaders in this sample perceived themselves as slightly more relations-oriented than task-oriented, and tended to associate this with taking a less active leadership role. The faculty members, however, perceived their leaders as characteristically exercising an active leadership role.

Bagley (1972) applied Fiedler's Leadership Effectiveness Contingency Model to 24 university graduate departments of physical education. In this study none of the departments was determined as having an unfavorable leadership situation, a finding comparable to Allen's report above. However, this variable did not seem to be an important one in determining the effectiveness of a department as measured in this study. Bagley also concluded that the human relations-oriented leaders were more effective in the favorable leadership situations that prevailed in this study.

A widely accepted concept in the social sciences is the concept of role; there is an extensive body of literature and research pertaining to it. The use of role concepts in administrative research in physical education and athletics, however, is a recent development.

Burkhart (1965) studied role expectations of the college director of physical education held by 14 department directors, their college presidents, and the 46 staff members in their departments. The findings showed that the directors were more accurate in their perceptions of the staff members' expectations than of the presidents' expectations for their role.

Dittus (1966) studied the expectations for the role of physical education director held by principals and physical education directors in senior high schools. There was disagreement within groups and among groups on the job expectations for the physical education director. Dittus concluded that there was a need for resolving such differences in the interest of better understanding and greater efficiency in administering physical education.

Wood (1971) studied the reciprocal role expectations of 10 university department chairmen and 102 faculty members using the role concepts of Neal Gross. Wood concluded that there is a wide range of agreement levels for the expectations for faculty members and an even wider range for the position of chairman. Wood also found that faculty satisfaction with the chairman's leadership was related to the accuracy with which the faculty member perceived the chairman's expectations for the faculty role.

Daniel (1971) studied the relationship between job satisfaction and the differentiated roles of the faculty members in the physical education departments of 10 Ontario universities. The findings indicated certain trends in job satisfaction that were related to role differentiation. Daniel concluded that "respondents whose roles tended to be more congruent with the expected roles of the academic community, and whose institutional recognition, therefore, tended to be more congruent with accepted and established institutional patterns, exhibited higher levels of job satisfaction." This conclusion appears to be consistent with one reported in 1955 by Small that "involvement in and satisfaction with the work of physical education departments tends to concentrate at the top of the prestige scales and to decrease with each lower position in the academic hierarchy."

Dannehl (1970) studied the organizational climate in college and university departments of physical education that were organized under four different types of administrative structures. The intrument used was the *Organizational Climate Description Questionnaire* developed by Halpin and Crofts. Dannehl concluded that perceptions of the organizational climate are significantly affected by the administrative structure, the type of appointment held, and by administrative positions held.

Flanigan (1973) studied the environmental characteristics of a college of physical education within a large university using the *College and University Environment Scale II.* He concluded that the faculty and students perceive the atmosphere or climate in significantly different ways in some areas and pointed out that such information can provide administrators with more insight about student withdrawals from the program. Using the same instrument (*CUS II*), Collins (1973) studied the environmental image of a small, private liberal arts college. His findings indicate perceptions of the climate by faculty and students that are considerably different than in the study reported above.

The studies reviewed in this chapter represent initial attempts to apply the concepts and methods of social science research to the administration of physical education and athletic programs. Only a small portion of the findings and conclusions could be presented in this brief review. It is clear, however, that there is great potential in this type of research. Future researchers should be very thorough in their review of the related literature and research to provide an integrated approach to administrative research studies.

REFERENCES [*]

Collins, G. W., 1973. An investigation of the environmental image of Ottawa University. Unpublished doctoral dissertation, University of Utah.

Cureton, T. K., 1949. Doctorate theses reported by graduate departments of health, physical education and recreation 1930-1946, inclusively, *Research Quarterly,* 20 : 21-59 (March).

Swerkes, B. S., 1972. A systems model for the development of the physical education curriculum. Unpublished doctoral dissertation, University of Southern California.

Zeigler, E. F., 1959. *Administration of physical education and athletics.* Englewood Cliffs, N.J.: Prentice-Hall, Inc.

Zeigler, E. F., and M. J. Spaeth, 1973. A Selected bibliography of completed research on administrative theory and practice in physical education and athletics. *Proceedings* of C.I.C. Symposium on Administrative Theory and Practice in Athletics and Physical Education. Chicago: The Athletic Institute 1973. Reprinted in Zeigler and Spaeth.

Zeigler, E. F., and M. J. Spaeth (eds.), 1974. *Administrative theory and practice in physical education and athletics.* Englewood Cliffs, N.J.: Prentice-Hall, Inc.

SUGGESTED READINGS

Barnett, M. L., 1979. The administrator as helper. *JOPER,* **50** : 42-43 (January).

Ehrle, E. B., 1979. Observations on the nature of deaning. *JOPER,* **50** : 38-39 (January).

Ilowit, R., and M. Soupios, 1979. There's got to be a better way. *JOPER,* **50** :38-39 (January).

---

*All references cited in the article but not included above may be located in the bibliography published by Zeigler and Spaeth 1973.

Parsons, T. W., 1979. What price prudence? *JOPER* **50** : 45 (January).

Richardson, H. D., 1979. Overview. *JOPER,* **50** : 35-36 (January).

Scott, P., 1979. The new administrator. *JOPER,* **50** : 40-42 (January).

Zeigler, E., 1979. The case for management theory and practice. *JOPER,* **50** : 36-37 (January).

76

Selected Research on Undergraduate Professional Physical Education Programs

Karl W. Bookwalter

In the 1950s a seminar in higher education in physical education was introduced in the school of Health, Physical Education, and Recreation at Indiana University. The author was assigned as the director of the seminar. Specific texts were either inadequate separately or did not exist in this field. A workshop approach was used with students taking a specific aspect of their interests or being assigned to areas not readily revealed in the literature.

In the later years class reports and projects were employed rather than examinations. Work in the seminar gradually led to interest in visitation to nearby institutions for group appraisals or utilizations of check lists. Subsequently, a score card evolved.

EVALUATING UNDERGRADUATE PROFESSIONAL PROGRAMS

Ross Townes (1950) was one of the first to evaluate physical education for men in black colleges in the United States. A checklist was constructed from findings in the literature that were documented and submitted to a jury of 12 authorities in the field. The investigator visited and interviewed department heads in 26 black colleges located in 11 southern states. All of the schools studied were accredited. One hundred percent had an established curriculum of professional education in physical education. Ninety-six percent were members of athletic conferences. All schools required a "C" average of graduates. Thirty-two percent of the faculty had only the baccalaureate degree. Seven percent of the enrollees were majoring in physical education. The faculty in these departments ranged from two to ten, an average of five. In summary, staffs were inadequate and curricula were less than desirable.

Several years later, Kerr (1955) evaluated nine institutions in New England, involving five states. He used a checklist based upon the standards revealed in the literature and upon validation by a jury. He found private institutions tended to have better library facilities for programs and better professional preparation programs than did the state-supported institutions. He found a general tendency for indoor facilities to be the weakest area. He concluded his study with specific recommendations for each institution.

Two years later Sauter (1957) using his own checklist, analyzed the undergraduate professional programs in institutions in Indiana. His checklist was derived from previously validated checklists or scorecards and reputable related physical education publications. A jury of 10 authorities in the field weighted the items, and item scores were derived. Twenty-one Indiana institutions, having undergraduate professional preparation programs in physical education, were visited and scored.

The institutions varied greatly in their ratings. Large schools were found to be superior to small schools, state supported schools outrated private schools, and universities outrated colleges—all on the average total score. Much variability was found among schools with regard to areas of the checklist. Faculty and staff standards rated highest, generally. Regarding curricula, the offerings in techniques (activities) rated lowest. Professional facilities rated lower than was desirable. Placement and follow-up procedures were quite inadequate as a rule. Facilities in general were lowest. The mean attainment on total score was 64.7 percent. *State* supported institutions, universities, and the *large* schools ranked highest relatively.

Errington 1958) developed a checklist by which to evaluate Canadian institutions. Standards for the checklist were determined, weighted, and scored by a selected jury of experts from Canada and the United States. (The two jury groups tended to agree.) The standards were applied by visits to 10 Canadian institutions having professional physical education programs. Canadian total programs averaged slightly higher than did the Indiana institutions in Sauter's study, although staffs rated highest in each study with Indiana rating the higher. Facilities rated lowest in the Canadian institutions. Professional education and facilities areas had the highest area of intercorrelation of .830. Item and area recommendations were made especially when attainments were below 50 percent.

With studies by Townes, Kerr, Sauter, and Errington as references along with literature in the field, students in the seminars in higher education in physical education set up standards for undergraduate professional physical education programs. These standards were changed into items for a scorecard with possible weightings. After much criticism and editing, the first edition of *A Scorecard for Evaluating Undergraduate Professional Programs in Physical Education* was published by Karl W. Bookwalter (1962).

Dollgener (1965) had been a student in a seminar in higher education in physical education and undertook to validate the first edition of this scorecard. This study was the first to analyze statistically the findings concerning Indiana institutions based upon the scorecard. Dollgener concluded that the Bookwalter scorecard was valid, reliable, and objective for its purpose. Internal consistency was found to be .661 (.796 according to the Spearman-Brown Prophecy Formula). An objectivity index of 95 percent was determined. His general findings were in high agreement with the previous study by Sauter (1957), who utilized a checklist. The mean of attainments indicated poor programs occurred within institutions with small enrollments, privately supported, liberal arts focused, and having a *department* of physical education. All 15 institutions had some strong areas and some weak ones. The *Teaching Act* ranked the highest. *Indoor Facilities* ranked lowest in the 10 areas in the scorecard. *Curriculum Policies and Practices* were rather uniform, in part due to state certification policies. This study led to the second edition of the scorcard with 10 areas, 40 subareas, 318 items, and 1000 points possible.

As a result of his study on the scorecard, Dollgener became coauthor of the revised scorecard (Bookwalter 1965). The scorecard contains essential standards for rating undergraduate professional programs of physical education. The 318 items permitted assignments of zero, minimal, good, and excellent ratings on each item. Subarea and item scores provided opportunities for short-range improvements. Area and total scores indicated major or general strength or weaknesses in the particular professional program. A pertinent bibliography was included. A percentile rating card in the third edition (Bookwalter 1967) of the scorecard permitted rating the institutions' areas and total scores in terms of national results.

A fourth edition of the scorecard (Bookwalter 1976) included a grid showing the effect of institutional types and enrollments upon total scores in terms of national results. A fifth edition is planned to include revision of some of the items and additional or improved devices for interpreting results.

Use of the Bookwalter-Dollgener Scorecard

A number of doctoral studies have been made using the Bookwalter-Dollgener scorecard. Most of these were done at institutions other than at Indiana University and many are available through University Microfilms, Ann Arbor, Michigan.

Livingston (1967) evaluated eight state-supported institutions of Alabama using the second edition Bookwalter (1965) of the scorecard. He found that universities came closest to meeting the scorecard standards and that institutions with larger enrollments generally made the higher scores. *Library-Audio-Visual* (area VII) ranked highest in attainment among the areas while the *Indoor Facilities* (area IX) ranked the lowest.

One hundred percent of possible was obtained on 10 items while four items had less than 10 percent attained on them. The item analysis led to detailed recommendations for each institution evaluated.

Buck (1968) used the second edition to evaluate 16 institutions in Oklahoma. Of the 16, five were privately supported and 11 were state supported. No significant difference was found between the private and public institutions. Private colleges generally had fewer volumes in their libraries, fewer facilities, and fewer staff members than did the public institutions of comparable enrollments.

The *Library-Audio-Visual* (area VII) was found to rank the highest while *Indoor Facilities* (Area IX) ranked the lowest. Recommendations to institutions were made on the basis of area and item analysis.

Marjorie Price (1968) evaluated 18 institutions in Missouri. She was the only one to evaluate both men's and women's programs, analyzing them separately and then as a group. She found Missouri institutions varied definitely as to the quality of their undergraduate programs. Some were found to be unqualified to offer a professional program. Men's programs tended to be slightly higher in attainment than did the women's programs.

Smaller, privately supported, liberal arts institutions tended to have the poorest programs while state-supported teachers' colleges more nearly met the standards of the scorecard. Accreditation was usually based upon the institution as a whole. The *Teaching Act* (area IV) ranked first in attainment while *Indoor Facilities* (area IX) rated last. *Staff Standards* (area II) best indicated good programs in undergraduate professional preparation in physical education.

Alfred M. Reece (1969) used the third edition of the Bookwalter-Dollgener scorecard to evaluate 26 institutions in Kentucky, Tennessee, and West Virginia. These institutions were selected randomly from an enrollment and institutional-type stratification of 58 coeducational institutions offering an undergraduate major. Two pilot institutions were visited previously to improve the objectivity and the reliability of the evaluation in the study. Above 94 percent agreement was attained in these pilot applications. Enrollment, type of institutional support, and accreditation status were determined and anonymity was maintained.

Marked differences were found. Schools having enrollments of 10,000 or more students, having a school or college of physical education, maintained by public funds, and nationally accredited, were superior to programs in other classes. The poorest programs were found in institutions enrolling less than 1000 students, liberal arts oriented, privately funded, and nonaccredited.

The area of highest attainment was the *Teaching Act* (area IV). (The evaluator felt this finding was somewhat suspect as to objectivity or validity.)

Indoor Facilities (area IX) were found to rank lowest of the 10 areas. The *Supplies and Equipment* (area VIII) was found to be the best single indicator of a good program.

A Spearman-Brown coefficient of consistency of .965 was found between odd-numbered and even-numbered items (total—318). This demonstrated very high internal reliability and was in high agreement with Dollgener's findings.

Reeves (1970) evaluated nine colleges and universities in Mississippi. The undergraduate professional physical education curriculum in each institution had been state approved. State colleges ranked the highest of the institutions. The *Library-Audio-Visual* (area VII) ranked highest among the 10 areas and the *Indoor Facilities* (area IX) ranked lowest.

The highest rho coefficient was found to be .533 between *Staff Standards* (area II) and the total score. Recommendations to each institution were based upon item analysis.

Like Reece, Douglas Wiseman (1969) did a detailed, interpretive study of professional physical education programs. He evaluated 17 institutions in New England (a population of institutions that offered an undergraduate major in physical education). Twelve of these institutions were state supported and five were privately supported. Those institutions with large enrollments tended to attain higher scores than institutions with lower enrollments. Ten institutions with schools or colleges of physical education averaged higher points than did the seven institutions with only departments of physical education.

The highest rho correlation between the area and total score was .898 for the *Service Program* (area V). The lowest correlation was in *Curriculum* (area III) with a correlation of .253, which was thought to be due to the state and national controls in this area. The area with the highest attainment was *Library-Audio-Visual* (area VII) while the lowest attainment was the *Indoor Facilities* (area IX). The highest subarea in attainment was *Institutional Affiliation* (IB) and the lowest subarea in attainment was *Housing for Students* (VIC). (Obviously a matter of costs.)

William M. McClain (1971) employed the third edition of the Bookwalter-Dollgener scorecard to evaluate 16 institutions in North Carolina. These institutions were found to be above the average of the national study. State supported institutions tended to have higher attainment than did privately supported institutions. The *Library-Audio-Visual* (area VII) ranked highest in attainment while the lowest ranking area was *Indoor Facilities* (area IX).

Edward C. Hanes (1971) limited his study to the evaluation of seven state-supported institutions in Kentucky, using the third edition of the Bookwalter-Dollgener scorecard. He reevaluated a few of the institutions formerly evaluated by Reece two years earlier. Six of the institutions were universities and one was a liberal arts college. All institutions had mean scores higher than the average of the national study. The highest attainment was in *Supplies and Equipment* (area VIII), while the area with the lowest attainment was *General Institutional and Departmental Practices* (area I). One institution had 100 percent attainment on 10 subareas and a second institution had 100 percent attainment on six areas different from the first. Institutions with larger enrollments tended to attain higher scores than did institutions with lower enrollments.

Isaac T. Moorehead (1973) used the third edition of the Bookwalter-Dollgener scorecard for a unique study at Alabama State College. His hypothesis was that the rating of the professional program in physical education would vary as the function of the status (class rank or faculty-staff) of the rater. At the same time, he hoped to provide information that would be useful in improving the professional physical education program at the university. He involved 22 sophomores, 37 juniors, 41 seniors, and 22 faculty-staff members. The subjects awarded points on the basis of the degree of compliance to which items measured up to the standards contained in the scorecard. A simple analysis of variance technique was used to compute the difference between the groups of raters for each of the 10 areas in the scorecard.

The hypothesis that the rating of the program would vary acording to the status of the rater was accepted (at the .01 or .05 level of significance) for four areas: *General Institutional and Departmental Practices* (I), *Student Services* (VI), *Supplies and Equipment* (VIII), and *Indoor Facilities* (IX). The hypothesis was rejected for the other six areas. Combined responses of the four groups did not support the hypothesis as the groups did not differ significantly. Detailed recommendations were made for the improvement of the professional program in physical education at Alabama State University. This study seems to justify self-evaluation by an institution using the Bookwalter-Dollgener scorecard.

Harry C. Stille (1974) evaluated five state-supported institutions and nine privately supported institutions in South Carolina as to their professional physical education programs for men and women. He used the third edition of the scorecard. He gave quite a complete coverage of the literature on professional preparation for physical education from 1920 on. Ten colleges were classed as liberal arts, three as universities, and one as a teachers' college. Six institutions had less than 999 students enrolled, seven had enrollments between 1000 and 4999, while one institution had an enrollment of over 10,000. Four institutions were predominantly black and 10 were predominantly white. All but one institution was coeducational. The exception enrolled only males.

Public-supported institutions tended to have better programs than did private institutions. Universities tended to be better than liberal arts colleges. Institutions with large enrollments tended to have better programs than did those with small enrollments. Predominantly white institutions tended to be better than predominantly black institutions. Among the areas, *Library-Audio-Visual* (area VII) ranked highest and *Outdoor Facilities* (area X) ranked the lowest.

James G. Pribula (1976) used the fourth edition of the Bookwalter-Dollgener scorecard to evaluate 13 institutions in Pennsylvania. State colleges and large state-supported institutions came closest to meeting the standards in the scorecard. The lower scores were attained by small, privately supported liberal arts colleges. The *Library-Audio-Visual* (area VII) ranked the highest among the areas in percent of attainment, and *Staff Standards* (area II) ranked the lowest. *Indoor Facilities* (area IX) was found to have the greatest variation between the highest and lowest raw scores. An item analysis was made within the areas below 50 percent attainment. Recommendations were made for each institution based upon the findings of the item analysis.

Beth Wray (1977) evaluated eight institutions in North Dakota and 10 institutions in South Dakota. She used the third edition of the Bookwalter-Dollgener scorecard. The means of both North Dakota and South Dakota were below the mean of the national study.

Analysis of National Findings

Most evaluators, who used the Bookwalter-Dollgener scorecard in their studies send their raw data sheets to the author of this article. Several professional workers in the field cooperated in evaluating some of the institutions and the author himself evaluated a number of institutions in the Midwest. In all, 197 institutions were evaluated. (See Fig. 76.1.)

The findings in this section of the national study were limited by the size of the groups and the opportunistic nature of the sampling.

Four of the states in the upper 10 states studied were in the Midwest (Wisconsin, Illinois, Michigan, and Ohio). Three others in the top 10 states were in the New England area (New Jersey, Massachusetts, Rhode Island). One southern state (Georgia) was in the top 10 states.

Four of the states in the lowest 10, in decreasing order (Mississippi, Tennessee, Missouri, and Alabama), were in the South. Two of the 10 lowest ranking states were in the North Central section of the country.

Eleven of the states were considered to have an inadequate sample and consideration should be given to evaluating more institutions in these states. (See Fig. 76.2.)

The *Library-Audio-Visual* (area VII) attained a percentage score of 76.93, and the *Teaching Act* (area IV) attained a percentage score of 76.31. These were the two top-ranking areas on the basis of their attained percents of possible scores. Admittedly, the evaluation of the *Teaching Act* (area IV) is largely a matter of personal opinion of the local evaluator. Higher officers at colleges and universities have little time for supervision of teaching.

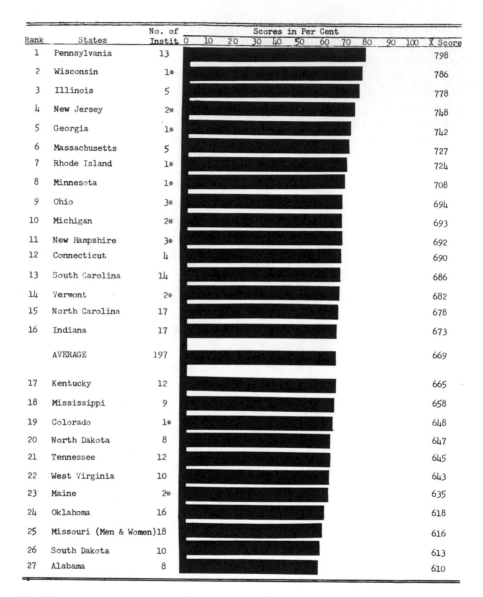

Rank	States	No. of Instit	Scores in Per Cent	X Score
1	Pennsylvania	13		798
2	Wisconsin	1*		786
3	Illinois	5		778
4	New Jersey	2*		748
5	Georgia	1*		742
6	Massachusetts	5		727
7	Rhode Island	1*		724
8	Minnesota	1*		708
9	Ohio	3*		694
10	Michigan	2*		693
11	New Hampshire	3*		692
12	Connecticut	4		690
13	South Carolina	14		686
14	Vermont	2*		682
15	North Carolina	17		678
16	Indiana	17		673
	AVERAGE	197		669
17	Kentucky	12		665
18	Mississippi	9		658
19	Colorado	1*		648
20	North Dakota	8		647
21	Tennessee	12		645
22	West Virginia	10		643
23	Maine	2*		635
24	Oklahoma	16		618
25	Missouri (Men & Women)	18		616
26	South Dakota	10		613
27	Alabama	8		610

Fig. 76.1 Rank order of 27 states on their undergraduate professional physical education programs as measured by the Bookwalter-Dollgener Score Card, 1965-1977. Institutions (197) and states (27) were sampled opportunistically.

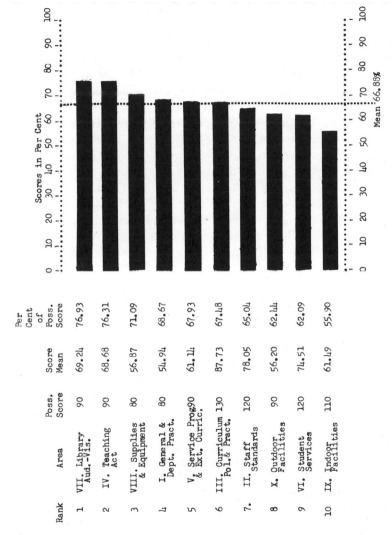

Fig. 76.2 Rank order of area attainment on the Bookwalter-Dollgener Score Card for evaluating professional programs by 197 institutions in 27 states, 1965-1977.

Judgments must be made, in part, upon student evaluation. Annual reports are of some value. Only those teachers whose behavior is reported voluntarily to the dean are noticed as a rule, and these reports are likely to be highly personal opinions, and at both extremes of the teaching spectrum. On the other hand, the *Library* and *Audio-Visual* items are quite observable. The budgets of schools or departments are probably much less for library and audio-visual equipment than for general facilities and equipment. Nevertheless, their use and need are matters of great importance to faculty and to students alike, and their use greatly enhances the quality of instruction for both. Thus, for a smaller annual outlay, as a rule, the educational functions are enhanced visibly. These facts may account validly for the position attained by this aspect.

At the lower end of attainment are *Student Services* (Area VI) with an attainment of 62.09 percent and *Outdoor Facilities* (area X) with an attainment of 55.90 percent. *Student Services* involve: (1) recruitment, selection, guidance, and counseling; (2) health services; (3) housing for students; (4) placement; and (5) follow-up and in-service education. These efforts have less visible effects, are not as uniformly accepted by students, faculty, or the public at large, and are quite expensive to maintain and to provide (due to their individual nature). These educational values, while presumably great, are actually difficult to prove. The problem increases somewhat as the number of graduates are added.

Outdoor facilities are predominantly a need of the physical education departments. When curricular demands increase, facilities are erected where woods, paths, and grass formerly existed. Modern-day transportation for students, faculty, and services must be as short as possible. Great parking spaces for faculty, staff, and students are demanded, and eventually an impasse occurs. The flattest, greenest spaces must go. Who uses these spaces most frequently? Students in athletics, intramurals, and class instruction! Eventually, we can't have what doesn't exist, so outdoor activities must either go indoors or not exist. Hence, this low score of 62.44 percent for outdoor facilities.

The rank order of attainment on the 40 subareas is found in Table 76.1. In rank order, the top five subareas in percentage scores are: IB. *Professional Affiliations* (86 percent); IVB *Personality of Instructors* (85 percent); VIIA *ment — Selection* (83 percent); and VID. *Placement* (80 percent). The reasons for these high scores are rather obvious.
reasons for these high scores are rather obvious.

In rank order, the bottom five subareas are: IIIB. *Foundation Sciences* (53 percent); IC. *Admissions* (50 percent); VIC. *Housing for Students* (48 percent); IXC. *Instructional-Recreational Facilities,* indoor (42 percent); and VIE. *Student Follow-up and In-service Education* (39 percent). Likewise, expenditures and demands on staff time and travel explained these low scores.

Table 76.1

Rank Order of the 40 Subareas in Undergraduate Professional Progams (N = 197) in Physical Education in 27 States as Measured by the Bookwalter-Dollgener Scorecard, 1965-1977

1.	IB	Professional Affiliations (12)*	86†		21.	IID	Teaching Load (26)	68
2.	IVA	Personality of Instructors (20)	85		22.	IIB	Staff Qualifications (22)	67
3.	VIIIA	Gen. Practices (Sup. and Equip.) (13)	84		23.	IIC	Staff Experiences (20)	67
4.	VIA	Recruitment, Guidance of Students (20)	83		24.	VC	Intercollegiate Athletic Programs (20)	66
5.	VID	Placement of Students (20)	80		25.	VA	Service Program (30)	66
6.	IA	Gen. Institutional Policies (24)	79		26.	VIB	Student Health Services (36)	65
7.	VIIA	Library (54)	79		27.	IXB	Indoor Administrative Facilities (23)	65
8.	IIID	Special Professional Theory (30)	78		28.	ID	Gen. Departmental Practices (22)	64
9.	VIIIB	Supplies (29)	78		29.	VIIIC	Equipment (38)	64
10.	IVB	Planning Teaching (18)	78		30.	IXD	Indoor Service Facilities (32)	61
11.	VIIB	Audio-Visual Aids (36)	75		31.	XD	Intercollegiate Athletic Facilities (22)	61
12.	IIE	Professional Status—Staff (22)	75		32.	XB	Facilities for Serv. and Prof. Tech. (27)	60
13.	IIIE	Special Prof. Techniques (32)	75		33.	XC	Outdoor Intramural Facilities (18)	58
14.	IVD	Evaluation of Teaching (17)	75		34.	IIIA	General Education (28)	53
15.	VB	Intramural Program (26)	72		35.	IIA	Number of Staff (30)	53
16.	IVC	Teaching Techniques (35)	71		36.	IIIB	Foundation Sciences (18)	53
17.	IIIC	Gen. Professional Education (22)	71		37.	IC	Admissions (22)	50
18.	XA	Outdoor Facilities—Gen. Feat. (23)	70		38.	VIC	Housing for Students (14)	48
19.	IXA	Indoor Facilities—Gen. Feat. (13)	69		39.	IXC	Instructional-Recreational Facilities (42)	42
20.	VD	Recreational Activities (14)	69		40.	VIE	Student Follow-up Services (30)	39

*Possible score.

†Percentage score.

Percentile scores. The percentile score equivalents (Table 76.2) for the total scores and area scores in this study have been revised several times due to additional samples of institutions and states. This present set of percentile norms is based upon a constantly increasing stability due to improved sample size.

Each increment from 86 institutions to 197, at this time, firmed up the *raw score* mean equivalents with respect to increments or decrements in percentile ranks. While appreciable increase in sample size could alter the distance between the percentile scores, they should not alter the *ranks* of earned raw scores when added to and recalculated for percentile raw score equivalents.

It is likewise obvious that the percentile scores have greater meaning than do their arithmetic equivalents to the average educator or administrator. The value of a score is often meaningless, especially with varying scores; whereas a rank from 100 to 0 appears to have constant meaning to the teacher or administrator.

Influence of types of organizations and sizes of enrollments. Repeated similar findings in all of the studies concerning the influence of increasing enrollment categories are merely statistical evidence as to the positive influence of enrollments in institutions upon professional physical education as a rule.

Likewise, the upward increment of scores with change in type of organization is not only logical but obvious. The *order* was set after the fact. Even single studies have found similar conditions to exist with more or less regularity.

Enrollments. The cell limits for enrollment categories vary from study to study. They were finally set as found in Table 76.3. The baseline cells for

Table 76.2
Percentile Norms for Total and Area Scores on the Bookwalter-Dollgener
Score Card for Evaluating Professional Physical Education Programs,
Based upon Scores from 197 Institutions in 27 States, 1965-1977

Percentiles	Total	I	II	III	IV	V	VI	VII	VIII	IX	X	Percentiles
99	875	73	106	121	89	83	104	89	79	101	85	99
98	825	71	104	117	88	81	102	87	78	99	81	98
96	818	69	101	112	85	78	99	85	77	95	77	96
94	804	67	99	110	84	76	96	84	76	93	75	94
92	793	66	97	105	83	—	95	83	75	91	73	92
90	784	65	96	103	82	74	93	82	74	89	72	90

88	775	64	94	102	81	73	92	81	72	87	71	88
86	768	—	93	101	80	72	91	80	71	85	70	86
84	761	—	92	100	—	—	89	—	70	83	69	84
82	754	63	91	99	79	71	88	79	69	81	68	82
80	747	62	90	98	78	70	86	—	—	79	67	80
78	741	—	89	97	—	—	85	78	68	77	—	78
76	735	61	88	96	77	69	84	77	67	75	66	76
74	729	—	87	95	76	—	83	—	66	73	65	74
72	723	60	86	—	—	68	—	76	—	72	64	72
70	718	—	85	94	75	—	82	—	65	71	63	70
68	714	—	84	—	—	67	81	75	64	69	—	68
66	709	59	—	93	74	—	80	—	—	68	62	66
64	704	—	83	—	—	—	—	74	63	67	61	64
62	700	58	82	92	73	66	79	—	—	—	60	62
60	695	—	—	—	—	—	78	73	62	66	—	60
58	691	—	81	91	—	65	—	—	61	65	59	58
56	687	57	80	—	72	64	77	72	—	63	58	56
54	685	—	—	90	—	—	76	—	60	62	57	54
52	678	—	79	89	71	63	75	71	59	60	—	52
50	674	56	—	88	—	—	—	—	—	59	56	50
48	664	—	78	—	—	62	74	70	58	—	55	48
46	661	—	77	87	70	61	—	69	57	58	—	46
44	654	55	—	86	69	—	73	—	56	57	54	44
42	647	54	76	85	—	60	—	68	55	56	53	42
40	643	—	—	—	68	—	72	—	54	55	—	40
38	638	53	75	84	—	59	—	67	—	54	52	38
36	633	—	74	83	67	—	71	—	53	53	51	36
34	628	52	73		66	58	—	66	52	52	—	34
32	623	51	72	82	—	—	70	—	51	51	50	32
30	616	—	—	81	65	57	69	65	50	50	49	30
28	610	50	71	—	64	—	68	64	49	—	—	28
26	603	49	70	80	63	56	67	63	48	49	48	26
24	597	—	68	78	62	—	66	—	47	47	47	24
22	591	48	66	77	61	55	65	62	46	46	—	22
20	585	—	65	75	60	54	63	61	45	45	46	20
18	578	47	64	74	59	53	62	60	44	43	45	18
16	571	—	63	73	57	52	61	59	43	42	44	16
14	563	46	62	72	56	51	60	58	—	41	42	14
12	555	45	61	71	55	50	58	57	42	39	41	12
10	547	44	—	70	53	48	55	56	41	38	39	10
8	539	43	60	68	51	47	53	55	40	36	36	8
6	530	42	58	67	49	45	49	53	39	33	33	6
4	520	40	55	65	44	43	45	50	35	28	30	4
2	503	38	52	61	41	42	42	44	31	25	29	2
1	491	32	50	59	39	38	41	34	24	19	23	1

increasing enrollment sizes reveal total score means of regularly increasing increments with the increments less, but positive, for the central columns.

The percentages, that column mean scores are of the population mean, increase regularly in direction, while the highest mean differences exist between categories I and II (80.29) and between categories IV and V (64.52). The smallest enrollment category mean score (582.13) differs from the largest enrollment category mean (798.56) by 216.43 points. These exceptions are regular for normally distributed large samples.

Institutional types. The vertical order of score results, by institutional types, was set to test the hypothesis that means of total score for institutions decrease regularly from schools or colleges of physical education to liberal arts colleges, with departments of professional physical education.

The institutions of school or college-of-physical-education-type, in the largest enrollment group (20,000 and up), and with a mean of 845.50, differ from the smallest liberal arts institutions with only departments of physical education ($\overline{X}$ = 581.15) by 31.26 percent of the earned scores. The former institutions are nearly a third better in score than are the latter on the average.

These schools or colleges, autonomous or under larger universities, had a total mean of 771.07 with seven cases. This was 115.28 percent of the grand mean of 668.83. *Universities* with departments of professional physical education and appropriate supportive departments averaged 709.03. This score was 106.01 percent of the grand mean of 668.83 and was based upon 71 cases. *Teachers' colleges* with departments of professional physical education and supportive departments (education, etc.) averaged 660.59 with 48 cases. This was 98.77 percent of the grand mean. *Liberal arts colleges,* usually privately supported and religiously focused, averaged 624.12 with 71 cases. This was 93.32 percent of the grand mean.

It is appropriate and sound to state that, in general and regularly (with one exception that could be explained) programs of professional physical education tend to rate higher on the average on the Bookwalter-Dollgener scorecard with the increase in order of total enrollments. Similarly, with the same single exception, better scores on the Bookwalter-Dollgener scorecard are associated with the institutional-type order—from the bottom to the top of the grid.

CONCLUSIONS

From pilot studies conducted by 12 researchers, the Bookwalter-Dollgener scorecard was found to be reliable and objective. Internal consistency on the first scorecard was found to be .796, but on the third edition of the scorecard the internal consistency was found to be .965.

States were found to vary in range of their mean attainment from 610 to 798, a difference of 188 points.

Area attainments by the 197 institutions ranged from 55.90 percent to 76.93 percent, a difference of 21.03 percent. Area VII, *Library-Audio-Visual,* was found to rank the highest while area IX, *Indoor Facilities,* was found to rank the lowest. The findings of seven researchers agreed with the ranking of area VII and nine agreed with the ranking of area IX. Subarea IB, *Professional Affiliations,* ranked the highest and area VIE, *Student Follow-up Services,* ranked the lowest.

When the 197 institutions were arranged in categories by type of organization and size of enrollment, the vertical array of cells with their sums of scores (ΣX), means ($\overline{X}$) and cases (N) provided evidence to establish the acceptance of the hypothesis that there will be, on the average, a regular increment in mean scores for type of organization of institutions and for sizes of enrollments in institutions. The arrangement in the grid was considered to be legitimate.

In no instance did a total enrollment group violate its logical order (based on the mean of the total scores). Nor did any institutional-type group deviate from the expected order on the basis of mean scores.

Only one school or college-of-physical education-type of institution was found below an enrollment of 5000. No independent liberal arts institution had an enrollment of over 10,000 in this study.

It was quite obvious that the superior organizational type of institution was the autonomous school or college of physical education and that institutions with enrollments of over 20,000 scored highest on the average on the Bookwalter-Dollgener score card.

The small (under 1000 enrollment) liberal arts college was apparently unable to meet the standards for quality professional preparation in physical education. The *mean* total score of the 197 institutions included in the study was 66.88 percent of possible score on the scorecard. The liberal arts colleges averaged only 624.12 points.

The column of total scores revealed a consistent increase in percent of the total mean achieved by the varied institutional types: liberal arts—93.32; teachers' colleges—98.77; universities—106.01; and schools or colleges of physical education—115.29. The percent the enrollment means were of the total mean also revealed a consistent increase from the lowest enrollment group to the highest enrollment group: 0-999—87.03 percent; 1000-4999—99.04 percent; 5000-9999—105.16 percent; 10,000-19,000—109.74 percent; and 20,000 and up—119.40 percent.

Table 76.3
Bookwalter-Dollgener Scorecard in Professional Education Mean Total Scores by Institutional Types and Enrollments for 197 Institutions in 27 States, 1965-1977

Types of Institutions	Institutional-enrollment categories					Totals	% type means are of total mean
	I 0-999	II 1,000-4,999	III 5,000-9,999	IV 10,000-19,999	V 20,000 and up		
School or College of Physical Education	N = 0	$\Sigma X = 786.00$ $\bar{X} = 786.00$ $N = 1$	$\Sigma X = 2162.00$ $\bar{X} = 720.67$ $N = 3$	$\Sigma X = 758.50$ $\bar{X} = 758.50$ $N = 1$	$\Sigma X = 1691.00$ $\bar{X} = 845.50$ $N = 2$	$\Sigma X = 5397.50$ $\bar{X} = 771.07$ $N = 7$	115.29%
University	$\Sigma X = 1841.00$ $\bar{X} = 613.67$ $N = 3$ ☆	$\Sigma X = 12877.50$ $\bar{X} = 677.76$ $N = 19$	$\Sigma X = 18380.50$ $\bar{X} = 706.94$ $N = 26$	$\Sigma X = 11746.25$ $\bar{X} = 734.14$ $N = 16$	$\Sigma X = 5496.00$ $\bar{X} = 785.14$ $N = 7$	$\Sigma X = 50341.25$ $\bar{X} = 709.03$ $N = 71$	106.01%
Teachers college	$\Sigma X = 2264.00$ $\bar{X} = 566.00$ $N = 4$ ☆	$\Sigma X = 22522.25$ $\bar{X} = 662.42$ $N = 34$ ☆	$\Sigma X = 6214.00$ $\bar{X} = 690.44$ $N = 9$	$\Sigma X = 708.00$ $\bar{X} = 708.00$ $N = 1$	$N = 0$	$\Sigma X = 31708.25$ $\bar{X} = 660.59$ $N = 48$ ☆	98.77%

Liberal arts colleges	$\Sigma X = 16853.25$ $\bar{X} = 581.15$ $N = 29$ ☆	$\Sigma X = 26082.00$ $\bar{X} = 652.05$ $N = 40$ ☆	$\Sigma X = 1377.50$ $\bar{X} = 688.75$ $N = 2$ ✓	$N = 0$	$N = 0$	$\Sigma X = 44312.75$ $\bar{X} = 624.12$ $N = 71$ ☆ 93.32%
Totals	$\Sigma X = 20958.25$ $\bar{X} = 582.13$ $N = 36$ ☆	$\Sigma X = 62267.75$ $\bar{X} = 662.42$ $N = 94$ ☆	$\Sigma X = 28134.00$ $\bar{X} = 703.35$ $N = 40$ ✓	$\Sigma X = 13212.75$ $\bar{X} = 734.04$ $N = 18$ ✓	$\Sigma X = 7187.00$ $\bar{X} = 798.56$ $N = 9$ ✓	$\Sigma X = 131759.75$ $\bar{X} = 668.83$ $N = 197$ 100%
% enrollment means are of total mean	87.03%	99.04%	105.16%	109.74%	119.40%	100%

☆ = Below mean   ✓ = Above mean

515

RECOMMENDATIONS

It is recommended that the states indicated as being inadequately sampled and those states not sampled at all be studied as to their ratings on the Bookwalter-Dollgener scorecard on adequate samples of institutions having professional physical education programs, for the sake of the state, and to complete the total state evaluation of professional preparation in physical education.

REFERENCES

Bookwalter, K. W., 1962. *A scorecard for evaluating undergraudate professional programs in physical education,* Author, Bloomington, Indiana.

Bookwalter, K. W., and R. J. Dollgener, 1965. *A scorecard for evaluating undergraduate professional programs in physical education,* revised edition, Authors, Bloomington, Indiana.

————, 1967. *A scorecard for evaluating undergraduate professional programs in graduate professional programs in physical education,* Third Edition, Authors, Bloomington, Indiana.

————, 1976. *A scorecard for evaluating undergraudate professional programs in graduate professional programs in physical education,* Fourth Edition, Authors, Bloomington, Indiana.

Buck, C. R., 1968. *An evaluation of the undergraduate professional programs in physical education in Oklahoma colleges and universities,* Ed.D. dissertation, University of Arkansas, Little Rock.

Dollgener, R. J., 1965. *A critical appraisal of a selected scorecard for evaluating undergraduate professional physical education programs in Indiana,* P.E.D. dissertation, Indiana University, Bloomington.

Errington, J., 1958. *An evaluation of undergraduate professional preparation in physical education for men in Canada,* P.E.D. dissertation, Indiana University, Bloomington.

Hanes, E. C., 1971. *An evaluation of the undergraduate professional preparation programs in physical education for state supported institutions of higher education in Kentucky,* Ed.D. dissertation, Indiana University, Bloomington.

Kerr, R. W., 1955. *The status of undergraduate professional preparation in physical education for men in New England colleges and universities,* P.E.D. dissertation, Indiana University, Bloomington.

Livingston, M. W., 1967. *An evaluation and analysis of undergraduate professional preparation programs in physical education for men in state colleges and universities of Alabama,* Ed.D. dissertation, University of Alabama, University.

McClain, W. M., 1971. *An evaluation and analysis of the undergraduate professional programs in physical education for men in colleges and universities of North Carolina,* Ed.D. dissertation, University of Alabama, University.

Moorehead, I. T., 1973. *An evaluation study of the undergraduate program in physical education at Alabama State University, 1972-1973,* Ed.D. disseration, University of Alabama, University.

Pribula, J. G., 1976. *An evaluation of undergraduate professional programs in physical education for selected colleges and universities in Pennsylvania,* Ph.D. dissertation, University of Maryland, College Park.

Price, M. A., 1968. *An evaluation of the undergraduate professional preparation programs in physical education in Missouri colleges and universities,* Ed.D. dissertation, University of Missouri, Columbia.

Reece, A. M., 1969. *A critical evaluation of undergraduate professional preparation in physical education in selected coeducational institutions in Kentucky, Tennessee, and West Virgiania,* P.E.D. dissertation, Indiana University, Bloomington.

Reeves, W. E., 1970. *An evaluation of the undergraduate professional preparation programs in physical education in selected Mississippi colleges and universities,* University of Alabama, University.

Sauter, W., 1957. *An evaluation of the undergraduate professional preparation in selected colleges and universities in Indiana,* P.E.D. dissertation. Indiana University, Bloomington.

Stille, H. C., 1974. *A comparison of the undergraduate professional physical education programs in colleges and universities in South Carolina,* Ed.D. dissertation, University of Alabama, University.

Townes, R., 1950. *A study of professional eduction in physical education in selected negro colleges,* P.E.D. dissertation, Indiana University, Bloomington.

Wiseman, D. C., 1969. *A critical evaluation of undergraduate professional preparation in physical education in selected colleges and universities for men and women in New England,* unpublished P.E.D. dissertation, Indiana University, Bloomington.

Wray, B., 1977. *An analysis and evaluation of undergraduate professional preparation in physical education in seventeen institutions of higher learning in North Dakota and South Dakota,* Ed.D. dissertation, University of Kansas, Lawrence.

77

Physical Education Facilities, Equipment, and Supplies

Roy J. Keller

Programs in physical education are dependent upon an availability of proper facilities, equipment, and supplies. As the myriad of programs are varied and far reaching, the necessary physical commodities include innumerable objects that must be obtainable if programs are to succeed.

Although the business aspects of purchasing and construction often take these tasks at least partly out of the hands of physical educators, the input of the program specialist whether it involves a teacher or researcher, is most desirable. Information offered here is designed to assist the physical educator in the wise planning for and purchasing of facilities, equipment, and supplies.

The areas within which the physical educator must obtain necessary accommodations would be inclusive of the program categories listed below; information offered here is designed to aid in the procurement of necessary materials and facilities.

Although it would be impossible to list all types of physical education equipment and supplies, it is incumbent upon administrators to procure at least the necessary equipment and supplies for the following program areas:

aquatics
gymnastics
wrestling
laboratory
track and field
field games
material reproduction machines
statistics laboratory
tennis courts
golf courses
concessions
training rooms
all-weather surfaces
ice activities
gymnasium activities
archery and/or riflery

lighting
equestrian
outdoor areas—
    parks and/or playgrounds
audiovisual equipment

The securing of equipment and supplies should ordinarily entail as a starting point the review of the *Thomas Manufacturers' Index;* this very precise system of indices provides a record of all products manufactured in the United States. In 11 volumes covering thousands of pages, the *Thomas Index* offers: (1) products and services listed alphabetically (volumes 1-6); (2) company names, addresses with zip codes, and telephone numbers listed alphabetically with branch offices, capital ratings, and company officials (volume 7); (3) brand names, index to products and services (volume 8); and (4) catalogues of companies appearing alphabetically and cross indexed in the first eight volumes (volumes 9-11).

Anyone interested in any products whatever, such as a diving board for example, could look this item up alphabetically and order the proper catalogue or request the necessary prices. *The Thomas Register* and *Thomas Register Catalogue File* is published annually and may be obtained by writing: Thomas Publishing Company; 461 Eighth Avenue; New York, NY 10001.

An example of a process that may be used in becoming more familiar with the availability of equipment, supplies and services would be to visit exhibitions provided at state, district, and national professional association conventions. The *National Conventioneer,* for example, which is issued at the national conventions of the AAHPERD, is a reference book that provides conferees with an organized compendium of suppliers' brochures, catalogues, and descriptive literature on products and services relevant to their fields of interest. Suppliers are given the opportunity to highlight their most innovative products and to educate the various registrants. This document may be obtained by writing: National Conventioneer; P.O. Box B; Allison Park, PA; 15101.

It is also possible to obtain helpful information from brochures and other documents provided by certain individual manufactureres and sellers of physical education or sports equipment and supplies. The information pertains to material comparison, maintenance, storage, and various logistical factors.

Another reference that warrants special mention is the publication by the Athletic Institute, which is listed with other references on the subject and includes detailed explanations of procurement, budgeting, accountability, and maintenance. The "calendar of buying" is part of this very pertinent information; dimensions of time and scheduling govern prices, availability, and delivery.

On of the specific areas mentioned previously, research, brings attention to two categories, those of research laboratory and research equipment. Cross reference is made here to another volume of this *Encyclopedia* where the research laboratory is fully described. In addition, reference is made to *Research Laboratory Equipment,* prepared annually by the Research Council of the AAHPERD.

Recommended books in the areas of facilities, equipment, and supplies are presented in the Suggested Readings below. The facilities referred to would include such accommodations as fields, gymnasia, playgrounds, and other areas.

SUGGESTED READINGS

AAHPER, 1977. *Planning facilities for athletics, physical education and recreation.* Washington, D.C.: AAHPER.

American Public Health Association, 1957. *Recommended practice for design, equipment, and operation of swimming pools and other public bathing places.* New York: American Public Health Association.

Athletic Goods Manufacturers Association, 1962. *How to budget, select, and order athletic equipment.* Chicago: Athletic Goods Manufacturers Association.

Athletic Institute, 1968. *College and university facilities guide for health, physical education, recreation, and athletics,* by participants in the National Facilities Conference, Chicago: The Athletic Institute.

————, 1960. *Equipment and supplies for athletics, physical education, and recreation,* Chicago: Athletic Institute.

————, 1965. *Planning areas and facilities for health, physical education, and recreation.* Chicago: Athletic Institute and AAHPER (NEA, Washington D.C.).

Baldwin, K. G., 1957. Take care of your athletic equipment. *JOHPER,* **27** :104 (January).

Bowerman, B., 1961. The track surface of the future, *JOHPER,* **32** : 67-68 (January).

Brewster, S. F., 1963. *Programming, planning, and construction of college and university buildings.* Provo, Utah: Brigham Young University Press.

Bronzan, R. T., 1974. *New concepts in planning and funding athletic, physical education, and recreational facilities.* St. Paul, Minnesota: Phoenix Intermedia, Inc.

Buikema, K. A., 1976. Centennial Education Park. *JOPER* 47 : 20 (September).

California State Department of Education, 1956. *Planning of shower, locker, and dressing facilities for California schools.* Sacramento: California State Department of Education, Bulletin No. 53 (November).

Canadian Red Cross Society, 1968. *Waterfront construction.* Ontario Division, Water Safety Services.

Council for National Cooperation in Aquatics, 1969. *Swimming pools; a guide to their planning, design, and operation,* edited by M. A. Gabrielsen. Fort Lauderdale, Florida: Hoffman Publications.

Council on Facilities, Equipment and Supplies, AAHPER, 1972. *Dressing rooms and related service facilities,* Washington, D. C.: AAHPER.

Crawford, W. H., 1963. *A guide for planning indoor facilities for college physical education.* New York: Bureau of Publications. Teachers College, Columbia University.

Delameter, J. B., 1963. *The design of outdoor physical education facilities for colleges and schools.* New York: Bureau of Publications, Teachers College, Columbia University.

Flynn, R. B., et al 1975. Focus on facilities. *JOPER* **46** : 23 (April).

Focus on facilities, 1962. *JOHPER,* **33** : 33-48 (April).

Illinois State Public Health department, 1970. *Sanitary requirements for swimming pools,* Springfield, Illinois: State of Illinois, Circular No. 4.102 (December 15).

Keller, R. J. Making the most of your facilities. *JOHPER,* **42** : 26-28 (June).

_____, 1973. *Modern management of facilities for physical education and athletics.* Champaign: Stipes Publishing Company.

_____, 1970. Planning collegiate tennis facilities, *Athletic journal,* **50** : 32, 110-111 (March).

Kenney, H. E., 1964. Facilities standards for physical education in colleges and universities, *Physical educator,* **21** : 151-152 (December).

Lynch, K., 1966. *Site planning.* Cambridge, Mass.,: M.I.T. Press.

Meyer, K. L., 1948. *The purchase, care, and repair of athletic equipment.* St. Louis: Educational Publisher.

Peterson, 1963. *A guide for planning the field house at a college or school physical education facility.* New York: Columbia University.

Planning and building the golf course., 1967. Chicago: National Golf Foundation.

Scott, H. A., and Westkaemper, R. B., 1958. *From program to facilities in physical education.* New York: Harper and Brothers.

Stanley, D. K., 1958. *References on facilities and equipment for health education, physical education, and recreation.* Washington D. C: AAHPER.

Terry, W. L., 1959. *A guide for planning the school and college swimming pool and natatorium.* New York: Columbia University.

Tips on getting the equipment and supplies you want under the bid system, 1969. *Physical education newsletter,* **2** : 2 (October 1).

United States Lawn Tennis Association, 1966. *Tennis courts: construction, maintenance, and equipment.* New York: The Association.

University of Illinois, 1960. College of Physical Education Building and Fields Committee. *A study of the present status, future needs, and recommended standards regarding space used for health, physical education, recreation, and athletics.* Champaign, Illinois: Stipes Publishing Co. (May).

78

A Model Physical Education Building

William A. R. Orban

Montpetit Hall is located at the University of Ottawa, Ontario, Canada, and has won two architectural awards for the category of educational buildings. It was functionally designed to provide for the conduct of a comprehensive academic program and to serve the sports and physical recreational needs of the university community and the community at large.

The primary consideration in designing the building was for academic needs, which would permit the conduct of academic activities without interference by its service function. Nevertheless, consideration was given to provide for sports and physical recreational needs within the academic scope of the design. The manner in which this was achieved is indicated below by some of the features of the building.

ACADEMIC ACTIVITIES

Research. The 5000 square feet of research laboratories provide an exclusive opportunity for research and graduate studies in the biochemistry, bio-mechanics, psychomotor learning, and exercise physiology subdivisions of the discipline. The laboratories are situated on the same level, adjacent to the professors' offices, and separate from the general public traffic using the building.

The open flexible design and the most up-to-date equipment available provide an opportunity to investigate physical performance under a variety of controlled conditions. Features of the laboratory include a sound-proof room with a one-view observation window to observe isolated performance, a special glass water tank to study aquatic activities, and a computerized treadmill installed in a floor well. In addition to the research laboratories for controlled observation, the entire building was designed to be a clinical laboratory that would provide the opportunity to study individual and group performance under natural, competitive conditions. This is achieved by providing special features in each of the activity areas, which are equipped with special apparatus to enable the recording of movement and physiological

Fig. 78.2 The front entrance to the building showing the windows of the offices and seminar rooms. Courtesy of Communications Center, University of Ottawa.

Fig. 78.2 Biokinetics laboratory, showing computerized treadmill and monitoring, recording, and analyzing equipment for measuring physical work capacity and physical stress. Courtesy of Communications Center, University of Ottawa.

Fig. 78.3 Biokinetic laboratory, showing the water tank which is used for measuring energetics of swimming, flotation, buoyancy, and body density. Courtesy of Communications Center, University of Ottawa.

responses and which can be transmitted to a central area for analysis. For example, the swimming pool has a mobile self-propelled apparatus that can follow a competitive swimmer from the pool deck taking four simultaneous and continuous visual recordings from different angles above or below the surface of the water. The apparatus can also be used to study various physiological parameters under competitive conditions.

Instruction. The 3000 square feet of demonstration laboratories contain basically the same equipment as the research laboratories but are less sophisticated and more durable to enable undergraduates the opportunity to gain the maximum benefits. Adjacent to this undergraduate laboratory is a demonstration amphitheatre into which various units such as treadmill, tanks, etc. may be moved for group demonstration purposes. Ten classrooms of different sizes and design are located close to the professors' offices, student lounges, and laboratories. Several classrooms are equipped with rearview projection screens to facilitate the study of movement. Every consideration has been given to provide the student with the latest devices for the learning of physical skills. For example, the 10 meter diving tower is equipped with a built-in bubbling machine, which provides a soft air cushion for the novice practicing his or her dives.

SPORTS AND RECREATION ACTIVITIES

Competitive sports. To ensure that the best performers could be observed and studied in the building, all indoor courts and areas were designed to meet international standards. Consequently this provides for all levels of competition in Canadian indoor sports. The three gymnasia, which can be separated by sound-proof motorized walls or used as one large area, provide for a combination of nine badminton, five volleyball, one basketball, one European handball, and one indoor tennis court, and palestra for gymnastics.

A seating capacity of 5000 is accommodated by portable bleachers that can be quickly changed by an air cushion carrier, thus providing a great deal of flexibility to the use of this space. These features and the fact that all activity areas, including a 50-meter swimming pool, a 10-meter diving tower, a weight training room, a combatives room, and six handball and squash courts are all located on the same level as the locker areas and the training room and completely separated from the academic levels, provide an optimum setting for control and conduct of the competitive program.

Physical recreation. The building was designed to provide a comfortable and pleasant atmosphere for all participants, to prevent the accumulation of odors common to locker rooms, and to provide a generally more comfortable temperature and humidity. To this end the high rate of air exchange in locker and activity areas and the dehumidification of the pool deck area with heated benches around the pool provide for the comfort of the participant. The bright and live color combinations found in every area from the locker room to the research laboratories create a pleasant atmosphere in the building. This is further enhanced by the openness of the spaces, particularly of the foyer corridors, that produces a kind of inviting, unlimited feeling of space and freedom and joy of physical effort.

79

The Administration of Athletics in American Colleges and Universities

Edward J. Shea

The administration of programs of athletics within educational institutions must rest upon the basic assumption that athletics have a legitimate place in the educational program; that if properly conducted under competent educational leadership, functioning within a framework of planned educational outcomes for the participant, and supported by the basic tenets of a democratic culture, they can be used to yield values that contribute directly in aiding institutions to meet their primary educational purpose.

The acceptance or rejection of this assumption constitutes the basis for extreme controversial issues that develop from and surround administrative practices in athletics. Acceptance of the assumption is based on the expectation that: (1) the purposes of athletics, when shown to be clearly educational, contribute to the purposes of education, and (2) the policies that guide the administration of athletics will be the same as, or similar to, those policies that guide other activities and programs of an institution of learning.

An overview of the literature reveals that the administration of athletics programs must be viewed within the context of the culture in which they function and within the totality of societal conditions that affect the administration of education at any particular level. The freedoms of the individual in a democratic culture, bolstered by the maintenance of a free and competitive

Fig. 79.1 Michigan Stadium reflects social, economic, and political forces of institutions of higher education. Courtesy of University of Michigan, Ann Arbor, Michigan.

enterprise system yet restrained by a moral and ethical code of conduct expected of citizens in that culture, represent the basic context within which the administrative process functions. The social, economic, and political forces of the culture that operate on the institution are certain to affect each of its constituent parts, including athletics.

The projection of literature related to the administration of athletics from research studies, athletics organizations, professional education groups, investigations and surveys, texts on administration in physical education and athletics, and administration in higher education, cluster around three major periods. These include: (1) the years following the 1929 Reports of the Carnegie Foundation For the Advancement of Teaching: (2) the 1952 Reports of The American Council On Education, the North Central Association of Colleges and Secondary Schools and other educational bodies; and (3) those of the early 1970s during which economic, social, and political changes took place throughout American life generally and educational institutions specifically.

It is of particular interest to note that widespread concern was expressed continually for the administration of athletics during the first three decades of the 1900s. The problems indicated by Sargent (1906) and by Hetherington (1907) were representative of those experienced constantly during the 30-year period. The appearance of these problems in the literature of athletics and educational organizations were to form the basis for comparison with the problems that existed throughout the ensuing century.

It was Savage's (1929, 1932) reports, however, that stimulated the production of a variety of research studies and other forms of publications. His investigation, conducted under the sponsorship of the Carnegie Foundation for the Advancement of Teaching, consisted of the most complete study related to intercollegiate athletics that has ever been published.

This report describes the growth of college athletics, the development of its modern amateur status, administrative control, participation and its results, the hygiene of athletics training, status of the coach, extramural relationships, recruiting and subsidizing, the press and its influence in athletics, and the values in athletics. The report revealed the continuing existence of the same conditions and problems indicated by Sargent and Hetherington earlier in the century. Its main conclusions were: (1) that colleges lacked a well-defined policy for the control of athletics; (2) that much extravagance was prevalent in athletics administration; (3) that there was poor control of scholastic eligibility; and (4) that faculty control, while ineffective, would still seem to be necessary.

Research studies utilizing an objective and systematic approach toward evaluating intercollegiate athletics standards and policies were published by Hughes (1932) and Galligan (1937). The refinement of standards and their application for evaluating administrative practices related to eligibility, business management, status of coaches, management of contests, athletics committee functions, schedules, and awards led to the establishment of recommendations to be used as guides for administration.

Master's theses by Wright (1935), Wagoner (1936), Robertson (1936), VanBibber (1937), and Bailey (1941), were concerned with the organization, administration, and control of intercollegiate athletics in specific institutions, or with general problems. These studies involved varying degrees of evaluation and were productive of standards and recommendations for improvement in the areas of budget, schedules, officials, staff, faculty committees, student managers, equipment, facilities, ticket sales, publicity, program of sports, awards, trips, and records.

Theses and dissertations tracing the organization, development, and functions of athletic conferences were written by Vickers (1938), Voltmer (1936), and Woerlein (1938). These productions were important in view of their relationship to efforts to regulate and control competition. They provided a comprehensive view of background material that contributed to a more extensive and proper perspective of the existence of problems from the beginning of the growth of athletics in colleges. They revealed the existence of early problems; the enforcement of policies that in content and meaning as early as 1906 were similar to those recommended and adopted in recent years; and the significance of the contributions of athletics conferences to education generally.

Reeves (1951) and Russell and Reeves (1933) surveyed the administrative practices in athletics programs of 35 church-related colleges and member colleges of the North Central Association of Colleges and Secondary Schools, respectively. The investigators offered primary recommendations based upon the principles of institutional or faculty control of intercollegiate athletics, the status and tenure of coaching personnel, protection from outside influences, and the moral conduct of the programs.

A voluminous quantity of textbook and periodical literature produced by physical educators followed the Carnegie Report. Almost without exception that literature presented recommendations or implications for recommendations for the proper educational conduct of athletics programs. Of particular significance were the writings of the joint authors of Williams and Hughes (1937) and Hughes and Williams (1944). These authors presented a most comprehensive treatment of the problems and place of athletics in education. Both presented lengthy lists of principles and policies with much documentation to substantiate them.

Other physical educators as a group remained steadfast in their recognition of the principle of establishing athletics as a part of a broad program of physical education complete with educational implications that such a status assumed. McCloy (1940), Mitchell (1948), Nash (1942), Voltmer (1949), Williams (1948), and Harmon (1940), are representative of that professional group in that earlier period.

The athletics scandals of the early 1950s stimulated the production of quantities of literature that rivaled the 1929 report of Savage and subsequent publications. The Report of the Special Committee on Athletic Policy of the American Council on Education (1952) opened the floodgates for research, surveys, and investigations, statements from authoritative athletic and educational professional groups, and articles and texts, all treating the subject of athletics administration.

The Report of the American Council on Education was adopted on February 16, 1952. The evaluative deliberations of the 11 college and university presidents who composed the committee were devoted to existent practices weighed subjectively in light of educational purposes. The report proposed remedies related to four primary objectives: (1) to relieve external pressures, (2) to insure institutional control, (3) to suggest general standards of acceptable practices, and (4) to invoke measures of enforcement as a guide for institutions desirous of upholding proper standards. The recommended remedies took the form of principles and policies pertaining to institutional control, status of coaching personnel, status of faculty athletics boards, admission standards, student progress toward achieving a degree, freshmen participation, procedures for disbursement of financial scholarships and grants-in-aid, release of data concerning athletic-playing personnel, limitations of playing and practice sessions, recruitment of athletes, provision of opportunity to all students for participation, and the scheduling of contests with comparable opponents.

The report that was accepted and approved by the Executive Committee of the American Council on Education, was recommended to the National Collegiate Athletic Association, the National Association of Intercollegiate Athletics, the regional accrediting associations, and the various athletics conferences. The report received widespread approbation from educators as a model toward which institutions concerned with the proper place and conduct of athletics might look for guidance and direction.

Various regional accrediting associations were prompted to action by the Report of the American Council on Education. Of primary importance were the statements of the Commission on Colleges and Universities of the North Central Association (1952). Its Revised Manual of Accrediting, in addition to the items covered in the American Council on Education Report, deals in greater detail with such factors as the place of intercollegiate athletics in education, standards of academic work, use of athletics prominence for public support, emphasis on winning teams, relationship of alumni and public to the administration of athletics, academic requirements as they relate to grades, influence of physical activity on study schedules and class attendance, health of students, sportsmanship, cooperation with athletic associations, and finally, relations with secondary schools.

Other regional accrediting associations, including the Middle States, New England, Western, Northwest, and Southern, produced similar statements of evaluation of athletics programs or acquiesced with statements of the American Council on Education.

The research studies of Barnes (1956) and Shea (1954) in this period are particularly noteworthy because they performed a critical evaluation of the policies governing intercollegiate athletics of a national scope. Unlike other research, which was limited to the study of analyzing administrative practices and policies in selected conferences or colleges, or which considered current practices controlling athletic administration, these two studies performed an in-depth task through the development of criteria for evaluation. Following the development of criteria, Shea critically evaluated the policies of 15 athletics conferences and the policies recommended for the control of athletics by educational professional groups. Additionally the latter study established principles to guide the formation of policies whose purposes would be compatible with the purposes of higher education.

These evaluative studies embraced, among others, the administrative policies of institutional control and responsibility, departmental status of coaching staff, admission standards, academic requirements, residence requirements, recruitment of athletes, financial aid and subsidization, limitation of sports seasons, control of the number and frequency of contests, scheduling, standards of conduct, relations with secondary schools, public relations, and years of competition.

The doctoral dissertations of Healey (1952), Irace (1958), and Pearson (1958) were concerned with a wide spectrum of administrative practices in athletics in selected colleges.

The research studies produced following the 1950s were varied in nature and purpose. Hoy (1966) and Powell (1964) were concerned principally with the influences of control factors, while the studies of Hohman (1971), Hutter (1970), Mears (1970), and Woodbury (1966) related to administrative policies in selected institutions, to attitudinal effects on the behavior of administrators of athletics, or to the philosophical relationships between athletics and physical education. McNutt's thesis (1967) is somewhat noteworthy in this period because it focused upon the intercollegiate athletic programs for women as a departure from the long line of research studies related only to the men's programs.

As would be expected, however, a tremendously large quantity of literature erupted immediately prior to and following the Report of the American Council of Education. These publications issued from educational professional organizations, athletic organizations and individuals acting singly or on behalf of an association or agency. The most pronounced were: the AAHPER (1959, 1961, 1962, 1963, Archer 1952, Duncan 1962), the National College Physical Education Association for Men (McDonough 1952), the Joint Committee of the National Association of Secondary School Principals, National Federation of State High School Athletic Associations, and the

National Association of Secondary School Principals (Elicker 1952), the American Council on Education (1952), the North Central Association (Aigler 1954, 1954: Hughes 1953), the National Education Association (Ed. Policies Comm. 1954), the Presidents Conferences of the Mid-American Conference (Mid-Am. Conf. 1952), Southern University Conference (1952) and Ivy League (Danzig 1954), the National Association of Collegiate Commissioners (1951), the National Collegiate Athletic Association (1965), the National Association of Intercollegiate Athletics (1965), and the National Federation of State High School Athletic Associations (1966). The literature emanating from these organizations is of extreme significance to students and researchers in the administration of athletics because it represents the foundation upon which educational programs of intercollegiate athletics are strongly recommended.

The textbook literature of Scott (1951, 1956) was significant during this period. He set forth in an educational frame the background upon which sound administrative policies, in practice as well as theory, were to be based to ensure viable programs of competitive sport within the broad program of physical education. Oberteuffer (1952), like Scott, contributed a sound philosophical basis for the educational operation of competitive sports.

The most comprehensive presentation of administrative policies and specific guidelines for administrative personnel who seek educational direction for college athletics was published by Shea and Wieman (1967). The policy statements were divided into 19 divisions, which appeared as separate chapters. All policy statements were supported with authoritative documentation.

The investigations and surveys of Edmonson (1954), Hughes (1953), and Mitchell (1954) assist in completing background information upon which decisions related to administrative practices must be formed.

It would be negligent for a treatment of the subject of administration of athletics not to include in the record the significant writings of individuals who contributed substantially to the periodical literature of this period. Highly related to the subject are the reports of Geiger (1953), Johnson (1953), Lumley (1953), Metcalf (1953), Nichols (1953), Randall (1953), Stetson (1953), and Turner (1953). These reports on individual college programs in actual operation were solicited and reported by the North Central Association. The reports of Aigler (1957, 1957, 1954, 1954, 1957) represent major contributions, particularly his reports as chairman of the committee on athletics of the North Central Association. Because of the significant representative position held by a number of authors, their writings are highly supportive of desirable administrative practices in athletics programs. These include Archer (1951, 1952, 1954), Corbally (1958), Duer (1960), Howes (1957), Pattillo (1952), Plant (1961), and Reeves (1951). Added weight is accorded their views and recommendations because of the authoritative, educational, and athletics organizations they represent.

In recognition of one of the fundamental factors involved in the administration of athletics, the Joint Committee on Phyiscal Education and Athletics of the AAHPER (1970), Havel (1953), Healy (1959), and Lawther (1965), projected studies on the professional preparation, qualification requirements, and the role and status of athletics coaches.

Finally evidence of the stirring of the souls of men was demonstrated in writings of Gardner (1960), Hein (1961), Hughes (1950), Marco (1960), Marsh (1952), Moore (1954), Reed (1963), and Williams (1937) all of whom treated the subject of the place of athletics in education.

The 1970s presented the administration of intercollegiate athletics with a set of problems somewhat different than those of previous years. The economic, political, and social conditions the nation encountered permeated into the functions of all institutions and programs. In a time when athletics experienced an unprecedented growth, its administration confronted financial constraints and demands for equalization in structural arrangements and in women's athletics.

The literature treating the administration of athletics in the 1980s will record these events and reflect the changes and solutions to problems in (it is hoped) a manner more consistent with educational objectives than formerly.

REFERENCES

Aigler, R. W., 1957. Control of intercollegiate athletics at Michigan, *The quarterly review of the Michigan alumnus* **43** : 317-327.

_____, 1957. Intercollegiate athletics and education, *The quarterly review of the Michigan alumnus,* **44** : 19-27.

_____, Chairman, 1954. Report of the committee on athletics to the Commission on Colleges and Universities. *The North Central Association quarterly* **29** : 189-196.

_____, Chairman, 1954. Memorandum regarding intercollegiate athletics: a tentative statement on intercollegiate athletics. *The North Central Association quarterly* **29** : 197-201.

_____, 1957. Amateurism and intercollegiate athletics, *The quarterly review of the Michigan alumnus,* **43** 185-196.

AAHPER, 1962, Athletic administration in colleges and universities, Washington, D.C., AAHPER.

_____, 1959. Athletic Directors National Conference, Washington, D.C., AAHPER.

_____, 1961. *Spectator sportsmanship: how to improve it.* Washington, D.C., AAHPER.

_____, 1963. Values in sport: a report of a national conference. Washington, D.C., AAHPER.

REFERENCES

American Council on Education, 1952. Council action on athletic policy; a report of the special committee on athletic policy, *The educational record*, **33** : 246-255.

_____, 1952. Improving the administration of intercollegiate athletics: a symposium, *The educational record*, **33** : 439-470.

Archer, J. K., Ed., 1954. Athletic policies in high school and college. *The bulletin of the National Association of Secondary School Principals*, **38** : 197-200.

_____, 1952. Standards in athletics for boys and girls: Report as Chairman Joint Committee on Standards for Interscholastic Athletics of the NASSP, the AAHPER, and the NFSHSAA, *The bulletin of the National Association of Secondary School Principals*, **36** : 322-325.

_____,1951. Chairman, Standards in athletics for boys in secondary schools; a report by the Joint Committee on Standards for Interscholastic Athletics for Boys in Secondary Schools, *The bulletin of the National Association of Secondary School Principals*, **35** : 74-82.

Bailey, J. W., 1941. Study pertaining to the organization and administration of intercollegiate athletics in colleges and universities for negroes. Springfield, Mass: Master's thesis, Springfield College.

Barnes, S. E., 1956. Criteria for evaluating the administration of intercollegiate athletics. Columbus: Ph.D. dissertation. Ohio State University.

Corbally, J. E., 1958. The problems of high school and college athletics, *The bulletin of the National Association of Secondary School Principals*, **42:** 127-129.

Danzig, A., 1954. Revised agreement among eight ivy colleges, *The New York Times*, February 11, p. 38.

Duer, A. O., 1960. Basic issues of intercollegiate athletics, *JOHPER*, **31** : 22-24.

Duncan, R. O., 1962. Chairman, Athletics in education: a platform statement of the Division of Men's Athletics of the American Association of Health, Physical Education, and Recreation, *JOHPER*, **33** : 24-27, 59.

Edmondson, J. B., and E. Youngert, 1954. Report on athletics submitted to the Commission on Colleges and Universities, *The North Central Association Quarterly*, **29** : 185-188.

Educational Policies Commission, 1954. *School athletics, problems, and policies*. Washington, D.C.: National Education Association.

Elicker, P. E., 1952. How to meet the unethical practices of colleges and alumni in soliciting star athletes in secondary schools, *The bulletin of the National Association of Secondary School Principals*, **36** : 198-199.

Galligan, G. E., 1937. A critical analysis of certain current practices in athletics for men in state teacher's colleges, New York: Ed.D. dissertation, New York University.

Gardner, F. H., 1960. The place of intercollegiate athletics in higher education, *The journal of higher education*, **31** : 364-368.

Geiger, I. J., 1953. The athletic program at Massachusetts Institute of Technology, *The North Central Association Quarterly*, **27:** 362-369.

Harmon, J. M., 1940. Educational principles in administering intercollegiate athletics, *Education* **60** (April) : 513-516.

Havel, R. C., 1953. The professional status of head coaches of athletics in colleges and universities. *Research Quarterly* **24:** 8-17.

Healey, W. A., 1952. An analysis of the administrative practices in competitive athletics in selected colleges of the midwest. Unpublished P.E.D. dissertation. Bloomington: Indiana University.

———, 1959. Educational qualifications of college coaches. *The Journal of Teacher Education* **10:** 455-457.

Hein, F. V., 1961. Athletics in education, *American Academy of Physical Education.* 7 : 17-28.

Hetherington, C. W., 1907. The organization and administration of athletics. Washington, D.C.: *National Education Association Proceedings.*

Hohman, H. R., 1971. An analysis of administrative policies of intercollegiate athletics in the rocky mountain states, Bloomington: P.E.D. dissertation, Indiana University.

Howes, R. F., 1957. Athletic scholarships are harmful, *Association of American Colleges Bulletin,* **43** : 464-467.

Hoy, J. T., 1966. Current practices in the control of intercollegiate athletics in selected conferences. P.E.D. dissertation. Bloomington: Indiana University.

Hughes, O., 1953. The recruitment of athletes: report of the activities committee of the commission on secondary schools, *The North Central Association Quarterly,* **28** : 218-228.

Hughes, W. L., 1932. The administration of health and physical education for men in colleges and universities. Unpublished doctoral dissertation. New York: Teachers College, Columbia University.

———, 1950. The place of athletics in school physical education program. *JOHPER,* **21** : 23-27 (December).

Hughes, W. L. and Williams, J. F., 1944. *Sports, their organization and administration.* New York: A.S. Barnes and Co.

Hutter, D. M., 1970. A study of the attitudes affecting the behavior of the administration of intercollegiate athletics. Columbus, Ohio: Ph.D. dissertation, Ohio State University.

Irace, S. C., 1958. Case studies in the administration of intercollegiate athletics for men with reference to the member institutions of the College of the City of New York. New York: Ed.D. dissertation, Teachers College. Columbia University.

Johnson, Henry W., 1953. The Harvard athletic program, *The North Central Association Quarterly,* **27** : 357-361.

Joint committee on physical education and athletics, 1970. Professional preparation of the administration of athletics, *JOHPER,* **41** : 19-23 (September).

Lawther, J. D., 1965. The role of the coach in American education, *JOHPER,* **36** : 65-66.

Lumley, A. E., 1953. Physical education and intercollegiate and intramural athletics at Amherst College, *The North Central Association Quarterly,* **27** : 349-353.

Marco, S. M., 1960. The place of intercollegiate athletics in higher education, the responsibility of the faculty, *The journal of higher education,* **31** : 422-427.

Marsh, A. W., 1952. The educational values of physical education including intercollegiate athletics, and their preservation, *The educational forum,* **16** : 409-419.

McCloy, C. A., 1940. *Philosophical bases for physical education.* New York: F.S. Crofts and Co.

McDonough, T. E., 1952. Chairman, Intercollegiate athletics: educational values and their preservation, special memo to presidents of colleges and universities, *College Physical Education Association Proceedings* (January 25).

McNutt, B. J., 1967. A study of the intercollegiate athletic program for women in the area served by the Midwest Association for Physical Education of College Women. Kent, Ohio: Master's thesis, Kent State University.

Mears, I. G., 1970. A study of the organization and administration of intercollegiate athletics in church-related colleges and universities of the United States. Los Angeles: Ed.D. dissertation, University of Southern California.

Metcalf, T. N., 1953. Athletics at the University of Chicago. *The North Central Association Quarterly* **27**: 340-345.

Mid-American Conference, 1952. A report of meeting of presidents of member institutions, *Special bulletin (February 16).*

Mitchell, E. D., and B.S. Mason, 1948. *The theory of play.* New York: A.S. Barnes and Co.

Mitchell, E. D., 1954. A survey of the athletic purposes of colleges of the North Central Association, *The North Central Association Quarterly,* **28** : 370-377.

Moore, H. J., Ed., 1954. What should be the relationship between high school and college in athletic policies, *The bulletin of the National Association of Secondary School Principals,* **38** :195-197.

Nash, J. B., 1942. *Building morale.* New York: A.S. Barnes and Co.

National Association of Collegiate Commissioners, 1951. Education and reform, *Mimeographed report on excerpts from minutes of meeting* (July 20-23).

National Association of Intercollegiate Atheltics, 1965. *Official Handbook,* Revised edition, Kansas City: NAIA.

National Collegiate Athletic Association, 1965. *The enforcement program.* Reprinted Edition. Kansas City: NCAA.

National Federation of State High School Athletic Associations, 1966. *Official handbook.* Chicago: NFSHSAA.

Nichols, J. H., 1953. Oberlin college sports program, *The North Central Association Quarterly,* **27** : 370-376.

North Central Association of Colleges and Secondary Schools, 1952. An interpretation of the revised policy on intercollegiate athletics of the North Central Association, *Special bulletin,* Chicago: Commission on Colleges and Universities.

Oberteuffer, D., 1952. Intercollegiate football, *College Physical Education Association Proceedings,* 12-18.

535

Patillo, M. J., 1952. The North Central Association and intercollegiate athletic reform. *American Association of University Professors Bulletin,* **38** : 209-219.

Pearson, C. E., 1958. An analysis of practices in the administration of intercollegiate athletics in selected colleges. New York: Ed.D. dissertation, Teachers College, Columbia University.

Plant, M. L., 1961. The place of intercollegiate athletics in higher education, faculty control, *Journal of higher education,* **32** : 1-8.

Powell, J. T., 1964. The development and influence of faculty representation in the control of intercollegiate sport within the intercollegiate conference of faculty representatives from its inception in January 1895 to July 1963. Champaign, Illinois: Ph.D. dissertation, University of Illinois.

Randall, R. E., 1953. Athletics at Haverford College, *The North Central Association Quarterly,* **27** : 346-348.

Reed, W. R., 1963. Big time athletics commitment to education, *JOHPER,* **34** : 29-30, 64-65.

Reeves, C. L., 1951. Standards and administrative policies for the interscholastic program. *The Bulletin of the National Association of Secondary School Principals* **35:** 69-74.

Robertson, A. J., 1936. The control of intercollegiate athletics. Ames, Iowa: Master's thesis. State University of Iowa.

Russell, J. D., and F. W. Reeves, 1933. *The organization and administration of the university.* Chicago: The University of Chicago Press.

Sargent, D. A., 1906. *Physical education.* Boston: Ginn and Co.

Savage, H. J. and others, 1929. American college athletics, New York: Carnegie Foundation For the Advancement of Teaching, *Bulletin 23.*

Savage, H. J. and others, 1931. Current developments in American college sports. New York: Carnegie Foundation for the Advancement of Teaching, *Bulletin 26.*

Scott, H.A., 1951. *Competitive sports in schools and colleges,* New York: Harper and Brothers.

_____, 1956. New directions in intercollegiate athletics, *Teachers college record,* **58** : 29-37.

Shea, E. J., 1954. A critical evaluation of the policies governing American intercollegiate athletics with the establishment of principles to guide the formation of policies for American intercollegiate athletics. New York: Ph.D. dissertation, New York University.

Shea, E. J., and E. E. Wieman, 1967. *Administrative policies for intercollegiate athletics.* Springfield: Charles C. Thomas.

Southern University Conference, 1952. Report of the committe on athletics, *Special bulletin* (April 9).

Stetson, W. J., 1953. Athletics at Swarthmore College, *The North Central Association Quarterly,* **27** : 354-355.

Turner, M. S., 1953. A re-emphasis on intercollegiate athletics: a report on the Johns Hopkins university athletic program, *The North Central Association Quarterly,* **27** : 334-339.

Van Bibber, E. G., 1937. The history and development of intercollegiate eligibility rules. Layfayette, Ind.: Master's thesis, Purdue University.

Vickers, E. F., 1938. A survey of intercollegiate athletic conferences and their contribution to education. Tucson: Master's thesis, University of Arizona.

Voltmer, C. D., 1936. A brief history of intercollegiate conferences of faculty representatives: with special consideration of athletic problems. New York: Ed.D. dissertation, Teachers College, Columbia University.

Voltmer, E. F., and A. A. Esslinger, 1949. *The organization and administration of physical education.* New York: Appleton-Century-Croft Inc.

Wagoner, M. E., 1936. Standards and policies in the administration of intercollegiate athletics at Kent State University. Columbus: Master's thesis, Ohio State University.

Williams, J. F., 1948. An analysis of the crucial issue in American college athletics. *College Physical Education Association proceedings.* 73-79.

Williams, J. F., and W. L. Hughes, 1937. *Athletics in education.* New York: A.S. Barnes and Co.

Woerlein, G. W., 1938. Intercollegiate athletic conferences, their history and significance. Columbus: Master's thesis, Ohio State University.

Woodbury, D. S., 1966. The administrative relationships between athletics and physical education in selected American universities. Salt Lake City: Ed.D. dissertation, University of Utah.

Wright, G. O., 1935. The administration of intercollegiate athletics in negro colleges. Ann Arbor: Master's thesis, University of Michigan.

80

Complying with Title IX of the Education Amendments of 1972 in Physical Education and High School Sports Programs

Marjorie Blaufarb

Title IX of the Education Amendments of 1972 is based on the principle that all activities in educational programs have equal value for both sexes. The regulations therefore state that physical education classes may not be conducted separately on the basis of sex, nor may participation in physical education programs be required or refused on the basis of sex. This principle has caused dismay in the minds of many administrators and teachers because for many years there has been a practice of offering instruction in physical skills separately beginning sometimes as early as grade 4 or 5.

It was not the intention of the people who framed the legislation, nor of those who wrote the regulations to effectuate it, to make the lives of the administrators and teachers more difficult than they are under normal circumstances. The legislation and the regulations arose from a demonstrated need to improve the opportunities of females in physical education and athletics along with all other areas of education. Those who cling to the sex-segregated programs state that they do so for reasons of safety and administrative and organizational convenience, because of physical, physiological, and psychological differences between the sexes, and because of differing teaching philosophies held by men and women.

The result of this practice of sex segregation has often been, even in those schools where facilities and equipment were comparable, that program opportunities for females avoided some of the "tougher" activities and concentrated on activities the teacher considered more suitable. But over the past decade there have been changes in this practice of sex segregation. In

---

This material was extracted from a longer article with the same title, published by AAHPER in 1975.

many schools some or all of the classes have been sex-integrated. In most cases where this has been attempted it has been welcomed enthusiastically by students and the teachers have found it worked well and improved the program for both sexes.

This chapter will attempt to examine some of the fears and practices and to offer some suggestions. Model curricula will not be suggested so as to avoid limiting activities that have been taught traditionally. There is no one best model for all the varying situations that influence programming in schools throughout the country. It cannot be said too often that any activities that have been offered traditionally in physical education classes may continue to be offered in a sex-integrated class.

In order to assist in an understanding of the Title IX regulations, it helps to define the components of a school program as they relate to physical activity. According to platform statements and position papers of the profession:

> Physical education is that integral part of the total education which contributes to the development of the individual through the natural medium of physical activity—human movement. In it, regular instruction and practices are provided in a variety of physical activities (leading up to and including athletics) that are suited to the nature and needs of the students depending on age and development and that ensure the development of an adequate level of physical fitness. (Secondary School P.E. Council 1976).
>
> The intramural program provides opportunities for students to utilize, in organized competition with their schoolmates, the knowledge and skills acquired in the basic physical education program. The interscholastic athletic program provides opportunities in secondary schools for students with superior athletic ability to develop and utilize fully this talent through organized competition with students of similar ability from other schools (AAHPER 1972).

This chapter has been divided into educational levels for convenience, but experienced teachers, coaches, and administrators will understand that many of the statements made about one level of school experience are applicable to all levels.

ACCESS TO COURSES IN PHYSICAL EDUCATION

Section 86.34 of the Title IX Regulation states that an institution or agency may not:

> . . . provide any course or otherwise carry out any of its education program or activity separately on the basis of sex, or require or refuse participation therein by any of its students on such basis, including health, physical education, industrial, business, vocational, technical, home economics, music, and adult education courses.

(a) With respect to classes and activities in physical education at the elementary school level, the recipient shall comply fully with this section, as expeditiously as possible but in no event later than one year from the effective date of this regulation. With respect to physical education classes and activities at the secondary and postsecondary levels, the recipient shall comply fully with this section as expeditiously as possible but in no event later than three years from the effective date of this regulation.

(b) This section does not prohibit grouping of students in physical education classes and activities by ability as assessed by objective standards of individual performance developed and applied without regard to sex.

(c) This section does not prohibit separation of students by sex within physical education classes or activities during participation in wrestling, boxing, rugby, ice hockey, football, basketball, and other sports the purpose or major activity of which involves bodily contact.

(d) Where use of a single standard of measuring skill or progress in a physical education class has an adverse effect on members of one sex, the recipient shall use appropriate standards which do not have such effect.

(e) Portions of classes in elementary and secondary schools which deal exclusively with human sexuality may be conducted in separate sessions for boys and girls.

In order to assess and evaluate and present compliance with the requirements of Title IX Regulation for nondiscrimination in physical education programs and to plan necessary modifications, HEW in 1976 outlined a self-evaluation, saying it is necessary to:

Review the following materials:
—copies of physical education requirements for students at all grade levels;
—copies of curriculum guides that outline the content, activities or instructional methodologies of all physical education programs;
—copies of all physical education course descriptions; and
—descriptions of all facilities and equipment used in physical education programs.

Collect the following data:
—name, description, and grade level of all physical education courses conducted on a coeducational basis and statement of facilities and equipment used;
—course enrollments by sex in physical education courses at all grade levels; and
—summary of program activities within each physical education course.

Determine compliance by answering:
—are physical education requirements the same for males and females?
—Are physical education classes conducted on a coeducational basis except during participation in contact sports?
—Do course descriptions make it clear that all physical education courses are open to male and female students according to nondiscriminatory criteria?

—Do course descriptions state the criteria for measurement of skills where these are used to group students?
—Are criteria used for measurement of progress within a physical education course or program explicit and free of adverse effects upon students of one sex?
—Are physical education class activities sufficiently diversified for achieving the range of physical education program goals and not concentrated only on contact sports?

If "no" is the answer to any of these questions, a school needs to undertake modifications and remedial steps to achieve compliance with Title IX.

SELF-EVALUATION FOR PHYSICAL EDUCATION

Self-evaluation is a process involving staff at all levels of the institution or agency. The following checklists provide general suggestions to personnel at the central administrative, building administrative, and building staff levels as to procedures and review questions that facilitate effective evaluation of compliance with Title IX requirements for nondiscrimination in physical education programs. (Note: These checklists are procedural only; substantive criteria for compliance evaluation are contained in the preceding paragraphs.)

Central Office Staff
—Has a policy statement been issued which affirms the right to every student to physical education without regard to sex?
—Has a policy directive regarding the specific implications of Title IX for agency and school physical education programs been disseminated to administrators and relevant staff?
—Have forms, procedures, and timelines been developed for submission of the following to the central office by building administrators:
    —list of enrollments by sex in all physical education courses with identification of the facilities used?
    —description of nondiscriminatory criteria used in assigning students to courses, classes, or ability groupings?
    —description of nondiscriminatory standards used in assessing individual progress in physical education courses?
    —statement of barriers (if any) to achieving immediate compliance with requirements of the Title IX regulation?
—Have district physical education requirements been received and modified where necessary to ensure that they are identical for males and females?
—Have district guidelines or requirements for physical education programs—including course outlines, instructional methodologies, class activities, and skills measurement criteria—been reviewed and modified where necessary to ensure compliance with Title IX?

—Have guidelines regarding procedures and/or criteria to be used in assigning students to physical education classes been developed and disseminated to administrative and relevant staff to facilitate compliance with Title IX requirements?

—Has every building administrator submitted all required data and assurances to the central office according to specified timelines?

—Have district plans been made for ensuring compliance with the Title IX Regulation requirements for physical education at the earliest possible date? Do they involve:

   —staff training?
   —program revision?
   —rescheduling?
   —renovation or construction of facilities?

Building Administrators (principals/supervisors)

—Has a policy directive regarding the specific implications of Title IX for school physical education programs been disseminated to all physical education staff?

—Have you requested that all building staff submit information regarding any instances of sex discrimination that they may identify in practices, policies, or materials relating to physical education?

—Has your school prepared the following for submission to the central district administration:

   —list of enrollments by sex in all physical education courses with identification of facilities used?
   —description of nondiscriminatory criteria used in assigning students to courses, classes, or ability groupings?
   —description of nondiscriminatory standards used in assessing individual progress in physical education courses?
   —statement of barriers (if any) to achieving immediate compliance with requirements of the Title IX Regulation?
   —description and assurances of immediate compliance activities where possible?

—Have plans been developed for ensuring school compliance with the Title IX Regulation requirements for physical education at the earliest possible date? Do they involve:

   —staff training?
   —program revision?
   —rescheduling?
   —renovation or construction of facilities?

Building Staff (instructors)

—Have you familiarized yourself with the implications of Title IX requirements for nondiscrimination in physical education courses or programs for which you have responsibility?

—Are all your physical education courses, classes, or activities (other than those involving bodily contact) provided on a coeducational basis?

—Have you reviewed the criteria you use in assigning students to classes or

ability groupings to ensure that they are objective and applied objectively?
—Have you reviewed the criteria you use in measuring student progress within physical education courses to ensure that they do not have an adverse effect on students of one sex?
—Have you submitted to your administrator or supervisor information regarding instances of sex discrimination that you have identified in practices, policies, or materials relating to physical education in your agency/school?

COMPETITIVE SPORTS, GRADES 7-12

Section 86.41 of the Title IX Regulation states that an institution or a district must develop and operate athletic programs—intramurals and interscholastics—according to the following specifications:

(a) General. No person shall, on the basis of sex, be excluded from participation in, be denied the benefits of, be treated differently from another person or otherwise be discriminated against in any interscholastic, intercollegiate, club, or intramural athletics offered by a recipient, and no recipient shall provide any such athletics separately on such basis.

(b) Separate Teams. Notwithstanding the requirements of paragraph (a) of this section, a recipient may operate or sponsor separate teams for members of each sex where selection for such teams is based upon competitive skill or the activity involved is a contact sport. However, where a recipient operates or sponsors a team in a particular sport for members of one sex but operates or sponsors no such team for members of the other sex, and athletic opportunities for members of that sex have been limited previously, members of the excluded sex must be allowed to try out for the team offered unless the sport involved is a contact sport. For the purposes of this Part, contact sports include boxing, wrestling, rugby, ice hockey, football, basketball, and other sports the purpose or major activity of which involves bodily contact.

(c) Equal Opportunity. A recipient which operates or sponsors interscholastic, intercollegiate, club, or intramural athletics shall provide equal athletic opportunity for members of both sexes. In determining whether equal opportunities are available the Director will consider, among other factors:

(i) whether the selection of sports and levels of competition effectively accommodate the interests and abilities of members of both sexes;
(ii) the provision of equipment and supplies;
(iii) scheduling of games and practice time;
(iv) travel and per diem allowance;
(v) opportunity to receive coaching and academic tutoring;
(vi) assignment and compensation of coaches and tutors;
(vii) provision of locker rooms, practice, and competitive facilities;
(viii) provision of medical and training facilities and services;
(ix) provision of housing and dining facilities and services; and
(x) publicity.

Unequal aggregate expenditures for members of each sex or unequal expenditures for male and female teams if a recipient operates or sponsors separate teams will not constitute noncompliance with the section, but the Director may consider the failure to provide necessary funds for teams for one sex in assessing equality of opportunity for members of each sex.

(d) Adjustment Period. A recipient which operates or sponsors interscholastic . . . club or intramural athletics at the elementary school level shall comply fully with this section as expeditiously as possible but in no event later than one year from the effective date of this regulation. A recipient which operates or sponsors interscholastic, club, or intramural athletics at the secondary or postsecondary school level shall comply fully with this section as expeditiously as possible but in no event later than three years from the effective date of this regulation.

Additional specifications and explanatory information regarding this portion of the Regulation are provided in the Memorandum regarding the "Elimination of Sex Discrimination in Athletic Programs," issued by the Director, Office for Civil Rights, HEW, in September 1975.

An extensive outline for self-evaluation of athletics programs (similar in format to that presented earlier for physical education) can be found in the HEW document (1976) regarding "Complying with Title IX: Implementing Institutional Self-Evaluation."

Interpretations and Suggestions Regarding Interscholastic Sports

The intramural program provides opportunities for all students to utilize, in organized competition with their schoolmates, the knowledge and skills acquired in the basic physical education program. The interscholastic athletic program provides opportunities in secondary schools for students with superior athletic ability to develop and utilize fully this talent through organized competition with students of similar ability from other schools (AAHPER 1972).

Athletics is credited with many magic properties by true believers but it is only recently that it has been acknowledged that females also could achieve the same benefits as males from athletic participation. A list of these benefits includes: fostering the physical, mental, emotional, social and moral growth of participants; development of increased physical fitness and vitality; and development of physical skills in movement that have potential for more efficient accomplishment of physical requirements of work and everyday living and more rapid response in situations demanding unusual strength, endurance, or coordination. Our common human heritage and a tolerance for the weaknesses and shortcomings of others and for economic, racial, or religious differences, together with the ability to lose gracefully are also included.

The degree to which all these benefits are achieved is open to question, but it is unquestionable that athletics is a valuable part of the school life of boys and girls and the Title IX requirement that students may not be excluded from athletic competition (intramural and interscholastic) on the basis of sex is a step toward making its values and desirable outcomes equally available to both sexes. In 20th century living men and women compete constantly in the fields of work, sport, and academics. Both men and women are exposed to situations demanding quick reflexes and reactions and all the other characteristics listed above.

A few areas of the country have offered varied competitive programs for both sexes for a number of years. High school athletic associations in these districts have arranged schedules to provide competitive opportunities in as many as 10 to 14 sports for girls and boys. Although the question of where the funds for enlarged programs are to be found is frequently raised, those districts and systems that have considered this level of competition for both sexes to be desirable have managed to get money for coaches and facilities and other support.

It is the difference in degree of competition that is the key factor distinguishing activities in grades 4 to 8 from the high school programs. There may be extramural opportunities in grades 7 and 8 but they are at a lower level of intensity than in situations of intolerable pressure. Title IX regulations do not speak to which sports should be part of the athletic program at any level—only to the fact that the selection of sports and levels of competition effectively accommodate the interests and abilities of both sexes.

All references in the HEW document to organized interscholastics should be interpreted to mean interschool athletic competition at the high school level (grades 9 to 12). Completion of the compliance review suggested will enable administrators and athletic directors to decide whether and where changes in interscholastic practices are needed. According to the Title IX regulations, neither equal aggregate nor equal per capita expenditures for males and females are required.

During the first year (prior to July 21, 1976) educational institutions operating athletic programs above the elementary level were required to determine the interests of both sexes in the sports to be offered by the institution. Where the sport is a contact sport or where participants are selected on the basis of competition, the relative abilities of members of each sex for each such sport offered should be determined in order to decide whether to have single-sex teams or teams composed of both sexes.

The determination of interest has raised some question in the minds of some administrators. How to go about the survey and how to interpret it have been cited as difficulties. It would be wise in developing the survey instrument to include questions that would indicate the degree of commitment of students. An indication could be given of the availability of coaches, equipment, and space, so that respondents could know whether an immediate response to their expressed interest is possible. Professional aid in framing the question-naire for students would be a help.

If a few students elect a sport not previously played at an institution and there is doubt about how strong the commitment is, a reasonable stand on the part of the administration might be to suggest trying to include the sport in the physical education curriculum for one year so that intending participants may get basic instruction. If enough students perservere to a reasonable skill level then, other things being equal, arrangements can be made to include the sport in intramural or club activities until it is well enough established to warrant a varsity team.

In cases where the traditional structure of one team to one school does not provide competitive opportunities to all students, administrators might look for innovative methods of meeting the needs. For example, two nearby schools could join to field a team in a hitherto little played sport or arrange extramural games until enough interest is shown for the high school activities association to act regionally or statewide. In situations where several small colleges have joined in a consortium, some teams are chosen on a consortium-wide basis and play in intercollegiate sports. High schools might be able to investigate a similar arrangement.

Interscholastic competition is regulated by state and local activities associations and it is important that these bodies should be responsive to the needs of female coaches and students. Until now the governing bodies of these associations have been primarily male; arrangements should be made for an equitable number of women to be in governance positions on boards of control at every level. (Conversation with director of Office of Civil Rights/HEW, May 20, 1976.)

The position of professional educators for many years has been that coaches should be properly certified and competent teachers. The coach needs far more than a technical knowledge of the game. It is not the intention of the Title IX regulations to change such philosophical and pragmatic positions formulated for the protection of students. In general, in making an adjustment to an enlarged athletic program at all levels, which will accomodate the interests of all highly skilled students, it helps to write detailed job descriptions for coaches and athletic directors and to resist the temptation to take as coaches individuals who have no qualification except that they once played the game.

Coaches have a responsibility to familiarize themselves with the rules governing athletics within their state or section and for being aware of rules of the Association for Intercollegiate Athletics for Women on recruitment and scholarships in addition to the rules of the National Collegiate Athletic Association. All students should be counseled that some institutions have athletic scholarships available for members of both sexes.

In various interpretations of the athletic regulations issued by the Office of Civil Rights, the vexed question of males on women's teams has been addressed. The regulations state that where a recipient sponsors a team in a noncontact sport for members of one sex but does not do so for the other sex, members of the excluded sex must be allowed to try out for that team if overall athletic opportunities have been previously limited. The fact that there has been no tennis team for female students does not automatically mean that they must be allowed to try out for the male tennis team. They must be permitted to try out for it, however, if opportunities to participate in competitive athletics generally (not just tennis) have previously been more limited for females than for males. Volleyball and field hockey have been two sports in which it has been feared that females would lose competitive opportunities because, since they are not contact sports according to Title IX, the males would wish to try out for them. However, according to the interpretation given above, males need only be allowed to try out if all their sports activities were previously more limited than those of the females in the school. At the present time it is an unusual school where this is the case (Director, Office of Civil Rights 1975).

There is one comment that can be made about this situation. In those schools that have always provided a fair competitive program for the female students, there are grounds to fear that the girls might lose out. The program for girls has usually included more noncontact sports than the boys' program. In many cases the only contact sport as defined by Title IX played by girls is basketball. There is great danger here that the program for girls might become unduly diluted and provide them with fewer opportunities than previously because there would be no legal basis to refuse opportunities to the males to try out for the teams in noncontact sports. This would be no less likely to happen to the boys' interscholastic program as boys traditionally play more contact sports. Although Title IX regulations do not require it, when the interest survey shows the need it might be a good idea to sponsor all-male teams in addition to all-female teams in some noncontact sports like field hockey or volleyball if enough interest is shown.

The interpretations also state that unitary teams (i.e., teams composed of members of both sexes) for which selection is based upon competitive skill may be sponsored only if, in doing so, the interests and abilities of members of both sexes are effectively accomodated. In other words, where a school decides that anyone, regardless of sex, may try out for a team, and there is substantial interest on the part of females in that sport but very few of them have skill sufficient to be selected, the sponsorship of the unitary team would not be sufficient to meet the interests and abilities of both sexes (Director, Office of Civil Rights 1975).

Students may not be excluded on the basis of sex from participation in a sport offered at the intramural or interscholastic team level, even though it may be a contact sport, or the basis for team selection is competitive skill, if sufficient interest exists among members of the sex that would otherwise be excluded to form a separate team, and if there are fewer opportunities for members of that sex to participate in athletics at the level of competition in question.

The September 1975 memorandum from the director of the Office of Civil Rights on elimination of sex discrimination in athletic programs, states that the fact a particular segment of an athletic program is supported by funds received from various other sources (such as student fees, general revenues, gate receipts, alumni donations, booster clubs, and nonprofit foundations) does not remove it from the reach of the statute and hence of the regulatory requirements (Director, Office of Civil Rights 1975).

Interpretations and Suggestions Regarding Intramurals and Club Sports

The varsity athletics teams in grades 9 to 12 accommodate a select group of highly skilled youngsters. The core of learning experience is in the physical education curriculum, and the skills learned in such classes can be applied by less highly skilled students in afterschool and noonhour intramural games. No matter on what basis teams are made up in intramurals, whether it is by skill, homeroom, grade level, or in any other way, persons may not be excluded on the basis of sex from participation in a sport, even though it may be a contact sport, if sufficient interest exists among members of the sex that would otherwise be excluded to form a separate team, and if there are fewer opportunities for members of that sex to participate in athletics at the level of competition in question. Intramural teams in noncontact sports, for which selection is based on interest rather than skill, may not limit membership to students of one sex.

Competition in intramurals should be as equal as possible, based appropriately on age, ability, height, weight, physiological maturity, and strength of participants. The same care for the safety of the participant should be taken as in interscholastics. In order to accommodate the great variations in sizes of children even in the same grade, it may be an advantage to rely more on ability, height, strength, weight, and physiological maturity than on grade level or age (AAHPER 1970).

In brief, school-sponsored intramural activities must meet the interests of both sexes and provide them with access to sports in which they display an interest. It was not the intention of the people framing the Title IX legislation nor of those writing the regulations to restrict opportunities for students in any way, so administrators are urged to look at total program opportunities available at all skill levels for males and females before curtailing any activities.

REFERENCES

AAHPER, 1972. Athletics in education, a platform statement by the Division of Men's Athletics, American Association for Health, Physical Education and Recreation. Revised 1972. Washington, D.C.: AAHPER.

_____, 1970. Essentials of a quality elementary school physical education program, a position paper of the Elementary School Physical Education Commission of of of the Physical Education Division of the American Association for Health, Physical Education, and Recreation. Washington, D.C.: AAHPER.

Director, Office of Civil Rights, Department of Health, Education, and Welfare, 1975. Memorandum to chief state school officers, superintendents of local education agencies, and college and university presidents (September).

Secondary School Physical Education Council of the National Association for Sport and Physical Education of AAHPER, 1976. Secondary school physical education, position statement drafted in 1976.

U.S. Department of Health, Education, and Welfare, 1976. Complying with Title IX: implementing institutional self-evaluation. Washington, D.C.: U.S. HEW, Office of Education (June).

SUGGESTED READINGS

Anonymous, 1975. Title IX: moving toward implementation. *Briefings,* **1** : NAPECW and NCPEAM.

Lopiano, D. A., 1976. A fact-finding model for conducting a Title IX self-evaluation study in athletic programs. *JOPER,* **47** : 26 (May).

81

Public Law 94-142 Rules and Regulations in Physical Education and Recreation Requirements

Julian Stein

Preliminary rules and regulations for the Education for All Handicapped Children Act (Public Law 94-142) were released through the Federal Register on December 30, 1976. Public hearings were conducted by Bureau of Education for the Handicapped personnel at six sites throughout the United States. Written testimonies were submitted by interested personnel and representatives of various organizations. The following information gives an overview of how this legislation and its associated rules and regulations affect physical education, recreation, and related activity areas.

Provisions of the law were implemented starting with the 1977-78 school year. State plans were developed with considerations given to local plans so that they were in full compliance with all aspects of the law. It was imperative that individuals interested and involved in physical education, recreation, and related activity areas be actively involved in the planning process. Only in this way could it be guaranteed that these areas were included and incorporated to the letter of the law and, most importantly, in ways that insured full participation by every child with a handicapping condition in programs and activities designed to meet his or her particular needs and to help him or her live the fullest life possible.

The Education for All Handicapped Children Act (P.L. 94-142) is designed to insure that all handicapped children have available to them a free, appropriate public education that includes special education and related services to meet their unique needs. In addition, the law insures that the rights of handicapped children and their parents are protected, provides assistance to states and localities in providing for the education of all handicapped children, and requires assessment to insure the effectiveness of

Adapted from *IRUC Briefings,* Volume 2, No. 2 (February) 1977, AAHPER.

efforts to educate these children. Instruction in physical education is the only curriculum area included in the defined elements of special education. Recreation is identified as one of the specified related services.

Rules and regulations provide the details for administering mandates of the law. Physical education includes special physical education, adapted physical education, and motor development, and it means the development of physical and motor fitness, fundamental motor skills and patterns, body mechanics, individual and group games, and sports skills to include intramural and lifetime sports, dance, and movement education. Recommendations have been made to add aquatics to this definition. Physical education must be made available to every handicapped child receiving a free, appropriate public education and be included in his or her individualized educational program.

In addition each handicapped child must be afforded the opportunity to participate in the regular physical education program available to nonhandicapped children unless the child is enrolled fulltime in a separate facility, or the child needs specially designed physical education as prescribed in the child's individualized education program, or the parents and public educational agency agree that the child should not participate in the regular program. If specially designed physical education is prescribed, the public agency responsible for the education of that child shall provide services directly or make arrangements for it to be provided through other public or private programs.

In addition, the public agency responsible for the education of a handicapped child shall take steps to insure that physical education provided to that child is comparable to services provided to nonhandicapped children. Other stipulations mandate that each state and local education agency shall provide nonacademic and extracurricular services and activities, special interest groups, or clubs sponsored by the state or local educational agency. Recommendations have been made to add intramural, extramural, and interscholastics as modifiers and desribers of athletics.

As a related service, recreation has been defined simply as including leisure education. However, recommendations have been made to expand this definition to include leisure education, therapeutic recreation, and recreation programs conducted in community settings. This expansion will provide a continuum of recreational services and opportunities more consistent with the varied needs of handicapped children and the real intent of the legislation itself.

Each state and local educational agency shall insure that an individualized educational program is provided for each handicapped child who is receiving or will receive special education regardless of what institution or agency provides or will provide special education to the child. Individualized educational programs must include:

1. a statement of the child's present levels of educational performance including academic achievement, social adaptation, prevocational and vocational skills, psychomotor skills, and self-help skills

2. a statement on annual goals describing the educational performance to be achieved by the end of the school year under the the child's individualized educational program

3. a statement of short-term instructional objectives that must be measurable intermediate steps between the present level of educational performance and annual goals

4. a statement of specific educational services needed by the child determined without regard to the availability of those services

5. the date when those services will begin and length of time the services will be given

6. a description of the extent to which the child will participate in regular educational programs

7. a justification of the type of educational placement the child will have

8. a list of individuals who are responsible for implementation of the individualized educational program

9. objective criteria, evaluation procedures, and schedules for determining on at least an annual basis whether the short-term instructional objectives are being achieved

Planning meetings, in which each child's individualized educational program is developed, are to include a representative of the local educational agency other than the child's teachers—a person qualified to provide or supervise the provision of special education; the child's teacher or teachers, special or regular or both, who have a direct responsibility for implementing the child's individualized education program; one or both of the child's parents; when appropriate, the child; and other individuals at the discretion of the parent or agency.

The law and its related rules and regulations specify populations who are to receive priority considerations in developing and providing services. First priority children means handicapped children who are not receiving any education. Second priority children means handicapped children within each disability with the most severe handicaps, who are receiving some but not all of the special education and related services specified in the individualized education program of those children.

The law mandated that all handicapped children three to 18 years of age have to have been receiving a free and appropriate education by September 1, 1977, and those three to 21 years of age by September 1980. An added incentive was built into the law to encourage state and local education agencies to provide services for children three to five years of age.

Among the other specific considerations of the law that have both direct and indirect implications for physical educators, recreation personnel, and other school staff, include delineation of due process procedures to guarantee and protect rights of both children and parents, assurances of confidentiality of information, specific evaluation protection against single or discriminatory diagnostic and assessment procedures, and delineation of least restrictive environment as containing a continuum of alternative placements.

SUGGESTED READINGS

Anonymous, 1976. Mainstreaming physical education. *Briefings,* **4** : NAPECW and NCPEAM.

Dirocco, P., 1978. Preparing for the mainstreamed environment: a necessary addition to preservice curriculums. *JOPER,* **49** : 24-25 (January).

Roice, G. R., 1977. Process for identification, assessment, planning, and placement of students into adaptive physical education, in compliance with Public Law 94-142. Office of the Los Angeles County Superintendent of Schools, Division of Special Education (September).

Stein, J., 1977. Physical education and athletics emphasized in rehabilitation act rules, regs. *IRUC Briefings* (May).

RELATED PROFESSIONS

Introduction

Why a section on the health or recreation profession in a physical education encyclopedia? First, to the reader who may not have been acquainted with either of these professions, such as a high school student contemplating a career, the mention of the terms health and/or recreation must be confusing and frustrating. Thus, chapters that explain the similarities and differences among these and other related professions seems appropriate. Second, it is understandable that a profession would wish to record its contributions to the development of other professions. This section attempts to do both.

Three chapters are devoted to the area of health, and a fourth, on gerontology, could be rationalized under community or public health. Staton outlines the traditional, at times almost indistinguishable, ties between physical education and health in the school setting. He mentions a number of physical educators who have nurtured the roots of health education. However, over the years the curriculum content of the two professions has become substantially different as the health profession concentrates more and more on such pressing societal problems as alcohol and drug abuse, human sexuality, mental health, acute and chronic disease, aging, etc., while the physical education profession concentrates predominantly on physical and motor development, sports skills, and physical fitness throughout life.

Though the professions may be drawing farther apart in health education curriculum content, they are certainly moving closer together in the area of community or public health, as the chapters by Montoye, Jokl, and La Salle will attest.

Montoye reviewed the works of scholars from many disciplines and established the historical interest in the relationship between exercise and health. He attempts to encapsulate what is presently known about the relationship between physical activity, or lack thereof, and such specific conditions as obesity, cardiovascular disease, cancer, aging, and others—conditions affecting enormous numbers of Americans today. The preponderance of interest seems to be in the potential of exercise as a preventive measure rather than as a cure. Unfortunately, with the possible exception of obesity, little solid scientific evidence is available to substantiate popular claims—although epidemiological information abounds in the area of cardiovascular disease.

Because national census data forecast a marked increase in older citizens in the 1980s and 1990s, the subject of the relationship between regular physical exercise and aging has taken on considerable import. Jokl approaches the question from the point of view of general physical development, general motor ability, and general physical fitness, as well as some specific physiological parameters. He uses interesting examples of documented performances of older champion athletes to help substantiate his contention that "training exerts a more determining influence on form and function than age." He concedes however that longevity, like physical and mental capacity, is largely a function of heredity, but insists the "transformation of these capacities in reality depends on 'nurture'."

The relationship of physical activity to mental health has long been of interest to physical educators, health educators, and psychologists. La Salle explores the role of games, sports, dance, and general play as a medium for enhancing emotional adjustment and equilibrium. Specifically she attempts to relate the positive effects of participation in physical activity upon such components of overall mental health as body-image, release of aggressions and hostilities, control of fear, aesthetic expression, and physical interaction with other human beings, singly and in groups. Although she is firmly convinced of the positive relationship between mental health and participation in games, sports, dance, and general play, she acknowledges that definite scientific verification has yet to be presented.

The field of recreation lays great claim to the general area of play. Sapora outlines the early relationships between recreation and physical education professions. He suggests that recreation as a separate profession grew out of the unwillingness or inability of the schools to absorb the rapidly growing recreation movement. Consequently public recreation became predominantly a function of municipal government and other agencies outside the public schools. He acknowledges the great contributions made by physical education leaders to the development of the recreation profession. Although the recreation profession has expanded to the point that it includes many areas outside the realm of physical education, he urges the continued interaction between the professions in the areas of sports, exercise, and dance.

The relationship of physical education to the field of safety is discussed in the articles by Ryan and Florio. The physical education profession has long been concerned with the safety of constituents particularly in the area of sports participation. Ryan produces a list of general and specific principles by which the hazards of sports participation may be reduced, if not eliminated entirely.

Florio identifies the relationship of physical education to driver education by suggesting that, when driver education emerged in the public schools in the early 1930s, many of the teachers already interested in accident prevention were physical educators and health educators. Many of these teachers were asked to assume the responsibility for driver education. Although driver education is considered a distinct field, the similarities of professional preparation of teachers in the two disciplines will insure a continued relationship for years to come.

Section Editor

James S. Bosco is also coeditor of this volume. See page vii for a biographical sketch.

82

Physical Education Related to Health Education

Wesley M. Staton

Like two children in the same family, physical education and health education have important interrelationships and similarities. They also exhibit significant differences and elements of independence. Though related and sharing certain historical commonalities, each field is unique in its philosophy, objectives, curriculum, methods and materials, teaching-learning milieu, and personnel.

ORIGINS AND DEVELOPMENT

The origins of physical education are clouded in the mists of antiquity. Human movement and the innate desire to improve skill, speed, endurance, strength, agility, and other physical qualities are as old as the beginnings of human existence. Bucher (1972), Gardiner (1930), Rice, Hutchinson, and Lee (1969), and Van Dalen and Bennett (1971) provide rich, detailed sources of the history of physical education.

As with physical education, human concern for health is rooted in our distant past. Prehistoric, pre-Christian, and subsequent civilizations have all left evidences of their interest in health and disease (Beck 1966; Hanlon 1969, 1971; Maple 1968).

"Health education" for these people took the form of family and trible rules of hygiene, codes based upon religious doctrine, witch doctor magic, superstitions and "old wives' tales," and the advice of physicians, friends, and relatives. Such health information was concerned primarily with the prevention or, more often, the cure of physical illness.

American physical education in the early part of the 20th century was a combination of personal dedication, physical fitness cultism, rigidly formalized programs, and a philosophy that placed physical culture and hygiene high on the scale of values for "the good life." The rather narrow, almost Puritanical, view of physical education at that time placed great emphasis on the physical and moral virtues of rigorous exercise. Social, emotional, recreational, and intellectual outcomes were not yet fully recognized (Bucher 1972; Rice 1969; Van Dalen 1971).

Health was proposed as far back as 1838 as an essential part of education by Horace Mann, "father of the public schools" in the United States. The suggestion was not accepted by educators of that era and little is recorded of actual instruction in health-related areas until the late 19th century though books on hygiene were available. At that time both elementary and secondary schools introduced a simplified anatomy and physiology into the curriculum. Implications for day-to-day healthful living were few and far between (Bucher 1971; Means 1962).

Physical education and health education both changed in parallel fashion as they gained increased recognition and emphasis in America's schools and colleges during the first half of this century. Except for the periods during and immediately following World Wars I and II, both fields took on a less didactic, more functional approach. Physical educators stressed the social, emotional, recreational, and intellectual outcomes along with physical fitness and motor learning. Health educators were beginning to move beyond the old "blood and bone" hygiene into a new era of concept-oriented education in health science (Anderson 1972; Hanlon 1971; Irwin 1945; Means 1962).

SIMILARITIES AND DIFFERENCES

Today's programs of health education and physical education continue to share similarities. Yet both are now established as essential but uniquely different facets in the kaleidoscope of general education.

Curriculum content for the two fields is substantially different. *Physical education* provides learning experiences in individual and dual sports, team games, aquatics, calisthenics and gymnastics, fundamental skills, and dance and related rhythmic activities (Bucher 1972; Irwin 1945). *Health education* seeks to develop knowledges, attitudes, and behavioral changes in the areas of mental health, drug use and abuse, consumer health, alcohol and smoking, health care, dental health, acute and chronic illness, nutrition, safety, vision and hearing, human sexuality, physical fitness, skin care, community health and environment, and first-aid and emergency care (Cal. Dept. Ed. 1972; Hoyman, 1973; Irwin 1945; Sinacore, 1971; Sliepcevich, 1964). All of this was in the interest of protecting, maintaining, and improving the health of the individual, the family, and the community. Fundamental differences in content are quite obvious. Still there are some significant similarities and interrelationships.

The curricula of physical education and health education exhibit several important points of co-identity and mutually reciprocal relationships. Clark Hetherington (1921) drew attention to the relevance of physical education objectives to those of public health. Rugen (1940) urged the acceptance of responsibility of physical educators for health instruction in schools. Later

Irwin (1945), Rugen (1951, 1952), and Sliepcevich (1961) delineated areas of common concern and pointed up opportunities for correlated teaching.

A number of topics offer rich opportunity for instructional interrelationships between the two fields. Areas of common concern include physical fitness, body dynamics, nutrition, drug abuse, alcohol and smoking, skin and foot care, mental and physical fatigue, sports safety, prevention and care of athletic injuries, exercise and heart health, sex differences in performance, sports and mental health, and the self-image (Bruess 1970; Hetherington 1921; Hondras 1969; Irwin 1945; Joint Comm. 1965; Oberteuffer 1972; Rugen 1951, 1952, 1940; Sliepcevich 1964, 1961).

Methods and materials for physical education and health education are fundamentally different. Health science is primarily an academic discipline conducted in the classroom. Physical education takes place in the setting of the gymnasium, the playing field or court, the natatorium, or the dance studio (Bucher 1972, 1971; Irwin 1945).

Both physical education and health education have benefited from the progress of research in the psychologies of learning. Both have increasingly used motion picture films, filmstrips, TV videotapes, recordings, cassettes, and, particularly in health teaching, much improved textbooks and workbooks (Anderson 1972; Bucher 1972; Cornacchia 1974; Joint Comm. 1973; Jones 1968; Mayshark 1972; Pollock 1974; Read 1971).

Professional preparation during the first half of this century in most colleges and universities was combined — or "homogenized" — under the aegis of "health and physical education." Such programs provided at best for one or two courses in health education for prospective teachers of physical education.

More recently there has been a trend toward increasing the health science background of students majoring in physical education (AAHPER 1962; Cornacchia 1974; Joint Comm. 1973; Mayshark 1972; Means 1962). Many universities today are encouraging physical education majors to minor in health education. School health education study data disclosed the fact that approximately 80 percent of health classes in junior and senior high schools are taught by physical educators (Sleipcevich 1964). This finding has provoked mixed reactions from health educators. Some "point with pride" while others "view with alarm," depending largely on individual background and experience. Yet with the growing number of professional students in physical education getting a better background in health education as a minor field or area of emphasis, there is more likelihood that some physical educators can serve effectively as health science teachers in our schools and colleges.

The history of physical education is replete with the names of leaders who also made major contributions to the field of health education. Clark Hetherington, Mabel Rugen, Leslie Irwin, Delbert Oberteuffer, Dorothy La

Salle, John Shaw, Pattric Ruth O'Keefe, James F. Rogers, Dr. Charles C. Wilson, Dr. Oliver Byrd, Arthur H. Steinhaus, Ruth Abernathy, Edward B. Johns, Warren Johnson, Dr. Margaret Bell, Carl Willgoose, and Elena Sliepcevich are just a sample of the "dual professional personalities" who worked to raise health education to its present level. Space limitations make it impossible to include here anything but an abbreviated representative list. Yet the point is clear: a significant number of erstwhile physical educators have demonstrated productive leadership in school and college health education.

Professional preparation of students majoring or minoring in health education has developed both in quality and quantity over the past 30 years (AAHPER 1962; Breuss 1970; Comm. on Phil. 1962; Cornacchia 1974; Means 1962; Pollock 1974). With the proliferation of research and content in the health sciences there has been necessarily a greater need for better *content* background of prospective health educators (AAHPER 1962; Anderson 1972; Cornacchia 1974; Oberteuffer 1972; Willgoose 1969, 1973). There has been growing concern in some quarters of the profession that modern health educators are sometimes long on method and short on scientific content (Cornacchia 1974; Willgoose 1973).

Increased emphasis in professional preparation has been placed on courses in genetics, research in health science, psychology, virology, immunology, public health and preventive medicine, health economics, health statistics, human sexuality, pharmacology, alcohol and other drugs, aging and health, maternal and child health, epidemiology, accident prevention, sociology, anthropology, environmental pollution, nutrition, and other significant content areas that undergird the health sciences. Perhaps this content emphasis will bring about a more realistic balance between methods and content.

CONTINUING RELATIONSHIPS

Although the trend to separate health education and physical education continues at the university level, the delineation of disciplines usually exists within a common administrative unit. Hence, both professional areas are recognized as distinct entities—departmental or divisional—functioning under the broader academic umbrella of a common school or college. Of course public health education programs are usually administered within schools of public health and generally have little liaison with physical education.

The future for health education is bright—as it is for physical education. New problems and challenges have set new dimensions and fresh approaches for school and college health education (Hoyman 1973; Joint Comm. 1973, 1965; Jones 1968; Pollock 1974; Willgoose 1973). Looking ahead several decades, it is probable that modern health education will attain a more independent identity. Yet old ties will inevitably remain, particularly when certain significant areas of content commonality continue to be regarded as important objectives of both fields.

REFERENCES

AAHPER, 1974. *Professional preparation in dance, physical education, recreation education, safety education, and school health education.* Washington, D.C. AAHPER.

_____, 1962. *Professional preparation in health education, physical education, recreation education.* Report of a national conference. Washington, D.C.: AAHPER.

Anderson, C. L., 1972. *School health practice.* St. Louis; C.V. Mosby Co.

Beck, J. B., 1966. *Medicine in the American colonies.* Albuquerque: Horn & Wallace Publishers, Inc. (Original printed in Albany, New York, 1850.)

Breuss, C. E., 1970. Approach to preparing health majors, *Journal of school health,* **40** : 545-546 (December).

Bucher, C. A., 1971. *Administration of health and physical education programs, including athletics.* St. Louis: C. V. Mosby Co.

_____, 1972. *Foundations of physical education.* St. Louis: C.B. Mosby Co.

California State Department of Education, 1972. *Framework for health instruction in California public schools.* Sacramento: the Department.

Commission on Philosophy, Division of Health Education, American Association for Health, Physical Education, and Recreation, 1962. A point of view of school health education, *JOHPER,* **33** : 24-26 (November).

Cornacchia, H. J. and W. M. Staton, 1974. *Health in elementary schools.* St. Louis: C.V. Mosby Co.

Gardiner, E. N., 1930. *Athletics of the ancient worlds.* Oxford, England: Clarendon Press.

Hanlon, J. A., 1969. *Principles of public health administration.* St. Louis: C. V. Mosby Co.

Hanlon, J. J., and E. McHose, 1971. *Design for health.* Philadelphia: Lea & Febiger.

Hetherington, C., 1921. Relationship of physical education objectives to public health. *American journal of public health,* **11** : 520-528 (June).

Hondras, T. H.,, 1969. Correlating health instruction with physical education. *JOHPER* **40 :** 75 (January).

Hoyman, H. S., 1973. New frontiers in health education, *Journal of school health,* **43** : 423-430 (September).

Irwin, L. W., 1945. *Curriculum in health and physical education.* St. Louis: C.V. Mosby Co.

Joint Committee on Health Education Terminology, 1973. *School health review.* **4** : 25-30 (November-December).

Joint Committee on Health Problems in Education of the National Education Association and the American Medical Association, 1961, *Health education.* Washington, D.C.: National Education Association.

Joint Committee on Health Problems in Education of the National Education Association and the American Medical Association, 1965. *Why health education.* Chicago: American Medical Association.

Jones, H. L., and Mileff, E., 1968. Health education. *Review of educational research* **38** : 512-527 (December).

Maple, E., 1968. *Magic, medicine and quackery.* London: Robert Hale Ltd.

Mayshark, C., and R. A. Foster, 1972. *Health education in secondary schools.* St. Louis: C.V. Mosby Co.

Means, R. K., 1962. *A history of health education in the United States.* Philadelphia: Lea & Febiger.

Oberteuffer, D., O. A. Harrelson, and M. B. Pollock, 1972. *School health education.* New York: Harper & Row.

Pollock, M. B., and D. Oberteuffer, 1974. *Health science for young children.* New York: Harper & Row.

Read, D. A., and W. H. Greene, 1971. *Creative teaching in health.* Riverside, New Jersey: Macmillan Co.

Rice, E. A., J. L. Hutchinson, and M. Lee, 1969. *A brief history of physical education.* New York: Ronald Press.

Rugen, M. E., 1951. Physical education's contributions to health education, *JOHPER,* **22** :25-28 (June).

Rugen, M. E. (ed)., 1951, 1952. The physical educator asks about health. *JOHPER* **22** : 11-14, 16 (December); **23** : 23-25 (January); **23** : 21-22, 38 (February).

———, 1940. The physical educator's responsibility for health instruction. *Journal-Lancet* 60 : 371-373 (August).

Sinacore, J. S., 1971. Basis of health education. *Journal of school health* **41** : 303-309 (June).

Sliepcevich, E. M., 1964. *School health education study; a summary report.* Washington, D.C.: School Health Education Study.

———, 1961. The responsibility of the physical educator for health instruction, *JOHPER,* **32** : 32-33, 70 (January).

Van Dalen, D. B., and B. L. Bennett, 1971. *A world history of physical education.* New York: Prentice-Hall, Inc.

Willgoose, C. E., 1969. *Health education in the elementary school.* Philadelphia: W. B. Saunders Co.

Willgoose, C. E., 1973. Saving the curriculum in health education, *Journal of school health,* **43** : 189-191 (March).

83

Physical Education Related to Community Health

Henry J. Montoye

The term "physical education" when used in its broadest sense includes programs for middle-aged and older people and even rehabilitative programs. Therefore this discussion is not confined to school physical education classes.

There are few if any good measures of health. A famous physiologist, Dr. Passmore of Edinburgh, when asked what he thought was a good sign of health, said, "On my way home my path leads across an open field. There is a bit of a brook and over it a small foot bridge. When I prefer to jump across that stream, I know I'm in good health" (Haun 1965). The *joie de vivre* certainly reflects health but is not a precise measure of health. A number of years ago Dr. David B. Dill (1933), distinguished exercise physiologist, expressed the view that one's capacity for physical work is a positive way of measuring health. There is abundant evidence that if inactive people undertake an exercise program, their work capacity improves. These changes as well as the physiological adjustments that make greater work capacity possible are well documented in the better physiology of exercise textbooks. (See Astrand and Rodahl 1970, for example.) However, some people argue that exercise (i.e., training) only better equips one to do more exercise and this is unrelated to the disease process.

BRIEF HISTORY

The question of whether the amount or intensity of physical activity in which one engages is related to the maintenance of health or the development of disease is not new. Hippocrates, in the fifth century B. C., in his treatise *Airs, Waters, Places,* stated:

> Therefore, on arrival at a town with which he is unfamiliar, a physician should examine its position with respect to the winds and the risings of the sun. . . the mode of life also of the inhabitants that is pleasing to them, whether they are heavy drinkers, taking lunch, and inactive, or athletic, industrious, eating much, and drinking little (Runes 1964).

Hippocrates in another treatise, *Regimen,* advocated exercise as preventive medicine:

> Exercise should be many and of all kinds; running on the double track increased gradually; wrestling after being oiled, begun with light exercises and gradually made long; sharp walks after exercises, short walks in the sun after dinner; many walks in the early morning, quiet to begin with, increasing till they are violent and then gently finishing (Hunter 1962).

There were many suggestions in the early middle ages and before that exercise is important to the maintenance of health. It was inevitable that, with the development of printing, these suggestions and observations were brought together in books published during the 16th century. The first was Mendez, (translated 1960) *Book of Bodily Exercise,* published in 1553, and the second by Mercurialis (1569) *The Art of Gymnastics Among the Ancients,* published in 1569. Both authors extolled the benefits of exercise; Mendez, from his own observations, and Mercurialis quoting many others. These works contained little in the way of scientific proof.

Ramazzini, an epidemiologist who wrote what is probably the first book on occupational disease more than 250 years ago, believed a sedentary life contributed to ill-health:

> All sedentary workers, tailors above all and women who do needlework in their homes day and night to make a living, suffer from the itch, are a bad color, and in poor condition. . . . These workers, then, suffer from general ill-health and an excessive accumulation of unwholesome humors caused by their sedentary life; this applies especially to cobblers and tailors (Ramazzini 1940).

In more recent times R. Tait McKenzie (1909), who wrote *Exercise in Education and Medicine* in 1909, typifies professional leaders of an era when medicine and physical education were closely related. It was common at that time for physicians to be chairmen of college physical education departments. The article by Steinhaus (1933) "The Chronic Effects of Exercise," and the little-known five-volume series edited by J.B. Nash (1933) are also classics of this period. In the latter reference the relation of exercise and health are reviewed by scholars in many disciplines. The fourth volume in this series is called "Physiological Health."

During the last few years several excellent references (AAHPER 1960; Franks 1969; Johnson 1960; Kraus 1961; Staley 1960) have appeared in which the relationship of exercise and health is the focus. Additionally there are some good summaries of research on particular diseases as they relate to physical activity.

With the increase in use of labor-saving devices and motorized transportation, the role of sedentary living as a factor in disease susceptibility has assumed greater significance. This is particularly true in recent years because degenerative diseases now appear more frequently as causes of death. Considerably less progress has been achieved in preventing these conditions, which are most closely correlated with habits of living, than in preventing or curing certain childhood diseases and acute infections.

PHYSICAL ACTIVITY: OCCUPATIONAL AND LEISURE

Occupational work and leisure-time activities are the only sources of physical activity. Leisure-time activities include sports, dance, and calisthenic-type programs, all of which constitute or are related to physical education. However, walking or riding a bicycle to or from work or for pleasure, gardening, and home repairs or construction, are also leisure-time activities but are not generally associated with physical education programs. Most of the direct evidence that exercise is a potent tool in preventive medicine is based upon epidemiological studies in which only occupational activity has been reported. There are obvious reasons for this. The effects of physical activity can be expected to be greater when the exercise is carried on six to eight hours a day, five days a week, as contrasted with a few hours per week of leisure-time physical activity. Additionally in most cases occupational activity is easier to assess because the job frequently defines the duration, frequency, and types of activities.

On the other hand, from a very practical point of view, it is the leisure-time physical activity that is most important. In the first place, many workers in highly industrialized societies have sedentary occupations. It is only the volitional, off-the-job pursuits that differentiate these people on the basis of physical activity. Secondly, from the standpoint of intervention programs, it is unlikely we will convince many bank executives that they should become carpenters in order to engage in more physical activity. Thirdly, with the trend for shorter work days and a four-day week, the average worker has more leisure hours available. Finally, in the study of old people, most of whom are no longer employed, leisure is the only source of physical activity.

Since there is appreciable evidence that physical activity in later life retards or prevents the development of certain diseases or disabilities, it is tempting to conclude that this is proof that physical education in the elementary or high school contributes to a longer and healthier life. If physical education during the school years is to affect health in later life, attitudes and habits must be developed that lead to leisure-time participation in physical activity later in life. That such attitudes and habits will be developed needs to be supported by good research evidence. Because this evidence is lacking, one should not infer that school programs are unimportant. On the contrary, insofar as health is concerned, they are probably most important for the following reasons:

1. It is likely easier to develop the habit of regular exercise in children than to change the life-styles of middle-aged people who have been sedentary for 15 to 20 years.
2. Interests and skills in sports are best developed at a young age. It is not that older people cannot learn new skills—there is clear evidence that they can—it is just that older people generally have less time and inclination to do so. Embarrassment due to awkwardness and fear of injury doubtlessly are factors.
3. Chronic diseases frequently have their origins early in life. For example, a heart attack may occur at age 50 but underlying atherosclerosis begins much earlier in life.

CAUSE AND EFFECT

In many ways physical education is similar to nutrition. The importance of each depends to a considerable extent on its relation to health. Good health requires good nutrition throughout life. It is not possible during childhood to consume and store sufficient minerals and vitamins to last a lifetime. Similarly, vigorous exercise taken only in our youth will have little effect in later life. The study of former outstanding athletes has made this abundantly clear (Montoye 1967). Also, like nutrition, exercise has three dimensions (frequency, duration, and intensity) that likely determine to some extent the health benefits of participation. A fourth dimension could be added, namely the conditions or environment in which exercise is conducted.

On the surface it would appear relatively simple to isolate the specific contributions of exercise to health. Actually this is rather difficult because habits of living are interrelated. People who are active tend to be lean; hence, is it the leanness, the activity, or both that is responsible? It is conceivable, for example, that sedentary occupations are psychologically more stressful and the stress may be the significant factor, not the lack of physical activity. When a middle-aged sedentary person undertakes a training program he or she may become more aware of breathlessness and give up smoking. One may argue that this may be academic. Indeed, from the viewpoint of the physical educator responsible for an exercise program, it may well be unimportant whether the effects of exercise are direct or indirect.

THERAPEUTICS

Physical education has a long history of an association with therapeutics, that is, treating patients using exercise in some way. Corrective and adaptive physical education programs in our schools are modern examples of this. It is common practice to have the cooperation of a physician in the conduct of such programs for the handicapped. There have been few medical-legal problems in these programs. In older subjects the problem is quite different. For example, in prescribing exercise for people who have already had a heart attack (called a secondary prevention program), the situation is more complicated. Quite aside from the exercise program, the patient is more likely to have a second heart attack than for a normal person to sustain one. When exercise is prescribed in these cases, it should be with the knowledge of and over the signature of a physician lest the physical educator be accused of practicing medicine.

In recent years a large literature has accumulated showing the benefit of exercise in patients—particularly heart patients. Many of these reports are observational studies. Also, in many instances other factors than exercise (diet, changes in occupation, smoking habits, etc.) are manipulated. Nevertheless, much useful data showing the effects of exercise have accumulated. This is not quite the same as preventive medicine (exercise) in essentially healthy subjects (sometimes called primary prevention), but the principles and even the results probably apply in most cases.

EXERCISE AND SPECIFIC DISABILITIES

Longevity. There is no solid scientific evidence, to the writer's knowledge, that exercise extends the longevity of people in general. There is suggestion that this might be true, as seen in animal studies. But these investigations are so limited and the application to human beings so questionable that the claim cannot be made with much confidence. It is difficult to show the effects of a sedentary life on longevity because people die from many causes. Most investigators therefore have wisely elected to study the effects of physical activity on the prevention or on the course of *specific* diseases—particularly those logically related to exercise—or on the "aging process."

Obesity. Sufficient evidence is available to conclude that exercise is a significant factor in maintaining desirable body weight. In some obese individuals and in some moderately overweight people, exercise is effective in reducing body fat. The mechanism may be more complicated than simply the energy expenditure in the form of work and heat exceeding energy intake in the form of food. Physical activity may depress the appetite, perhaps by raising the temperature of the hypothalamus. Also the basal metabolic rate is elevated in some people for a considerable time after the exercise. There appears to be no evidence that "spot" reducing is possible through exercise. Gadgets of various kinds seem to be effective only in the proportion to the degree they require people to expend energy. The usefulness of vibrators, stimulators, or weight belts are governed by the same principle. Since they generally require the subject to expend little energy they are, in most instances, ineffective. Mayer (1968) is probably the best reference in the area of exercise and weight control.

Cardiovascular disease. A number of summaries and collections of papers on the role of exercise in heart disease have appeared in recent years (Fox 1972; Karvonen 1967; Montoye 1962; Proceedings 1967). Most of the evidence that sedentary living contributes to the early development of cardiovascular disease is based on epidemiologic studies of occupation. This evidence together with the results of other kinds of studies shows that the high incidence of coronary heart disease in relatively young adults is in part due to a sedentary life. Although in animal studies atherosclerosis (the underlying factor in most coronary heart disease) has been retarded and even reversed, data from studies on human beings indicate that the development of atherosclerosis is probably not much affected by physical training. On the other hand people who are active seem better able to live with atherosclerosis and are able to avoid or survive a heart attack than are less active persons. The most promising explanation for this lies in the increased vascularization of the myocardium as a result of regular exercise. However, habitual physical activity or training probably to some extent also lowers resting and exercise blood pressure, serum total cholesterol, and serum triglycerides. There is also the possibility that exercise has favorable psychic affects that tend to prevent or delay heart attacks. Additionally there is some evidence of favorable influences of exercise on blood coagulation time (decreased) and fibrinolysis (increased).

Childbirth and menstruation. A number of observational studies have been reported, particularly in Europe, in which habits of regular physical activity among women is believed to result in less complications during childbirth. However, no well-controlled studies have been done. There is evidence that low back pain following pregnancy in some women is associated with low levels of physical activity. This may be part of a general low back pain condition in middle-aged men and women. Certain exercises and regular physical activity appear to be effective in the management of dysmenorrhea, but here again additional careful studies are needed.

Cancer. Animal studies suggest beneficial effects of exercise in delaying the onset and progress of mammary cancer. However, the effects may be indirect through control of body fatness. Careful investigations of the relationship of physical activity to cancer development in human beings have not been reported, as far as is known to this reviewer.

Osteoporosis. Demineralization of bones occurs almost universally, and especially in women, beyond middle-age. Whether a sedentary life is partially responsible for this is not known. Almost complete inactivity (bedrest, space flight, immobilization) results in marked loss of cortical bone even in young people. However, only a minimal amount of weight-supporting activity may be all that is necessary to maintain normal bone density. The question of whether regular vigorous activity reduces the degree of osteoporosis in older individuals is an important one because of the large numbers of older people who sustain a hip fracture, which in turn is related to osteoporosis. Hip fracture in this age group carries with it many other problems associated with loss of mobility.

Aging. The study of the effects of physical activity on rate of aging is particularly difficult for several reasons. In the study of populations, most people are less active as they become older. To what extent then are the changes due to aging and to what extent are they the result of a more sedentary life? Aging is generally a slow process; hence longitudinal and experimental studies are beset with difficulties. The application to humans of studies in animals whose life span is short is always open to question.

It is clear that exercise or physical training in later life preserves work and metabolic capacities and maintains strength and flexibility, at least to some extent. Furthermore, almost invariably the changes in structure or function that result from a program of physical exercise are in the direction characterizing youth.

REFERENCES

AAHPER, 1960. *Research quarterly,* **31** : 261-375 (Part II) (May).

Astrand, P. O., and K. Rodahl, 1970. *Textbook of work physiology.* New York: McGraw-Hill Book Company.

Dill, D. B., 1933. A measure of health—the capacity of an individual for work, part II, section 4 in *Interpretations of physical education, Vol. IV,* of *Physiological health,* Nash, J. B. (ed.) New York: A.S. Barnes and Company.

Fox, S. M., and J. L. Boyer, 1972. Physical activity and coronary heart disease, *Physical fitness research digest,* Series 2, No. 2 (April).

Franks, D. (ed.), 1969. *Exercise and fitness.* Chicago: The Athletic Institute.

Haun, P., 1965. *Recreation: a medical viewpoint.* New York: Teachers College, Columbia University.

Hunter, D., 1962. *The diseases of occupations,* Boston: Little, Brown and Company.

Johnson, W. (ed.), 1960. *Science and medicine of exercise and sports.* New York: Harper and Brothers.

Karvonen, M. J., and A. J., Barry, (eds.), 1967. *Physical activity and the heart.* Springfield, Ill: Charles C. Thomas.

Kraus, H., and W. Raab, 1961. *Hypokinetic disease.* Springfield, Ill. Charles C. Thomas.

Mayer, J., 1968. *Overweight: causes, cost, and control.* Englewood Cliffs, N.J.: Prentice-Hall Inc.

McKenzie, R. T., 1909. *Exercise in education and medicine.* Philadelphia: W. B. Saunders Co.

Mendez, C., 1960. *Book of bodily exercise,* translated by Geurra, F. and edited by Kilgour, F. G., New Haven, Conn.: Elizabeth Licht.

Mercurialis, G., 1569. *The art of gymnastics among the ancients.*

Montoye, H. J., 1962. Summary of research on the relationship of exercise to heart disease. *J. sports med. and physical fitness* **2** : 35-43.

———, 1967. Participation in athletics. *Canadian Medical Association journal* **96** : 813-820 (March 25).

Nash, J. B. (ed.), 1933. *Interpretations of physical education,* 5 volumes. New York: A.S. Barnes and Company.

Proceedings, International Symposium on Physical Activity and Cardiovascular Health, 1967. *Canadian medical association journal,* vol. **96**, no. 12 (March 25).

Ramazzini, B., 1940. *De morbis artificum* (1713), translated by W. C. Wright. Chicago: University of Chicago Press.

Runes, D. D., and T. Kierman, (eds.), 1964. *Hippocrates: The theory and practice of medicine.* New York: Philosophical Library.

Staley, S. C., T. K. Cureton, L. Huelster, and A. J. Barry, 1960. *Exercise and fitness.* Urbana, Ill.: University of Illinois.

Steinhaus, A. H., 1933. Chronic effects of exercise, *Physiol. rev.,* **13** : 103-147.

84

Physical Education Related to Gerontology

Ernst Jokl

The yearning after perennial youth is one of the eternal dreams of mankind, vividly expressed in Lucas Cranach's painting "Fountain of Youth." It shows old women being brought to a wondrous pool that restores youthful vigor and beauty so that once more they can partake in the pleasures of life.

The picture raises a question modern science has tried to answer, namely that of the alterability of the aging process. The question has broad implications in that, until not so long ago, life's chronological progress was thought to be designed as a fixed sequence of patterns much as Shakepeare has described them in "As You Like It":

> All the world's a stage,
> And all the men and women merely players:
> They have their exits and their entrances;
> And one man in his time plays many parts,
> His acts being seven ages. At first the infant,
> Mewling and puking in the nurse's arms.
> And then the whining schoolboy, with his satchel,
> And shining morning face, creeping like a snail
> Unwillingly to school. And then the lover,
> Sighing like furnace, with a woeful ballad
> Made to his mistress' eyebrow. Then a soldier,
> Full of strange oaths, and bearded like the bard
> Jealous in honour, sudden and quick in quarrel
> Seeking the bubble reputation
> Even in the cannon's mouth. And then the justice,
> In fair round belly with good capon lin'd,
> With eyes severe, and beard of formal cut,
> Full of wise saws and modern instances;
> And so he plays his part. The sixth age shifts
> Into the lean and slipper'd pantaloon,
> With spectacles on nose and pouch on side,
> His youthful hose wel sav'd a world too wide
> For his shrunk shank; and his big manly voice,
> Turning again towards childish treble, pipes
> And whistles in his sound. Last scene of all,
> That ends this strange eventful history,
> Is second childishness, and mere oblivion,
> Sans teeth, sans eyes, sans taste, sans everything.

Recent physiological and clinical studies with athletes have revealed that "the seven stages of man" are not fixed rigidly. That youth is not necessarily characterized by physical and mental immaturity, has become evident since many competitors as young as 14 reach Olympic finals in swimming, ice-skating, gymnastics, and other sports. The biographic literature contains a number of individual descriptions of outstanding young musicians, chess players, and performers in other fields. Mozart played before Empress Maria Theresa when he was seven. However, such cases are uncommon.

Several other determinants of human phenotypes were shown to be amenable to major changes through intensive physical training, among them the status of women. Simone de Beauvoir (1953) scornfully entitled her famous book "The Second Sex." Today, women's record performance standards in all branches of sport are beyond the reach of the majority of men. Another revision of established concepts became necessary when athletic excellence was achieved by large numbers of persons afflicted with irremediable physical handicaps. Finally entire population groups whose social advancement had been held back arbitrarily initiated their emancipation through sport. It is one of the most worthwhile achievements of the United States sports movement to have given special impetus to the emancipation of the nation's black citizens.

PHYSICAL ACTIVITY AND AGING

The scientific community has become concerned specifically with yet another problem whose reevaluation became necessary when more and more well-trained old men and women made their appearance in athletic contests: the problem of physical activity and aging. In the 1950s a comprehensive study of structural and functional changes in men and women between 30 and 90 years of age was conducted by the National Institutes of Health. The investigators described a consistent trend of decline over the years of the following parameters: basal metabolic rate, work rate, cardiac output, vital capacity, maximum breathing capacity, nerve conduction velocity, body water content, filtration rate of kidney, and kidney plasma flow (Strehler 1962) (see Fig. 84.1). Similar findings relating to single physiological parameters had been noted previously: Professor Sid Robinson (1938) of the Harvard Fatigue Laboratory reported that the capacity of the heart to accelerate during exercise declines with age. Professor Hollman (1963) of Cologne noted a steady reduction with aging of maximal oxygen intake capacity, a generally accepted indicator of physical endurance.

In sharp disagreement with these studies were observations of large numbers of middle-aged and old men and women who participated in sports. Textbooks of physiology and medicine took no cognizance of these observations until recently. In 1952 the writer compiled the following list to show that the then generally accepted view that "aging" is invariably accompanied by a decline of physical power was untenable.

Dr. Savolainen of Finland won a bronze medal in the horizontal bar competition at Helsinki in 1952 at the age of 45; the Swiss 10-km. walking champion Schwab, was 48 at the time of his start at the 1948 Olympic Games; the third in the 50-km. walk, Johnson of Great Britain, was 48; the second in the marathon,

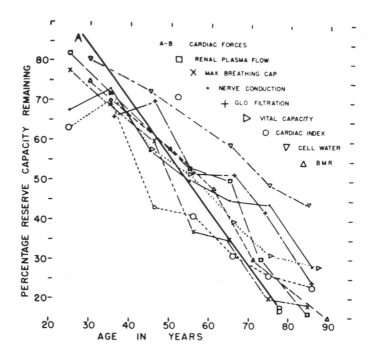

Fig. 84.1 Decline of body functions with age.

Richard, 49; the hurdler, Finlay, 40. The French tennis champions Borotra and Cochet, both close to their middle 50s, were finalists in several international tournaments in 1952. When he was 47, Tilden beat the 24-year-old champion, Don Budge. The British oarsman, Jack Beresford, five-fold Olympic winner in rowing, participated in a boat race on his 50th birthday. The Swiss mountaineer, Chevalier of Geneva, climbed the Jungfrau when he was 74 years old. The 49-year-old Tibetan, Dawa Tondu, was chief carrier for the British Everest Expedition. Two former world record swimmers, Arne Borg of Sweden and Johnny Weismuller of the U.S., swam the 100 m. around 60 sec. when they were 50 years of age.

These observations indicated the need to conduct systematic investigations of the problem of physical activity and aging. In 1952 the writer examined all of the 1704 participants of the German National Festival for Senior Gymnast (Jokl 1954). Each carried out prescribed gymnastic exercises, such as those shown in Fig. 84.2, as well as track and field activities. The results of these investigations, reported in a monograph that appeared in 1954, left no doubt that trained old people are more fit than untrained young people. Once this fact was established, the question of nature and scope of the effects of sustained physical training upon the "aging process" offered

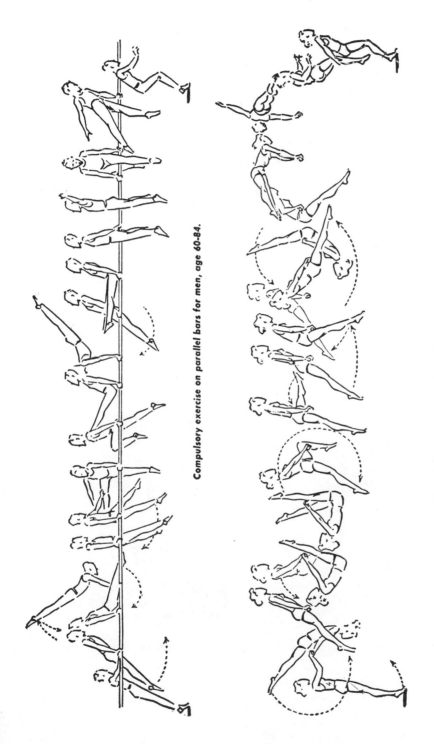

Compulsory exercise on parallel bars for men, age 60-84.

Compulsory exercise on horizontal bar for women, age 32-52.

Fig. 84.2. Compulsory apparatus exercises for senior gymnastic festival (men 60-84 and women 32-52).

itself for analysis. Since 1950 the writer has devoted several studies to its clarification. The present state of our knowledge can be summarized as follows:

1. Training inhibits the decline with the years of "form," specifically loss of lean body mass and increase of surplus fat—a common trend in our affluent society. The change in the appearance of the well-trained wrestler in Fig. 84.3 at age 25 and again after 30 years of overeating and physical inactivity, speaks for itself (Jokl 1955).

2. Training inhibits the decline with the years of a variety of *functional* parameters such as those demanded from all participants in the 1952

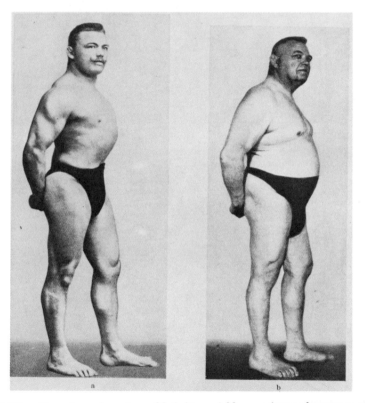

Fig. 84.3 Wrestling champion at age 25 (left), and 30 years later after years of inactivity (right).

Gymnastic Festival. The implications of physical fitness thus documented are far-reaching. They include physiological, psychological, and social adjustments whose beneficial influence on the status of "the old" has been demonstrated in much detail through comparative studies of "senior athletes" and inmates of old-age homes.

3. Training protects against a number of illnesses believed to be "naturally" associated with "the aging process," chief among them the ischemic heart diseases.*

RECENT RESEARCH INFORMATION

Fig. 84.4 shows two effects of training upon muscle tissue—hypertrophy and capillarization. Both are reversible. Discontinuation of training causes "inactivity-atrophy" as well as reduction of blood supply. Another ubiquitous accompaniment of physical inactivity is deposition of surplus fat. With rare but noteworthy exceptions "fatness" and "fitness" are mutually exclusive attributes (Cureton 1969). Most well-trained male endurance athletes carry not more than 5-7 percent fat. By contrast, the body of the average American male at age 50 consists of 20-25 percent fat. In this context it is well to realize that on the whole obesity is not genetically programmed. Fig. 84.5 shows tracings of soft-tissue roentgentograms of chest and abdominal walls of monozygotic triplets, that is, of three adult individuals whose "design" is identical. The differences in the thickness of fat layers are due to different activity and eating habits. Hypotheses of hereditary control of deposition of excess fat are clearly not tenable (Garn 1963).

Another parameter of physique modifiable through exercise is the water content of the body referred to previously in connection with the findings in the "aging" study of the U.S. National Institutes of Health. Figure 84.6 shows results of analyses of blood volumes of "normal," obese, and lean men and women—also of trained athletes (Jokl 1972). The data are relevant to geriatrics since a reduction of blood volume accompanies "aging" in sedentary subjects. Vascularization of the brain is reduced in most old people (Fig. 84.7). It is not as yet known whether this latter trend can be influenced through training (Jokl 1970). In 1956 the writer reported that systolic contraction power of the heart is greater in trained than in untrained men and women (Fig. 84.8). Since a decline of systolic contraction power was at that time considered an inevitable accompaniment of aging, ballistocardiograms of old athletes at rest

---

* It is a matter of major interest that two summaries of the problem of aging do not deal with the subject of modifiability through physical training: Simone de Beauvoir's voluminous monograph on aging published in 1971, and W. Ferguson Andersen's contribution to the book *The Biology of Affluence* (1972). The issue has been fully discussed in a book, *Physical Activity and Aging,* by D. Brunner and E. Jokl (1970).

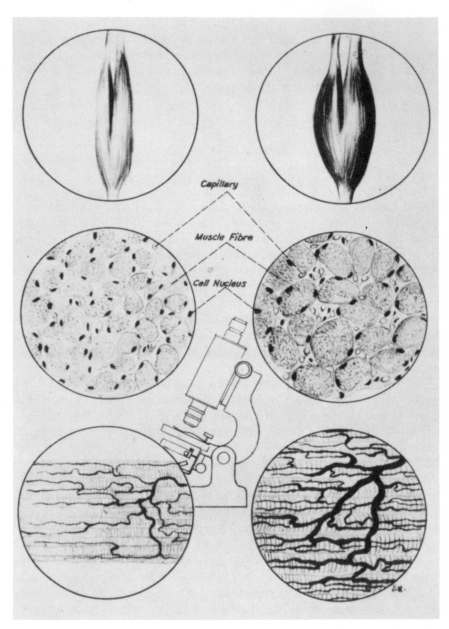

Fig. 84.4 Untrained (left) and trained (right) muscle showing hypertrophy and increased capillarization.

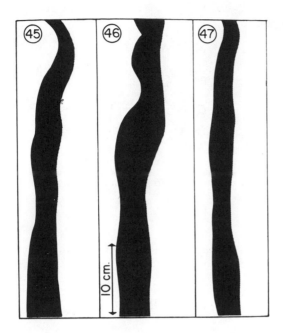

Fig. 84.5 Soft-tissue roentgentograms of a set of monozygotic triplets.

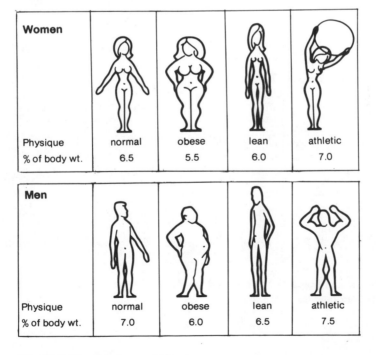

Fig. 84.6 Blood volume analyses.

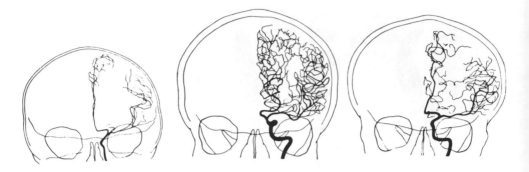

Fig. 84.7 Normal cerebral arteriogram of one-year-old child (left), young adult (middle), and 75-year-old man (right).

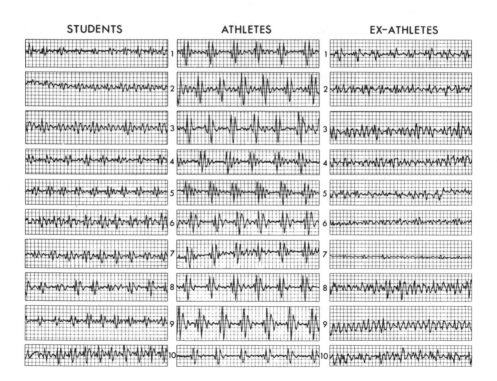

Fig. 84.8. Ballistocardiograms of untrained and trained athletes, and of former athletes out of training.

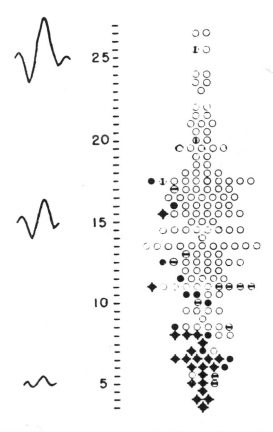

Fig. 84.9 Long-term implications of ballistocardiographic amplitudes.

Legend: o no heart disease developed;
           ● those who developed undoubted heart disease
           ✦ those who died from heart disease
           ⊖ those who developed a doubtful cardiac status
           ⊙ those who developed hypertension without evidence of heart disease

rest as well as after exercise were examined. The favorable effect of training on cardiac power proved to be the same in old and young subjects. Professor Isaac Starr of Philadelphia has since presented data demonstrating that variants of myocardial quality, identifiable through ballistocardiography, are not only of physiological but also of clinical significance. Middle-aged men whose ballistocardiographic tracings at rest were characterized by large systolic amplitudes remained free of heart disease during the ensuing 20 years; contrariwise, most of those whose tracings showed small deflections became victims of coronary or myocardial afflictions (Fig. 84.9). An epidemiological finding of interest in this context was obtained by Professor Yudkin (1957) of London, who noted parallel increases of incidence of coronary mortality and of numbers of radio and television licenses in England between 1940 and 1960 (Fig. 84.10). Both trends reflected the extent to which lack of physical activity affected the bulk of the populations in all western countries during these two decades.

Figure 84.11 summarizes the results of exercise tests conducted with fat and lean boys. The latter's performance capacity was significantly superior

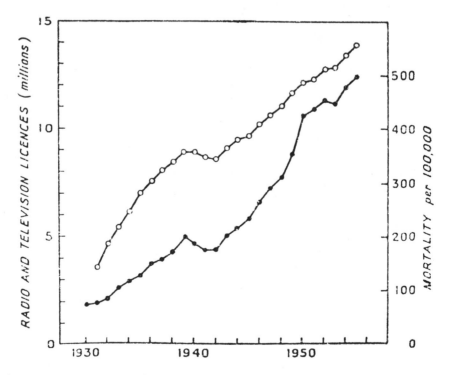

Fig. 84.10 Coronary mortality and radio and TV licenses in England, 1940-1960. (After John Yudkin.)

FAT GROUP MEAN FIT GROUP MEAN

Mean weight	156 pounds	125 pounds
PULL-UPS	.3 ————————	9
SIT-UPS	36 ————————	82
PUSH UP	14 ————————	47
SOFTBALL THROW	125 ft. ————————	188 ft.
STANDING BROAD JUMP	5 ft. 1 in. ————————	6 ft. 4 in.
50 YARD RUN	8.6 sec. ————————	6.4 sec.
SHUTTLE RUN	10.8 sec. ————————	9.4 sec.
600 YARD RUN	2 min. 44 sec. ————————	1 min. 59 sec.

Fig. 84.11. Comparison between results of U.S. President's Council of Youth Fitness test conducted with fat and lean schoolboys age 13 years.

(Jokl 1973). Differences of the same kind and magnitude can be demonstrated in exercise tests with adult and old subjects. The general statement is justified that *training exerts a more determining influence on form and function of the body than age* (Strandell 1964).

Excess fat after 25 years of age is a "coronary risk factor," one of several that has been identified in epidemiological studies conducted with large numbers of subjects, such as at Framingham, Massachusetts (Kinch 1964). Likewise, high cholesterol concentrations in blood and electrocardiographic anomalies, such as inversion of the T-wave in several leads, were implicated. The evidence was derived from retrospective analyses of files of patients after they had suffered attacks of coronary infarction.

Medical observations of athletes do not always fit into the above concept. Three examples show this. First, during a study of physiological responses to exercise of women athletes, a 21-year-old physical education student was found to have a serum cholesterol concentration of 445 mg./100 ml. Medical examination excluded the presence of cardiovascular illness. Her father's blood cholesterol was 190 mg.; her youthful-looking mother, 390 mg. The latter's parents, both alive and well in their eighth decade, likewise had markedly elevated blood cholesterol readings—390 and 344 mg./ 100 ml., respectively.

Second, electrocardiograms obtained from an internationally renowned soccer player during a routine examination showed T-waves that were inverted in multiple limb and precordial leads, at rest as well as after exercise. The tracings were indistinguishable from those recorded from patients with myocardial infarction.

Third, routine medical examinations of athletes have identified several fat champions, among them marathon runners, channel swimmers, weight-lifters, shot putters, ice hockey players, and wrestlers.

The general relevance of these observations is that protection afforded by sustained physical training against ischemic heart diseases is not necessarily mediated through elimination of or reduction of "coronary risk factors." Such protection becomes effective through physiological modalities, all of which as yet are not known. The pathogenic role of the "coronary risk factors" that are currently discussed in cardiology must be evaluated specifically in reference to the fact that they were derived from retrospective analyses of records of victims of coronary infarction.

It is a matter of major practical and theoretical importance to point out at this stage that physical training does not bestow resistance against malignant tumors and against infectious diseases. Otto Warburg and Gerhardt Domagk considered the former possibility in the 1940s, arguing that the improvement through training of the oxygen supply to the tissues of the body may conceivably prevent the metabolic transformation of normal cells into carcinomatous cells that grow "irregularly" because of their ability to derive energy anaerobically. However, this hypothesis has been proved untenable. Also, it is now generally known that athletes are as susceptible to infections as nonathletes, at times even more so.

Geriatric medicine is confronted with the problem of the effectiveness of a sustained exercise regimen as a prophylactic modality against ischemic heart disease, the most common cause of death in the United States today; while a sustained exercise regimen is ineffective against the second most common cause of death, the malignant tumors. It is also ineffective as a prophylactic modality against communicable illnesses.

INTELLECTUAL AND ARTISTIC PERFORMANCE

Recent studies have demonstrated a genetically designed interrelationship between intellectual and motor endowment. Whether these endowments develop depends entirely upon the environment in which the individual is placed. In light of new knowledge of a hidden linkage of the above two qualities, there is a need to initiate studies designed to elucidate the implications of the fact that many old persons excel in intellectual and artistic sectors. It is likely that many of them may possess motor capacities much greater than is presently supposed. If the validity of this assumption can be proved, a number of public policy changes would be called for.

Examples of intellectual and artistic performances of an exceptional quality by old persons are: (1) during the ninth decade of his life, the Italian painter, Titian (1477-1576), presented some of his best works; (2) at an age of 95, Sir Chalres Sherrington (1857-1952) revised his book "Man on his Nature"; and (3) Arthur Rubinstein continued with his concert appearances at the age of 85.

Longevity, like mental and physical capacity, is determined as part of each individual's hereditary endowment. The transformation of these capacities into reality depends upon "nurture." To exemplify, the genetic "driving force" for longevity has not changed during historical times, but the average European and American now lives more than 30 years longer than his forebears did a century ago. Resources for the acquisition of knowledge and skills are available today more readily than ever before. But programs aiming at the improvement of the mode of living of the old do not as yet include efforts to maintain an adequate level of physical fitness.

Life is finite. However, the manner in which old people arrange their "declining years" reflects a great variety of choices of their own.

In Israel in 1966 the writer witnessed an annual event, "The 3-Day-March" to the nation's capital, in which more than 25,000 people participated. Among the walkers was a 100-year-old man who was asked after his arrival, "Isn't it remarkable that at your age you joined in this strenuous venture?" He replied: "What better death could I have than to die on the way to Jerusalem?"

REFERENCES

Beauvoir, S. de, 1953. *The second sex.* New York: Alfred A. Knopf. 1953.

Brozek, J., 1965. *Human body composition.* Oxford: Pergamon Press.

Brunner, D., and E. Jokl, 1970. *Physical activity and aging.* Basel: S. Karger.

Cureton, T. K., 1969. *The physiological effects of exercise programs on adults.* Springfield, IL: Charles C. Thomas.

Garn, S. M., 1963. Human biology and research in body composition, *Ann. N.Y. Acad. Sci.,* **110** :429-446 (September 26).

Hollmann, W., 1963. *Hochst- und dauerleistungsfahigkeit des sportlers.* Muchen: Johann Ambrosius Barth.

Jokl, E., 1954. *Alter und leistung* (monograph). Heidelberg: Springer Verlag.

————, 1970. *Alter und physiotherapie* (ed. V. Bohlau). Stuttgart & New York: F. K. Schattauer Verlag.

————, 1955. Deceleration of aging, *JOHPER,* **26** : 28-30 (April).

————, 1966. Exercise, training and cardiac stroke force. In: Raab, W. (ed.), *Prevention of ischemic heart disease.* Springfield, Ill: Charles C. Thomas.

————, 1972. Korperliches training und altern, *Proc. sci. congr.* 1972, Olympic Games 1972. Munich: Boehringer, Mannheim.

————, 1970. *Physiology of exercise* (2nd edition). Springfield, Ill: Charles C. Thomas.

————, 1973. Physique and performance, *Amer. Corr. Ther. J.,* **27** : 99-112 (August).

Kinch, S. H., A. M. Gittelsohn, and J. T. Doyle, 1964. "Prospective study of degenerative cardiovascular disease," *J. Chron. Dis.,* **17** : 503-514.

Robinson, S., 1938. "Experimental studies of physical fitness in relation to age, *Arbeitsphysiologie,* **10** : 251-323.

Starr, I., and F. C. Wood, 1961. Twenty-year studies with the balistograph, *Circulation,* **23** : 714-732 (May).

Strandell, T., 1964. Circulatory studies on healthy old men, *Acta med. Scand.,* Supplement 414.

Strehler, B. L., 1962. *Time, cells and aging.* New York and London: Academic Press.

Yudkin, J., 1957. Diet and coronary thrombosis, *Lancet,* **2** : 155-162.

85

Physical Education Related to Mental Health

Dorothy La Salle

The increasing amount of emotional maladjustment in American society highlights the fact that mental health programs at state and local levels must be both expanded and improved. The publicity given to problems of mental health seems to indicate that within the 1980s the public will be so aroused as to be willing to give adequate financial support so that good programs can be developed. When that time comes, physical education must be ready to show the part it can and should play in such programs. This statement is a summary of our knowledge of the effect of physical activity on the psyche.

Throughout the literature there are repeated references to the desirability of physical education and its contributions to the wholesome development of personality. These references, although in the main based upon scientific investigation, indicate only a promising beginning. They offer leads for increased investigation toward the realization of a deeper understanding of the significant contributions that physical education can make in the maintenance of emotional equilibrium of boys and girls and of men and women.

Physical education in the form of vigorous daily exercise is a basic physiological need of the human organism. Its importance is equal to that of food and sleep. It is a means of integration. It produces a benign effect on the body that results in feelings of satisfaction and well-being. According to Hopkins (1937) the feeling of satisfaction indicates a low level of tension in the body, which improves its stability and unity. This mild, stimulating feeling is a biological necessity for normal, integrating functions (Hopkins 1937). The resultant condition of integration relaxes the individual, and for the time being at least frees a person from tensions and anxieties. All of us have seen with what joy children run. All of us have seen children enter a gymnasium and immediately start moving rapidly across and around it. We know how exhilarated they look as they run or skip. We know with what difficulty we restrain them and, when restrained, how hard it is to engage their interest in something else. Plant (1937) tells us that "the major education of the visceral system . . . occurs through the play life." Physical activity is natural and extroverting and produces desirable feeling tone in the child. This physiological need must be met; this authority of the body must be recognized if the individual is to be emotionally well-adjusted.

THE SELF-IMAGE

Basic to all else is the development of the self because self-acceptance is an essential of mental health (Jersild 1952). The growth of the self is complex. It does not come readymade; it is acquired and influenced by relationships with other people. An important factor in the development of the self is the attitude toward the body. The body is the symbol of the self, not only to the individual but to the world at large. Speaking in terms of the complete unity of the organism, the body is the self. It is the sum-total of all that a person is. Whatever self one may have, whatever personality or character one may have, are manifested through the body. These are not evident in the appearance only. They are evident in facial expressions, in wrinkles, in gestures, in the voice, the movements, the excitement shown in pleasure, the anger or control in frustration, and through all of the gamut of daily living experiences. The body then is the symbol of the self (Murphy 1947).

Physical education therefore should help each child develop a positive body image. It can and should improve the physical characteristics of the body so that the general image is one that is agreeable and acceptable in our culture. It cannot of course change hereditary characteristics, but it can help the individual gain increasing body control. It can help develop a body that is well-proportioned and pleasing to the eye. It can help the child increase skill in games, sports, and dance. All of these aid in developing a positive body image—a positive self-image—and therefore tend to increase self-acceptance. The body is the instrument with which we interact; it is the means through which we experience. It is essential that it be an instrument at the ready command and desires of the self (Wiles 1956).

PLAY AND THE CHILD'S PERSONALITY

Vigorous and joyous play helps to offset the strains our culture places upon children. The environment, as it impinges upon the personality, causes the individual to create a protective wall early in life. This protective wall, which Plant (1950) calls the envelope, occurs as early as two to three years of age and helps to hide from those about the child the turmoils, the conflicts, and the insecurities within. In play this wall disappears and an individual loses oneself in an engrossing situation. All experienced teachers have seen this phenomenon occur. They are familiar with the timid, quiet child who in a game laughs and shouts; with the shy male adult who in a square dance enters into the spirit of the dance, vigorously beating time with hands or feet, swinging his lady into the air, and shouting with zest.

Mental health literature is replete with references to the pleasant emotions that occur in connection with body functioning, particularly with the rapid expenditure of energy after periods of conflict or frustration. In relation to the child, Isaacs (1933) says: "Play is supremely the activity which brings him psychic equilibrium."

Teachers of physical education are deeply concerned with the continued marked reduction in opportunities for expansive play in our cities and suburbs. To a large extent in these areas, all of our wide-flung games of running, hiding, and seeking are barred. The games formerly played as children, games that involved moving considerable distances at a rapid pace, around barns, behind sheds, over fences, creeping from tree to tree—these exciting activities are no longer possible to the average child. The ideational content of the child's life produced by the radio, movies, television, and comics has little or no physical outlet. No longer can the ideas be played out in spirited running, fearless searching, or cautious stalking. The city child is too often restricted to running up and down the sidewalk, shouting and waving a toy gun. As our culture becomes more technological, the psychological health of our children needs increased protection. This protection requires a deeper understanding of children's play, particularly of those ages five to ten. It is in this period that we are in danger of introducing children too rapidly into our adult culture (Gesell 1946). There is need for more use of the simple, unsophisticated forms of play life that keep children close to nature and give them ample opportunity for vigorous physical activity. A rich mental content for the child, without its physicl concomitants, can produce traumatic intro-version (Plant 1937). Play, through its integrating function, can help to improve emotional adjustment. As Cowell (1949) says, "It is a great protective mechanism for syphoning-off dammed-up tension."

Not only is play a means of reducing tension, but it is also a medium for promoting a feeling of worth. It is children's chief means of social contact. Through play they become acquainted with other children; through play they develop friendships. "No child can enjoy an adequate social life unless he has learned the ability to play with other children. Play is the area where . . . he learns to hold his own with his peers" (Bettleheim 1950).

To be able to play well is of major importance in developing social acceptance. Physically developed children with well-coordinated skills are sought by their peers. They are chosen leaders of their games. Probably no other single factor contributes so much to a boy's feeling of adequacy as the ability to play games well with his group. According to Meek's study (1940) among boys, physical prowess is preeminent in establishing prestige with other boys. To a lesser degree this is true also of girls, especially in the preadolescent stage. Because of this, motor skill becomes an important component in developing an individual's feeling of confidence and of pride.

The fact that the ability to play well contributes so significantly to personality growth puts a premium on skill development. Educators should be deeply concerned that children and youth develop play skills so that they are beyond the "dub" stage. Careful instructional guidance in skills should be a main component of every physical education period.

Through play children are helped to understand the world about them; they can move from the known to the untried and unknown. In play, they can be something they are not; they can do what they may not in actuality do. They can change their age and sex. They can change weaknesses into strengths. They can be a fox, a horse, a bear, a tree, an automobile, a fire-engine, a jet bomber. They can be the sun, the rain, the wind, the thunder. They can create a world that they can manipulate. As children play, they project their personalities when they become the sly fox, the warm sun, the sympathetic mother; through this identification they develop greater under-standing and deeper appreciation of the world about them.

AESTHETIC EXPRESSION

Aesthetic experiences in the arts, drama, and dance are widely accepted by mental hygienists as: (1) desirable means of expressing emotions and beliefs that, though they cannot be put clearly into words, are felt vividly; (2) catharsis for relaxing emotional tensions; and (3) tonic for restoring morale (La Salle 1954). Since movement ranks high as a nonverbal instrument for conveying meanings, creative dance is among the most beneficent of all aesthetic activities. Both for children and adults it is a channel of communication and a means of developing a richer, fuller, more integrated personality. Through it the individual shares feelings, fears, longings, beliefs and joys. It is another medium through which individuals can speak vividly and with conviction and bring to the surface their ideas and emotions (La Salle 1946).

For the hyperactive, hostile, or aggressive child, rhythmic experiences seem to have a salutary effect. Children tend to be soothed, relaxed, and less tense. Their interest is challenged; their explosive behavior is provided with an outlet. Likewise the shy, withdrawn child is enabled to maintain closer relationships with peers during rhythmic activities. The stimulation of the music, the relaxed atmosphere, and structured sounds all seem to have a reassuring effect that helps to withstand attacks on the ego and to reach out to others. When people are happy and active, they are in a favorable condition for making positive group contacts (Hartley 1952).

OUTLET FOR AGGRESSIONS AND HOSTILITIES

The growing-up process in our present-day society, with its countless restraints, inconsistencies, and lack of freedom, inevitably thwarts the child and thus creates frustrations. These in turn arouse feelings of aggression and hostility. Even the most cordial love relationships between children and parents, between siblings, between children and other adults, will be tinged by the aggressive impulse system. Our present-day culture increases the sum-total of aggression. Sociologists and anthropologists as well as mental hygienists have documented the hatred-producing power of poverty, social inequality, and slum living (Redle 1952).

Direct expressions of hostility and aggression usually take one or more of the following outlets: (1) death wishes and their equivalents, (2) retaliation in kind, (3) open spite, (4) verbal rejection, (5) ridicule, or (6) destructiveness. Because our culture frowns upon the overt display of aggressions, the outlets appear in various disguises. They may be buried in vague states of uneasiness, irritation, or depression. They may stimulate action, such as to hit, to run, or to move against one another. Naked hostility toward grown-ups is looked upon with such disfavor in our society that the average child finds it dangerous to express aggressiveness openly. Retaliation coming from the grown-up can be too overwhelming.

What recourse then have children from feelings of anger against adults? Their main outlet for expressing feelings in desirable and acceptable ways is through play. In many respects, play is a dramatization of the life and death struggle. To catch means to prove superiority, to "show up," to punish, or to kill. All tag, "it," and hiding-seeking games are examples of the dramatization, the acting-out in fantasy, of the death wish. When to this fantasy are added vigorous running and dodging, the therapeutic effect upon the emotions is readily apparent.

Such fantasy in the play of the younger child has its emotional parallel in many games of the older child. Striking, hitting, pounding, kicking, and throwing all offer excellent opportunities for the release of hostile emotions. Games in which an object is struck by the hand, fist, or bat, such as batball, handball, or softball, can aid in draining off feelings of anger and hostility. Kicking games, such as kickball, soccer, touch football, or activities involving physical struggle, such as rooster fight, stick wrestle, Indian wrestle, horse and rider, and individual sports, such as punching a bag, also provide opportunities for releasing hostilities (La Salle 1954). Likewise, pounding or kicking the water, thrashing in it, jumping into it, especially if preceded by a spirited run, have strong mental health values.

All sports similarly give the youth and adult excellent occasions for expressing negative emotions and for draining off aggressions. The rules of the game and the skills involved permit the expression of hostile feelings that, thus acted out, free the individual from the need to express them in social contacts where they would be unacceptable. Children can "sock" the ball with a bat, racket, or club. They can throw their entire strength into a tackle. They can tag the runner out with the ball. They can catch another player between bases. They can outwit by use of strategy. They can keep opponents "on the run" by skillful placement of the tennis ball or badminton bird. In team games the group is pitted against a common enemy. In these the individual has the experience of working with others to depose and defeat the opponent.

Mental health literature stresses the desirability of exploration and adventure in furthering good emotional adjustment. Games and sports provide excellent vehicles for risk, thrill, and adventure. In these the elements of stalking and surprising adversaries, jumping out at them, pouncing on, outwitting, and dodging them will help to satisfy the need for adventure. The more highly organized games are adventurous, exciting experiences that challenge the player. The tactics and strategy of the game, directed toward diverting and outmaneuvering the opponent, help to satisfy the desire for risk and thrill (La Salle 1954).

ATHLETIC SKILL AND PERSONALITY RATING

At least two research studies indicate that athletic skill and personality adjustment have a significant positive correlation. Sperling (1943) found that varsity and intramural athletes rated higher than a nonathletic group in personality scores, ascendance, and extroversion. Athletes with the greatest experience had more favorable adjustment scores than did those with less experience. Cabot's (1938) study of body build and personality reveals that boys of the athletic type are more likely to be ascendant and to take the lead in social situations.

Ronald Lippitt, Norman Polansky, Fritz Redl, and Sidney Rosen (1953), in a study of two camp groups, obtained similar results. In this study they sought to determine, among other things, the characteristics of certain influential boys. They found that these "high power" boys had physical superiority. They were not necessarily larger but they were more skillful in the use of their bodies and had great "fight potentiality."

FEARS

Jersild (1935) of Teachers College, Columbia University, and his associates, in a study of children's fears, found that lack of motor skill was an important reason why children were afraid. Children in the study who exhibited much fear were described as being overprotected and lacking in neuromuscular skills. Rough games, fear of being struck with a ball, and fear of tackling and fighting, were some of the reasons children themselves gave for being afraid. Considerable decline in fear was observed with increasing physical abililty. The authors said:

> Case studies in the main body of this investigation illustrate the importance of skills in relation to fear behavior. The child who has never learned to climb or to engage in rough and tumble games, who has been helped too much in caring for his own needs, who has not learned to manipulate objects—catch a ball, dodge a missile, or hold his own in tussles with other children—is likely to be insecure in many ways and to be more susceptible to fears of the falls, fights, and hurts of everyday life.

ADOLESCENCE AND BODY MOVEMENTS

The satisfaction that comes from bodily movement not infrequently forms a sound basis on which the adolescent increases self-confidence. Greater emotional security may stem from increased sense of the body's adequacy. Physical eduction plays a large part in this adjustment. At a time when young people are beset with many anxieties, the fact that they can control body movements with reasonable ease, that they can walk into a room without fear of stumbling, that boys can escort girls across the dance hall without bumping them into several persons, or that, in the dance studio, girls find release from tension, as well as scope for the creative use of their bodies through expressive movement, all help to make them less uneasy.

THE EFFECT OF THE GROUP ON PERSONALITY DEVELOPMENT

Since most physical education is group oriented, the effect of the group upon personality development is quite significant. The group has the potentiality for producing constructive effects that further personality growth. Among these are: (1) the feeling of belonging and status, (2) the protection from real or fancied threat, (3) the enhancement of self-esteem, (4) the loosening of the facade of defensive mechanisms and the opportunity for testing the self against reality, (5) the proper conditions for sublimating basic drives, (6) the curbing of infantile desires and behaviors, and internalization of group standards in exchange for the love and protection received, and (7) the diverting of undue aggressiveness and its use for purposes of self control and defense (Scheidlinger 1953).

A group of course does not *per se* yield these results. It must be a cohesive group with common interests and planned goals, and so guided that the outcomes are educationally sound. Difficulties arise in the planned use of groups for personality development. One is the danger of promoting undue dependence when protection and support are offered. The problem of extreme jealousy may arise. Last but not least, an overcompetitive attitude may threaten desirable outcomes.

CONCLUSION

We have seen that physical education (particularly play , sports, and dance) has a significant role in the wholesome emotional adjustment of boys and girls and of men and women. In many ways it contributes to psychic equilibrium. In many ways it helps children understand the world about them and to build friendships. In many ways it acts as a therapeutic agent and catharsis. Perhaps play experiences are uniquely invaluable because they provide a bridge between inarticulate, subjective impressions, and the structured language and prescribed conduct of social communication in our culture. The child uses play to disguise conflicts or to relieve tensions and anxieties. For all people movement can be a direct, powerful mode of transmitting emotions and ideas.

In the 1980s we hope we have some definitive studies by physical educators that will demonstrate even more conclusively the significant contributions physical education can make to the mental health of children and youth. If this is done, we can look toward the day when good physical education instruction is an essential in every school curriculum, when it is recognized by all educators for what it is: a superb tool for personality development.

REFERENCES

Bettlehaim, B., 1950. *Love is not enough.* Glencoe, Ill,: The Free Press.

Cabot, P., 1938. The relationship between characteristics of personality and physique in adolescents, *Genetic psychology monographs,* **20** : 3-120.
Quoted in: English, H. B., *Child psychology.* New York: Henry Holt and Co., 1951.

Cowell, C. C., 1949. Mental hygiene functions and possibilities of play and physical education, *Elementary school journal* **50** : 196-203 (December).

Gesell, A., and F. Ilg, 1946. *The child from 5-10.* New York: Harper and Row.

Hartley, R. E., L. K. Frank, and R. Goldensen, 1952. *Understanding children's play.* New York: Columbia University.

Hopkins, L. T., et al., 1937. *Integration.* New York: D. Appleton-Century Company.

Isaacs, S., 1933. *Social development in the young child; a study of beginnings.* New York: Harcourt Brace and Co.

Jersild, A., 1952. *In search of self.* New York: Bureau of Publictions, Teachers College, Columbia University.

Jersild, A. T., and F. D. Holmes, 1935. *Children's fears.* New York: Bureau of Publications, Teachers College, Columbia University.

La Salle, D., 1954. Looking ahead. In *Children in focus.* Washington, D.C.: AAHPER.

———, 1946. *Guidance of children through physical education.* New York: A. S. Barnes & Company.

Lippitt, R., N. Polansky, F. Redle, and S. Rosen, 1953. Quoted in Cartwright, D., and A. Zander, *Group dynamics.* Evanston, Ill.: Row, Peterson & Co.

Meek, L. H., et al. 1940. *Personal-social relations of boys and girls.* New York: Progressive Education Association.

Murphy, G. 1947. *Personality; a biosocial approach to origins and structure.* New York: Harper & Bros.

Plant, J. S., 1937. *The envelope.* New York: The Commonwealth Fund, 1950.

———, *Personality and the cultural pattern.* New York: The Commonwealth Fund.

Redle, F. and D. Wineman, 1952. *Children who hate.* Glencoe, Ill.: The Free Press.

Scheidlinger, S., 1953. Freudian concepts of group relations. In: Cartwright, D., and A. Zander, *Group dynamics.* Evanston, Ill.: Row, Peterson & Co.

Sperling, A. P., 1943. Relationship between personality adjustment and achievement in physical education activities, *Research quarterly,* **13** : 351-363 (October).

Wiles, K., C. Brown, and R. Cassidy, 1956. *Supervision in physical education.* Englewood Cliffs, N. J.: Prentice-Hall, Inc.

86
Physical Education Related to Recreation
Allen V. Sapora

The word *recreation* has had and still conveys a variety of meanings. The word was first used in this country in the 1890s when the industrial revolution began to affect seriously the lifestyles of people in the United States. The Puritan ethic prevailed in our early society in which the primary goal was *work*. But with the industrial revolution came a change in work habits. Production in the home was moved to the factory, and people worked long hours. Time off from work, not used for rest and recuperation, was directed toward purposeful activities that enhanced the individual's ability to return to work refreshed and ready to engage effectively in more work. Activities such as play and leisure pursuits were accepted only on the basis that they would *recreate* one's physical and mental resources expended in work. From this connotation, the word *recreation* became popular and was accepted broadly by 1910 as the word describing this broad range of human behavior.

HISTORICAL BACKGROUND

Recreation programs of various types began to be identified specifically in what Rainwater (1922) called the recreation (play) movement in the United States. The playground, unique to this country, was created through experimental programs in Boston, New York, Chicago, and other large urban centers between 1895-1910. Simultaneously there was a nationwide effort to develop public parks, indoor facilities such as field houses, community centers, and school recreation centers, and voluntary agencies (i.e., YMCA) built industrial, private, commercial, and other recreation facilities. Program opportunities and services were offered in these facilities through a variety of auspices. Recreation then evolved through the recreation movement and has grown to have at least four meanings:

1. For the individual it means experiences engaged in voluntarily during leisure time and motivated primarily by the satisfaction or pleasure derived from these experiences.

2. The name of a relatively new profession with 215,000 professionals and over 900,000 fulltime personnel currently employed in the field. In 1970, there were 13,000 students registered in four-year curricula leading to the B.S., M.S., or doctorate in recreation and park administration. In 1975 there were over 26,000 registered in these programs.

3. A network of organized and informal recreation programs, facilities, and services that have become an integral part of a complete community master plan for living now and in the future.

4. An area of study in institutions of higher learning, with its primary focus on the study of leisure behavior of people and the physical resources directly associated with this behavior.

Physical education and recreation have been closely related since the early history of the recreation movement. It was the Turnvereins, Settlement Houses, the YMCA, sports clubs, gymnastics societies, and similar groups in the 1880s that gave significant impetus to the development of informal sports activities outside of the public schools, which offered only the formal gymnastics program. The Charlesbank Outdoor Gymnasium was opened in 1889 and, although its program included only formal types of physical education, offered suggestions about how outdoor areas might be adapted to informal recreation. In 1888 under the leadership of Luther Gulick and Henry Curtis, the New York City public school department of physical education opened its doors for informal play and recreation. Summer vacation schools were operated in Boston, Chicago, Rochester, and other cities, sponsored in many instances by physical educators who included a variety of sports and informal play programs for all ages.

From 1900 to 1920 there were many attempts to involve the public schools, and particularly physical education, in the rapidly growing recreation movement. However, except in a few states, public schools generally rejected the responsibility for conducting total community recreation programs and services. Consequently public recreation became predominantly a function of municipal government and a variety of other agencies and groups outside the public schools. This trend can be attributed for the most part to the facts that:

1. Public school systems were not willing or in many cases were unable to assume the expense involved in administering recreation programs.

2. There was increasing evidence of the complexity of providing total public park and recreation services with which school systems were hesitant to deal.

3. There was lack of flexibility and innovation in teacher preparation programs, including physical education, to prepare teachers or other college graduates specifically to assume community park and recreation leadership.

4. A rapidly growing group of individuals with diverse backgrounds who identified themselves as community recreation professionals opposed to public schools as appropriate legal and functional units to administer community park and recreation programs and services.

Despite the fact that many physical educators entered the recreation field and the functions of recreation and physical education overlapped in some areas, an information and communication gap in relationships between physical education and recreation developed between 1920 and 1940. The period following World War II found physical educators occupied with increasing student enrollments caused by the population explosion and by the popular demand to teach sports skills with tremendous emphasis upon interschool competitive athletics. Correspondingly professional recreators were engulfed with the spectacular growth of recreation and park development, again predominantly outside of school auspices. The two areas developed their own identity in the new postwar society, and an urgently needed closer cooperation between the two fields was not achieved.

Special note should be made of the forward-looking concept regarding recreation adopted by a number of physical education leaders in institutions of higher learning immediately following World War II. Departments of physical education were in most cases the sponsors of new curricula for the B.S. degree in recreation and park administration. As in the case of health, safety education, dance, and similar new academic program areas, this was a significant contribution to recreation by the field of physical education. The relationship still exists today in view of the fact that most professional preparation departments of recreation and park administration are located in colleges of health, physical education, and recreation.

The review of the relationship of physical education to recreation in the past indicates that interaction between the two disciplines has been the result of technological, economic, social, and cultural forces that have markedly changed the needs of people in our society. Much has been learned from leaders in physical education and recreation as they reacted to meet these needs. The economic development of the United States has produced trends that have interacted to generate massive social problems. While industrialization has produced affluence and leisure, it has also produced urbanization and the automation of work. Thus many contemporary workers are faced with the progressive depersonalization of their work experiences. To offset this, their affluence and increase leisure hold major promise for the amelioration of the problems resulting therefrom. The wise use of leisure seems to be a critical resource available to a person seeking to achieve individual fulfillment in contemporary society. By 1980 it was the major category in the time-use budget of Americans. Leisure as a resource has the potential to exert a massive influence on the American scene. Problems inherent in delivering leisure services to a vast urban population must be mastered if such promise is to be realized.

In this changing world, children walk less, do fewer chores, and engage in limited physical activities. Adults are becoming more sedentary as a result of automation and other physical changes in our life styles and the environment; and the need for active, vigorous exercises and physical recreation are more important than ever before to the health and welfare of people. Citizens have the obligation to themselves and to their country to do their utmost to become and to remain healthy, alert, vigorous, and productive. The benefits of the formal physical education program and physical recreation (informal physical activities) are already well documented. The objective now is to coordinate the efforts of these two disciplines to provide learning experiences and opportunities to participate in physical activities that maximize these benefits.

CURRENT RELATIONSHIPS

Recreation professionals look to a number of disciplines for basic information to guide them in decision making in the development of recreation programs and services. Recreation administrators in the community, as well as the recreation educators and researchers, are much like the urban planners, social workers, or landscape architects. They act as catalysts, coordinators who synthesize information from their own as well as from a wide variety of disciplines, and translate this information into theories, principles, programs, and services that relate to the behavior of people during their leisure. Thus the recreator depends a great deal upon professional specialists for scientifically sound information and program leadership from disciplines such as music, drama, art, crafts, physical education, and sports, as well as additional theoretical knowledge from psychology, sociology, geography, landscape architecture, urban planning, and other disciplines.

More specifically then, the recreator looks to the physical educator for the following professional relationships:

1. A body of knowledge about sports, exercise, and dance. The recreator is not only interested in programs that provide *fun* but also in what happens to people in many other ways as a result of participation in recreation activities. Therefore, the recreator is interested in, and needs interpretation from the physical educators, about physical fitness, the psychology of motor learning, exercise physiology, the social aspects of sport and exercise, and scientifically sound information about the administration and operation of sports programs.

2. An organized sequential physical education program in the school that includes instruction in a wide variety of sports skills and physical exercise. At various ages, students should experience sports and exercise activities that are most beneficial for immediate as well as life-long needs of each individual. Knowledge about the relation of sports and physical exercise to the individual's abilities, health, and enjoyment is also significant; and the development of attitudes in the school program toward sports and exercise is of tremendous importance. From this basic education, the recreator and the physical educator can cooperate to promote the most effective out-of-school, informal community sports and physical exercise programs for the entire community.

3. Develop professionally prepared physical education personnel to conduct community-wide programs in sports, exercise, and dance. As already indicated, the recreation administrator and others interested in the conduct of sports programs need assistance and cooperation from specialized personnel to conduct a variety of recreation and leisure-time programs in the community. Schools preparing professional physical educators should insure that young men and women, interested in careers in conducting sports and exercise programs outside school settings, are prepared to conduct and direct these programs in public recreation agencies, industries, voluntary agencies, and a variety of private sports enterprises and services. These specialists, increasing in demand, need special preparation to promote, lead, and administer vast existing sports programs, to explore new program areas with recreators, and meet even greater needs for sports and exercise programs that are predicted for the future.

4. Provide a basic philosophy of sport, exercise, and dance for the nation and for the world. Sport, like music, drama, and similar art forms, has tremendous impact upon the development of positive social and cultural values in any civilization. This fact is borne out by history of past civilizations as well as by obvious evidences in our present society. Parents, public recreation administrators, and agency and private entrepreneurs of sports activities seek basic principles and concepts that

Fig. 86.1 Recreation and park planning. Courtesy of the Department of Leisure Studies, University of Illinois, Urbana-Champaign.

Fig. 86.2 The recreation consultant. Courtesy of the Office of Recreation and Park Resources, Department of Leisure Studies, University of Illinois, Urbana-Champaign.

Fig. 86.3 Developing modern physical activity play facilities. Courtesy of the Department of Leisure Studies, University of Illinois, Urbana-Champaign.

should be followed to achieve the greatest values from the conduct of sports and exercise programs. Physical educators have an important relationship to the recreation profession and other interested persons to provide this overall philosophical framework based on a sound scientific foundation.

THE FUTURE

National, state, and local recreation resources are being coordinated to meet the massive demand for sports as well as participation in recreation activities during leisure time. Public recreation and park agencies are developing reciprocal programs such as city-school, or park-school programs, with definite written policies designating joint sponsorship and functional operations. School sports facilities, often closed in earlier years, are being utilized for community sports and exercise programs; park, playground, community center, and camp facilities are being planned jointly and operated by recreation and physical education personnel. Professional preparation curricula in physical education and recreation in institutions of higher learning, although differing sharply, are becoming more integrated. The role of the physical educator in recreation enterprises is becoming more clearly defined, and physical educators are constantly playing a more expanded role in intramural sports and many specialized sports and exercise programs conducted in the community. These relationships between physical education and recreation now and in the future are too important to be anything but cooperative, based on a mutual understanding of function.

The conduct of physical education programs in schools and the development of informal sports and exercise programs in the community have significant importance to the health, effectiveness, and pleasures of every individual. The relationships of physical education to recreation, whatever directions they may take, should maximize the effectiveness of each field to help meet the important needs of individuals to sharpen skills, generate appreciation, develop interests, establish values, and enjoy participation in vigorous physical activities.

SUGGESTED READINGS

AAHPER, 1974. *Professional preparation in dance, physical education, recreation education, safety education and school health education.* Washington, D.C.: AAHPER.

Bannon, J. J., 1972. *Problem solving in recreation and parks.* Englewood Cliffs, N. J.: Prentice-Hall, Inc.

Brightbill, C. K., 1966. *Education for leisure centered living.* Harrisburg, Pa.: Stackpole Books.

Bull, C. N., 1971. One measure of defining a leisure activity, *Journal of leisure research,* **2** : 120-126 (Spring).

De Grazia, S., 1962. *Of time, work and leisure.* New York: The Twentieth Century Fund.

Dulles, F. R., 1965. *A history of recreation.* New York: Appleton-Century Crofts.

Dumazedier, J., 1967. *Toward a society of leisure.* New York: The Free Press.

Ellis, M. J., 1973. *Why people play.* Englewood Cliffs, N. J.: Prentice-Hall.

Fabun, D., 1966. The theory of the leisure masses. In: *The dynamics of change.* Kaiser Aluminum Series.

Kaplan, M. and P. Bosserman, (ed.), 1971. *Technology, human values, and leisure.* New York: Abington Press.

Krause, R., 1971. *Recreation and leisure in modern society.* New York: Appleton-Century-Crofts.

Leisure today: education for leisure, 1976. *JOPER,* **47** : 25 (March).

Leisure today: the leisure revoluation, 1976. *JOPER,* **47** :25 (October).

Merril, Lynch, Pierce, Fenner and Smith, 1968. *Investment opportunities in a $150 billion market.* New York: Securities Research Division.

Neumeyer, M. H., and E. S. Neumeyer, 1960. *Leisure and recreation.* New York: Ronald Press.

Rainwater, C. E., 1922. *The play movement in the United States.* Chicago: University of Chicago Press.

Recreation and park education in the United States and Canada, 1974. *Parks and recreation.* National Recreation and Park Association, **9** :32-35 (January).

Recreation research, 1965. Washington, D. C.: AAHPER.

Sapora, A. V., and E. D., Mitchell, 1961. *The theory of play and recreation.* New York: Ronald Press.

Zeigler, E. F., 1964. *Philosophical foundations for health, physical education and recreation education.* Englewood Cliffs, N. J.: Prentice-Hall, Inc.

87

Physical Education Related to Safety in Sports

Allan J. Ryan

No sport is entirely free from the occurrence of injury. Those sports commonly practiced at the school, college, and professional levels are characterized by vigorous, and sometimes violent, physical activity. They frequently involve actions accurately described as "unsafe," and often require that these actions be repeated many times in the course of a practice or competition. It is a wonder therefore not that injuries occur in sports, but that the relative occurrence of serious, disabling, and fatal injuries is so small in comparison with the number of competitors.

We lack accurate statistics regarding the numbers of injuries occuring in most sports, primarily because the accumulation of such figures would require funds and personnel not presently available. Small sampling studies have been made, more often in football than any other sport. From these, certain trends have become apparent, and in some instances these findings have led to the establishment or confirmation of preventive measures. The value of the dental mouthguard and the face bar or mask in reducing facial and dental injuries in high school football was clearly demonstrated, for example, by the continuing study of reported injuries in Wisconsin high schools carried out by the Wisconsin Interscholastic Athletic Association.

Although the knowledge of the actual occurrences of sports injuries is essential to the evaluation of control measures, the types of injuries that will occur in any particular sport can be predicted quite accurately by a conceptual analysis of the types of actions involved, the nature of the sports environment, the persons involved, the implements used, and the rules governing play. This type of analysis coupled with the practical experience of coaches and players has led in the past to the development of safety measures in the form of protective equipment, preventive conditioning, rules modification, and other precautionary steps.

In addition to those injuries that are to some extent preventable, such as those due to direct traumas, heat and cold stress, changes in barometric pressure, near drownings, and toxic reactions, there are injuries that occur as the result of actions of athletes themselves without the direct influence of an outside source. These may be of an acute or chronic nature. Normally sports skills are practiced repeatedly, thus imposing a stress not manifested clinically with one repetition, but whose cumulative effect is responsible for many of the injuries that appear to arise spontaneously or come on gradually over a period of time. The injury may become chronic in spite of adequate therapy because the athlete may not be able to change the circumstances that produced the original injury.

Injury may also arise within the athletes as the result of unskilled or mistimed actions or from a failure to prepare their bodies by warming up properly before attempting maximum efforts. It may also occur because of a predisposing condition associated with a systemic illness, such as the rupture of a spleen that is enlarged and friable due to infectious mononucleosis, or with incomplete healing of a previous injury.

The realization of safety in sports then depends on the constant attention to detail in applying a lengthy series of general and specific principles to the practice of each sport. No one person, no matter how knowledgeable in these areas, can assume complete responsibility for sports safety. The athlete, coach, trainer, sports director, and physician must share this responsibility. The success that will be achieved depends on how well they appreciate the role they must play in this team effort and how the efforts of each individual are coordinated to produce the most favorable outcome.

GENERAL PRINCIPLES

Careful screening of aspirants for sports by means of physical examination, laboratory tests, functional capacity tests, and psychological evaluation will help to eliminate those who may be inordinately susceptible to injury in particular sports activities. Defects that are remediable may be identified and corrected. Sports activities suitable for the handicapped may be prescribed. Classification of participants by age, height, weight, or other pertinent measures can be established clearly.

Proper conditioning measures for each sport should be outlined. These may involve the development of strength, endurance, speed, balance, coordination, flexibility, and perhaps other qualities necessary to insure safety. The timing and appropriate levels of these conditioning activities should be specified as to preseason, intraseason, and postseason. Immediate preactivity warmup exercises should be specified and should be mandatory.

Uniforms and equipment should be specified in such a way that they do not pose any hazard to the contestant, teammates, or opponents. Where protective equipment is used, its quality should approach as closely as possible maximum protective requirements while still being reasonably light in weight and not bulky or cumbersome. It should be capable of use again without significant loss of its protective factors, properly fitted to the individual, maintained in excellent condition, and replaced when it can no longer afford the requisite protection.

Coaching should seek to maximize the skillful and fluid performance of skills so that the occurrence of injury due to awkwardness, deficient perception or poor timing will be minimized. Under no circumstances should coaches teach techniques inherently dangerous beyond the ordinary risks involved in the sport, but should try in every instance to teach methods that combine reasonable safety with efficiency. Motivation to athletes should be positive and not enforced by physical threats or other forms of coercion.

Rules should be drawn and revised periodically as necessitated by evolutionary changes in the game, so that the safety of the players is a primary consideration, but with due regard to maintaining the essential character of the game. They should be enforced by officials who are well prepared and paid adequately for their work, and who are particularly alert to observe the early signs of injury in a player, and will act promptly to prevent aggravation of such an injury.

The facilities for sports must be constructed and maintained in such a way that hazards to players and spectators are minimized. When natural sites, such as ski slopes or open water courses are used, they must be patrolled carefully to avoid unwanted incursions which might endanger participants.

The control of spectators requires a constant vigilance on the part of athletics directors and their staffs to prevent intrusions onto playing areas, to protect athletes and officials from the attacks of spectators, and to protect spectators from each other.

Provisions should be made for medical supervision at appropriate times, for emergency first-aid and medical care at all times, and for early definitive treatment and adequate rehabilitation of all sports-related illness and injury. In this way disability can be minimized and potentially disastrous consequences prevented.

SPECIFIC PRINCIPLES

Each sport has particular hazards associated with it. Careful analysis of these hazards in advance should lead to specific precautionary measures to minimize or eliminate them.

When it becomes apparent immediately before or during the course of a sports practice or event that circumstances beyond the complete control of those in charge pose an unreasonable hazard to the players or spectators, action should be taken immediately to stop the activity and either await the resumption of more favorable conditions, transfer the activity to a more favorable environment, or postpone it until it is safe to resume at a future date.

Safety rules or a safety code should be established for each sport embodying the particular precautions to be taken under all conditions in which the sport might be practiced. Knowledge of these rules should be obligatory for all athletes, coaches, and supervisors engaged in these sports. Violations of these rules should be penalized. These rules must be reviewed periodically and revised according to the needs of the sport.

CONCLUSIONS

The prevention of illness and injury as the result of sports participation is a very complex matter. Injuries can never be eliminated completely, but with thoughtful planning and execution they can certainly be minimized. Even if it were possible to completely eliminate all hazards of injury from sports, this might require such drastic modification of their practices that all enjoyment for both athlete and spectator would be lost.

The athlete, coach, trainer, directors, physician, and spectator must share their knowledge and work together to minimize the occurrence and effects of sports injury and illness. In any event, persons undertaking a principal responsibility for sports safety often find themselves in an unpopular role since so many external factors have to be provided for, and people prevented from doing many things they find interesting and exciting.

SUGGESTED READINGS

Allman, F. L., Jr., and A. J. Ryan, 1973. *Sports medicine.* New York: Academic Press.

Clarke, K. S., (ed.), 1971. *Fundamentals of athletic training.* Chicago: American Medical Association.

Novich, M. M., and B. Taylor, 1970. *Training and conditioning of athletes.* Philadelphia: Lea and Febiger.

Olson, O. C., 1971. *Prevention of football injuries.* Philadelphia: Lea and Febiger.

Yost, C. P. (ed.), 1970. *Sports safety.* Washington, D. C.: National Education Association.

———, 1967. Football mask and dental guard study, *Wisconsin interscholastic athletic association bulletin.* (November 11).

88

Physical Education Related to Driver Education

A. E. Florio

No documented evidence describes why many physical educators are involved in driver education. No exact figures illustrate the number or percentage of driver educators also involved in physical education and athletic coaching. But historically some of the pioneers in accident prevention were individuals whose background and professional preparation were in the area of sports and physical education. From this early concern for accident prevention in sports and physical education came the development of a broader concept of safety. This concept was also ingrained into the professional preparation of health educators who in many instances were also at one time involved in physical education.

When driver education started in the early 1930s, there was a natural interest in this specific area of safety by those already concerned with accident prevention. Many of these individuals were physical educators and/or health educators. Departments of public instruction began to include driver education under the overall umbrella of health education, physical education, and recreation. Today this organizational structure still exists in many state and local jurisdictions. In many instances the director of physical education has also the direct responsibility for administering, conducting, and supervising the driver education program.

In a study by Norman Key concerned with the status of driver education, in which he discussed titles and preparation and experience of professional personnel in driver education, it was illustrated that, more than any other discipline, the responsibility for driver education programs was in the state department of health education and physical education. In the same study, more *local* supervisors and administrators of driver education were also supervisors of health education and physical education.

Although in recent years there has been a general trend for driver education to be a separate discipline, there is still evidence that many teachers of this subject are also teachers of physical education.

Probably the closest relationship of the two disciplines lies in the fact that they are dealing with young people and are concerned with their physical, mental, and emotional characteristics as they relate to everyday activities. Some characteristics related to both disciplines that are potentially conducive to reckless behavior, may become assets rather than liabilities if students are properly motivated by the concerned teacher.

The ability to establish a close rapport with adolescents through the types of activities conducted by both physical educators and driver educators seems to bring these disciplines closer together in their relationships. The relevancy of perception, reaction time, neuromuscular skill, fatigue, kinesthetic factors, stability, and health are all concerns of both disciplines. The nature of psychomotor activities in driver education and physical education also point up the natural relationships between these fields. This is not to imply that other educational disciplines are not concerned, but there seems to be a more direct bond between the two areas. This may be due to the similarity of professional preparation of teachers in the two disciplines as they involve the humanities, social, and natural sciences, and their relationships to physical, mental, and emotional development. Many advisors and counselors in professional preparation programs for physical education guide students into driver education because it provides an excellent second teaching area.

While there is similarity in purposes and procedures of these two fields, it should be recognized that they are two distinct and separate disciplines. Today there is a general trend for traffic safety education to be a specific, separate department both at the high school and teacher education level. As both programs play a vital part in preparing people to live safe and healthy lives there should be no encroachment of one area over the other.

SUGGESTED READINGS

AAHPER, 1974. *Professional preparation in dance, physical education, recreation education, safety education and school health education.* Washington D.C.: AAHPER.

Key N. 1960. *Status of driver education in the United States.* Washington, D.C.: National Commission on Safety Education, National Education Association.

Maynard, Z. and S. Rinaldi, 1964. *State school laws and regulations for health-safety-driver-outdoor and physical education.* Washington, D.C.: U.S. Department of Health, Education, and Welfare. National Commission on Safety Education, 1964. *Policies and guidelines for teacher preparation and certification in driver and traffic safety education.* Washington, D.C.: The Commission, National Education Association.

———, 1965. *Policies and practices for driver and traffic safety education.* Washington, D.C.: The Commission, National Education Association.

Stack, H. J., 1966. *History of driver education in the United States.* Washington, D.C.: National Commission on Safety Education, National Education Association.

AFFILIATED
ORGANIZATIONS

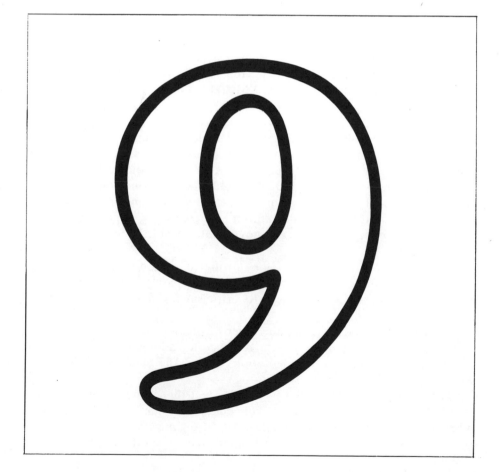

Introduction

Throughout this volume, especially in Section 2, various organizations have been mentioned in connection with the physical education profession. Some of them have been professional (e.g., the AAHPERD), some public (e.g., PCPFS), and some quasi-public (e.g., YMCA).

The purpose of Section 9 is to present selected organizations "affiliated" with the physical education professions, and to sensitize the reader to the fact that millions of people engage in physical education outside the school or military settings. The word affiliated in this case is not used in the formal sense, but rather it is meant to encompass *all* organizations that support, conduct, or are associated with, physical education (including exercise, games, sports, and dance) programs. Private organizations are included to acknowledge this growing national trend. Increasingly large numbers of physical education professionals are moving into so-called commercial physical education.

Obviously coverage of all of the "affiliated" organizations—assuming they could all be identified—would require a separate volume. Thus this chapter will necessarily be subject to criticism for omitting the reader's favorite organization.

Articles were solicited from a number of organizations (we hope representative of the various types), with requests for addresses. The reader is warned, however, that many organizations change their addresses with regularity.

A final word of explanation is due the fact that some chapters in this section do not identify the author. This occurred when the individual who submitted the material (usually an officer of the organization), did not deem it ethical to take credit for material that might have been developed by committees.

Section Editor

Harold T. Friermood recently retired as the executive director of the Council for National Cooperation in Aquatics. He received his B.P.E. from George Williams College, the M.A. from the University of Wisconsin, and the Ed.D. from New York University. During his professional career he was associated in varous capacities with YMCA programs in Indiana, Illinois, and Ohio. He served the National YMCA as director of health, physical education, and sports, 1943-1968. He is a Life Member of AAHPERD and two national YMCA societies in addition to a number of other professional organizations. He is a Fellow of the American Academy of Physical Education. He was very active in establishing the initial groups associated with the YMCA Health Service Clinic and the YMCA's Society of Health Service Directors. He has also been very active in the United States Volleyball Association, the United States Olympic Committee, and the International Council for Sport and Physical Education. He was a cofounder of the Council for National Cooperation in Aquatics. His articles have appeared in publications that represent a wide cross-section of readers both in this country and internationally. He has authored or edited numerous books and manuals and has contributed to the *Encyclopedia Britannica* and the *Encyclopedia of Sports Sciences and Medicine.*

89
American Alliance for Health, Physical Education, Recreation, and Dance

George F. Anderson

HISTORY

The American Alliance for Health, Physical Education, Recreation, and Dance (AAHPERD) was founded in 1885 by a group of 49 people interested in the promotion of physical education. Called together by William G. Anderson at Adelphi Academy, Brooklyn, New York, they elected as first president Edward Hitchcock, M.D., of Amherst College, founder of the first college department of physical education in the United States.

The original name, the Association for the Advancement of Physical Education, was changed in 1896 to the American Association for the Advancement of Physical Education and in 1903 to American Physical Education Association. In 1937 the association became affiliated as a department of the National Education Association (NEA) with the title of American Association for Health and Physical Education. A year later, its expanded interests were indicated with a change in name to the American Association for Health, Physical Education, and Recreation. In 1974 the AAHPER reorganized and became an alliance. On September 1, 1975, with the implementation of a new NEA constitution, the Alliance became completely independent. At the annual conference in New Orleans in March, 1979, the Alliance Assembly voted to add "Dance" to the title of the alliance.

Today, AAHPERD is an alliance of voluntary professional associations totaling 50,000 individual members and, through the Association of Intercollegiate Athletics for Women, the governing body for women's intercollegiate athletic programs, more than 800 colleges and universities are institutional members.

Purposes of the alliance are to support, encourage, and provide assistance to member groups as they seek to initiate, develop, and conduct programs in health, leisure, and movement-related activities for the enrichment of human life.

Alliance members share a common mission of promoting and educating in the related areas of health education, safety, physical education, recreation and leisure education, dance, and sport.

Through its local, state, district, and national membership networks, the alliance reaches into more than 16,000 school districts, more than 2000 colleges and universities, and over 10,000 community recreation departments.

The alliance includes teachers, administrators, and students, and serves members working in professional organizations, state departments of education or health, colleges and universities, schools, and other community agencies.

PROGRAM

The alliance provides numerous vehicles for growth and dissemination of the knowledge base of the allied professions. *Update* is the monthly newsletter for members and freinds. The *Research Quarterly, Journal of Physical Education and Recreation,* and *Health Education* are professional journals for practitioners. The alliance publishes about 40 new titles on film and in print each year.

The AAHPERD *Journal of Physical Education and Recreation* has been the major journal of the profession for nearly 50 years. The *Research Quarterly* has been published since 1930. *Completed Research in Health, Physical Education, and Recreation,* is an annual publication. *Health Education* has been published since 1969. The annual convention of the Alliance provides continuous reporting of current research, with abstracts available in an annual volume since 1970.

The national convention is held annually in conjunction with one of the six district associations on a rotating basis. The convention program initiates professional meetings, workshops, and clinics, and an extensive products display of sports equipment and clothing, play and gymnastic facilities, and media. Five other district conventions, state conventions, and numerous regional and national conferences are scheduled each year.

AAHPERD is project-oriented and conducts projects on its own or in cooperation with others.

The Physical Education Public Information (PEPI) Project, utilizing a network of members working with the media, has helped the public understand the "new physical education."

The Alliance Unit on Programs for the Handicapped, with funding from the U.S. Bureau of Education for the Handicapped and other groups, has developed an Information and research Center (IRUC) to serve personnel working in recreation and physical education for the handicapped.

National awareness of the contribution of lifetime sports to health and fitness began in the 1960s with the AAHPER Lifetime Sports Project.

The AAHPERD Fitness Program has motivated millions of children and youth with a system of evaluation and awards topped by the Presidential Physical Fitness Award.

The Outdoor Education Project is a venture with business and industry to promote environmental education along with camping and recreational skills.

A Boating Safety Project in cooperation with the U.S. Coast Guard developed the plan for a national certification of recreation boating educators.

The alliance is committed to facilitating research in human movement, fitness, and health. Informational services under alliance auspices are in progress of integration to become a central data base for the allied fields.

ORGANIZATION AND GOVERNANCE

Geographically the alliance is divided into six district associations: Central, Eastern, Midwest, Northwest, Southern, and Southwest. Each district elects its own officers, including a representative to the alliance board of governors. There are 53 state and territorial associations.

The *Alliance Assembly* is the governing body of the alliance. It is charged with the responsibility of electing officers, making changes in the constitution and bylaws, approving resolutions and position statements, and initiating other Alliance business. With some 350 members, the assembly is made up of the alliance officers and representatives of the national, district, and state associations.

The *Board of Governors* is the executive arm of the alliance and, with the support and approval of the assembly, initiates and transacts alliance business. The 18 members of the board meet twice a year, in the fall and in the spring at the time of the annual convention. The board is composed of the president, past president, president-elect, presidents of the seven national associations, and representatives of the six district associations. The chairperson of the finance committee and the executive director are ex-officio members.

Board members are the policy makers of the alliance and assume responsibility for making policy decisions during their terms of office. The *Executive Committee,* consisting of the alliance president, past-president, president-elect and executive vice-president, meets several times a year to carry on the operations of the alliance between board meetings.

The *Committees* carry on a large share of the alliance program of work, and serve as a means by which individual members may assist in planning, recommending policy, and otherwise giving direction to alliance affairs.

The *Headquarters Staff* of more than 70 people carries on the vast amount of alliance work that cannot be undertaken on the volunteer basis. Tasks handled by staff members include keeping financial and budget records; processing and maintaining memberships; editing and production of publications and periodicals; promotion and distribution of publications; organizing conferences and conventions; providing informational and public relations services; and conducting project and program efforts. Staff includes the executive secretaries of the seven national associations that make up the alliance.

AAHPERD is a founding member of the International Council of Health, Physical Education, and Recreation (ICHPER) and of the U.S. Collegiate Sports Council (USCSC).

The national associations now making up the alliance are:

American Association for Leisure and Recreation (AALR). It promotes school, community, and national programs of leisure services and recreation education.

American School and Community Safety Association (ASCSA). It emphasizes safety in sports and other safety concerns such as education for injury control, safety education, highway safety, and first aid and emergency care.

Association for the Advancement of Health Education (AAHE). This organization works for continuing, comprehensive programs of health education. Position papers are developed on such health topics as certification, drug education, and sex education.

Association for Research, Administration, and Professional Councils and Societies (ARAPCS). It coordinates the following special interest structures: aquatics: college/university administrators; city and county directors; outdoor education; facilities, equipment, and supplies; international relations; measurement and evaluation; physical fitness; research; therapeutics; and student members.

National Association for Girls and Women in Sport (NAGWS). This serves those involved in teaching, coaching, officiating, athletic administration, athletic training, club sports, and intramurals at the elementary, secondary, and college levels.

National Association for Sport and Physical Education (NASPE). It provides leadership opportunity in sports development and competition, consultation, publications, conferences, research, and a physical education public information program.

National Dance Association (NDA). The association promotes the development of sound policies for dance in education through conferences, convention programs, special projects, publications, and cooperation with other dance and arts groups.

Headquarters of the alliance and constituent national associations are at 1900 Association Drive, Reston, VA 22091.

90

The American Academy of Physical Education

Louis E. Alley

In 1930 after five years of preliminary organization, 29 charter members adopted a constitution, elected R. Tait McKenzie as president, and officially founded the American Academy of Physical Education. The academy was committed to the goal of advancing the cause of physical education, which was considered to include health education and recreation. To this end the academy cited as one of its major functions the election to membership of persons with established records of distinguished service and outstanding contributions to these fields.

Today the document of governance of the academy reaffirms these original purposes with the declaration that its purposes are "to incorporate and promote the study and educational application of the art and science of human movement and physical activity, and to honor by election to its membership persons who have directly or indirectly contributed significantly to the study and/or application of the art and science of human movement and physical activity."

The academy strives for the advancement of the profession through such activities as: (1) organizing and encouraging the continued scholarly and professional productivity of its individual Fellows; (2) synthesizing and transmitting knowledge about human movement and physical activity at annual meetings and via the publication of *The Academy Papers;* (3) formulating philosophical considerations of the purposes, values, and issues related to human movement and physical activity; and (4) annually bestowing honors for outstanding contributions to the fields of health education, physical education, recreation, and/or dance.

The governing body of the academy is comprised of Active Fellows, limited to 125 in number, who are currently employed in—and have made significant contributions to—the fields of physical education, health education, recreation, and/or dance. Active Fellows must be nominated and elected by the active members of the academy; Associate Fellows are persons in related fields and professions who contribute through their work to the improvement of the fields with which the academy is directly concerned; Corresponding Fellows are elected from countries other than the United States in recognition of their outstanding contributions to the fields of concern to the academy. The academy designates former Active Fellows who have retired as Fellows-Emeriti who serve as active participants and counselors in the academy, but do not hold office.

Further information may be obtained from the current secretary-treasurer of the academy, whose name and address may be obtained by writing to the Executive Vice-president, American Alliance for Health, Physical Education, Recreation, and Dance, 1900 Association Drive, Reston, VA 22091.

91

American College of Sports Medicine

The American College of Sports Medicine is a unique professional organization composed of physicians, basic scientists, and educators who share a common interest in sports medicine. The college was incorporated in 1955 and has a membership of over 2300. The policies of ACSM are determined by a board of trustees elected by the membership.

The objectives of the college are: (1) advancement of research concerning the effects of sports and other physical activities on the health and well-being of individuals; (2) cooperation with other organizations having allied interests; (3) furtherance of postgraduate educational offerings in the various sciences related to sports medicine; (4) correlation, integration, and dissemination of information from the allied sciences with sports medicine application; and (5) publication of a journal pertaining to the various aspects of sports medicine.

Sports medicine is a perspective, easier to describe than define. It involves sports but is not limited to organized athletics. It involves health but is not limited to medical supervision. Essentially it is the study of the health implications of people in activity.

Sports medicine has the task of clarifying and emphasizing for immediate utilization as well as future evaluation some guiding principles relating to particular aspects of people in activity. Such utilization and evaluation warrants an acknowledgement of and sensitivity to the combined influences of physiological, psychological, and cultural forces.

There is no single profession defined in sports medicine. The task requires the involvement of a number of professions, each in accordance with its respective competencies and interests. It draws from various professions but does not absorb them. Mutual understanding and respect among all professions is necessary. To summarize, the meaning of sports medicine is its responsibility to share, respect, and sythesize the interprofessional implications of all its components. The objectives of ACSM can only be met if the membership is professionally heterogeneous. The college is neither to duplicate nor replace the roles of organizations already serving the respective profession.

The college publishes a quarterly scientific journal, *Medicine and Science in Sports*. A quarterly *Newsletter* keeps members informed of ongoing college activites. In 1971 ACSM in cooperation with the University of Wisconsin completed work on a comprehensive *Encyclopedia of Sports Sciences and Medicine*, published by the Macmillan Company in New York.

The college conducts annual scientific meetings, usually in May. Regional meetings are held as the interest of members dictates. At both annual and regional meetings, scientific papers are presented and discussed. Annual meetings also feature symposia on timely topics and a special lecture relating to clinical medicine. In recent years three regional chapters have been granted provisional status within the national organization. They are: The Mid-West Regional Chapter; The Central States Chapter; and The Sports

Medicine Association of Greater Washington, D.C.

The American College of Sports Medicine is located at 1440 Monroe Street, Madison, Wisconsin, 53706.

92

American Corrective Therapy Association, Inc.

Warren C. Smith

The American Corrective Therapy Association is a national, incorporated professional organization, operated for educational and scientific purposes, to maintain and advance the standards of medically prescribed corrective therapy and adapted physical education in cooperation with approved educational institutions and medical specialties. Corrective therapy and adapted physical education are allied professions that apply the principles, tools, techniques, and psychology of medically oriented physical education to assist the physician and client in the accomplishment of prescribed objectives.

Membership in the American Corrective Therapy Association is available in seven categories: Active, Past-active, Associate, Life, Student, Member Emeritus, and Honorary. The association provides for and encourages the certification of its members through an examination process and has advanced an accrediting system for the selection of universities to provide trainees for the profession.

There are approximately 520 corrective therapists working in Veterans Administration hospitals throughout the country, 275 employed in miscellaneous health care facilities, and 400 working as adapted physical educators in the secondary and collegiate-level school systems. Corrective Therapy, with the support of the American Society of Allied Health Professions, will gradually expand its services to the point where it may not be predominantly government-hospital oriented. The need for additional therapeutic exercise for the multiple-handicapped, preschool child, the entire age-range of the mentally retarded individual, and the geriatric population—away from in-hospital care and into the community itself will expand. Outpatient and home-care facilities should provide considerable outlets for employment and/or counseling by tomorrow's corrective therapist. It is also feasible that involvement can be initiated and intensified into the programs of other rehabilitation agencies, such as Goodwill and Easter-Seal Foundation.

The administrative organization of the association is composed of eight elected, noncompensated officers: president, president-elect, three vice-presidents, secretary, treasurer, and past-president; and a paid executive director.

The association's professional publication is the *American Corrective Therapy Journal,* 4910 Bayou Vista, Houston, Texas 77091. The *Journal* is published every other month. National educational and scientific conferences are held annually in July at preselected sites throughout the country.

The executive director (and permanent mailing address) of the association is: Kirk Hodges, Box 128, Mountain Home, Tennessee, 37684.

93

American School Health Association

Glenn R. Knotts

The ASHA has approximately 20,000 members—professional people of all sorts who together make up the "school health team." Established in 1927 as the American Association of School Physicians, the ASHA strives to promote comprehensive and constructive school health programs—health instruction, health services, and healthful school living.

The association constantly conducts professional and promotional work, and maintains a cooperative informational service for its membership. Inquiries concerning special problems are referred to members with professional and practical experience for accurate and helpful replies. Informative materials are distributed in an effort to improve all phases of school health and to benefit the school child. The ASHA works closely with local, state, and national organizations in behalf of all school health personnel.

The association operates through an executive committee and governing council. Special committees are active and provide services for those members interested in specific areas of school health. As an example, one of the latests publications of the ASHA is a curriculum guide, *Teaching About Drugs.* This guide is the product of the Committee on Drugs of the American School Health Association, and of the Pharmaceutical Manufacturers' Association.

Members of the American School Health Association receive *The Journal of School Health* each month except July and August. *The Journal* provides a wide variety of articles on problems and programs concerned with the child in school. Its diversity is reflected by some recent titles: "The Brain-Injured Child," "A Drug Educational Program," "Behavioral Objectives in Health Instruction," "Issues and Answers in Sex Education," "Assessment of Programs in Dental Health Education," "The Diabetic Child and the School Nurse," "Skin Disease and the Adolescent," "Developmental Dyslexia," and "Distribution of Health Services."

Articles are contributed by physicians, educators, nurses, psychologists, school administrators, dentists, sociologists, pharmacists, and physical therapists. Special features include "Research of Interest," and "How We Do It" columns, which appeal particularly to those who wish to share specific experiences with others in programming.

The Journal serves also as the official repository of the annual reports of the study committees of the association. These reports include jointly prepared statements on a variety of program problems; examples of such reports are "Research and Standards in School Programs for the Visually Handicapped," "Standards for the Preparation and Activities of the School Nurse," "Suggested Courses of Study for the Curriculum and Health Instruction," "Patterns of Administration in the Total Program of School Health Education," "The Role of the School Physician in School Health Education," "Family Life and Sex Education," "Drug Abuse Education," and "Standards for the Activities of the School Dentist and Dental Hygienist."

The Journal publishes selected abstracts of papers presented at the association's annual convention during the meetings of the ASHA research council. Researchers in all disciplines concerned with school health participate in these meetings.

Members receive as membership benefits special supplements published by the ASHA. *Mental Health in the Classroom; The Nurse in the School Health Program: Guidelines for School Nursing; Health Instruction: Suggestions for Teachers;* and *Growth Patterns and Sex Education: A Suggested Program, K-12* are titles of published supplements. The *ASHA Newsletter,* a quarterly, is sent to all members to keep them informed about activities at the national headquarters, professional employment opportunities, and other newsworthy information.

At its annual conventions the association conducts seminars, lectures, and discussion panels involving all aspects of school health.

For further information write to Glenn R. Knotts, Executive Director, American School Health Association, 107 South Depeyster Street, Kent, Ohio, 44240. Contributions to the *Journal of School Health* are welcomed by the editorial staff and should be sent to Editor, *The Journal of School Health,* at the same address.

94
American Youth Hostels, Inc.

Thomas L. Newman

American Youth Hostels, Inc., is a nonprofit membership organization whose aims are to encourage young people of all ages to enjoy outdoor recreational "under-your-own-steam" activities, help them to travel simply, and to establish inexpensive overnight accommodations called hostels.

The hosteling idea was conceived by a German elementary school teacher, Richard Schirrman, who established the first hostel in 1909. There are now 48 countries with hostel associations in the International Youth Hostel Federation, and there are some 4400 hostels round the world, operating under the rules and regulations of the federation and supervised by houseparents.

The American organization was founded by Monroe and Isabel Smith, scout leaders and school teachers, who became interested in the movement while on a Europen hostel tour. They established the first American hostel in Northfield, Massachusetts, in 1934. President Franklin D. and Mrs. Roosevelt, were the first honorary presidents of AYH, and Dr. Paul Dudley White, the famous heart specialist and bicycling-for-health enthusiast was honorary president for life. Lyman Moore of the National Heart and Lung Institute is president, and Thomas L. Newman is executive director.

There are more than 115 hostels in the United States, some in national and state parks, more than 80,000 members and hostel passholders, and 28 local councils throughout the country, whose active members carry on a year-round hosteling activities program. There are more than 100 hosteling clubs in the country, in schools, churches, and other organizational groups, which specialize in one or more hosteling activities for their members.

These are affiliated with AYH local councils and are chartered annually by the parent organization.

The national organization supervises annual summer travel programs for hostelers traveling in small groups, led by prepared and experienced leaders in hiking, biking, canoeing, and utilizing hostels for overnight stays, wherever possible. There is a wide variety of trips in the United States, Canada, Mexico, Japan, Israel, Hawaii, and Europe.

Fig. 94.1 Bikers and hostelers. Courtesy of American Youth Hostels, Inc.

For many years, AYH has conducted leadership preparation courses in some of its hostels in the East, Mid-West, and the West Coast. These courses are designed for people who can ultimately lead AYH trips, with all expenses paid, and for youth-serving agencies and organizations who need this type of leadership. An increasing number of colleges, offering courses in recreation, have included the AYH training program as part of their curricula and have given college credit to the trainees.

American Youth Hostels, Inc., is located on a 62-acre site 60 miles west of Washington, D.C., in the Blue Ridge Mountains.

For information about AYH and its programs, write American Youth Hostels, Inc., National Campus, Delaplane, Virginia, 22025.

95

The Athletic Institute

Don E. Bushore

As innovator and stimulator in the area of physical fitness, the Athletic Institute has served physical educators, school administrators, and teachers charged with the responsibility for the physical development of youth.

Continued growth of the Athletic Institute has been due to the popularity of its publications. The *How to Improve Your Sport* (HTIYS) series is a set of 35 handbooks designed and written under the direction of an authority in the sport. Step-by-step picture demonstrations on how to improve form and skill instruct the reader. The *HTIYS* handbooks have been revised and released under a new series title, *Sport Techniques*. In still another area are publications provided to colleges and municipalities with information on how to construct efficient facilities economically.

Motion picture production has figured prominently in the Athletic Institute's planning. Early endeavors in this field resulted in three color, sound, 16mm motion pictures. The institute also undertook a color filmstrip series, "Beginning Sports," illustrating fundamental sports techniques. Each slide film was produced under the technical direction of experts in the field. Covering 36 sports areas, these slide films have had wide use in schools, colleges, and communities.

The Athletic Institute initiated the first extensive series of sports films in 1951. These training films permitted students to analyze the step-by-step performance of champion athletes for a better understanding of fundamentals. In 1966 the Athletic Institute introduced a new sports film series called "Sports Techniques," with a new format and improved teaching techniques. This 8mm loop film series was developed under the direction of Don Bushore, executive director, who combined teaching and coaching experience with a feeling for visual presentation. A "Sports Techniques Loop Film Guide" accompanies each cartridge unit. Students may view the films and use the guide to learn basic techniques while the instructor is free to comment and emphasize key techniques. Each loop presentation employs regular and slow motion to analyze complicated movements. Stop action or freeze frames are utilized within each sequence to point out the most critical actions of the movement. Diagrams and captions superimposed on the film also assist instructors in identifying key techniques.

More information may be obtained by writing the Athletic Institute, 200 Castlewood Drive, North Palm Beach, Florida 33403.

96

Boy Scouts of America

The purpose of the Boy Scouts of America, incorporated on February 8, 1919, and chartered by Congress in 1916, is to provide for boys and young adults an effective, educational program designed to build desirable qualities of character, to train the responsibilities of participating citizenship, and to develop personal fitness.

The BSA accomplishes this purpose by making its program available in partnership with existing groups having compatible goals, including religious, educational, civic, fraternal, business, labor, governmental bodies, corporations, and professional associations.

THE CUB SCOUT PROGRAM

The Cub Scout program is a family and home-centered program for boys who are 8, 9, and 10 years old.

In 1930 the Boy Scouts of America designed a new program for boys younger than Scout age. It was called Cub Scouting. Since then, it has grown to be the largest of the three BSA programs (the other two are Scouting and Exploring). It is a year-round, home-centered program emphasizing involvement between boys and their parents, boys and their leaders, and boys and their friends. In the multidimensional program of the Boy Scouts of America, Cub Scouting is where it all begins.

Cub Scouting has a number of purposes. It influences a boy's character development and his spiritual growth; develops habits and attitudes of good citizenship; encourages good sportsmanship and pride in growing strong in mind and body; improves understanding within the family; strengthens a boy's ability to get along with others; fosters a sense of personal achievement by developing new interests and skills; shows a boy how to be helpful and do his best; provides fun and exciting new things to do; and prepares him to be a Scout.

Team sports and other competitive events occur within the pack and at the interpack level. Some of the standardized activities that have become favorites over the years are Cub Scout shows, pet shows, pinewood derbies (minature car racing on tracks), regattas, kite-flying contests, summer Olympics, and father-and-son cake-baking contests.

THE SCOUT PROGRAM

The Scout program is a program for boys ages 11 through 17, designed to achieve the BSA objectives primarily through outdoor programs.

On July 29, 1907, two men and 21 boys landed on Brownsea Island, located in a sheltered bay off England's southern coast. They set up a campsite along the shore where they would stay for two weeks. Unknown to the boys— maybe even to the men—they would make history. They were the first Boy Scout troup in the world.

One of the men was Lord Baden-Powell, British hero of the Boer War, who envisioned a new and different kind of activity for youth, one based on his own experiences in Africa that brought him into close contact with methods of survival in the African forests and savannahs. Some of the activities were founded on British military experience—the uniforms, camping, signaling, and organization. But much of what Baden-Powell taught his boys came from his own observations of African lore learned from his native guides.

The boys came from the streets of England; some from exclusive schools. They never knew they were Scouts until Baden-Powell had tested his vision. Two weeks later, Scouting was born.

In 1910, a Chicago publisher named William D. Boyce was in England on business. One day he lost his way in the fog. As he groped to find his way, a boy materialized to ask if he might be of service. Boyce explained his predicament and the boy helped him to his destination. The boy refused a shilling tip, explaining that he was a Scout and could not accept a fee for doing a Good Turn. Intrigued, Boyce wanted to know more about these Scouts. The next day he interviewed Scouting's founder. When he boarded the steamer for home, he brought with him to America Baden-Powell's dream. On February 8, 1910, Boyce incorporated the Boy Scouts of America in Washington, D.C. A Federal Charter from Congress was granted on June 15, 1916.

It is the purpose of the Boy Scouts of America to provide for boys an effective program designed to build desirable qualities of character, citizenship, and personal fitness, thus to help in the development of American citizens who: are physically, mentally, and emotionally fit; have a high degree of self-reliance as evidenced in such qualities as initiative, courage, and resourcefulness; have personal and stable values firmly based on religious concepts; have the desire and skills to help others; understand the principles of the American social, economic, and governmental systems; are knowledgeable about and take pride in the American heritage, and understand America's role in the world; have a keen respect for the basic rights of all people; and are prepared to fulfill the varied responsibilities of participating in, and giving leadership to, American society and forums of the world.

In 1969 Congress challenged the BSA to reach more boys in the disadvantaged rural and urban communities of America. In response the BSA launched the Boypower '76 program designed to reach a representative one-third of all boys. "Representative" means reaching more blacks, Puerto Ricans, chicanos, American Indians, and poor whites. To this end it was necessary to increase the professional staff by recruiting men from the communities they were to serve. To meet these goals, the Boypower campaign was launched. By January 1973 over $25 million had been raised and 300 additional men were employed, most of them in critical areas.

Part of the Boypower '76 program was devoted to making sure Scouting was relevant to the times. After several years of research the improved Scouting program was launched in 1972. Features of the program include a flexible advancement program with more options; easy adaptation to any local environment; emphasis on modern skills such as communications, space exploration, personal management, and decision making; streamlining the interpretation of the Scout law; new emphasis on sports leadership development and personal growth.

Early motivation for achievement takes the form of skill awards that a Scout can earn as soon as he joins the program. They are: camping, citizenship, communications, community living, conservation, cooking, environment, family living, first-aid, hiking, physical fitness, and swimming.

Scouting's emphasis is still on vigorous outdoor activity. The BSA currently maintains 640 camps operated by local Scout councils. There are additional high-adventure camps: Philmont Scout Ranch and Explorer Base in New Mexico; Chalres L. Sommers Wilderness Canoe Base in Minnesota; Northern Wisconsin National Canoe Base; Maine National High Adventure Area; and the Florida-Bahama Treasure Hunt, an underwater experience.

THE EXPLORER PROGRAM

The Explorer program is a contemporary program for young men and women, ages 15 through 20, that provides realistic opportunities to explore adult-like roles and vocational opportunities.

The purpose of Exploring is to provide a program that will meet the needs, desires, and concerns of the next generation of citizens. It achieves its purpose through a planned program of action that brings young adults voluntarily into association with adults. These adults are selected and prepared carefully and, by example of their character, citizenship traits, knowledge, and physical and mental fitness, are a positive force in shaping the lives of youth. Today Explorers are the youth of America. Tomorrow they will be its custodians.

Exploring helps young people find their present and future roles as individuals in society and the world of work through emphasis in six experience areas: *Social* activities are designed to bring all kinds of people together—other explorers, adults, friends and those who will be friends; *vocational* activities allow Exploreres to look ahead at potential careers and vocations; *outdoor* adventure helps Explorers develop their skill in sports and their respect of the environment; *personal fitness* means developing self-reliance through physical, mental, and emotional growth; *service* projects allow Explorers to give help to other people—these experiences develop the quality of unselfish leadership; *citizenship* is what Exploring is really about—it enables one to participate as a member in the home, school, religious institution, and community.

Working closely with the U.S. Olympic Committee and the President's Council on Physical Fitness and Sports, Exploring sponsors a national Olympics program that regularly attracts over 2,000 young people to the annual Explorer Olympics.

In the fall of 1972 the Fourth Annual Exploring Grand National Safe-Driving Road Rally was held in Detroit, Michigan. Ninety Explorers comprising 45 two-person teams competed for trophies and $7000 worth of scholarships. These state teams were selected from 20,000 young people who participated in local safe-driving rallies throughout the year. Other national sports events include a National Exploring Surfing Conference and an Annual Sailing Championship.

Additional information concerning this organization may be obtained by writing: Boy Scouts of America, North Brunswick, New Jersey 08902.

97
The Boys' Clubs of America

John W. Owen

Founded in 1906 and chartered by Congress in 1956, Boys' Clubs of America is one of the fastest growing youth service movements in the nation, serving over one million members through 1100 Boys' Clubs. Boys' Clubs are designed to give boys 7 to 18 years of age responsible adult guidance and to fill a need that is frequently not met either at home or in school.

It seems obvious that this country needs to provide methods and opportunities for youth to increase their participation in physical activity. Such activity is important. Not only does it contribute to healthy body growth and functioning, but it also relieves emotional strains and lessens pressures.

In programming for physical fitness, we keep in mind all of the components that contribute to the total person. This includes the spiritual, mental, emotional, social, and cultural, as well as the physical. Therefore, any emphasis on the physical element of youth development takes into consideration the interelationships of all these factors.

It is of little value, for instance, to help an individual to good physical health if, along the way, he doesn't learn to respect other people's rights, is emotionally maladjusted, or his code of behavior is contrary to accepted moral and ethical principles.

PHYSICAL FITNESS—ALWAYS OUR CONCERN

As one of the afterschool youth services Boys' Clubs are in an especially strategic position to be an effective aid in the development of physical fitness.

Fig. 97.1 Downside up.

Boys' Clubs work intensively with boys in their early formative years, providing them with constructive programs in health, social, educational, vocational, and character development. In addition, we operate our own buildings, often with very good physical education facilities, which are available daily to all boys. This helps guarantee a continuity of day-to-day experiences.

Despite our commendable efforts in the development of strong, healthy bodies, the facts concerning the physical fitness of American youth in general should be very disturbing to all of us. It is now common to see boys transported to and from the Boys' Club in their parents' cars or by public conveyance. There was a time when practically all members walked to and from their Boys' Club regardless of the distance. Our gymnasiums and swimming pools now allow for more and more spectator space, sometimes at the sacrifice of valuable area for activity. It is also true that the members of a Boys' Club reflect the attitudes and habits of the larger community regarding physical activity. Some club members tend toward obesity. They are avid television fans and suffer generally from "spectatoritis."

Do physical activities compensate for the increase in comfort and leisure and the decrease in physical exertion needed to perform daily tasks? This challenging question needs to be answered if we are to fulfill our obligation to provide for the development of the total boy in today's world.

Each Boys' Club gives serious consideration to ways and means of contributing to the fitness of youth in its particular community. This implies concerted action to make maximum use of physical facilities, provide challenging programs and activities geared to the various age groups served, and increase opportunity for fostering positive attitudes among the boys and their parents.

WHAT WE ARE DOING NATIONALLY

Boys' Clubs of America has accepted the physical fitness problem as a continuing concern. It studies the annual program reports submitted by member clubs. A compilation of the data indicates trends developing in the program, and the findings form a basis for determining which areas of the health and physical education programs require emphasis in the future.

In order to stimulate interest in physical activities, sectional basketball, swimming, and "Olympic" tournaments have been revised and extended to include greater participation by Boys' Clubs and by individuals. The programs in aquatics and physical goals have been revised for easier and more efficient use. Their formats make these programs attractive to boys.

Publications such as *Fit for Fun* have been developed. Articles in *Keynote* help to keep clubs abreast of ideas and activities developed in the area of physical fitness programming. With the help of committees, Boys'

Fig. 97.2 Pro.

Fig. 97.3 Seven-year-old sport.

Clubs of America continues to conduct further research, develop projects and articles and to give help and encouragement in order to strengthen and improve physical fitness programs in Boys' Clubs.

Through trained, concerned leadership and behavior and attitude guidance, a Boys' Club attempts to help youth grow into mature, constructive adults able to participate fully in both the benefits and responsibilities of American society.

Boys' Clubs strive to attain this objective by offering members a wide variety of programs geared to individual interests and needs. These include such activities as job orientation and development, educational supplementation and enrichment, cultural programs, citizenship and leadership development, library, and health and physical education activities.

Because of the age group served, health and physical education comprises a large part of the programs of Boys' Clubs throughout the country. Since each club has complete facilities, opportunities are provided for a variety of sports and athletics on a daily, on-going basis with emphasis on every boy and not just on varsity sports.

The Boys' Clubs of America Swimming Program, which is adapted from the American Red Cross, each year teaches thousands of youth from disadvantaged neighborhoods to swim and to be safe in and about the water. In addition, many more thousands of boys qualify and receive fitness certificates for their performance in physical fitness tests. Outdoor activities and camping are also heavily stressed.

Providing support and leadership to the 1100 Boys' Clubs are over 80,000 members of board of directors, and over 3000 fulltime workers aided by a large staff of parttime workers and close to 50,000 volunteer workers.

For more information, write the Boys' Clubs of America, 771 First Avenue, New York, New York 10017.

98

Camp Fire Girls, Inc.

Carol A. Bitner

Camp Fire Girls, Inc., a not-for-profit volunteer membership organization, was founded in 1910 by Dr. and Mrs. Luther Halsey Gulick. Dr. Gulick, a leader in the field of health, physical education, and recreation, had been the first director of physical education for the public schools of greater New York and director of the Department of Child Hygiene of the Russell Sage Foundation.

The traditional emphasis of the Camp Fire program has always been on the small group under skilled, caring adults, making use of informal education, and recreation, and group-work principles and techniques. This program, which is divided into four program levels, Blue Bird Clubs, Adventure Clubs, Discovery Clubs, and Horizon Clubs, focuses on learning by doing, developing a positive self-image, responsibility and creativity, gaining decision-making and planning skills, and learning to appreciate, care, and work with others. The program builds opportunities for personal and social learnings—life skills—and works to reduce sex-stereotyping.

In November, 1975, the then 68-year-old organization adopted "A New Day." This design included a total agency renewal process involving program, membership, finances, structure, local-national relationships, bylaws, and even the basic corporate purpose. The purpose is to provide, through a program of informal education, opportunities for youth to realize their potential and to function effectively as caring, self-directed individuals responsible to themselves and to others; and, as an organization, to seek to improve those conditions in society that affect youth.

Camp Fire is no longer a one-program agency; rather, it is a multi-program, multiservice organization. The client/membership group has been expanded to include youth of both sexes from birth to 21 years, while retaining the fundamental policy of openness without regard to race, economic status, or national origin. The primary target continues to be girls 6 to 18 years of age.

The new program flexibility is intended to enable the local council to be responsive to community youth needs, unmet by other agencies. Local councils will continue the traditional club program, but will also provide such diverse activities as preschool programs, latch-key programs, drop-in centers, juvenile justice programs, career education projects, family life education classes, etc. Camping and outdoor activities continue to be a popular program focus.

Programs are determined by the 345 local councils. However, all programs must carry out the corporate purpose and must meet national policies and standards. Councils are serving over 500,000 members (adults and youth) in rural, urban, and suburban areas. There are Camp Fire programs in over 35,000 communities.

Chartered councils are the corporate members of Camp Fire Girls and meet as a congress (an exciting convention atmosphere with over 1000 in attendance) every other year to elect the National Board of Directors, establish broad objectives for the biennium, amend bylaws, and carry out other business as may come before it. In the alternate years, councils meet as zones to elect zone chairmen who sit on the national board of directors and conduct seminars, workshops, etc., for the councils in the zone. Current president of Camp Fire Girls is Dr. Faith LaVelle. Current chairman of the board is Jon Dee Lawrence. The organization's national professional staff is headed by national executive director, Dr. Hester Turner.

The new corporate headquarters of Camp Fire Girls at 4601 Madison Avenue, Kansas City, Mo. 64112, develops materials for national and local use and prepares, advises, provides consultation, and supports those involved with Camp Fire programs thoughout the country. The Camp Fire Supply Division, 450 Avenue of the Americas, New York, N.Y. 10011, sells service costumes, awards, ceremonial gowns, books, and other items to stores and councils.

99

Canadian Association for Health, Physical Education, and Recreation

C.R. Blackstock

The Canadian Physical Education Association (CAHPER) was founded in 1933. The present title was assumed in 1948 and the association received a federal charter in 1951. It is incorporated as a nonprofit, voluntary membership, educational organization.

The purposes and aims are to: (1) assist in the improvement and extension of programs for Canadians of all ages, (2) seek the improvement of professional preparation of teachers and leaders, (3) take part in the effort to disseminate information and knowledge of good practices in health, physical education, and recreation, and (4) cooperate with other organizations with similar purposes.

Membership has never been very large, but through the efforts of the presidents and the several boards of directors the association has exerted a very positive influence in both public and private agencies. Various interest and action committees have undertaken studies and projects, making the results available to the membership and the public.

The biennial convention has been held in cities from coast to coast and is an undertaking of the CAHPER branch in city selected. These meetings bring together people from all over Canada and from other countries, at which time there is an exchange of ideas, techniques, research findings, and philosophy.

CAHPER joined with the Canadian Medical Association in fostering the formation of the Canadian Association of Sports Sciences (1967). With the same association it had a small part to play in placing the Mill of Kintail, R. Tait McKenzie's summer place and studio at Almonte, Ontario, into the public domain (June 1972).

The publication of the *Bulletin* from 1933-1952, and *the CAHPER Journal* from 1952 to the present, have been the most consistent projects of the association. The national office was established in 1960 at which time it initiated a book service for members, which included most of the American Alliance for Health, Physical Education, and Recreation titles. The association has published Canadian fitness-performance and work-capacity tests together with national norms.

CAHPER assisted in the development of the first *Physical Fitness Act of 1943,* and the second, the *Fitness and Amateur Sport Act of 1961.* The association has always enjoyed a good relation with the federal Department of National Health and Welfare and the American Alliance for Health, Physical Education, Recreation, and Dance. Branches in the provinces have brought the influences of the association to the local level. They also sponsor clinics, workshops, and conferences in their regions.

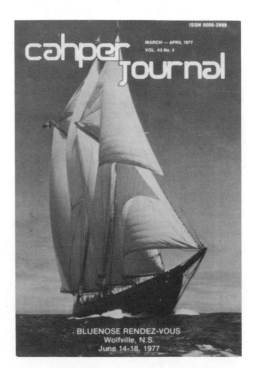

Fig. 99.1 Cover of a *CAHPER Journal,* Courtesy of the Canadian Association for Health, Physical Education, and Recreation.

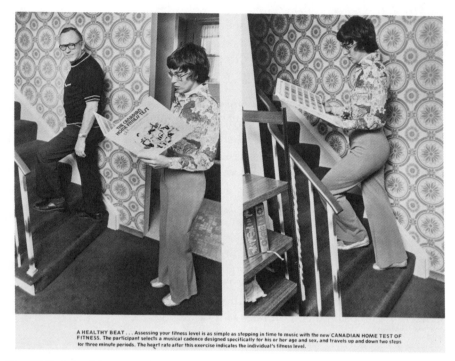

Fig. 99.2 A healthy beat. Courtesy of the Canadian Association for Health, Physical Education, and Recreation.

Fig. 99.3 Community involvement.
Courtesy of the Canadian Association for
Health, Physical Education and Recreation.

Dr. A.S. Lamb, McGill University, guided the formation of the association and was the president for the first six years. Miss Florence Somers, Margaret Eaton School of Physical Education, was the first woman president. Dr. J.H. Crocker, J.G. Lang, Miss Iveagh Munro, and Morrie Bruker were other early leaders. The newer generation of leaders who have done much to expand the influence of the association are M.L. Van Vliet, G.A. Wright, M.L. Howell, D.W. Smith, J.F. Passmore, M.S. Yuhasz, and W.A.R. Orban.

National offices of the association may be contacted by writing: Executive Secretary, 333 River Road, Vanier City, Ontario, Canada KIL 8B9.

100
Council for National Cooperation in Aquatics

Harold T. Friermood

The original purpose of the Conference for National Cooperation in Aquatics, now called the Council for National Cooperation in Aquatics (CNCA), was to provide a setting in which official representatives from national organizations could come together to report on individual agency programs, plans, and projects, to share and discuss common problems, and to plan ways of working together on agreed-upon projects. Planning and working together on appropriate and well-defined tasks brings about a greater understanding among national voluntary organiztions, professional societies, and governmental agencies, making it possible to serve a larger number of people more effectively. Such cooperative effort, added to the independent work carried on continuously by the various national groups, was expected to help advance the entire field of aquatics.

The idea for expanding cooperative aquatic efforts at the national level was originated informally on March 24, 1945. Following two years of discussions and successful preliminary meetings in November 1947 and January 1948, a period of inertia was interrupted by the Korean conflict. This stimulated a planning meeting during the early summer that brought about the organization of CNCA, as now known, in the fall of 1951. From the very beginning the AAHPER (general staff) and NAGWS representatives took an active part in the planning and leadership of CNCA.

CNCA was incorporated legally as a national, nonprofit, educational, public service organization in the state of New York, August 13, 1964. The official bylaws of CNCA, Inc. are shown in the appendix of the report of the 1972 International Aquatic Conference entitled *Waters of the World—Use and Conservation.*

Since 1951 general meetings have been conducted. For the first dozen years, 1951 to 1962, an annual meeting was held. Then a general meeting every two years to permit committee and project work to move forward without the pressure to plan and conduct a large event every year. Closed workshops were conducted during each intervening year to work on designated projects. From the general meetings and workshop projects have come CNCA publications.

A six-page cumulative chart gives the sequence of the national conferences. Included in the chart are program topics of general sessions, workgroups, demonstrations, and lists of elected officers. The nature of each conference report is described concisely. CNCA National Honor Award recipients, beginning in 1960, are listed. Three honorary chairmen have served since 1954. (See the 1972 CNCA Conference Report #17 for details.)

The following 32 national organizations presently constitute CNCA:

Amateur Athletic Union of the United States (AAU)
American Academy of Pediatrics (AAP)
American Alliance for Health, Physical Education, Recreation, and Dance
— General representation (AAHPERD-Staff)
— Aquatic Council
— National Association for Girls and Women's Sports (NAGWS)
American Camping Association (ACA)
American National Red Cross (ARC)
American Public Health Association (APHA)
American Swimming Coaches Association (ASCA)
Athletic Institute, Inc. (AI)
Boy Scouts of America (BSA)
Boys' Clubs of America (BCA)
Camp Fire Girls, Inc. (CFG)
International Swimming Hall of Fame (ISHOF)
Joseph P. Kennedy, Jr., Foundation (JPKJF)
National Assocition of Intercollegiate Athletics (NAIA)
National Association of Underwater Instructors (NAUI)
National Board of the Young Women's Christian Associations (YMCA)
National Collegiate Athletic Association (NCAA)
National Council of Young Men's Christian Associations (YMCA)
National Federation of State High School Athletic Associations (NFSHSAA)
National Jewish Welfare Board (JWB)

National Recreation & Park Association (NRPA)
National Safety Council (NSC)
National Surf Lifesaving Association of America (NSLSA)
National Swimming Pool Institute (NSPI)
President's Council on Physical Fitness & Sports (PCPFS)
Underwater Society of America (USA)
United States Public Health Services (USPHS)
United States Swimming Foundation (USSF)
Women's National Aquatic Forum (WNAF)

Member groups and all new national organization applicants (no individual may apply for or be accepted into membership) are checked against the following criteria:

1. has expressed an interest in and a desire to support the purpose of the council
2. has a membership constituency, or is a federal agency, involved in the promotion of aquatics
3. conducts or participates in aquatic programs, or has aquatic facilities to operate
4. employs professional personnel and uses volunteer leadership in aquatics.

Each related national member organization specifies its official representative to serve on the board of directors.

CNCA was not intended originally to be an operating entity but rather an interpretive, stimulative group of responsible, capable, representative persons seeking to advance aquatics throughout the country. CNCA depends upon the related member groups to carry on specific aquatic functions with their own constituencies through their own national channels. The materials and publications encouraged or created by CNCA are prepared as a service to aquatics in general. Their widespread use by all groups and individuals is encouraged. Because of the expanded organizational and management functions that had developed by 1967, the CNCA board of directors defined responsibilities and selected Harold T. Friermood as its first executive director in 1968. He was instructed to select a location and establish a national headquarters where operations and services could be centralized and materials and records maintained. This enabled the officers, committee, and board personnel to devote their time and efforts to policy and program rather than administrative-operational matters.

A ten-point statement adopted some years ago was updated, reorganized, and rephrased periodically as follows:

1. Aquatic activities provide some of the best recreational pursuits for the entire family.

2. Swimming is a healthful activity in which almost everyone can participate, including both sexes, the young, the aged, persons with physical handicaps, and those with mental limitations.

3. Under competent leadership, swimming and other aquatic activities can contribute to physical, mental, emotional, and social fitness.

4. The primary objective of water safety instruction is to help the individual become safe while in, on, or near the water.

5. Everyone should have the opportunity to learn water safety and be encouraged to improve aquatic skill regardless of age, sex, racial, or cultural background.

6. The reduction and elimination of water accidents should be a goal of every community aquatic program.

7. Existing aquatic facilities (private and public) should be utilized to the maximum.

8. Every community has a responsibility to develop adequate facilities and provide competent aquatic leadership.

9. Education in aquatics should be included in the program of every school system, and swimming ability required for high school graduation.

10. A more effective aquatic program can be achieved in a community and throughout the nation when all interested groups and individuals cooperate in working for clearly defined, agreed-upon goals including conservation and wise use of natural resources.

This gives a foundation upon which to project plans and programs locally or nationally on a cooperative basis.

Publications and aquatic materials developed by CNCA are recommended and available for purchase and use.

Scholarship plans have been established to honor former CNCA leaders and to encourage the thorough preparation of volunteer and professional aquatic leadership. Information about the scholarship program is available through the AAHPERD Aquatic Council and NAGWS representatives, and from the other member organizations of CNCA. The CNCA scholarship program should stimulate member groups and others to establish their own plans for upgrading standards of aquatic leadership. The watchword of CNCA is *Progress is Made Through Cooperation.*

The executive director is Bernard E. Empleton, 220 Ashton Road, Ashton, MD 20702. Phone (301) 924-3771.

SUGGESTED READINGS

Bullock, D. L., (ed.), 1962. *Advanced aquatic skills in synchronized swimming activities.* Ashton, Maryland: CNCA.

CNCA Headquarters, 1951, 1952, 1953, 1954, 1955, 1956, 1957, 1958, 1959, 1960, 1961, 1962, 1964, 1966, 1968, 1970, 1972, 1974, 1976. Nineteen CNCA Conference Reports on microfilm for library purchase and reference use. Ashton, Maryland: CNCA. Eugene, Oregon: Microfilm Publications, College of Health, Physical Education and Recreation, University of Oregon.

Empleton, B. E., (ed.), 1974. *action in aquatics.* Conference Report.

———, 1977. *First aid for skin and scuba divers. Conference Report.*

———, 1973. (early editions: 1957, 1959, 1962, 1964, 1968, 1970). *New science of skin and scuba diving.* New York: Association Press.

Friermood, H. T., (ed.), 1970. *Aquatics in the 70's—challenges and changes.* Sixteenth Conference Report. Ashton, Maryland: CNCA.

———, 1972. *Waters of the world—use and conservation.* Seventeenth Conference Report, Ashton, Maryland: CNCA.

———, 1968. *Wide world of aquatics.* Fifteenth Conference Report. Ashton, Maryland: CNCA.

———, 1972. "How CNCA began and it progress ' *Journal of physical education,* **69** : 72-78. (Jan.-Feb.).

——— (coordinator). *Out-of-print aquatic classics.* Ann Arbor, Michigan: University Microfilms International.

Gabrielsen, M. A., (ed.), 1969, revised 1972. *Swimming pools—a guide to their planning, design and operation.* Fort Lauderdale, Florida: Hoffman Publications.

Howes, G. T., (ed.), 1973. *Lifeguard training, principles and administration.* Out of print.

Stein, J. U., (ed.), 1969. *A practical guide for teaching the mentally retarded to swim.* Washington, D.C.: AAHPER.

Yates, F. W., (ed.), 1968. *Swimming and diving—a bibliography.* New York: Association Press.

101

Girl Scouts of the United States of America, Inc.

Melba M. Ferguson

Girl Scouts of the U.S.A. is the largest voluntary organization for girls in the world. It is open to all girls ages 6 through 17 (or in grades 1 through 12) who subscribe to its ideals as stated in the Girl Scout Promise and Law. It is a part of a worldwide family of girls and adults in 94 countries through its membership in the World Association of Girl Guides and Girl Scouts.

Girls Scouts of the U.S.A. has more than three million members—2.6 million girls (one of every nine girls, ages 6 to 17, in the United States) and 557,000 adult members (women and men)—volunteer leaders, consultants, board members, and staff specialists in the areas of child development, adult education, outdoor education, and administration.

The Girl Scout program encourages participation in sports activities for sound physical and mental development, for maintenance of a healthy existence, and for recreational enjoyment.

Fig. 101.1 Backpacking the Girl Scout National Center West, Big Horn Basin, Ten Sleep, Wyoming.

On the troop level, Girl Scouts, in partnership with their adult leaders, may plan sports activities. Depending on their interests, camping, swimming, boating, bicycling, and individual and team sports may be included in their plans.

Girl Scout councils have initiated sports days, council-wide "Olympics" and local recognitions for participation and achievement in sports.

For further information write: (Mrs.) Frances R. Hellelbein, Executive Director, 830 Third Avenue, New York, New York 10022.

102

Health Clubs

Paul Hunsicker

Health clubs in one form or another have a long history. At least the concept of a place to go for bathing, massage, and exercise was in existence in imperial Rome.

From the days of Pompeii and the Stabian baths, which combined the baths, a palaestrum, areas for exercise and recreation, to emperor Caracalla's famous baths, these edifices occupied a central portion of Roman life.

More recent forerunners of today's health clubs were the European Spas so famous in the 18th and 19th centuries. In the United States, the Battle Creek Sanatorium was a pioneer in introducing strength-testing and electromechanical exercise devices into the health field in the late 19th and early 20th centuries.

It is not the purpose of this chapter to examine the historical background of health clubs but the writer wanted to acknowledge the fact that these institutions have been a part of the scene for centuries. The main thrust of the chapter will deal with health clubs in the present era.

Anyone faced with the task of describing the work of health clubs soon recognizes some obvious difficulties. Some insights into the problem follow. There is no national professional association of clubs similar to the American Alliance for Health, Physical Education, Recreation, and Dance or the American Public Health Association. There are health clubs that are nationwide in terms of their locations, but these are not united to any professional association. Many clubs are strictly local or even one-unit operations with no affiliations. There is no single definition of a health club. It is extremely difficult to secure data covering the total health club picture to include personnel involved, clients served, or total money spent in this sector of the economy. State laws regulating the certification of personnel working in health clubs are practically nonexistent. In most instances people can work in a health club with little or no prior formal education in the field of physical education or health.

To assist in limiting the coverage of this chapter it might be useful to offer an operational definition or framework of "health clubs" as perceived by the writer. By and large the coverage will extend to clubs whose clientele are free of any known pathology but are interested in their fitness level because of health, cosmetic, or recreational reasons, or who view their experiences at the club as sound preventive medicine. An effort will be made to describe different kinds of health clubs but no attempt will be made to include all operations. This would be a hopeless task. While the writer exercised judgment in selecting representative clubs for inclusion, no evaluative criteria were applied to either the practices employed or the kinds of information dispensed by the clubs.

While precise statistics are difficult to obtain, certainly agencies such as the YMCA, the YMHA, or the Jewish Community Centers serve a tremendous number of health club members. The YMCA operation will be described in some detail as representative of a social agency health club.

The general supervision of the club is administered by a qualified physical director. Under his direction are a corps of technicians who supervise and/or administer message, baths (shower, steam, sauna, whirlpool), ultraviolet irradiation (artificial and natural sunlight), infrared heat, instruction in relaxation, and personally directed exercises.

A recent study of YMCA health clubs recommended: (1) they should be designed for 300 male members, (2) they should provide for 100 females or there should be a separate women's club for not less than 150 members, and (3) space should be available for a 50 to 100 percent expansion in five years.

Currently YMCAs have over 400 actual clubs in operation, and register well over 200,000 members. The member has access to the customary activities associated with the Y, such as handball, swimming, combatives, exercises with or without weights, jogging, yoga, and others. In recent years, a greater emphasis has been placed on personalized fitness testing and counseling.

The facilities in most private clubs are, by gymnasium standards, plush, and feature wall-to-wall carpeting, an attractive swimming pool, chrome-coated exercise devices plus sauna, steam, solarium, hot mineral whirlpool, and ultraviolet sun room. In most clubs separate facilities are available for men and women. The private health clubs are similar to the agency health clubs in their publicity releases. Both appeal to the desire to control weight, improve physical fitness, slow the process of aging, and enhance physical appearance. Services and facilities are generally a direct reflection of the fee paid. Since these are private enterprises with no government support, a large share of their personnel effort must be directed toward enrolling new members. Rewards in terms of commissions are based on the ability to secure new participants. By virtue of economic necessity the better paying jobs are directed at the membership challenge rather than at directing exercise programs. But one must not lose sight of the fact that the club has to be sensitive to the needs and desires of its membership. At the end of three months, after a trial membership, or at the end of the year, the member decides to continue his affiliation or drop it. The moment of truth is inevitable. The health clubs are well aware of it and try to be genuinely responsive to the members.

Another kind of facility is the spa, connected with a hotel. This type of health club, which is part of a hotel complex, exists, although not always in such a luxurious setting, in most resort cities. The facilities and programs offered are fairly standard with emphasis on massage, baths of various types, and exercise programs. The one major difference stems from the fact that participants are usually on a vacation and, consequently, transient. Their commitments are on a daily basis. Programs of this kind have been in existence for many years without any radical changes.

A few hotels have health centers with a multidisciplinary approach utilizing medical specialties, physical education, physical medicine, and counseling. A typical program might include a preexercise physical examination, which includes a thorough cardiopulmonary evaluation under stress, as well as measurements of other parameters such as blood chemistry and motor ability. As a result of this examination it is possible to plan an individual activity program based on physical capacity and needs. This is carried out for the next four days. Exercise dosages are prescribed and can be executed on specially designed machines that monitor the intensity of the workout and keep the subject within the prescribed limits. At the conclusion of the five-day session participants receive a report describing their physical condition together with specific recommendations for personalized activity programs, including diet, that can be continued at home.

The entire complex might encompass a lounge, medical exam rooms, x-ray room, laboratory, a physical fitness lab, a central gym for group exercises, passive exercise equipment, separate fitness gyms for men and women, physical therapy and massage rooms, outside whirlpool, special exercise pool, jogging tracks, and a seminar room for group discussions.

This type of health center represents a revival of interest on the part of selected physicians in the therapeutic and preventive values of exercise. The importance of cardiac stress testing is recognized as an important adjunct to the customary resting-state EKG.

Recently there has been a wave of physical fitness centers employing stress testing and prescribing exercise as preventive measures against coronary heart disease. Typical of these installations is Dr. Kenneth Cooper's in

Dallas and Dr. Fred Allman's in Atlanta. These institutions are continuing at an operational level equal to the operations of university physiology of exercise laboratories, and mark a hopeful outlook for future health clubs.

Although the coverage here has been primarily concerned with health clubs in the United States, one might observe that in the Soviet Union, Austria, Germany, and Switzerland, both the government and industry sponsor and support reconditioning centers for workers. The programs of most of the European reconditioning centers consist of systematic calisthenics, breathing exercises, running, swimming, bathing, and ball games during the forenoon, and an hour or two of relaxation after lunch. More games, hiking, and climbing occupy the afternoon. In fact, the hiking follows the famous Oertel Terrain Cure, a series of walks graded in intensity, developed by Dr. Oertel in the 19th century.

The late Dr. Wilhelm Raab of the University of Vermont tried for years to interest both the United States government and various industries in following the pattern of support given in these countries. He personally observed the benefits of these programs and hoped he could persuade America to follow suit. As a final word, let us hope his pleas were not in vain!

SUGGESTED READINGS

Encyclopedia britannica, 1965. Vol. 18, p. 201-5.

Hadas, M., 1965. *Imperial rome*. New York: Time Inc.

Kraus, H., et al. *Hypokinetic disease*. Springfield, Ill.: Charles C. Thomas.

McKenzie, R. T., 1923. *Exercise in education and medicine*. Philadelphia: W.B. Saunders.

Van Dis, J., 1970. YMCA health club facilities and equipment, Paper presented to Health Service Directors Society Clinic, New Haven, (July 21).

103

International Olympic Academy

Harold T. Friermood

The International Olympic Academy (IOA) is situated 200 miles west of Athens, Greece, in the locality called Elis, near the village of Ancient Olympia. The academy site occupies several acres on which modern facilities and attractive buildings have been constructed. Down the hillside just across the main highway, excavations completed nearly a century ago by French and German workers have reclaimed the setting of the original Olympic Games—first recorded in 776 B.C. Removal of silt, laid down over 2000 years by the restless, course-changing Alpheaos and Kladeos rivers, has opened new vistas for the study of sport history. The relevance of ancient practices and ideals for contemporary society, through the medium of modern sport, is the challenge. For three weeks in July each summer this general subject brings together 200 men and women from many countries.

This gathering of serious-minded people, the majority ranging in age from 18 to 35 years, meet with great athletes and world famous lecturers, recognized authorities in their fields of sport history, archaeology, sociology, psychology, physiology, sports medicine, coaching, training, skill techniques, literature, the information media, and other fields. General lectures, given in the three official languages (Greek, French, and English) with simultaneous electronic interpretation, provide the background for small group seminars, personal study, and informal discussions. Visitations, sports, and many types of social recreation round out the busy daily program.

When Dr. Carl Diem from Germany visted Greece in 1934 to arrange the first torch-lighting, relay-carrying ceremony for the 1936 Olympic Games in Berlin, he met John Ketseas, a businessman and sports enthusiast, in Athens. Both men were great admirers of Baron Pierre de Coubertin, leader in establishing the modern Olympic Games. Diem and Ketseas conceived and developed the idea of the IOA, presented it to the International Olympic Committee (IOC) in London at the time of the 1948 Olympic Games and were deeply gratified when, a year later, the IOC approved the plan.

It took 12 years to plan, organize, and conduct the first session of the IOA in 1961. For the first several years, the participants lived in tents. Lectures and discussions were carried on under the trees. Financed by the Greek government, the academy now has modern living facilities for students and lecturers, recreation building, lecture hall, dining room, library, administrative offices, post office, bank, medical services, large athletic field, all-weather courts for volleyball and basketball, and a fine outdoor swimming pool.

As now conceived the purpose of the IOA is to:

1. Assemble young people from around the world to consider, under mature leadership, the purpose of the Olympic Games and the Olympic Movement.
2. Explore the values of sport and recreation for all people.
3. Emphasize the need and opportunity for international cooperation in preparing young leaders to share these concepts and their academy experiences through sport, educational, recreational, and other national organization channels.

IOA PROGRAM

The session starts each year with assembly in Athens, visits to the Acropolis with its impressive Parthenon, the national archeological museum, and other points of interest in the city. The formal opening occurs shortly before sunset with the group seated on Pnyx Hill, looking toward the Acropolis while a band and a chorus provide background music. Short speeches set the tone and provide a genuine welcome to visitors from the many lands represented. The evening is completed with a reception and dinner provided by the Hellenic Olympic Committee.

Early next morning chartered buses transport the entire group to Ancient Olympia. Days are filled with work at the academy, trips, sports, recreation, and social evenings where movies are shown and games, dances, and music are demonstrated and taught to fellow students.

Because of the increasing importance of the work of the academy, with its continual emphasis upon total development of all persons, the academy's popularity has grown. Formerly each National Olympic Committee was allowed up to 10 participants; this has now been reduced to only five, with further reductions anticipated. Selective procedures in the USA are designed to help insure that the summer academy experience will be carried back home and utilized in the sports and educational groups where USA candidates for the Olympic Games are developed. This, it is hoped, will make the ideals of Olympism a continuing influence rather than a dramatic spectacle that occurs only every fourth year.

WHO IS ELIGIBLE?

USA candidates, men and women, must be citizens of this country. First consideration is given to persons 18 to 35 years of age who meet selection criteria and rate well on the announced grading plan.

Each applicant must be related to one of the designated national Olympic sport, educational, or national youth organizations.

Application forms and information must be secured from, and correspondence about the academy carried on with, the liaison person specified. (Any person related to an educational organization or institution interested in the academy may secure information and file an application through the designated AAHPERD staff liaison office or person.)

From September 15 to November 15 applications for the following year's IOA summer session may be sent to the proper sports or group representative.

From November 15 to December 5 respective liaison persons grade, score, and rate applications, determine the top one or two candidates in each group, and transmit basic information, rating sheets, and personal evaluations to the USOC-IOA Committee.

After careful review and consultation the USOC-IOA Committee selects and submits, by January 10, its final recommendations of up to five USA student participants, plus alternates, for approval by the USOC officers and board of directors.

The final successful candidates and alternates are notified of the board's action by the USOC-IOA committee on or before February 15. If any candidates decline, alternates are invited and finally, the full quota from the USA is selected. After making necessary adjustments in personnel and securing proper material from each approved candidate, the USOC-IOA committee transmits credentials to the Greek IOA committee in Athens by March 31.

RESPONSIBILITIES OF USA STUDENT PARTICIPANTS

Candidates understand that if selected they must (1) attend a two or three day orientation program in New York City, and/or Athens just prior to the start of the IOA session in Greece; (2) pay a portion of the travel and related expenses from home-base to New York, to Athens, and back home*; (3) clear

---

* The USOC will provide each USA student participant with a scholarship that will cover his/her expenses during the academy session, including food, housing, and bus travel. The USOC will also share one-third of the round-trip excursion rate air fare, going to and returning from Athens. The participant and his/her sponsoring agency will pay the other two-thirds.

all travel plans and secure tickets through the USOC coordinator of transportation, Olympic House, N.Y.C.; (4) prepare an approved plan for making effective use of the academy experience upon return; and (5) submit a written report by September 1 evaluating the academy experience and outlining final plans for making effective use of the experience—this report to be submitted to the USOC-IOA committee.

SPECIAL SESSIONS

Because of the fine facilities and attractive setting provided by the academy, special short-term sessions may be planned and announced from time to time. These are studied by the USOC-IOA committee and, when found to be of sufficient value to have USA representation, steps are taken to announce them and secure suitable candidates.

Additional plans have been developed to provide involvement with the purposes of the IOA. Beginning in 1977 USA National Mobile Olympic Academy Sessions were authorized. Such designated events are conducted on university campuses. Each is expected to provide a background based upon study and discussion of the purpose and conduct of the ancient Olympic Games, the revival of the modern games in 1896, and the subsequent 80 years of performance. With this perspective established, the main thrust is the examination and analysis of the contemporary domestic and international scene as it relates to recreation, fitness, amateur sport, interpersonal relations, and an integrated philosophy of life. Approved sessions may be conducted over a five-day to two-week period or concentrated in a three-day weekend. With proper academic standards maintained, some host universities may arrange to give college credit for satisfactory work accomplished. USOC national sports groups, community agencies, the media, historians, writers, Olympic team candidates, as well as college faculty members and students will make up the major part of the attendance. Experiences gained during 1977, 1978, and 1979 were used to set standards for future operations. The Mobile Olympic Academy Sessions will help prepare thousands of leaders to supplement the limited few that go to the IOA in Greece each year.

The USOC-IOA committee has also proposed arranging traveling educational seminars with several days spent on the IOA campus in Greece, with academy faculty members participating.

The Greek IOA committee selects the lecturers it wants for each summer session or special sessions. These experts and recent Olympic participants are contacted directly about their participation. When agreement is reached the Greek IOA committee clears on topics and material to be prepared to support the summer session theme and also enable lecturers to present their specialties. Agreements are also reached about travel expense, hospitality arrangements, and other details that need to be negotiated. From time to time the USOC-IOA committee makes recommendations about qualified USA lecturers, but final selections and negotiations are carried on by the Greek IOA committee.

USOC OFFICIAL BOARD REPRESENTATION

One USOC board member is selected each year to be the official USOC representative at the summer session. This person conducts the New York City or Athens orientation program, serves as "Chief of the Mission" (leader of the USA group of participants), reports to the USOC-IOA committee and the board of directors, and serves on the USOC-IOA committee for the balance of that quadrennial.

A printed report is issued several months after each IOA annual summer session. Each participant receives a copy. Others may secure copies for a fee directly from the Greek IOA committee in Athens.

Upon recommendation of the AAHPERD executive officer, the AAHPERD liaison-contact person, appointed by the USOC-IOA committee is: Dr. Raymond A. Ciszek, International Relations, AAHPERD/USOC-IOA, 1900 Association Drive, Reston, VA 22091. Educators, physical educators, and AAHPERD members may secure information and correspond about the IOA with Dr. Ciszek.

104

National Association for Physical Education of College Women

Joanna Davenport

The National Association for Physical Education of College Women is a nonprofit organization founded formally in 1924; however, it began many years before. In 1910, at the invitation of Amy Morris Homans, the directors

Editor's Note: In June 1978 this organization merged with the National College Physical Education Association for Men to form the National Association for Physical Education in Higher Education (NAPEHE).

of physical education departments in the women's colleges of New England met at Wellesley College to discuss mutual problems. Convening annually, they formed a permanent organization in 1915 known as the Eastern College Women's Physical Directors Society. Two years later the college women physical directors in the Mid-West formed a similar organization. A third group was founded in 1921 by the women physical directors in the colleges of the West. The three bodies united in 1924 to form the national organization known then as the National Association of Directors of Physical Education for College Women. In 1935 a southern group organized and joined the larger body. In 1936 a fifth district was formed in the central part of the country and merged with the national association. These same five district associations are still affiliated with NAPECW. The district associations and NAPECW cooperate with each other by extending the work of the respective groups and coordinating activities.

The early name indicates this national organization was limited originally to women directors of physical education departments. In 1942 this restriction was eliminated with a resultant increase in the number of members. Membership is now open to any woman college or university faculty member whose reponsibilities are in physical education. An active member of NAPECW must first hold membership in her district association. From 16 members in 1924, the association now has a membership of over 1200.

NAPECW has cooperated on many projects with the men's college organization, NCPEAM; the most notable venture has been the joint publication of *Quest*.

The purpose of the association is to promote instruction, related services and research in physical education for college women, and to provide a professional affiliation of women concerned with all aspects of women's physical education in two and four-year colleges.

Further information may be secured from Marianna Trekell, University of Illinois, Urbana, Illinois 61820.

105
National College Physical Education Association for Men
Fred B. Roby

The National College Physical Education Association for Men was founded in 1897. The aim of the association is to further the advancement of physical education and sport in institutions of higher education. The objectives are: (1) to improve the contributions of physical education, intramurals, sport, and athletics, and when appropriate, the related fields of health education and recreation to higher education; (2) to identify and define major issues and problems confronting the profession, particularly those of higher education, and encourage and organize research including the gathering, analyzing, and interpreting of data in an effort to resolve these issues and problems; (3) to develop interdisciplinary relationships with kindred fields of knowledge for the insights they may be able to contribute on the nature of values of physical education, such as anthropology, history, philosophy, physiology, psychology, sociology, sports medicine, and other disciplines, and (4) to improve public relations through increasing public awareness and understanding of the nature and purposes of physical education.

The association functions by: (1) conducting annual meetings that primarily deal with physical education's body of knowledge, professional preparation in physical education, and sport and leisure in higher education; (2) producing four different publications for members and nonmembers of the association; (3) maintaining 14 standing committees, president's committees, continuing committees, and joint committees with other associations; and (4) maintaining effective liaison with related professional groups.

Membership is open to men actively engaged in physical education—teaching, research, or administration in higher education—or to male physical education graduate students or to men associated with allied fields.

Editor's Note: In June 1978, this organization merged with the National Association for Physical Eduction of College Women to form the National Association for Physical Education in Higher Education (NAPEHE).

Members are entitled to a copy of the *Proceedings* of the annual meeting, two copies of *Quest* per year, the association's *Newsletter,* and copies of *Briefings.*

The *Proceedings* is a volume containing the papers presented at the annual meeting. These represent the most recent thinking about physical education in higher education. This publication makes a significant contribution to the professional literature of the field. *Quest* monographs are published jointly by the National College Physical Education Association for Men and the National Association for Physical Education of College Women. *Quest* has received a certificate of merit from the American Academy of Physical Education for its excellence in content and style. *Newsletters* are published in October, February, and May, and report on the affairs of the association. *Briefings* also are published jointly by the National College Physical Education Association for Men and the National Association for Physical Education of College Women. This publication is designed to address a specific issue facing the profession of physical education and to be published and distributed relatively fast; one or more issues are published each year.

For further information write C.E. Mueller, Secretary-Treasurer, 108 Cooke Hall, University of Minnesota, Minneapolis, Minnesota 55455.

106
National Federation of State High School Associations
John E. Robert

The National Federation of State High School Associations (NFSHSA) consists of 50 individual state high school athletics and/or activities associations and the association of the District of Columbia. Also affiliated are the high school athletics association of the Philippine Islands and eight interscholastic organizations from Canadian Provinces. The NFSHSA membership represents more than 20,000 high schools and approximately 9.5 million secondary school students. The legislative body is the National Council, which consists of one representative from each member association. Each representative must be an officer or a member of the state board of control. The executive body is the Executive Committee consisting of eight members, one from each of the election sections.

Fig. 106.1 Basketball. Courtesy of National Federation Press Service.

Fig. 106.2 1976 Volleyball. Courtesy of National Federation Press Service.

The activities of NFSHSA are based on the belief that strong state and national high school athletics organizations are necessary to (1) protect the activity and the athletics interest of high schools; (2) promote an ever increasing growth of the type of interscholastic athletics that is educational in both objective and method, and which can be justified as an integral part of the high school curriculum; and (3) to protect high school students from exploitation for purposes having no educational implication.

State associations have pooled their efforts through NFSHSA in a nation-wide program of athletics experimentation. Each year the sport in season is carefully observed and experimental proposals for improvement are tested in laboratory schools throughout the nation. Included in this experimental program is a thorough evaluation at the end of each sport season to determine the sentiment of high school leaders and to gather the best thoughts about possible improvement. As an example, NFSHSA was the first to require the use of face protectors on helmets and the use of mouth and tooth protectors, which greatly reduced football injuries.

The rules-writing activity of NFSHSA includes over 50 publications ranging from rules books to early season questions. More than 2.25 million copies are printed annually. Rules books are written in baseball, basketball, field hocky, football, girls' and boys' gymnastics, soccer, softball, swimming and diving, track and field, volleyball, and wrestling. Other teaching aids include case books in baseball, basketball, football, and swimming and diving, officials' manuals in baseball, basketball, football and wrestling, and hand books in basketball and football. In addition, NFSHSA publishes for football and basketball, "Rules—Simplified and Illustrated." It uses cartoons and diagrams to explain situations otherwise difficult to comprehend, and is useful in physical education classrooms and officials' interpretation sessions.

The National Federation Press Service includes a collection of materials selected as a source of supply for the editors of state and national publications. Subjects include administration of athletics departments, athletics rules revisions, book reviews, and comments on the medical aspects of sports.

National Federation Sports Films, Inc., a wholly owned subsidiary of NFSHSA, produces annually a new 16mm, 28-minute motion picture designed specifically to provide coaches, officials, players, and spectators with a better understanding of the rules and officiating procedures in football, basketball, baseball, and track and field. In addition, shorter films for wrestling, swimming and diving, and volleyball have also been produced. Distribution of the films in each state is through the state high school athletics association or an approved agency.

NFSHSA has also established the Mutual Legal Aid Pact, which makes available judgments on court cases to which member state associations may refer when their rules or standards are questioned. NFSHSA conducts and subsidizes a national inservice program for high school directors of athletics.

The annual conferences attract large numbers of directors of athletics and provide a forum for interaction with some of the nation's most knowledgeable experts on problems of athletics department administration.

NFSHSA prints and distributes free of charge 20,000 copies of the complete proceedings of each national conference.

For further information, contact Brice B. Durbin, Executive Director, 400 Leslie Street, P.O. Box 98, Elgin, Illinois 60120.

107

National Intramural-Recreational Sports Association

H. Edsel Buchanan

Dr. William N. Wasson is recognized as the founder of the National Intramural-Recreational Sports Association (NIRSA). Until 1975 NIRSA was known as the National Intramural Association. Wasson's completed research at Dillard University, New Orleans, entitled *A Comparative Study of Intramural Programs in Negro Colleges* resulted in the formation of NIRSA in 1950.

Since 1950 NIRSA has experienced growth at a steady rate characterized by diversity in individual, institutional, and male-female membership. The NIRSA membership is available to all individuals working and/or concerned with intramural-recreational programs of institutions both on a national and international basis, regardless of sex, creed, or race. The membership categories include: (1) institutional membership with the fee structured upon enrollment size, (2) professional membership for individuals working within the various areas concerned, (3) an undergraduate student membership, and (4) emeritus membership available to professional people who have retired with a minimum of 10 years membership in NIRSA. Honorary membership is also available to individuals who have made outstanding contributions to the profession but are not members of the association. Annually NIRSA recognizes an outstanding professional member in the form of the NIRSA Honor Award. NIRSA publishes a quarterly journal, *NIRSA Journal,* with the publication offices located at Leisure Press, P.O. Box 3, West Point, New York 10996.

The objectives of the association are to: (1) promote and encourage the growth and development of intramural-recreational programs on all educational levels; (2) meet annually to conduct its business, exchange information and ideas, and plan ways and means of furthering its objectives; (3) carry on, sponsor, and publish research relative to intramurals; and (4) work in close harmony with any organization that is concerned with intramurals, physical education, health, recreation, and athletics.

The goals of the association are to: (1) provide members with the opportunity to grow professionally; (2) assist members in enriching their present program; (3) keep members informed of the research being carried out in intramurals, and entitle members to possible funding of research projects that are regional and/or national in scope; (4) permit members to participate in programs aimed at the betterment of intramurals throughout the nation; (5) make members aware of job opportunities in junior high and senior high schools as well as in colleges and universities; (6) give members access to the names of persons who are interested in obtaining new positions in intramurals; (7) afford members the support of other members when members seek offices in other organizations; (8) acquaint members with the efforts of affiliated organizations in behalf of the intramural movement; (9) permit members to attend the annual conference of the association where members receive three days of program planning and discussion about intramurals; (10) allow members to run for NIRSA offices after two consecutive years of membership.

A foundations and a Special Projects Program is supported strongly by the NIRSA for the purpose of producing revenue for two important programs. One of the programs involves a work-study program related to actual internship-type work designed for the purpose of attracting to, and involving individuals in, the professional area of intramurals and recreational sports including both administration and programming. Another major thrust of NIRSA is to fund as many work-study program opportunities as possible for new, young members.

Each year the association allocates $900 for research grants to members with worthy projects. All research proposals are submitted through a permanent research committee, which recommends for approval specific research projects that are national, regional, and local in scope.

The National Intramural-Recreational Sports Association offices are located at Oregon State University, Dixon Recreation Center, Corvallis, Oregon 97331.

108

National Jewish Welfare Board

Lionel Koppman

Created by the American Jewish community to meet special needs, JWB is an association of more than 400 Jewish community centers and YM and YWHA's with branches and camps in the U.S. and Canada, which serve more than one million Jews. Each of them has extensive health and physical fitness programs. The board is a government-accredited agency for providing religious, cultural, social, morale, and welfare services to Jewish military personnel, their families, and veterans in VA hospitals. It sponsors the Jewish Book Council, Jewish Music Council, JWB Lecture Bureau, and other programs to enhance Jewish cultural life in America and build stronger bridges with Jews in Israel and throughout the world. It also sponsors national and regional tournaments in basketball, volleyball, swimming, and other sports, and health and physical education institutes.

To help improve the quality of Jewish living in America and to develop a sense of community and a sense of Jewish peoplehood, JWB services its constituents through: (1) *consultations* with Jewish Community Center and Federation executives, boards, and committees to assess the needs in their particular communities and to provide specialized assistance to help meet these needs; (2) *program development and research,* which identifies key issues and problems of immediate concern to Jewish community centers with an eye toward charting program directions and developing and monitoring research projects; (3) *statistical data* on JCC membership, finances, program and personnel, camping, and other areas; (4) *training institutes and seminars* to develop communal leadership, prepare professional personnel, demonstrate and develop innovative programs to meet changing needs; (5) *publications from A —administration to Y —young adults covering a wide variety* of subjects of particular interest to Jewish Community Centers and Jewish communities, Jews in the armed forces, and persons interested in Jewish culture; (6) *intercommunity* projects in a variety of areas; (7) *liaison with the United States government* in relation to matters in which Jewish Community Centers and JWB are especially interested; and (8) *representation on national and international bodies* such as the National Conference on Soviet Jewry, the Conference of Presidents of Major American Jewish Organizations, Uni-

Fig. 108.1 Basketball is a popular sport at the Jewish Community Center. JCCs and Ys affiliated with JWB seek to provide physical fitness opportunities for all ages. Courtesy of JWB. The Association of Jewish Community Centers, Ys and camps in the United States and Canada.

ted Service Organizations (USO), National Assembly for Social Policy and Development, the Veterans Administration Voluntary Service, the American Camping Association, the United States Committee on Sports in Israel, the United States Olympic Committee, the Amateur Athletic Union, the President's Council on Physical Fitness and Sports, the United States Mission to the United Nations, and the Council on Social Work Education.

On behalf of the American Jewish community, JWB serves Jews in the U.S. armed forces, their families and hospitalized veterans during a critical time in their lives, offering them spiritual comfort, providing for their cultural and recreational needs, and giving them a sense of community.

The majority of Jewish men in the military are married and have their wives and children with them. They want and deserve a quality Jewish education for their children, social outlets for their wives, and Jewish cultural programs for the entire family.

JWB fulfills its obligations to the American Jewish community and to the U.S. government to serve the religious, cultural, recreational, and social service needs of Jewish military personnel, their families, and hospitalized veterans through its Commission on Jewish Chaplaincy, local armed forces and veterans services committees, its Women's Organizations' Services, the USO-JWB Community Services, and the Military Lay Leadership Program.

JWB has become a major force in deepening an awareness and appreciation of the Jewish cultural heritage. Hundreds of Jewish lecturers and performing artists are signed by Jewish communities for their programs through the JWB Lecture Bureau. More than 2000 local Jewish groups annually celebrate the Jewish Book Month and the Jewish Music Fesitval with the stimulation and materials provided by JWB's Jewish Book Council and Jewish Music Council.

More American Jews are buying and reading Jewish books and enjoying Jewish music than ever before. Programs of adult Jewish education featuring performing artists and lecturers are attracting greater numbers.

Through its World Service Committee, JWB conducts a variety of programs and projects that build bridges between American Jewry and Israel and Jews around the globe.

More information about this organization may be obtained by writing: National Jewish Welfare Board, 15 East 26th Street, New York, New York 10010.

109
National Jogging Association

Gary K. Olsen

The National Jogging Association was founded in 1969 by Richard L. Bohannon, M.D., who had recently retired as Surgeon General of the U.S. Air Force, and a group primarily of medical professionals. It was the concept of this group to promote jogging as a means of preventive medicine and to establish jogging as an activity beyond a fad. In the years since the association was formed, over 25,000 individuals have enrolled as members.

These individuals are drawn from all walks of life, from all areas of the nation (and the world), and from all age groups (the oldest current member is

Fig. 109.1 NJA joggers on Saturday, a.m., all ages.

107, the youngest is age six). Members receive a tabloid newsletter, *The Jogger,* which contains medical information and motivational-type articles and news about members and jogging events. In addition NJA provides incentives for members and nonmembers through several award and achievement programs. In 1976 over 5000 persons jogged in the NJA's popular Bicentennial Program for 76 or 200 or 1776 miles; subsequent programs for 1977 and 1978 have added 5000 more entrants to NJA's annual Challenge events. Motivation is also provided locally in over 200 communities throughout the country by groups that have met or jogged together during National Jogging Fortnite in October of each year. National Jogging Day is the second Saturday of each October.

Other association publications include the 164-page book, *Guidelines for Successful Jogging;* a special four-page tabloid, *Successful Jogging,* which was distributed to nearly 200,000 joggers in 1977 alone; and the *NJA Fitness Bookshelf.* The association also conducts surveys of exercise facilities and jogging-oriented podiatrists and physicians.

For further information write the National Jogging Association, Washington Medical Center, 919 18th Street N.W., Suite 830, Washington, D.C. 20006.

110

President's Council on Physical Fitness and Sports

C.C. Conrad

Richard Nixon, on September 25, 1970, by virtue of his authority as President of the United States, gave Executive Order #11562 as follows:

Section 1. Program for physical fitness and sports. The Secretary of Health, Education, and Welfare (hereinafter referred to as "the Secretary," shall, in carrying out his responsibilities in relation to education and public health, including specifically the health of children and youth, develop and coordinate a national program for physical fitness and sports. The Secretary shall: (1) enlist the active support and assistance of individual citizens, civic groups, professional associations, amateur and professional sports groups, private enterprise, voluntary organizations, and others in efforts to promote and improve physical fitness and sports participation programs for all Americans; (2) stimulate, improve, and strengthen coordination of federal services and programs relating to physical fitness and sports participation; (3) encourage state and local governments in efforts to enhance physical fitness and sports participation; (4) seek to strengthen the physical fitness of American children, youth, and adults by systematically encouraging the development of community-centered and other physical fitness and sports participation programs to encourage innovation, improve teacher preparation, and strengthen state and local leadership; (5) develop cooperative programs with medical, dental, and other similar professional societies to encourage and implement sound physical fitness practices; (6) stimulate and encourage research in the areas of physical fitness and sports performance; and (7) improve school health and physical education programs for all pupils, including the handicapped and the physically underdeveloped, by assisting educational agencies in developing quality programs to encourage innovation, improve teacher preparation, and strengthen state and local leadership.

Section 2. President's Council on Physical Fitness and Sports. (a) There is hereby established the President's Council on Physical Fitness and Sports (hereinafter referred to as "the Council"), which shall be composed of the President's Consultant on Physical Fitness, who shall be the Chairman, and 14 other members appointed by the President. The Council shall meet on the call of the Chairman.
(b) The members of the Council shall receive no compensation from the United

Fig. 110.1 Physical fitness. Courtesy of President's Council on Physical Fitness and Sports.

States by reason of their service on the Council, but shall be reimbursed for travel expenses, including per diem in lieu of subsistence, as authorized by law for persons serving the government without compensation (5 U.S.C. 5703).

Section 3. Functions of the Council. (a) The Council shall advise the President and the Secretary concerning progress made in carrying out the provisions of this order and shall recommend to the President and the Secretary, as necessary, steps to accelerate progress.
(b) The Council shall advise the Secretary on matters pertaining to ways and means of enhancing opportunities for participation in physical fitness and sports activities and on state, local, and private action to extend and improve physical activity programs and services.

Section 4. Conference on Physical Fitness and Sports. (a) There is hereby established a Conference on Physical Fitness and Sports (hereinafter referred to as "the Conference"), which shall be composed of 100 members whom the President may, from time to time, appoint. The Conference shall meet on the call of the Secretary to assist him in carrying out his responsibilities under this order.
(b) The members of the Conference shall receive no compensation or expense allowances from the United States government by reason of their service on the Conference.

Section 5. Assistance by Agencies. (a) The Secretary and the Council are authorized to request from any federal department or agency information or assistance deemed necessary to carry out their functions under this order and each department and agency is authorized, to the extent permitted by law and within the limits of available funds, to furnish such information and assistance to the Secretary and the Council.

(b) The Secretary shall appoint the Executive Director of the Council. Subject to law: (1) the Department of Health, Education, and Welfare shall furnish necessary staff, supplies, facilities, and other administrative services for the Council: (2) expenses of the Council shall be met from funds available to the Secretary; and (3) the Department may provide staff assistance to the Conference.

Section 6. Continuity. The Council established by this order shall be deemed to be a continuation of the Citizens Advisory Committee on Physical Fitness and Sports which has heretofore existed under Executive Order No. 11398 of March 4, 1968, as amended.

(b) The seal prescribed by Executive Order No. 10830 of July 24, 1959, as amended, shall be the seal of the President's Council on Physical Fitness and Sports as reconstituted herein.

Section 7. Revocations. Executive Order No. 11398 of March 4, 1968, and Executive Order No. 11492 of October 30, 1969, are hereby revoked.

Section 8. Construction. Nothing in this order shall be construed to abrogate, modify, or restrict any function vested by law in, or assigned pursuant to law to, any federal department or agency or any officer thereof.

At its May 26, 1971, meeting, the President's Council on Physical Fitness and Sports adopted the following formal "Statement of Basic Beliefs":

1. All school children in grades K-12 should be required to participate in daily programs of physical education emphasizing the development of physical fitness and sports skills.

   a. Medical authorities recommend unequivocally regular vigorous exercise during school years, since it is essential to healthy development of individuals.

   b. In order to enjoy a sport, master the necessary skills and participate safely, a person must be physically fit. The popular slogan, *Get Fit by Playing,* should be: *Get Fit to Play Safely.*

   c. Within the educational context of physical education programs, students should develop knowledge of the effects of activities for conditioning as well as the relation of activities to various aspects of health throughout life. Students need to understand the basic elements of physiology of exercise and the value of participating in regular vigorous activities. The need to continue activities in adulthood should be stressed at an early age and throughout the school physical education experience. Knowledge, understanding, and participation should result in the development of desirable attitudes concerning the values of participation in regular vigorous physical activity.

   d. Special programs of physical education should be provided those pupils with orthopedic problems, obesity, perceptual-motor problems, and other health-related problems. Such students must first be identified, along with those who may suffer from physical underdevelopment, malnutrition, or inadequate coordination.

e. Physical education programs should be planned to include physiological fitness goals along with other educational aims needed to meet the developmental needs of children; thus, activities must be adapted to individual needs and capacities and be vigorous enough to increase energy utilization and heart rate significantly.

f. The school physical education program should include a core of developmental and conditioning activities appropriate for each grade level. Activities should be identified and stressed in progressive order. Demonstration standards for survival activities, particularly swimming, should be established and competence maintained by periodic testing and training.

g. Every pupil should have continuing supervision by the family physician and dentist, including periodic examinations and correction of remedial defects. Through these resources, supplemented wherever necessary and feasible by school and community services, the health appraisal procedures should include:

   1) Identification of pupils with correctable orthopedic defects and other health problems, and subsequent referral to medical authorities.
   2) A posture check, including foot examination; pupils with acute problems should be referred to medical authorities.
   3) Height and weight measurements, interpreted in terms of individual needs; pupils who are obviously obese, underweight, or malnourished should be identified and referred to medical authorities.

2. College/university students should be required to participate in physical education programs emphasizing the development of physical fitness and sports skills and should be provided opportunities to participate in intramural, recreational, and intercollegiate sports.

3. Public school sports facilities belong to the people and should be available for community use when not being used for school activities. School sports facilities—gymnasiums, swimming pools, tennis courts, etc.—should be available for public use when not being used for school programs and functions.

4. Provision of sports and recreation facilities should be a part of all land development and construction for residential purposes.

5. Adults should get one hour of vigorous physical activity (through work, play, planned exercise, or a combination of these) each day. Regular vigorous exercise during adulthood improves appearance and performance and may prolong life.

6. Public and private employers should provide facilities, time, and encouragement for employees to participate in supervised fitness and sports programs.

7. Communities should organize, with medical backing, to provide for the organization, promotion, and instruction of adult physical activity and fitness

programs; for the dissemination of appropriate resource information regarding individual programs such as jogging, cycling, swimming, etc., and for the provision of physical fitness classes, etc.

a. Opportunities as well as motivation should be provided for the continuance of appropriate physical activities into and through the adult years when the full impact of increasingly sedentary patterns of living become manifest.

b. Activity programs should be extended to the preschool child in nurseries and day-care centers.

c. Physical activity programs should also be extended to those groups in institutional settings such as hospitals, penal institutions, nursing homes, institutions for emotional and mentally disturbed, as well as for the mentally retarded.

d. Adapted physical activity programs aimed at specific types of general cardiovascular conditioning, strength, and skill development for children and adolescents, must be planned and conducted by personnel prepared in specialized physical education or health dynamics programs.

e. Community recreation departments should provide a wide range of programs, particularly in the areas where school programs are inadequate.

f. Eductional programs should be provided older people, that would place proper emphasis on physical activity, weight control, nutrition, and other aspects of healthful living.

g. Public authorities should plan and provide facilities for adult physical activity and fitness programs. Often this may require only a simple alteration of the school's plans for a physical education facility.

8. Physicians should become leaders in recommending and implementing physical fitness programs for their patients, schools and communities.

For further information write: President's Council on Physical Fitness and Sports, Room 3030, Donohue Building, 400 Sixth Street, S.W., Washington, D.C. 20201.

111
Phi Epsilon Kappa
Rollin C. Wright

Phi Epsilon Kappa is a national professional fraternity for men and women who are engaged in or are preparing themselves for professional work related to health, physical education, or recreation. Regardless of the profession for which individuals prepare themselves, becoming a member of the national fraternity of one's profession is an important indication of one's interest in that profession and one's seriousness of purpose. Phi Epsilon Kappa is selective on the basis of scholarship, character, and future promise. Being invited to become a member of a national professional organization dedicated to the promotion of all that is highest and best in the profession should arouse a feeling of pride within the individual.

Phi Epsilon Kappa was founded on April 12, 1913, at the Normal College of the American Gymnastic Union. The major objectives of the fraternity are to elevate the standards, ideals, and ethics of individuals engaged in teaching health, physical education, and recreation; to provide a medium whereby students, faculty, and alumni can work together on an equal basis; and to improve the scholarship and the general quality of work in the profession.

From its somewhat meager beginning in 1913 the fraternity has experienced a steady growth to where it presently has 60 collegiate chapters and 12 alumni chapters. Since its establishment over 24,000 members have been initiated.

The fraternity's major publication is *The Physical Educator,* which is no longer just a fraternity magazine but is recognized as a national professional publication with subscribers and readers all over the world. This magazine is issued quarterly. The fraternity also publishes several monograph series.

The fraternity maintains a foreign literature exchange with more than 40 foreign journals. The initial monograph series began in 1955 when the fraternity published the first volume of *Index and Abstracts of Foreign Physical Education Literature.*

In 1966 the fraternity published the first monograph of *Physical Education Around the World,* which contains a description of physical education programs in selected foreign countries. During the time since the first monograph was published there has been an ever increasing interest in international physical education and sport. This series has played an important role in furthering this widespread interest. Some 32 countries are represented in the first four issues.

In 1970 the fraternity published a five-volume series titled *An Introduction to Measurement in Physical Education.* This series has been developed primarily for use in college undergraduate courses in tests and measurements. Seventeen authorities contributed in their respective areas of expertise to present this comprehensive series.

In 60 years PEK has clearly demonstrated that a professional organization has a needed function to serve, and the contributions made to individuals and institutions are invaluable. The fraternity has an enviable record of noteworthy accomplishments and its roster includes many of the leaders in the profession.

For further information write: Phi Epsilon Kappa, 6919 East Tenth Street, Suite E-4, Indianapolis, Indiana 46219.

112
Private Sports Organizations

Numerous private organizations promote instruction and provide competition in physical education activities. Currently there are about 13,000 clubs of all different types. In addition 1200 more are either new or under construction and, as a result, have no reported history. Of about 11,000 clubs, 5800 are considered full-service country clubs, 2500 are city organizations 115 are affiliated with universities and an equal number are classed as athletic clubs. There are approximately 900 luncheon clubs, 600 fraternal organizations, 1400 military groups, and 550 yacht clubs.

Under the country club classification some 5800 have golf courses, 4600 have swimming pools, and 3000 have tennis courts. In the city club classification, over 400 have swimming facilities and 250 have tennis courts. Among the fraternal organizations, almost 200 have swimming pools and 40 have tennis facilities. In the military grouping, 181 have swimming pools and the same number have tennis courts. Among the yacht clubs, over 300 have swimming pools and 250 have tennis courts.

There are about 30,000 private swim and/or tennis clubs throughout the United States. This totals some 35,700 swimming pools and 15,500 tennis facilities operating. This number has quite an impact on the development of swimming, tennis, and golf activities for the membership of these private clubs. In addition to these activities, many have other sporting facilities offering skating, bowling, curling, squash, handball, racquetball, and skeet shooting.

Most clubs operate with a golf professional, a swimming professional, and a tennis professional. Organized private and small group lessons for young and old are provided by most clubs. Age-group competition is promoted between clubs of similar status in all these sports. Training and coaching sessions are held especially for the swim groups; usually these sessions are scheduled in the early morning, five days a week, with competitive events held on weekends or late afternoons. Instruction in diving, lifesaving, and scuba supplement the program.

Ordinarily toward the end of the summer competitive season, each club has its own intramural competition in swimming and diving, tennis, and golf, all regulated by age and sex classification. Medals and trophies are common awards for place winners. In addition to age-group events most clubs have events for adults, especially in tennis and golf, and these are promoted usually in conjunction with evening social events.

113

The Society of State Directors of Health, Physical Education, and Recreation

Simon McNeely

The Society of State Directors of Health, Physical Education, and Recreation is composed of state leaders in those fields of education and their associates.

The purposes of the Society are to: (1) promote effective, comprehensive school health and safety programs, sound programs of physical education, including appropriate athletics at preschool, elementary, secondary, and postsecondary school levels, and worthwhile school and community recreation programs; (2) strengthen preservice and inservice education of personnel employed in these fields; (3) study problems affecting the quality of programs and to implement procedures for their solution; (4) provide opportunities for interchange of ideas, experience, and successful, innovative practices among members of the society and their constituents; and (5) cooperate with other organizations, agencies, and individuals in the fields of education, health, medicine, physical education, physical fitness, athletics, safety, recreation, outdoor education, and other disciplines, in the development of programs designed to advance the health and well-being of Americans, young and old.

Active membership in the society is open to the state directors or consultants of health, physical education, and recreation, or the person certified by the chief state school officer as being primarily responsible for state programs in these fields. The District of Columbia and outlying areas of the United States are considered as individual states. In states where there are separate and parallel directors in one or more of these fields, each is eligible for active membership. *Associate* members are those who have duties in health, safety, physical education, athletics, recreation, outdoor education, or related fields in state departments of education, the U.S. Office of Education, state and federal health, fitness, and recreation agencies, and the staff of other public and professional organizations, teacher education institutions, and voluntary associations concerned about these fields. Others who are interested in the purposes of the society may also be elected to associate membership. *Honorary* memberships are also awarded from time to time to worthy persons. Membership numbers about 150 individuals from all the states, the District of Columbia, and the outlying areas.

During and following World War I the people of the United States evidenced a growing concern for the health and physical fitness of all citizens, and most particularly of youth. School programs of physical and health education, developing since the introduction of various European systems during the latter half of the 19th century, took on increasing importance. The immediate warborn objective of military preparedness was soon subordinated to broader purposes reflecting the physical, social, and psychological concerns of an educational force suited to a dynamic democratic society.

State education legislation reflected the intense public interest. Prior to 1915 three states had laws requiring physical education in the elementary and secondary schools. During 1915-1918, eight additional states enacted such legislation. By 1922, 28 states had laws on physical and health education and this number increased to 36 in the next eight years. Since the 1940s, 48 states, the District of Columbia, and two outlying areas have had laws and/or regulations requiring the teaching of health education and/or physical education. State educational legislation does not, of itself, insure good school programs. The improvement of educational opportunities for children and youth requires dedicated and competent leadership at both state and local levels. This need for state leadership in physical and health education was as evident as the need for legislation. The first state director of physical and health education, Thomas A. Storey, M.D., was appointed in New York State, February 1, 1916. By the mid-1930s about 35 states had fulltime personnel working in these fields. The number has grown steadily. Currently 44 states have one or more persons working fulltime in health education, physical education, and recreation. In the other six states there are persons who have specific responsibilities for these fields, in connection with other duties.

A professional person seeks the exchange of experience and insights, and the inspiration of mutual sharing with other professionals who have similar interests and problems. There were 16 such professional people and their associates—state directors of physical and health education who had met informally in the post-World War I years. In 1926 at New York they organized the Society of State Directors of Health and Physical Education. Dr. Carl L.

Schrader, Massachusetts state director of health and physical education, was its first president. James E. Rogers, director of the National Physical Education Service, National Recreation Association, was elected secretary and served continously in this capacity through 1940. Dr. James H. McCurdy, Secretary of the American Physical Education Association, and Dr. James F. Rogers, U.S. Bureau of Education, were associated with the society for many of its early years and their successors have continued this association. Membership in the society then as now included incumbent state directors, their professional assistants, past directors and other associates.

During the depression days of the 1930s the society successfully fought to preserve programs of health education and physical education, more needed than ever before, and to protect children from the loss of vital experiences that some would have eliminated as ill-afforded frills. One of the important works of that period was the succinct analysis of a desirable program in the schools, prepared by a committee headed by Bernice R. Moss, Utah, and W.H. Orion, California. Their published report and its subsequent updated versions continue to be among the most widely used and influential documents in the literature.

In the 1940s the word "Recreation" was attached officially to the name of the organization, this action representing an increasing scope of interest and size of membership. Society members assisted with the preparation of two important yearbooks of the American Association of School Administrators, one in health education, the other in safety education.

The emergencies of World War II and Korea brought renewed emphasis on physical fitness. Many state directors answered the call to the armed forces, many helped set up vast programs of physical training, recreation, welfare, and rehabilitation in various military branches. Those directors who remained on the job, and those who stepped into militarily vacated spots, gave heroic service in civilian physical fitness programs and civil defense, finding and preparing replacements for a depleted teaching force, bolstering faltering school programs, and taking on many other necessary duties related to running a school system in wartime. The society proved a potent medium of mutual assistance to both military and civilian segments.

Educators were faced with new challenges in the unfolding world of space and atoms of the postwar years. Those years of the 1950s brought explosive increases in school enrollments, overcrowded schools, an insufficient supply of adequately prepared teachers, and new physical and mental health problems. Three biennial workshops, each in an informal camp setting, were focused on searching "self-improvement through self-study." Preparatory to the workshops, several task forces made preliminary studies and provided cogent materials for discussion and action. The workshop reports became useful tools not only for the director and his associates in their day-to-day jobs but also for teacher educators, administrators, and supervisors in various general and specialized educational fields. The society has continued to hold an annual workshop in addition to its yearly national meeting. The reports of proceedings, special publications, and projects of these meetings have continued to be used widely to upgrade programs.

For many years the society has held its national meeting in conjunction with the convention of the American Alliance for Health, Physical Education, Recreation, and Dance. It has also collaborated with that association and other agencies and organizations in sponsoring conferences and study projects. These included such subject areas as youth fitness, school-community recreation, outdoor education, elementary and junior high school athletics, professional preparation, interagency cooperation in both health and recreation, and many others. Members of the society played a vital role in conferences and activities related to the President's Council on Youth Fitness and the President's Citizen's Advisory Committee on Fitness of American Youth, both established by executive order in 1956. They have continued to work cooperatively with the staff and leadership of subsequent modifications of that agency, currently the President's Council on Physical Fitness and Sports.

Emphasis from the sixties on reflect societal concerns and particularly an increasing federal influence. State directors give added attention to physical fitness objectives and programming during this period when many Americans are living sedentary lives, becoming overweight, and are prone to coronary heart disease and other chronic health conditions. There are also special programs dealing with smoking and health, sex education, venereal disease, and drug abuse. State leaders in health, physical education, and recreation are heavily involved in improving programs for the educationally disadvantaged and the handicapped, and in developing innovative approaches to program improvement and educational reform at all levels.

Over the years, the society has issued numerous proclamations, resolutions and proceedings that have had an impact on school, college, and community programs. Its major publication is *A Statement of Basic Beliefs— The School Programs in Health, Physical Education, and Recreation*. First published in 1938 and revised several times, this statement of basic principles and guidelines has been used widely for program improvement. The society has collaborated with a number of national professional organizations on the preparation of yearbooks, reports, and other publications on pertinent subjects. A *Newsletter* is issued to society members periodically.

National offices of the Society of State Directors of Health, Physical Education, and Recreation may be contacted through: Simon A. McNeely, Secretary Treasurer, U.S. Office of Education, BESE/OAC, 400 Maryland Avenue, S.W., Washington, D.C. 20202.

SUGGESTED READING

Robinson, M. C., and W. H. Jubb, 1976. Fifty years of leadership: the Society of State
Directors of Health, Physical Education, and Recreation. *JOPER*, **47** : 21 (June).

114

United States Volleyball Association

Harold T. Friermood

Thirty-three years after the USA sport of volleyball (first called "mintonette")
was invented in 1895, in Holyoke, Massachusetts, YMCA by William G.
Morgan, the United States Volleyball Association (USVBA) was organized.
The purpose of the USVBA was to standardize the rules, encourage many
organizations to use and enjoy the game, promote it widely because of its
health and recreational values, and point out the opportunities for women
and girls as well as men and boys to participate. Prior to the organization and
during the first 45 years of the USVBA, the YMCA played a dominant role in
the organization and development of the game.

In June 1896 William Morgan was invited by Dr. Luther Halsey Gulick to
demonstrate his new game at a YMCA physical directors' conference. Morgan took two five-man teams from his businessmen's class from Holyoke to
Springfield. During the conference, held at YMCA Springfield College, the
demonstration and explanation were received with keen interest, but after
observing and listening, professor Alfred T. Halstead pointed out the batting
or volleying phase of the activity and proposed the name of "volley ball." This
name was accepted by Morgan who turned over his game to the YMCA
Physical Education Society for development. The name has continued
throughout the years with only one slight change: in 1952, the USVBA board
of directors voted to spell the name as one word, "volleyball."

A committee was appointed by the YMCA Physical Directors Society to
study the rules and guide progress and promotion of the new sport. William
E. Day, physical director in Dayton, Ohio, chaired the rules committee for
several years. Rules were printed in an 1896 YMCA periodical and were also
included in a handbook of the Athletic League of the YMCAs of North
America (ALYNA). This handbook was issued in 1897 by the National
YMCA office under the direction of Dr. Gulick. He served as national

Fig. 114.1 William G. Morgan, YMCA Physical Director, Holyoke, Mass., inventor of volleyball, 1895. (Credit: Historical Library, National Council of YMCAs)

Fig. 114.2 George J. Fisher, M.D. First President of the USVBA, served from 1928-1952. (Credit: Picture provided by, G. Gordon Fisher).

YMCA secretary of physical education as well as director of the professional Physical Education Training School at Springfield College. The handbook was published several years for the ALYNA in the *Spalding Sports Guide* series.

The game was introduced throughout the United States and Canada and to other countries by YMCA physical educators. It was included in the first Far Eastern Games conducted in 1913 by Elwood S. Brown, with the Philippine Islands, China, and Japan participating. Although used by recreation departments, industries, schools, women's groups, and clubs during the first 20 years, the YMCA volleyball committee believed the game should be integrated more actively into the college men's sports program. Accordingly, a dual relationship was worked out by Dr. George J. Fisher, successor to Dr. Gulick in the national YMCA physical education office, and by professor LeBaron R. Briggs of Harvard, president of the NCAA. Committees were named by both groups to reach agreements. In 1916 the *Spalding Volleyball Guide and Rule Book* was issued by the joint committee.

During and immediately following World War I an extensive sports, fitness, and recreation program was developed and conducted by the YMCA in army camps and naval stations as well as overseas with the American and allied troops. The 391-page *YMCA Army and Navy Athletic Handbook,* prepared in 1918 and printed by Association Press early in 1919, was distributed in the thousands. It contained a concise statement on the philosophy and purpose of sport, conditioning, physical recreation, organization and conduct of mass activities, leagues and tournaments, and rules of many games. Volleyball rules were included with the footnote, "These rules were adopted as the official rules by the Physical Directors' Society in June 1912, amended May 1915, again in May 1916, and copyrighted 1916 by the Joint Rules Committee."

In 1922 the joint committee was enlarged to include representatives from the Playground and Recreation Association of America and the Boy Scouts of America (Dr. Fisher went to the national office of the Boy Scouts near the end of 1919 and he was succeeded by Dr. John Brown, Jr., in the National YMCA office). To expand volleyball contacts further with national organizations, the newly formed National Amateur Athletic Federation (NAAF) in 1923 requested the joint committee to serve as its volleyball committee; the 1923-1924 annual volleyball guide, *Blue Cover Series,* was issued under the sponsorship of the NAAF. The guide first appeared in the 1926-1927 Spalding, American Sports Publishing Co. *Red Cover* Series. At about the same time, the joint committee considered the possibility of initiating steps to secure International Olympic Committee recognition of volleyball for inclusion in the Olympic Games.

During the New York City, May 14, 1928, annual meeting of the joint volleyball rules committee, consideration was given to organizing a National Volleyball Association. The special committee named to explore and implement the idea invited 372 key persons from many organizations to participate in the organization meeting. Held on June 22, 1928, at the Yale Club, the conference recommended that the joint volleyball rules committee change its name to the United States Volleyball Association, adopt a constitution and bylaws that would make provision to enlarge the committee personnel and functions, and that the new association should affiliate with the NAAF, assume responsibilites for revision of the rules, for publication of the *Annual Guide,* and represent volleyball interests nationally and internationally.

On July 9, 1928, during the special meeting of the joint volleyball rules committee, the above recommendations were approved, a subcommittee was named to develop a constitution and bylaws and also submit a plan to enlarge the organization. At that time the following national groups were represented on the joint committee and became the member groups of the newly formed USVBA: Young Men's Christian Association, National Collegiate Athletic Association, Playground and Recreation Association of America, Boy Scouts

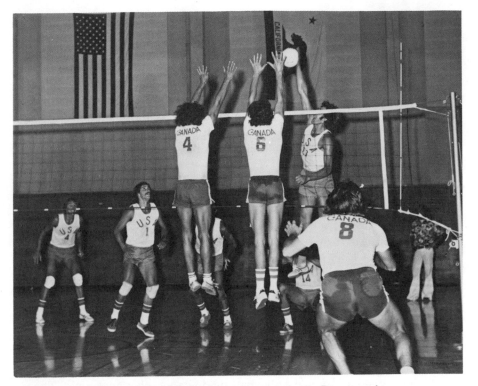

Fig. 114.3 Canada and USA Men's teams compete in the Pan American Games. (Credit: Dr. Leonard B. Stallcup, Los Angeles, Photo).

of America, Women's Division of the National Amateur Athletic Federation, high schools, industrial organizations, U.S. Army, and U.S. Navy.

The YMCA conducted its first annual national volleyball championship in 1922 at the Brooklyn Central branch with 27 teams. Upon the formation of the USVBA, it received a rotating trophy from Herbert Lee Pratt, to be awarded through an open tournament; the YMCA was asked to conduct this open division championship in conjunction with its closed event. Although the USVBA was not formed until after the 1928 National YMCA championship, the Pratt Trophy was inscribed to begin retroactively to show as its first recipient, the national YMCA championship winner.

Elected as first president of the USVBA was Dr. George J. Fisher (deceased) who continued to serve until 1952 when he was succeeded by Dr. Harold T. Friermood. Wilbur H. Peck, Indianapolis, Indiana, became president in 1971.

The first jointly published guide was issed in 1916 and, with only a few interruptions during and following WW I, it has appeared regularly. The first

Fig. 114.4 Aggressive team play in USVBA National Women's Championships. (Credit: Dr. Leonard B. Stallcup, Los Angeles, photo).

editor was Dr. George J. Fisher, New York City (1928-1949), and the present editor is Marvin Veronee, Chicago, Illinois (1974 to the present).

To preserve fast-disappearing, original historical resource references, the USVBA archives, history and records committee spent five years in assembling a complete set of annual volleyball guides and other materials. These were put on microfiche cards and encompass more than 9000 pages. They are available through Microform Publications, College of HPER, University of Oregon, Eugene, Oregon 94403. Additional materials are included in phases two, three, and four.

During the first 45 years of USVBA existence, all phases of organization and operation were carried on voluntarily by the officers, board of directors, committees, and through the program of national member groups. A major share of the load was carried by the YMCA's lay and professional force, but significant developments took place that required fulltime professional leadership. Among these developments were: great expansion of the game during WW II; formation of the International Volleyball Federation in 1947, with the USVBA one of the 14 charter members; addition of a women's division in the 1949 National USVBA Championships held in Los Angeles; worldwide cooperation of volleyball leaders to secure 1957 IOC approval of volleyball to be conducted for women and men in the Olympic games program beginning in Tokyo in 1964; greatly expanded international contacts through the International Volleyball Federation (FIVB) meetings, team and coach visits and exchanges, Pan American Games, world championships, and zonal qualifications for the Olympic games.

In mid-1973, the board selected Albert M. Monaco, Jr., to be the first USVBA executive director. National headquarters were established at 557 Fourth Street, San Francisco, California 95201 (Phone 415-982-7590).

Three years later a national training director was added—Val Keller, 15691 Aulney Lane, Huntington Beach, CA 92647—to supervise national team programs (training center for women at Pasadena, Texas—for men at Dayton, Ohio), regional coaches certification, and volleyball summer camp training.

This brief resume of the growth and development of the USVBA and the part it has played in bringing all national groups together to plan, initiate, and conduct important projects and events, and to establish and maintain international contacts, suggests the scope of this recreative and competitive sport. It could not reflect developments in each of the USVBA member organizations. Nor does it record the personal enjoyment of the game resulting from skill improvement, recreative release from daily tensions, fitness and health developed, friendships made, and opportunity for volunteer service of many types. These benefits are deeply implanted in the lives of the participants.

Volleyball is a game that belongs to all people. This sense of proprietorship is present in the player, teacher, coach, manager, official, spectator, reporter, man, woman, boy, or girl. Each says, "This is my game."

SUGGESTED READINGS

"Rules of Volleyball." Association Athletic League Handbook, 1897. (Official Handbook of the Athletic League of the Young Men's Christian Associations of North America.)

Friermood, H. T., 1955. Sixty years of volleyball. Souvenir program U.S. National Volleyball Championships, sponsored by YMCA, Oklahoma City, Oklahoma.

Game of volley ball. *Physical education,* July 1896, (reproduced in the 1916 volleyball rule book). Selected annual volleyball guides: 1916 to 1973.

Welch, J. E., 1969. *How to play and teach volleyball.* Associated Press. Revised.

Morgan, W. G., 1916. How volley ball was originated. Official (guide) volley ball rules. (Adopted by the Young Men's Christian Association Athletic League and the Collegiate Athletic Association. Guide edited by Dr. George J. Fisher). Spalding Athletic Library, Group XII, No. 364. American Sports Publishing Co., New York, N.Y.

115
Young Men's Christian Association

Harold T. Friermood

The National Council of Young Mens' Christian Association is headquartered in New York and has a chief administrative officer. The 1825 accredited local units, incorporated by the states in which they function, elect representatives to serve as members of the National Council of YMCAs, a body of 300 persons. Meeting annually, the council elects the national board, with 50 to 60 members, to carry the legal and management responsibilities of the movement organization. At least two-thirds of each of these organizations are laymen.

Although each local YMCA has autonomy, it must meet agreed-upon standards to be recognized by the national movement, submit annual reports, outline its purposes in harmony with those specified by the National Council and the World Alliance of YMCAs, employ staff members that meet educational and professional standards, and provide a portion of its annual budget in support of the movement structure and general administration. Working in coordination with the headquarters staff, more direct contact with local units is provided through six regional offices: Northeast, Middle Atlantic, Southern, Great Lakes, Mid-America, and Pacific.

The New York headquarters provides general administrative services, guides field operations, human resources (personnel services and records), research and development, international relationships, program and urban action, specialized constituencies such as armed services, students, transportation, and services such as publication (Association Press), fund raising, purchase of equipment and supplies, and expert counsel in planning and designing buildings and facilities. National guidance and leadership in health, physical education, recreation, and sports are centered in the Program and Urban Action Division.

At the end of 1973 Earle R. Buckley, editor of *YMCA Yearbook and Official Roster* reported that of the 1825 local YMCA units, 1215 conducted physical education, sports, and physical recreation programs for men, women, girl, and boy constituents. With 5,824,573 registered members and 2,171,780 additional registered program constituents, a total of just under eight million registrants were related directly to YMCA programs. "More than 60 percent of all enrollees in registered groups," said Buckley, "participated in physical

Fig. 115.1 YMCA gymnasium in the Tremont Building, Boston, 1872-1183. Equipment is characteristic of the period. (Credit: Historical Library, National Council of YMCAs)

activities." Organized classes, interest groups, clubs, instruction, organized leagues, tournaments, supervised recreation, individual activities, body building, testing, and committee and community service gave point and purpose to this great volume of activity.

With its 2500 gymnasia, 1000 swimming pools, 3000 handball, paddleball, and squash raquets courts, 1200 special exercise rooms, 600 resident camps, hundreds of professional leaders, and thousands of volunteers, YMCAs are equipped and staffed to serve effectively the communities that endorse and support them voluntarily. The YMCA as a community asset, working cooperatively with schools, churches, other voluntary organizations and public community agencies, with a major focus on the needs of youth and the education of parents, has a history of 135 years.

Started June 6, 1844, in London, England, by George Williams, the YMCA came to North America (Montreal, Canada, and Boston, Massachusetts) late in 1851. Three years later the newly formed International Committee of the YMCAs of Canada and the USA met in Buffalo, New York. The next year, 1855, less than 100 young men from 12 countries met in Paris and the World Alliance of YMCAs was formed. Physical education received its first official attention during the third meeting of the International Committee in 1856 at Montreal. A spokesman from Washington identified the need for supervised physical activity, but preoccupation with the Civil War delayed attention to this program.

YMCA buildings with special provision for physical education programs were opened in 1869 in San Francisco,Washington, D.C., and New York City. Lack of trained personnel hampered the early work. Persons with the professional background and understanding of YMCA purposes were not available or did not exist. Two schools were organized to produce such leaders: Springfield YMCA College (1885) and George Williams College (1890); later, a third school was established in Nashville, Tennessee, but was discontinued during the depression of the 1930s. Graduates of many colleges have entered the ranks of professional YMCA directors over the years.

Boston YMCA physical director Robert J. Roberts made an early impact because of his systematic program, his dedication to YMCA purposes, and development of the first leaders' clubs (1884). From the ranks of his club members were recruited many of the early YMCA physical directors before college-trained men were available. Medical doctors were also recruited; they established the need for physical examination of members before starting activity programs and use of anthropometric measurements and records as the basis for determining developmental progress.

Dr. Luther Halsey Gulick, the first person to serve in the national office as Physical Education Secretary, International Committee of the YMCAs (1887-1903), was the philosopher, developer of the "why" of YMCA physical education, and originator of the YMCA emblem, an equilateral triangle, symbolic of the harmonious development of body, mind, and spirit. More importantly he created an educational concept of the interrelatedness of activities and experiences affecting all aspects of human personality. Dr. Gulick's thinking, speaking, and writing made a profound impact within the YMCA and with other groups and organizations. Through intensive study he developed a philosophy about the psychology of play in a country that was becoming increasingly urban. He made many contributions to the recreation and playground movements. In addition to duties as national YMCA physical education secretary, Dr. Gulick also served as director of the department of physical education at Springfield (YMCA) College.

The first YMCA swimming pool was opened in the Brooklyn Central YMCA in 1885, a second opened the next year in Detroit, and, by 1909 there were 293 YMCA pools. In 1900 there were 507 YMCA gymnasia and 272 physical directors.

Volleyball was invented in 1895 in the Holyoke, Massachusetts YMCA by William G. Morgan, the physical director, and spread quickly around the country and to foreign lands. The Athletic League of the YMCAs of North America was formed in 1896 with Gulick as executive secretary, and the official *Handbook* was published the next year. Articles of affiliation with the Amateur Athletic Union were signed, and the AAU adopted the YMCA basketball rules in 1897. George T. Hepbron, a YMCA physical director, was

Fig. 115.2 Luther Halsey Gulick, M.D. National Director, YMCA Physical Education, 1889-1903. (Credit: Historical Library, National Council of YMCAs)

Fig. 115.3 John Brown, Jr., M.D. National Director, YMCA Physical Education, 1919-1939. (Credit: Historical Library, National Council of YMCAs)

Fig. 115.4 Lloyd C. Arnold, Ed.D. National Director, YMCA Physical Education, 1968 to the present. (Credit: Historical Library, National Council of YMCAs)

Fig. 115.5 G. Gordon Fisher Chairman, National YMCA Physical Education Education, 1943-1968. (Credit: Historical Library, National Council of YMCAs)

named secretary of the basketball committee. As a part of the Universal Exposition of 1904, held in St. Louis, Missouri, an extensive "physical culture" program was held; this included the Olympic Games and national YMCA sports championships. Olympic lectures were given related to "development of the human body" and education through sports programs. Many contemporary leaders presented papers. The American Physical Education Association, the newly formed Physical Directors' Society of the YMCAs of North America, and other national groups held conferences and conventions.

A publication, *Physical Training,* was started in the fall of 1901 with Gulick as the editor. Dr. George J. Fisher became the National YMCA secretary for physical education in 1904 and served for 15 years. During that period he also served as editor of *Physical Training.* Martin I. Foss was editor from 1920 to 1924 and was succeeded by Dr. John Brown, Jr. The name of the magazine was changed to *Journal of Physical Education* in September 1927. Started as a publication to reflect organization policies, it became the official publication of the Physical Education Society of the YMCAs of North America when that group was organized in 1903. It continues as such, and is the medium through which the professional group shares ideas, stimulates study and research, and interprets YMCA physical education to other groups domestically, as well as to readers in 30 to 40 other countries.

Elected as the first president of the Physical Directors' Society of the YMCAs of North America, in 1903, Dr. George J. Fisher continued to serve through his 15 years as senior secretary for physical education in the national headquarters, 1904 to 1919.

Dr. John Brown, Jr., was national director for physical education for 20 years (1919-1939). The position was vacant until the end of April 1943 when Harold T. Friermood was selected. He served for 25 years until April 1968. After a six-month interval, Lloyd C. Arnold was installed.

In 1924 the National Council of YMCAs was formed and the general movement organization was changed. The executive committee of the Athletic League of the YMCAs of North America became the National YMCA Physical Education Committee with John R. Brooks as the first chairman and John Brown, Jr., the executive secretary. Brooks continued as chairman until 1939 and functioned on call until 1944, when the committee was reorganized completely, with Dr. Frank S. Lloyd, chairman, and Dr. James Harold Fox, associate chairman. For the first time, a woman, Dr. Josephine Rathbone, was included in the committee structure.

During one of several national reorganizations from 1967 to the present, the long-standing National YMCA Physical Education Committee and other national program committees were eliminated. This meant that a strong lay organization made up of the national Physical Education Committee, its subcommittees, a National Physical Education Council, and 17 area/state committees—a total group of 500 to 600 interested and capable persons scattered throughout the United States—was disbanded. Emphasis was placed upon operating councils for aquatics, scuba diving, volleyball, physical fitness, gymnastics, etc., but without a superior, coordinating body to give general guidance and leadership. This role was assumed by the professional leadership in the regions and in the national office.

During World War I many YMCA physical directors were called into service. Many of these men gave leadership in the war training camp programs as physical training experts and physical recreation leaders. Following the war dozens of experienced YMCA physical directors were called to Europe to give leadershipo in establishing health and physical education programs at the national level, in educational systems, and in the military structures. One man, Elwood S. Brown, who had served the National YMCA of the Philippines, conceived and, working closely with the USA military, helped direct the great Inter-Allied Games in June 1919. Money raised by the YMCA built the Pershing Stadium outside Paris, the scene of the games, sometimes called the "Military Olympics." Preparation for the games, qualification for the various teams, and actual conduct of the championships involving 18 to 20 countries kept thousands of men occupied constructively. Early in 1914 the historic "standardization conference" was held in Lakehurst, New Jersey, and from this came the book *Physical Education in the YMCAs of North America.* Following World War I concern was registered about trained men moving from physical education into the general administration of the YMCA. The Studer Commission worked for three years and reported at a national conference in 1924. Implementation of a number of its recommendations helped to emphasize and stabilize YMCA physical education.

William H. Ball, serving on the national staff with responsibilities in leaders' club work and the YMCA aquatic program, saw the close relationship between the YMCA and the Red Cross in first-aid training and certification; he recommended that the Red Cross establish a program of lifesaving. His work resulted in a program that has been of tremendous service throughout the country ever since.

Dr. Henry F. Kallenberg, while serving on the central region staff in the mid-1920s, developed a YMCA manual on lifesaving; he also fostered the concept of the natatorium or swimming pool as a "water gymnasium" and suggested many activities to stimulate greater use of this valuable facility.

National YMCA sports championships were launched vigorously during the 1920s: volleyball, 1922; swimming and diving, 1923; followed by handball, track and field, the hexathlon, individual achievement for various age groups scored on a team basis, and a national four-year study program for enrolled leaders' clubs. The YMCA cooperated in the organization of the National Amateur Athletic Federation, gave major leadership in the formation of the

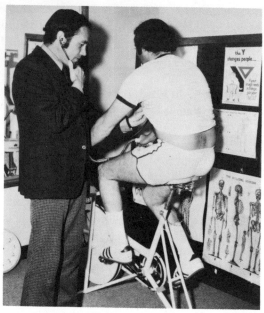

Fig. 115.6 Fitness testing lab. Downtown YMCA, Nashville, Tennessee. (Credit: Building and Furnishings Service, National Council of YMCAs)

Fig. 115.7 Well planned, attractive YMCA buildings with modern equipment, now serve total family: men, boys, women, and girls, in neighborhood settings, similar to this north suburban branch in Northbrook, Illinois. (Credit: Building and Furnishings Service, National Council of YMCAs)

United States Volleyball Association, and worked to reestablish relationships with the AAU that had been discontinued in 1913. Dr. George G. Deaver and Dr. Henry F. Kallenberg gave new direction to the YMCA individual health service and to the program in YMCA athletic clubs. Major emphases during the late 1920s and early 1930s were: research in YMCA physical education, character education through sports and physical education, coed and family programs, increasing the range of physical recreation programs during the depression years, the McCurdy study resulting in the book, *The New Physical Education in the YMCA,* and perhaps most significant of all, the planning and conduct of the first national YMCA Aquatic Conference. Preceded by more than a year of intensive study and research by 17 separate commission or committee groups, the conference was held in May 1937 at George Williams College in Chicago. Authorized by the National YMCA Physical Education Committee, upon recommendation of the Metropolitan Sports Council of the Chicago YMCA, a small steering committee made up of John W. Fuhrer, John Brown, Jr., and Thomas K. Cureton guided the project to a successful conclusion. Dr. Cureton, then on the faculty at Springfield College, directed the research effort. It was this conference that redirected the YMCA's aquatic program with new publications, new plans for leadership training and certification, and a field organization designed to stimulate and implement the program. Following the conference Cureton was appointed chairman of the National Aquatic Committee and served dynamically for 25 years.

World War II made new demands upon the YMCA. Many facilities were in use 16 to 20 hours per day. Recreation and fitness programs were planned for swing-shift workers, and service for enlisted men enlarged dramatically in response to the invitation, "Your uniform is your membership card." Soon after Friermood went to the national staff, a Wartime Aquatic Conference was conducted at Lake Geneva, Wisconsin, and the following year a National Fitness Conference was conducted at the same place; Dr. Cureton was the chief resource at both events. He also conducted hundreds of local YMCA and district fitness clinics or institutes. Summer leaders' schools were scheduled at traditional YMCA conference spots: Silver Bay, Lake George, New York; College Camp, Lake Geneva, Wisconsin; Blue Ridge, Black Mountain, N.C.; Association Camp, Estes Park, Colorado; Seabeck Conference in the Seattle, Washington locality; and the Canadian leaders' school at Geneva Park, north of Toronto.

In late summer 1943 the Second National YMCA Health Service Directors' Clinic was conducted in Dayton, Ohio. Growing out of actions suggested the year before, a specialized organization was formed made up of the local directors of YMCA health service sections.

Upon conclusion of hostilities, postwar programs were initiated with greater emphasis given to cooperative efforts within communities and at the national level. The National YMCA Physical Education Committee called a first meeting of its National Physical Education Council in Illinois, and the essential elements for a competitive sports policy were identified; this resulted in National YMCA sports championships being assigned and conducted on the basis of nondiscrimination.

After 12 years, a Second National YMCA Aquatic Conference was conducted in 1949; the *New Lifesaving Book,* prepared by Charles E. Silvia, was distributed for use. Dr. Cureton again served as chief resource and conference chairman.

Following the 1948 World YMCA Consultation on Health and Physical Education in London at the time of the Olympic Games, plans were made to conduct similar events each four years: Helsinki, Melbourne, Rome, Tokyo, Mexico City, Munich, and Montreal, consecutively.

An idea first considered in 1945, worked on by a number of people during a six-year period, became a reality in the fall of 1951 when the Conference for National Cooperation in Aquatics (now known as the Council for National Cooperation in Aquatics—CNCA) came into being. This brought representatives from more than 20 national organizations into a forum situation where agency plans and programs could be shared and common projects developed. The work of CNCA has helped to advance the entire field of aquatics in the intervening years. Rosters that appear in the printed conference reports show YMCA participation in the planning and conduct of CNCA ongoing work.

When the president's conference on Physical Fitness of Youth was scheduled by President Eisenhower, the YMCA planned a follow-up in late 1955; this was conducted in spite of the fact that the president's event had to be postponed a year. The national YMCA Fitness Clinic started a program that has gained momentum during the intervening years. Selected YMCA physical educators were encouraged to go to the University of Illinois Fitness Laboratory and take graduate work under Dr. Cureton. National YMCA scholarship financing was secured as a further stimulus. Over a period of 10 years between 60 and 75 professional practitioners took such work, and their efforts, added to those of other students who went to Kent State University and other schools, have resulted in a widely scattered group of capable persons doing outstanding work in the field of adult and youth fitness. A national fitness conference conducted in Philadelphia, planned and directed by Clayton R. Myers in 1971, gave further dimensions to this specialized work.

Dr. Leonard A. Larson was chairman of a study committee in the mid-1950s that established a design, developed a study document, collected data, and carried on consultations that resulted in a report to the National Council and a book, *A New Look at YMCA Physical Education.* This committee set directions and created expectancies that have influenced YMCA programs during the years from 1959 to the present. A second book by Friermood and J. Wesley McVicar, *Basic Physical Education in the YMCA,* was built upon the philosophical base laid down by the Larson study, as reported by Richard E. Hamlin, and presented the practical work developed through years of experience in Canada and the United Staes.

A third book, *History of YMCA Physical Education,* is authored by Elmer L. Johnson.

YMCA physical educators have contributed to the culture of many countries by serving as world service workers under the auspices of the International Committee of the YMCAs of North America, upon request from the country involved. They were faced with the task of building an indigenous movement abroad in the face of many obstacles brought on by racial, social, ethnic, and religious differences. Despite these obstacles YMCA secretaries pushed forward into the unknown to accomplish basic purposes. They had visions that penetrated beyond ethnic and religious differences and the distrust they encountered frequently as foreigners in alien lands. They saw the YMCA as a means of reaching people and serving the fourfold nature of man: physical, spiritual, social, and intellectual. They believed that each YMCA could influence the quality of life for future generations. The list of such YMCA physical education "ambassadors" includes many illustrious names.

To motivate a progressive plan of self-improvement and continuing study, the Physical Education Society established a titles, grading, and recognitions program. Points were earned for summer school and institute courses, satisfactory service and job continuity, reading and reporting on specified books, and preparation of professional papers. Periodic listing in professional publications of standards required and those who had achieved recognition encouraged others. The society awarded "instructor" and "director" of physical education titles when requirements had been met. At one time, the title "senior director of physical education" was provided, but standards were high and only two were granted. A select group, Society of Fellows in YMCA Physical Education, was formed into which only those who had achieved the title "director of physical education" were invited. The highest YMCA honor, the Roberts-Gulick Award, has been given annually since 1930 for distinguished leadership and contributions as an administrator, researcher, and writer.

Recently reorganized and nationally staffed phases of health and physical education programs include: National Aquatic Program, New York City, Robert Orozco, director; the National Youth Basketball Association, New York City, New York, John H. Farrell, director; the National YMCA Scuba Research and Training Center based at Key West, Florida, Robert W. Smith, director; Cardiovascular Health Program, New York City, Clayton R. Myers, director; Back Conditioning Program, San Mateo, California, Alexander

Melleby, director and Hans Kraus, M.D., advisor/consultant; and Swimming for the Mentally Retarded and Physically Handicapped, Longview, Washington, Grace D. Reynolds, director. When each of these program areas is carefully interpreted, promoted, and buttressed by a strong advisory committee, membership and community service will be significantly expanded.

A definition for physical education used in the YMCA for many years has challenged its professional and volunteer leaders to encourage all participants to achieve their full potential within the concept of the triangle (body, mind, and spirit), or as Dr. Steinhaus explained, "Achieve the wider life dimensions of a balanced, inverted pyramid." He added that "physical eduction is that which sees in measures insuring bodily health and the right amount and kind of motor activity, an avenue of approach through which the whole individual may be influenced for good in mind and character as well as in body. The word physical denotes the means and not the end." Movement education, individual initiative, and creativity, social responsibility, an opportunity for all, fair play and good sportsmanship, idealism and spiritual development are all a part of physical education and achievable with the right leadership.

New tools in the form of specialized programs, books, and materials, based on sound objectives, are being put to work by modern leaders in the YMCA. The need is greater than ever. The future is bright!

For more information write to YMCA, 291 Broadway, New York, New York 10007.

SUGGESTED READINGS

Fisher, G. J. (ed.), 1914. *Physical education in the YMCAs of North America.* New York: Association Press.

Friermood, H. T., and J. W. McVicar, 1962. *Basic physical education in the YMCA.* New York: Association Press.

Friermood, H. T., 1967. Physical education—its role in YMCA service to man, booklet edited by David E. Misner, YMCA physical education for the '70s. Report of *a National Consultation on Health and Physical Education in the YMCA.*

Friermood, H. T., (ed.), 1950. *Principles, rules and administration of YMCA amateur sports.* New York: Association Press.

Hamlin, R. E., 1959. *A new look at YMCA physical education.* (The report of a national study.) New York: Association Press.

McCurdy, J. R., Chairman, Study Committee, 1938. *The New YMCA physical education in the YMCA.* New York: Association Press.

116
Young Women's Christian Association

Sandra Fonger

The Young Women's Christian Association (YWCA), founded in London in 1855 and active in the United States since 1858, has from its inception been concerned with meeting the needs of women and girls and advancing the cause of peace, justice, freedom, and dignity for all people.

The YWCA was actively involved in the suffrage movement in the early 1900s and it supported legislation regulating the hours and wages of working women. Provision of housing for women coming to the cities to work and for newcomers to America was also an early development. Today the YWCA's concern about such social issues as day care, health and environment, and legal protection reinforce the organization's commitment to its one imperative: the elimination of racism wherever it exists and by any means necessary. This imperative was adopted at the 1970 triennial convention and reaffirmed in 1973. Concurrent with the aims of the imperative, the YWCA is working for a society that assures the empowerment of women, youth, and the Third World people, greater social and economic justice, and a more human environment.

Over the years the YWCA has offered a wide range of programs and services for women and girls. Sewing, cooking, and pottery classes now exist side by side with classes in woodworking, plumbing, and auto mechanics. The Job Corps-YWCA is a government-funded, extension residence program offering transitional living experience to girls completing Job Corps training and preparing to work. As a member agency of the USO, the YWCA serves military men, women, and their families here and abroad. Through the National Student YWCA college and university women, the YWCA's One Imperative and Program for Action are carried out on their respective campuses. The Resource Center on Women (established in 1970) focuses the many varied resources of the YWCA of the United States on serving the needs of women and girls, individuals and groups, oriented toward effecting far-reaching social change.

The health program of the YWCA is designed to help the individual achieve total fitness through generating an interest in her state of health and how to improve it, informing her of the existence of community health services and motivating her to use them, providing information enabling her to discriminate between quackery and scientific health care. The YWCA is also cognizant of the fact that special attention should be given to the extension of health services to minority, rural, and other groups needing such benefits, since there is an interdependence between health and environment in terms of one's economic status, education, religion, personal and family relationships, etc. However, to implement any health program so that total fitness may be achieved, it is necessary not only to teach physical skills, but also to provide opportunities for the use of such skills in recreational activities.

The YWCA offers a varied physical education program primarily focusing on such individual sports as tennis, golf, yoga, judo, and karate; exercise and dance classes are also featured. Many local YWCAs offer day and resident camping acommodations. However, swimming activities continue to attract the greatest number of individuals to the YWCA. Instructions are given for all age levels in the following kinds of swimming: recreational, life saving, competitive, and synchronized; aquagym classes (swimming exercises), and pool shows are also featured. Skin diving and scuba lessons are offered when qualified instructors are available.

Currently the YWCA is at work in more than 6000 locations in the United States and in more than 80 countries worldwide.

The National Board of the YWCA of the U.S.A. has headquarters at 600 Lexington Avenue, New York, 10022. The World YWCA is headquartered in Geneva, Switzerland.

Biographical Appendix

Louis E. Alley is professor and head, department of men's physical education, University of Iowa. He earned a B.S. in education from Central Missouri State University, the M.S. from the University of Wisconsin and the Ph.D. from the University of Iowa in 1949. He is a past president of the National College Physical Education Association for Men, American Alliance for Health, Physical Education, Recreation, and Dance, and American Academy of Physical Education.

Fred L. Allman, Jr., is director, Sports Medicine Clinic and orthopaedic consultant to Georgia Technical University and the Atlanta, Georgia, public schools. He is author and/or coauthor of several books on sports medicine. He is past chairman of the American Medical Association's Committee on Exercise and Physical Fitness. He received the National Physical Fitness Leadership Award, awards from the National Football Foundation Hall of Fame, and the National High School Coaches Association.

George F. Anderson was executive director of AAHPERD from 1974 to 1980. Prior to this appointment, he served as associate executive secretary for 23 years. He has an undergraduate degree from SUNY Cortland, and an M.S. and Ed.D. from Syracuse University. He has taught and coached in the public schools of New York State and Syracuse University. He is a member of Cortland's Hall of Fame and received honor awards from the AAHPERD Eastern District and the Society of State Directors of HPER.

Robert J. Antonacci graduated from Indiana University and received M.S. and Ed.D. degrees from the University of Michigan. He has taught and coached at major universities and was director of health and physical education for the Gary, Indiana, school district. He is presently professor of physical education at Temple University in Philadelphia, Pennsylvania. He has received national and international honors and commendations for his children's books dealing with sports and fitness.

Kate R. Barrett received her undergraduate degree from Boston-Bouve College (Northeastern University), and the M.S. and Ph.D. degrees from the University of Wisconsin-Madison, and has studied in England. She is professor of physical education at the University of North Carolina at Greensboro, teaching at both the undergraduate and graduate levels. She has conducted research in the areas of curriculum theory/implementation, teacher behavior, and analysis of specific ideas of leaders in the field of movement and dance as traced through their writings.

Lawrence Benjamin is an assistant professor in the school of health, physical education, and recreation at the Ohio State University, Columbus. He is teaching in the graduate and undergraduate programs of teacher education. His research interests are in the area of teacher behavior and in the design, development, implementation, and evaluation of curriculum.

Carol A. Bitner is associate national executive director of the Council Services Division of Camp Fire Girls, Inc. In this role she serves as a member of a three-person team responsible for the total management of this national youth organization. As the director of this division, she is responsible for development and execution of youth program development, field consultation, training, new council organization, government relations, camp administration, council management, publications communications, and membership development.

C.R. Blackstock is a well-known Canadian physical educator and one of the pioneers in the field in his country . Now in semiretirement, he is a consultant at the National Sport and Recreation Centre in Ottowa. He edited and published the Canadian Association's *Journal of Health, Physical Education, and Recreation* for many years and was its first fulltime executive director. He was the recipient of the Canadian Association's Honor Award and Honorary Life Membership. He is the author of many articles dealing with camping and outdoor education.

Marjorie Blaufarb was editor of *AAHPERD Update* and director of public affairs for the American Alliance for Health, Physical Education, Recreation, and Dance. She spearheaded the alliance effort in equal opportunity and human rights during a critical period when Title IX was greatly discussed. She has written many articles on the subject in an effort to assist teachers and administrators to adjust to the differing requirements of the legislation.

James S. Bosco is coeditor of this volume and editor of Section 7—Related Professions. See page vii for a biographical sketch.

Karl W. Bookwalter received the A.B. degree from Denver University, the M.A. from Teachers College, Columbia University, and the Ed.D. from New York University. He taught in the Denver public schools for nine years. For 39 years he taught at Indiana University where he served as director of the bureau of service and research. He also was chairman of the graduate division in the school of health, physical education, and recreation at Indiana University.

John L. Boyer is a medical doctor and a Diplomate of the American Board of Internal Medicine. He is a Fellow of the American College of Physicians and an Associate Fellow of the American College of Cardiology. He is the medical director of the Exercise Physiology Laboratory and Adult Fitness Center at San Diego State University, San Diego, California. He is also a professor in the graduate school of the college of professional studies at that university. He also serves as the director of medical services, Cardio-Pulmonary Rehabilitation Institute in San Diego. During 1977-78 he served as president of the American College of Sports Medicine. He is also the chairman of the American Medical Association's Committee on Exercise and Physical Fitness.

H. Edsel Buchanan was secretary of the National Intramural Recreational Sports Association (NIRSA) in 1964 and 1965. In 1968 Buchanan served as president of NIRSA. From 1971 through 1973 he served as executive secretary of this organization. In 1975 he proposed that the name of the association be changed to its present title. He was honored by NIRSA in 1974 as the recipient of its highest award, the Honor Award.

Donald E. Bushore, executive director of the Athletic Institute, received an M.S. from Brigham Young University after serving the profession as a high school principal, coach, and teacher. In 1965 he was an associate professor at New Mexico State University, and then became a public relations person for the Athletic Institute in 1966. In 1971 he assumed his present position. He is a member of the Advisory Council of the United States Sports Academy, a director of CNCA, and a member of Phi Delta Kappa, AAHPERD, NCPEAM, and other professional organizations.

C. Carson Conrad received the B.A. from the University of California at Santa Barbara and the M.A. from California State University, Sacramento. He was named executive director of the President's Council on Physical Fitness and Sports in September 1970. Prior to this appointment he was a professional staff member in the California State Department of Education for 24 years, the last 16 years as chief of Health Education, Physical Education, Athletics, and Recreation. He received the National Physical Fitness Leadership Award in 1966.

Raymond A. Ciszek is acting executive vice-president, American Alliance for Health, Physical Education, Recreation, and Dance. Dr. Ciszek has been a key figure in that organization since 1962. Prior to that he was Chairman of Health, Physical Education, and Recreation at Western Washington State College. He received his Ed.D. from Boston University. He has been the prime mover and motivating force from AAHPERD in the publication of this *Encyclopedia*.

Chalres B. Corbin earned the Ph.D. degree from the University of New Mexico and the M.S. from the University of Illinois. He is currently professor of health, physical education, and recreation at Kansas State University where he directs the Motor Development Research Laboratory. Dr. Corbin has authored six books and more than 40 research and professional articles. He has been instrumental in the development of the "concepts" or foundations approach to physical education at both the college and high school levels.

Thomas K. Cureton, Jr., is chairman of the *Encyclopedia* committee and series editor. See page v for a biographical sketch.

Paul W. Darst received the B.S. and M.S. degrees at the University of Akron and the Ph.D. from the Ohio State University. He has specialized in the areas of teacher preparation, curriculum development, and teaching methods. He has taught at both the secondary and university level and is presently teaching at Arizona State University.

Joanna Davenport is associate professor of physical education and women's athletic director at Auburn University, Auburn, Alabama. She received the B.S. degree at Skidmore College, her M.S. at Smith College, and the Ph.D. at the Ohio State University. Active in many professional organizations, she has been president of the National Association for Girls and Women in Sport, and historian-archivist of the NAPECW since 1969.

Charles J. Dillman is presently an associate professor of physical education and director of the Biomechanics Research Laboratory at the University of Illinois, Urbana. His major research interests are in the biomechanical aspects of human performance as related to sport activities.

Anna M. Doudlah is a research scientist, Perceptual-Motor Development Research Section at Central Wisconsin Center for the Developmentally Disabled in Madison. She received the Ph.D. in physical education from the University of Wisconsin-Madison in 1967. Dr. Doudlah's primary research interest is in the motor development of infants and the effects of "developmental" programs on the motor development of infants considered to be at risk.

Helen M. Eckert is professor of physical education at the University of California, Berkeley. She has contributed numerous articles to various professional journals. She has also served as an associate editor of the *Research Quarterly* since 1967, coauthor of *Motor Development*, and author of *Practical Measurement of Physical Perfor-*

mance. She is listed in *Who's Who of American Women* and is a Fellow of the American Academy of Physical Education.

Anna Espenschade is a Fellow of the American Academy of Physical Education, the American College of Sports Medicine, the American Psychological Association, and the Society for Research in Child Development. She is an Honorary Member of the National Association for Physical Education of College Women, the United States Field Hockey Association, and both the American Alliance and California Association for Health, Physical Education, Recreation, and Dance. She has served as associate editor of the *Research Quarterly* and as a field reader for the United States Office of Education's Bureau of Research. Her major research and writing has been in the fields of child development, physical growth and abilities, and motor development.

Arthur A. Esslinger, now deceased, served as one of the editors of Section 3. See page 102 for a biographical sketch.

Marvin H. Eyler is coeditor of Section 4. See page 256 for a biographical sketch.

A.E. Florio is emeritus professor of safety education and program director of driver education, department of health and safety education at the University of Illinois. He received the B.S. and M.A. degrees from the University of Illinois and the Ed.D. degree from Columbia University. He is a pioneer in teacher education preparation in safety and driver education and has written in these areas extensively. He is a past president of the American Academy of Safety Education and the Illinois Association for Professional Preparation of Teachers of Health, Physical Education, and Recreation. He also served as vice-president of the Safety Division of AAHPERD. He is a Fellow of the American Academy of Physical Education.

B. Don Franks is an editor of Section 3. See page 101 for a biographical sketch.

Harold T. Friermood is editor of Section 9. See page 613 for a biographical sketch.

Reuben B. Frost is Buxton Professor Emeritus at Springfield College, Masschusetts. He received the A.B. degree from Luther College, the M.A. from the University of Iowa, and the Ph.D. from the University of Oregon. He coached, taught, and administered programs at all levels of education during his professional career, which spanned 1928 to 1974. He is past president of AAHPERD and a recipient of its Honor Award. He also received the Massachusetts Association and AAHPERD Central District Honor Award. He is general editor of Volume III of this *Encyclopedia.*

Ellen W. Gerber was formerly an associate professor at the University of Massachusetts, Amherst. She received the Ph.D. degree from the University of Southern California. She coauthored *The American Woman in Sport* in 1974 and has authored numerous books and articles, with particular emphasis on the history of women in sport. She is a committed feminist and presently serves as staff attorney for the Legal Aid Society of Northwest North Carolina.

William Gilmore is the public relations director for American Youth Hostels, Inc. This organization was founded in 1934 and is a member of the International Youth Hostel Federation. It is a nonprofit association organized as a community service to provide year-round opportunities for outdoor recreation and inexpensive educational travel through hosteling.

Billy E. Gober is the coordinator of health and physical education for the DeKalb County School System, Georgia. From 1965 to 1968 he served as supervisor of health, physical education and athletics for the DeKalb school system. He taught at the University of Georgia and Temple University prior to his return to public school work. He is a member of the Comprehensive Health Education Committee for the Georgia PTA and the Georgia Medical Association's Task Force on Health Education in Schools.

Michael Goldberger is presently an associate professor at Temple University. He designed and now coordinates the Temple CBTE program. He received his graduate education at the University of Pittsburg and has studied with Professor Muska Mosston at the Center on Teaching. Currently he is studying the effectiveness, in terms of learner outcomes, of various models or styles of teaching.

Joseph J. Gruber received the Ph.D. from Purdue University. He taught and coached in high school, YMCA, college, and military settings. He has been on the faculty at Purdue University and is now at the University of Kentucky where he has served as chairman of the department. He is the coauthor of three books and 30 articles. He was the recipient of a research and scholarship award on two occasions at the University of Kentucky. He currently serves on the editorial board of the *Research Quarterly*.

Richard A. Haas is a physical education instructor and coach at Stout Junior High School, Dearborn, Michigan. He received the B.A. degree from Michigan State University and M.A. from Eastern Michigan University. Mr. Haas has been the intramural director at Stout Junior High School for 12 years. He has coached football, basketball, swimming, and track.

Frank J. Hayden is director of the school of physical education and athletics at McMaster University, Hamilton, Ontario, Canada. He has worked in the field of adapted physical activity for 17 years. He was a director at the Joseph P. Kennedy, Jr., Foundation in Washington, D.C., and created its International Special Olympics program. In 1968 he received the St. Coletta National Award for Outstanding Contributions to the Field of Mental Retardation. His current research concerns the work capacity, body fat, and physical activity characteristics of retarded children.

Leona Holbrook edited Section 1. See page 4 for a biographical sketch.

Agnes M. Hooley is professor emeritus of the physical education and recreation department of Bowling Green State University. She attended the University of Bridgeport (Arnold College), Teachers College, Columbia University, and the University of Wisconsin, where she attained the Ph.D. degree. She has taught all levels in health, physical education, and recreation with her specialties being in adapted physical education and recreation. She is the author of 30 articles, coauthor of *Physical Education for the Handicapped*, and has edited several professional books.

Paul A. Hunsicker, now deceased, received the B.S. degree from Syracuse University, the M.P.E. from Springfield College and the Ph.D. from the University of Illinois. He was professor of physical education at the University of Michigan. He served in many capacities in state, district, and national professional associations. He authored or coauthored four books and a large number of technical reports. He worked extensively in the areas of tests and measurements and physical fitness.

Robert J. Janus graduated from Lock Haven State College with a B.S. in health education and received the M.S. in physical education from the University of Maryland. He is currently a motor development specialist for the special education department of the Prince George's County Public Schools, Prince George's County, Maryland.

Warren R. Johnson is an editor of Section 3. See page 100 for a biographical sketch.

William P. Johnson is an associate professor and team leader in physical education at Brookdale Community College, Lincroft, New Jersey.

Dr. Ernst Jokl, M.D., a native of Germany, teaches medicine at the Universities of Kentucky and of Berlin, Germany. He is the founder of sports medicine in the United States, a member of the executive committee of the UNESCO International Council of Sport and Physical Education, and a Fellow of the American College of Cardiology. Among his numerous scientific publications are 15 books and over 100 articles. The Harveian Society of London awarded him the Buckston Browne British Commonwealth Prize and Medal for Medical Research; and the president of the Federal Republic of Germany bestowed upon him the Grand Cross of Merit of Germany in 1972.

Leonard H. Kalakian received the bachelor's and master's degrees in physical education from Southern Illinois University. The Ph.D. degree was completed at the University of Utah with emphasis in special physical education. Dr. Kalakian is professor of physical education at Mankato State University where he has been a faculty member since 1965. He is the author or coauthor of four texts in physical education, among them, *Movement Experiences for the Mentally Retarded and Emotionally Disturbed*.

Roy J. Keller edited Section 7. See page 490 for a biographical sketch.

Barbara L. Kerch received the B.S. from the University of Illinois and the M.S. degree from the University of Wisconsin. She has been the consultant for physical education, K-12 in Granite City, Illinois since 1952. She has been involved in all levels of educational instruction. She has served both AAHPERD and the Illinois Association in positions of leadership. She has been the recipient of a number of awards, including the AAHPERD and Illinois Honor Fellow awards. She has served as committee chairperson and editor for two elementary physical education publications developed for the state of Illinois.

William R. Kilpatrick has been the coordinator of health, physical education, and athletics for the Dearborn, Michigan, public schools since 1967. He was a physical education and health teacher, coach, and athletics director, prior to becoming the coordinator. He received the B.S. and M.S. degrees in physical education from Bowling Green State University.

Clark King went to Virginia Military Institute as an assistant football coach in 1952 after a second tour with the U.S.M.C. In 1963 he became head of the department of physical eduction. He holds the bachelor's degree from Kearney State College, a master's degree from Wyoming University, and the doctorate from the University of Virginia.

Karl K. Klein, D.C.T., is a professor in the department of health and physical education at the University of Texas at Austin. He also serves as coordinator of physical rehabilitation and consultant in physical rehabilitation to the student health center at that university. He holds degrees from several institutions including Indiana University and Springfield College. He is a member of AAHPERD, American Corrective Therapy Association, American College of Sports Medicine, American Congress of Rehabilitation Medicine, National Athletic Trainers Association, Phi Epsilon Kappa, and Phi Kappa Phi Honor Society.

Richard P. Kleva is an assistant professor of physical education at Brookdale Community College, Lincroft, New Jersey.

Marian E. Kneer, Ph.D., University of Michigan, is an associate professor of physical education at the University of Illinois, Chicago Circle. She is a curriculum and instruction specialist. Her background includes secondary teaching experience, university student teaching supervision, and currently she is director of graduate studies. She is coauthor of *Physical Education Instructional Techniques: An Individualized Humanistic Approach* and *Softball—Fast and Slow Pitch.* In addition she has contributed articles for various publications. She has served physical education and sports organizations as a leader, speaker, and demonstrator.

Brigadier General Frank J. Kobes, Jr., was professor and director of physical education from 1953 to 1974 at the United States Military Academy. His views and studies on the fitness of American youth have appeared in numerous magazines and newspapers. He has contributed greatly to the President's Council on Physical Fitness and Sports. He is frequently asked to serve as a consultant on physical education and athletics. As director of the Academy of the International Council of Military Sports, he earned an international reputation in sports training. He was active in the YMCA and other major physical education associations.

Lionel Koppman is the public information director of the National Jewish Welfare Board and a former editor, author, and newspaperman. He is the coauthor of *American Jewish Landmarks: A Travel Guide and History*. He received the National Jewish Book Award and the Outstanding Filmstrip of the Year Award.

Hans Kraus graduated from Vienna University in 1930. He was an associate professor of physical medicine and rehabilitation, New York University until his retirement in 1968. He has served as a medical consultant to the President's Council on Physical Fitness and Sports. He has authored several books and written over 100 papers.

Fernand Landry received the B.A. (Labal) and B.S. (Ottawa) degrees and obtained both the M.S. and Ph.D. from University of Illinois. He was formerly the director, school of physical education, University of Ottawa, and director, department of physical education, Laval University. He is a past-president of the Canadian Association of Sports Sciences, and the Scientific Commission of the International Congress of Physical Activity Sciences. He has served as vice president for North America, International Council for Sport and Physical Education (NGO status A, UNESCO). He has written articles for scientific publications in French, English, and German in the biological aspects of physical activity.

Dorothy LaSalle is presently professor emeritus at Wayne State University. She received the B.S., M.S., and Ed.D. degrees from Columbia University. She was a teacher in private and public schools and an administrator for 10 years serving the New Jersey public schools as director of health and physical education. She has written numerous books and articles on health and physical education topics. She is a Fellow of the American Academy of Physical Education and has received Honor Awards from the American Alliance and Michigan Associations for Health, Physical Education, Recreation, and Dance, and the Michigan School Health Association.

George Leonard served as a senior editor for *Look* Magazine for 17 years. He is author of *Education and Ecstasy, The Transformation,* and *The Ultimate Athlete.* He is a student and teacher of aikido, in which he holds black belt rank, and is widely known as a lecturer and workshop leader.

Barbara D. Lockhart received the B.S. and M.A. degrees from Michigan State University and the Ed.D. from Brigham Young University. At Temple University she has been director of women's athletics, assistant dean of the college of health, physical education, recreation, and dance, and presently is an associate professor. She has served as president of the National Association of Sport and Physical Education of AAHPERD. Her competitive career was highlighted by participation in the 1960 and 1964 Olympics as a speed skater for the United States Olympic Team.

Gilbert A. Magida is the coordinator of physical education in Park Ridge, Illinois. He is also the director of the Golf Maine Park District in Des Plaines, Illinois. Throughout his career he has held positions in both physical education and recreation. He has served as a supervisor-consultant for student teachers from the University of Illinois, Champaign, and as instructor in the graduate school of the National College of Education, Evanston, Illinois.

Benjamin H. Massey is coeditor of Section 4. See page 256 for a biographical sketch.

Chalres H. McCloy was born in Marietta, Ohio, in 1886 and died in Iowa City, Iowa, in 1959. He was research professor of physical education at the State University of Iowa, 1930-1954. He received the Ph.B. and M.A. from Marietta College, Ohio, and the Ph.D. from Teacher's College, Columbia University. During his career he served in many capacities in the United States, China, and Japan and lectured in South America, Canada, and Europe. He was a prolific writer and his works were published throughout the world.

Lynn W. McCraw is an editor of Section 3. See page 101 for a biographical sketch.

King J. McCristal has served the profession of physical education in many ways during the past 50 years. He received the bachelor's and master's degrees from the University of Illinois and the doctorate from Columbia University. During a 24-year career at Michigan State University, he served as professor and department head. He returned to the University of Illinois in 1961 as dean of the college of physical education and served in that role until retirement. He was president of the Michigan Association for HPERD, the Midwest District of the AAHPERD, and the American Academy of Physical Education. He has published widely and received many honors.

Betty Foster McCue was associate dean of the college of health, physical education, and recreation at the University of Oregon. She was president of the Midwest Association of Physical Education of College Women, vice-president for Girls' and Women's Sports of the Ohio Association and AAHPERD. She is chairman of the advisory board for *Quest,* a member of the editorial boards for *JOPER* and the *Journal of Sport History,* and is the author of two books and several research articles. She is a Fellow of the American Academy of Physical Education.

Asbury C. Moore is coeditor of Section 2. See page 44 for a biographical sketch.

Henry J. Montoye received the B.S. from Indiana University and M.S. and Ph.D. from the University of Illinois. He is currently head of the department of physical education and dance at the University of Wisconsin, Madison. He has published over 150 research articles in scholarly journals, and is the author or coauthor of four books and nine chapters in various books. Honors include a citation from the University of Toledo, Ohio, and the American College of Sports Medicine. He has received Honor Awards from Phi Epsilon Kappa, AAHPERD, and was the First Alliance Scholar, AAHPERD.

Thomas L. Newman was most recently director of the mid-Atlantic field office for the Nature Conservancy. Prior to this he conceived and designed the "Urban Justice

Program" for the Chicago bar association and board of education. He was director of educational development teams of the Amhurst Project of the Committee for Study of History and supervisor of training at the University of Illinois Circle Campus-Chicago. He also was director of a coed private boarding school in Stockbridge, Mass.

Timothy J. Nugent is editor of Section 6. See page 418 for a biographical sketch.

Delbert Oberteuffer was most recently professor emeritus of the Ohio State University. He was a Fellow of the American Academy of Physical Education from whom he received the Hetherington Award. He received both the Gulick Award and the Howe Award. He was also the recipient of the Distinguished Service Award of the American Association for Health Education and a Special Honor Award from the Society of State Supervisors of Health and Physical Education. He was the former editor of the *American Journal of School Health*. His articles and books contributed much to the fields of physical education and health education. He was professor of physical education at the Ohio State University from 1932 to his retirement in 1966, and was active in the field until his death in 1981.

Gary K. Olsen received the B.A. from Haverford College and pursued graduate courses at Baylor, Stanford, and American University. He is the founder and president of the American Society of Association Executives. He is presently the executive director of the National Jogging Association.

William A.R. Orban received the Ph.D. from the University of Illinois. He is the author of the RCAF 5Bx Fitness Program. At present he is a professor of kin-anthropology at the University of Ottawa, Ontario, Canada. He has been involved in research and has published in the area of exercise physiology.

John W. Owen is a member of the national staff of the Boys' Clubs of America located in New York, New York. The article was authored by several members of the staff.

Clyde Partin is chairman of the division of health, physical education, and athletics at Emory University, Atlanta, Georgia. He is a past-president of the Georgia State Association for Health, Physical Education, Recreation, and Dance. He has also served the Southern District of AAHPERD as president. He has been active in civic and community affairs and the author of articles published in professional journals.

Russell R. Pate is a graduate of Springfield College (B.S.) and the University of Oregon (M.S., Ph.D.). Currently he is an assistant professor at the University of South Carolina where he teaches and conducts research in exercise physiology. He chaired the committee that constructed the South Carolina Physical Fitness Test, a recently implemented test of health-related fitness. He received the AAHPERD Mabel Lee Award in 1981.

James J. Perrine is a biomedical research consultant. During the past 15 years his work has centered around the development and application of the isokinetic muscle-loading principle. He has designed several isokinetic dynamometers, ergometers, and specialized training devices. Current professional associations include the U.C.L.A. Neuromuscular Research Laboratory, and the National Athletic Health Institute, Inglewood, California. He has authored several articles on muscle testing and training, and maintains an active schedule of lectures and seminars.

G. Lawrence Rarick received the Ph.D. from the State University of Iowa and is professor of physical education, University of California, Berkeley. His research has been published in some 25 research and professional journals and 12 technical reports. He has contributed to a number of books and monographs and edited and authored several books. Dr. Rarick has held several offices within AAHPERD at both the national and district level. He received the AAHPERD Honor Award and is a Fellow of the American Academy of Physical Education and the American College of Sports Medicine.

Philip J. Rasch was educated at the University of Southern California, where he earned the A.B., M.A., M.Ed. and Ph.D. degrees. He served in the United States Navy during World War II and retired with the rank of Lieutenant Commander. He was the chief of the physiology division of the Naval Medical Field Research Laboratory. He authored or coauthored *Kinesiology* and *Applied Anatomy, Sports Medicine for Trainers, Weight Training, What Research Tells the Coach about Wrestling,* and numerous articles.

Edward R. Reuter received the B.S. degree from Washington State University and the M.S. and Ph.D. degrees from the University of Illinois. He taught at the University of Illinois and the University of Washington before going to the University of Oregon in 1959, where he is presently an associate professor in physical education. For five years he served as chairman of the physical education basic instructor program at that university.

Allan J. Ryan is editor of Section 5. See page 294 for a biographical sketch.

Allen V. Sapora is a graduate of the University of Illinois with a B.S. and M.S. in education. He later received the Ph.D. from the University of Michigan. He joined the faculty of the University of Illinois, department of leisure studies in 1946. He was head of this department from 1946-1951 and from 1966-1973. He was acting dean of the college of physical education, University of Illinois, 1973-1974. He is a Fellow of the American Park and Recreation Society, Society for Park and Recreation Educators, and Illinois Park and Recreation Society. He is a member of the American Association for Leisure and Recreation and a Fellow of the American Academy of Physical Education.

Vern Seefeldt received the Ph.D. from the University of Wisconsin in 1966. He is the coordinator of a recently completed 10-year study of the interrelationship between biological maturation, physical growth, and motor skill acquisition. He is a faculty member of the department of health, physical eduction, and recreation at Michigan State University.

Captain Carl Selin is director of physical education at the U.S. Coast Guard Academy, where he also coached and served as director of athletics. Earlier in his career he taught physical education and coached at Aurora College and the University of California in Riverside. His undergraduate education was completed at Northern Illinois, and he has advanced degrees from the University of Illinois and the University of Iowa. Each summer he directs the Maine Wilderness Canoe Basin/Deer Isle Sailing Center and Les Chalets Francais.

Dr. Edward J. Shea holds degrees from Springfield College, Emory University, and New York University. His professional experience has included positions as director of athletics at the Atlanta Athletic Club, associate professor and head swimming coach at Emory University, director of athletics at Philips Academy, Andover, Massachusetts, and 23 yars as chairman of physical eduction for men at Southern Illinois University. His record of service on state, regional, and national educational professional organizations and agencies in physical education and sport has been extensive.

Uriel Simri received the Ed.D. from West Virginia University with prior degrees taken at Physical Education Teachers' College, Tel Aviv, and City College of New York. He is presently director of the department of instructional media, Wingate Institute for Physical Education and Sport, Nethanya, Israel. He has published 11 books and 54 articles in the United States, Canada, Israel, and other countries. He was president of the Society on the History of Sport and Physical Education in Asia.

Warren C. Smith has spent the past 20 years as a practicing corrective therapist. He initiated his career as a staff therapist in Indianapolis, Indiana, in 1957; became a clinical training supervisor in 1964; chief of a therapy section at Brecksville, Ohio in 1967; and assumed the position of Chief, Corrective Therapy in the Veterans Administration Central Office in 1973. He has been active in and president of the American Corrective Therapy Association.

Marcia J. Spaeth is associate dean of health, physical education, and recreation education at the State University College at Cortland, New York. She received the B.S. and Ph.D. degrees from the University of Illinois. She has taught physical education and community recreation at the State University College at Oswego, New York. Her administrative positions include professional work in the Girl Scouts-USA and two years as acting dean of the division of health, physical education, and recreation education at Cortland.

Elba Stafford is presently a faculty member at the University of Wisconsin-Madison. She received the B.A. and M.A. degrees from Chico State College, Chico, California, and the Ed.D. from the University of Oregon. Her teaching experience includes elementary through university levels. Her professional interest centers on curriculum development at the elementary school and middle school levels of education.

Wesley Staton is coordinator, health education, at the University of Lowell, Lowell, Massachusetts. He previously taught and conducted research at University of California, Los Angeles, University of Florida, Wayne State University, and New Mexico State University. During 1967-1971 Dr. Staton was chairman, department of health, physical education, and recreation, University of Alabama, Tuscaloosa, Alabama. He is a member of AAHPERD's Research Council and has published widely.

Louis C. Steele is director of the United States Coast Guard physical education and recreation program at the Coast Guard Training Center, Alameda, California. He has contributed to the development of the physical fitness standards for this branch of the military. He has conducted research studies for the U.S. Coast Guard in aquatics and fitness. He has organized summer youth programs for the underprivileged and received an award for meritorious achievement in this area from the federal Department of Transporation.

Julian U. Stein has served as consultant, unit on programs for the handicapped at AAHPERD since 1966. Since 1972 he has directed Physical Education and Recreation for the Handicapped: Information and Research Utilization Center (IRUC), which is a comprehensive information center dealing with physical education, recreation, and related activity areas involving special populations. Previous experiences include teaching at all levels as well as coaching at the secondary level.

Patricia W. Tanner was born in England and graduated from Dartford College of Physical Education in 1948. She earned the B.A., M.Ed., and Ph.D. degrees, the latter from the Ohio State University. Initial teaching experiences in England and South Africa spanned K-12 grades. During two six-month tours she served as a representative field hockey coach from England to Australia in 1958 and America in 1960. Her major focus has been in the area of elementary physical education, highlighting movement education through film loops, publications, and workshops.

L. Budd Thalman joined the Buffalo Bills football organization as vice president for public relations in 1973 after 11 years as sports information director at the U.S. Naval Academy. A native of Wheeling, W. Virginia, he is a 1957 journalism graduate of West Virginia University. He worked for one year in the Associated Press Bureau at Huntington, West Virginia, before entering the army where he served from 1958-60 as public information officer for Fort Jay, Governor's Island, New York. Thalman returned to the AP in 1960, transferring to the Annapolis, Maryland, bureau in January 1962.

Marianna Trekell is coeditor of Section 2. See page 44 for a biographical sketch.

Mary Ann Turner is coeditor of this volume. See page viii for a biographical sketch.

Janet A. Wessel received the B.A. from MacMurray College, the M.S. from Wellesley College, and the Ph.D. from the University of Southern California. She earned a certificate in physical therapy in 1948. She is a member of AAHPERD and Midwest and Michigan Associations for HPERD. She is a Fellow of the American College of

Sports Medicine and is noted in *Who's Who of American Women.* She is a member of the National Advisory Committee of Physical Eduction and Recreation for the Handicapped USOE-BEH. She served as chairman of the Michigan State Board of Education-Vocational Rehabilitation Advisory Committee and vice chairman, Michigan Council on Physical Fitness. She was an associate editor of the *Research Quarterly.* She is now serving on the National Advisory Committee on the Handicapped. She is a faculty member at Michigan State University.

J. Stuart Wickens received both the B.S. and the M.P.E. degrees from Springfield College. He received an M.A. degree from Yale University and Ph.D. degree from the University of Oregon in 1958. He taught at Springfield College and Yale University prior to assuming the position of head of the health and physical education department, Groton School, Groton, Massachusetts. He retired as head emeritus from this position in 1971. He is an author of numerous research articles, a member of AAHPERD, a Fellow of the American College of Sports Medicine, and a member of the board of governors, and past-president of the New England Preparatory School athletic council.

Dr. Philip K. Wilson is executive director of the La Crosse Exercise Program and professor of physical education at the University of Wisconsin-La Crosse. He is on the board of directors of the American College of Sports Medicine, and is actively involved in adult fitness and cardiac rehabilitation programs.

Rollin G. Wright is presently professor and head of the department of physical education at the University of Illinois. He is a life member of Phi Epsilon Kappa and has served in a number of roles including national president. He was a charter member of Alpha Rho Chapter and was a recipient of the Scholarship Award and the National Honor Award.

Earle F. Zeigler has taught and coached at Yale University, University of Western Ontario, London, Ontario, Canada, University of Michigan, and the University of Illinois. In 1977 Dr. Zeigler completed a six-year term as dean, faculty of physical education, the University of Western Ontario. A former president of the Philosophic Society for the Study of Sport, he is a Fellow of the American Academy of Physical Education and the Philosophy Education Society. In 1969 he was elected to membership in the American Philosophical Association, and in 1975 was granted the LLD degree from the University of Windsor. He is the Second Alliance Scholar of AAHPERD.

Helen M. Zimmerman is an editor of Section 3. See page 101 for a biographical sketch.

709

Index

Adapted physical education, 295-296
  defined, 420
Administration
  intercollegiate athletics, 525-532. *See also* Athletics
  policies, 531
Administration research, summary, 491-498
Aesthetic expression, and physical education, 592
Affective domain, 208
Affective learning, 198-200
Aggression, 6
Aging
  and athletics participation, 575-579
  and physical education, 570, 572, 573-587
Amateur Athletic Union, 49, 52, 84, 662, 684
American Academy of Physical Education, 4, 51, 618-619, 656
American Alliance for Health, Physical Education, and Recreation, 203, 206. *See also* American Alliance for Health, Physical Education, Recreation, and Dance; American Association for Health, Physical Education and Recreation.
American Alliance for Health, Physical Education, Recreation, and Dance, 4, 7, 8, 42, 54, 203, 519, 520, 614-618, 637, 645, 651, 675. *See also* American Alliance for Health,

Physical Education, and Recreation; American Association for Health, Physical Education and Recreation.
American Alliance for Health, Physical Education, Recreation, and Dance Aquatic Council, 642
American Association for the Advancement of Physical Education, 48, 51, 614
American Association for Health and Physical Education, 614
American Association for Health, Physical Education and Recreation, 11, 389, 390, 428, 473, 530, 538, 544, 562, 563, 567, 639. *See also* American Alliance for Health, Physical Education, Recreation, and Dance
  Committee on Adapted Physical Education, 420
  Task Force on Programs for the Mentally Retarded, 428
American Association for Health, Physical Education and Recreation Fitness Tests, 341
American Association for Health, Physical Education and Recreation Research Council, 491
American Association for Leisure and Recreation, 617
American Association of School Administrators, 674
American Blind Bowling Association, 460

711